RUINS OF DESERT CATHAY

RUINS OF DESERT CATHAY
PERSONAL NARRATIVE OF EXPLORATIONS IN CENTRAL ASIA AND WESTERNMOST CHINA

BY

M. AUREL STEIN

WITH NUMEROUS ILLUSTRATIONS, COLOUR PLATES, PANORAMAS, AND MAPS FROM ORIGINAL SURVEYS

IN TWO VOLUMES
VOL I

Published by

Gyan Publishing House
5, Ansari Road
Daryaganj, New Delhi-110002
Phone: 011-47034999, 9811692060
E-mail: books@gyanbooks.com

Distribution Network
gyanbooks.com
India, USA, Canada, UK, Australia, France

© **Publisher**

ISBN : 978-81-212-2160-3 (Set)
ISBN : 978-81-212-2159-7 (PB)
First Published, 1912

2nd Impression 2021

Printed at: Gyan Press, Delhi.

Ruins of Desert Cathay, Vol. I
Author: M. Aurel Stein

RUINS OF
DESERT CATHAY

PERSONAL NARRATIVE OF EXPLORATIONS IN
CENTRAL ASIA AND WESTERNMOST CHINA

BY

M. AUREL STEIN

WITH NUMEROUS ILLUSTRATIONS, COLOUR PLATES, PANORAMAS,
AND MAPS FROM ORIGINAL SURVEYS

IN TWO VOLUMES

VOL. I

MACMILLAN AND CO., LIMITED
ST. MARTIN'S STREET, LONDON

1912

ANCIENT BUDDHIST PAINTING ON SILK, SHOWING VAISRAVANA, DEMON-KING OF THE NORTHERN REGION, MOVING WITH DIVINE HOST ACROSS THE OCEAN. DISCOVERED AT THE 'CAVES OF THE THOUSAND BUDDHAS,' TUN-HUANG.

(CHAP. LXVIII. SCALE, TWO-FIFTHS).

TO THE MEMORY

OF

MY PARENTS

IN UNCEASING LOVE AND DEVOTION

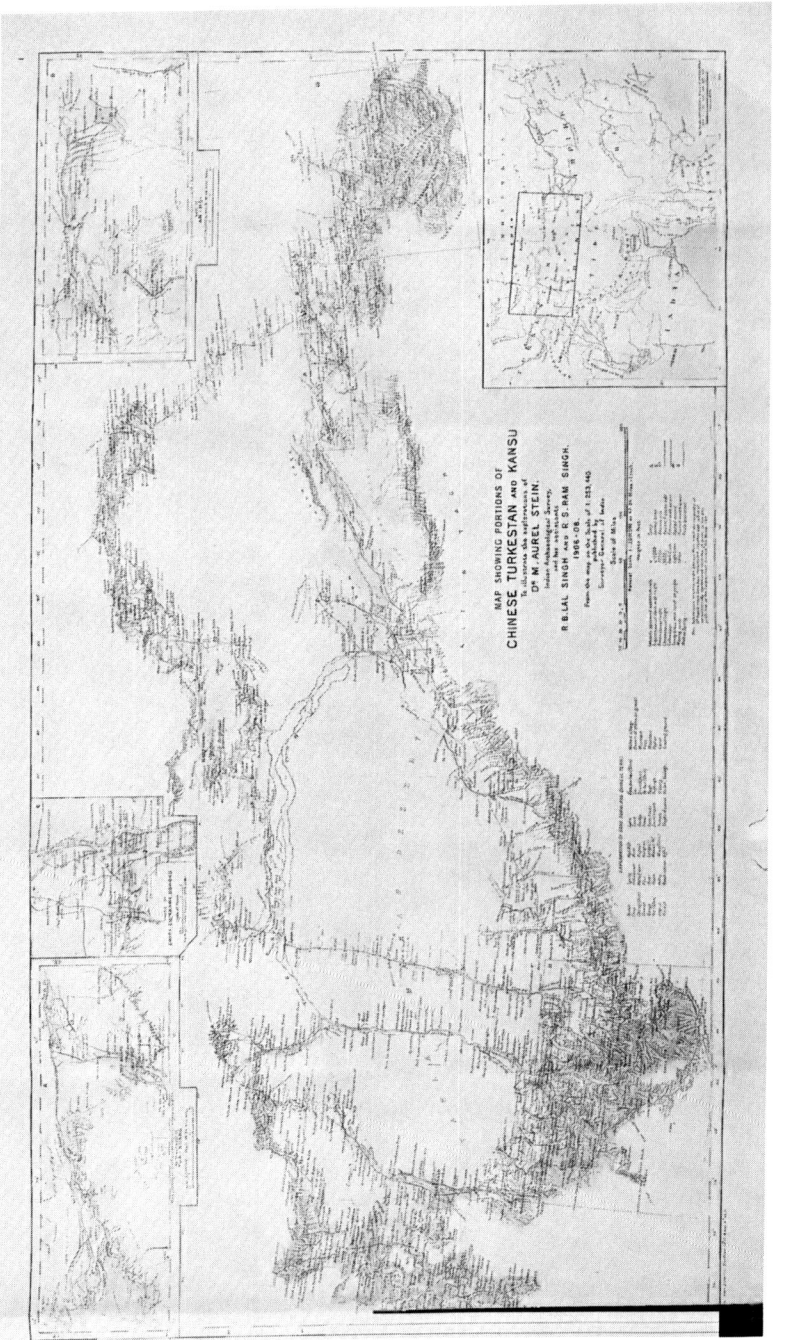

MAP SHOWING PORTIONS OF
CHINESE TURKESTAN AND KANSU
To illustrate the explorations of
Dr M. AUREL STEIN.
Indian Archaeological Survey.
1906-08.
From the surveys of
R.B. LAL SINGH AND R.S. RAM SINGH.
Scale of Miles

PREFACE

THE purpose of these volumes is to furnish the general reader with a personal record of the archaeological and geographical explorations which, during the years 1906-1908, I carried out under the orders of the Government of India in remote parts of Central Asia and westernmost China. The plan of these explorations was based upon the experiences and results of my earlier journey in Chinese Turkestan, during 1900-1901, of which my *Sand-buried Ruins of Khotan*, first published in 1903, contained a popular account. In the Introduction to that book I explained the manifold historical and other interests which first attracted me to pioneer work in what was then practically a virgin field for antiquarian research. When subsequently publishing the Detailed Report on the scientific results of that journey in my *Ancient Khotan* (Oxford University Press, 1907, two vols. quarto), I had occasion to dwell more fully upon the singular fascination possessed by the ancient remains of a region which once served as the main channel for the interchange of the civilizations of India, China, and the classical West, and also upon the geographical interest of the deserts which have helped to preserve those relics. There seems therefore no need to detail here the general aims which guided me in the plans of my second journey.

A kindly Fate allowed me to carry through my programme in its entirety and with abundant results.

The extent of these explorations is sufficiently indicated by the length of time spent over constant travel and field-work, more than two years and a half, and by the aggregate marching distance of close on ten thousand miles. As to the importance of the results achieved, it will be enough to mention that it was recognized by the Royal Geographical Society, soon after my return at the commencement of 1909, with the award of the highest distinction in its gift, the Founder's Gold Medal. Owing to the abundance of interesting discoveries made on this expedition, it will take years to complete the full scientific publication of its results in spite of the help afforded by the collaboration of a large number of savants. Even then such a Detailed Report will, by reason of its bulk and cost, necessarily remain beyond the reach of the general public.

I fully realize the necessity of enlisting the interest of this wider public for a field which has yet much to reveal as regards the far-spread influence exercised by the ancient civilization, religion, and arts of India— a field, too, in which British scientific enterprise was rightly the first to assert itself. I feel, therefore, grateful for the permission accorded to me by His Majesty's Secretary of State for India to publish independently the present narrative. I have endeavoured to make it not merely a descriptive record of my personal experiences and observations amidst some of the most forbidding deserts and highest mountain ranges of Asia, but to give in it also the first-fruits of the abundant 'finds' which came to light from ancient sites abandoned for long centuries to the desert sands. I hope the photographs and panoramic views here reproduced from among the many taken by me, the colour plates showing specimens of ancient art objects, and the well-executed maps indicating the surveys effected over wide regions by my Indian assistants and myself, will help the reader to visualize some of the results of my explorations and also the conditions under which they were achieved.

My excavations in 1900-1901 at ruined sites in the Taklamakan Desert around Khotan first revealed fully the great historical interest of that ancient culture which, as the joint product of Indian, Chinese, and classical influences, once flourished in the oases of Chinese Turkestan. They also showed the remarkable state of preservation in which even the humblest relics of a civilization extinct for long centuries might survive under the sands of a region vying with Egypt in its extreme dryness of climate. By my second journey I succeeded in extending these systematic explorations farther eastwards for nearly a thousand miles in a straight line. There, along routes which from the last centuries B.C. onwards linked China with the kingdoms of Central and Western Asia and the classical world, are scattered ruins which yielded up plentiful relics throwing light on the early history, arts, and every-day life of regions the past of which, except for rare references in the Chinese Annals, seemed lost in darkness.

But many reasons led me to devote quite as much attention to the things of the present as to those dead and buried. Nowhere, probably, in Asia is the dependence of historical development on physical conditions so strikingly marked, nor the secular changes of these conditions so clearly traceable by archaeological evidence, as in those barren basins of innermost Asia. This observation is of particular importance with regard to the much-discussed problem of progressive desiccation or general drying-up of the climate. Hence the characteristic physical features of the regions traversed, and their influence on the economic and social conditions of the scattered settlements met with, were bound to claim a large share in my observations of travel.

My story starts from the valleys of the Indo-Afghan

border, where Graeco-Buddhist art first endeavoured to use classical forms for the figures and scenes of Indian religious worship. Thence it takes the reader across the snowy range of the Hindukush up to the cradle of the River Oxus on the Pamirs, the 'Roof of the World,' and down into the great basin drained by the Tarim River which finally dies away in the marshes of Lop-nor. Explorations in the Kun-lun Range, framing this basin south and west of Khotan, show the forbidding nature of the glacier-clad mountains which feed the Tarim's greatest tributary. Then a succession of expeditions to ruined sites in the desert far beyond the extant oases east of Khotan helps the reader to realize the archaeological attractions as well as the serious difficulties of that dreaded Taklamakan Desert, where want of water raises constant obstacles and risks, and where work is possible only in the winter.

At the fascinating ruins of the Niya Site, amidst the remains of ancient dwellings abandoned since the third century A.D., and still surrounded by their dead arbours, hundreds of wooden documents were discovered, in Indian script and language, but often bearing classical seal impressions. Then north-eastwards to the wind-eroded dead wastes and the salt-encrusted dry lake-beds round Lop-nor. Plentiful discoveries rewarded my explorations carried on in this desolate region under exceptionally trying conditions; but I may allude here only to two. From ruins now situated at a distance of fully a hundred miles from the nearest supply of drinkable water, I recovered conclusive evidence that the use for administrative purposes of the same early Indian language I had found in the oldest records of the Khotan region, extended in the first centuries of our era as far as this most remote corner of Central Asia. At the same time, the discovery of fine wood-carvings in Graeco-Buddhist style, and of beautiful frescoes quite classical in style that once adorned Buddhist shrines offered unexpected testimony to the powerful influence exercised by Hellenistic art even on the very confines of true China.

After crossing the great desert by the track which Marco Polo, like early Chinese pilgrims before him, had followed on his journey to Cathay, I found myself rewarded by a big and fascinating task after my own heart. It was the discovery and exploration of the long-forgotten western-most portion of that ancient frontier wall, or *Limes*, with which the Chinese Empire guarded the chief line for its political and commercial expansion towards Central Asia and the West against the raids of the Huns during the centuries immediately preceding and following the time of Christ. The line of the ancient wall, with its watch-towers and stations, found often in wonderful pre-servation, was explored for over 200 miles. Having remained undisturbed by the hand of man in the solitude of the gravel desert, it yielded a rich harvest of early Chinese and other records of historical interest, along with many curious relics of the life once led along this most desolate of borders.

Not far from Tun-huang, the chief oasis still surviving within this western extremity of the ancient 'Great Wall,' lies the sacred site of the 'Thousand Buddhas.' Buddhist piety of early times has here honey-combed the rock walls of a true Thebais with hundreds of cave temples, once richly decorated with frescoes and stucco sculptures, and still objects of worship. Here I had the good fortune in the spring of 1907 to gain access to a great deposit of ancient manuscripts and art relics which had lain hidden and perfectly protected in a walled-up rock chapel for about nine hundred years. The story how I secured here twenty-four cases heavy with manuscript treasures rescued from that strange place of hiding, and five more filled with paintings, embroideries, and similar remains of Buddhist art, has been characterized by a competent observer as a particularly dramatic and fruitful incident in the history of

the prospective archaeological 'finds.' Recognizing the
services rendered by this great institution in the past
towards Oriental researches, it is gratifying to me to think
that it has been possible for me to bring back a collection
of antiques which has made this share, even from a
financial point of view, a very profitable investment.

When the time came in 1906 for the start on my
journey the kind interest shown in my enterprise by Lord
Minto, then Viceroy of India, was a great encouragement. It continued through the whole course of my travels,
as shown in the letters of my old friend Colonel (now Sir
James) Dunlop Smith, then the Viceroy's private secretary.
I shall always remember with sincere gratitude the effective
support which my subsequent efforts to secure adequate
leisure for the elaboration of my results received from
Lord Minto.

For the execution of my geographical tasks the help of
the Survey of India Department has proved, as before, of
the utmost value. Under the direction of Colonel F. B.
Longe, R.E., it readily agreed to depute with me one of its
trained native surveyors, and to provide by a special grant
for all costs arising from his employment. Colonel
S. Burrard, R.E., F.R.S., then Superintendent of Trigonometrical Surveys and now Surveyor-General of India,
lost no opportunity to encourage and guide our labours in
the field and to facilitate the preparation of their cartographical record in his office. It is mainly due to his
unfailing help that our geographical results are now worked
out and embodied in an Atlas of ninety-four map sheets,
on the scale of four miles to one inch, which await
publication with my Detailed Report. In Rai Ram Singh,
the excellent Surveyor who had accompanied me on my first
journey, and in his equally experienced and hard-working
colleague Rai Bahadur Lal Singh, who subsequently
relieved him when considerations of health necessitated
the former's return to India, I found not only most

efficient topographical assistants, but also willing and always reliable helpers in many other practical tasks. The story of our travels as recorded in these volumes will bear ample testimony to the great value of their services and to the trying physical conditions in which they were cheerfully rendered.

Quite as valuable for my geographical work was the moral support which, in addition to the loan of a number of instruments, the Royal Geographical Society gave me. Those who like myself have to struggle hard for chances of achieving their scientific aims in life, will appreciate the encouragement I derived from the Society's generous recognition of the results of both my Central-Asian explorations. Whether in the course of solitary travel across the desert plains and high mountain ranges of innermost Asia, or struggling with the difficulties of the labours which the results brought back imposed upon me in more commonplace and often less congenial surroundings, I always felt the vivifying touch of the friendly interest and unfailing sympathy of the Society's incomparable secretary, Dr. J. Scott Keltie. I must also record here my special thanks to the Royal Geographical Society for having enabled me to make the results of the surveys effected by my topographical assistants and myself more accessible; in its *Journal* have been published three maps presenting on a reduced scale the main contents of the Atlas prepared at the Indian Trigonometrical Survey Office, Dehra Dun. With the Society's kind permission and the publishers' ready concurrence it has been possible to reproduce these maps here.

Once beyond the Indian political border I knew well that the success of my undertaking would depend very largely upon the view which the local powers would take of my plans and upon their readiness to countenance them. I could not have wished in this respect for a more encouraging sign at the outset than when H.M. Habibullah, King

of Afghanistan, readily gave me permission to cross his
territory on the uppermost Oxus on my way to the Pamirs,
and most effectively provided for my passage along an
ancient route of very great interest, but difficult at the time
and quite closed to European travellers.   For this gracious
consideration and hospitality on the part of the ruler of
those regions, towards which my scholarly interests have
been turned with special keenness ever since my youth, I
wish to record here my deep gratitude.

After crossing the Chinese frontier on the Pamirs the
fields of my exploratory work consisted almost entirely of
deserts and inhospitable mountain wastes.   But just there
I could realize more than ever how absolutely essential
was the active co-operation of the Chinese administrators
for the execution of my plans.   Without their efficient
help it would have been impossible to secure the transport and labour indispensable for my expeditions into
the dreaded deserts where 'old towns' had to be searched
for, or to obtain what was needed in animals, men, and
supplies for prolonged explorations in forbiddingly barren
mountains.   My narrative will show how fortunate I was
in meeting with invariable attention and willingness to
help among the Mandarins of all the oases which served
successively as my 'bases of operation.'   At most of the
Ya-mêns I soon found trustworthy friends and scholars
keenly interested in my archaeological aims and 'finds.'

Among many to whom my thanks are due, I must
content myself with specially naming Ch'ê Ta-jên, the
Amban of Khotan; Liao Ta-lao-ye, who helped me from
his dreary place of exile near Lop-nor where he afterwards died; Wang Ta-lao-ye, the learned magistrate, and
Lin Ta-jên, the military commandant of Tun-huang, who
both did their best to remove difficulties from my explorations along the ancient 'Great Wall.'   But most of all
I owe heartfelt gratitude to my old friend P'an Ta-jên
(the Pan-Darin of my former narrative), then Tao-t'ai of

Ak-su, who, cherishing a kindly recollection of my work and person from my former journey, did all he could from a distance to use the influence of his high office for smoothing my paths.

But what secured to me from the outset the benevolent disposition of the provincial administration of Chinese Turkestan was the influence exercised on my behalf by my old friend Mr. G. Macartney, C.I.E., for many years the representative of the Indian Government at Kashgar, and now H.M.'s Consul-General for the 'New Dominions.' Throughout that wide region his name and character are held in high respect by officials and people alike. I owe to him a heavy debt of gratitude for the most effective help which he was ever ready to extend to me from afar; for all the hospitality and kindness I enjoyed during my stay at his residence in Kashgar; and, last but not least, for the watchful care with which he assured the safe transit of my antiquities and my mails when distances up to a thousand miles and more lay between us.

But it was a service of quite as great importance as any just mentioned, and one which I shall always remember most gratefully, when he recommended to me an excellent Chinese secretary in the person of Chiang-ssŭ-yeh. Since I had not been able to equip myself by a serious study of Chinese, the help of a qualified Chinese scholar was of the utmost importance for my tasks. I found in Chiang-ssŭ-yeh not merely a zealous teacher and secretary, but the most eager of helpmates, always cheerfully sharing labours and hardships for the sake of my scientific interests. My narrative will show how much of the success attending our work on purely Chinese ground was due to his invaluable services. How often have I longed since we parted for my ever alert and devoted Chinese comrade!

The rapid sketch given above of the aims, extent, and

character of my explorations will convey some idea of the heavy tasks which the elaboration of their over-abundant results has laid on my shoulders since my return. When so much detailed research had to be started on new materials likely to need scholarly application for years, it seemed doubly important that I should work out my own observations and conclusions in broad outlines and make them available as soon as possible. I realized from the first that the publication of a general narrative like the present offered the most suitable place for their early record. Hence these volumes were to serve not for the mere reproduction of diary leaves or first impressions of travel, but, apart from any personal interest they may possess, also as a prelude, and in some respects a necessary complement, to my Detailed Scientific Report.

This close connection has made the preparation of the present book a more responsible task than may appear on the surface. It also imposes upon me the duty of recording, however briefly, the manifold help without which it would have been impossible to reap the true results of my efforts in the field. Most of all do I owe gratitude to the Government of India, which, with the approval of H.M.'s Secretary of State, sanctioned my being placed on 'special duty' in England for a period of two years and three months, in order that I might be able to devote myself to these tasks within easy reach of my collection of antiquities. I hope that when it will be possible to make this accessible to the public by a temporary exhibition, and still more when the publication of my Detailed Report, as sanctioned by H.M.'s Secretary of State, in four quarto volumes, will be completed, the value of the official help thus extended to me will be fully appreciated.

It would have been quite impossible for me to accomplish within a reasonable time all the manifold labours connected with the arrangement and description of my collection and the study of its *embarras de richesse* in remains of ancient art had I not enjoyed once again the invaluable assistance of my old friend and chief helpmate, Mr. F. H. Andrews, late Principal of the Mayo School of Art, Lahore. Prolonged study on the spot of Indian art in all its aspects, coupled with his own high artistic gifts and his wide experience of Eastern crafts in general, has made him an expert, unsurpassed in this country, for all questions touching the arts and industries of ancient Central Asia. I shall never cease to feel deepest gratitude for the enthusiastic devotion which induced him to sacrifice to our common tasks what hard-earned leisure he could spare from educational duties elsewhere.

Besides his constant co-operation in matters of art and technical interest, the present book has benefited greatly by the special care which Mr. Andrews has bestowed upon its illustrations. Thus I owe to his artist's hand the black and white drawing reproduced in the vignette on the title-page, which shows a faithfully restored enlargement of the figure of Pallas Promachos, as seen in several of the ancient seal impressions on clay recovered by me from the desert sand. In addition to Mr. F. H. Andrews' guidance, the work of arranging and classifying my finds has derived much advantage also from the trained and zealous help of several young classical archaeologists, Mr. J. P. Droop, Miss F. Lorimer, Mr. H. G. Evelyn-White, and Mr. L. C. Woolley, who conjointly or successively have filled the posts of assistants at my collection during the last two and a half years. To them, too, I wish to record my grateful acknowledgments.

Ever since temporary accommodation was secured for my collection at the British Museum its Director, Dr. F. G. Kenyon, and the Keepers of the Departments directly concerned, especially Dr. L. Barnett, Sir Sidney Colvin, Mr. C. H. Read, have done all in their power to facilitate my labours by valuable advice and support. For the help thus received and for the very useful information placed at my disposal on subjects of special enquiry by the

Assistant-Keepers and Assistants, Messrs. J. Allan, R. L. Binyon, L. Giles, R. L. Hobson, T. A. Joyce, R. A. Smith, I may be allowed to express here my sincere thanks.

A number of distinguished savants have helped me towards producing the present work by collaborating on the materials brought back from my journey. On the artistic and technical side my hearty thanks are due, in the first place, to my old friend Monsieur A. Foucher, Professor at the Paris University, the leading authority on all that relates to Graeco-Buddhist art. To his exceptional knowledge of Buddhist iconography I owe the correct interpretation of some of my most interesting frescoes and paintings. Professor Percy Gardner has generously allowed me to draw upon his wide archaeological knowledge for the elucidation of objects of classical art. Professor J. Strzygowski, of the Imperial University of Vienna, has been good enough to afford similar guidance as regards the links which connect the ancient art of innermost Asia with that of the late classical world. In respect of Tibetan art remains my friend Colonel L. A. Waddell, C.B., C.I.E., gave me welcome assistance from his wide experience of Tibetan Buddhism. Sir Arthur Church, F.R.S., allowed me to profit from his life-long researches for an analysis of the materials used in the ancient paintings, frescoes, and relievos. To Professor J. von Wiesner, of the Imperial Academy of Vienna, a great authority on plant-physiology, I owe illuminating investigations on the substance and technical character of my ancient papers and textiles. My old friend, Professor L. de Lóczy, head of the Hungarian Geological Survey, did his best to help me in the elucidation of interesting geological questions suggested by my desert explorations.

Among my philological collaborators my heaviest debt is due to M. Éd. Chavannes, Membre de l'Institut, the eminent Sinologist and the leading authority on Chinese sources of information concerning early Central-Asian history. Immediately after my return he charged himself with the detailed study and publication of all early Chinese records excavated by me, and subsequently very kindly allowed me to utilize the results of his painstaking labours for the present volumes. The perusal of almost any chapter dealing with ancient sites will show to what extent my interpretation of their past must depend on the materials thus made available to me. It is a special satisfaction to me to know that M. Chavannes' volume dealing with these early Chinese 'finds' will soon be ready for publication in advance of my 'Detailed Report.' M. Paul Pelliot, Professor at the Sorbonne and the successful leader of a French archaeological mission to Central Asia, has put me under a great obligation by undertaking the inventory of the thousands of old Chinese texts and documents from the Caves of the Thousand Buddhas.

Dr. A. F. Rudolf Hoernle, C.I.E., the pioneer of Central-Asian studies on the British side, has rendered me very valuable help by his preliminary analysis of all manuscript 'finds' in Indian Brahmi script, which are in one or other of the 'unknown' languages of Chinese Turkestan. It is reassuring for me to know that the analysis of the ancient wooden records in Kharoshthi script discovered on my second journey has been undertaken by the same highly qualified scholars, Professor E. J. Rapson, M. É. Senart, and the Abbé Boyer, who had already bestowed so much critical acumen and labour on the corresponding 'finds' of my first expedition. To the Abbé Boyer I am indebted besides for the decipherment of certain important Kharoshthi inscriptions. In regard to my Sanskrit manuscript materials I have enjoyed equally competent assistance from my friends Dr. L. Barnett and Professor L. de la Vallée Poussin.

For the analysis of the plentiful Tibetan records I had the good fortune to secure the collaboration of an exceptionally qualified expert, Dr. A. H. Francke, of the Moravian

Mission, Ladak, while the catalogue work on the Tibetan Buddhist texts, started by Miss C. M. Ridding with the help of Dr. F. W. Thomas, the learned Librarian of the India Office, has also benefited my own task. Professor V. Thomsen, of Copenhagen, the veteran Orientalist and decipherer of the famous Orkhon inscriptions, has done me the honour of examining and interpreting my early Turkish manuscripts in Runic Turki writing. To Dr. A. von Lecoq, of the Royal Ethnographic Museum, Berlin, who carried on exceptionally fruitful excavations at Turfan, I am indebted for the full edition of an important Manichaean text in old Turkish; and to Dr. E. Denison Ross, Assistant Secretary to the Government of India, for a preliminary investigation of Uigur Buddhist manuscripts. Professor F. W. K. Müller, Director of the Royal Ethnographic Museum, Berlin, has helped me by an analysis of the manuscript materials in the Sogdian language which he was the first to decipher. Even earlier relics of this interesting Iranian language have come to light in certain documents of an 'unknown' script resembling Aramaic, to which my friend Dr. A. Cowley, Fellow of Magdalen College, Oxford, and subsequently M. R. Gauthiot, of the École des Hautes Études, Paris, have been kind enough to devote much learned labour.

This long record of much-needed scholarly help cannot make me forget that for the purpose of the present book it was, perhaps, even more important to bring the results of my labours graphically before the eyes of the reader than to determine in all cases their exact scientific bearing. So I feel particularly grateful for the liberality with which my publishers have allowed me to provide illustrations so numerous and varied. My special thanks are due also to Messrs. Henry Stone and Son, of Banbury, who, by dint of much skill and care, have succeeded in making the colour plates worthy and true reproductions of the specimens of ancient art work.

I have left it to the last to record my heartfelt gratitude
to those kind friends who have bestowed their personal
care on these volumes. Mr. J. S. Cotton, late editor of
the *Academy*, did me the great favour of revising my
manuscript with regard to the needs of the general reader ;
he also readily charged himself at the publishers' request
with the preparation of an appropriate Index which, I
trust, will also be found useful as a glossary of Eastern
terms. Mr. P. S. Allen, Fellow of Merton College, Oxford,
spared time from absorbing scholarly labours of his own,
and, assisted by my friend Mr. J. de M. Johnson, of
Magdalen College, cheerfully sacrificed it to a very
thorough revision of the proofs. His letters, which
followed me everywhere on my travels, had been a
constant source of encouragement amidst difficulties and
trials. That I was able to complete this narrative in
Oxford and in surroundings both inspiriting and congenial
was a special boon assured to me by the kind hospitality
of the Warden and Fellows of Merton College. The
peaceful retreat for work which they granted me under
their historic roof will always be remembered by me
with sincere gratitude.

But whether working by the banks of the Isis or in
British Museum basements, amidst the condensed humanity
of London, I never ceased to long for the deserts and
mountains which had seen my happiest years of labour.
How gladly should I forget all the toil which the results
brought back from this journey have cost me, could I but
feel sure of freedom for fresh explorations, in old fields and
in those to which my eyes have, as yet vainly, been turned
since my youth !

M. AUREL STEIN.

MERTON COLLEGE, OXFORD,
November 3rd, 1911.

CONTENTS

CHAPTER I

CHAPTER II

CHAPTER III

CHAPTER IV

CHAPTER V

CHAPTER VI

CHAPTER VII

CONTENTS

CHAPTER VIII

CONTENTS

CHAPTER XVII

CHAPTER XVIII

CHAPTER XIX

CHAPTER XX

CHAPTER XXI

CHAPTER XXII

CHAPTER XXIII

CHAPTER XXIV

CHAPTER XXV

CHAPTER XXVI

CHAPTER XXVII

CHAPTER XXVIII

CHAPTER XXIX

CHAPTER XXX

CHAPTER XXXI

CHAPTER XXXII

CHAPTER XXXIII

CHAPTER XXXIV

CONTENTS

CHAPTER XLIV

CHAPTER XLV

CHAPTER XLVI

CHAPTER XLVII

CHAPTER XLVIII

CHAPTER XLIX

ILLUSTRATIONS

CHAPTER I

BETWEEN HYDASPES AND INDUS

EVER since, in 1901, I returned from my first journey into Chinese Turkestan, happy recollections of successful labour among its mountains and deserts kept my mind fixed upon the hope of fresh explorations. By the excavations I then effected it was my good fortune to bring to light for the first time authentic remains of that ancient civilization which, as the joint product of Indian, Chinese, and classical influences, had once flourished in the oases fringing the Tarim Basin. There was every reason to hope that explorations renewed over a wider area, and with a more liberal allowance of time and means, would be equally fruitful. But the very abundance of the results which had rewarded my first effort retarded the attainment of that eagerly sought chance. Their scientific elaboration had to precede a fresh journey, and to assure that elaboration in a manner befitting pioneer work in a new field involved a task of exceptional difficulty. It was not enough to record and illustrate in full detail discoveries so ample and varied; the very novelty and the remoteness of their region laid it upon me to become their interpreter also from whatever historical and geographical light could be gathered.

The task was doubly heavy for one who had to struggle for leisure from exacting official duties. So it was not until the summer of 1904, while employed as Inspector-General of Education on the North-West Frontier, that I was able to submit to the Government of India detailed proposals about another journey which was to carry me back

B

to my old archaeological hunting-grounds around the Takla-makan desert, and thence far away eastwards to within the Great Wall of China.   Owing to the kind interest shown by Lord Curzon, then Viceroy of India, and the help of devoted friends able to realize how closely the proposed explorations touched the sphere of India's histori-cal interests, my scheme obtained, in the spring of 1905, the approval of the Indian Government and the Secretary of State.   Their favourable decision was facilitated by the Trustees of the British Museum, who agreed to con-tribute two-fifths of the estimated cost of the expedition, £5000 in all, against a corresponding share in the pro-spective 'archaeological proceeds,' as official language styled them.

I had originally tried hard for permission to start during the summer of 1905.   But my efforts were frustrated by the difficulty of securing that freedom from routine work which I needed for the completion of my scientific Report on the former journey.   At last by the 1st of October 1905 I was released from administrative duties.   Rarely have I felt such relief as on that day when I could set out from my alpine camp in Kaghan, the northernmost corner of the Frontier Province, to Kashmir.   There six months of 'special duty' were to enable me to complete in strict seclusion my scientific Report, and also to make the multi-farious preparations indispensable for the fresh explorations before me.

It seemed quite a holiday, and at the same time like an appropriate training, when, by six days' hard marching, largely over mountain tracks which probably never before had seen any laden traffic, I managed to move my camp with its respectable array of book boxes across the high passes above the Kishanganga into Kashmir.   It was pleasant, too, to find myself, after an enforced absence of over five years, again in the beloved Alpine land to which many seasons of congenial antiquarian labour had attached me.   Yet soon those happy summers seemed as if passed in a previous birth.

Incessant desk-work, more fatiguing to me than any hard marching or digging, kept me imprisoned in my little cottage above the Dal lake near Srinagar from morning till dusk. Had it not been for my solitary walks in the evening, I should scarcely have had time to observe how the glowing tints of the Kashmir autumn gave way to the dull mists and muddy snows of the valley's cheerless winter. It was a period of great strain and anxious labour; for a variety of practical considerations which cannot be detailed here, made it a matter of the utmost concern that I should be free to start for Turkestan as early in the spring as the high passes northward were at all practicable. But in the end the unbroken exertion of those trying six months bore fruit. Towards the close of March, when the sun had at last begun fitfully to smile again upon the Alpine land, which Hindu mythology represents as Himalaya's favourite daughter, my *Ancient Khotan* was practically completed. Thanks to the help of self-sacrificing friends far away, the greater portion of its two stout quarto volumes had safely passed through the University Press in distant Oxford.

Nor had the many preparations for the long and difficult travels before me been neglected. Correspondence had settled all details about the two native assistants whose services were to be placed at my disposal by the Survey of India and the Military Department. What stores, scientific instruments, and other equipment were needed from London, Calcutta, and elsewhere had been ordered in good time. In Srinagar itself willing hands of faithful old Kashmiri retainers had busied themselves over the furs, felt boots, and other articles of personal outfit which were to protect us against the climatic rigours of Central-Asian mountains and deserts. Their care, too, had effected what repairs were needed in my little Kabul tent, supplied by the Cawnpore Elgin Mills in 1900 for my first journey, and ever since my only true home, to make it thoroughly fit for another three years' campaigning.

For my entry into Chinese Turkestan I was eager to use a new route, singularly interesting for the student of early geography and ethnography, but practically closed by political difficulties to the European traveller. It was to take me from the Indian administrative border

near Peshawar through the Pathan tribal territory of
Swat and Dir into Chitral, and thence across the Hindukush to the uppermost Oxus Valley and the Afghan
Pamirs. My lamented chief and friend, Sir Harold A.
Deane, K.C.S.I., that truly great Warden of the Marches,
then Chief Commissioner of the North-West Frontier
Province, whose kind help and interest never failed me,
had readily agreed to my project. A political obstacle
which I had reason to consider very serious was removed
more easily than I had ventured to hope; for H.M.
Habibullah, King of Afghanistan, on being approached
through the Indian Foreign Office, had granted me, with
a promptness for which I shall always retain sincere
gratitude, permission to cross a portion of his territory
not visited by any European since the days of the Pamir
Boundary Commission.

    But before reaching Afghan soil beyond the Hindukush
I should have first to get into Chitral, and the misgivings
entertained locally as to the possibility of safely crossing
with baggage the difficult Lowarai Pass, leading from Dir
to Chitral, then deeply buried under snow, still interposed
a formidable barrier. I had the strongest reasons to
apprehend the results of any delay in this crossing; for
if I could not reach the headwaters of the Chitral River
before May ended, I should run a very serious risk of
finding its narrow uppermost gorges above Mastuj, which
give access to the Oxus watershed on the Baroghil, closed
completely to traffic by the melting snows of the spring.
The official correspondence on this subject continuing for
months had grown imposing. In the end its file was
quite bulky, though much of it consisted of telegrams
on the thinnest paper! So when April arrived without
any assurance as to an early date being allowed for the
Lowarai crossing, I felt it high time to leave Kashmir for
the Frontier and to make personal efforts to clear the way
for an early start.

    A truly bright day, the first of the season, preceded
my departure from Srinagar early on April 2, 1906. But
the trees and fields I passed on the road down to Bara-
mula, Nature's ancient 'Gate of the Kingdom,' were still

in their wintry bareness. For the sight of the first iris I
hoped in vain. As the clattering tonga carried me down
through the narrow forest-clad gorges of the Jhelam there
were plenty of broken bridges and other obstacles to distract attention. So I can scarcely tell exactly at what
point spring coming up the Hydaspes and I hurrying down
had a passing encounter by the roadside.

After the gloomy cold of a Kashmir winter I was quite
ready to appreciate the signs of the approaching hot
weather which greeted me on arrival in the Punjab plains.
My first days there were claimed by Lahore, once my
official 'station' for eleven years, whither the wish to say
good-bye to old friends and the more prosaic necessity of
having my teeth looked to before protracted travels 'in
the wilds' were now calling me. A few peaceful days
under the hospitable roof of my friend Mr. E. D. Maclagan,
then Chief Secretary to the Punjab Government, gave the
brief relaxation which I was not likely to meet with again
for a long time. These happy days sped past only too
fast. Yet, what with long-missed familiar faces and sights
all round me and the pleasant memories revived by visits
to some delightfully neglected old gardens in the Lahore
Campagna which used to be my favourite places of refuge
during long years of strain and unceasing exertion, I could
say farewell to my kind hosts with a feeling as if I had
lived through again much that had cheered me in my
Indian past.

At Peshawar, to which I proceeded on April 10th,
there was plenty to keep my thoughts fully occupied with
the present and immediate future. An auspicious chance
had so willed it that Lord Minto, the new Viceroy, was
to pay his first visit to the capital of the Frontier Province
just before the time I was planning for my start from the
Peshawar border. It was important for me to interest
His Excellency in the explorations before me, and the
intercession of his Private Secretary, Colonel (now Sir
James R.) Dunlop-Smith, K.C.I.E., C.S.I., whom old
friendship has ever prompted to smooth things for me,
had already assured to me the desired interview. I could
not have revisited my old headquarters on the Frontier

under more pleasant aspects. Peshawar was deliciously cool, and displayed all the spring glory of its gardens with their exuberance of roses and irises. Recent rain had cleared the atmosphere, and the great semicircle of trans-border ranges, dominated by the towering mass of Mount Tartara westwards, raised its barren outlines above the vast arena of the smiling Peshawar Valley with a sharpness truly fascinating. The coming visit of the Viceroy was drawing Frontier officers from all parts of the border into Peshawar, and every hour brought cheerful meetings with old friends. There was plenty to do in my office, not this time with papers and files, but with the packing of my too numerous books, which a timely 'burial' in tin-lined cases was to save from white ants and other risks during my long absence.

On April 12th I first saw the new Lord of the Indies when the 'Administration' of the Frontier Province gathered at the Peshawar railway station for his official reception. A pleasant meeting at the same time with Sir Louis Dane, K.C.S.I., then Indian Foreign Secretary and since Lieutenant-Governor of the Punjab, gave me the welcome impression that H.M. the Amir's ready permission for my passage through Upper Wakhan, just conveyed in an imposing Firman of the 'God-created Government,' was regarded with much satisfaction in diplomatic quarters of the Indian Olympus.

Two days later I had the honour of being received by Lord Minto. The kind interest he showed in what I had to tell him of the results of my past Central-Asian efforts, of official obstacles encountered and overcome, and of the difficulties and risks besetting the tasks now before me, soon reassured me that I might reckon upon what support the personal sympathy of the head of the Indian Administration could give. Often during the long lonely travels which followed, when worrying uncertainties oppressed me whether I should ever succeed in securing the leisure needed for working up my scientific results, or the still more eagerly desired chance of freedom for exploratory tasks in the future, I looked back with sincere gratitude to the encouragement which the appreciation of my aims by that statesman of the true *grand-seigneur* type had given me in the start.

With the Viceroy in residence at Government House and many important affairs of the Frontier to settle, Sir Harold Deane yet found time for a quiet talk with me on the morning of my departure. How grateful I feel now for having had this chance of saying in person my farewell words of thanks to him who had always been my truest friend and patron! I felt deeply the parting from the protective aegis of the noble soldier - administrator, so alive to all the historical interest of the Frontier, who had never missed an opportunity of giving me scope for archaeological exploits within or without the border. I was aware that it might be a parting for longer than the time of my journey. And yet there was nothing to warn me that within little more than two years this born ruler of men, whose strength of body and mind impressed the most turbulent tribesmen, would succumb to the ceaseless strain of guarding the peace on the Frontier.

For the mobilization base, as it were, of my expedition I had selected Abbottabad, the pretty sub-alpine head-quarters of the Hazara District, which offered coolness and seclusion for the busy time of final preparations. When I reached it on the morning of April 17th I had the satisfaction to find the array of mule trunks containing equipment safely arrived from Kashmir. The cases with stores and outfit which had been ordered from England and down-country places of India also awaited me at the comfortable new Circuit House. But when could I really hope to make all these impediments move off northwards? I had long before decided that my start from the Frontier ought to be effected by the last week of April. But even while at Peshawar I had been confronted by tantalizing doubts as to whether the local help, without which the crossing of the snow-covered Lowarai Pass could not be attempted, would be forthcoming at the right time.

The local reports sent on by the Political Agent in charge of the Swat-Chitral route continued to represent the avalanche risks as so great, owing to abnormally heavy snowfalls, that any attempt to pass with heavy baggage needing a large number of load-carrying men would be likely to result in serious loss of life. Vainly did I assert that my Alpine experience would necessarily make me take all needful precautions. As a last resort, I had told Colonel Dunlop-Smith of my difficulty, and that kindly *deus ex machina* offered to write a note in the right sense to the cautious Guardian of the Passes. Whether it was this friendly note from the Viceroy's camp or a mere lucky coincidence, I had scarcely been at Abbottabad for twelve hours when a long telegram announced the receipt of good reports from Chitral. They seemed to have cleared away, as if by magic, most of those formidable snow barriers on the Lowarai and of the still more cumbersome responsibilities.

It was as well to have my mind eased on this point; for the work awaiting me at Abbottabad was heavy for the short time in hand. There was the checking of all equipment articles, instruments, and stores; their safe distribution and packing into mule trunks to make loads of the right weight for the difficult tracks ahead; the preparation of exact lists; not to mention writing work of all sorts which an Indian official can never hope to escape from—not even in Central-Asian deserts. It scarcely meant any lessening of this initial strain that I was now being joined by my Indian assistants. The first to arrive was worthy Naik Ram Singh, the fine-looking Sikh corporal of the First (Prince of Wales's Own) Sappers and Miners, who, through the kind offices of my friend Colonel J. E. Dickie, R.E., Commanding Royal Engineers on the N.W. Frontier, had been allowed by the Military Department to volunteer for my expedition. When he had paid me a visit in my Kaghan camp the previous summer, his look of physical strength and cheerful disposition, and his hereditary skill as a ' Mistri ' or carpenter, seemed to show him specially suited to act as ' the handy man ' whom I should need. I had taken care to make it clear to him that the task for which he had volunteered, and for which he was to receive substantial compensation in the shape of a salary about five times as big as what he would be entitled to in the way of pay and allowances even when employed on field service outside India, implied serious hardships and possible risks. But he cheerfully stuck to his offer, and the effective special training which the regimental authorities of his distinguished corps had subsequently provided, qualified him also to help me in the development of photographic negatives, drawing of plans, and similar technical tasks.

A day or two after I was joined by Rai Sahib Ram Singh, the skilful native Surveyor who had accompanied me on my former journey. The Survey of India Department, now under the direction of Colonel F. B. Longe, R.E., willing as ever to assist me in the execution of my geographical tasks, had readily agreed to depute him with me and to bear all costs arising from his employment. Since we parted in 1901 the Rai Sahib had had the good fortune to add extensively to his survey experiences in Central Asia by accompanying Captain Rawling and Major Ryder on their successful expeditions in Tibet. I was heartily glad that there came again with him honest Jasvant Singh, the wiry little Rajput who had acted as his cook on my first Turkestan journey. Never have I seen an Indian follower so reliable in character, so gentlemanly in manners and bearing, and so cheerful under hardships and trying conditions of all sorts.

I had every reason to regret from the start that his high caste as a Mian Rajput of the bluest blood precluded his giving to myself the benefit of his ministrations. For the Indian Muhammadan whom I had managed, not without difficulty, to engage at Peshawar as my cook for the journey, soon proved to be a failure professionally as well as incapable of facing prolonged hard travel, even when fortified by clandestine drink and doses of opium. I had been obliged to have recourse to this worthy, since young Aziz, the Ladaki whom a friendly missionary had sent down from Leh in the autumn in response to my request for a cook with experience in rough travel, had displayed sad ignorance of European cookery and rooted inability to acquire its rudiments even when professional teaching was provided to fit him for my requirements, modest as they were. But otherwise he was willing, trained by former employment to look after ponies, and in any case a

'hardy plant,' and fairly intelligent, like most of his fellow-
Shalguns, cross-bred of Kashmiri and Tibetan. So I
decided to take him along, with the fond wish that his help
as cook's understudy might not often be needed. Our
small party further included my faithful old caravan man,
Muhammadju from Yarkand, who had braved the wintry
passes in order to join me, and had narrowly escaped with
his life at the close of March when an avalanche swept
away and buried half a dozen of his fellow-travellers on the
Burzil.

Rai Sahib Ram Singh had brought up a small armoury
of surveying instruments from the Trigonometrical Survey
Office, and also a few carbines and revolvers with ammuni-
tion which prudence demanded we should take from the
stores of the Rawalpindi Arsenal. The equipment provided with much care by the workshops of the First
Sappers and Miners at Roorkee was also necessarily bulky,
including as it did tools of all sorts for the Naik, and a
raft of special design floated by numerous goatskins, which
were to be utilized also for transport of water in the desert.
By dint of much overhauling, elimination, and arrangement
I succeeded at last in reducing the whole of our baggage
to fifteen mule-loads, one less than the train with which I
had started on my first expedition. Three among them,
with articles not likely to be required until the autumn, were
to go by the Kara-koram trade route to Khotan. Taking
into account that our equipment comprised indispensable
stores of all kinds, calculated to last for two and a half
years, and among them the great and fragile weight of
close on two thousand photographic glass plates, I felt
satisfied with the result of my efforts at compression.

Fortunately Abbottabad presented itself to me not
merely in the light of a 'Transport and Supplies' base.
I found there a number of kind friends and—spring in all
its hill glory. Banks of white and blue irises stretched
over the slopes of the pretty 'Station' gardens. The
thoroughly English-looking bungalows were covered with
masses of roses, among them that pride of the Frontier,
the large-petalled Mardan rose. All along the quiet
shady lanes of the little cantonment the scent of blossom-

ing trees recalled England, and to my mind dear Hampshire.

The personal *milieu* was equally cheerful. Friends whom I had last welcomed in my mountain camp of Kaghan competed in offering pleasant evenings after the day's toil. There was encouraging company in the person of a genial 'Padre,' the Rev. G. A. Campbell Bell, an earlier occupant of the Circuit House. We had scarcely had more than a meal together when he eagerly enquired whether I could not take him to Turkestan as my chaplain! I wondered, if my spiritual needs could have been provided for in that good old fashion, whether he would not have found the desert too lonely a region for his sociable spirits, nurtured at St. Edmund's Hall, Oxford. But even with all this to brighten the last busy days in civilization, I felt heartily glad that they were drawing to an end.

CHAPTER II

On April 24th, 1906, all the heavy baggage in charge of the two Ram Singhs had been started ahead to Fort Chakdara, where our journey was to commence in earnest. Two days later, in the evening of the 26th, the tonga carried me, too, down from Abbottabad after a cheering send-off by kind friends. Little did it matter that a sudden storm drenched me and my light baggage before we had got fairly clear of the foot-hills. The swollen Haro River was crossed without much trouble and the midnight train duly caught at Hassan Abdal; but I vainly kept the train waiting for some time in the hope that my Peshawar cook would also arrive. He had started four hours before me, but the heavy downpour would, of course, suffice as an excuse for delay. So my old Pathan orderly had to be left behind to catch the belated and probably not too willing traveller, with orders to deliver him safely, as early as possible, at Chakdara.

Long before daybreak we had crossed the Indus at Attock. As the narrow-gauge train was carrying me slowly through the breadth of ancient Gandhara, the classically barren hill ranges towards Swat and Buner greeted me in the early morning. From far away to the east the great mass of Mount Mahaban sent its farewell just as the sun rose, a familiar vision to me, and yet quite as imposing as in the days before I had set foot on its heights in 1904 as the first European to explore the alleged site of Alexander's Aornos. The rain of the night had laid the dust all over the big fertile valley and beautifully cleared the serrated outlines of the rugged ranges which stand guard over it against the trans-border.

1. VIEW FROM MALAKAND FORT, LOOKING NORTH INTO THE SWAT VALLEY.

Open ground below, on left, marks the position of Crater Camp.

From the little station of Dargai, where the railway line fitly ends within a fortified outwork, the tonga carried me up rapidly to the Malakand Pass, now crowned by frowning forts and walls. The Political Agent's Bungalow, where Major S. H. Godfrey, C.I.E., hospitably received me, was full of cherished reminiscences from visits I had paid there to Colonel Deane before and after the last great tribal rising. Major Godfrey's kind forethought had arranged all details of transport and escort for the crossing of Swat and Dir. So there was little to discuss now, and plenty of time left to enjoy the glorious view which opens from the steep bare hillside into the rocky defile north of the Malakand and across the rich Swat Valley beyond (Fig. 1).

In all clearness I saw again the blood-drenched gorges and slopes covered with huge boulders where the Pathan tribes had in that fateful summer of 1897 delivered their desperate attacks night after night. Crater Camp, then so heroically held in the face of overwhelming odds, has long ago been abandoned, death-trap as it was in truth. But delightfully mediaeval towers, with machicoulis and all the defensive contrivances which 'tribal-proof' fortification has resuscitated, crown the rocky crests around; they would render a repetition of those frantic onslaughts impossible, whatever waves of fanaticism may pass in the future over Swat and the wild hill tracts beyond.

That civilization had set in fast on the Malakand was brought home by the conspicuous appearance of its true pioneer on the Frontier, 'the British Baby.' Mrs. Godfrey's charming little children played about on the verandah with all the frankness and freedom of officially accredited babies. I heard that now even regular children's parties might be seen on the Malakand, where, in 1897, the existence of ladies and children had to be strictly kept from official knowledge. Other aspects of life, too, had softened. Beautiful roses and sweet peas were growing in little beds cut out with no small trouble from the rocky slopes near the Political Agent's Bungalow, and excellent strawberries were placed before me as proud produce of Malakand gardens!

After a final consultation about the Lowarai crossing,

I bade farewell to Malakand and its hospitable 'political' guardian. The nine miles down to Chakdara, by the splendid military road quite Roman in its breadth and solidity, were covered within an hour. Glimpses only could I get of those sites of hard fighting in 1895-97 near Khar, Batkhela, Amandara, and of the pretty side valleys of Shahkot and Charkotli, where I had once explored interesting old ruins. Chakdara Fort (Fig. 2), on the grim old rocks which Nature has set to guard the passage across the Swat River, had changed little since I last enjoyed its shelter soon after the siege. But instead of the Afridis and Sikhs who had then so bravely defended it, I found stalwart men from Oudh, the 7th Rajputs, forming its garrison. Hospitable reception awaited me here, too, in spite of short notice and the exceptional demands upon the limited accommodation available. General Sir Edmund Barrow, commanding the Peshawar Division, with his staff had just arrived on inspection. My evening passed most pleasantly in the Mess, a simple room but gorgeously adorned with the regiment's 'art acquisitions' from Peking. If any, the brave Rajputs who first relieved the Legations had a right to display such exquisite loot. To me it seemed like an invitation from the distant Cathay I was bound for. Heartily glad, too, I was for the chance which had allowed me at this outpost to meet again the distinguished and far-travelled general who had more than once shown kind interest in my explorations. I owed gratitude to him, also, as the original author of that excellent guide to all the mountains between Oxus and Indus, the confidential *Hindukush Gazetteer* of the Indian Intelligence Department.

The morning of April 28th found me busy with letters from daybreak and then supervising the distribution of the twelve mule-loads to which our baggage was to be restricted. By 11 A.M. the wretched much-belated cook was at last safely delivered under a Levy escort from Dargai, alive and well, but looking distinctly crestfallen. Half an hour later my caravan filed out of the Fort gate, and I, too, soon cantered after it, buoyed up by kind wishes of luck and by thoughts of the freedom before me.

2. CHAKDARA FORT, SWAT VALLEY, SEEN FROM NORTH.

3. SHIKARAI HAMLET ABOVE DIR, WITH DIR LEVIES ON ROAD.

My journey was to take me not only to distant regions but also far back in the ages. So it was doubly appropriate that its first march should lead over ground full of ancient associations. I knew that in the open fertile valley of Uch, through which I was riding northward, the much-injured ruins of Buddhist Stupas and monasteries were dotting the low spurs, just as at so many points of ancient Udyana along the Swat River. But there was no time now to revisit them.

Soon as the road turned to the west towards the Katgala Pass which divides the Swat and Panjkora drainage, my eyes were delighted to catch sight again of the picturesque ruins of ancient towers and dwellings rising above the scrub-covered slopes on the left. In the burning afternoon sun they looked, indeed, what their local Pashtu name, 'Saremanai,' derived from the colour of the sandstone material, calls them, 'the red houses.' That a thousand years at least has passed over these remains of Buddhist Udyana is certain. But more fascinating vistas rose before me as, hurrying on through the oscillating glare of the first hot-weather day, I thought of the tempting suggestion, discussed only the night before with General Barrow, that Alexander on his way from the Kunar Valley to Gandhara and to Aornos must have marched by this route. Broad geographical facts lend support to this association. Yet, alas, just as in the search for Aornos, the extant accounts of the Macedonian's Indian campaign fail to furnish conclusive topographical evidence for this part of his route.

A glorious view from the Katgala Pass over the broad Talash Valley and across the deep-cut course of the Panj-kora made up for critical misgivings of this nature. Far away to the west the snow-covered ranges above Bajaur and Pashat closed the horizon. Between them and the green fields of Talash stretched a picturesque jumble of well-wooded low hills, ideal ground, it seemed, for those adventurous raiding parties which Bajaur used to send forth, and which are still a tangible danger for this part of the Dir-Chitral route. The numerous posts held here by Dir Levies along the road showed that the risk of such little exploits is kept in view at all times. But the frequent patrols and pickets we passed this afternoon were probably a special safeguard provided by the active Levy Jamadar of Chakdara who rode with my party.

The smart soldierly bearing of the men was evidence of the progress made during the last eight years in the organization of this useful local corps. Raised originally partly with a view to give occupation to selected 'Badmashes' of these tracts and to keep the more fiery young spirits out of mischief, the Levies had taken their share in the fighting of 1897 round Malakand and Chakdara—needless to say, on the wrong side. The composition of the corps can scarcely have changed very much; yet the Martinis they now carried showed the increased reliance placed on them. The Native Assistant for Dir, who was to see me through to the Chitral border, proudly assured me that since the new armament some two years before no rifle had yet been abstracted. In appearance I was glad to see the men still looked the tribesmen they are. With the exception of fluttering white shirts, evidently washed for once in my honour, and brand-new Pugrees of red and khaki, there was no trace of a uniform.

Considering our late start from Chakdara, the march to Sarai, the usual first halting-place, would have been enough for the day. But good reasons had decided me to push on to the Lowarai by double marches. It was getting on towards 5 P.M. when we passed the Levy fort of Sarai; yet I could not forgo my intention of using what remained of the day for my first piece of archaeological survey work. At the hamlet of Gumbat, some two miles to the south-west of Sarai, I had found in 1897 the comparatively well-preserved ruin of an old Hindu temple, closely resembling in plan and style shrines I had, in times gone by, surveyed in the Salt Range of the Punjab. There had been no time then to effect a proper survey, and now, too, Fate willed that the work had to be done in a hurry. Luckily, Naik Ram Singh was now riding along to assist me.

As our ponies scrambled up the terraced slopes of the hillside, along the lively little stream which spreads fertility here near the grove of Jalal Baba Bukhari's Ziarat, it amused

5. RUIN OF KARWAN-BALASI NEAR BOZAI-GUMBAZ, LITTLE PAMIR.

Ghujub Beg (Karaul Begi) on left; Muhamad Shah (Ak-sakal) on right.

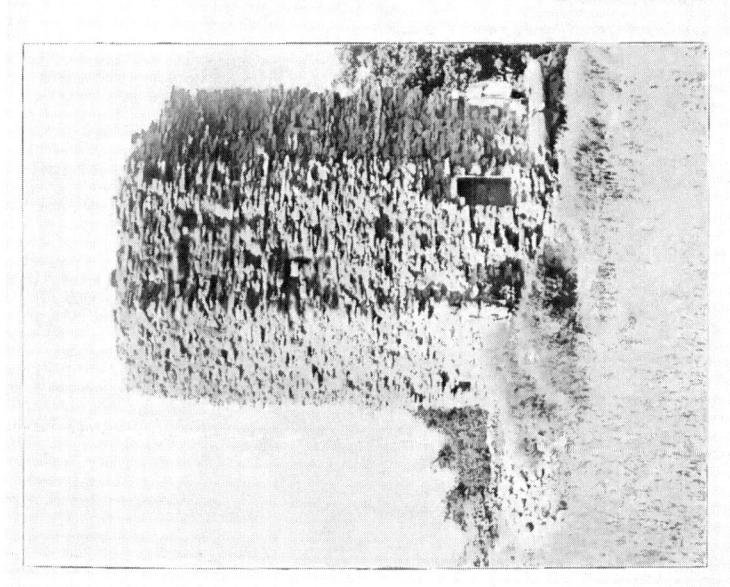

4. RUIN OF OLD HINDU TEMPLE, GUMBAT, TALASH VALLEY.

me to think how here, too, the worship of an orthodox Muhammadan saint was manifestly but a survival from the days when the ruined Hindu shrine attracted its pious pilgrims. Approaching the picturesque hamlet with its houses scattered under fine walnut-trees, vines, and Chinars, I came unexpectedly upon massive walls of Gandhara construction, reaching in places to fifteen feet in height. Some seemed to have belonged to ancient dwellings, but the majority, no doubt, had been built to support terraces of cultivation. The present Pathan settlers, quite incapable of such structures, had been content to profit by the terraces. But the ancient dwellings they had long ago quarried away, to build their huts and enclosures out of the materials.

The temple itself to which the hamlet owes its name of 'Gumbat' or dome, had, alas! suffered badly (Fig. 4). Already by 1897 most of the well-cut sandstone facing its walls had been removed, and now it was sad to find the stripping almost completed by the villagers, a strange handwriting on the wall, as it were, by approaching 'civilization.' Luckily the interior construction of the cella and the dome rising above it to a height of some twenty-seven feet was massive enough to permit of essential measurements. The arrangement of the trefoil-arched porch and what remained of the outer architectural decoration showed close relation to the style, classical in its ultimate origin, of which the temple ruins of Kashmir of the seventh to the ninth century A.D. are the best-known illustrations.

In spite of Naik Ram Singh's manful help it was getting well towards sunset before, with ground plan and elevation completed, I could hurry down through the orchards and rice-fields to the road where the main body of the escort were waiting. Luckily much of the ground before us was still level enough to be covered at a canter. The young moon, too, gave light as we rode more cautiously up the winding bridle-path towards the Kamrani Pass giving access to the Panjkora Valley near Saddo, which was our destination. Not far from the top of the pass, at times a favourite place for waylaying exploits, we were met by a party of sturdy Levies from the Saddo post

whom the Jamadar's forethought had ordered ahead. By
9.30 P.M. the mud-built little stronghold safely received us
and our baggage equally belated.

Double marches for the next two days took us up the
Panjkora Valley to the capital of the Khan of Dir. His
authority, somewhat doubtful in Talash and nearer to
Bajaur, was, for the time being, well established above
Saddo. Hence there were no small towers and Levy
patrols en route to remind us of the force which keeps the
road clear between Swat and Chitral. Yet at the posts held
by the Levies along it special precautions for the European
traveller's safety were still thought needful. The sentry
posted outside the door of the room I occupied seemed,
indeed, harmless. But the other placed outside under
the window might well have attracted the rifle thief
during the night instead of increasing one's safety. Nor
was it altogether convenient to find oneself shadowed at
every step outside the walled enclosure by a couple
of Levies. The posts themselves which served for the
nights' halts or else for my brief half-way rests, curiously
reflected in their construction the stage of political settlement reached in this region. Against raiding parties from
outside the Khan's territory they would, no doubt, offer
useful shelter; but in case of a general tribal rising their
defence could not be attempted. Seeing that the Levies
themselves are raised entirely from the Khan's men, and
scarcely as yet proof against fanatical outbreaks, it would
be manifestly risky to provide them with strongholds
such as guard Frontier routes entrusted to more reliable
elements.

The road we followed offered pleasant glimpses of
the snow-covered ranges towards Asmar and Swat, and
here and there views of picturesque fort-villages. But of
striking scenery there was little until we drew close to
Dir. The green of the corn-fields, covering the broad
alluvial fans and terraces capable of irrigation, looked
delightfully vivid below the brownish slopes of bare rock
on the spurs running down to the river. Spring at an elevation gradually rising from 3000 to 4000 feet was already
far advanced, and red poppies brightened all the fields.

From the post of Robat passed en route on April 29th I could see long streaks of snow still descending the pine-covered heights of the Laram. At Warai, where I halted for that night, I watched with misgivings clouds gathering on the snowy peaks visible far away to the north. To attempt a crossing of the Lowarai in bad weather was out of the question, and the advent of it would threaten awkward delay. So the imposing mercurial mountain barometer included in our Survey equipment was set up and anxiously consulted. It showed no fall in the morning, and the sun shone bright enough at first to make the twenty-two miles' walk I indulged in, a fairly hot business. Yet when in the afternoon I crossed, below Chutiatan Fort, the eastern main branch of the Panjkora coming from the Swat highlands, clouds had overcast the sky and the air was close in spite of the increased elevation.

The first drops of rain greeted us some five miles farther when in view of the Khan's fort and the cluster of terraced hamlets forming the Dir capital. The Levy post half a mile beyond, where the Dir Valley narrows to a gorge, offered shelter just as the downpour set in. But even if I could have indulged in hopes of a rapid change of the weather, the aspect of this shelter would have sufficed to depress me. Squeezed in between high cliffs and the left bank of the tossing river, the mud-built quadrangle was scarcely large enough for its garrison of some forty Levy Sepoys and the postal establishment working the line of Dak runners across the Lowarai. The advent of my party and of the Native Assistant's following filled the place to overflowing. Still more gloomy than the surroundings was the room set apart for my use. Though quite a recent addition to the structure, it showed already marks of rapid decay. The plastering of the rubble-built walls had come down some weeks before, and its débris littered the corners. The barred windows high up on the walls let in but a dim light, while the low-lying floor was kept soaked by steady percolation from a stream of rain-water flowing past the door and east wall.

All about me there was the sensation of imprisonment,

and for fully forty-eight hours the pouring rain continued with more or less violent thunderstorms. More depressing even than the actual discomforts of a badly leaking roof and sodden mud floor was the uncertainty as to the length of this detention. To move to the foot of the pass, one march ahead, would have been worse than useless. Any attempt to cross while such weather continued or immediately after its cessation would have meant imminent avalanche risks. So there was nothing for it but to use the time as well as I could for accounts and plenty of 'office' work still remaining, and to collect what local notes could be gathered. I managed to get hold of some Kohistanis from Garwi, still speaking one of the little-known Dard dialects which have receded to the high valleys about the head-waters of the Panjkora and are fast disappearing before the onset of Pashtu, and to secure, not without difficulties, my first measured 'heads' in anthropological interests. Old coins, too, going back to Indo-Scythian times, were obtained from a Hindu trader.

But my thoughts were ever travelling ahead to the pass and to Chitral, from which it barred me. On the evening of May 2nd there came at last a short break which I used to escape for a walk up the valley. But the rain had not damped the watchfulness of the sentries, and I had scarcely emerged from my shelter when two of the Levies faithfully attached themselves to my heels. Heavy clouds still filled the side valleys and prevented any view of the pass and its approaches. All the more delighted was I, when turning into the wretched courtyard about midnight, to see the mist completely lifted and the stars shining brightly. The sturdy little mules which had brought up my baggage were picketed close by, and it was easy to arrange for a start early next morning.

6. PATHAN AND GUJAR CARRIERS COLLECTED AT KOLANDI, ABOVE DIR; DIR LEVIES ON FLANKS.

CHAPTER III

ACROSS THE LOWARAI

MAY 3rd, when I escaped from my prison-shelter at Dir, was a gloriously clear day, and as we drew nearer to Gujar, the last summer grazing-ground at the foot of the Lowarai Pass, some 7800 feet above the sea, my spirits rose rapidly. In the tiny hamlets lower down the fruit-trees and hedges were just in blossom, while above the first shoots of grass were only beginning to sprout near the banks of avalanche snow (Fig. 3). To Mirga, the last hamlet, where Captain Knollys, the Assistant Political Agent for Chitral, was caught early in December of the previous year by an avalanche and, though nearly buried himself, by heroic exertions saved his party, the inhabitants had not yet returned. But I had already been met by a large contingent of willing carriers from Kashkar, Kolandi, Miana, who were to help in taking the baggage across (Fig. 6).

I had been warned of the grave reluctance with which the local people attempt a crossing before June. But in reality everything seemed to show that, with the peculiar indifference or ignorance which clings to Pathans in all matters of snowcraft, these hillmen would not have needed much temptation even for a crossing two days earlier, had I been prepared to indulge in so foolish a venture. It was but a fresh instance of the different aspect 'local opinion' on the Frontier assumes, according to whether it is tested on the spot or reported from a distance for official consumption.

Gujar consisted only of a tiny Levy post and some wretched huts half-crushed below that year's snow (Fig. 7). All men of the valley agreed that the snowfall had been exceptionally heavy, but were confident that loads could now be taken across safely. In spite of this local attitude I was resolved not to forgo any of the precautions I had kept in view ever since my struggle for a passage over the Lowarai commenced. Every load was lightened so as not to exceed forty pounds, or else two men were detached for carriage in turn. To reduce risks I divided the whole train of carriers into three detachments, in charge of myself and the two Ram Singhs. With each detachment I detailed four men without loads, but provided with spades and ropes to come to the rescue of any who might be in trouble. Each detachment was to keep fifteen minutes' or so walking distance from the next, to prevent too heavy a weight being brought on any treacherous snow-slope. Finally, I kept to my programme of crossing at night, and getting clear of all avalanche shoots on the north side long before the morning sun could set the snow moving.

These arrangements kept me busy all through the afternoon, and as the start was to be made by 1 A.M. I was glad enough to turn in for a few hours just as it was getting dark. By 11.30 P.M. I was up again to start the next day's work, and after a hasty 'Chota Hazri' which my cook was determined to treat as a 'supper,' I was ready to set my detachments in motion. Thanks to the previous evening's arrangements all men were quickly at their loads, and the moon shone just long enough to make it easy to keep the detachments apart. Shortly after 1 A.M. I set out with the first party of twenty men, trusty Muhammadju looking after those in the rear. By the movement of the lanterns behind I could see that Naik Ram Singh started the second detachment with military punctuality, followed by the Surveyor's party after another fifteen minutes' interval. Close above Gujar the valley bottom completely disappeared under snow. How deeply it lay was clear from the fact that no sound of the streams flowing beneath this continuous slope of snow bridges ever reached me. Huge avalanches had swept down at intervals from the steep spurs and gorges on either side for months past, leaving their tracks marked by

7. VIEW OF LOWARAI PASS FROM GUJAR POST.

The arrow indicates position of pass and snow-filled gorge leading to it.

moraine-like banks of hard snow. For the sake of the load-carrying men steps were cut in these banks by the spare men ahead with me. The advance was very slow work. But the time thus spent in ascending allowed me to realize how well the Lowarai deserves its evil reputation.

The ascent throughout lay in a narrow gorge flanked by precipitous spurs which would send their gliding masses of snow right across to the opposite side (Fig. 7). From avalanches there was here no possible place of safety. But the time for the great spring avalanches had passed by, apparently a fortnight earlier, and from any falls of fresh snow we were protected by the bitter cold of the night, which had frozen the surface hard. When the first flush of dawn showed over the spurs eastward the narrow saddle of the pass came in sight, and a little before 5 A.M. my party gained the top, *circ.* 10,200 feet above the sea.

Previous descriptions had prepared me for the abrupt fall of the northern face. Nevertheless, I was surprised to find myself at the brink of a real snow wall, some 80 to 100 feet high, and resting below on a remarkably steep slope where any heavy object once in movement would be swept irresistibly down. Where this snow wall joined on to the flanking height south-westwards, the Dak runners' track descended abruptly in narrow zigzags, the steps trodden into the hard snow being often at three or four feet vertical interval.

It was on the firmness of these steps that safety in descending depended; for any break might set the adjoining parts of the snow wall moving, though luckily it showed no signs of being corniced. No heavy loads had as yet been carried over it, and with anxiety I watched my coolies descending. It required much care on my part and a great deal of shouting to prevent over-crowding; but I felt heartily glad when at last I could start down and escape the icy wind sweeping the crest. Khan Muhammad Kuli Khan, the Native Assistant for Chitral, whom Captain Knollys had kindly sent to meet me, had carried his attentive care to the point of ascending the pass from Ziarat, the first Levy post on the north side. Not being encumbered with baggage he had reached the crest just before me, and his Chitralis were most useful in helping my men down.

There was little temptation for any of them to tarry long on the precipitous snow slope which lay below the crest wall and only some 1200 feet farther down assumed an easier gradient. They all knew that in this avalanche couloir there lay buried the twenty-four unfortunate men who had been overwhelmed by falling masses of fresh snow in the preceding December, when the Mehtar of Chitral, returning from the Prince of Wales's reception at Peshawar, had insisted upon crossing in the face of a snowstorm. The loss of the seventeen ponies which perished on the same occasion appealed, perhaps, even more to the men's imagination; for human lives have never been valued high in this region. About half-way down this incline, which seemed almost too steep for glissading, we came upon the trail of a quite recent avalanche. According to the Native Assistant's statement it had descended early on the previous afternoon—just as I had expected might happen after the two wretched days spent in Dir.

Where the formidable snow-shoot from the pass was joined by some smaller gorges and the meeting masses of snow had thrown up a mighty barricade, I halted to let the whole convoy assemble. A dangerous place, the Chitralis called it, earlier in the season; but now the coagulated dark surface here and lower down in the gorge showed that it lay well beyond the actual avalanche zone. While I refreshed myself with cold tea and a hurried breakfast of sorts, the watching of the straggling parties behind afforded amusement. I only wished the light of the early morning in this confined debouchure had been strong enough to permit of a snapshot at my new cook. With three nimble Chitralis to support him he was brought down more like a log than an animate being.

The next three miles' descent to Ziarat seemed easy, though snow choked the bottom of the gorge to a great depth. The high snowy range which divides the main valley of the Chitral River from the Bashgal portion of Kafiristan, rose in glorious tints before me. The sides of

8. GORGE NEAR ZIARAT, BELOW LOWARAI PASS.

the gorge became more and more wooded, and the many fine fir-trees and pines which avalanches had swept down into the snow-bed, delightfully scented the air (Fig. 8). How often had I enjoyed this avalanche perfume in the gullies descending from high forest-clothed Margs in Kashmir and Kaghan! As we approached Ziarat my Chitrali guides pointed out the huge avalanche which four weeks earlier had swept down a precipitous side valley and almost overwhelmed the block-houses of the Levy post.

It was a comfort to view this snow monster, recalling by its furrowed contortions the dragons drawn in old maps of the Alps to mark glaciers—and to think that we were safe now from risks of this kind. But still greater was the relief as I counted men and loads all complete before the smoke-begrimed log walls. After the endless writing, etc., it had cost me to secure my passage through Chitral, I could not help looking back with some triumph to the pass now safely behind me. The great obstacle had been taken without running any needless risks. I hastened to send off this news to friends on the Frontier through a runner who carried my telegrams to 'wire end' at Fort Drosh.

Soon after 8 A.M. the loads were transferred to the Chitrali carriers kept ready at the post, and the Pathans from the Dir side were paid off with a liberal Bakhshish into the bargain. It was delightful to feel in a new region, and pleasant also to realize by the mere look of the men who had greeted me on the Chitral side that the need of carrying a revolver lay behind me for good. As we descended rapidly towards Ashret, the first Chitral village, bits of the well-made road to the pass emerged here and there from the snow-beds (Fig. 9). At last where luxuriant jungle growth clothed the mountain sides some 6000 feet above the sea the snow was finally forsaken for the road. Curiously enough it offered here more chances of accident than where completely effaced. The wire of the telephone line connecting Ziarat with Fort Drosh had, of course, broken down during the snowy season, and now lying dishevelled across the road, it formed in places regular wire entanglements.

In Ashret village, 4800 feet above the sea, it felt
quite warm, and the hour or so it took to pack our loads on
a miscellaneous crew of lean mules and ponies was anything but a rest.   The Native Assistant had done his best
to raise local transport.   But in a territory where the
maintenance of about two hundred Commissariat mules
practically exhausts all available fodder resources, privately
owned animals must have a bad time until the summer
grazing on the mountains commences.   Most willing and
polite the Chitralis seemed compared with the sullen or
jaunty Pathans whom we had been in contact with during
the previous days ; but all their bustling attention could
not make loads stick on rickety riding saddles when every
rope seemed to break.   More than one of the poor animals
would have broken down on the sixteen miles still to be
covered to Drosh, or else have deposited its load down the
' Khud,' had not the Mehtar's officials sent to escort me
managed always to produce some willing ' hands ' to keep
the loads going.

   That I had stepped into a different world, racially and
politically, was brought home to me by the interesting
figures of my new local attendants.   There was the
energetic and lively son of the Hakim or governor of
Drosh, with the looks of a somewhat unkempt young Celt,
whose good-natured hustling and pushing the country folk
seemed always ready to receive with respect and humility.
Except for his curled-up felt cap, the national head covering of all ' Dards,' he had donned clothes cut in the
European fashion but of Chitral homespun.   Old Kurban,
a regular factotum and guide for all Sahibs whom duty
brings to Chitral, still wore the wide flowing brown Choga
of the Chitral gentry and high red leather top-boots of
local make (Fig. 17).   But he had attached himself too
long to the ' Sirkar's ' interests—he had fought with Sir
G. Robertson's escort during the Chitral siege—not to
adopt divers Indian importations in the form of Sam Browne
belt, etc.   More useful for me was it that he had learned
to talk, not fluently, it is true, but intelligibly, that queer
jargon, the Sahibs' Hindustani. I readily attached him to my
side as interpreter and fountainhead for local information.

9. SNOW-BEDS OF AVALANCHES FROM SIDE VALLEY OF
BUZAGOL, ABOVE ASHRET.

10. IN TANGI-TAR GORGE BELOW TAR-BASHI.

Line of holes cut into foot of rock (p. 100) is seen on left.
Kirghiz riding on yaks in foreground.

However great my interest in Chitral and all the petty hill states around it where the 'Dard' tribes have dwelt from the very dawn of Indian history, I had never found time to study Khowar, the language of Chitral, or any of its kindred dialects for practical purposes. Hence Kurban's presence was, indeed, a boon from the very first hour. He seemed to know every rock and field by the roadside, and his relationship to the Mehtar, rather distant as it may seem to us—he prided himself upon being the husband of the foster-mother of the ruler's eldest son— assured him unfailing authority among the country folk.

It felt hot and close in the Ashret Nullah, and perhaps I failed in consequence to pay as much attention as Kurban expected from a lover 'of old things' to the precipitous rock face from which the bloodthirsty Kafirs raiding across the Chitral River used to swoop down of yore on travellers from and to Dir. At the latter place I had found the terrors of these Kafir raids, the last of which apparently preceded the Chitral Relief Expedition by a few years, still vividly remembered. But when I had turned the rocky spur at the debouchure into the main Chitral valley, all heat and fatigue was forgotten. Enclosed between mighty ranges still crowned with snow, the valley wound away northward with imposing breadth and a variety of striking vistas. At the point where I had first struck it, the picturesque fort of Mirkandi, built on precipitous cliffs some two hundred feet above the river and for ages the frontier guard station towards Asmar, formed a fit gateway.

Whether it was the view of the huge bare detritus slopes descending for thousands of feet from the flanking ranges, or the curious light blue of the sky so different from its Indian aspect, or perhaps only the wide expanse of rock-strewn waste with its tiny oases of green dotted over alluvial fans, the sensation came over me that I had already regained Central Asia. With joy I greeted the familiar scent of the wild-thyme-like scrub which covered patches of less stony ground by the roadside. It brought back vividly happy days of travel through barren valleys in Sarikol and in the T'ien-shan. On the move since midnight, I felt the wearisome slowness of the nag I was riding and kept looking out eagerly for Drosh Fort. When at last it came in sight from a projecting small spur, the wonderful clearness of the air wholly deceived me as to the distance, still fully six miles.

Galkatak, the first village we passed, delighted my eyes with its large grove of Chinars and its Ziarat full of quaint mud-built tombs and fluttering flags, a true Turkestan sight. But gladder still was I when I rode up to the trim west wall of Fort Drosh and learned from an amiable note of Captain Wordell, the Station Staff Officer, of the hospitable reception awaiting me among the officers of the Chitral garrison. Soon I was met by its writer, who, with the same friendly care I had so often experienced in out-posts of the North-West Frontier, lost no time in looking after my comfort and that of my men. Rai Sahib Ram Singh found a cousin to welcome him among the men of the 39th Garhwal Rifles, who formed the majority of the garrison. Naik Ram Singh was entrusted to the care of the Jamadar of the Sappers' and Miners' detachment as a comrade in arms, and I myself finally conducted to the Mess for tea and to the room reserved for me in the officers' quarters. They occupy the topmost part of the steep slope enclosed within the fort, and to reach them meant a great pull for the straggling baggage animals. So it grew late before I could indulge in the much-delayed tub of the day.

From Colonel R. H. Twigg, commanding the 39th Garhwal Rifles, and his officers I met with the kindest attention. Their Mess looked quite a centre of civilized comfort. Apart from the few detached officers in Chitral, I was the regiment's first guest since its arrival some eight months earlier. But this undeserved distinction would scarcely account for the friendly interest which my hosts showed in my journey and plans. It was easy to recognize the fascination which the Pamirs and other Central-Asian regions just beyond the mountain walls must exercise upon every British officer whom duty brings to this outlying bastion of the North-West Frontier. The regret which more than one of my hosts at the Mess table expressed at not being able to join my party was genuine enough, I could see. So it was a comfort to feel that Chitral with its splendid shooting of ibex, markhor, etc., practically reserved for this dozen and a half of officers, had compensations to offer even to the most eager among them.

I shall not easily forget the cheerful hours I passed among these keen soldiers and sportsmen, or the stirring performance of Highland airs by the regimental pipers marching round the Mess table. Fatigue was soon forgotten in such animated surroundings. Yet I felt grateful for the rest to which at last I could retire about midnight, after having had only a couple of hours' sleep since first dawn of the day before. From Gujar I had covered a distance usually reckoned as three marches, and a good portion of it over snow on a pass unusually trying.

CHAPTER IV

IN CHITRAL

In spite of the strongly pressed offers of further hospitality, I set out in the forenoon of May 5th from Drosh for the double march to the Chitral capital. I was eager to meet there Captain E. Knollys, the Assistant Political Agent, and to commence my antiquarian and anthropological enquiries. It was a long day's ride, some twenty-six miles by the road, and lengthened still further by the visit I paid to an inscribed rock on the left river-bank beyond Gairat. The sun shone from a specklessly clear sky all day, and its power was strong ; for Kala Drosh lies only 4300 feet above the sea and Chitral but 600 feet higher. But in spite of the heat I could not have wished for a more enjoyable introduction to ground and people in Chitral proper.

At Kala Drosh the presence of a relatively large garrison with its Commissariat lines, Bazar, etc., imparts a certain Indian air to what was before 1895 only a cluster of hamlets scattered over a broad alluvial plateau. In the fine grove of Chinars just below the fort I had even passed the whitewashed structure of the 'Victoria Reading Room,' a curious proof of the presence in strength of those worthy Babus whom the non-combatant branches of an Indian force are bound to drag with them to the remotest outposts. But once beyond the rifle ranges constructed in the little plain where the Shishikuf Valley with mighty snow-clad peaks in the background joins in from the north-east, I had true Chitral to myself. Bare and bleak the rocky spurs rose on either side, with broad talus shoots along their faces where falling stones are a frequent danger after every fall of rain or snow. Yet the great difficulty which this main route of Chitral presented before the good bridle-path was made, could be realized only when we turned round the precipitous rock face near the little hamlet of Kes. A five-foot bridle-path cut into the rock wall or carried over well-constructed galleries and supporting walls was a comfortable track to look down from into the river tossing some three hundred feet below. Reminiscences of the Hunza 'Rafiks' and all their amenities rose before me as I pictured to myself what this route meant some ten years ago. For animals, even unladen, it must have been practically impossible whenever the rising water of the river closed the narrow track over boulders and sand-banks far below by the water's edge.

The boldly projecting spur of Gairat a mile or so beyond had often served as a barrier against invasion from the south. During long and anxious weeks in 1895 the Chitral Mission's escort endeavoured to stem here the threatening tide of Pathan invasion and Chitrali disaffection abetting it. The only visible marks left of that stirring episode were small stone heaps once formed into Sangars. Past the small fort since built behind this natural gate or 'Darband,' I hurried on northward to where the rock-cut inscription was said to exist. The first sight of Tirich-mir, the highest of Chitral peaks, was the main reward of this détour (Fig. 13). In imposing grandeur and isolation towered the giant, over 25,400 feet in height, far away in the north, completely closing the background of the broad Chitral Valley and dwarfing all lateral snowy ranges. The line of glacier-clad summits culminating in the Tirich-mir Peak owes much of its grandeur to this apparent isolation and the symmetry of their disposition on either side of the spire-like central peak. A worthy rival to Rakiposhi this serrated ice massif appeared to me, and a worthy theme for all the legends with which Chitral folk-lore surrounds its inaccessible summit.

The inscription I was seeking occupied a magnificent rock face rising precipitously to at least a hundred feet above the river, fit to receive the records of a 'King of Kings,'

like those of Darius on the Behistun rock. But, alas! what
a Chitrali ruler of the eighteenth or nineteenth century
had thought fit to engrave here was only a few rhetorical
couplets in Persian, turned apparently after the model of
Jehangir's famous line in the Great Moghul's palace at Dehli.
Their presence had attracted still more modern scribblings,
and, as a mark of the religious propensities of the honest
Gurkhas usually forming the Chitral garrison, plentiful
signs of Siva's trident. Hastily we rode back to Gairat; for
the afternoon was advancing, crossed the wire suspension
bridge between two almost vertical rock spurs, and then
hurried on over the narrow zigzagging path towards Chitral.

Elsewhere it might be thought a test for one's nerves
to trot along such a precipitous track with the river
hundreds of feet below. But one soon learns to share the
Chitralis' unbounded confidence in their ponies. Even
my apprehension about the cameras gaily jolting along on
the back of mounted Chitral Levies was allayed by the
remembrance how one of them had tumbled down with
his pony from the path on the opposite bank close to the
inscribed rock without the camera sustaining any damage.
The fall luckily had been only of five or six feet, though it
made the Sowar insensible for a few minutes. On a large
alluvial fan formed by the river draining the Bambureth
and Kalashgum valleys we passed a series of pretty
hamlets collectively known as Ayun (Fig. 11). Ensconced
in groves of walnut and Chinars each looked a rural
picture; but there was time only for rapid glances at the
lovely green swards stretching between hamlet and hamlet.

Pleasant, too, were the meetings with villagers in
groups, lounging under the trees or returning from their
fields. Their bearing seemed at all times polite and full
of good-natured ease. Ten years of British control have
sufficed to teach young and old a relatively smart imitation
of the military salute. Well built and slim in gait, these
Chitralis impressed me as the most taking representatives
I had as yet met of the Dard race (Fig. 12). With their
clear, sharp-cut features, fair complexion and hair, they
reminded me of types common at the Italian foot of the
Alps. Seeing how close the affinity in language and race is

11. BASHGALI KAFIRS SETTLED AT AYUN, CHITRAL.

12. CHITRALI VILLAGERS COLLECTED FOR ANTHROPOMETRICAL
EXAMINATION.

between the Chitralis and the Galcha tribes north of the Hindukush, those typical representatives of the 'Homo Alpinus' in Asia, this resemblance is not difficult to account for. Something in the long ample garments, usually of brown wool, the round caps with upturned brims, and the rich locks hanging down to the neck, seemed to project these figures into Southern Europe of the late middle ages.

Callous and born conspirators Chitralis have often been called, and the tangled web of intrigue, murder, and treachery which constitutes what is known of the modern political history of the little mountain state seems fully to support this description. But with all the vices which these kaleidoscopic usurpations and betrayals reveal in the leading classes, good manners and cultured ways of enjoyment do not appear to have suffered. Pliability and polished discretion were, no doubt, needful for all when the chances of sudden misfortune were so constant and near. Every palace revolution threatened property and life of the petty aristocracy, the Adam-zadas, while the Chitral chiefs' practice of selling their subjects as slaves into neighbouring hill states from personal spite or for financial profit must have carried insecurity into the humblest household. Perhaps the lightening of the struggle for life which such checks on the population brought about has helped the Chitrali to retain much of good-natured humour and fondness for all pleasures of existence.

The last eight miles into Chitral showed little but barren slopes of rock and detritus. But from the height of the Atani spur Tirich-mir came into view once more, a glorious mass lit up in red and gold tints by the setting sun. It was getting dark when, rounding the great boulder-strewn spur opposite Chumarkhon, we emerged upon the broad valley containing the Chitral 'capital.' As I cantered ahead between the fields I was met by Captain E. Knollys, the Assistant Political Agent, who had come to offer kind welcome. Once only had we seen each other far away on the Bannu border; but the mile or so we rode slowly along engaged in cordial talk sufficed to

make me feel quite at ease in the grand place which now
hospitably received me. In the midst of a fine old garden
there rose on terraced ground the Chitrali house which
had served as the Political Agent's residence before the
upheaval of 1895. How delightful it was to be ushered
into a suite of rooms—from their size they might almost
be called halls—which with all Western comfort combined
unmistakable proofs of genuine local architecture. Beautifully carved pillars of deodar disposed in a rectangle supported the roof, where a cleverly constructed sky-light
served as a modern but unobtrusive substitute for the
light-and-air hole of the usual Chitrali type. The large
room which was to form my quarters looked doubly
inviting by its wealth of fine carpets. With delighted
surprise I discovered among them several that had come
from Khotan, my old haunts I was longing to revisit.
Still more strangely familiar seemed to me the ornamental
wood-carving on the pillars; for many of its early Indian
motifs looked as if copied from the carved columns and
other architectural pieces in wood which my excavations
had brought to light at ancient sites of the Khotan desert.

A pleasant dinner-party, to which my kind host had
invited the two officers of the detachment garrisoning the
fort, closed a day full of novel and fascinating impressions.
It was well that a multitude of tasks obliged me to choose
Chitral for a three-days' halt; for I could thus in good
conscience take the first real rest since I had set out from
my gloomy Dir prison. With its amiable host, its spacious
ease, and all the facilities resulting from the beneficent
presence of a 'Mulki Sahib' (political officer), the Chitral
Agency struck me from the first as an unexpected anticipation, in a beautiful mountain setting, of Chini-bagh, my
cherished Turkestan base. I could not have wished for
more prompt or thorough arrangements to enable me to
collect the information and materials I needed.

Already on the morning after my arrival picturesque
crowds of Chitralis gathered on the lawns of the garden
to supply me with anthropometrical data. They had been
sent by the Mehtar to be measured, etc., and strange as
my proceedings must have appeared to these honest folk

Tirich-mir Peak, 24,310 ft.   Yarkhun River Gorge.

13. TIRICH-MIR PEAK, SEEN FROM BELOW CHITRAL AGENCY.

from outlying mountain hamlets, there were plenty of willing dignitaries at hand, from a former State Councillor downwards, to enforce discipline and impress all the victims with the importance of the occasion. By hours of demonstration on living specimens Surveyor Ram Singh was drilled into the mysteries of 'taking heads' for anthropological purposes. When I could let him continue the practice on specially selected men, under the safeguard of occasional checks, the development of photographs in the dark room improvised by Naik Ram Singh absorbed much of my time and attention.

What with these labours, the record of local traditions, adjustment of accounts, repairs, etc., my three days were, indeed, kept full to overflowing. Only to a few episodes can I briefly refer here. On the afternoon following my arrival I first met the Chief of Chitral as his guest at a game of polo played on the picturesque ground a little below the offices of the Agency. It was a pleasure to watch the plucky play of riders in whose valleys the noble game has been the honoured pastime for many centuries.

Still more interesting was the opportunity for a long talk with the ruling Mehtar, Shuja-ul-Mulk, who had succeeded to the blood-stained 'Takht' of Chitral after the events of 1895. Already in the descriptions of the Chitral siege in which he shared as a passive spectator ten years old, I had read of the excellent manners of the young chief. None of his ancestors could have displayed more of Eastern good breeding and grace than he now showed—in spite of his European clothes. We talked in Persian of the past of his land, of the relations that once bound it to the dominions of the distant 'Khakan-i-Chin,' the 'Great Khan of Cathay,' whose power asserted itself in these inaccessible valleys as late as the eighteenth century. Chitral has never enjoyed the distinction of a written history. Traditions, too, have survived only in vague outlines even for the late Muhammadan period. Hence manifest interest was aroused by what I could tell of the occasional glimpses of Chitral history which the Chinese Imperial Annals reveal from the seventh century onwards.

Tea and cakes served in true European fashion

refreshed us while the match proceeded at a rate which would have tired out any but the wiry hill ponies that Chitral still manages to secure from neighbouring Badakhshan in spite of Afghan export prohibitions. Half the population of the villages which make up the capital seemed to be gathered on the green slope behind to watch its progress. When at last the conclusion of the match was announced with great din by the local band on long curiously shaped horns and kettle-drums, there followed the dance of the defeated side for the delectation of the victors and onlookers. Needless to say that the performance, prescribed by ancient custom, is little cherished by those who have to partake in it, and a few capers perfunctorily gone through was all to which we were treated. The Chitráli dances by selected young men which followed were far more interesting. There was plenty of rhythm and verve in the movements, which at one time seemed to recall the steps of the Hungarian Csárdás, at others again the gyrations of a Khattak sword dance. An avowedly Pathan dance closed the entertainment, clearly suggesting that influence from the south may well have had its share in shaping this national pastime.

But for the presence of the small group gathered round the Mehtar's tea-table, all before my eyes, I felt, might have been witnessed by a visitor to Chitral centuries ago. The airy beings with which popular belief fills all the valleys and heights of Chitral seemed to have felt the same; for plenty of fairies were said to have been seen flitting round the polo-ground at the previous match played two days before in Captain Knollys's presence. Their appearance was the great topic of Chitráli talk, being held to forebode deaths and violent events at the Mehtar's castle. But this has at all times held factions divided by bitter feuds, and the young Mehtar himself was not shy in talking composedly about the fairies' latest visit. If it was to bring evil to those around him, might it not fall on those least desirable in his *entourage*?

The same evening I had an opportunity of appreciating the young Mehtar's sociable adaptation to European ways at Captain Knollys's dinner-table. It was pleasant to chat

14. MOSQUE IN GROVE OF CHINARS (BAZAR-MASJID), NEAR CHITRAL AGENCY.

at ease about themes time-honoured in Chitral. Yet the forces and currents now at work in shaping its political destinies are not to be fathomed and gauged even in this seeming intimacy. I learned enough to realize that the use to be made of the full powers recently bestowed upon the Mehtar means something of a problem, if not for him, perhaps, at least for those called upon to watch their effects on the people.

Ten years' administration virtually under British guidance must necessarily have produced deep-going changes even among the most conservative hill-men. A return to the patriarchal despotism of former Mehtars seemed all the more fraught with risks as the presence of a British garrison effectively closes that traditional safety-valve, murder or usurpation by a conveniently handy rival. The very *pax britannica* must earlier or later raise grave economical problems ; for the population, no longer checked by slave-selling and feudal fighting, is bound to increase rapidly, while the reserve of arable land still unoccupied is likely to be exhausted within a measurable period. The problem is how to allow due scope to the chief's legitimate wish to rule in fact as well as in name, without at the same time rendering the people discontented with the power which has indirectly brought about all these changes. May it be solved by forethought and without bitter experiences on either side !

My return visit to the Mehtar gave an opportunity of seeing his castle, the site of the memorable siege of 1895. It still retains the high square towers, then the mainstay of the defence, and around it the groves of old Chinars from which the Afghan sharpshooters found it so easy to harass the garrison. But various alterations and additions to the great pile of rubble and timber made it difficult to locate all the incidents. The mosque and open galleries in the outer court of the castle still show plenty of quaint old wood-carving. Curious, too, is the high iron-plated gate through which more than one successful pretender has forced his way to the blood-stained ' Takht ' of Chitral. Outside it, near a praying platform shaded by magnificent Chinars, there rises a small structure, ugly in its unmistakable imitation of Indian 'Public Works' style, and significant for its purpose—the Mehtar's new school. How grateful I felt that I could with a good conscience forgo the inspection !

During most of my stay in Chitral the weather was cloudy and threatening. Yet after the day's 'rush' and toil I always managed a short excursion to one or other place in the close vicinity where remains of antiquity were reported. More instructive than these remains themselves were the rides that took me there. For some miles above and below castle and Agency the valley is a closely cultivated oasis, one hamlet with its orchards and avenues almost touching the other (Fig. 14). In Dawawish, under luxuriant walnut-trees, I was shown a roughly built house supposed to date back to the times of the 'Kafirs.' Outside it looked like a large heap of stones; within I found a large central room elaborately panelled in deodar black with the smoke of ages. Here, too, the decorative motives clearly recalled Gandhara work, though far more primitive in execution. The owner of this gloomy old house was a Mullah, practising also as a carpenter. Proudly he claimed the original Kafir builder of it as a fellow-craftsman. The scanty remains of old fort walls at Jughor and Uchust had little to teach me; for their materials were only unhewn stones, scarcely distinguishable in their laying, etc., from the rough walls common at present in this region. But the views across the green valley, with the barren mountain slopes behind rising abruptly to thousands of feet, were in each case lovely.

On the last day of my stay I had the good fortune to measure and photograph a number of Kafirs of the Bashgali tribe who had found a refuge in the Mehtar's territory when forcible conversion threatened them after the annexation of their old homes by the Afghans. Some two hundred families are said to be settled now in Bambureth and other nullahs above Ayun (Fig. 11), and the Mehtar had obligingly ordered a representative set to come in for measurement (Fig. 15). Quiet and harmless the men looked, in spite of their old reputation for savage cruelty in the days of independence. Only the shaven fore-part of

15. BASHGALI KAFIRS, ANTHROPOMETRICALLY EXAMINED AT CHITRAL AGENCY.

the head and the hair hanging down behind in wild tresses suggested the semi-barbarian. The anthropometric data I could collect were mainly of interest as proving the close affinity of these Kafirs with the more civilized Dard tribes farther east, as already suggested by linguistic evidence. But what a rich harvest could be gathered here by the student of old customs and folk-lore ! Most of the refugees still adhere to their old 'heathen' creed, an inheritance probably from the days when the Dard tribes separated from the Iranian race, to be 'shelved' as it were for ever in the inaccessible valleys of the Hindukush.

Want of time and of knowledge of their language rendered it impossible for me even to touch this rich mine of anthropological lore so temptingly ready at hand. But by Captain Knollys's kind care I was treated on the eve of my departure to a Kafir dance, in some respects the weirdest spectacle I have ever witnessed. It took place late at night in a grove near the Agency, by the light of a huge bonfire. The dance was performed by about fifty men and youths, some clad in their proper dancing robes of deep red, others just as the Mehtar's summons had found them. All carried small axes, the rhythmical twirling and switching of which is an essential accompaniment of the dance. How I wished I were possessed of sufficient choreographic knowledge to have kept a record of the quaint steps and gyrations which followed each other with almost automatic precision ! Whether moving forward and backward in a big circle, filing off into rows which swung round the bonfire, or resolving into pairs as in the chain of Lancers, the men kept wonderfully exact time.

Yet the music seemed scarcely to mark any change, consisting of the simplest set of tones curiously recalling a pheasant's call. For days this 'melody' haunted my ears ; but quite unmusical as unfortunately I am, I cannot attempt to describe it more closely. Performed in their own villages on specially constructed sounding-boards the effect must be still greater. For nearly an hour the dance went on, practically without the men ever stopping. By the glittering eyes and the growing *abandon* of the dancers one could watch the exciting effect of the performance. There was, alas! nobody to tell me what each phase of the dance was supposed to symbolize, or of the feelings of the men. Was it with dances of this kind that the safe return from victorious raids on their Muhammadan neighbours was celebrated? All I could learn from those who had witnessed similar dances before was the numbers of human victims the more prominent performers could claim. There were a few jovial-looking men who enjoyed credit for having slain from forty-two 'enemies' downwards. That the number of 'heads' included in each case women and children, for which Kafir raiders never had any mercy, was a detail scarcely calculated to bring these heroes humanly nearer.

With the Afghan subjugation completed within the last ten years or so, the struggle carried on by the Kafirs for so many centuries against their Muhammadan neighbours north and south has probably now closed for good. Thinking of the untold misery that must have accompanied this unrelenting savage warfare, one cannot regret the end. Yet the thought was oppressing that I had witnessed a scene which after a generation or so will never be seen again, and that with this ancient race now doomed to absorption much old-world lore was passing away which no amount of scholarly acumen could ever recover. May this last settlement of true Kafirs yet find its student before it is too late!

CHAPTER V

THROUGH MASTUJ

It was hard to tear myself away from Chitral, so full of interesting people and things, and from my accomplished host, brimful of the local knowledge needed to explain them. But apart from my eagerness to approach Turkestan quickly, there was another strong reason for an early start northward. Already on my arrival I had been greeted by the news that four messengers from Wakhan had reached Chitral to report that all arrangements had been made at Sarhad for my reception on Afghan soil. Under the orders of the general commanding in Badakhshan an Afghan colonel with a company of infantry and some cavalry was said to be waiting to see me safely through the Amir's territory. Though His Majesty's 'Firman' authorizing my passage had reached me in April, nothing had prepared me for so much friendly attention. It was clear that the Afghan authorities had expected me earlier —they knew, of course, nothing of my struggle for crossing the Lowarai—and that to keep the colonel and his band waiting would imply more hardship for them and for the scanty hill hamlets obliged to feed them. So on the morning of May 9th I said farewell to the hospitable shelter of the Chitral Agency. After a thunderstorm the previous evening the sky had cleared, and I was able to sight once more and photograph Tirich-mir in its full glory (Fig. 13).

Three fairly long marches were to carry me and my *impedimenta* to Mastuj, the chief place on the upper Chitral river, here known as the Yarkhun. The route of some sixty-seven miles abounds in natural difficulties; for the valley is really nothing but a succession of more or less formidable defiles, rarely broken by alluvial fans which alone offer room for cultivation. In spite of the new bridle-path maintained by the Military Works on this important line of communication to Gilgit, the risks to the baggage from projecting rock corners and talus slopes forming natural stone shoots were not to be regarded lightly. The kindness of Colonel Twigg had allowed me the hire of trusty Commissariat mules. Yet even they with trained drivers managed to knock off loads on every one of the marches. Luckily none fell far down, and the losses were confined to supplies laid in at Chitral. Moroi, a pretty village ensconced in orchards, was our first halt after a day spent in passing gloomy gorges. From there I crossed to the right bank to examine a rock-carved inscription opposite the hamlet of Jomshili, while the baggage continued the second march by the main route along the left bank.

It proved a long day's work for me and my little party. Our trying path zigzagging up and down precipitous spurs spun out the distance to fully thirty miles, and was in places too bad even for led ponies. The interest of the inscription, however, and of the rock-carving above it amply repaid me for the trouble. The former, neatly cut in a great granite boulder by the side of the narrow track skirting the steep spur known as Pakhturinidini, proved to contain a dedicatory Sanskrit record in Gupta characters of about the sixth to eighth century A.D. Above it I found to my delight the carefully engraved representation of a Stupa, showing in accurate detail the identical architectural proportions which I had again and again observed in the ruined Stupas of Kashgar and Khotan. There were the three bases, the drum and the dome exactly conforming to the traditional precept followed by the Buddhist builders of Eastern Turkestan.

The sun, in spite of an elevation of over 6000 feet, beat down mercilessly during the hours which were needed to make a paper cast of the inscription and to prepare the rock carving for photographing. Its outlines had first to be 'picked out' from the black ground of the granite boulder, and with nothing but hard pebbles at hand this was slow work. Then the badness of the track winding along excessively steep slopes of rock or detritus retarded progress. Beyond the little village of Parpish we had to cross extensive mountain faces of gliding talus, forbidding in its absolute barrenness, and many hundreds of feet above the river. From such ground the vividly green fan of the village of Reshun, on the opposite bank at the mouth of a deep gorge coming down from a glacier-crowned peak, looked singularly inviting. The bird's-eye view we had of it showed clearly the verdant sward of the polo-ground, and by the side of it the rubble-built dwelling in which Edwardes and Fowler with their hand-ful of men had made so heroic a stand in 1895. Even the gap in the wall enclosing the polo-ground from which the two young officers had watched the game which was to end with their treacherous capture and the massacre of their men, could be made out exactly.

There was nothing about Reshun with its smiling orchards and fields to suggest such a tragedy. But the wild and desolate Kuragh defile, entered some distance above it, seemed by Nature designed as a scene for blood-shed. We passed its four or five miles of rocky wilderness in the gloom of the falling evening. There was not a tree or shrub to relieve the sombre brown of the precipitous spurs, and of equally forbidding ravines between them. Not far from its upper end had been enacted the bloodiest episode of 1895, the destruction of Ross's detachment of the 36th Sikhs. We saw from across the tossing river the shallow caves or rather grottoes by the water's edge in which that small body of doomed men had taken refuge for several days. Just a little higher up were the stone-shoots descending from almost inaccessible cliffs which the Chitralis with goat-like agility had climbed to bar retreat to the relatively open ground of Kuragh village.

I fancied I could recognize the steep rock slope up which the men, worn out by days of starvation, had tried one night to effect their escape. Was it surprising that a seemingly unscalable rock face barring their track had stopped the men from the plains of the Manjha and driven them back to their ill-chosen refuge ? When at last forced by hunger the hapless Sikhs turned to run the gauntlet of those terrible stone-shoots, the task of destruction was easy for the Chitralis high up on the crags and their Pathan allies holding Sangars across the river.

Charrun, my night's camp, seemed near enough on the map to the scattered homesteads of Kuragh; but the impossibility of getting back to the left bank without previously crossing the big tributary river of Drasan forced me to a long and weary détour. It was dark before we passed the rickety cantilever bridge of native construction near Kosht, which few but Chitrali ponies would care to face. Then a canter of a couple of miles over a boulder-strewn flat at the confluence of the Drasan and Yarkhun brought us to the ford through the latter. Grateful I felt for the torches which some villagers sent from Charrun had lit to show us the passage; for with the melting snows the Yarkhun river was a serious obstacle so low down. The cheerful shelter of my little tent was not reached till 10 P.M.

From Reshun upwards the left side of the Yarkhun Valley forms part of Mastuj, a mountain tract still as in the old days politically separated from Chitral proper. So at Charrun I was received by worthy Khan Sahib Pir Bakhsh, who with the official status of Hospital Assistant of Mastuj combines the functions of adviser and guide to the Governor of the territory (Fig. 18). Twelve years of continuous residence in these mountains have made this pleasant Punjabi familiar with almost every one of the thousand odd households which make up the population of the Mastuj or Khushwakte chiefship, as it is generally known from the race of its hereditary rulers.

So my ride to Mastuj on May 11th gave ample chance for collecting useful local information. The morning hours were spent in taking copies and photographs of a Sanskrit inscription and a rock-carved Stupa representation closely resembling those of Pakhturinidini. The large boulder on which both are engraved was brought to light in a field near Charrun only some eight years ago. Yet the lingering recollection of an earlier worship was still strong enough to induce the villagers, good Muhammadans as they have been for centuries, to treat the infidel rock-

16. OXUS VALLEY NEAR SARHAD, WITH RANGE TOWARDS GREAT PAMIR,
SEEN FROM KANSIR SPUR.
The fields of Sarhad on alluvial terrace above right river bank.

17. VILLAGERS OF BUNI, MASTUJ, WITH KHAN SAHIB PIR BAKHSH AND KURBAN
ON EXTREME RIGHT.

carvings with reverent awe and to protect them by the construction of a rude hut.

The day's march was made pleasant at intervals by villages charmingly situated on alluvial fans in the course of the rock-bound valley. Buni, with over a hundred houses, is the largest of them, and looked most inviting with its apricot and other fruit trees still in bloom. A deputation of grey-beards received me at the first fields with an offering of well-preserved pears (Fig. 17). I contented myself with touching and remitting this present —rare at this season—only to succumb to the tempta- tion of buying the same fruits when we had ridden on a short distance, as the last I was likely to see for months.

Through the pretty hamlets of Avi, Mem, Miragram, all ensconced by the side of glacier-fed rivulets which rush down from the sides of the hoary Buni-zom Peak, over 21,000 feet high, I reached in the afternoon Sanoghar. This large village abounding in orchards, where the noble Chinar trees still thrive in spite of a glacier background, forms the summer training-ground for the Chitral Scouts. This most promising local corps is organized after the fashion of the Militia raised in the Khyber, Kurram, and elsewhere along the North-West Frontier. Captain Sawyer, their commandant, hospitably offered me tea in the simple but comfortable homestead taken up as his office and residence. Much talk we had about the rugged but fascinating mountains which form such a splendid Alpine training-ground for his men, and of the still more interesting regions beyond towards the Oxus.

Then I was taken to inspect the newly-raised Mastuj company on the long-stretched polo-ground which serves for their drilling-place. It was a pleasure to see this body of lithe, alert hill-men embodied only a week ago and full of martial keenness. With men who are born cragsmen and sharpshooters, two months' initial training must go a long way, and the annual training of one month which follows seems ample to assure increasing experience. I saw here realized what I had hoped for years before when passing through Hunza : the military employment of these mountaineers whom Nature itself seems to have bred for the defence of the Hindukush ramparts. With the men so eager to show their new training, I almost regretted the antiquarian zeal which had induced me to scale previously the rugged ridge overlooking the river and known as the site of the Sanogharo-noghor, the old fort of Sanoghar. Ancient potsherds of remarkable hardness showed that the position had been occupied from an early date. It offered additional interest by commanding a full view of the Nisar-gol plateau opposite, where Colonel Kelly in 1895 had fought his successful action and cleared the way for the relief of the Chitral garrison.

At a mighty avalanche stretching right down to the river about a mile above the village I said good-bye to Captain Sawyer. Then crossing the gloomy river gorge below the wall-like cliffs of Nisar-gol I hurried on to Mastuj. It was close to nightfall when I came in sight of the capital, a cluster of tiny hamlets spread over the bare stony plateau where the Yarkhun river is joined from the south by its first main affluent, the river of Laspur. At the bridge leading back to the left bank old Bahadur Khan, the actual ruler of Mastuj and a cousin of the Chitral chief, awaited me in person with two youthful sons (Fig. 18). Though close on eighty years, the portly white-haired chief seemed still full of vigour and genuine enjoyment of life and its pleasures. He had loyally stood by the British side when the Chitralis and Umra Khan's Pathans invested Mastuj Fort, and the staunchness he then showed as governor has secured for him practical independence from Chitral. His straightforward, simple ways, full of old-fashioned courtesy withal, have made him a favourite with all European officers in Chitral.

He insisted now on conducting me to my tent, pitched in one of the few modest groves of fruit-trees of which Mastuj can boast. On the lawn around the hardy small kind of iris which has become my old friend from Kashmir and the Turkestan valleys, raised its delicately scented pale blue flowers in plenty. White plum blossoms, too, strewed the ground. Glad was I for the peace and seclusion of my little orchard, with abundance of work to

18. BAHADUR KHAN, GOVERNOR OF MASTUJ, SEATED IN CENTRE WITH HIS TWO SONS: KHAN SAHIB PIR BAKHSH ON HIS RIGHT, AND MASTUJI ATTENDANTS.

be done during my single day's halt.   The advantages of
the last telegraph office I was to see for a long time were
not to be lightly forsaken; for by its use I could send
news and instructions to far-away Europe with a saving of
nearly two weeks.   It is at the last outposts of Indian
civilization that one appreciates most the boon of 'post-
registered' telegrams *via* Bombay — and the general
cheapness of the Indian telegraph system.

From Mastuj I sent ahead two of the Wakhis from
Sarhad to announce my approaching arrival on the Oxus.
I myself, still escorted by the attentive Khan Sahib, set out
on the morning of May 13th for the journey northward.
The Yarkhun Valley, so difficult during the summer months
when the melting snows render the route by the river-bed
quite impracticable, proved owing to the early season still
easy in its nearest portion.   A double march that first day
brought me past barren rocky slopes, descending from
ranges with a crest-line of about 17,000 feet, to the hamlet
of Miragram.   At Mastuj I had said farewell not only to
the glittering pinnacles of Tirich-mir but also to the last
Chinars.   Yet in the midst of all the rugged waste of rock
and detritus the scattered hamlets along the route showed
blossoming fruit-trees, with a first crop of spring flowers
in their stony little fields.

At Brep I surveyed the remains of an ancient fort, built
of large sun-dried bricks on a small hillock of conglomerate
rising over the rubble-strewn debouchure of the Brep
stream.   Local tradition ascribes the structure vaguely to
the time of the 'Kalmak' or Chinese domination.   Judging
by the size and make of the bricks, and the hardness of
the potsherds mixed up with them, the trapezoid-shaped
fort, measuring 180 by 130 feet, might well go back to some
earlier Chinese occupation than that of the middle of the
eighteenth century.   But how could one hope to recover
datable relics at old sites in valleys which until a few
years ago knew not the use of coined money, nor could
ever have possessed many objects in metal or other hard
materials capable of artistic ornamentation?   Of the arrow-
heads said to have once been found here, I could not secure
a specimen.

At Miragram, a hamlet as pretty as its name sounds, I found a delightful camping-ground in the large orchard of the Sub-Hakim of the uppermost Yarkhun Valley (Fig. 19). By the side of Obaidullah Khan's house, with a shady stone-paved praying platform, I pitched my tent on a sward that, strewn with fallen plum blossoms, looked as if sprinkled with snow. The evening air was still and mild, and all aided the illusion that I was once more in one of the favoured little oases by the edge of the Turkestan desert. Obaidullah's house, modest rubble-built hovel as it looked from the outside, within proved a museum of local architectural ornament and household art. There were delightfully quaint bands of fresco decoration in terra-cotta, black and white, on the walls of verandahs, with motifs of the lotus, the Chakra, and four-petalled flower, looking exactly as if derived from the frescoed walls of the ancient halls I had excavated in 1901 at the Niya site. The parlour and living-room of the house showed panelled walls and carved pillars of excellent workmanship, with a display of graceful Aptabas, Chaugans, and other house-hold utensils such as I had never suspected behind the modest exterior (Fig. 20).

What with Chitral and Badakhshan carpets, an old inlaid flint-lock, and other details, I had before me a picture arranged as it were by the brush of an old Dutch painter. I did my best by camera and notes to retain a record of all that went to make up this old-world interior, while Naik Ram Singh's pencil was busy in sketching the antique designs reproduced in the wood-carving. Gladly would I have acquired the whole of this state room, if only I had had the means to move the *ensemble* and somewhere to set it up again. But to accept the carved Mihrabs, which the owner was ready to remove from the panelled walls when I examined and admired them, would have been an act of vandal destruction. For this self-restraint I had my reward when my host, evidently prompted by his women-folk who were watching from behind screens, proceeded to exhibit before my eyes the contents of the family jewel-box. The amulets, ear-rings, necklaces, etc., all showed how faithfully the silversmith's art had retained in these

19. OBAIDULLAH KHAN, WITH HIS SONS AND VILLAGERS, MIRAGRAM.

20. PARLOUR IN OBAIDULLAH'S HOUSE, MIRAGRAM.
Ceiling with sky-light of characteristic construction ; below this, open fire-place ;
carpets of local make.

far - off valleys the decorative designs and the taste of ancient India.

Shuyist, which I reached on the evening of May 14th after a long march from Miragram, was the place where the final arrangements were to be made for the move into Wakhan. At the tiny hamlets of Jhopu, passed en route after long barren slopes of rock or detritus, the bleak fields and the almost total absence of fruit-trees showed plainly the harsher climatic conditions prevailing in the upper Yarkhun Valley. Then followed the gloomy defile of Darband, flanked on either side by huge unscalable spurs (Fig. 21); decaying watch-towers helped to emphasize the great defensive strength of this natural gate of Mastuj. Where the valley beyond broadened, tracts of jungle and scrub appeared at its bottom, a clear indication that land for cultivation was not sought for here as much as lower down. Thus I was fully prepared to find Shuyist, the last village of the valley, a place devoid of resources. The few terraced fields and low stone huts I could see from my camp pitched by the sandy scrub-covered river-bank did not belie this expectation. But all the more surprised was I by the ample array of ponies and coolies which the forethought of worthy Khan Pir Bakhsh had assembled here.

There was no time for enquiries on the morning of May 15th when this modest but thoroughly capable representative of British authority in Mastuj took his leave. But when, after busy hours devoted to my last mail from Indian soil, I followed the baggage up the valley, the relative ease with which ponies and men had been secured here very soon explained itself. Instead of narrow strips of boulder-strewn ground or shingle slopes, such as the previous marches had taken me past in depressing monotony, I found myself crossing a succession of broad alluvial plateaus where arable land was plentiful. Signs of new cultivation met the eye everywhere, jungle clearings, scattered homesteads, and fields as yet unenclosed. From these new colonies of Imkip, Chitisar, Abdullah-lasht had come most of the animals and men collected at Shuyist. Yet the land actually taken up here seemed but a very small proportion, perhaps not one-tenth, of the area awaiting cultivation.

It did not take me long to realize that I had here before me by far the most extensive stretch of fertile ground within the whole of the Yarkhun Valley, offering room for settlements quite as large as, if not larger than, those forming Chitral proper. The information I gathered from the intelligent Hakim of Miragram and other local attendants clearly indicated that these recent colonists had reclaimed ground of earlier cultivation, and the sight of old-terraced fields above the fertile strips of ground taken up first by the new settlers fully confirmed it. As I rode for miles past these abandoned village lands now gradually undergoing reclamation, the sight brought back forcibly to my mind a passage of the Chinese Annals which mentions *A-shê-yü-shih-to* as the chief place of the small mountain territory of Shang-mi, or Mastuj, in the eighth century A.D. There could be no doubt that this name, which I had long vainly tried to locate, was but the Chinese transcription of an earlier form of the name *Shuyist* still applied to the whole of this large stretch of arable land.

My guides, including Kurban, were disposed to attribute the former abandonment of these lands to the increasing cold brought about by the advance of the glaciers. And the latter, indeed, began to play from here onwards a very prominent part in the landscape. Just opposite to Abdullah-lasht a huge river of ice, known as Shayos, was pushing its dark snout almost down to the river-bank. Even without this chill neighbour the climate of Shuyist, about 10,500 feet above sea, was bound to be cold, though barley and oats would grow well. But whether or not this part of the Mastuj Valley has been affected by important climatic changes during the last twelve hundred years, there remains the interesting fact that the main cause now leading to the reoccupation of this tract where cultivation had ceased for centuries, was the incipient pressure of the population, a direct result of the British pacification of the country.

Another equally extensive glacier, stretching down from a peak over 21,000 feet high, faced us from the south

26. DEFILE OF DARBAND, YARKHUN VALLEY, WITH RUINED WATCH-TOWERS, SEEN FROM NORTH.

when we pitched camp in the jungle-covered little plain of Kankhun-kuch. Just before reaching it I had sighted the glittering crest-line of the main Hindukush range, which forms the watershed towards the Oxus, and had felt elated by the thought that the Pamirs were now drawing so near.

CHAPTER VI

FROM Kankhun-kuch only two marches remained to the Baroghil Pass, that remarkable saddle in the Hindukush range which at a height of only 12,400 feet gives access to the uppermost Oxus. But before I could cross it there was another task to be accomplished, upon which I had set my heart in the face of manifest difficulties. The Darkot Pass, which leads over the glacier-crowned great range south of the highest part of the Yarkhun Valley, at an elevation of about 15,400 feet, did not lie on my route. Yet from the first I had decided to visit it; for the record preserved in the T'ang Annals of the memorable exploit by which the Chinese general Kao Hsien-chih in 747 A.D. led his force over it for the successful invasion of Yasin and Gilgit, had long ago attracted my interest to every detail of its topography. The Darkot, with its six to seven miles of glacier slope on the north face, is a trying pass even during the few summer months when it is supposed to be practicable for men and unladen animals. But at so early a season as ours, Mastuj opinion stoutly maintained that its passage had never been attempted, and was sure to prove particularly difficult that year owing to its exceptionally heavy snowfall. Fine weather was an indispensable condition for the ascent, and as I had no time to spare for patiently awaiting this good chance, I was anxiously watching the clouds which soon began to envelop the mountains after my arrival at Kankhun-kuch.

The night from the 15th to the 16th May brought rain, and though this troubled us but little at the relatively low elevation of 10,700 feet, it raised doubts about an early

visit to the pass; for I knew that the softening of the snow
brought about by such weather would greatly impede the
ascent. The march to Vedinkot, the summer grazing-
ground at the foot of the Darkot Pass, from where the
ascent was to be attempted, was short; so it mattered little
that with the rain continuing well into the morning we set
out late. The sky remained overcast, and as we ascended
the narrow gloomy valley, crossing and recrossing the
river-bed where the water was still low, I vainly watched
for a fresh breeze to clear the atmosphere for the morrow.

Fortunately there was a succession of imposing glacier
views to distract attention. From the mighty range to the
south, crowned with peaks from 21,000 to over 22,000 feet
in height, glaciers were seen descending in every side
valley and ravine. The one known as Kotal-kash has
pushed its high snout of dark ice down close to the left
river-bank, and its steady advance threatens to block
before long the course of the river itself. Just opposite
to it the path on the right bank is obstructed by precipitous cliffs rising amidst slopes where mighty boulders
are heaped up in wildest confusion. Here all loads
had to be taken off and carried by the men for some
distance. The water in the river was fortunately still low
owing to the cloudy cold weather prevailing, and repeated
crossings saved us the difficult climbs over rocky spurs
and intervening glaciers which during the summer months
practically close this part of the route to laden animals.
Yet even here at the debouchure of several gorges from
the south, terraced fields of an earlier time were recognizable amidst the desolate streaks of detritus, stretching
down from the end of the ice streams.

Where the grand Chatiboi Glacier came in view on the
south I was surprised to find a little bay of open ground on
the left bank occupied by fields actually under cultivation.
They belonged, as my Shuyist guides explained, to four
Wakhi families who had settled down here some six
or seven years ago to struggle with these semi-arctic
surroundings. Other patches of ground capable of cultivation and now claimed by these hardy immigrants were
sighted when we crossed the broad grassy shoulder of

Vedinkot facing the foot of the glacier. Behind it, in a bleak but sheltered little glen, is the usual camping-place. But I was eager to get my night's rest as close as I could to the Darkot. So the river was crossed just where it emerges from a deep-cut and narrow rocky gorge above the Chatiboi Glacier. It flows here as a raging torrent hemmed in by boulders and cliffs, and for the sake of my baggage I felt glad to find that the rough bridge thrown across it just a little above the glacier was still intact. That the latter has steadily advanced during recent years there could be no doubt; for its terminal wall, which Kurban had seen still washed at its foot by the river, on the occasion of Lord Kitchener's visit to the Baroghil in 1903, has now pushed completely across to the right bank with the river flowing in a tunnel below it.

Within full view of the glacier's right flank, as shown by the panoramic view (Plate I.), I pitched my camp on a small plateau overlooking the ice-filled ravine in which the stream from the Darkot finds its way to the river. It was a bleak spot, and the ground, still covered with large patches of snow, showed no sign of approaching spring. The clouds hung persistently low in spite of cold blasts up the valley; and when, to reconnoitre the Darkot, I ascended the spur behind, known as the Rukang Pass, 12,000 feet or so above the sea, over which the track to the Baroghil leads, there was little visible but the terminal moraines of its glacier and a forlorn little tarn which lower down receives its waters.

It required some optimism to make preparations for the ascent under such unpromising conditions. The men who were to help in the attempt had never visited the pass so early in the season and did not disguise their apprehensions about the venture. The depth of the snow overlying the glacier route to the pass was bound to be exceptional this year, and its surface would be softened by the bad weather of the last few days. I was hence in no way surprised when Kurban and the Shuyist headmen did their best to dissuade me. However, they were not expected to take a personal share in the attempt, and as a prolonged wait at the foot of the pass would only have increased the hard-

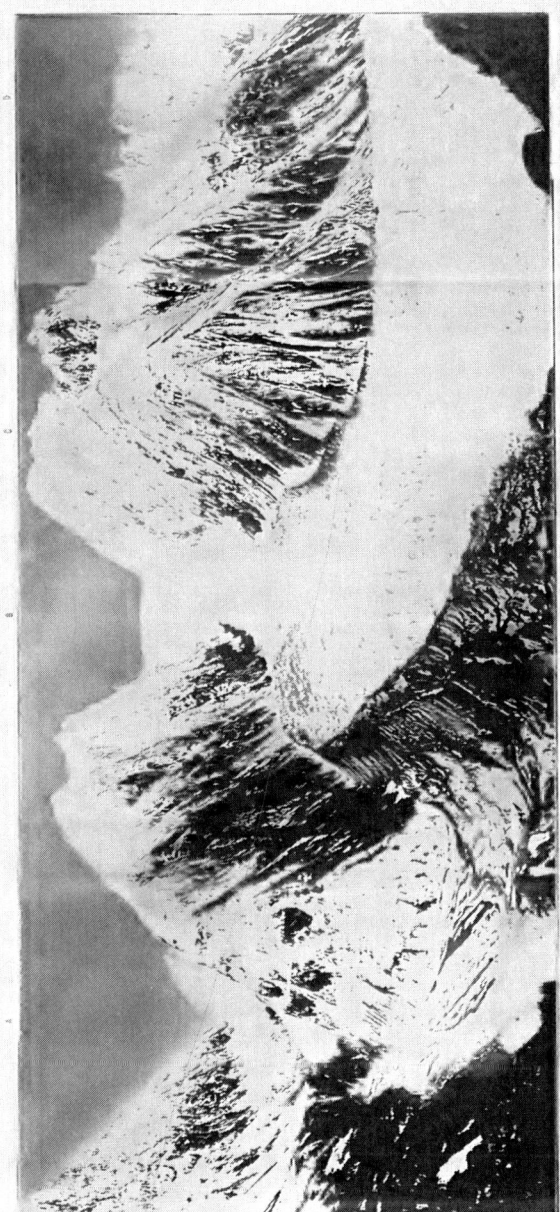

PANORAMIC VIEW OF THE GARNET AND CHATURU GLACIERS TAKEN FROM THE FOOT OF THE BURANG SPUR, LOOKING SOUTH AND SOUTH-WEST.

The scale is such that a coarse Glacier may take in the scene as the Hubbard Pass on Mt Rainier. The western of the glaciers (a, b) p. 67, broken up for part of its course at (b), in middle, that Chaturu Glacier, with its Baghra picture system at Kilimanjaro is to one, p. 68. On the right of the Garnet Glacier (g), over (d) descending from a bergschrund descending lava at the summit; the snowy span (dd) beyond Hut Peak (14,780 feet).

ship for their men and ponies, they were forced in the end to admit that it was best to let me try at once. They probably also realized my firm determination not to expose the men to any avoidable risks. In order to be prepared for any accidents arising from bad weather, I decided to carry supplies for two days and whatever else was absolutely needed to permit of our spending a night or two on the glacier without immediate danger from exposure. With a view to keeping the individual loads of food supplies, rugs, and fuel as light as possible, I fixed the number of men at twelve. Among them I included two of the sturdy Wakhis who had joined me at Vedinkot, and who from their knowledge of Persian were to me specially useful.

What with selecting the men, inspecting their kit and food supplies, and testing the ropes to be used on the glacier, it was late before I could retire for a few hours' rest. By 12.30 A.M. I got up to find not the rain or snow I had feared, but the clouds still low and a stillness in the air that gave little promise. It took some time before my Hindustani cook in these unwonted surroundings managed to produce what he persisted in calling my supper. But just then a breeze rose, and after a while the first stars showed through a break in the clouds. This sufficed to settle the question of a start, and by 3 A.M. our party was winding its way up the Rukang spur. We found the top still covered with snow, and soon realized how much its softness would delay our progress. At the relatively low elevation the cold of the night was not sufficient to freeze the surface, and wading through soft snow three to four feet deep, with occasional dips into little streams hidden below it, proved a slow and trying business.

Surveyor Ram Singh had readily offered to accompany me, though apart from a hoped-for observation of the height of the pass by mercurial barometer there was no specific topographical task for him to accomplish. But while the spirit was thus willing enough, the body of my worthy companion was bound to give trouble. Since his last great tour in Tibet, up from Gyantse to Lake Mansarowar, Ram Singh had had ample time to acquire once more the pronounced *embonpoint* which invariably distinguishes him during periods of quiescence at Survey headquarters. He had persistently stuck to his pony all the way from Chakdara, and, of course, now found the double work of ascending and wading a serious tax on his organs of breathing. In order not to let him fall behind too far, I had again and again to check our progress and make halts.

I knew that we should have to pass close below snow-covered slopes to the north of the Darkot Glacier (see Plate I.) before continuing our ascent on the glacier itself, and as risks from avalanches were likely, I had tried to get beyond them as early as possible. But the rising sun found us still in front of these steep slopes. Evidence of recent avalanches having swept down in places was plentiful, and though this sight had its effect on the experienced Surveyor, who also now endeavoured to hurry on, it was not till 7 A.M. that we got past the danger zone. The ascent over snow-covered moraines was slow work, but quite safe, in spite of the soft snow that made us sink in deep when getting too near to some hidden boulder.

An hour later we could take to the broad expanse of the glacier; but even without the warning of our intelligent Wakhi guides there was no mistaking the closely packed crevasses which furrowed its surface. The deep snow still covering the ice formed convenient bridges and proved hard enough to bear our weight. But roping was now a necessary precaution. So I proceeded to divide the men into four small parties, each on a separate rope. None of the Mastujis or Wakhis had ever climbed roped, though they must often have crossed ice slopes before and thoroughly knew their dangers. Yet it was a pleasure to watch how quickly these born mountaineers grasped the object of our alpinistic contrivance and the assurance it gave. All the way the rope was kept tight between the men, and I soon found that they could tie it into loops which would hold, far more quickly than I could myself.

The slope over which our ascent now led looked easy enough, almost like a plain between the high snowy walls emerging from the mist on either side. Though the sun had begun to shine with considerable force through the light clouds, the snow still kept reassuringly firm. Yet with all these advantages in our favour the distance of some six miles to the top of the pass cost the hard toil of nearly five hours. As soon as the worst zone of crevasses lay behind us, I pushed ahead without waiting for the Surveyor. The clear atmosphere did not last long, but sufficed to deceive us thoroughly as to the distance and slope. What again and again I took for the crest of the glacier-filled valley proved but a shoulder on that easy but seemingly never-ending slope. I began to understand the story of Kao Hsien-chih's crossing, the dismay and confusion of his Chinese troops when, brought face to face with the precipitous descent on the south side of the pass towards Yasin, they realized to what height they had ascended. As long as the sky kept clear, the high glacier-crowned range which flanks the Darkot Pass from the west, with its pinnacles of spotless white, was a vision never to be forgotten. Its central peak, close on 23,000 feet high, keeps watch over the Chatiboi Glacier on its western face, and was subsequently visible in all its glory also from the Baroghil (Fig. 24).

But the sun could not long exert its full power. White mists settled on the slopes above us, and even the spurs nearest to the glacier showed only in veiled outlines. With the mist there mingled soon a fine spray of snow particles driven down by strong gusts of wind from the pass. At first I felt glad for the coolness they brought; for the reflection of the sun had irritated eyes and skin in spite of goggles and ointment. But soon the effect of this cutting wind made one wish for some shelter or better protection than a wrap round the head could afford. It was only during the following night, when I woke up with a face badly swollen and blistered, that I realized how intense the reflection must have been from the snow of the slopes and from the glittering silvery spray. As we got higher and higher the men began to complain of the 'poisonous air' and the headaches which it caused them. Their loads were light, but the soft snow lower down had sorely tried them.

At last some time after mid-day the rocky knob came in view which rises close to where the Shawitakh Glacier branches off from the Darkot to the north-east. We were nearing at last the summit of the pass, and the broad expanse of snow became almost level. As we halted where my guides located the 'Kotal' (Fig. 22) the veil of mist lifted south-eastwards for a short while, and the rocky mountain walls flanking the uppermost part of the Yasin Valley showed up in their barren grandeur across what looked like a lake of brooding vapour. The depth of the valley below us remained hidden, except for some moments when the wind from the north of the pass gained the upper hand and cut a rift through this vapour. The change was too brief to permit of locating the south foot of the pass near the little hamlet of Darkot over 6000 feet lower down. But even this glimpse sufficed to impress one with the striking contrast which the precipitous descent here presents to the broad snowy expanse on the north.

My thoughts went back to what the Chinese Annals tell us of Kao Hsien-chih's adventurous march over 'Mount T'an-chü,' and the stratagem he had to resort to in order to get his three thousand troops to complete their successful crossing. I have related the story elsewhere. For me it was no small satisfaction to see now with my own eyes how closely the actual conditions of the Darkot agreed with the scene of the exploit of Kao Hsien-chih, the able Corean general who for the first, and perhaps the last, time led a real army across the Pamirs, and successfully pierced the great mountain rampart that defends Yasin and Gilgit from northern invasion. I could not mark my admiration for the feat by putting up the humblest cairn to his memory; for there was nothing but snow and ice for many feet below us. But I could not refrain from writing a note on the spot to my friend M. Chavannes, the great Paris Sinologist, whose learning had first revived the story of that memorable expedition, and from telling him how in my thoughts I had performed 'kotow' here to the memorial tablet of its hero.

Despite these thoughts, I could not altogether forget the troubles of my humble but faithful companions. In spite of 'poisonous air' and their loads all of them had stuck to me and now lay tired out in the snow. Some had

22. TOP OF DARKOT PASS, LOOKING TO NORTH-WEST ACROSS DARKOT GLACIER TOWARDS INDUS-OXUS WATERSHED.

Small specks of black on glacier below arrow indicate Surveyor's party.

23. ON THE BAROGHIL SADDLE, LOOKING TOWARDS OXUS VALLEY.

Wakhi carriers relieve a floundering pony of its load.

suffered badly from headache and other symptoms of mountain sickness. But the tea I carried in my large water-bottle proved a powerful 'Dawai,' and a few mouthfuls of it for each of the patients sufficed to restore better spirits, though it was respectfully observed that my medicine tasted bitter. By the time the Surveyor had struggled up we all sat contented in spite of a cutting wind and occasional drifts of light snow. The mercurial barometer was safely set up and its reading observed (17.45 inches at 44° Fahr.) which was to give us the exact height of the pass. It had been before estimated approximately at 15,400 feet.

At 3 P.M. we set out for the downward journey, pleased that we had gained our goal in the face of such forbidding conditions. Though the snow even near the top of the pass was now giving way far more than a few hours earlier, we gained the badly crevassed part of the glacier by 5 P.M. From here, however, the speed of our descent sadly slackened. Care was needed to thread our way between the gaping crevasses no longer covered by safe snow bridges. In a few places men sank in the softened snow down to their armpits, but with the support of the rope they were soon extricated. More troublesome still was the descent over the slippery crest of the snow-covered moraine, where it was impossible now to dodge sharp-cut boulders. From reasonable apprehension of avalanches and impassably soft snow my Wakhis now fought shy of the slopes we had skirted in the morning and took us instead down straight over the huge bare moraines. It was slow work to pick one's way over these confused masses of rock, tired out as our knees were by the day's climb. I felt more and more nails from my Alpine boots going, and envied the Mastujis their moccasins of stout but pliable leather.

Just as we reached the foot of the lowest moraine close to the glacier snout and were beginning to climb up once more to the Rukang spur, the clouds descended for good and soon enveloped us in thickly falling snow. Luckily Kurban had thought of my return, and correctly ascertained the route we should follow. So ponies had been sent ahead to meet me and Ram Singh, whom this first climb after more than a year's ease had wellnigh exhausted. Covered with soft snow and half wet still from wading in glacier mud and slush, I reached my tent by 8 P.M. cheerful enough. I had snatched my visit to the Darkot from the obstacles created by an exceptional winter snowfall, the early season, bad weather, and want of adequate time, and could take my rest at its close with the comforting assurance that none but unavoidable risks had been run. A sheep and ample libations of tea, this time sweetened by that cherished luxury sugar, provided a great feast for those who had shared the day's climb. The songs from the camp fires told me that contentment reigned supreme this night in spite of a steady fall of snow and the great glacier's chilly vicinity.

On the morning of May 18th I was up before sunrise, with a face so badly blistered and swollen that I thought even my best friends could not have recognized it; but the sight of a gloriously clear sky made up for all discomfort. The snow which had covered my tent in spite of repeated clearings was hard frozen. So the baggage could not be sent off towards the Baroghil until 8 A.M., when the sun had melted the hard crust. The ponies and spare men had been employed the day before to clear a track through the soft snow covering the Rukang Pass to a depth of three to four feet. Yet in spite of this pioneering it took more than three hours to get the baggage over the four miles of otherwise easy slopes separating our Vedinkot Camp from the open Maidan known as Baroghil-yailak, where the route for Wakhan strikes off from the main valley of the Mastuj river. Here, at an elevation of some 11,000 feet, snow still covered the greater part of the easy Pamir-like valley which during the summer forms a favourite grazing-ground for Wakhi shepherds from Sarhad.

Pushing on to Chikmar-robat, one of their usual camping grounds, we had no more than four miles of open valley between us and the Baroghil saddle, that remarkable depression of the Hindukush range where the watershed between Indus and Oxus drops to only 12,400 feet.

Approach to Darkot Pass.   Kalandar-ghum Glacier.   Koyo-zum Peak, 22,600 ft.

24 VIEW FROM APPROACH OF BAROGHIL SADDLE TO SOUTH-WEST, TOWARDS DARKOT RANGE.

But the attempt to reach the saddle that day soon proved hopeless, as I had feared. The warmth of that brilliantly clear day had made the snow so soft that after a mile or so walking became most difficult even for men, while the laden animals stuck helplessly after a few hundred yards. There was nothing for it but to pitch camp at Chikmar-robat, and to try to open a track for the morrow by sending ahead all ponies unladen, with every available man that could be spared.

From the easy slope above our camping-place I enjoyed a glorious view of all the high peaks which flank the Darkot, and of the mighty ice streams descending from them (Fig. 24). Chatiboi was visible in its full length, with the needle-like Koyo-zum Peak rising behind its topmost névé beds. The highest part of the glacier, known as Kalandar-ghum, and an object of Mastuji legend, has so steep a fall that it looked from this distance almost like a huge frozen cascade. The route to the Darkot lay mostly hidden. But even without the previous day's experience the glittering walls of snow and ice rising on either side would have sufficed to give an idea of the difficulties which must attend its crossing at all times. Here, too, as in Hunza, it is not the main watershed range but the mountain chain south of it which forms the true rampart against northern invasion.

In spite of the messengers sent ahead from Mastuj there was no sign yet of the hoped-for men and transport from the Afghan side coming to meet us. As the evening drew on news was brought that the ponies had exhausted their strength in pushing through the snow to the 'Kotal' and could not advance down the Wakhan side, where the snow lay equally deep. The prospect of making the same tired animals cross laden next morning seemed slight, indeed, and the available number of men was far too small to give a chance of effecting the transport by their means without spending some days on the pass. So the outlook was decidedly gloomy until late in the evening, when a letter arrived from the Afghan Colonel of whose presence I had heard already at Chitral. It promised fresh ponies and all needful help for the morrow. The lively young

Wakhi, Ghajab Beg, who had brought the Colonel's message and who introduced himself as the ' Karaul Beg,' or chief of the local frontier guards, had plentiful details to relate about all the arrangements made weeks before to receive and help me onwards.   So the spirits rose rapidly in my camp, while I felt more grateful than ever for H.M. the King of Afghanistan's friendly permission which had opened to me the easiest route to the Oxus.   When to cross the open saddle of the Baroghil required such special help, how could I have hoped to get my worn-out Chitral transport over the far higher Khora-bhort Pass and the glacier barriers between it and the Yarkhun Valley—the route I should have had to attempt in the absence of such formal permission !

CHAPTER VII

IN AFGHAN WAKHAN

The night preceding our passage to the Oxus proved bitterly cold, the minimum thermometer showing 5° Fahr. So when on May 19th we started at 6 A.M. for the pass under a specklessly clear sky the snow was hard frozen. It was a delightful change to see the long string of baggage animals move now over the glittering surface without needing the track which had been ploughed by them the day before with such efforts. But the growing intensity of the sunshine, doubly felt by me with a face still blistered from the Darkot, warned us to hasten on. By 7.30 A.M. we reached the level plain of the saddle where in the summer the waters divide almost imperceptibly between Indus and Oxus. Now the snow lay everywhere to a depth of not less than five or six feet. The descent for the first two or three miles was equally easy, though in places one or other of the more heavily laden ponies would break through where the snow covered small watercourses (Fig. 23). But by 9 A.M. the surface had already softened badly, and with the animals constantly floundering the help of the fifteen sturdy Wakhis who had met us on the saddle proved most welcome. It would have been quite impossible to get the animals, even unladen, through the snow-choked gorge into which the Baroghil drainage passes farther down. So with a good deal of trouble they were dragged up to the crest of a shale-covered side spur where the snow had partially melted, while parties of good-natured Wakhis carried up load after load.

It was a relief to sight at last at the bottom of a small side valley the first bit of fairly dry ground with signs of vegetation. It was grass land with some terraced cultivation belonging to the Zartighar hamlet, and there I decided to halt while the baggage was slowly being brought down in driblets. Scarcely had I begun to refresh myself with a modest breakfast when Kurban and my Indian followers came up in a great flurry to announce the arrival of two Afghan officers. Painfully aware as I was of my sadly neglected appearance, the result of the last day's toils, and of the increased regard which, once beyond the farthermost limits of Indian authority, Oriental notions of propriety had a right to claim from me, I hastened to don *en plein air* my best travelling suit, brought down by forethought in a saddle-bag. I could not have wished for a heartier welcome on the soil of the last true Eastern Kingdom than that which worthy Risaldar Abdullah Khan, commanding the Colonel's mounted escort, and jovial Mubarak Shah, the Wakhi Ak-sakal ('white-beard') or headman of Sarhad, came to offer me in the name of the military and civil dignitaries awaiting my arrival on the Oxus. They invited me to ' Dastarkhan' or refreshments at the Top-khana or watch-tower of Zartighar, a couple of miles lower down in the main valley.

It was a glorious day full of sunshine, and as I sat with my hosts and their Wakhi attendants on a much-worn Khotan carpet spread out below the ruined watch-tower, my eyes revelled in the brilliant colours presented by the light blue sky, the snows, and my gay Central-Asian *entourage*. The barrenness of the landscape seemed only to heighten their effect. My thoughts were buoyant too. For everything around brought up visions of Turkestan, to which I was now happily returning after years of separation. Had I not at last succeeded in making my way to that valley of the Oxus which had attracted me ever since my early youth, and of which I had before had to content myself with a single glimpse from its glacier sources on the Wakhjir? The repast was modest, indeed : a weak infusion of green tea, some terribly tough chops, and oat-cakes. I should, however, scarcely have noticed this, had there not been some apologetic hints at the poverty of Upper Wakhan and the strain involved upon its scanty resources by the prolonged presence of the Afghan escort awaiting me. What at the time I felt like a jar on my feelings was the polite refusal of my two Indians to partake of the offered collation. Of course, I knew well that hard-and-fast caste rules would allow neither Surveyor Ram Singh, the Hinduized Gurkha, nor Naik Ram Singh, the Sikh, to partake of impure Mlecchas' dishes. Yet this little commonplace incident made me realize, on the very threshold of Central Asia, that the distant region I was now re-entering after years of absence lay in many ways much nearer to our European horizon than familiar and yet ever-inscrutable India.

When the baggage had turned up under faithful old Kurban's care, we rode in an imposing cavalcade down the steadily broadening valley towards its junction with the Oxus. Near the scattered homesteads of Pitkhar I was delighted to get my first information of ancient walls on the steep spur overlooking the debouchure from the west; for just at this point the Chinese record of Kao Hsien-chih's famous expedition had made me locate that fortified line by which in 747 A.D. the Tibetans attempted to bar his advance from the Oxus to the Baroghil.

There was no time now for further investigation, as I was soon met on my way by gallant old Colonel Shirin-dil Khan, who, mounted on a fine Badakhshi and in full uniform, had galloped ahead with a crowd of horsemen to receive me. He had been sent up from Badakhshan by Prince Nasrullah, brother of the Amir and General Command-ing in the Oxus Provinces, to assure my safe passage through the Afghan territory on the Pamirs. After patiently waiting for me at Sarhad for over four weeks he now offered me the warmest of welcomes. From the very first his soldierly bearing and evident kindliness of dis-position, coupled with a certain rough frankness, struck me most pleasantly. With his six feet of height and burly figure he looked an active Warden of the Afghan Marches north-eastwards, in spite of his years, probably close on sixty, and manifest traces of a hard life. The Russian-looking uniform with a sort of black busby suited him well, better, perhaps, than a somewhat similar get-up did his civil coadjutor in the honours of my reception, Hakim Mansur Khan, governor of Upper Wakhan. He, too, showed me thereafter all possible attention. A typical Kabuli Afghan by birth and manners, he had spent long years of exile in India, could speak Hindustani well, and knew a good deal, too, about the ways and works of the 'Sahibs.' And yet somehow it was not so easy to forget the Oriental in him as it was with the bluff old Colonel.

On we cantered at the head of quite a respectable cavalcade to where, on the sandy plain opposite to the main hamlet of Sarhad (Fig. 16), two companies of foot with a squad of cavalry, close on two hundred men in all, were drawn up as a guard of honour. Hardy and well set up most of them looked, giving the impression of thoroughly serviceable human material, in spite of a manifestly defective drill and the motley appearance of dress and equipment. They belonged, so the Colonel explained to me afterwards, to a sort of militia drafted from the local population of the Badakhshan valleys and Wakhan into the regiments permanently echeloned as frontier guards along the Russian border on the Oxus. Apart from the officers, the proportion of true Pathans among them was slight. Yet I could well believe from all I saw and heard that, properly led and provided for, these sturdy Iranian hillmen might give a good account of themselves. Did not Marco Polo speak of the people of 'Badashan' as 'valiant in war' and of the men of 'Vokhan' as 'gallant soldiers'?

The stripling Oxus, which we had to cross to camp after inspecting the men, was spreading itself over the broad valley bottom in several wide branches. Its water was still so low that from the back of my pony I had some difficulty in laving my hand in it as a pious salute to the great river touched at last after many years' waiting. It was delightful to have reached the head-waters of the Oxus, and to feel that I had got again a step nearer to the fascinating regions lower down its course upon which my eyes had been fixed since early youth. Access to them was still barred for me, as it has been during many years for all Europeans. But for moments I could almost forget this as I sat on the carpet in the Colonel's neat tent during the long hours it took for my baggage to arrive, and, refreshed by tea and Wakhan dainties, listened to all my host would tell, in a ready flow of sonorous Persian, of his cherished home in beautiful Badakhshan and of his varied experiences up and down the Oxus. For Fortune so willed it that the appointment, which, some seven years before my visit, put Shirin-dil Khan in command of the Afghan frontier garrisons from Badakhshan upwards, had brought the old warrior after many years of arduous soldiering in distant parts of Afghanistan back to ground he knew and loved from his youth. So from this our first meeting a bond of common local interest made him eager to satisfy my curiosity about those lands of ancient Bactria which, by their historical past and their very inaccessibility, will never cease to attract me.

The presence of this delightful and well-informed old soldier would alone have been an inducement to tarry by their threshold on the Oxus. But when my camp had at last been pitched in the evening, at some distance above that of the Afghan commando, and I was free after ceremonial visits from the local head-men to review the situation in quiet, I could not fail to recognize that, apart from my own eagerness to gain rapidly the fields of labour awaiting me in Eastern Turkestan, serious practical con- siderations urged me onwards. There was reassuring evidence that, for my progress eastwards to the Chinese border on the Pamirs, every help which the scanty resources of barren Upper Wakhan would permit had been provided under the Amir's orders. But it was equally certain that the military force which those charged with their execution had seen fit to send up for my sake to the highest permanently inhabited part of the valley, had been exposed already far too long to serious hardships from the rigours of the climate and from inadequate shelter.

Still more I owed consideration to the discreet but touching applications which reached me in the privacy of my tent from the representatives of the peaceful Wakhi villagers upon whom this host had been mainly subsisting all these weeks. There was only too much reason to believe that their reserve supplies were wellnigh exhausted, and with snow-bound mountains all around and practically no sign of spring as yet, I could judge for myself how far off the hope of a fresh harvest was for poor Sarhad. So I had reluctantly to content myself with a single day's halt before starting on the march to the Pamirs.

At nightfall the fine-looking, genial Ak-sakal of Sarhad (Fig. 30), with some grey-bearded elders of the village tract, turned up again to plead another earnest prayer in the quaint thick-spoken Persian of Wakhan, curiously recalling the Welsh accent. Would I allow a few trusty villagers to keep watch during the night near my tent—not as a safeguard against their own people, who were all honest enough, but as a protection against anything going wrong with the Afghan guards posted at my camp? I could not feel sure, of course, whether the Wakhis' cautious request was prompted as much by interest for my personal safety as by the fear of being victimized whoever the aggressor might be. But for my first nights on Afghan soil it did not seem wise to refuse this sort of double insurance.

May 20th, the day of our halt at Sarhad, was anything but a rest for me. Our motley transport and attendants from the Mastuj side had to be paid off, and what with the elaborate rates specified by benign 'Political' solicitude and my wish to make extra largess commensurate with individual merits, the accounts were complicated enough. That all such payments throughout my journey had to be made with my own hands is a detail which for travellers of Oriental experience would scarcely need mention. The task of securing formal receipts in all cases for the satisfaction of the Comptroller of India Treasuries had fortunately been simplified by keeping printed receipt forms ready, which only needed filling in with figures and names before their attestation with smudgy finger-prints. The despatch of a last Dak *via* Chitral, arrangements for the fresh supplies and transport we needed on the Pamir journey before us, and a friendly exchange of visits and presents with my Afghan hosts kept me busy till the evening. Only then could I find time for a ride with the communicative Karaul Beg round the nearest of the small hamlets which, scattered along broad alluvial terraces above the right bank of the Oxus, or Ab-i-Panja as it is here called, make up the present Sarhad, reckoned altogether at some 130 households.

There was little about the low grey houses, or rather hovels, of mud and rubble to indicate the importance which from early times must have attached to Sarhad as the highest place of permanent occupation on the direct route leading from the Oxus to the Tarim Basin. Here was the last point where caravans coming from the Bactrian side with the products of the Far West and of India could provision themselves for crossing that high tract of wilderness 'called Pamier' of which old Marco Polo rightly tells us : " You ride across it for twelve days together, finding nothing but a desert without habitations or any green thing, so that travellers are obliged to carry with them whatever they have need of." And as I looked south towards the snow-covered saddle of the Baroghil, the route I had followed myself, it was equally easy to realize why Kao Hsien-chih's strategy had, after the successful crossing of the Pamirs, made the three columns of his Chinese army concentrate upon the stronghold of Lien-yün, opposite the present Sarhad. Here was the base from which Yasin could be invaded and the Tibetans ousted from their hold upon the straight route to the Indus.

Both Colonel Shirin-dil Khan and Hakim Mansur Khan declared themselves bound by their instructions to accompany me personally across the Afghan Pamirs to the Chinese border. But my well-meaning military protector gave way, not altogether reluctantly I thought, to my earnest representations, and agreed to send the bulk of his little force back to Kala Panja and to take only a portion of his mounted men along. Though he had taken the precaution to establish supply depots at suitable points ahead, I knew that manifold preparations would delay the start of our little column for the first march. So I was doubly glad when the gallant old

Colonel agreed to let me examine in the morning of May 21st the ruined fortifications reported on the steep spur overlooking the debouchure of the Baroghil route on the west, while he himself would look after the starting of baggage and escort.

So with Naik Ram Singh and a few Wakhis, including the Karaul Beg and Talmish, a versatile follower of his who quickly attached himself to me as a sort of local factotum (Fig. 30), I rode off to the south for three miles across the level plain of sand and marsh over which the Baroghil stream spreads out towards the Oxus. Just where the mouth of the valley narrows to a width of about half a mile at the bottom, it is flanked by precipitous rocky ridges, the last offshoots of spurs which descend from the main Hindukush watershed. Protected by these natural defences the position seemed to correspond accurately to that which the Chinese Annals describe as having been occupied in 747 A.D. by the Tibetans when they endeavoured to bar Kao Hsien-chih's advance to the Baroghil and Darkot. Posted at a distance of fifteen Li, or about three miles from the river, to the number of eight or nine thousand, they are said "to have taken advantage of the mountainous ground to erect palisades." This time-honoured Tibetan scheme of defence, to await attack behind a wall erected across the open ground of the valley, had the same results then as when repeated in 1904 against the British Mission force at Guru and on the Karo-la. For the Chinese general having gained the heights, i.e. turned the fortified line, engaged the defenders in a fight which ended in their complete defeat with heavy loss.

Of the palisades I could not well expect to find visible traces after the lapse of centuries. But how Kao Hsien-chih had turned the Tibetan position I could see quite clearly when, starting a short distance south of absolutely impracticable rock faces, I climbed up to the top of the western spur after an hour's hard scramble over steep slopes of rock and shingle. There, beyond a stretch of easily sloping ground, rose the old fort of Kansir my Wakhi informants had spoken of, at the extreme north end of the crest. Between the narrow ridge occupied by the walls and bastions and the continuation of the spur westwards a broad dip seemed to offer an easy descent towards the hamlet of Karkat on the Oxus.

It was manifestly for the purpose of guarding this approach that the little fort had been erected on this exposed height. On the north and east, where the end spur falls off in unscalable cliffs to the valleys of the Oxus and Baroghil some 1600 feet below, structural defences were needless. But the crest slope of the ridge and the narrow neck to the south had been protected by a bastioned wall for a distance of about 400 feet. Three bastions to the west and the one at the south end still rose in fair pre- servation, in parts to a height of over thirty feet. The connecting wall curtains had suffered more, through the foundations giving way on the steep incline. Of buildings inside the little fort, if the limited ground, scarcely 200 feet across at the broadest, and the rocky surface had ever admitted of such, there remained no trace. But some antiquarian indication was supplied by the construction of the walls. Outside a core of closely packed rough stones they showed a solid brick facing, four to six feet in thickness, with regular thin layers of brushwood separating the courses of sun-dried bricks.

The size of the bricks, about eight by seven inches and four inches thick, furnishes no definite evidence. But in the use of the brushwood layers I could not fail to recognize a peculiarity with which ancient Chinese construction in the Tarim Basin had made me familiar. It was, no doubt, intended to assure greater consistency, and must have been used, as my subsequent explora- tions much farther to the east showed, from the very commencement of Chinese expansion into Central Asia. But later discoveries in the Lop-nor region and else- where have proved also that the Tibetan invaders of the T'ang period, when building their own forts, did not neglect to copy this constructive expedient of their Chinese predecessors and opponents in this region. So, in the absence of other remains, it can scarcely now be decided whether the construction of the Kansir walls was due to the Chinese while they held for a few years the route to Yasin and Gilgit, or to the Tibetans when they returned after Kao Hsien-chih's final retirement and were, perhaps, anxious to guard against any repetition of that successful move which had outflanked a favourite defensive position.

What with the examination and plotting of the ruined fort there scarcely remained time to enjoy the glorious view commanded by the height we had climbed. Across the broad valley to the north there rose like a huge unbroken wall the high snow-covered range separating the Ab-i-Panja from the Victoria Lake branch of the Oxus and the Great Pamir (Fig. 16). Westwards my eyes followed wistfully the wide-spreading bed of the Oxus where it flows down to Kala-Panja and on towards Badakhshan. But for better or worse my course now lay to the east, and there the narrow gorge in which the river-bed disappeared not far above Sarhad gave a warning of the difficult marches before us. So I hurried to scramble down after mid-day to where the ponies had been left by the Baroghil stream. By 2 P.M. we rejoined Colonel Shirin-dil Khan, waiting for me where the Ab-i-Panja debouches from its confined gorge near the junction with the Daliz-darra.

The marches before us were bound to be exceptionally trying, owing to the fact that the winter route in the Oxus bed was already closed by the flooded river, while impracticable masses of snow still covered the high summer track which avoids the deep-cut gorge altogether by crossing a succession of side spurs at relatively great elevation. For about four miles we followed the cliffs and steep detritus slopes of the right bank by a narrow difficult path which, but for the example set by the gallant old Colonel and his hardy troopers, I should have thought in most places quite unfit for riding. It was wonderful to watch the agility with which our Badakhshi ponies scrambled up and down precipitous rock faces. Riding myself a splendid grey pony which Shirin-dil Khan had kindly lent me, I did my best to display full confidence in its prowess. But I confess the pleasure would have been greater without having to take one's own share in these acrobatic performances.

Then we had to cross the tossing river, with its water reaching well above the ponies' girths, for a track quite as bad on the left bank. Heavy avalanches here choked the mouths of side gorges. Three times more had we to repeat these crossings in greyish-green water dashing against boulders, until I got thoroughly drenched at the last ford. Then a steep zigzag track led us up a spur overlooking the Shaor stream, where for a short distance we got easier going on the summer route leading down from the Daliz Pass. Soon after the sharp eyes of our Wakhi guides sighted a herd of Ovis Poli on a narrow ledge high above the left river-bank opposite, and in the fading light of the evening the old Colonel, keen sportsman as he is, vainly tried a long-range shot at them with his Martini.

Finally we dropped down again to the river, where a sandy reach, covered with stunted trees and brushwood, and known as Baharak, offered a convenient camping-place for the night in the midst of these gloomy defiles. The baggage on hardy Wakhi ponies, though started well ahead and with an adequate number of Sarhad men to watch and help it on, did not struggle through till hours later. But thanks to the cheerful company of Shirin-dil Khan and the hospitable solicitude of his Afghan attendants, who had spread a felt rug on the ground and got tea ready long before mine would bestir themselves even to light a fire, I scarcely noticed the long wait.

It was delightful to listen during these hours of common marching and camping to all this amiable warrior could tell me of the varied experiences of an active lifetime spent among the old-world conditions which political seclusion has helped to preserve in Afghanistan. He had fought through all the troubled times preceding and immediately following Amir Abdurrahman's succession, and had gained the present congenial billet in his beloved Badakhshan after much hard service in far less attractive regions. He had fought against Turkoman rebels and in the rugged mountains of the Hazara. For years he had struggled to maintain order on the barren border of Khost and Mangal against wily Wazir tribes.

I found him not only full of interesting information

about ancient remains in Badakhshan and old Bactria, the regions which he knew so well and to which my own thoughts were ever eagerly turning, but himself also, as it were, a fascinating historical record. Was it not like being shifted back many centuries to find myself listening to this considerate and gentlemanly old soldier, who in his younger days had helped to build up pyramids of rebel heads just to establish order in the time-honoured fashion of Central Asia? Of course, much of our talk used to turn on things of the past, for which a lucky dispensation had endowed my friend with real interest and a great deal of shrewd practical observation. Yet quite as enticing was it to listen to his enthusiastic descriptions of all the charms of Badakhshan, its well-watered valleys with shady groves and abundance of all fruits, and its extensive Alpine plateaus offering rich grazing and cool retreats for the summer. Ever there rose before me, during such converse in these bleak wintry valleys, pictures of my cherished Kashmir, and I wondered when the time might come for me to see its Central-Asian *pendant.* May kindly old Shirin-dil Khan be still there then to welcome me!

Our onward march on May 22nd proved difficult in its first half. The crossing of the big snow-fed stream dashing down the side valley of Baharak involved much trouble and risk for the baggage (Fig. 26), and the fifteen hundred feet ascent to the Bashgaz spur which followed had to be effected in many places over steep and slippery rock faces. Without the energetic assistance of our Afghan protectors the baggage which had to be unloaded again and again would never have been hauled up, in spite of the additional Wakhi carriers brought from Sarhad. By a narrow track which kept winding along steep slopes high above the impassable river-gorge, and in a few places passed small alluvial plateaus, where patches of ground looked as if terraced for cultivation in ancient times, we reached camp at Langar in the evening. The little mud-domed structure which has given the place its name, meaning 'rest-house' in Turki, was uninviting; but the broad gravel 'Dasht' on which we camped, with its easy slope towards the river, gave promise of easier ground before

25. KIRGHIZ SHIFTING FELT TENT AT GUMBAZ-ÖTEK.

26. AFGHAN ESCORT WITH BAGGAGE PREPARING TO CROSS BAHARAK STREAM.
Colonel Shirin-dil Khan on extreme right.

us. Our poor baggage animals needed it badly; for the fatigues of the previous marches had almost exhausted them, and the bleak exposed plain over 12,000 feet above the sea, on which the snow had only just melted, offered neither grazing nor shelter.

CHAPTER VIII

TO THE SOURCE OF THE OXUS

THERE could be no doubt about our now nearing the Pamirs when, after a cold night with the thermometer sinking to a minimum of 25 degrees below freezing-point, we started across stony and partly marshy ground for the low saddle known as Dasht-i-Mirza Murad. By crossing it the route cuts off a southern bend of the now much broadened Oxus Valley. A ten miles' ride over alluvial plateaus still retaining snow in great patches brought us to a low spur from which I first sighted north-eastwards the rolling downs of the Little Pamir. In the clear air of this high elevation our day's goal, the Kirghiz camp at Bozai-gumbaz, seemed quite close. There the head-waters of the Ab-i-Panja meet the stream coming from Lake Chakmaktin on the Little Pamir. In the distance far away to the east I rejoiced to greet again the snowy peaks guarding the approach to the Wakhjir Pass and the source of the Oxus.

But at this point of my return to the 'Roof of the World' there was an archaeological object to claim my attention. The fairly well preserved little structure of which I had heard before is known as Karwan-balasi, from the local tradition which believes it to have been built as a tomb for a merchant's son who had died here in old times. The ruin shows a small cella, about nine by ten feet outside in ground plan, solidly built of flat slabs set in mortar and at a height of about twelve feet surmounted by a now broken dome (Fig. 5). The orientation of the cella towards the south-west, *i.e.* the direction of Mecca, with a doorway from the side opposite, makes it practically certain that it was erected in Muhammadan times. All the more interesting to me was the observation how closely all its constructive features—the three outer stories divided by projecting cornices, the dimensions, etc.—corresponded to the little Stupa of Thol, the last Buddhist remains I had seen in 1900 south of the Hindukush, when approaching the Pamirs from the side of Gilgit and Hunza. The adaptation of an ancient architectural model of Buddhism to Muhammadan use could not have been illustrated more strikingly.

We reached Bozai-gumbaz in glorious sunshine soon after mid-day and yet were glad to seek shelter from the keen air of these breezy altitudes in the felt tents or Kirghas which Muhammad Isa, the head-man in charge of the Kirghiz grazing on the Afghan Pamirs, had caused to be erected for our reception. Once inside, it seemed hard to realize that fully six years had passed since I enjoyed Kirghiz hospitality on the 'Roof of the World.' So familiar appeared the gay-coloured felt rugs spread out on the ground, the brightly woven nettings along the foot of the tent walls, and the other simple fittings which long tradition and the absence of all variety in local resources have helped to standardize in these nomadic homesteads.

There were the same harsh Tartar faces, too, darkened by constant exposure and with features as if roughly hewn out of wood, and the same blunt but hearty hospitality. To listen again to the high-pitched guttural Turki of our Kirghiz hosts was a treat for my ears. But what they had to relate over tea and plentiful bowls of hot milk was by no means cheerful. The snowfall of the winter had been exceptionally heavy and late, and with the snow covering the ground in the valleys to a depth of six feet and more instead of the usual maximum of about three, the yaks had for weeks found it hard to get at their accustomed grazing. So the losses among these beasts, which form the most valued stock of the Kirghiz, had been terribly heavy all over the Pamirs. Their sheep had suffered almost equally. It was easy to realize that the advent of so large a party of official guests from Wakhan was bound to appear that season in the light of an additional hardship.

I was anxious to make this infliction as short as possible ;

yet a day's halt at Bozai-gumbaz was for several reasons
indispensable. The Wakhis, whose help was necessary for
crossing the pass, badly needed a rest after their preceding
exertions ; the collection of fresh baggage animals from the
scattered Kirghiz camps would cost time ; and, lastly, it was
important to send Kirghiz ahead to the Chinese side to
make sure about the transport we should require after
crossing to the Taghdumbash Pamir. Months before I
had informed M. Sher Muhammad, the ' British Political
Munshi' in Sarikol, of my planned route and of the help I
expected in the matter of transport. Again from Chitral
and Mastuj I had used the convenient wire to Gilgit in
order to communicate to him *via* Hunza the approximately
exact date of our coming. And now after all these precautions it was disquieting to find at Bozai-gumbaz that
for months past no news whatever had come through from
the Taghdumbash Pamir.

I used our halt on May 24th for a ride to the west shore
of Lake Chakmaktin, at a distance of about twelve miles
from Bozai-gumbaz, and to the Little Pamir. Our way took
us past a ruined watch-tower on a low plateau, known as
Karaul-dong, and a warm and slightly sulphurous spring
close below it. Then we crossed, almost without per-
ceiving it, the low and flat saddle which separates the
Ab-i-Panja Valley from the drainage of the Murghab or
Ak-su, the other main branch of the Oxus. By a geo-
graphically interesting bifurcation which I was glad to
verify closely, the stream of the Chilap Jilga which
debouches on this saddle from the range to the north sends
its waters partly towards Bozai-gumbaz and the Ab-i-
Panja and partly into Lake Chakmaktin, the head-waters
basin of the Murghab. It was curious to think that, while
some drops in the Chilap stream would reach the true
Oxus bed within a couple of hours, others from the same
melting snow-bed would have to travel over three hundred
and fifty miles through the Russian Pamirs and the
gorges of Roshan before becoming reunited.

From where we touched the shore of Lake Chakmaktin the broad basin of the Little Pamir spread out to
the north-east, a *morne* waste of half-frozen marsh and

27. VIEW ACROSS LAKE CHAKMAKTIN TOWARDS AK-TASH, LITTLE PAMIR.

A   B   C

28. IN THE FELT TENT OF MUHAMMAD ISA, KIRGHIZ HEAD-MAN OF AFGHAN PAMIRS.
A, B. Afghan Officers. C. Muhammad Isa.

bare glacis-like slopes still showing no sign of spring (Fig. 27). The impression of height in the snow-covered ranges on either side, though they reach to points over 18,000 feet, was largely discounted by our own elevation, just over 13,000 feet according to the Pamir Boundary Commission's triangulation. And yet there lay over the whole a sensation of vastness which made me feel here, as years before on the heights of Muztagh-ata, that I was looking, indeed, across the 'Roof of the World.' For close on fifty miles to the north-east along the course of the Ak-su the eye could travel quite unhindered, and at a still greater distance beyond I could recognize bold icy pyramids, close on 21,000 feet in height, which overlook the valleys of Tash-kurghan and Tagharma.

In spite of the bright sky a bitterly cold wind blew all day from the south-west. So I was glad on the return ride to accept Muhammad Isa's invitation to visit his own encampment in a sheltered little hollow near the debouchure of the Chilap Jilga. It was a delightfully cosy Kirgha, carpeted with bright felt rugs (Fig. 28). Plenty of embroidered cushions and other fineries imported from Farghana attested the owner's wealth and comfort. Deliciously creamy milk was boiling in the big cauldron over the fire kept up with the roots of Teresken, instead of the usual pungent dry yak-dung. From behind the gaily woven reed Purdah the chief lady of the household would emerge with cherished cups of china and polished copper tea jugs to do honour to the festive occasion—and to have a good look at the stranger. No European had been seen in these parts since 1895, the time of the Pamir Boundary Commission. Much useful information could I gather from Muhammad Isa about the hundred odd Kirghiz families which then crossed from the Russian side to the Afghan Pamirs and have continued to graze them. The official tax annually gathered for the governor of Wakhan, one sheep in every ten, seems light enough. But I wondered whether the natural independence of the Kirghiz, aided by the ease of changing to the Russian or Chinese side, has availed to keep off other less official imposts.

It was interesting, too, to learn that the ancient trade route up the Oxus from Badakhshan to Sarikol and to Yarkand is still frequented during the summer months by enterprising Bajauri traders. That the total amount of merchandise carried was represented by only about one hundred pony loads each way in the year scarcely surprised me, seeing how trade between Afghanistan and Chinese Turkestan is handicapped by present economic conditions in both regions and powerful competition from the Russian and Indian sides. But Hakim Mansur Khan talked of the Amir's intention to have Sarais built at all stages along the Oxus to the Wakhjir in order to facilitate transit, and even without them I could well imagine trade reviving by this old and direct route if only immunity were afforded against fiscal and other exactions west of the Pamirs. The natural obstacles seem small, when compared with those which Indian traders have to face on the route from Kashmir across the Kara-koram and Kun-lun.

I was busy writing late at night in my own camp when to my relief a messenger from the Chinese side arrived. The letter he brought from Munshi Sher Muhammad contained only a query about the route and date of my crossing. Rather belated I thought it after all the trouble I had taken to indicate them well in advance and to keep to them. Still I was now assured of the contact, and within half an hour two hardy Kirghiz rode off in the dark of the night to carry my reply across the Wakhjir and urge timely succour from the other side. How often have I wished on less trying ground for such tough and untiring despatch-riders as are ever ready at hand among Kirghiz nomads!

Fresh snow fell overnight to a depth of two inches, and the drying of our tents delayed our start in the morning. But the march up the Ab-i-Panja to Gumbaz-ötek, our next stage, was only twelve miles, and the track, mostly over alluvial plateaus two to three hundred feet above the river, was quite easy. A number of Kirghas, pitched in advance by our Kirghiz hosts (Fig. 25), were badly needed to afford shelter for all our following. Though the baggage had now been transferred mostly to Kirghiz yaks, our Afghan protectors wisely insisted on taking all the Wakhis along for help in the crossing before us. The snow on the northward slopes of the valley still lay to a level even below our camping-ground, some 13,300 feet above the sea, and higher up the snout of a hanging glacier from the Hindukush main range faced us. Yet in spite of these chilly surroundings and fresh snow descending in the evening, I enjoyed my last peaceful converse with Colonel Shirin-dil Khan. In vivid colours he painted all the glories of springtime in his beloved Badakhshan, the flower-carpeted meadows of the Koh-i-daman, and the fruit-trees now blooming in the valleys. How near and yet how distant it all seemed here by the Oxus head-waters!

On the morning of May 26th we shifted camp to the last point below the Wakhjir Pass, where a patch of flat ground clear of snow was obtainable, at an elevation of about 14,000 feet. Mist and low clouds hid the head of the Ab-i-Panja valley when we started. But slowly the sun broke through, and by the time we were approaching our final camp on Afghan soil, the junction of the great glaciers eastward in which Lord Curzon has, I think rightly, recognized the true source of the Oxus, came clearly into view (Fig. 29). So leaving my Afghan friends to seek shelter from the keen east wind, I ascended the steep stony slope on the right bank for some five hundred feet until a wide panorama opened before me. To the south there extended a splendid array of glaciers clothing the slopes, and filling the gorges between the succession of bold spurs which descend from the high Hindukush watershed towards the newly born Oxus. I had first sighted these glaciers nearly six years before when, on July 2nd, 1900, I made my rapid raid across the Wakhjir to catch a glimpse of the uppermost Oxus, and, thanks to the photo-theodolite panorama brought away then and since published, the details remained fresh in my memory. But now the spectacle was still more imposing; for I was much nearer to some of the fine hanging glaciers, and the ancient moraines and extensive detritus slopes below them, then bare, were still covered by almost continuous snow-beds (Fig. 31).

In our bleak camp it was a busy and anxious time for me. Our Kirghiz and Wakhis did not disguise their fears about the difficulties to be faced in crossing the pass with heavy baggage. I myself felt constrained by previous experience to believe what they said, and knew that without our Afghan protectors' emphatic orders the men could never be got to make the attempt. So it was a great assurance that Shirin-dil Khan's support allowed of no objections, and that, besides an ample number of yaks, we were to have the help of every available Wakhi and Kirghiz to get the baggage across. But would the weather permit the attempt on the morrow? Driving showers of snow descended at intervals through the afternoon, damping the men's spirits still more.

Inside my Kirgha I was busy completing Persian versions of my letters to H.M. the King and Prince Nasrullah, which were to convey my genuine gratitude for the whole-hearted assistance received while on Afghan soil. Colonel Shirin-dil Khan and the Hakim of Wakhan, to whose excellent arrangements I had not failed to give amply deserved praise, were naturally eager to possess authenticated translations for their own assurance. Accounts, too, for supplies and the rest were settled with the Wakhi and Kirghiz head-men ; for to my special satisfaction it was understood from the outset that, notwithstanding the special protection afforded, I should be allowed to settle all expenses of my journey through His Afghan Majesty's territory in a business fashion. That, in addition to the official presents delivered on arrival at Sarhad, I was able to leave now a few articles from my own equipment as personal souvenirs to Shirin-dil Khan and the governor, was an attention mutually appreciated.

In my last quiet chat with the kindly old Colonel the wistful hope for a chance yet to come of seeing him in Badakhshan was the main theme. To a minor point of regret we could only allude with discretion. I had been eager to provide myself with a hardy Badakhshi for the long travels before me. The Colonel's spare mount, the excellent grey I had ridden all the way up from Sarhad, had greatly taken my fancy, and I understood from a

29. OXUS SOURCE GLACIERS SEEN FROM MOUTH OF WAKHJIR VALLEY.

30. WAKHI HEAD-MEN AND CARRIERS AT KÖK-TÖKÖK.
Mubarak Shah, 'Karaul Beg,' Talmish, and 'Dash' in foreground.

reliable quarter that a 'deal' would have been equally welcome to the owner. But how to effect the transaction in the face of the Amir's strict prohibition against all export of Badakhshan ponies? We both respected the law; but I never ceased to regret afterwards that there was no conveniently irresponsible Kirghiz smuggler at hand to relieve us of loyal scruples.

Knowing that the great difficulty before us was from soft snow, I was anxious for a start as early as possible on the morning of May 27th. At 3 A.M., when the yaks had been loaded, a thick mist full of floating ice-particles was hanging over the valley. So a party of men had to be sent ahead to search out and mark the right track. With the fresh snow hiding boulders and shallow water-courses the yaks' progress was terribly slow. Though the atmosphere steadily cleared, the foot of the proper ascent to the pass was not reached until full daylight. There I bade a hearty farewell to Colonel Shirin-dil Khan, who with the Hakim and his principal followers had insisted upon accompanying us thus far. As I took a parting look at his features, I found it hard to believe that scarcely more than a week had passed since our first meeting. And when might be the next? To our Wakhis and Kirghiz he repeated his injunctions, under threat of severe penalties and in a tone which admitted of no trifling, not to show their faces again on the Afghan side unless they could bring my written acknowledgment of all baggage having been safely delivered across the pass. And to make quite sure of the effect and to be ready for help if needed, he declared his intention to await their return in our last camp.

The snow ahead lay so deep that soon my Indians, who had torpidly stuck to their yaks, had to dismount. In spite of a minimum temperature of 25 degrees below freezing-point in camp that morning, only the surface of the snow was hard frozen, and that rapidly softened under the rays of the sun when he rose after 7 A.M. above the broad gap of the pass north-eastwards. The unladen yaks, which were pulled and driven ahead through the soft snow to beat down a track for the rest, before long floundered hopelessly

and proved of no further use. For about half a mile onwards, the men pushing ahead, first in single file for short
distances, and then returning each time to the baggage,
managed to drag the laden yaks on, three or four helping
each animal.

But as their heavy bodies kept sinking helplessly
into the soft snow, which gave no hold even for these
wonderfully sure - footed animals, the procedure soon
proved too exhausting for beasts and men alike. At a
point which, from my recollection of the ground and the
map, I estimated to be still fully two miles from the watershed, the last of the powerful Kirghiz yaks had to be left
behind and all the loads transferred to the men. Their
total number was close on thirty. But in such snow and
at an elevation well over 15,000 feet even the lighter
baggage articles required frequent shifts, and the heavier
boxes three or four men at a time. So the transport had to
be effected by instalments over short distances, the men
then returning to fetch the remainder. It was painfully
slow work, and but for the energy and watchfulness of the
Wakhi head-men and the care of my experienced Yarkandi
Muhammadju the risk of packages getting left behind in
the snow would have been serious.

As long as our track skirted the steep slopes looking
south near the debouchure of the Wakhjir stream, there
was danger from possible avalanches ; but this grew
less after we could take, about 10 A.M., to the deep
and almost flat snow-beds filling the broadening valley
as it gently rises towards the pass. Pushing ahead
with the two Ram Singhs and a couple of Wakhis, who
carried the precious cameras, I struggled through the
snow in which we often sank waist-deep. Grateful was I
for the light mist which settled after mid-day, and somewhat relieved the intense glare which added pain to this
toil. At last towards 2 P.M. we gained the flat expanse of
snow marking the top of the Wakhjir. My hypsometrical
readings of 1900 had given a height of about 16,200 feet
for the watershed ; but how deep this now lay buried
under snow it was impossible to determine. Even the
high glacier tongue with beautiful stalactites of the purest

31. HEAD OF AB-I-PANJA VALLEY, LOOKING TOWARDS WAKHJIR PASS AND OXUS SOURCE GLACIERS.

ice, which I had then observed within a few hundred yards
north of the pass, was now completely effaced. Only the
top of one huge boulder emerged from this deep snow
mantle, and on it we few were glad to crouch for a short
rest. Nothing impressed me more with the toil these long
hours of ascent had cost us than the subdued whining of
'Dash,' my inseparable little companion. For him, with
his irrepressible young fox-terrier spirits, the month's
hard travelling from the Swat border had seemed so far
but an enjoyable outing. Nor were snow slopes any
novelty for him; for had he not two years earlier when
quite a young puppy by his delight of romping on the
snow-beds of the Kaghan mountains earned his full-
fledged Turki title of 'Kar-dash Beg' ('Sir Snow-
Friend'), which I bestowed upon him for his incognito
on prospective Central-Asian travels? Now he was eager
to huddle up under the lap of my fur coat, and to forget
all the stress of this day in a short nap.

When at last the first of the load-carrying men struggled
up to us, we could leave this desolate watershed between
Oxus and Tarim and begin our descent on the Chinese
side. It proved far more trying than I had expected.
Whether it was due to further softening of the snow—the
sun had broken through again and was showing up the
valley before us in the brightest afternoon glow—or to the
cuttings effected below the surface by more numerous side-
streams, progress was stopped again and again by portions
of snow-beds where one would sink in to the armpits. It
became necessary to seek for firmer snow on the slopes,
or try to advance along snow-covered old moraines. All
this meant wearisome détours and halts for us pioneers.
Of the small lakes which in July 1900 I had passed in
this valley no trace could be discovered now.

Some four miles from the pass the valley began to turn
to the east, and an encouraging vista opened towards the
head of the Taghdumbash Pamir lit up by the setting sun
in glorious tints of red and purple. But of succour in the
shape of yaks and men, for which we were all anxiously
looking out to help the poor fellows left with the loads on
or behind the pass, there was no sign yet. At last, when

turning a rocky spur near where the Wakhjir route is joined by a side valley from the north-west, the keen eyes of Ram Singh, the Surveyor, caught sight of little black specks moving up slowly across the white bottom of the main valley. They were a drove of yaks which Munshi Sher Muhammad with a few Wakhi herdsmen from the Taghdumbash was endeavouring to hurry up to our rescue. So, after all, this strategic concentration of transport which I had endeavoured to assure weeks before, over such distance and ground, had not failed altogether.

Half an hour later I had the pleasure of shaking hands again with the 'Political Munshi,' representing the Sirkar in Sarikol. He was still the same fine-looking big Punjabi I remembered from our first meeting in these parts in 1900. But my assurance about all trouble being at an end vanished, when he reported how he had expected me to cross by the Kök-török Pass, and how he had left all supplies and spare men at the mouth of the Kök-török Valley while hurrying up now to meet me by the Wakhjir. It was not easy to account for the Munshi's original mistake about my route, nor for his own camp being left behind what I knew to be nearly a day's march. That old Indian force — or rather weakness — 'Dastur' or routine, was probably the only explanation. The Kök-török Jilga is the valley towards the Afghan Pamirs where the few European sportsmen coming from Gilgit always go up to shoot, and its mouth their regular camping-ground fixed by custom. So an Indian subordinate, having due respect for tradition, would necessarily expect a Sahib from the Afghan side also to come by that valley and to pitch camp at that orthodox spot, even though his written communications might explicitly indicate a different intention.

If Sher Muhammad's yaks had only been utilized for bringing up some dry fuel, we might have remained for the night close to where we had met them, uninviting though the ground was. But without any means to light fires for drying ourselves and for cooking, there was nothing left but to try and push on to Kök-török. When the advance party of Wakhis with light loads had at last struggled down after us by nightfall I set out with my Indians. Sher Muhammad gallantly insisted upon remaining behind to see the baggage safely down that night or by daybreak. The route at the wide valley bottom being one continuous shallow marsh of melting snows, progress was wearily slow. There was only the choice between wading in icy water or risking frostbite for one's feet while sticking to our sluggish yak mounts in the bitter cold of that night. Luckily the temper of yaks allows something in the way of gymnastic exercises on the part of the rider to shake off incipient numbness. This and the attention needed by 'Dash,' who was mounted in front of me, alone kept me from falling asleep on this dismal ride.

At last, after midnight we heard a dog barking, and soon could rouse from their sleep Sher Muhammad's attendants and some Sarikolis. The shelter of the three small Kirghas left standing here for long years was filthy to a degree. But how welcome it seemed that night to us weary people! Of food, all I could get was some cups of hot tea, and the several-weeks-old attempt of Sher Muhammad's Wakhi cook to bake a 'Wilayeti' cake. Pungent smoke from the fire of half-wet yak dung filled the felt tent; but glad enough was I to warm myself by it after exposure to the bitter cold of a night at some 14,000 feet elevation. Then I stretched myself out on the focusing-cloth from my camera, the only clean thing within reach, and fell into a sleep fitfully broken by dreamt noises of baggage arriving.

Next morning the baggage began to come in reality by slow instalments; but my gratification at its safety was damped by the fact that the loads containing supplies and cooking things were brought last. It was mid-day before I could get some modest apology for the meals missed on the previous day. While waiting all through the morning there was ample time to get satiated with the surroundings at this my first camp on Chinese soil. Already in 1900 when I descended here from the Kilik Pass, the Kirghas left standing at the mouth of the Kök-török Jilga, probably ever since Lord Curzon's Pamir visit, were sad things to behold, judged unfit for resumption by their original Wakhi owners. Since then established custom seems to have inveigled or forced every Sahib coming from Gilgit for Ovis Poli shooting to establish his camping-base at this same dreary patch of bare gravel. All round the dry bones and offal of the animals skinned here or slaughtered strewed the ground thickly, while the tattered and mouldering felt tents had become infested by a resident population of vermin which the bleakness of the surroundings seemed to have rendered only the more bloodthirsty. Altogether I felt convinced that this ' Dastur '-decreed halting-place was the filthiest spot on all the Pamirs.

So I was anxious to escape from it as soon as our baggage was complete. An urgent message sent down the valley had brought up my old Wakhi friend and host, Muhammad Yusuf, now Beg of the Taghdumbash valley, with ponies and more yaks. Our helpers from the Afghan side, who had overcome the fatigues of that crossing so manfully without harm to themselves or the baggage, were paid off with ample gratuities (Fig. 30). Then after a hearty farewell to the Wakhi head-men from Sarhad, whom I entrusted with a letter for my kind protector, the old Colonel, I set off for Muhammad Yusuf's encampment at Tigharman-su. With regret I thought of the shortness of that chapter now closed behind me on the Oxus. But there was the cheering assurance that the road to distant and new fields eastwards now lay open.

CHAPTER IX

FROM SARIKOL TO KASHGAR

THE journey down the Taghdumbash Pamir, on which I started on May 28th from Kök-török, took me over ground already familiar from 1900, and therefore my account of it may be brief. After a refreshing night's rest at Tigharman-su, where Muhammad Yusuf Beg's clean and comfortable Kirgha might almost have tempted me to forsake my own little tent, we rode down in a long march to the Karaul or watch-station of Bayik. It was pleasant to listen en route to all my host had to tell. Things had fared well with him since our first meeting, and now as the happy owner of a thousand sheep (Fig. 32) and dozens of camels and yaks the jovial Sarikoli was a man of substance fully equal to the dignity of Beg, newly won or rather purchased from the Chinese Amban of Tash-kurghan. With his tall figure, fair hair, and blue eyes, he looked the very embodiment of that Homo Alpinus type which prevails in Sarikol. I thought of old Benedict Goëz, the lay Jesuit, who when passing in 1603 from the Upper Oxus to 'Sarcil' or Sarikol, noted in the looks of the scanty inhabitants a resemblance to Flemings.

At Mintaka Karaul, where the route to Hunza branches off southward, I had the good luck to catch the two Dak runners carrying the mails despatched by Mr. Macartney some ten days earlier from Kashgar (Fig. 33). Of course, I did not hesitate to detain ' H.M.'s Mail' for a couple of hours, in order to use this chance of early conveyance to India and Europe for a rapidly-written-up mail-bag of my own. How often did my rather bulky correspondence thereafter add to the burden which these hardy and fleet hill-men of Hunza carry cheerfully three times each month across the snowy pass and through the awful river-gorges behind it !

Icy blasts from the south accompanied us all the way to Bayik, and still pursued us next morning when we continued the march downwards to where the Taghdum-bash river makes its sharp bend to the north. There I was able to investigate the remains of an ancient strong-hold which, though of considerable historical interest, had by an unfortunate chance escaped me on my former passage. Hsüan-tsang, the famous Chinese traveller, on whose track I was happy to find myself again, had, when returning about 642 A.D. from long pilgrimages to Buddhist shrines of India, passed from Badakhshan across the Pamirs into Sarikol. Of the royal family of the latter region he relates in his Memoirs a curious legend.

According to old popular tradition it traced its origin to a princess of the Chinese Han dynasty who had been betrothed to a king of Persia. On her progress towards her royal spouse she had reached Chieh-p'an-t'o, or Sarikol, when the roads east and west became blocked by robbers. For safety she was placed by her escort on an isolated mountain peak protected by precipitous cliffs. But there the well-guarded princess received visits from the sun-god, and, being found *enceinte* when the road became again open, was induced by her escort to remain in Sarikol and to establish her reign there. From her miraculously born son the chiefs ruling that mountain region were supposed to have sprung.

Already in 1900 I had heard, but too late for a visit, of remains of ancient walls perched on precipitous cliffs on the left bank of the Taghdumbash river near the bend already referred to. A story commonly known to Sari-kolis and Kirghiz that King Naushirwan, an ancient Persian ruler, had once placed his daughter there for safety, clings to the ruins and accounts for their popular designation, 'Kiz-kurghan,' meaning in Turki 'the tower of the princess.' This story was plainly a genuine relic of the fuller tradition current in Hsüan-tsang's days, and

32. WATCH-STATION AT FOOT OF MINTAKA PASS WITH SARIKOLIS.

33. HUNZA DAK RUNNERS (ON LEFT) AND SARIKOLI FRONTIER GUARDS,
WITH THEIR CHILDREN, AT MINTAKA KARAUL.

consequently I was eager to survey the site and the ruins where it is still localized.

Kiz-kurghan proved to be situated on the extreme eastern end of a rugged high spur which descends from the north-west to the river exactly at the entrance of the narrow defile extending from Ghujakbai to Dafdar. The end of the spur as we approached it from the south by the steep river bank, presents an almost isolated rock promontory falling away in nearly perpendicular cliffs on the south and east, and raising its top ridge some 700 feet above the Taghdumbash river. Our subsequent survey showed that equally unscalable rock walls protect it on the north and west towards the narrow and wildly twisting valley known as Kiz-kurghan Jilga.

Only from the south-west a low and narrow neck connects this frowning rock fastness with the spur behind it, and to that I climbed up with Surveyor and Naik under much difficulty. The ascent led over a steep fan of detritus and subsequently through a still more precipitous couloir of rock débris. The young guide accompanying us had never ascended before, superstitious fears keeping Sarikolis in general from visits to the ruins. Plentiful débris of ancient-looking juniper wood, or 'Archa,' strewing the higher slope gave me an inkling of the construction of the old walls of which we caught glimpses above us. When we had reached the neck, only fifteen to twenty feet across, and clambered up an equally narrow rocky arête for some 150 feet, I found my antiquarian surmise verified ; for the old walls rising before us (Fig. 35), along what proved to be the west rim of the highest of a series of terraces forming the top of the promontory, showed the curious structural peculiarity of twigs and brushwood embedded in regular layers between courses of sun-dried bricks. A massive bastion some twenty-five feet square barred approach from the neck and narrow crest. But we managed to scramble over its ruined side and to cross along the top of the decayed wall, some sixty feet long, which connected this bastion with the main defences ; the crumbled state of the wall and the precipices below made this rather nervous work.

Then we stood on the line of walls which was meant to defend the rim above mentioned. For a length of some 450 feet the walls could be traced first running from south-east to north-west and then, near a massive corner bastion, taking a turn due north. Rising still to over twenty feet where in fair preservation, elsewhere decayed almost to their foundation, they once protected completely that portion of the isolated rock top facing westwards on which alone an attack could be attempted. But even here, excepting the narrow neck we had followed, the slopes were far too steep to be climbed by armed men in any numbers. Everywhere else sheer walls of rock descending for hundreds of feet formed unscalable natural defences. From the west rim the top of the hill sloped to the north and east in a series of terraces which must have afforded ample space for structures of shelter. But these, having probably been built of rough stone, were traceable only in much-decayed heaps of rubble. In two places I recognized the positions of small reservoirs intended to collect water from melting snow or rain.

The solid construction of the bastioned walls would alone have sufficed to prove for the site high antiquity. They showed an average thickness of sixteen feet, and, apart from large rough slabs used in the foundations, consisted of remarkably regular and closely laid brick-work. The bricks, sun-dried yet solid enough, were about five inches thick and measured on the average fifteen by twelve inches. Neither the material, a fine clay plentifully mixed with pebbles, nor adequate water for making them could have been obtained on the spot, and their transport to this height must have greatly increased the trouble of construction. Both here and at Kansir the conjecture suggested itself that the insertion of thin layers of twigs and brushwood (here from the juniper growth which is still to be met with in some of the neighbouring side valleys) was primarily intended as a substitute for an adequate supply of wet plaster to set the bricks; want of water at such a height must have rendered this difficult to obtain. And the observations subsequently gathered along the ancient Chinese border wall

34. CHINESE FORT OF TASH-KURGHAN SEEN FROM NEAR LEFT BANK OF RIVER.

35. RUINED WALL AND BASTION OF KIZ-KURGHAN SEEN FROM SOUTH-WEST.

in the desert west of Tun-huang fully supported this opinion.

But whatever the origin and purpose of this peculiar constructive feature may be, I felt certain that the old fastness was the same which Hsüan-tsang had seen or heard of. The way in which he records the ancient legend then clinging to it leaves no doubt about its having become ruined long before his own time. The local tradition he had heard ascribed the stronghold to the Han times, the earliest period of Chinese influence in the Tarim Basin ; and I felt not a little pleased to think that here, at the very first point where I had touched his Central-Asian route, archaeological evidence on the spot confirmed afresh the often-proved trustworthiness of my Chinese patron-saint. But how striking, too, was the evidence afforded by the ruins for the dryness of the climate which prevails in these mountains, and which alone could account for their survival in so exposed a position from so early a date !

When, after making a rapid plan of the ruins, we had safely descended and were continuing our march in the failing light, I felt more than ever impressed by the natural strength of the Kiz-kurghan position. The narrow track leading by the left bank of the river was completely commanded by rock walls ; these towered so sheer above it that some contrivance of ropes would have enabled the defenders to gain direct access to the river water. Close investment of the fastness was impossible either from the river or the winding gloomy gorge of the Kiz-kurghan Jilga, forming a huge natural fosse with precipitous rock scarps on both sides hundreds of feet high.

Proceeding down the gradually widening defile of the Tash-kurghan river, I passed old terraced fields with traces of canals from the side valley of Kara Jilga, and was thus able to realize that Kiz-kurghan had once guarded not only the great route from the Pamirs but also the old western limits of Sarikol cultivation. At Pisling, where we halted for the night near two mud-built huts and some felt tents permanently tenanted by Sarikolis, I found fields tilled quite recently. The complaint here as at Dafdar, a small settlement of Wakhan immigrants across the river, was that the ripening of the oat crops was very uncertain owing to the rigorous climate.

There was, indeed, no sign of spring yet in the air or on the ground when next day, May 31st, we did our long march of forty miles down the wide, open valley to Tash-kurghan. Still the extensive stretches of ground terraced and prepared for irrigation which we passed on the left river bank down to the mouth of the Taldekul Jilga, a distance of some eight miles, and with widths up to half a mile, gave evidence both that cultivation is possible in this elevated portion of central Sarikol and that a steady growth of population makes the need of it felt. When I passed down the right bank in 1900 I could not fail to note clear traces of the desolation which a long succession of raids from Hunza down to 1891 had worked. By rendering all permanent occupation in the valley insecure they had greatly reduced its population, and land once manifestly occupied had passed out of cultivation.

Since 1900 the tide of returning prosperity had grown stronger, and there was reason to think that the reclaimed areas which I saw now, and which for the present were being sown only in turn every third or fourth year by Tash-kurghan people, would in time be brought under annual tillage. On the right bank, in fact, enterprise already asserted itself in the shape of a new canal dug at considerable expense by one of the Ihsans who represent the Aga Khan's authority among the Mullai sect widely scattered in these regions. It was to bring the river water to the fertile meadows of Ghan which in 1900 I had seen as a mere summer grazing-ground.

But once we had left behind a succession of fertilizing side streams which descend from the high snowy range westwards, the ground along the left bank of the river changed into a dreary waste of gravel 'Dasht' fringed by light dunes. The sky had become overcast as if to harmonize with the barren landscape, and the last twenty-four miles of our ride had to be done with an icy north wind blowing in our faces. So I had little attention to bestow on the precarious cultivation started some five miles above Tash-kurghan, which owed its existence to a new canal dug under official Chinese auspices. But for the latter I felt all the more grateful when on arrival I found a neat little rest-house of the orthodox Chinese type ready to give us the shelter we badly needed.

Preceding fatigues and the arrangements needed to assure a rapid onward journey to Kashgar detained me for two days at the modest village which forms the traditional capital of Sarikol. The ruins of the old walled town, which occupy a conspicuous plateau of conglomerate cliffs rising above the left river bank, exactly as Hsüan-tsang and an earlier Chinese Buddhist pilgrim, Sung Yün, describe it, together with the modern Chinese fort built in one corner of the ancient site, remained just as I had seen them six years before (Fig. 34). But otherwise the interval had brought some significant changes. A little before the outbreak of the Japanese war the Russian Consul-General of Kashgar succeeded in planting a small Cossack garrison at this dominant point of Sarikol, for better control of trade or smuggling operations to the Russian Pamirs. The provincial Chinese administration, uneasy about the purpose of this move, thought it best to meet it by the significant expedient of withdrawing the military commandant who previously with a handful of harmless soldiers had alone represented Chinese authority on this westernmost border of the empire, and of turning Sarikol, at least on paper, into a regular administrative district under a civilian 'Amban.'

It is true neither the scant population of these valleys which before had its affairs and taxation managed entirely through its local head-men, nor the unfortunate Amban, planted in this poor mountain tract with its forbidding climate and devoid of all fiscal resources, had reason to rejoice at the change. But anyhow there was now a miniature 'Ya-mên' of the regular type set up in the Chinese fort, while at the other end of the half-ruined site there rose the neatly whitewashed walls of the Russian fortified post with a captain of the Turkestan Staff to share the delights of residence with some forty Orenburg Cossacks. Munshi Sher Muhammad, formerly the solitary 'Political' representative at this meeting-point of three empires, had somewhat suffered from the drawbacks of honourable isolation. Now the presence of those rival dignitaries supplied a stimulating sense of diplomatic competition, besides society of some kind and increased responsibilities.

For myself I had reason to feel grateful for the newly built official rest-house by which the latest nominee to the Sarikol Ambanship had marked his desire for public improvements. A little Bazar, too, consisting of a row of mud-built booths just below Sher Muhammad's modest house, attested the Amban's good intentions. But their execution, plus certain financial recompenses exacted for his official exile in such a region, had cost money to poor Sarikol, and just then the Amban had found it prudent to take leave to Kashgar and meet local complaints before higher authority in person. So when I returned at the Ya-mên the visit his secretary had paid me, I had to content myself, instead of the Amban's presence, with viewing the proofs of his up-to-date tastes in the shape of photography, Russian colour prints, a gramophone, and the like. Strangely out of place they seemed in the grim and confined fort quarters; but manifestly the world was moving, even on the Pamirs.

I gained brighter impressions when I went with Sher Muhammad to pay my respects to Captain Bobusheff commanding the Russian garrison. The space inside the small post, a sort of defensible barrack square, was here confined enough. But the captain, a fine-looking, fair-haired young officer, and his lady, who did not seem to have suffered much from their exile in such depressing surroundings, gave me the friendliest welcome. The mid-day meal I shared with my hosts and the 'Feldscher' or military assistant surgeon, passed very pleasantly; for luckily the captain and myself could make up for our mutual linguistic deficiencies by fluent conversation in Turki. The captain was looking forward to be relieved from this solitary post in a few months. Yet in spite of all the privations in the way of comforts and society to which they had been exposed for over two and a half years, neither he nor his wife seemed to bear Sarikol a grudge.

Only when I quoted the old local saying which credits Sarikol with nine months of winter and three of summer, I was asked with a resigned smile to observe that their summer had already commenced. With the biting north wind still sweeping the valley and no leaf as yet on the few solitary poplars and willows, it seemed hard to believe in the reality of this Sarikol summer. My hosts had two little boys who, in spite of all drawbacks, were flourishing; and when on the eve of my departure Madame, prompted by true kindness and an intuitive perception of the weakest point in my camping arrangements, sent me two huge loaves of excellent Cossack bread, I was glad to return this valued gift by a tin of compressed chocolate which I knew would be welcome to the youngsters.

At Tash-kurghan I divided my party. Rai Ram Singh had to be left behind, to start systematic survey work by triangulation from its vicinity. He was then to carry it down a portion of the Tash-kurghan river valley hitherto unexplored, and subsequently to extend it northward across the eastern buttresses of the great Muztaghata range. I myself was anxious to reach Kashgar as early as possible, in order to push on there the organization of my caravan, before my old friend and helper, Mr. G. Macartney, C.I.E., the Indian Government's representative, should leave for his summer camp in the hills.

The most direct route to Kashgar was the caravan track which crosses the great spurs radiating from Muztagh-ata to the south and south-east, and as it had not been touched by me before and presented several points of antiquarian interest, I was glad to follow it now. Only I made up my mind to cover its ten regular marches in six days in spite of the baggage. Early on June 3rd I set out from Tash-kurghan and, after selecting with Ram Singh a convenient triangulation base for measurement near Tiznaf, marched down the river through a gloomy and twisting rock defile known as Shindi. This, as well as the still narrower side gorge into which the route turns northward at the small hamlet of Shindi, becomes impassable as soon as the snows melt in earnest, and access to the

Chichiklik plateau has then to be sought over the high pass of Kök-moinak.

This year deep snow was said still to cover the latter, and so I felt glad to be able to avoid it by continuing on June 4th from Kara-kapa, our night's camp, the ascent along the stream which drains the Chichiklik. But progress in the gorge soon became terribly difficult, owing to the confused masses of boulders which choke it and the steepness of the rock slopes on its sides. At several points the baggage had to be unloaded and carried by the pony-men. So it was not until 2 P.M. that we gained at about 14,000 feet the easy detritus slopes leading up to the Chichiklik Maidan or plateau.

It was curious to find at that height an almost level plain, about two and a half miles long from north to south and over a mile across, bordered all round by snowy ridges, and to see with my own eyes how closely its appearance agreed with Hsüan-tsang's description of the level space comprising "some thousands of acres" which he saw on his route to Kashgar and at two days' marching distance from the Sarikol capital, "in the midst of the four mountains belonging to the eastern chain of the Ts'ung-ling mountains." The pilgrim has recorded the severe troubles encountered by merchant caravans on this desolate high plateau, where "both during summer and winter there fall down piles of snow, and the cold winds and icy storms rage." He has also related an 'old story' how once a great troop of merchants, with thousands of followers and camels, perished here by wind and snow. A saintly man of Sarikol was supposed to have collected the precious objects left behind by the caravan, and to have built with the proceeds a hospice for the shelter of travellers.

The topographical indications given by Hsüan-tsang had before induced me to identify this locality with the Chichiklik Maidan, and the accounts I heard from Muhammadju, my experienced Yarkandi caravan-man, and my Sarikoli followers were convincing as to the losses which this desolate high plateau, exposed to the winds and snows, claims annually in animals and at times in men, too. But now I had the additional satisfaction of tracing on a low knoll near the centre of the plain the foundations of a square enclosure, some thirty-five yards on each side, built with rough but massive stone walls. It seemed likely to mark the remains of the ruined hospice which my Chinese pilgrim guide had referred to, and the decayed graves I thought I could trace inside supported the conjecture. For had I not found elsewhere on my Central-Asian travels the continuity of local worship illustrated so often by the preference with which pious Muhammadans buried their dead at sites already sacred to Buddhist tradition? But there was matter-of-fact evidence, too, of the spot being suited for a hospice, in the shape of two huts erected under Chinese orders some two hundred yards away. Though dating only since Sarikol had received an Amban, the huts looked already half-ruined.

After our experiences across the Baroghil and Wakhjir the snow-beds encountered on the Chichiklik Maidan, relatively firm under a grey heavy sky, did not impress me so much as they might otherwise have done. Yet I could not help realizing the trials presented at other times by this bleak plateau close on 15,000 feet above sea, as I recalled here the account left by Benedict Goëz, the worthy lay Jesuit, whom missionary zeal had sent in 1603 from the court of Akbar in search of fabled Cathay. From the hamlets of "the province of Sarcil," *i.e.* Sarikol, he and the large Kafila of merchants to which he had attached himself for safety, reached in two days "the foot of the mountain called Ciecialith (Chichiklik). It was covered deep with snow, and during the ascent many were frozen to death, and our brother barely escaped, for they were altogether six days in the snow here. At last they reached Tanghetar (Tangitar), a place belonging to the kingdom of Cascar."

By nightfall we struggled down to Tar-bashi, some 3000 feet lower, where a Kirghiz Beg offered us comfortable shelter in his felt tents. Next morning we entered the deep-cut defile eastwards, appropriately known as 'Tangi-tar,' *i.e.* 'the narrow gorge,' through which the winter route passes eastwards. For over two miles it leads in the stream bed itself between high frowning rock walls, overhanging in places, which in case of a sudden rush of flood-water would leave no escape. Luckily the snows were late in melting, and with the help of the Kirghiz yaks we got our baggage safely through. At a particularly confined point, where deep pools of tossing water between big slippery boulders obstruct progress, I noticed large and well-cut holes in the rocks on either side evidently intended for a bridge (Fig. 10). The work looked decidedly ancient. But there was for me another memory of old times haunting this forbidding passage which in the spring and summer becomes altogether impassable. This was in all probability the narrow defile where Hsüan-tsang's precious elephant, brought all the way from India, got lost in the water during the confusion caused by an attack of robbers, as duly related in his biography.

Where the defile widens lower down we came upon the first shrubs and flowers near the Kirghiz grazing-ground of Toile-bulan (Fig. 37), and after making our way up another steep valley and across the loess-covered Tor-art spur reached our night's halting-place at Chihil-gumbaz. Apart from a number of ruined Kirghiz tombs which account for the name 'Forty Domes,' the valley bottom shelters a few fields of oats. Leaving the route to Yarkand which here branches off south-eastwards, we ascended on the morning of June 6th to the long-stretched ridges of the Kashka-su Dawan (Fig. 36). Thickly covered with loess and in parts quite of down-like appearance, these ridges, in spite of their elevation of probably close on 13,000 feet, seemed to offer excellent grazing, the most extensive I had yet seen on the rims of the Tarim Basin. I was delighted to greet familiar flowers again, small white daffodils and a hardy sort of iris common in Kashmir.

Glorious was the wide view to the south reaching the high snowy range between the Tash-kurghan and Zarafshan rivers, those two great feeders of the Tarim. But there lay fascination for me also over the far less imposing vista which spread out east and north-eastwards. A succession of absolutely barren transverse ridges,

36. OUR TRAIN OF YAKS AND PONIES CROSSING THE KASHKA-SU DAWAN. VIEW TO SOUTH.

37. KIRGHIZ HEAD-MEN AND FOLLOWERS IN FRONT OF FELT TENT, TOILE-BULAN.

fantastically serrated and fading away in a yellow haze : the farthest edge of that great desert plain which had been drawing me back with force, and which was now soon to greet me once more.

The Kashka-su Dawan was our last pass, and the route to the plains now lay open before us. Between bare and much-eroded rock spurs we followed the easy valley north-eastwards, down to where a large Kirghiz camp, near the side valley of Pokht-aghzi, offered us shelter and supplies for the night's halt. There was a good deal of grazing in the well-watered bottom of the valley, and I was not surprised at the Kirghiz 'Bai,' who hospitably received us, claiming fully a thousand sheep, a hundred yaks, and some dozen of ponies as his own. But both physique and ways of living showed a falling-off from the standards prevailing among the hardier Kirghiz of the Pamirs.

The ponies for which we exchanged our yak transport at Pokht-aghzi allowed us to effect a big march of over thirty-five miles on the next day. For the first part plentiful clumps of wild poplars and frequent patches of brushwood growing near the banks of the shallow river tempered the barrenness of the hill slopes. But as the valley descended and widened, the young green of isolated bits of cultivation was the only relief for the eye. Over the yellowish bareness of the much-broken hillsides and the broad wastes of rubble beds in the valley there brooded already the glare of a Turkestan summer day. Below Aktala, where the stream from the Ghijak Pass joins in, the valley contracts again between mighty sandstone cliffs. Some compact masses, to which erosion has given a fantastic castle-like look, tower to fifteen hundred feet or more above the river-bed. It is the last natural gate of these mountains. After a few miles' hot ride along the stony river-bed now rapidly spreading out to a couple of miles' width, we reached the first small permanent settlement at Kichik-karaul, 'the Little Watch-station.'

One or two modest mud houses of Turki cultivators, ensconced among groves of high Tereks (or white poplars) and fruit-trees, and with green fields extending along

carefully irrigated terraces : that was all. Yet how
delightful it seemed to halt for a short while in the grateful
shade and, after all those long marches amidst barren
wastes of snow, rock, and detritus, to rest my eyes upon
this familiar picture of a tiny Turkestan oasis. If anything can approach the fascination of reaching new ground
long vainly sought for, it is to regain by a new route a
region endeared by former labours and still full of interests.
A lucky chance would so have it that Kichik-karaul had
served only a year earlier as the Macartneys' 'hill station'
during the hottest weeks of the Kashgar summer. So
when the kindly housewife of the nearest hut hospitably
sent out to me a bowl of cool milk by her ruddy good-
looking boy and asked for news of my friends, I had the
welcome touch of a personal *accueil.*

Some four miles lower down at the 'Big Karaul'
another reception awaited me as if from a far-distant age.
The sun declining behind us lit up in bold relief long lines
of battlemented wall, stretching along the low detritus
ridges on either side of the valley : picturesque ruins of
defences by which Yakub Beg, the successful chief of the
last Turkestan rebellion, had thought to guard the approach
to his kingdom. This quaint attempt at a 'Chinese Wall'
system, barely forty years old, seemed like a hint at the
very threshold to assure me of all the old-world lore still
surviving in this innermost portion of Central Asia. I had
ridden through the big crumbling gateway and received
friendly greeting and tea from the humble Turki scribe
who is supposed to keep watch here over wayfarers, when
a cluster of horsemen, including the Yüz-bashi or head-man
of Ighiz-yar, galloped up to conduct me to the first real
oasis.

The village of Ighiz-yar, where I was to halt for the
night, was cheerfully spoken of as 'quite near.' But I
scarcely minded when the distance stretched out to some
eight weary miles. Before me extended a view, wonderfully impressive in all its barrenness, across the most
perfectly regular alluvial fan I have, perhaps, ever beheld.
The absolutely bare gravel glacis sloped away unbroken
to the north and north-east. There was by a fortunate

chance scarcely any of the usual dust haze. The oases scattered over the huge grey cone of Piedmont gravel showed up clearly as distant dark patches. Of the river which accounted for their vegetation there was scarcely a trace left. Such water as had not sunk into the thirsty soil of stone and pebbles was carefully caught in narrow canals and conducted away for irrigation. Here and there I could see rising above the uniform slope small boldly crested pyramids, the last remnants of rocky spurs worn down by ceaseless erosion and half buried by the débris constantly accumulating around them. Far away on the horizon north-eastwards the eye caught lines of yellowish-red waves lit up by the last rays of the sun: it was the real sea of drift sand, the big dunes I had crossed in 1900 on my march from the desert shrine of Ordam-Padshah.

It seemed as if the *genius loci* of the whole Tarim Basin had wished to welcome me back with a vast view embracing its most typical aspects. From the little arbour of a solitary Mazar, passed soon after leaving the crumbling watch-station, came the sweet fragrance of flowering Jigda or Eleagnus trees, bringing back faint impressions of early childhood days spent under silvery olives. Strangely near all seemed in space and in time during that ride in the fading light—but it would need another pen to express it.

After a short and sultry night's rest passed at the Yüz-bashi's farm in Ighiz-yar village I set out early on June 8th for the final ride to Kashgar. I had somewhat rashly announced to the friends there my arrival for that date, and was eager to keep the appointment, even though I knew the distance to be reckoned at three full marches or, as it turned out in the end, well over sixty miles. I started at 4.30 A.M. with my young Ladaki and a few indispensable things on saddle ponies, while the heavy baggage under Naik Ram Singh's care was to follow by easier stages. In spite of the early morning the heat and stillness of the air felt oppressive as we rode across the bare gravel Dasht for some ten miles to Suget, a long-stretched collection of hamlets where the mulberries were just ripening. All view of the hills had now vanished.

Then followed another long stretch of waste, hard loess

left sterile through want of irrigation, and salty soil with plentiful Kumush or reed beds, until we reached cultivation again at the village of Kara-bash. Its irrigation proved to be supplied not by canals from the Ighiz-yar river but by springs of 'Kara-su' (literally 'black water') in which the water sunk into the gravel beds higher up on the alluvial fan comes to light again.

Soon we struck the high road from Yarkand some three miles before it enters Yangi-hissar, and were met there by an imposing cavalcade. The two dozen odd Hindu money-lenders settled in that flourishing district town had learned of my approach overnight and had ridden out to bid me welcome. Their wish to offer attention to an officer of the 'Sirkar' which protects them in this land of highly profitable exile was quite genuine, and the hospitality offered by old Hira Lal, their Ak-sakal or head-man, acceptable enough after the weary ride in heat and glare. Yet as I looked at the brave show of my *cortège* on prancing ponies I thought of all the mischief resulting from these hardy Shikarpuris being allowed to fasten themselves on Turkestan soil and leech-like to suck by their usury the substance of its cultivators.

White-haired Hira himself was quite an interesting person to talk to. As a path-finder for the whole money-lending fraternity he had come to Yangi-hissar by way of Bokhara as long ago as 1870. Since then he had seen the population of the district and the area of its cultivation fully doubled, mainly a result of the peace and order established by the Chinese after the troubled times of the Muhammadan rebellion. How much Hira himself had benefited by this economic development I could have guessed from the fine house and garden to which he welcomed me in the main Bazar of the lively town, even if I had not heard long before of the Lakhs of rupees he had remitted to his family in distant Sind.

But there was scant time to gather information from this far-travelled and successful representative of the Indian money-lending profession. When, during an hour's halt in Hira Lal's shady garden, I had refreshed myself with a wash and some tea and secured a change of ponies, I resumed my ride towards Kashgar. The route was not new to me; for I had followed it five years before on my return from Khotan. All the more interested was I to observe repeated proofs that cultivation had been steadily extending since then. The considerable areas of reed-covered waste or open drift sand, which the road to Yapchan, the next stage, had then crossed at intervals, seemed greatly reduced by new cultivation. I was never out of sight of trees and fields. Yet the horizon was greatly restricted by the dust haze which, raised by a steady north wind, tempered the intensity of the mid-day sun.

In my eagerness to move ahead I had left Yangi-hissar without waiting for the Ya-mên's Darogha who was to have joined us. In the absence of this modest dignitary serving as the visible mark of the support of official authority, the 'Ötangchis' who at the postal station of Yapchan ought to have furnished a change of our hired ponies, proved dilatory beyond their usual practice. An hour was lost before a change was secured, and even then the beasts produced looked so poor that I preferred to trust myself to the pony which had brought me from Yangi-hissar.

Progress over the twenty miles of dusty high road still before us was thus bound to prove wearily slow. But the increasing force of the Shamal blowing into our faces now added to the discomforts. From six o'clock onwards I was riding in blinding clouds of dust and sand, and often found it hard to keep to the right track, broad as it was. The baggage ponies had lagged far behind when at last in the dusk I found myself in front of the high clay walls enclosing the 'New City' of Kashgar with its Chinese cantonment. I knew that the high road to the 'Old City,' still seven miles off, where shelter was awaiting me with my friends, wound round this big square of walls looming through the dimness. Not a soul was stirring in the howling dust-storm for me to ask the right way, nor was it surprising that I mistook my bearings and rode on by a road almost at right angles to the direction I ought to have followed. It led me before long to marshy ground, and when at last, with the help of a young cultivator whom

I succeeded in unearthing from a hovel and enticing outside by the promise of a glittering silver piece, I had regained the high road thick darkness spread round about me.

Slowly I groped my way onwards, my worn-out pony stumbling in the ankle-deep dust. Grateful I felt for such guidance as the trees of the avenue gave with which we came in collision, and for the slight glimmer of light which at fitful intervals filtered through the murky air from humble booths occasionally passed by the road-side. The desolation of this great thoroughfare, which I remembered so busy in daytime with traffic between the 'New' and 'Old' cities, seemed almost uncanny and its length never-ending. At last when I had safely crossed the Kizil-su bridge and was getting among the silent suburbs of the 'Old Town,' the force of the Shamal slightly abated. Too wary now to trust to short cuts in such darkness, I kept steadily on till I struck the city walls—just on the side most remote from the Macartneys' residence. The city gates had been closed hours before for the night, and but for the howling of the dogs it might have been a city of the dead along the walls of which I was wending my way.

With the poor pony almost collapsing from fatigue and myself fairly worn out by the long day and the choking dust, I found myself at last, about 10 P.M., in the lane leading between gardens and fields to the Macartneys' house. What a relief it was when I recognized the familiar gate of Chini-bagh and found it still open! My shouts in the spacious outer court were soon answered by Turki servants who remembered me well, and a few moments later the heartiest welcome greeted me from my friends who had waited and waited and given me up at last. It took some time before I could clear off sufficiently my crusts of dust to allow me to sit down at a civilized dining-table, and midnight had long passed before the steady flow of news and talk after such long separation would let me seek rest. Yet it was cheerful, then and since, to look back on the hard ride which had brought to a fit close that journey of six weeks' 'rush.'

CHAPTER X

THE days in Kashgar which followed that night of my arrival in the midst of a dust-storm were as pleasant as the kindness of old friends and the varied comforts of the hospitable shelter they offered could make them. After five years' absence Chini-bagh still showed all the attractions which had so often made me look back with longing regret to my previous stays there, and which I have endeavoured to describe in the account of my previous journey. The British representative's residence, which Mr. Macartney's patient skill had evolved out of the modest nucleus of a native garden house, had been greatly enlarged in the meantime, and recalled more than ever an English home created somewhere in Eastern Europe. The garden still offered the same delightfully commanding vistas over the winding Tümen Darya and the fertile village lands which skirt the river's high loess banks. The trees along its shady avenues and walks were already putting on that profusion of fruit which made me remember my first long stay in August and September 1900 as a period of unbroken feasting.

But little had I then foreseen how greatly the brightness of Chini-bagh, with the old setting faithfully preserved, would be added to by the advent of a new master, the British Baby. Eric, the Macartneys' little son, who when barely six months old had proved himself a born traveller by doing the long journey from London to Kashgar at a tryingly early season without a day's illness, had long ago discarded the quaint conveyance, half perambulator, half sledge, in which I had seen him last in London preparing for his first travels. It was a joy to see the lively little boy running about in the garden, climbing its mud-built parapets whenever the protecting eyes of mother or nurse were turned, and otherwise enjoying the glorious freedom of a residence so spacious and a season so genial.

How memories revived of my own early childhood, of days quite as sunny spent in gardens which then to youthful eyes seemed as vast as a kingdom! But Master Eric, the happy possessor of this Kashgar kingdom, had for a few months enjoyed the additional good fortune of a baby sister to admire and to play with—the first British Baby which had made bold to see the light in innermost Asia. Ever smiling and cheerful, the little ruddy-cheeked maid was a constant visitor to the garden, imbibing robust health and good spirits with its fresh air.

I was anxious to start my desert campaign from Khotan as early as the abating heat of the plains would permit; and what with all the work planned elsewhere during the few intervening summer months, I could not spare more than a fortnight for Kashgar. So the 'rush' of the preparations to be got through there was necessarily great. Mr. Macartney's unfailing help and forethought did much to lighten their worries, and the gratifying way in which one of my old myrmidons after another turned up to resume his place in the rapidly forming caravan, to some extent simplified arrangements. Yet in spite of all the advantages which my hosts' inexhaustible kindness and local influence assured, the days slipped past far too rapidly before I was ready to move southwards. Within a week of my arrival, however, I managed to secure a set of eight camels, which looked big and well seasoned, from a trading convoy setting out to Almati across the T'ien-shan northward. The price I had reluctantly to pay for them, 88 Taels per animal, or about rupees 220 at the rate of exchange then prevailing, seemed high. But it was only an illustration of the great rise in the cost of most commodities which has taken place since 1900 through the rapid economic development of the whole region. This rise necessarily made itself particularly felt at Kashgar, the central emporium for the flourishing trade with Russian Turkestan and southernmost Siberia. Luckily the dozen ponies needed for followers and light baggage could still be picked up at reasonable prices, varying from rupees 35 to 50, on successive visits to the weekly horse market.

Strangely enough, the increased cost of living had in no way affected the leisurely or, to put it plainly, lazy and idling habits of the Kashgar artisans. Picnics in suburban gardens still appeared to them, as to the rest of the inhabitants just above the verge of downright indigence, the only legitimate occupation for the summer. The fruit season had set in about a week before my arrival, with delicious apricots in plenty, mulberries of several sorts, and the rarer cherries, all to be indulged in almost for nothing. Hence it proved a somewhat exasperating task to catch the leather-worker, carpenter, blacksmith, and tailor needed for the outfit of my caravan. One after the other of these worthies brought from the Bazar by Mr. Macartney's Chaprassis with kind words or a little gentle pressure, after a few hours' playing at work disappeared on the flimsiest pretence or escaped without even offering one. Not until many failures could sufficiently tame specimens be discovered, who by sheer apathy or force of habit condescended to turn up regularly for their easy tasks and generous wages when market-days and other local distractions did not prescribe a legitimate *dies festa*. More than ever I learned to appreciate the happy conditions of life in cases where pressure of population has not yet begun seriously to make itself felt, and to admire also the infinite patience and perseverance which it must have cost my kind hosts to create a home so well appointed and furnished as Chini-bagh.

So in genial ease the artisans progressed slowly with the numerous repairs which the baggage required, with the new saddlery ordered, and with that accumulation of little tasks which in more business-like regions might be disposed of in a day or two, but in Turkestan are apt to spread themselves out over weeks in oppressive fashion; and all the while I was hard at work in my shady garden quarters on proofs of *Ancient Khotan*. The accumulation of these well-printed quarto sheets from the Oxford University Press had been a heavy burden on my conscience ever since the 'rush' of my journey from the Peshawar border had made it a physical impossibility for me to 'eat up' the weekly consignments of proofs with which that distinguished *officina* supplied me regularly whenever a Dak could reach us. The Russian post *via* Farghana, now still further accelerated by the opening of the Tashkend-Orenburg Railway, furnished a quick means of transit for the return of the corrected sheets, and twice every week I sent packet after packet to the letter-box of the Russian Consulate to catch the despatches.

But apart from the chance of clearing off a literary obligation, what a luxury it seemed at Kashgar to be within nineteen or twenty days' post of dear friends in the Far West! All through the two years of travel which followed, my mail bags sent over steadily growing distances from the East carried brief communications for transit by the Russian post, while the bulk of my letters, especially those of any importance, were for safety's sake directed by the far longer but 'all-British' route *via* Hunza and India.

At the Russian Consulate I met from the first with the friendliest reception. The Anglo-Russian agreement seemed at Kashgar happily anticipated, at any rate in personal relations. M. Kolokoloff, who had succeeded Consul-General M. Petrovsky about two years before, proved an officer exceptionally well acquainted with things Chinese and full of interesting information about the Far East. He had been Russian Consul at Mukden during the first period of the Japanese War, and the description of his experiences brought the scenes of those historical events strangely near. Nor could I fail to be impressed with admiration for the patient heroism of Madame Kolokoloff, who had been forced to leave Mukden for St. Petersburg with her youngest child only nine days old immediately after the outbreak of hostilities. That weary journey of close on two months must have been an experience to try strength, physical and mental, more perhaps than many a long journey of exploration.

Close to the Consulate the local agency of the Russo-

Chinese Bank, just established at Kashgar when I left in 1901, had reared for its abode quite a 'Europe' structure. It is true that the spacious rooms with big glass panes, swinging doors, and other Western luxuries seemed to have their peace but rarely disturbed by business. As I walked in the well-shaded little lane leading from the Bank to the Consulate past houses and gardens of the Russian colony, I had somehow the feeling as if a little corner of Europe had been reproduced here more thoroughly than it ever could be in India, even in a hill station. But then here, just as practically throughout the whole of Russian Turkestan, there was no insidious climate and no rigidly separated ethnic environment to be reckoned with, and—the Europe reproduced was an unmistakably Eastern Europe.

The first days after the dust-storm which had swept across the oasis on the day of my arrival were relatively cool, and after a light shower or two on June 11th the air cleared so remarkably that for a whole long summer day I could enjoy the glorious view of the great snow-clad range far away to the south-west, bordering the Pamirs and familiar to me from my first journey. The huge dome of Muztagh-ata itself, that point of convergence for the classic Imaos, is hidden from view at Kashgar. But the line of high glacier-girdled peaks which radiates from it northward was perfectly visible, and I much regretted Ram Singh's absence in the mountains, as the opportunity would have been excellent for a fresh triangulation and fixing of the position of Kashgar.

But the summer dust-haze soon reasserted itself, the heat steadily rising. At last even the nights became sultry, though I took to spending them in my tent pitched under some big trees. Meanwhile my preparations were advancing at as rapid a rate as Kashgar ways would permit. The money supplies I wished to take with me at the start, in the shape of Chinese silver and a less bulky reserve of Russian gold roubles, had been secured at last by selling to Hindu money-lenders Supply Bills on Indian Treasuries. Their rate of exchange (Tangas 6 Dachins 10 for the Rupee) was slightly less detrimental than the one which the Russo-Chinese Bank, negotiating *via* St. Petersburg-London-Bombay, could offer.

The provision of what I may call the human sinews of war for my caravan was a matter for even more careful consideration. I knew that camels would be the mainstay of my transport, and I had learned by experience that for the safeguarding of these inscrutable animals, so hardy and at the same time so fastidious, there was no other course but reliance on a carefully selected expert. Now real camel-men must be born and bred, being products as much of inherited knowledge as of constant practice; and as almost all who prove capable and trustworthy, get in Chinese Turkestan permanently attached to big traders owning camel trains or become themselves carriers along the main trade-routes into Russian territory, the chance for a passing traveller of picking up the right sort of man is extremely limited.

So I felt heartily glad when on the very morning after my arrival Hassan Akhun, the lively young camel-man whose irrepressible inquisitiveness had proved to me so useful in the course of my former desert explorations, turned up claiming re-engagement (Fig. 38). Besides his good points I knew well the bad ones : his quarrelsome temper, his explosive pugnacity, his terribly sharp tongue, which made him enemies among all. But he was ever full of energy, always knew his own mind and what was good for his beloved camels ; and, best recommendation of all, I felt instinctively that it was the true spirit of adventure, so rare among Turki people, which made him look out for a fresh chance of desert travel with me. So quicksilvery Hassan Akhun was duly appointed to the chief command of my 'ships of the desert,' even before they were bought. In spite of many a petty tribulation thereafter, which justified my misgivings about the risks implied to the peace of our travelling household by Hassan Akhun's presence, I never regretted the choice.

It was, perhaps, even more difficult to secure at Kashgar a cook. It was true, I had managed to bring across the Hindukush and Pamirs worthy Nur Khan, that queer representative of the 'Khansama' type of Northern

38. HASSAN AKHUN, MY HEAD CAMEL-MAN.

Indian cantonments, whom in Peshawar I had been obliged to fall back upon as a last resource. But his physique was manifestly not equal to the fatigues of such travel, and besides, the occasions had been painfully frequent when he failed to produce digestible food, even of the simplest sort. He persistently ascribed his failure to want of ways and means for the due execution of those culinary rites which orthodox Khansama practice in Indian 'stations' ordains. It was wholly beyond my power to produce such regulation conditions as he claimed; and as the Macartneys were then without a proper cook, and their fully equipped kitchen just the place which he declared that he needed for giving proper scope to his talents, I was glad to leave Nur Khan behind at Kashgar.

The only available substitute was Ramzan, a young Kashmiri, clever but otherwise far from prepossessing, who a few years before had drifted up to Turkestan with a party of Sahibs, and with the versatility of his race had during periods of service with the Swedish missionaries picked up there a practical knowledge of Western cooking sufficient for my needs. My long acquaintance with Kashmiris has, in spite of all my attachment to their land, always made me fight shy of employing any of them for personal service, and I soon realized that Ramzan possessed more than an average share of such racial failings as fickleness, churlish temper, and ingrained habits of dirt. While still at Kashgar, he lost heart more than once at the prospect of dreaded hardships and tried to back out. But there was the encouraging example of my old men, all safely brought back from the Gobi and now eager to take service again, and probably a sneaking hope of cutting the rope whenever he might have had enough of travelling—and a more than liberal pay. In my own mind I was determined to keep him to his contract wherever I might go, and to assure myself through him the food I needed for full fitness. The contract was kept, indeed, to the end, but the worries from the start were greater than I now care to recall.

There had been another applicant for the post in the familiar person of Sadak Akhun, my former Turki cook, and for the sake of old times and from regard for his undoubted skill I should have gladly taken him again into my service. But, alas! the natural development of the baneful propensities which had turned him before into a frequent source of anxiety, made this course quite impracticable. His 'Charas' habit, which had disturbed the peace of his mind more than once in the Taklamakan, had steadily grown since I said farewell to him at Osh in 1901. From a spell of Russian service, which was said not to have been exactly calculated to raise his moral tone, he had taken to keeping an opium shop—an occupation most suited to indulgence in his own cherished enjoyments. His haggard looks and unsteady eyes told a painful tale of decay far advanced. Was it for me to attempt his reclamation, an almost hopeless task, and to face the risk of being left stranded in the desert with a cook incapacitated by too heavy doses, or possibly liable to running amuck at the slightest provocation?

Scarcely different was the case of Niaz, my old Chinese interpreter, the humorous Tungan, who also immediately after my arrival came to ask to be re-installed in his old functions. I remembered only too well all the troubles which had arisen from his gambling habits and the systematic blackmailing he had practised on the former journey whenever he had passed out of my immediate control. As I expected, he had ruined himself completely after his new marriage at Khotan, and had long ago sunk to the ranks of that nondescript fraternity of 'Kamarbaz' or professed gamblers which haunts all Turkestan towns. To employ him again would have meant burdening myself in an aggravated form with cares I had learned to estimate properly. So a liberal present of silver was all I could give as a solace. I learned, of course, very soon that it had been offered in sacrifice to the 'God of the Dice,' to use the old Indian phrase. Ahmad Akhun, a Chinese-speaking Kashgari, who was recommended by one of the local Mandarins for employment, proved a safe though by no means too intelligent or energetic substitute for that troublesome old retainer.

But far more important than all the rest put together

was a qualified Chinese secretary. For the tasks before me the help of a Chinese scholar had from the first appeared indispensable. Having always had to carry on my labours in India amidst struggles for leisure, I had never had a chance of adding to my philological equipment by a serious study of Chinese, however much I realized its importance. And with plans of exploration which were to take me so much farther east and right into China proper, the sense of this great gap weighed heavily upon me. Though I had long before my start informed Mr. Macartney, that most helpful of friends, of my anxiety to secure a competent Chinese assistant, I knew that it would be no easy matter to find one fitting my peculiar requirements.

In view of probable finds of Chinese records and other remains of Chinese origin needing antiquarian elucidation on the spot, I was obliged to look out for a *literatus* with regular training. In order to find my way quickly into the rudiments of colloquial Chinese, and to make the most of such scanty lessons in the language as I might find time for in the saddle or in camp, it seemed important to secure a teacher acquainted at least with the elements of Turki or some other language which might serve as a medium of interpretation. Finally, I could not think of taking any one with me who was not willing and physically fit to face the hardships of travel. *Literati* of any attainments are rare enough in that land of exile, the 'New Dominion,' and they generally manage to find snug posts in the Ya-mêns with fair prospects of future promotion. The outlook of prolonged wanderings far away from the flesh-pots of official headquarters has nothing enticing for the 'Ssŭ-yehs,' the gentlemen-clerks and office candidates, whose ranks were alone likely to contain a suitable man.

It was hence a pleasant surprise to me when Mr. Macartney on my arrival informed me that he had already a likely aspirant *in petto*,—a friend of the Chinese Munshi to the Agency whom Macartney had heard of at Yarkand. He was promptly written for to present himself in person, and duly arrived some ten days later. Yin Ma Chiang, or Chiang-ssŭ-yeh (Fig. 39), to give him his familiar title, impressed me at once very favourably by his lively ways, frank and kindly look, and an unmistakable air of genial reasonability. His terms seemed at first by no means low, amounting, with allowances for a servant, to 50 Taels or about rupees 120 *per mensem*. But in view of the high rates of remuneration prevailing for Chinese clerical employment throughout this outlying province, there could be no questioning on that score.

Chiang-ssŭ-yeh cheerfully assured us he was prepared to face the 'Great Gobi,' and something in his round jovial face and in the alert gait of his slight but wiry body gave me hope that he would know how to shift for himself even on rough marches and among the discomforts of desert camps. Mr. Macartney, whose knowledge of everything Chinese is profound, and who can read human character in general with rare penetration, found Chiang both clever and straight, and thought he might do some day as a successor to the Agency Ssŭ-yeh. This hope would, of course, act as an inducement to my Chinese assistant and mentor to stick to me, and was therefore confidentially hinted at.

Chiang's stock of Turki was extremely slight, in spite of some seventeen years' stay in the country, and at first sounded scarcely more intelligible to me than Chinese. It was the queer lingo which has grown up in the 'New Dominion,' by a constant process of clipping and transmogrification in Chinese mouths unable to pronounce the consonantal combinations of real Turki or to use its elaborate inflectional system. Still, we soon managed to make intelligent guesses as to our mutual sayings, and within a few hours from our first interview Chiang was formally attached to my establishment and busily helping to check Chinese names in my proofs. How I then wished that years of Sinologist study could have provided, for intercourse with my new Chinese assistant, that common stock of scholarly interests which my knowledge of Sanskrit had given me from the start, for work with my Pandit friends in Kashmir!

But it did not take long, once we had been thrown together in the constant intercourse of daily travel, before

39. CHIANG-SSŬ-YEH, MY CHINESE SECRETARY AND HELPMATE.

I began to realize how much gratitude I owed to Mr. Macartney for his thoughtful choice. It was a piece of real good fortune which gave me in Chiang, not merely an excellent teacher and secretary, but a devoted help-mate ever ready to face hardships for the sake of my scientific interests. His vivacity and inexhaustible flow of conversation lent attractions to the lessons I used to take in the saddle while doing long marches, or else in camp whenever it was pitched early enough in the evening. Once I had mastered the very rudiments of colloquial Chinese, his ever-cheerful companionship became a great resource during long months of lonely travel and exertion.

From the very first his unfailing care, good manners and tact assured me that I had not merely a faithful helper by my side, but a gentleman and true comrade. Very soon, with the true historical sense innate in every educated Chinese, he took to archaeological work like a young duck to the water. With all his scholarly interest in matters of a dead past, he proved to have a keen eye also for things and people of this world, and his ever-ready flow of humorous observations lightened many a weary hour for us both. But what it took time to make sure of, and what always surprised me afresh, was the cheerful indifference and the physical toughness with which Chiang could bear up against privations and discomforts. Often as I look back on all we went through together, I have wondered to what merits (of a previous birth, perhaps?) I was indebted for this ideal Chinese comrade of my travels!

To secure from the start the goodwill of the provincial Chinese government for my fresh explorations was, of course, an important object of my stay at Kashgar. In this direction, too, Mr. Macartney's kind offices, supported by his personal influence, were of the utmost value. A recollection of my previous archaeological labours about Khotan had helped to prepare the ground favourably, even though, with the kaleidoscopic shuffling of appointments which forms so essential a feature of the Chinese adminis-trative system in Turkestan, I could not expect to find any of my old Mandarin friends still actually on the scene. Official visits paid during the first days of my stay put me in touch with the Tao-t'ai and other local Mandarins, and Mr. Macartney's company made me, as of old, feel quite at home in their Ya-mêns.

The amiable and learned old Tao-t'ai, who five years before had shown such kind interest in my efforts to trace the footsteps of my Chinese patron-saint Hsüan-tsang, had passed away within a year of my bidding him farewell. But his successor, though a man evidently with a far keener eye for the good things of this world, was in no way behind him in attention and readiness to oblige. The first visit I paid him was promptly seized for a cheerful lunch party, which was shared by the genial superintendent of foreign trade affairs. Though only a small informal feast, this lunch ran into some eighteen courses, but all so neatly served and relatively so wholesome that my apprehensions as to its results on one long accustomed to simple diet proved wholly unjustified. Of course, we had swallows' nests, preserved fish and fruit from China, and other expensive delicacies; for our host had known how to make his pile (he was credited on the best authority with having sent the year before a million of roubles in gold to his Chinese home *via* Hunza and India), and did not hesitate to make free use of his savings for a little display and high living.

At his table I first realized how much the attitude of the Chinese official class in the 'New Dominion' towards Western, in this case specially Russian, customs and imports had changed during the few years since my previous visit. There were clean well-ironed napkins, instead of the damp hot towels, for use during the meal. My conservative feelings received a shock when I was asked to seat myself at a table spread in white, that colour of mourning formerly tabooed on all festive occasions. Knife and fork were handled with perfect familiarity by our convives, and eating-sticks seemed to lie on the table merely out of deference for time-honoured convention. It was curious to recognize in such changes small but significant effects of that great historical movement of Chinese 'reform' to which the Russo-Japanese War has given the final impulse. The menu, however, was still so thoroughly

Chinese that even Mr. Macartney confessed himself puzzled as to the real character of certain savoury dishes.

In spite of all the causes making for delay, I pushed on my preparations sufficiently to allow me to fix the time of my start southward for June 23rd. Two days earlier I indulged in a hot midsummer day's outing, in order to visit a ruined site beyond the northern edge of the Kashgar oasis which had escaped me during my previous stay. The ruins of Och-merwan, 'The three windows,' had never been mentioned to me before, probably just because they were familiar to most Europeans stationed at Kashgar. Leaving Chini-bagh by the great route which leads north towards the Artush Valley and the passes across the T'ien-shan, I found the ruins where the barren gravel-strewn Dasht of Chamalik Sai skirts the right bank of the Artush River. A much-decayed Stupa, built in sun-dried bricks of large size, rises to a height of some thirty-two feet above a low loess mound, which seems to owe its existence to wind erosion having lowered the adjacent open ground. The much-scoured appearance of the absolutely barren foot-hills beyond the broad and almost wholly dry river-bed, and of those lining its debouchure from the south, bore ample evidence to the great erosive force which the desert winds must exert here even so close to the edge of a large cultivated area.

The outer surface of the solid brick structure had suffered so badly as to render impossible an exact comparison of proportions, etc., in its dome and base stories with those of the Mauri Tim Stupa I had surveyed six years earlier to the north-east of Kashgar. But the size of the bricks and the manner of construction left little doubt about its belonging approximately to the same period. This relic of Buddhist worship sufficed to determine that the ruined walls enclosing two small forts of irregular oblong shape a little to the north-west (Fig. 40), and known locally as Khakanning-shahri, 'The town of the Khakan (or Great Khan),' were also of pre-Muhammadan date. The narrow ridge of clay and gravel which these walls occupy, rises to forty feet and more above the level Dasht southward, and, falling off on the opposite side in precipitous cliffs towards the deep-cut river-bed, offers a natural position of defence. Within the crumbling walls, which are built of bricks of practically the same size as those of the Stupa (fifteen by twelve inches and about four inches thick) and have a thickness varying from three to five feet, there appeared no structural remains inviting excavation. Nor was there much hope of relics of interest, such as written records, surviving to any extent on ground bare of the protecting cover of drift sand, and particularly exposed by its slope to the effects of such downpours as this north-western rim of the great basin from time to time knows.

So, after completing a plane-table survey of the ruins under a burning sun, I rode on north-westwards where the road to Artush skirts on its left a long sandstone terrace rising with an almost vertical rock face above the flat riverine Dasht. There, carved into the rock at an elevation of about fifty feet above the top of the débris slope which has accumulated at the foot of the terrace, and about as much below the overhanging brink of the latter, gaped the three niches close in line which are known as Öch-merwan. The doorways, carefully carved from the rock within shallow recesses, showed slightly slanting jambs, and seemed to measure about eight feet in height and about six feet across. I could easily make out at the back of the shallow central niche the painted head of a seated Buddha with hair-knob and halo, which Mr. Macartney appears to have been the first to notice.

The two side niches seemed much deeper, and suggested a connecting passage behind, which would permit the orthodox circumambulation or 'Pradakshina' of the sacred image in the small central shrine. Square holes cut into the rock at irregular intervals below the niches had once served to support the scaffolding needed for access to this little cave temple. To clamber up to it with the help of a rope let down from above proved impossible, and there was no time to improvise a rope-ladder such as I understood had been used by the Cossacks, who first visited the caves. Since they had been examined subsequently also by the members of the German archaeological mission which spent some time

40. RUINS OF OLD FORT, KHAKANNING-SHAHRI, ABOVE RIGHT BANK OF ARTUSH RIVER.

41. MUHAMMADAN SHRINE AND CEMETERY ON ROAD TO KASHGAR.

at Kashgar during the preceding autumn, I could rest content with what my glasses showed me.

The ride back in the evening was delightful. Even before we reached the oasis, the weary desolation of the baked grey Dasht was relieved by the steady flow of mounted village folk returning from the Kashgar Bazar day. As soon as we passed the edge of the irrigated area, all senses felt revived by the fresh air, the brilliant colours, and the life pulsating around us. As I rode in the grateful shade of big poplars and mulberry-trees along the winding high road, my eyes never stopped feasting on the pictures which the yellow expanses of ripening corn, broken by deep green groves of orchards and the gleaming white cupolas of half-ruined cemeteries (Fig. 41), presented in the warm glow of the evening sun. The endless succession of villagers' parties riding gaily homewards on ponies and donkeys seemed like a rippling human stream, and the road, which traffic has worn into the soft loess soil to a depth of several feet below the adjoining ground-level, like a canal specially made to receive it. To the hardy little animals, which in the morning bring to market their masters mounted above heavy loads of country produce — for no Turkestan cultivator ever walks if he can help it—this return home in the evening with much-lightened burdens must seem a positive treat.

Of course, market day in town is the right occasion for the display of fine clothing, and the large proportion of well-dressed figures among the peasants, and especially their women-folk, was a striking proof of the prevailing prosperity. The bright red gowns of loose cut which local fashion favoured among these Kashgarian ladies, supplied splendid patches of colour, and the fine peaked fur caps in more sombre hues which completed the costumes looked both picturesque and imposing. But I could not help pitying their wearers on such a trying summer day. The young folk manifestly shared my feelings; for wherever the road crossed canals we saw them full of frolicsome children splashing in the chocolate-coloured water. The Tümen River, where we forded it in view of the Russian Consulate grounds, spread out its evening flood in a wide sheet of reddish brown. With the crowds crossing and the bathers on both banks it presented a wonderfully gay scene. Never had Kashgar appeared to me so full of colour as on that evening, nor its peaceful comforts more enticing than when after nightfall and a refreshing meal I sat with my kind hosts enjoying the cool air and repose from the terraced roof of my Chini-bagh quarters.

It was the last quiet evening I could hope to enjoy in the society of my kind and ever - thoughtful Kashgar friends. But we little thought that my start would be preceded by a leave-taking from the friend who for them was the last link with what Mr. Macartney used to call old Kashgar times. Notwithstanding the rapid extension of trade relations towards Russian Central Asia and the marked rise in economic conditions generally, Kashgar has scarcely at all changed in the appearance of the town and of its native inhabitants. But the small European colony has altered its composition so completely, even since my first visit, that of the Kashgar which Mr. Macartney had known when he first came there to watch over Indian interests, there remained no one but old Father Hendricks, that quasi-international link for all the divergent sections of Kashgar European society.

The genial old ' Abbé,' as he used to be called, whom chance had drifted to Kashgar nearly eighteen years before, found there a quiet, yet sufficiently sociable *milieu* and was content to remain. But for half a year past he had been steadily declining in health. His friends and protectors were soon aware that cancer was shortening his life; but the old priest in his semi-Chinese costume still continued assiduously to pay his daily round of visits impartially to British, Russians, Swedes, Chinese. Painfully I saw him struggling to Chini-bagh, drawn by force of habit and perhaps by that irresistible thirst for social intercourse which had made the lively old gentleman act as a living newspaper for Kashgar.

Yet none of us realized how near the end was. For some days before my departure his familiar figure was missed by my hosts, and when on the morning of June 22nd Mr.

Macartney proceeded to Father Hendricks' humble abode within the city walls not far from the 'Water Gate,' he discovered the poor sufferer relieved of all further pains by what seemed to have been a nervous stroke. Alone in his ramshackle house he had persistently rejected all offers of nursing and help. So there was no one to witness the end. It was a pathetic close to a life which was strangely obscure even to the old Abbé's best friends. Nothing definite was known at Kashgar of his original home and relations, except that he had been born in Holland and reached Turkestan after some years of work as member of a Catholic missionary congregation in Manchuria. After a consultation with Mr. Macartney as the deceased's oldest friend and protector, the Russian Consul-General charged himself with the arrangements for the burial, no easy task in Kashgar, where European convention asserts itself although the means for satisfying its prescripts in this mournful direction are of the scantiest.

Though the intense heat of the day would have counselled an early start, I postponed my departure for Yarkand on June 23rd until after the funeral. When, after busy hours since daybreak spent in starting the baggage and settling petty accounts of artisans and the like, I followed with Mr. Macartney what we took to be a summons to the funeral, we found M. Kolokoloff and some of his officers still sitting at the carpenter's shop where the coffin was being got ready. It was to have been finished the evening before; but neither the incentives of life nor the call of death can disturb the ineradicable slackness of the Kashgar 'Ustad.' So there was nothing for the good-natured Consul but to assure the completion of the coffin by personal supervision of the labour. Weary hours passed over this. We soon found the air of the little shop stifling, and retired to the shelter of a neighbouring Sarai to talk in peace of the strange life now ended and—the tasks which the future had for me. Periodical visits to the shop showed us the gentlemen of the Russian colony partaking of a much-needed collation, and smoking by the side of the coffin now being completed with the help of some sturdy Cossacks. It was a picture in chiaroscuro, which with its contrasts deeply impressed itself on my memory.

At last towards noon the coffin was finished. The whole of Kashgar's European colony followed it through the narrow dusty lanes to the modest dwelling which the goodwill of the Chinese officials had let Father Hendricks occupy for years past as a matter of charity. The body rested alone in the locked-up house, but the grizzly-haired Chinese shoemaker, the solitary convert whom the old priest claimed, had faithfully kept watch on the house-top. The two rooms where the poor 'Abbé' had led his quaint domestic existence looked as dim and dusty as ever. Books, maps, *paperasse* of all sorts mingled in utter confusion with household objects and implements used for his chief practical occupation, the making of Kashgar wine. There was the humble altar at which he used to say his solitary masses, and not far from it the open trap-door giving access to the roughly dug cavity which served as wine-cellar and laboratory.

Not easily shall I forget this odd collection of litter, accumulated in the course of years and mingling with successive layers of Kashgar dust. It was like a cave by the seashore where the play of the waves had deposited strange débris from distant coasts. While the body, terribly reduced by long sufferings, was reverently transferred by Cossack hands to the coffin, I thought of the strangely faithful reflex which these surroundings offered of the departed's mental world. Learning, indeed, he had in plenty and experience of many people and lands; yet orderly use of this knowledge was as difficult as quick discovery of any particular object in this accumulation. But what only personal intercourse could reveal was the old priest's child-like kindness of heart and warm interest in all whom chance had brought near him.

The cortège which followed his remains to the grave was as large as European Kashgar could furnish. Orenburg Cossacks, tall strong-looking fellows from Vernoye, carried the coffin, while the rest of the Consulate guard marched in front. Bare-headed they did the slow journey to the small Russian cemetery, about a mile away, between the river and Chini-bagh, and did not seem to fear the mid-day sun beating down with painful intensity. Russians in Central Asia evidently get acclimatized far more thoroughly in some respects than Europeans ever can in India.

For me it was comforting to see the poor old 'Abbé' carried to his rest by men whose ruddy cheeks, fair hair, and general bearing were just those one might have seen among Slavonic peasants anywhere in Eastern Europe. The hymns they began to sing on nearing the cemetery were full of that sweet melancholy which lends charm to the national music of Russia. They were the only substitute for a burial service. There was no pope to read it according to the rites of the Greek Church, and to let the Swedish missionaries perform any religious functions on ground consecrated for orthodox Russians would apparently have raised objections among the Cossacks. Even for the mere burial of a Catholic the latter's permission had specially to be asked by the Consul. So there was nothing for us but to say farewell to the weary wanderer in reverent silence, and to trust that a tombstone which Mr. Macartney was preparing to raise would soon mark his last resting-place.

CHAPTER XI

TO YARKAND AND KARGHALIK

EARLY in the afternoon of the same day, June 23rd, I took leave of my kind hosts and the friendly shelter of Chini-bagh to start for Yarkand, my first *étape* on the long journey south-eastwards. It was not without a feeling of regret that I cast a farewell look over the sun-lit terraces of the garden and the stately poplar avenues which give shade to its walks. I could not say this time whether my return journey would bring me again to Kashgar, and anyhow an interval of two years seemed a long time even in Central - Asian conditions of life and travel. The Macartneys by their hospitality and unceasing care had made my stay a time of real rest in spite of all hurried labours. On saying good-bye to them I felt as if I were parting with the last living link, too, which bound me to dear friends left behind years before in distant Europe.

The journey which brought me in five days to Yarkand lay by the main road I had followed in parts during 1900-1901, and again on my ride from Ighiz-yar. But there was a marked change in the conditions of travel. After the trying heat of that afternoon and evening spent on the first march between Kashgar and Yapchan I realized that my travelling would have to be done mainly at night, both for the men's sake and for that of the animals. To take shelter during the day in a small tent such as mine was out of the question. So I had to abandon the thought of camping in the gardens which had offered peaceful retreats on former journeys, and instead to look out for a more solid roof to rest under during the heat of the day.

There were the official Chinese rest-houses or ' Kung-kuans' to receive me, spacious enough to accommodate us all. But their state of cleanliness left much to be desired, in spite of the notice carried ahead by Daroghas; and what with inquisitive Chinese caretakers and other travellers already established there, I found it difficult to secure peace and privacy. These Kung-kuans, intended in the first place to accommodate Mandarins when travelling between their stations, are invariably built after the plan of a Ya-mên, with an outer and inner court separated by those typical double-folding gates which open only for the honoured few while the ordinary mortal passes by the side. The central set of rooms, three in number, always faces this gate and, fronting regularly to the south as Chinese tradition in such buildings requires, is exposed to the full heat of the sun. Of shade under trees or otherwise the wide courtyards offer none, as my camels soon found when stabled there.

So after one red-hot day spent over proofs in the Yangi-hissar rest-house, I preferred to seek refuge in the houses of well-to-do villagers. Again I was struck by the degree of comfort to be found there, far higher than anything in corresponding conditions in India. At Kizil I was delighted to find my former visit remembered, and quarters prepared for me in the house of the Yüz-bashi whose orchard had offered such a pleasant camping-place in September 1900. The trees were now laden with ripening apricots and the ground splashed with big white and black mulberries. But the air was burning hot, fully 105° Fahr. in the shade, and even while sleeping outside in the open court of the house until midnight, it was difficult to get a breath of fresh air. Luckily the sky next morning was laden with yellow haze and clouds, and we managed to cover the twenty-four miles or so across bare stony Dasht to Kök-robat on the northern edge of the Yarkand oasis before 9 A.M. The mere sight of the green fields gave relief, and while working at my proofs all through the day under the mud-covered roof of a villager's loggia, I enjoyed the benefit first of the cooling gusts of an incipient dust-storm and then of a few minutes' rain. The shower was barely enough to lay the dust; yet in a region so exceptionally dry one learns to feel grateful for such favours.

The march of the next day, June 26th, which carried me to Yarkand city, proved unexpectedly pleasant. A little more rain fell before we started at 2 A.M. and the air cleared wonderfully. The snowy range towards Muztagh-ata showed distinctly at sunrise. Soon we were riding through the extensive tract generally known as Kara-kum, which a canal newly constructed by the late energetic Amban Liu Ta-jên has recovered from the desert sands. When I passed here five years before, the colonists were still engaged in levelling the slopes of the sand-hills and in cutting the distributing channels or Ariks; except at a few advanced spots no sowing had yet taken place. Now an expanse of fresh green stretched almost as far as the eye could reach. But to my surprise I realized that, apart from a strip of corn or lucerne fields here and there, only luxuriant rank growth was covering the carefully terraced fields and the banks of the Ariks.

The story told by Muhammadju, my Yarkandi servant, solved the puzzle. The fertilizing waters of the new canal had brought salts of the ground to the surface in most of the low-lying parts. The failure of one crop sufficed to drive back to their old homes the colonists whom the well-meaning Amban's 'Hukm' had forced to take up land here, though all of them knew that this saline outcrop was to be expected for the first few years. After five or six years, continued cultivation, or even the mere growth of rank grass and scrub, will have cleared the ground of all salts and the fields now deserted will be eagerly sought after.

But such is the ease of life prevailing in all these under-populated oases, that the effort of extending cultivation on such ground will not be persisted in except under continuous administrative pressure. This continuity is most difficult to assure under the prevailing administrative system, which practically farms out districts to rapidly changing Chinese officials. Liu Ta-jên, who had made the canal and who was able to start the new colony by his personal energy, had left the Yarkand Ambanship more than five years before. None of his successors had seen much advantage to himself in keeping up his efforts. Thus it was left to time and the growing pressure of population to attract these colonizing pioneers back to their fields too hastily abandoned.

In the meantime the rapid spread of wild plants and shrubs over this virgin soil of fertile 'sand,' or rather fine alluvial sediment, had created a sight such as rarely greets the eye of the traveller by a Turkestan roadside. There was a profusion of flowers and grasses such as I had never seen before in a land where irrigation is restricted to tilled fields or gardens and no moisture is available for soil not actually under cultivation. The hardy Kumush, a sort of reed and an old acquaintance from the desert outskirts, predominated in luxuriance. The large pools formed by canals that had not received proper cleaning were thickly covered with water-plants. Everywhere vegetation given this exceptional chance seemed to indulge in high revels. Even the sandy ridges, once dunes arrested in movement, which had not yet been levelled, were being clothed by a thick coat of bright green Kumush growth. So far is fertility spread by the abundant subsoil water now brought here. The young trees, too, planted by the settlers, were flourishing mightily in spite of the forsaken state of the fields which they were intended to line. Farther on by the roadside poplars and willows only three or four years old were giving thick shade, and showing a bulk such as trees of the same class in the less favoured soil of the Punjab would attain only after ten or more years. Naik Ram Singh, my authority for the statement, had a carpenter's keen eye for all tree growth.

Nearer Yarkand we passed miles of ground lying somewhat higher, also fertilized by the new canal. Here the initial difficulties seemed to have been less or to have been overcome with more vigour, owing, perhaps, to Liu Ta-jên's energetic presence. The comfortable big homesteads with their neat woodwork, the newly built clean Sarais and other features put me in mind of the great canal colonies of the Jhelam and Chinab, which have in the last two decades so completely transformed agricultural conditions in the Western Punjab. What changes and development these oases in the Tarim Basin might witness,

in spite of all 'desiccation' of climate, if only the modern
irrigation engineer were given a free hand and his efforts
backed up by a Western administration!

Once again I crossed the big Opa Darya, an old irrigation canal but now broad like a true branch of the Yarkand
River, by the bridge of Bigil.   In front of it there cantered
up to me and hastily dismounted a burly figure, honest
Tila Bai, of Badakhshi descent, the best of my old caravan-
men.   He had followed my summons from his village up
the Yarkand River, in order to exchange once more the
humdrum life of the settled petty landowner for the more
exciting experiences of the traveller's camp.   He, too,
must have felt dimly at times the call of the desert.   I
greeted him with a feeling of grateful relief; for under his
quaint broad figure, his jaunty gait, and at times bluff
manners I could be sure of a stout heart and absolute
reliability.   Besides he was an expert in ponies, and under
his care I knew that my animals would always get a fair
chance.

Some four miles outside Yarkand City, by the side of
one of those Pao-t'ais or brick-built square towers which
along the main Chinese high roads in Turkestan mark the
roughly measured distances of 10 Li (circ. two miles), the
whole body of Hindus in Yarkand, with Pandit Butha Mal
at their head, gave me a solemn welcome (Fig. 42).   No
money-lenders this time but hardy and respectable traders,
mostly from Hoshiarpur, to whose enterprise India and
British commerce owes most of its exports across the
Kara-koram.   It was again a grand cavalcade, like that
which in 1900 had conducted me to the old country
residence of Niaz Hakim Beg, once Yakub Beg's powerful
governor; and as I knew now what cool palatial quarters
were awaiting me, I did not mind that my loyal Punjabis
made the most of the occasion and led me by circuitous
routes through one principal Bazar after the other.   It was
a manifest satisfaction to them to display their Sahib to as
many people as possible in this flourishing trading centre.

I found the suburbs of Yarkand more verdant than
ever, and noticed once more in the many fine poplars and
elms unmistakable indications of a climate more genial than

42. RECEPTION BY HINDU TRADERS AT EIGIL, NEAR YARKAND.
Pandit Butha Mal fourth in front, from left.   'Pao-t'ai' in background.

43. BAZAR GROUP BY CANAL BANK, NEAR KARGHALIK.

that of Kashgar. The attractions of the Yarkand Chini-bagh, where I again took up my quarters, had in no way diminished. Often I had from afar recalled to my mind the picture of its spacious halls, and it was now cheering to make sure that the picture was true in all details. Plentiful Khotan carpets had been spread in all the main rooms, and I felt almost like the owner of all this grandeur coming back to his own place. Anyhow, the real possessor of this villeggiatura, Niaz Hakim Beg's son, was as obliging and anxious to efface himself as of yore. My only regret was that financial pressure had obliged him to sacrifice the delightful wilderness of the neglected old garden to prosaic wheat crops. Yet there still rose the fine big fruit-trees and the high enclosing walls to ensure seclusion.

The refreshing cool air of my lordly quarters and the unwearying help of the worthy Ak-sakal, Pandit Butha Mal, made it easy to use my four days' stay at Yarkand to the full. Additional ponies were secured after a good deal of trial and bargaining, among them a good-looking young bay horse for my own use, which passed as of Badakhshi blood. It proved with experience as hardy a mount as I could wish for, indefatigable on the roughest ground and quite inured to the privations of deserts without grazing. So, in spite of its unsociable temper, ' Badakhshi' in time became dear to my heart as a constant companion, though never quite near enough to rival my little canine comrade whom he at times obliged with a ride. Either Sahibs could still command more willing labour here than at Kashgar, or else the local picnic parties of Yarkand were less of an attraction—anyhow, tailors, tinners, etc., were secured for the remaining needs of my establishment. Surveyor Ram Singh now joined me, after having effected much useful new survey work along the eastern buttresses of the Muztagh-ata Range between the Tash-kurghan River in the south and the Kara-tash River towards Yangi-Hissar ; and, of course, after all the roughing undergone his equipment needed many repairs.

Chiang, my genial literatus, had a busy time, too, at Yarkand, where long employment at the local Ya-mên had given him many friends and local ties of another sort requiring attention before his departure on our travels. Chinese officials big and small are accustomed to carry all their worldly possessions about with them while in Central-Asian exile, and the amount of Chiang-ssŭ-yeh's proposed baggage in consequence looked distinctly alarming. That in spite of my inability to give adequate expression to my motives, I succeeded in convincing him of the need of great reductions in the baggage and in making him part even with the bulk of his cherished little library, was a first proof of his practical reasonableness. But I need not disguise the fact that, as he grew more experienced in the conditions of travel before us, he found scope for further reductions thereafter. On the other hand I managed to obtain for him at Yarkand a small tent of very light Indian make, and to improvise for it that warm inner lining without which it could not have given him adequate protection against the bitter cold of our winter campaigns in the desert. As an illustration of the influence exercised far away in Central Asia by modern facilities of travel I may mention that the most useful of our Yarkand craftsmen was a young tailor of local birth but Kashmiri extraction, who had already done his Mecca pilgrimage and by a year's residence in Stambul had also profited in his professional training.

Friendly intercourse with Pên Ta-jên, the Amban of Yarkand and a dignitary of prominent rank, also absorbed a good deal of time, but proved instructive and profitable owing to the keen interest shown by him in things historical. The search for old Chinese local names of these regions, in the works of Hsüan-tsang and other pilgrims of which I could show him the texts, lengthened not inconsiderably his return visit. I was duly rewarded for this when at a small dinner-party next day the Amban presented to me an interesting batch of old Chinese coins, chiefly of the early Sung dynasty (tenth to eleventh century), which had recently been found in digging foundations close to the 'Yangi-shahr' of Yarkand. They supplied the first definite indication that Yarkand occupies approximately the site of the ancient *So-chê* with which Chinese official nomenclature nowadays identifies it. But antiquarian topics did not occupy us entirely during the lavish and yet *recherché* feast to which the kindly old administrator treated my jovial Ssŭ-yeh and myself. Pên Ta-jên told me a good deal about his favourite son, who had been for two years a student in Japan and was now holding a good administrative post near Shanghai. He had never seen him since he was a small child. But the telegraph from Kashgar kept father and son in touch, in spite of the enormous distance, which letters by official Chinese post still took half a year or more to cover.

The Amban, in spite of his own strictly traditional learning, was full of admiration for Japanese success, but seemed inclined to attribute it mainly to the solid foundation which Confucian philosophy as studied in Nippon had prepared for it! Buddhism, I was sorry to gather, seemed to him too closely associated with superstitions of all sorts to deserve serious study, though out of regard for my revered patron-saint he politely refrained from putting this quite plainly. But the most pleasing item of converse was the news that P'an Ta-jên, my old friend and supporter in Khotan, had just been appointed from Urumchi to the office of Tao-t'ai at Ak-su. As the Lop-nor region was included among the districts attached to his new charge, his friendly influence was likely to assist my fresh labours even from afar. So his appointment at this opportune juncture seemed, indeed, an auspicious omen.

Visits to Mr. Raquette, the Swedish missionary, and his wife, old acquaintances in Kashgar now transferred to Yarkand, gave me occasion for evening rides through the Bazars and the winding lanes of the 'Old Town.' They looked far more picturesque and pleasing than those of Kashgar, a result mainly due to the plentiful presence of fine shady trees and of tanks which, to the eyes at least, were refreshing. But I wondered whether their water, stagnating probably for a great part of the year, was not largely responsible for that prevalence of goitre which old Marco Polo had noticed among 'the inhabitants of Yarcan.' Hidden away at the end of a narrow lane in a quiet part of the city, the Raquettes' house was quite a surprise by its neat and well-furnished European interior. Within eighteen months of their arrival the cheerful Swedish couple had managed to fit up their residence with whatever seems needful for a simple European household. There were well-made tables and cupboards, framed pictures on the walls, and a table laid out hospitably with all orthodox comforts. Mr. Raquette's widely appreciated work as a medical missionary gave him special opportunities for mixing with all classes, which he was using to compile a Turki dictionary on the basis of local materials. There is much about Yarkand to recall an Indian city, the relative luxuriance of its vegetation and the large colonies of Kashmiris, Baltis, Afghans comprised in its population. So when taking the air of an evening in the Raquettes' little garden, ensconced between silent walls of neighbouring houses, I felt as if I were being entertained by Mission friends in some native city of the Punjab.

My four busy days seemed almost too short a time for hunting up specimens of that old Chinese and Turkestan art ware which survives among the numerous old families of Yarkand as a sediment from more prosperous days, and the supply had manifestly diminished. Yet I managed to secure half a dozen fine 'Aptabas,' some hand-basins, jugs, etc., characteristic relics of the elaborate 'open' brass-work which once flourished among the crafts of Khotan. What with accounts of all sorts to settle, the debts of my Yarkandi servants to adjust with their creditors —debts are almost indispensable as marks of respectability in these parts,—and similar tasks to tax my reckoning faculties not yet fully accustomed to the intricacies of the local currency, it was difficult to snatch a few hours' rest during the night preceding my start.

The immediate objective of the journey on which I set out by daybreak on July 2nd was Karghalik, only two marches off to the south. But I intended to use the move also for a visit to the site of Kiziljai, from which a few old manuscript records, apparently in early Turki or Uigur, had been brought to Mr. Macartney some two years before. I knew that the remains there were insignificant, but all the same I wished to satisfy my archaeological conscience in regard to them. No definite indication could be secured as to the position of the locality, except that it lay beyond the Yarkand and Tiznaf rivers eastwards. So it was difficult to prevent the officious Beg and Darogha deputed to escort me from extending the march to Bagh-jigda, the nearest inhabited place to the site, over two days. However, I did not feel sorry for this, though the distance proved only sixteen miles ; for the slowness of our progress allowed me to get a good picture of parts of this fertile oasis and of ground on to Karghalik which had never been surveyed before.

The first day's march took me through richly irrigated country, and across the Yarkand River, filling then a single bed about a quarter of a mile broad, to the village of Tata. Here I found in the house of the local Yüz-bashi excellent quarters, all the more welcome since a much-delayed big mail had to be got ready for Kashgar. The adjoining orchard was exceptionally large and shady, the apricot-trees bending under their loads of luscious pink and yellow fruit, and the ground strewn with apples which had fallen before ripening.

It was just the season to make me realize fully the advantages of the 'Aiwan,' that prominent feature in well-to-do people's houses throughout the southern oases. It is a kind of square central hall or Atrium, having a roof well raised over the central area and provided with clerestory openings on all four sides. Sometimes on one or two sides the upper wall portion shows merely a grated wooden framework, freely admitting light and air. Thus during the hot summer months the Aiwan gives not only cool shade but access for any fresh breeze. Rooms or passages opening from this Atrium communicate with the rest of the house. One or two rooms, close to the entrance from the outer court, form the usual guest quarters known as 'Mihman-khanas.' Gay cotton prints hung as dados round the walls and Khotan carpets spread on the floors make them look quite cosy. But as light and air are admitted only by a small opening in the mud roof, the Aiwan itself makes far more inviting summer quarters. Raised platforms extend along all its walls, broad enough for rest or for work, and, as the position can be varied, what sunshine and heat passes in may be dodged.

For day and night such a spacious Atrium—and those I resided in usually measured from thirty to over forty feet square—seemed delightfully adapted to the climate. Again and again in my subsequent excavations I discovered exactly the same architectural arrangement in the ancient residences of sites abandoned to the desert, and always felt sure from personal experience that much of the daily life, long dead and buried, must have passed in those ruined Aiwans.

Whatever the owner's wealth, the modern country residences of the oases show little or no art about their construction ; whether the walls are of stamped clay as about Yarkand, or of plastered timber and wattle as in the Khotan region. But an enticing air of comfortable simplicity always pervades them, symbolic, as it were, of the lives of nonchalant ease which they witness. A very moderate income suffices to make one a ' Bai ' or capitalist in Turkestan ; and as long as there is plenty of food and something to spare for fine clothing, these favoured ones of a materialistic race see no reason to trouble much about things of the past, present, or future.

On the night of July 2nd there fell a shower of rain. No meteorological station could have measured its quantity ; yet with a fresh breeze from the north-east it was sufficient to render pleasant the short march next morning to the right bank of the Tiznaf River. The village lands of Kuma, Khan-arik, Öch-köl passed on the route seemed exceptionally fertile, and the grand avenues of poplars and almost equally high willows were a feast to the eye. The Tiznaf River, which flows here for a considerable distance parallel to the river of Yarkand before being absorbed in it near the large oasis of Merket, was in flood, and the crossing by the single small ferry-boat took hours for the baggage. The river flowed in a narrow but rapid channel, about one hundred and twenty feet broad, with a velocity of about two yards a second. Its depth was from ten to over fifteen feet. Yet, as we subsequently discovered, there was a ford scarcely a mile off where the spread-out waters would allow even laden donkeys to cross; but the slippery mud bottom would have made it unsafe for the camels.

Beyond the Tiznaf we were in Bagh-jigda, a narrow tract of cultivation between the river and the desert dunes clearly visible eastwards. The whole, though extending over eleven to twelve miles in length, is reckoned as one village, forming the domain of Nasir Beg, a rich landowner of Yarkand whom my informants credited with landed property amounting in the aggregate to some sixty thousand acres, a good deal of it, no doubt, as yet unreclaimed. At the residence of Musa Dogha (Darogha) I found a comfortable and cool shelter, worthy of the representative and land agent of so big a *seigneur*.

The 4th of July was devoted to a visit to Kiziljai, the locality where the Uigur manuscripts had been found. As it proved well beyond the extreme limit of the culti-vated area and on the very edge of the open desert of drift sand, the excursion of some twenty miles would have been a tryingly hot affair, had not the sky shown consideration for the promptings of my antiquarian conscience. Another shower of rain overnight, preceded by a mild dust-storm, had once more cooled the air, and a canopy of greyish-yellow clouds towards the east gave protection until towards mid-day. At 4.30 A.M., when we started, the horizon westwards was delightfully clear, and the high snowy ranges north and south of the Yarkand River were clearly visible, though fully fifty miles away in a straight line.

The first five miles lay through cultivation or rather large enclaves of it surrounded by ground which Kumush and other wild plants growing in luxuriance seemed to claim as their own. Yet there were canals large and small quite equal to a full reclamation of the whole area. Liu Ta-jên's energy had pushed on irrigation here too. But disputes about the water had arisen with the colonies of Merket fringing the right bank of the Tiznaf lower down, and a great commission of the Ambans of Karghalik, Yarkand, and Maral-bashi, whose districts adjoin here, had settled that the new canal of Bagh-jigda was to receive water only every third year.   Boundary ' Pao-t'ais ' marked now the extreme limit up to which Bagh-jigda could reclaim desert land.   But with the reduced allotment of water, cultivation of the many acres newly levelled had not proved sufficiently attractive, and so the luxuriant vegetation of the riverine jungle was allowed to step in and annex them.   Of course, it protects them almost equally well against the drift sand of the desert, for the benefit of future generations whom prospective pressure of population may force to turn their labour to such land.

While the observations here and in a few miles of young Toghrak jungle, carefully preserved by Nasir Beg for the sake of its fuel, were interesting, the antiquarian results of my visit proved scanty.   The first owner of the Uigur manuscript, a Bagh-jigda tenant, pointed out as its find-spot one of those curious tamarisk-covered sand-cones which form so typical a feature on the edge of the Takla-makan.   It turned out that more than ten years had passed between the discovery and the presentation of the manu-script fragments to Mr. Macartney.   How the several portions were found at greatly varying depths, as the original owner asserted, seems difficult to explain, seeing that these sand-cones are of relatively slow growth, and not likely to cover up parts of the same manuscript at periods separated by centuries.   But here, as in the case of almost all chance discoveries of this kind in Turkestan which have not been followed up at the very time, the critical verdict can only be : *non liquet.*

Two miles to the north of this place, and beyond a belt of fine Toghraks known as Kiziljai Mazar, I found numerous ruins of mud-built houses scattered over an area which, by its clearly traceable irrigation channels, its terraced fields and similar indications, was marked as having been occu-pied down to a not very distant period.   Mr. Macartney had visited this locality, called Koilogh-ata, earlier in the year and, stimulated by the find of the Uigur manuscripts, had the rubbish in one or two of these humble dwellings cleared.   But the only discovery rewarding his excavation was part of a leather slipper, and the chronological fixing of remains of this kind in Turkestan is as yet beyond the archaeologist's ken, unless indeed they are found together with dated relics, such as coins or ancient documents.

Two long marches on July 5th and 6th brought me to Karghalik. The barren yellow sands of the desert edge remained ever in view as we moved south along the right bank of the Tiznaf River. The holdings of the village of Kona-Tatar spread out in a narrow belt over a distance of fully seventeen miles, large areas between the patches of cultivated ground being abandoned to luxuriant reeds and riverine jungle. Considerable stretches of pebble Sai and barren loess steppe also intervened, and after crossing one of these it was doubly cheerful to find our quarters prepared at a substantial farm. Mihman Bai must have done well by the tiny oasis of about 200 acres on which he had grown old. His house with its fine Aiwan and numerous outbuildings, including a mosque, seemed the very type of a well-to-do ' Dehkan's ' residence, and I did not fail to get a plan made of it by Naik Ram Singh.

In the orchard close to the courtyard the trees were bending low under their fruit. On a single branch a little over one yard long I counted forty-five luscious apricots glowing in their glossy amber skins just like small oranges. There was the arbour, too, with its square central area enclosed by a double row of poplars, to serve as an *al fresco* feasting-place, or as a 'spare bedroom' in the summer. The mosque not far off looked a spot quite inviting for rest, with its well-raised hall open on all sides except the south-west, the direction of Mecca, and shaded by a wooden roof with quaintly carved posts of Persian style.

Increasing prettiness in the simple rural scenery marked our approach to Karghalik. More than in any other Turkestan oasis I have seen, the soil and climate of Karghalik seem to favour tree growth. All through the thickly populated village areas of Sultan-arik, Shorok, Dafdar, through which we rode in succession, fine avenues of poplars, mulberries, and willows, often of imposing size, gave shade and coolness. It is true the latter was also provided by a light fall of rain during the night, and by a pleasant breeze from the cloud-hidden mountains.

The slight undulations of the ground, and the increasing frequency of terraced banks for fields told that we were nearing the foot of the Kun-lun. Is it possible that Karghalik owes its luxuriant trees to a climate rendered slightly less dry by remnants of monsoon moisture passing here across the mountains from Baltistan and the great Muztagh glaciers? However that may be, it was a special pleasure to find all impressions of my first visit to this tract revived so faithfully. I always enjoy greatly revisiting familiar places—old friends, as it were, of a geographical order; but I like to approach them by new routes. So, too, old friends who have never been absent from one's mind seem dearer still when regained after long wanderings in new fields.

An imposing posse of Hindu money-lenders which received me some three miles from the town showed that the business of these sharp Shikarpuris flourished more than ever. Since 1901 their community had increased by some thirty per cent of new arrivals. I cannot pretend to any personal regard for these Shylocks from the lower Indus, who even in their best clothes have an undefinable air of meanness and clammy dirt about them. But their hardy ways and perseverance must exact a certain grudging respect. On seeing these lank, weak-looking figures I can never forget how Shikarpuris had worked their way all through Central Asia, in spite of Muslim contempt and fanaticism, long centuries before British power was established throughout India to give them protection.

When Forster, about 1782, travelled through from Bengal to the Caspian he found them flourishing and evidently long established throughout Afghanistan and far to the north of the Oxus. In Bokhara and Samarkand large colonies of them used to thrive until recently. Did they reach there only in Muhammadan times, or is it possible to conjecture that Sogdiana already knew these irrepressible leech-like seekers of Mammon when Alexander conquered the northernmost outposts of ancient Iran? The thought came naturally to me, since among the Shikarpuris who subsequently in a solemn deputation came to pay their respects at my temporary quarters, there was one who had drifted to Karghalik from Bokhara some twenty years before. He was a queer-looking old man with the face of a harpy, more than a match for the cleverest of Turki debtors who may fall into his clutches. He had brought a good number of old Bactrian, Arsacidian, and other Greek coins with him from Bokhara,—or had since been supplied with them by friends left behind there. Most of the silver pieces proved to be forgeries, and this, together with the big prices asked, prevented a business transaction.

The Amban of Karghalik had not yet returned from a visit to Kashgar, whither enquiries into certain alleged fiscal defalcations of his predecessor had called him. This saved me a halt and those formal visits which seemed to have grown more exacting since the style of my new Chinese passport from the Wai-wu-pu had promoted me to the rank of a Ta-jên or ' Excellency.' The modest little suburban house where I took up my quarters, conveniently near the Bazar and the Ya-mên, gave pleasant shelter for a busy day. My residence consisted mainly of a kind of loggia, with a carved wood front giving on a small but picturesque garden. I was delighted to find in it real European flowers—nasturtiums, a kind of phlox, and some other old acquaintances which to me, alas, remain anonymous. Otherwise the garden was of the typical Indian style, a miniature jungle crossed by rectangular paths.

My Chinese secretary's visit to the Ya-mên soon secured all arrangements needed for the stay I had planned at Kök-yar. There, at an elevation of about 6400 feet, I hoped to find a cool and peaceful spot to dispose of the tasks still burdening me in connection with *Ancient Khotan*. The little oasis where the summer route from the Kara-koram Pass debouches from the mountains, with its local resources, seemed just suited for this purpose, and in the hills close by my camels and ponies could get good grazing, and prepare for the hard work before them.

CHAPTER XII

In the early dawn of July 7th I started from Karghalik southwards. There was just light enough as we rode through the Bazars to observe the gaily decorated cook-shops and a stately Mosque and Madrasah with polychrome woodwork. Karghalik once again reminded me of some small town in Kashmir, probably on account of its fine trees, the abundance of running water, and the plentiful use of timber in its houses (Fig. 43). Scarcely two miles from the town we left cultivation behind us, and were moving over the bare gravel Dasht of a huge alluvial fan which slopes down unbroken from the foot of the outer hills. Only along the canals fed from the Tiznaf River and the stream of the Ushak-bashi, on the right and left of the route, but too far to be clearly sighted, stretched patches of fertile ground. A dreary landscape like this, made drearier still by a glary haze, was easy ground for the plane-table.

It was also singularly adapted for taking peregrinating lessons in Chinese from my worthy Ssŭ-yeh. With nothing to distract attention it seemed easier to grasp the explanation of phrases, grammatical matters, etc., which he never tired of pouring forth in an uninterrupted flow of Chinese and the queerest of Turki, almost as difficult to follow as the former. But his lively talk and expressive gestures and the intuitive contact created by common philological instincts helped me in comprehension, in spite of the difficulties arising from the eel-like perplexity of Chinese phonetics and the terrible snares of tonic accents, so hard for unmusical ears to distinguish. My own efforts

at Chinese conversation were grasped with a quickness
which spoke volumes for Chiang's sympathetic penetration,
and plenty of time on the road made up for the want of
regular desk-work.   If only Sinologist industry had provided a handy pocket-book on sound Ollendorfian methods
—and if only Chiang's broad Hunanese accent had not
made his spoken Chinese so difficult to recognize in the
orthodox transcriptional system of my available books!
It took a little time before I realized that 'Fu-lan,' the
name by which I grew accustomed to hear of his beloved
native land, was the province usually spelt Hu-nan; that
'Bue-jin' represented Pei-ching, 'the Northern capital,'
our familiar Peking, etc.   Of course, it ended by my
learning to pronounce my modest stock of colloquial
Chinese 'as we talk in Fu-lan.'

Chiang, to my great relief, seemed fully to relish his
new functions and took easily to our wandering life.   He
was always laudably ready for the start in the morning,
learned by gradual deposits to reduce his baggage to a
very modest allotment, and yet managed invariably to
turn up in neat clothes befitting his (brevet) rank and
his position as a Ta-jên's secretary and mentor.   His
garb gave a touch of colour to the greyest *ensemble*
of dust, sand, and gravel.   A dark blue silk jacket,
exchanged at times for a maroon one, harmonized well
with the bright yellow silk overalls which he wore when on
horseback.   The high and substantial Chinese saddle which
he acquired for his outfit, bore a comfortable cushion of
the brightest scarlet, while the broad black leather flaps
below were gaily decorated with yellow and green
embroidery, as if in niello.   But I never could look at
this heavy horse millinery and the terribly massive
stirrups, each weighing some three pounds and of truly
archaic type, without feeling sorrow for his mount.   Of
course, I took care to let him have the hardiest of our
animals, a bony but trustworthy black pony.   Against the
heat Chiang used to protect his head by putting a light
blue silk cloth under his small travelling cap, the pigtail
being used to fix this substitute for a 'Sola Topi.'
The eyes were shaded by the usual detachable peak of

strong paper made in sections showing all colours of the rainbow.

There was no want of due dignity and appropriate display whenever Mr. Secretary Chiang proceeded to pay visits to Ya-mêns on my behalf, nor of punctilious neatness when he penned epistles to Ambans on neat pink paper, carefully retaining 'office copies' for my assurance. Yet the cheerful way in which he did his marching, and the humorous contentment with which he would settle down in whatever quarters we could get, gave me hope from the first that I should find in him that field literatus I had fondly wished to discover. It was pleasant, too, to notice how kindly he took to my Indians, and how well he could impress them with the fact of his being a gentleman. Indian attendants are quick to appreciate such a fact, knowing from experience that the utility or importance to their Sahibs of native clerical assistants is by no means a guarantee for respectability and good manners.

We broke the journey at Besh-terek, a modest mud hovel with a tiny patch of cultivation by the roadside. But there was water from springs, and the green of reed beds gave relief to the eyes. The poky little hole reserved for me was anything but inviting, and for pitching a tent it was far too hot. So I was heartily glad to establish myself in the humble mud-built loggia which does for a mosque. Of course, I enquired from the jovial old 'Langarchi' whether my stay there would cause any religious qualms. But of such there is no real thought among Turki people, ordinarily free from all fanatical prejudice.

All the same I did not fail to administer first a solemn warning to 'Dash' that he was not to follow me into the shady retreat of the 'Jamat.' Having thus satisfied my conscience I took no special notice when my little terrier promptly ignored the injunction as soon as my bed was spread and ready to afford him the accustomed place of rest. After all, the Mosque was open to the invasion of stray dogs. So who was likely to trouble about the presence of so privileged a creature as the 'Ulugh Mihman's' ('the great guest's') far-travelled canine friend and companion? I could not help thinking then, and on many an occasion afterwards, of the curious contrast between all this good-natured indifference to religious propriety and the fervour with which pilgrimages to Muhammadan sanctuaries, and if possible to Mecca, are indulged in by everybody in the country. There is scarcely a village now without a proud 'Haji' or two, the enormous journey, *via* Baku, Stambul, Egypt, completely absorbing the savings of all but the wealthiest of these pilgrims. How difficult it would be for a future historian or ethnographer to believe that all this zeal for religious pilgrimages existed side by side with the utmost slackness in practising the prophet's tenets.

The remaining march to Kök-yar led over ground if possible even barer. But the greater elevation attained on the gravel glacis of the mountains made itself perceptible by decreased heat, and the nearest hills to the south gradually emerged from the haze. After sighting the oasis of Yül-arik in the distance, we turned towards the wide debouchure of a valley descending from the southwest, and at Ürük-langar reached the first cultivation. There a large convoy of camels with some Yarkandi traders was waiting to march to the Kara-koram Pass by the route which was then about to open for traffic along the upper Yarkand River. A couple of miles beyond we entered the oasis proper. The sight of this long expanse of green fields, hemmed in by absolutely barren greyish-yellow hills on either side, was as refreshing as the cool air which I found here. Past orchards and detached farmhouses we rode to the central hamlet of Kök-yar. There a most hearty reception awaited me from the Chinese petty official who is supposed to act as guardian of the route, and from his colleague who holds similar charge of the Raskam Valley towards Hunza, but prefers to reside in Otan-su, the last hamlet of Kök-yar.

Then I was taken to Chavash Beg's house which had been selected for my quarters. I found it quite a substantial residence, with plenty of rooms and a good deal of fine old wood-carving on posts, door-jambs, and beams. But at first I feared the noises of the village, close enough on one side. So under the guidance of a fine old Haji, who in the Yüz-bashi's absence did the honours of the place, I rode forth to inspect other well-to-do cultivators' houses and gardens. I failed to find any suitable for so large a party as ours, but this lordly house-hunting gave me at least an excellent idea of local domestic architecture. Our reception everywhere was of the friendliest, however unexpected may have been such an invasion.

Having satisfied myself, after the inspection of a dozen or so of "desirable residences," that Chavash Beg's house was the best I could choose for my stay, I settled down in it with additional pleasure. Substantial as it was and over a hundred years old, I found it easy to make alterations in the arrangement of the rooms to suit my needs. To let the servants pass through the large loggia, which in this cooler climate does for an Aiwan, was, of course, out of the question. So in less than ten minutes a passage was broken through the mud wall of one of the rooms to give another exit to the kitchen. The garden, which was to serve as my safest retreat, contained only rows of fruit-trees and some fields of lucerne. But even without flowers I preferred its shady and green open air to dark rooms or a loggia fully exposed to the morning sun.

Grateful I felt for the seclusion Kök-yar offered and the comparative coolness; for the tasks to be disposed of were so heavy that it took fifteen long days of constant labour from 6 A.M. until dusk before I managed to get clear of them. Appendices of all kinds to my *Ancient Khotan*, descriptions of some two hundred plates, and finally an introduction had to be prepared, copied, and sent off to distant Oxford, where self-sacrificing friends were to see all these tiresome parerga through the press. It was no small relief when I found that in my little camp despatch-box all needful materials had safely arrived with me.

Happy summers of hard work on Alpine plateaus of Kashmir and Kaghan had spoilt me in regard to quietness of my surroundings. With my little pony corps and my camel detachment close by there was little hope of such peace as I needed. So it was a double gain when I could despatch my transport to convenient grazing-grounds a march or so up the valley, where the animals could have rest and grow fat—without cost to my exchequer. After a couple of days' topographical work in the neighbourhood Rai Ram Singh, too (Fig. 44), left me with a qualified Darogha and guide for surveying tasks along the Kun-lun main range between Karghalik and Khotan. There was a real *terra incognita* to be mapped in the difficult mountain region within the great bend of the Kara-kash River, and it cost me an effort not to set out for it myself.

With some little trouble a place had been found where my tent could be pitched, under the closely planted apricot trees of the garden, and thanks to their shade I could work there the whole day without feeling the heat too oppressive. Almost every afternoon a strong breeze swept up from the plains to bring refreshing coolness—and a load of fine dust which descended steadily in layers for hours after the wind had subsided. I could not have had a better demonstration how all the loess beds forming the fertile bottom of these valleys had originated, and that they were still growing by such aerial deposits. On either side of the green irrigated strip of ground which extends for some four miles between the extreme points of the Kök-yar oasis, there was nothing to be seen but barren yellow hills with broad pebble slopes skirting their foot. On them there was neither moisture nor vegetation to retain the fertile loess dust which the winds let fall on them daily.

On my evening walks I soon saw how confined was the cultivation which, aided by the flourishing felt manufacture, maintains the two hundred odd homesteads of Kök-yar. Nowhere more than about a quarter of a mile broad, the oasis can easily be content with the single road, mostly shaded by fine willows and poplars, passing up its whole length. Seeking for variation I tried many a by-path along the little 'Ariks' which distribute the water between the fields, only to find that none was really practicable in comfort for Chiang, the regular companion of my walks. Peripatetic Chinese lessons were the motive necessitating his company, and bravely he followed me in spite of dainty slippers and waving silk garments over the narrow canal embankments and through the thickets of luxuriant Kumush edging the fields of wheat or oats. Yet his discreet allusions left no doubt that the high road seemed to him a more reasonable line of progression for people of rank and culture.

As I always used to chat with the country folk on these evening walks, the number of my Kök-yar acquaintances soon grew large in spite of the seclusion of my day's work. Comfortable farm-houses lay scattered along most of the road from my quarters to Otan-su, some two and a half miles up the valley. There were fruit-trees near all of them, though only in small walled-in spaces, and scarcely a farm was without its loggia where the women and children seemed to spend most of the summer day. A peep into the living-room for the winter showed invariably huge piles of carefully folded felt rugs, cushions, and fur coats, evidence of the comfortable provision made against the rigours of the winter season. Kök-yar is famous throughout Turkestan for its excellent felts, and a good deal of the manifest ease prevailing in these homesteads was, no doubt, derived from the profits of this flourishing industry.

Pretty was it to see the tall, waving poplar groves of Otan-su against the yellow background of the rugged cliffs which there line the valley. The maze of narrow lanes in this village, with the apricot and mulberry trees peeping across every mud wall, had its picturesque places, too. Great was the amazement of the good people of Otan-su when they first saw me paying a visit on foot. Ponies were dragged out in haste, and invitations to mount them were many and pressing. But after a time the shock wore off, and I was allowed to indulge in my queer taste for trudging along on my own feet. Otan-su was the place where Li Ta-lao-ye, the convivial little Chinese official who was supposed to guard the Raskam border, had taken up his unauthorized residence. His work was *nil* from morning till evening, but loneliness evidently oppressed him, and invitations to my Ssŭ-yeh for lunch and supper parties

A   B

44. SURVEYOR RAI RAM SINGH (A) WITH JASVANT SINGH (B) STARTING FROM KÖK-YAR.

45. PAKHPU HILLMEN ANTHROPOMETRICALLY EXAMINED AT KÖK-YAR.

were a natural consequence. I myself escaped with frequent and, to confess the truth, often welcome offerings of fresh vegetables, with which the 'Lao-ye' was kept supplied by his friends at Karghalik, and which it was easy to return with little presents of my own.

While day after day passed in busy work the fruit was ripening even at my 'hill-station.' Delicious little apricots began to drop around my tent, and their glow of yellowish pink among the leafage was a joy for the eye. In my egotistic seclusion I never realized that I was keeping my host's children from a perpetual feast, until one evening, returning earlier than expected, I found the garden invaded by a swarm of boys who were busy gorging themselves on the trees. After that I arranged that there should be a daily shaking; yet ripe apricots were ever falling as the wind rose, and I soon grew accustomed to hear them drop on my tent fly and to see them roll down gently among the lucerne growing around me. I wonder whether I did not appear to the parties most interested like the snake of Indian legend, guarding jealously a treasure which he himself refrains from enjoying.

My days at Kök-yar were, however, not wholly devoted to desk-work. After a few days' wait I had the satisfaction to see little troops of Pakhpu folk arrive, those hill-men from the Tiznaf head-waters in whose racial type and origin I had long been interested (Fig. 45). Their small semi-nomadic settlements scattered in five grazing valleys lie far away from all main routes and had never been examined. It had cost special efforts on the part of the Darogha sent to their Beg residing in Chukshü to make these hill people come down for examination. At first they fought terribly shy of leaving their high valleys, just as if real live heads were to have been taken instead of mere measurements and photographs with perfectly harmless instruments. But my authority seemed great under the orders from Karghalik; and the Pakhpus sent down by their Beg faced the swollen streams, the relative heat of the lower valleys, and the fearsome mysteries of anthropological measurement. Of course, I took care to relieve their feelings by arranging for hospitable entertainment and paying into each man's hand appropriate compensation.

I found them very interesting, in their physical features, which closely approach the Homo Alpinus type of the Iranian tribes of the Pamir region. Most of them were fine-looking men, the frequency of fair eyes and hair, and other racial characteristics clearly showing that Alpine isolation had preserved in them direct representatives of that Iranian stock which in ancient times appears to have extended right through to Khotan and even farther east.

But their alleged distinct language proved a fiction, or at least a thing of the past; for neither the offer of reward, nor the fear of further enquiries I might be induced to conduct in their own hills, would induce my Pakhpu visitors to acknowledge that they knew aught but their 'Taghlik' or hill Turki dialect. They were hugely amused when I soon spotted the chief features of their faces, etc., which distinguish them from the people of the plain oases; for with a little practice I was able to pick out any Pakhpu from the midst of local villagers who crowded to watch the proceedings. Later on came the turn for the 'Kök-yarliks'; and as after a time I could leave the specific measurements which take up most time to the care of my handy corporal, who like most Indians loved a mechanical task and tabular statements to fill up, my collection of 'heads' soon assumed a respectable size,—in the packet of slips which record them and in the photographs taken.

Two days before the date fixed for resuming my journey towards Khotan there arrived a long-expected Dak from Kashgar, with the postal accumulations of nearly a month. Then I had the satisfaction to see the last of my book tasks done, down to the exhaustive Introduction which was to mark their successful conclusion. But how grateful I felt to those distant friends who were ready with unfailing devotion to assure the careful reproduction of all this writing! By July 24th camels and ponies turned up from their holiday, and when all my things, which had been allowed to 'spread themselves' during this fortnight, had once more been compressed into mule trunks, I was free to return the attentions of my Chinese friends of Kök-yar and

Otan-su by a little tea-party. I was delighted to see my jovial Ssŭ-yeh doing the honours of the modest feast with all the assurance of a man of learning whom travel and intercourse with strange foreign people has made feel at home even outside a Ya-mên.

CHAPTER XIII

ALONG THE FOOT OF THE KUN-LUN

On the morning of July 25th I said farewell to Kök-yar and its obliging people just as the dawn broke. I had thought to have taken leave of my 'Ta-lao-yes,' too, the evening before. But, lo, as I approached the outlying farm of Újmelük Langar, where the valley turns to barren Dasht, I found them awaiting me with a farewell Dastarkhan of tea and eggs, spread out on red felts in orthodox fashion. Considering how averse Chinamen of easy circumstances seem to be from early rising, I was pleasantly touched by this final mark of goodwill and politeness. In return I wished my Chinese hosts the speediest progress on the official ladder up to the Futai-ship of the 'New Dominion.'

Instead of the high road leading from Karghalik along the edge of the desert, I had decided to make my way to Khotan by the little-known route which passes through the barren outer hills of the Kun-lun, and would give me a chance of fresh surveys. Our first march was easy and pleasantly varied. After surmounting the bleak conglomerate ridge eastwards near the little Mazar of Saskan Khoja, there spread out before me the fertile debouchure of the valleys of Yül-arik and Ushak-bashi, with a cluster of long-stretched oases along the streams which are fed by the snowy range about the Karlik Dawan. As we crossed one fertile strip after another, Yül-arik, Rowush, Yawash, and Ushak-bashi, I feasted my eyes on beautiful groves of fruit-trees and rich fields between. Yül-arik and the neighbouring villages are famous for their apricots, melons, and walnuts. Even grapes ripen in sheltered places in spite of the elevation of about 5800 feet. Dastarkhans awaited me on the edge of every village area, and as these all consist of narrow belts stretched along the canals and scarcely a mile broad, my diagonal progress eastwards was necessarily much interrupted.

Before Ushak-bashi I crossed the Ulugh-Ustang, here a rapid mountain stream some forty yards broad and flowing in a picturesque bed of boulders deeply cut into the alluvial fan. In the little Bazar beyond I found two Shikarpuri Hindus, established three years before and manifestly thriving on a field for usury previously unexploited. Through shady lanes I reached Rais Akhun's house, a pleasing country residence of some pretensions, far away from the village noises and adjoined by a large and beautiful orchard. Its Aiwan, where I soon settled down to work, showed vines trailing over the open centre and a rustic attempt at a 'hanging garden,' i.e. flower-beds raised on rough posts to a height of some five feet above the verandah floor. The owner was evidently a man of taste and eager to embellish his home ; for in the ' Mihman-khana,' where I had my bath and a change, the walls were neatly decorated with plaster plaques of coloured flower designs, quite the most tasteful ornamentation I had seen since Yarkand. Pretty polychrome patterns of Svastika emblems decorated the ceiling.

To the rustic charms of Ushak-bashi the desolate pebble Sai, which I crossed next day for a distance of about twenty miles eastwards, formed a striking contrast. Over such absolutely bare ground it would have been difficult to get exact ' fixings ' for my plane-table, had not the outer hills to the south and a forbiddingly desolate ridge on the northern rim of the broad glacis-like plateau over which we were passing, shown their outlines just in sufficient clearness. The haze was too great to allow me to sight the high snowy range southwards, and before we were nearing the tiny oasis of Hassan Boghra Khan, our halting-place, a light dust-storm spread a veil even over the nearest hills.

Hassan Boghra Khan proved a pleasant surprise ; for though it consists only of a modest Ziarat with a Sheikh's house and two or three holdings, there was a large shady orchard with beautiful old trees and some approach to a real lawn to afford me an inviting camping-ground. It was watered by a small canal fed by the Kilian River during the summer months. During the busy hours spent there over work, and all through the night, the ripe apricots were dropping on and around my tent. For days past nobody seemed to have troubled to collect this profusion, the housewives of these parts evidently not caring to lay in stores of dried fruit for the winter.

An easy and cool march brought me on the morning of July 27th to Kilian. One learns after the glare and heat of these deserts to appreciate a sky covered with clouds and a breeze fresh from the snow-covered mountains. Of the latter, great peaks showed from time to time between the grey masses of rolling cloud. The Kilian Pass, some three or four marches up the valley, forms one of the approaches to the Upper Kara-kash and the trade-route which leads thence across the Kara-koram to Ladak. So, when I sighted the oasis of Kilian from a broad conglomerate ridge guarding the debouchure of the valley, there was the thought of the high passes southwards to give additional interest to the landscape.

But Kilian itself was a pleasing sight, with its green fields and orchards set between barren yellow cliffs and the sombre grey mountains as a background. The river, too, which we had to ford some two miles below the main oasis, showed by its greyish-green water and its respectable volume that it had come down from perpetual snows. In the orchard which I selected for my camping-ground I lighted upon the traders of a small caravan just about to start with Charas, that precious but mischievous hemp-drug, for Ladak. So while my tent was being pitched I promptly wrote a letter to my learned Tibetan collaborator, the Reverend Mr. Francke, of the Moravian Mission in Leh. It was pleasant to think that my news would thus reach him by the most direct route, even though it would take four weeks or more in transit. When I asked the head trader, a jovial fat Yarkandi, to be sure and take care to deliver the letter, he assured me with a mien of self-satisfied dignity that he was a 'Saudagar' or trader, and thus pledged to a

faithful discharge of all such obligations. How cheerful
was it to feel shifted back into the centuries, seemingly
so far off, which knew no postal service, and to realize in
practice that safe opportunities were available then, too,
for friendly communications over great distances.

A host of writing tasks obliged me to make a busy
day's halt at Kilian. A short evening walk along the
track, deep in soft loess dust, which leads up to the southern
edge of the Kilian oasis, counting in all some four hundred
or five hundred homesteads, was my only diversion. Next
day the completion of my heavy mail would not allow me
to follow my baggage started eastwards until after mid-
day. This delay brought its due punishment. After
a dreary march of some seventeen miles, mostly over
desolate ridges of sand and gravel stretching down from
equally barren hills southward, I arrived at the tiny spring-
fed stream of the Sulagh-aghzi Valley, the only place where
water could be obtained for a night's halt. Then I found
to my dismay that by a mistake of my men the baggage
had been moved down to a distant Langar on the Sanju-
Karghalik trade-route. What had induced the men thus
needlessly to increase the day's march, I could not learn,
unless it was the 'Kirakash' instinct, which drew them
back to the high road familiar from many journeys to and
from the Kara-koram.

It was dusk by the time I reached the few homesteads
established in a tiny oasis near the source of the Sulagh-
aghzi stream, and the weary march in complete darkness
down the valley for some seven miles seemed endless. The
flat glacis-like Sai on which it debouches stretched away
in absolute bareness, and the absence of any marks to
indicate our goal made the distance seem still greater.
Sulaghaz Langar, reached by 10 P.M., proved a cluster of
wretched mud-hovels, and the short night's rest, passed
by necessity in the stuffy hall of one of them, was anything
but refreshing.

The heat would have sufficed to send me back to the
route I had intended to follow through the hills, even if
there had not been the necessity of resuming my survey
at the point where darkness had before stopped it. So,

while the baggage moved on to Sanju by the main road, I turned back to the head of the Sulagh-aghzi stream and thence struck across the rising ground eastwards. It was a dreary ride between long-stretched conglomerate ridges, with not a drop of water in the broad valleys of scrub-covered loess between. The breeze, for which I felt grateful at first, soon developed into a dust-storm equally trying to eyes and throat. So I was heartily glad when at last the appearance through the haze of the curious flat-topped hill, known as 'Kizil-bash' from the red colour of its clay, marked the approach to the Sanju Valley.

A steep descent brought us down to the edge of the valley bottom, here about a mile and a half across, and refreshed by a welcome Dastarkhan of tea and fruit, sent ahead to a desolate little Langar, I hastened towards the oasis. The storm had dropped by the time we reached it, and the ride of some four miles through fields and orchards stretching along both banks of the river was cheering in spite of the thick dust-haze. The greyish-green water, filling in rapid flow a bed over sixty yards broad and some three feet deep, showed the great extent and near neighbourhood of the snows which feed the river.

The oasis of Sanju, divided into the four villages of Sawu, Saidulla, Baskak, and Dombak, is reckoned at a thousand houses. But from the extent of the irrigated area and the crowds I met returning from the weekly Bazar, this estimate appears distinctly too low. The Sanju Valley serves as the most frequented approach to the Kara-koram route, and its main oasis must derive substantial profit from the supplies taken for the Ladak caravans coming and going. I found some Hindu traders from Yarkand just preparing to set out for India, but vainly inquired about any arrivals from that direction, a proof how late is the opening of regular trade across the high Kara-koram passes. In order to reduce my baggage on the difficult journey *via* Chitral and Wakhan, I had despatched from Abbottabad three pony-loads *via* Ladak in charge of Musa, Muhammadju's companion. They contained my new water-tanks for the desert, spare photographic stores, survey instruments, and, among other important equipment, the skins which were to serve both for a raft and for water transport in the desert. That after three months Musa had not yet arrived at Sanju was a source of considerable concern to me. But there was comfort at least in the thought that I had myself avoided serious loss of time by not taking this trade-route.

The official rest-house close to the Bazar of Saidulla-kenti, which the attentive Chinese officer in charge of the route had prepared for my accommodation, proved anything but a peaceful abode ; and as the heat was also perceptible, I resumed my journey on July 31st without regret. I was now within a day's march of Zanguya on the main Karghalik-Khotan high road ; but the wish to complete my survey of the route farther south decided me to move on to Duwa, the last of the small oases among the foot-hills of the Kun-lun, west of Khotan. The distance, about thirty-five miles, was too great to be covered in one day. So after a short march I had to halt at Puski, the only valley *en route* where water was obtainable. I found there a narrow strip of cultivation extending in patches for some six miles along the bed of a stream which is fed by springs but also serves as a flood channel for the melting snows of the hills.

There would have been no inducement to stop at this little oasis of some forty homesteads surrounded by the most barren of hills, had I not learned soon after my arrival of a ruined mound or ' Tim ' some distance farther down. The men of Puski estimated it at about a Pao-t'ai, *i.e.* roughly two miles. But when I rode out in the afternoon to visit it, I soon realized through my glasses that the distance would be nearly four times as much and the ruin could not be reached before dusk. So the survey of it had to be left for the next day. The heat at Puski was great, 90° Fahr. even after nightfall, and the ride to the ruined Stupa—for as such I could recognize it even from a distance—next morning anything but refreshing.

The structure of sun-dried bricks, originally dome-shaped and resting on a square base, proved greatly injured by diggings for ' treasure.' Yet a careful survey convinced me that in dimensions and arrangement it must have closely agreed with the Stupa of Topa Tim I had discovered six years before between Guma and Moji. Its lowest base seems to have measured about thirty-four feet square. It was curious to note that, in spite of the complete destruction of the outer facing of masonry, the rows of small sticks of willow and tamarisk which once supported plaster mouldings could be traced over a considerable portion of the base. Nowhere around the mound could I find any mark of ancient habitation. The bare gravel Sai showed not even fragments of old pottery, those most lasting indications of early occupation. Hence it is clear that the Stupa must have risen then as it does now on the bare Dasht between Puski and Zanguya. Half a mile to the east of it flows the stream of Puski, and just across the latter stands a modest mud-built Mazar, evidently the inheritor of the worship once paid to the Stupa.

That the area of cultivation could not have changed greatly in this neighbourhood is proved by the débris-strewn Tati which I found extending for about three-quarters of a mile below the fields of Jangal-bagh, the northernmost of the tiny oases which constitute Puski. The ground, a soft loess, is here thickly covered with fragments of ancient pottery, mostly of fine texture and remarkable hardness. More of this Tati had been reclaimed for cultivation when the new colony of Jangal-bagh was established here some twelve years before my visit; and as there is ample water for further irrigation, it can only be a question of time before the rest of the Tati disappears again under fields—and the deposits of loess dust which accumulate over all cultivated areas.

The torrid heat of the day passed at Puski was made bearable by the satisfaction I felt on finding after my return to camp that Musa and his loads had just arrived safely from Sanju. He had crossed the Kara-koram with the first caravan of the year. The carrier who had under-taken to deliver my loads at Khotan at a freight charge of sixty rupees per pony-load from Kashmir to Khotan, had lost half of his animals on the passes, and only with great difficulty had they been replaced by freshly hired ponies from the Kirghiz encampment of Suget. Just before

Sanju the carrier had come to the end of his resources ; and but for the fortunate chance which made my passage through Sanju almost coincide with Musa's arrival, the latter would have found himself stranded at some five marches' distance from his destination.   The case seems an apt illustration of the exceptional difficulties which attend the use of the Kara-koram for a trade-route.

The march of August 2nd from Puski to Duwa proved very trying for the baggage animals.   The dreary plateaus of gravel over which most of the march led, were intersected by a succession of four barren valleys, all cut in with steep scarps to a depth of several hundred feet.   None of them now held any water, though there was plentiful evidence of the destructive erosion worked by occasional rain floods. It was curious to notice that the western slopes of these valleys showed always a deep cover of sand, while the eastern ones displayed their steeply-scoured conglomerate surface.   Up the last of these valleys, the Kum-koilagan Jilga, we had to wind our way for nearly four miles, until its bottom gorge narrowed to a mere fissure.   There was a perfect maze of little side gorges, while the red sandstone ridges high above showed fantastically - eroded formations, curiously recalling in miniature the weird gorges through which I had first approached the Kashgar Plain from the side of the Tokuz-dawan in 1900.

The whole way we had not met a single human being, and I was wondering how far we might have yet to travel through this wilderness of stone and dust, when suddenly from a ridge above the head of the gorge the topmost part of the Duwa oasis came into view at the bottom of a broad valley.   At Sanjagiz Langar we reached the Duwa stream flowing rapidly with its cool greyish-green water in a bed about a hundred yards broad but now only half-filled.   Then a three miles' ride past well-cultivated fields, where the wheat was just ripening, brought me down to the central part of the village.   Green swards such as I had not seen for a long time, lined both banks of the river where we crossed it to a Bai's house and garden which were to afford quarters.   The many fine walnut-trees in the neighbouring lanes and the quaintly carved woodwork

in a number of houses and mosques again recalled distant
Kashmir. The Bai's house was an old one, and in the
profuse carving covering the pillars and architraves of its
hall and its gate-posts, I recognized a number of decorative
motives and patterns with which my first excavations of
ancient residences at desert sites in Khotan had made me
familiar. It seemed like a gratifying assurance that I was
now close to the westernmost border of the old Khotan
kingdom—and my own field of antiquarian work.

Duwa, in spite of the lowness of the conglomerate
hills flanking the valley, proved a cool halting-place. So
after a peaceful night spent under the high poplars and
elms of the orchard, I started refreshed for the long march
which was to carry me on August 3rd to the very confines
of Khotan. A straight cut across the glacis-like Sai from
Duwa to Kum-rabat Padshahim would have sufficed to
make a long day. But when I asked my Darogha to
secure guides for this route, the good men of Duwa urged
difficulties of all sorts. The high dunes of moving sand,
the many steeply cut 'Yars' to be crossed, and the absolute
want of water over these twenty-five miles or so, seemed
to frighten them thoroughly. Loss of animals and even
of men from the heat to which this shelterless desert
would expose them, was predicted as a serious danger.
So there was nothing for it but to resign myself to the
equally hot and still longer route which leads first to
Pialma, the terminal oasis of the Duwa stream, and thence
by the Khotan high road through the desert. As I had
decided to relieve my camels, which the work in the
summer heat had severely tried, by the hire of ponies,
consideration for local opinion was all the more needed.

The first few miles down the banks of the Duwa Darya
were pleasant enough in the early morning. As far as
cultivation extended, narrow strips of greensward lined the
river course. But soon the route left the stream where it
debouches between steep conglomerate cliffs near the last
fields of Lamus and took to the most barren of Dashts, with
nothing but gravel and dust. Pialma, the last of the oases
on the high road to Khotan, was approached by mid-day;
but to save a little distance I only skirted its easternmost

fields. A tank of greenish water at an outlying farm gave a refreshing drink to the ponies, and then we set out in the burning heat of the desert for the remaining twenty-two miles. The glare over this great waste, successively changing from bare loess steppe to gravel and sand, was intense. But luckily a steady breeze from the Taklamakan northward helped to make the heat bearable through constant evaporation. I felt glad once more to be on that ancient route which had seen Hsüan-tsang, Marco Polo, and so many other old travellers on their way to Cathay, and to let my thoughts wander back freely to my own first approach to Khotan nearly six years before.

Ak-langar, the well-built rest-house of Yakub Beg's days, with its deep well of brackish water, looked as shunned and forlorn as ever. The sun was already low when we passed it ; but the breeze had died away, and the heat given out by the ground seemed quite as bad as at mid-day. Slowly our animals dragged themselves over the curious stretch of red loess which extends for over a mile beyond. This suggested to me a possible folk-lore origin for the legend of a great battle which Hsüan-tsang relates in connection with the story of the sacred rats, still located, though in Muhammadan guise, at the shrine of Kum-rabat Padshahim. Glad was I when the rising dunes told me that we were getting near to 'My Lord of the Sands' Station,' which was to give shelter for the night's halt : and gladder still for the sake of animals and men worn out by a march of some thirty-six miles over such ground, when I recognized the high poles and modest huts of the 'Pigeons' Shrine' amidst patches of reeds and tamarisk, growing between the dunes.

The sacred birds which now receive the wayfarers' worship, instead of the sacred rats of Buddhist days, had retired to rest when we reached the spot by nightfall. So there was nothing to disturb the delicious peace of the desert which had always lingered so alluringly in my recollections of that happy winter campaign in the Taklamakan. Two young Sheikhs were alone present at the shrine. Warned of my coming by the Darogha sent ahead from Pialma with fodder for the ponies, they had made themselves useful by collecting a little fuel from the few tamarisk-trees growing along the depression to which the sacred spot owes its shallow well. The full moon had risen by this time, and true to Indian poetic notions seemed to spread coolness with its bright light.

It took nearly two hours more before the last of the baggage ponies had come in. A number of the Duwa men with them lay prostrate on the rapidly cooling sand, too weary to look after their animals. But all had safely arrived, and to my relief my party had not added its quota to the bones of perished beasts of burden which mark the whole route from Pialma. Even two small foals which, without my noticing it, had been taken along with their mothers, had survived this long march; but I felt grieved at having unwittingly inflicted upon them such an experience so early in life.

CHAPTER XIV

THE night among the dunes near the shrine of 'My Lord of the Sands' proved unexpectedly pleasant, the quick radiation of the drift sand helping to emphasize the change from the day's heat. Dinner did not appear until close upon midnight. But what was the long wait compared to the happy feeling of being once more on the very border of 'the Kingdom,' and enjoying also a foretaste of the peace and freedom of the desert! When I rose next morning at 4 A.M., later than usual in those days, the air was still fresh, the thermometer showing 60° Fahr. While the baggage was getting ready I made my food offering to the sacred pigeons, a duty which my old followers would on no account have allowed me to neglect (Fig. 46). In their eagerness to secure the holy birds' goodwill for the long journey before us, they had caused some additional Charaks of grain to be brought along from Pialma. So the winged host which inhabits the Mazar enjoyed a good breakfast long before I came up from my own. It was nesting-time for the pigeons, and as no calls of the Sheikhs would induce the mothers to leave their eggs, I had to enter the little rooms in order to realize that the multitude of birds was as numerous as ever. Steps had to be careful to avoid crushing eggs; so closely was all available ground covered by nests.

The day which brought me back to 'the Kingdom' will long live in my memory as one of the happiest I spent in Khotan. It is always delightful to revisit scenes to which one's thoughts have longingly returned for years past, and still more delightful to find that the memory of one's self still lives among those scenes. This was now my happy experience. Already late on the previous night a messenger brought intelligence to my camp that arrangements had been made for over a week past to receive me at Tarbogaz, the lonely Langar which forms Khotan's frontier watch-station, as it were, westwards. So I was not surprised when, on my passage through the curious sand-hills which stretch east of the 'Pigeons' Shrine,' I was met by quite a cavalcade of Begs sent from the Amban's Ya-mên with their attendants. In one of them, Roze Beg, I recognised the favourite interpreter of P'an Ta-jên who five years before had been deputed to escort me on my departure by this very route.

Green and smiling looked the rural scenery from Tarbogaz onwards. Land that I well remembered as a sandy waste with scrub and reeds, had been reclaimed for cultivation by a new canal; a reassuring proof at the outset that the old oasis could still carry on its fight against the desert — in spite of 'desiccation.' I had much to ask from my escort about old friends, big and small; and before I had finished my queries, I found myself riding past Zawa-kurghan, the quaint quadrilateral stronghold by which the last 'king of Khotan,' Habibullah 'the Haji,' in 1864-66 had thought to ward off all invasion. In the Bazar close by all looked gay and cheerful, just as when I had bid farewell here to honest old Turdi, my desert guide,—as Fate willed it, for ever. For over two years now the old 'treasure-seeker' had gone to his rest, alas! from the prison gate. The absence of his familiar figure was the only shadow cast on this bright day.

At Zawa I found the neat little official rest-house by the road-side gaily decked with red cloth, and refreshing tea and fruit ready on the raised central platform of the courtyard. Fresh evidence, too, of the Amban's attention came in the form of pony-loads of fodder for my animals and provisions for myself, offered as a special sign of regard at my entrance into the district. The Kara-kash River, now swollen by the melting snows, could not be crossed on the high road that leads straight to Khotan town. Boats were to be found only at Kara-kash town, some ten miles farther down, and

46. FOOD OFFERINGS TO THE SACRED PIGEONS AT SHRINE OF KUM-RABAT PADSHAHIM.

47. MOSQUE AND AVENUE OF POPLARS NEAR BORACHE, KHOTAN.

thither my party was to be conducted. It meant a
day's delay on the road, but I did not grudge it; for the
route from Zawa to Kara-kash was new to me and proved
an excellent sample of all that these rich tracts watered
from the Kara-kash river could offer in rural beauty.

The whole of the cantons of Kuya, Makuya, Kayash
through which I rode in succession, looked like a big park,
with fertile fields to take the place of pastures. The love of
the Khotanese peasantry for fine avenues to line the roads
and for shady clumps of trees to mark off each small holding, has always appealed to me as a mark of old-established
civilization, and the scenery passed on to-day's route illustrated it to perfection (Fig. 47). With every bit of ground
intensively cultivated, this concession to the picturesque
in rural surroundings seems doubly deserving of note.
The road led through thickly populated tracts. Yet so
plentiful is the tree growth that only rarely could the eye
of the passing traveller catch sight of the cultivators'
mud-built houses scattered in small hamlets. But open
vistas were provided by the green valley-like stretches
where the big canals of Kuya, Makuya and Bahram-su
rolled their muddy waters northward between deep-cut
loess banks.

At the 'Wednesday Bazar' of Borache, a local market
town as yet undiscovered by me, Roze Beg owned a country
house. So a liberal Dastarkhan awaited us here as a
matter of course. Gaily-coloured cloth canopies had been
stretched across the road and hundreds of villagers thronged
in front of them, evidently happy to take their share in the
festive reception. The house was quite new, and its
Aiwan with clean poplar-wood roofing and neatly plastered
walls made a delightfully cool retreat. Melons of all sorts,
peaches and grapes formed the bulk of the collation to
which my travel-stained followers settled down in most
business-like fashion. I always enjoy seeing animals—or
men—absorbed in hearty feeding, and knowing that feasts
of this sort would not come their way every day, I did not
grudge my people the time needed for a thorough disposal
of all this hospitable treat. When they emerged from the
side room where they had conducted operations, their

faces bore an expression of happy satiation which deserved
to be caught by the brush of an old Dutch painter.

The seemingly endless row of booths, probably quite
half a mile long, in the Bazar street (Fig. 48), though empty
this day, was the best proof of the agricultural wealth
and the busy production of this neighbourhood. Not less
was the industrial importance of Khotan brought home to
me by the constant succession of caravans, made up mostly
of droves of sturdy donkeys, carrying silk, cotton fabrics,
felts and other manufactured goods westwards. I thought
of the day, happily still far off, when Khotan will have
its railway, and when all this busy life of the road will be
transferred to stations and trains.

As I approached Kara-kash, my escort was joined by
the local Beg, a person of consequence, looking grand in his
blue silk coat and official Chinese cap with crystal button
and horse-tail. As etiquette makes all such dignitaries
insist on riding in front of one, in due order of rank, there
was plenty of dust to be swallowed in return for such exalted
attention. But, I confess, that day I gladly submitted to
all this display, from a feeling that after all it was my
return to ground to which by hard work I had established
a scholarly claim. It may be weakness and vanity, but it
pleased me to see how well I was still remembered throughout the oasis. The Amban had passed the town in the
morning, having been obliged to proceed to a village of
the Zawa canton for urgent investigation of a murder case.
Though he was expected to return for the night, nothing
would do for the accommodation of the ' Ulugh Mihman,'
my humble self, but the recently constructed official
residence of the Amban, a kind of ' Sessions House,' to use
the Anglo-Indian term. So to it I had to proceed, though,
if a choice had been possible without causing much trouble,
I should have greatly preferred to take up my quarters
again in the quiet country house of my old host of 1901,
Karim Akhun Beg.

My misgivings were justified; for when I entered the
large Ya-mên-like building at the meeting of three fine
poplar-lined roads just outside the west gate of Kara-kash,
I found that the building operations which were needed to

48. ENTRANCE TO BAZAR OF BORACHE, KHOTAN OASIS.

49. T'ANG TA-JÊN, MILITARY AMBAN OF KHOTAN, WITH HIS CHILDREN AND ATTENDANTS.

transform the old 'Baj-khana' or octroi and revenue office into a spacious residence, had not yet been quite completed. Everything in the large apartments and verandahs enclosing the inner court looked clean and well-planned. But there had been no time to cover the wooden roofing with the usual layer of stamped clay, or to put up the lattice-work which would shut out the glare from the courtyard. So the heat was great in my palatial rest-house, and the noise too from the host of Daroghas, retainers of the Beg, and townsfolk who thronged the outer court and entrance hall as a matter of right. Two harmless-looking public executioners in red caps and robes, whom the Beg had thought fit to post at the gate of 'my Ya-mên,' were no protection against the good-natured intrusion authorized by local custom.

The local Beg of Kara-kash, an officer of importance and evident wealth, proved a most attentive host. I was interested to learn that his family enjoyed a hereditary connection with the Chinese Imperial court, through the office of 'Wang' or local chief. It is, of course, a purely nominal charge, though it causes one of its members to proceed to Peking every five years, the journey to and fro with residence at court extending in all over some twenty-two months. I did not succeed in ascertaining from what period of effective local rule this charge of quasi-mediatized chiefship was derived. But my informants all agreed that the 'Gung-luk' or Wang-ship of the family had been maintained for over three centuries, and that formal enquiries in the Imperial archives had re-established its claim after the old papers relating to the charge had been lost during the troubled times of the usurper Habibullah. The account of this office recalled to my mind the frequent references in the Chinese dynastic Annals from the fifth century onwards to princes and nobles from Khotan who, coming with embassies of 'tribute,' received honourable posts in the Imperial guard and household employment, no doubt, as easily discharged by occasional visits as the 'Gung-luk' of Hafiz Beg. The annual salary drawn by the latter in virtue of his court charge was said to amount to forty horse-shoes of silver, equivalent to

2000 Taels, or roughly rupees 5000, quite a big sum for these regions.

My short stay at Kara-kash was brightened by the arrival late in the evening of Islam Beg, my old Darogha of the Karanghu-tagh and Dandan-oilik expeditions, whose excellent services P'an Ta-jên had at my recommendation rewarded by the Beg-ship of the 'Ming' or canton of Kayash in the Kara-kash district (Fig. 71). The news of my arrival was quick to reach him, and now he hurried to greet me and assure me of his gratitude. That in spite of Chinese administrative methods in the ' New Dominion,' which for reasons of fiscal policy and—private advantage—favour frequent changes in the native *personnel,* he had retained his charge without a break, was more than he or I could reasonably have hoped for when we parted.

It was evidently efficient work and popular esteem to which he owed this special consideration on the part of successive Ambans, of whom Khotan had seen not less than four in the five years since P'an Ta-jên. But Islam Beg politely insisted in attributing his good luck to my protection, or rather to the impression my advocacy had left behind at the Ya-mên. It was anyhow gratifying that he now claimed the privilege of sharing my campaign in the mountains. This task, for which his previous experience no doubt fitted him, was sure to imply also renewed hardships. However, in spite of a fat post and a comfortable income from his inherited land, Islam Beg had kept fit in body and full of quiet energy. So I gladly accepted his offer, provided the Amban would agree to this 'deputation.'

A march of some sixteen miles on August 5th brought me back once more to the Khotan capital. It was a day of trying heat, but full of most cheering impressions. Chance had so arranged it that it should be a Sunday, the weekly market-day of Kara-kash town, and that the road leading to this thriving local centre from Khotan should be enlivened by a continuous stream of mounted traders and country folk bringing merchandise and produce. So again a great portion of the curiously mixed community of petty traders — Bajauris, Afghans, Andijanis, men descended from Kashmiri immigrants, etc., passed me as it were in review.

The crossing of the Kara-kash river, now in full flood, took us a long time; for though there were two fairly big ferry-boats available for our party and baggage, the rapidity of the current flowing at over one yard in the second, and still more the sand-banks, sorely tried the modest skill of the 'Suchis' or watermen. We crossed about a mile and a half below the town, where the river flowed in two branches about 60 and 150 yards broad. The depth of the water in the middle and towards the east bank, where the current was setting, was up to eight or nine feet. As far as Khan-arik we crossed a well-cultivated tract belonging to the Sipa canton. Then followed a belt of marshy ground, and farther on towards Lasku the sands of Balamas-kum, an inlet from the true desert on the north which irrigation is now slowly reconquering.

It was in the midst of this glaring waste, where the thermometer at 10 A.M. showed a close approach to 100° Fahr. in the shade, that I was solemnly received by my old friend Badruddin Khan, the chief Afghan trader of Khotan (Fig. 50), and some representatives of the Indian community. It was a large gathering, showing curiously how much the general economic advance of Chinese Turkestan has brought Khotan also nearer. In addition to Afghan traders chiefly from Kabul, Pishin, and Bajaur settled here years ago, there appeared two Hindus, and even a full-fledged 'native doctor' in the shape of M. Abdul Aziz, late Hospital Assistant at Kashgar. The last, a much-travelled Muhammadan from the vicinity of Delhi, had during his temporary stay at Khotan found a big field for practice with all the varied chronic diseases prevailing in the oasis. But he complained, with good reason, no doubt, of the backward notions of his well-to-do patients, who were slow to realize that they owed him more substantial rewards than words of gratitude and offers of prayers.

But more interesting to me than this Aesculapius, who dressed in Franco-Turkish fashion—he had lived for some time in Mecca and Bushire—and talked English of sorts, was worthy Chandu, the first Shikarpuri money-lender who had ventured to exploit the virgin soil of Khotan. With that community thriving so well elsewhere, it was strange to find Khotan five years before wholly clear of their activity. The field for usury must have been exceptionally tempting; yet the sharp Shikarpuris had been content to abandon it wholly to their Chinese confrères. Among the reasons I heard, the most prominent and, perhaps, the only real one was a virtuous dread—of the women of Khotan and their easy morals. In view of many testimonies reaching back to early Chinese records, it would be impossible to assert that the popular reputation enjoyed by Khotan for the independence of its women - folk and its licence is altogether unfounded. I ought, therefore, to note, perhaps, of the first brave settler from Sind that he faced this danger under the protection of advanced age and a flowing white beard.

I had been riding for nearly two hours in the smothering cloud raised by my big cortège past a good deal of new cultivation in the Lasku and Givos tracts, when news unexpectedly arrived of the official welcome prepared for me under the Amban's orders some two miles outside Khotan town. I had never been treated before in so grand a fashion, and could not now think of putting on a black coat, etc., to be equal to the occasion; for the baggage was miles behind. I almost envied the Beg of my escort, who did all that was needful by taking his official cap, with button, red tassel, and the rest, from the head of an attendant, whom so far he had allowed wear it with the risk of catching a bad headache under this inadequate covering. Even the little dusting I attempted proved futile.

At the reception-hall built by the road-side I found a pompous gathering of Chinese officers in flowing silk robes, and an array of picturesque figures with swords and halberds representing a selection from the garrison. A crowd of followers of all sorts surged after us into the open hall and prevented all study of details. The military Amban who did the honours (Fig. 49) received me with a great show of friendly animation, while the portly chief of the police on my left was a figure refreshing to look at in his

50. BADRUDDIN KHAN, 'AK-SAKAL' OF INDIAN AND AFGHAN TRADERS AT KHOTAN.

51. AHMAD ISHAN (ANDIJANI 'AK-SAKAL'), AND ABDULLAH KHAN (AFGHAN TRADER) AT KERIYA. See p. 262.

easy *bonhomie*. After such a long, hot ride it was rather
tantalizing to sit with a cup of fresh tea by my side and
exchange conventional compliments instead of allaying my
thirst. But Chinese etiquette on such formal occasions
makes the sipping of the tea immediately offered a mark of
approaching departure, and one learns to exercise patience.

Badruddin Khan had prepared quarters for me at Niaz
Hakim Beg's old garden palace, Nar-bagh, where in 1901
my last stay in Khotan had been spent. It was only when
I passed through its shady Aiwans and halls into the
familiar garden with its central pavilion, where I again
established myself, that I felt fully assured my longed-for
return was a reality. My thoughts for the last five years
had so often turned to these scenes, and the difficulty of
ever revisiting them had appeared so great, that it seemed
almost strange to verify on the spot how exact my recollections had been. Nothing seemed changed in the many-
windowed pavilion which had seen my long cross-examina-
tions of Islam Akhun and the clever forger's final confession.
The garden was the same green wilderness refreshing to
the eyes, only the layers of dust were thicker on every leaf
and twig.

Time had dealt kindly, too, with old friends left behind.
Already the first afternoon dear old Akhun Beg, whose
garden had sheltered me on my first visits to Khotan,
came to greet me. Hajis and traders from Khotan, of
whom I had enquired after him during their passage
through Kashmir and Peshawar, had brought him news
how well I remembered him. When, next day, I returned
his visit, I had the satisfaction to convince myself how
faithfully every little incident of my stay was remembered
by the burly old gentleman (Fig. 52).

Many and pressing were his invitations to take up
again forthwith my residence in his house and garden.
But regard for the heat which would not allow of a stay
under canvas, and a wish to avoid an invasion of the house
itself which might disturb the inmates, obliged me to put
off this renewal of old associations until my return from the
mountains. In the meantime I accepted hospitality for my
camels, which were to recover from the hot work of the last

weeks on Akhun Beg's grazing-grounds in the mountains above Hasha. The glowing description he gave me of his flocks of sheep, of his herds of yaks, ponies, etc., was a proof that in spite of increased age my old host still kept a keen eye on the development of his rural wealth.

Ch'ê Ta-jên, the Amban of Khotan, returned from his tour of criminal investigation late on the day of my arrival. The fatigue which must have attended his rapid journeying did not keep him from a formal visit on the following morning. I had, of course, intended to pay the first call myself. But my genial Chinese secretary, whom I had entrusted with the needful announcement as well as with my official presents—a binocular and a piece of fine yellow Liberty brocade which always pleases Chinese taste —had not thought time of special importance in this case, and was still preparing himself by a prolonged visit to the barber when the Amban arrived in full state.

I was delighted to find him a very amiable and lively official, showing by his ways and conversation unmistakable energy and intelligence. His chief interpreter had been in office under P'an Ta-jên, and being thus well acquainted with my former work and travels in this region, was able to explain quickly and clearly what I stated about the objects of my renewed visit. The plates of my *Ancient Khotan* were of great help in demonstrating the results of my former labours; and though the Amban modestly refused to put himself in the same category with so learned a man as P'an Ta-jên, it was easy to see from his questions that his historical sense was equally keen.

But what pleased me even more was Ch'ê Ta-jên's evident interest in matters geographical. I badly needed his help for the renewal of my explorations in the Kun-lun range south of Khotan. Our surveys of 1900 had left interesting problems unsolved as to the uppermost course of the Yurung-kash River far away to the east and of the glacier sources of its main feeders from the south. To force our way up those difficult gorges, which form the only approach to the true head-waters of the great river, was a task I had long kept before my eyes. Without strict orders from the Amban the passive resistance of the wily

52. 'HAJI' AKHUN BEG, MY HOST AT KHOTAN.

hill-men of Karanghu-tagh was sure to baffle all efforts in that direction. With so much wholly unexplored ground before us and the certainty of exceptional physical difficulties to be encountered, it was very reassuring that Ch'ê Ta-jên quickly grasped my aims and the way in which I wished to attempt their realization. Though he had come to Khotan only a few months before, his acquaintance with the general topography of the district and those adjoining it eastward seemed surprisingly good. He followed my explanations on the map of our previous surveys without any difficulty and readily promised all help in his power.

When in the afternoon, accompanied by Chiang-ssŭ-yeh, I returned the Amban's visit at the familiar Ya-mên, I was received not only with a tasteful collation and all possible marks of honour, but with the information that all the various official orders needed to assure effective assistance were already drafted and ready for my secretary's perusal. There could be no possible doubt as to the Amban's eagerness to offer help, and I appreciated this assurance all the more since I still vividly remembered the caution and reservations with which six years before P'an Ta-jên had met my corresponding requests. I wondered whether in the meantime the dread of the unknown Tibetan uplands, where the Yurung-kash was vaguely supposed to take its rise, had diminished in the eyes of Chinese officials, and why. Or was it only Ch'ê Ta-jên's geographical instinct which roused his personal interest in the plan for which I had asked his assistance?

My hope of successful explorations in the Khotan mountains received additional encouragement when two days later Rai Ram Singh safely joined me from the difficult expedition for which I had detached him from Kök-yar. His success in the tasks I had entrusted to him was complete, and I could congratulate him on a really remarkable exploit. He had surveyed the hitherto very imperfectly known part of the Kun-lun between Kök-yar and the Kilian route, including the head-waters of the Yül-arik River about the Karlik Dawan. He had then made his way over the Pass of Kilian still deeply covered by snow to the upper Kara-kash course, and had thence

successfully pushed across the glacier-covered Hindu-tash
Pass, some 17,400 feet above the sea, into the high valley
of Pusha.

For nearly half a century the latter has figured in
our maps as almost the only local name within the blank
of *terra incognita* left between Karanghu - tagh and the
middle course of the Kara-kash river. But nothing was
known of the position of Pusha, nor of the topography of
the valleys and mountains around it which fill the great
bend of the Kara-kash river; for in 1862 Schlagintweit,
the only European who had approached this difficult
region, had turned back from the north foot of the Hindu-
tash Dawan, and had not been able to record what
observations he may have gathered there before he was
murdered at Kashgar.

The advance of a big glacier on the north side has
since so effectually barred access over the Hindu-tash Pass
that among the Kirghiz of the upper Kara-kash Ram
Singh could find only a single man who ten years earlier
had visited Pusha. He had grown old and lame, and
could do no more than indicate from the watershed the
general line he remembered having followed down the
steep and much-crevassed glacier, over six miles long. It
was an adventurous descent which Ram Singh effected
here, and though from his usual taciturnity it was not easy
to extract a detailed description, the risks he and his few
Kirghiz companions had run were only too evident. In
spite of my warnings he had neglected the precaution of
roping when crossing the glacier, with the result of more
than one narrow escape from hidden crevasses.

Sheltered behind the great icy barriers of the main
range, and accessible from the Khotan side only by exe-
crably bad mountain tracks, he had found an Alpine valley
singularly rich for these parts in water and grazing-grounds.
The abundance of flowers greatly struck the Surveyor, and
also the thriving condition of the flocks owned by the
Taghliks of Pusha. Lower down he had come upon
scattered homesteads and cultivation. When subsequently
he crossed the succession of deep-cut side valleys which
descend to the right bank of the Kara-kash east of the

Pusha Valley, the flooded condition of all streams was a source of great risks to both men and baggage. If only for the sake of fuller descriptive details, I greatly regretted that my Kök-yar work and other reasons had prevented my sharing this tour. But Ram Singh's topographical work had been effected very thoroughly, and the plane-table sheets he brought back left little to fill up in the blank space which my previous detailed map of the Khotan region prominently displayed in its south-west corner.

For the sake of giving Ram Singh and his plucky myrmidon Jasvant Singh a minimum of time for rest and the many repairs which their sadly battered equipment required, I had to extend my stay at Khotan to five days. The manifold preparations I had to push on, both for our expedition into the mountains and for the archaeological campaign to be commenced in September, made these days seem far too short. Only for an hour or so could I emerge in the evening from the busy workshop of Nar-bagh. In one of the tanks in its arbours we put together and successfully tried our raft of inflated skins (Fig. 53). There were constant interviews with 'treasure-seekers' whom Badruddin Khan had hunted up to gain information as to any possible sites awaiting excavation. Since my explorations of 1900-1901 the ancient profession of searching for 'treasure' in the Taklamakan seemed to have languished.

Even old Turdi, my faithful guide of that winter, was said to have only once subsequently visited the desert; some three years before my return he was so ill advised as to smuggle a Beg of Khotan, who had reason to fear the wrath of the Amban, through the desert to the lower Keriya River. The malcontent Beg thence pluckily made his way right through the Taklamakan to Shahyar, only to be caught there by his pursuers and brought back in ignominy. Poor Turdi himself naturally fell into disfavour for this exploit. For six months he was kept imprisoned on a trumped-up charge of cattle theft in which he got implicated through some relatives of shady character. What knowledge, if any, he had of the latter's doings human justice will never clear up; for Chinese criminal procedure in these parts knows no elaborate *dossiers*, and my honest 'treasure-

seeking' guide had died some two weeks after being
released from his fetters. It was poor consolation to me
to know that he had died at his modest home, and that
until that fateful desert trip the small post I had secured
for him had kept him in peace and in fair comfort.

Young Roze, Turdi's step-son and acolyte, who had
been with us to the ruins of Dandan-oilik, had after his
master's death settled down as a cultivator in the Yurung-
kash tract, and confined his 'treasure-seeking' to occasional
visits to the neighbouring débris areas known as 'Tatis.'
The antiquarian spoil he could now offer for purchase was
slight, consisting only of a miscellaneous collection of
ancient coins, cut stones, and other small objects. But
he brought also the fragment of a well-modelled Buddha
figure in terra-cotta, which he had found among the remains
of a 'But-khana' or temple recently left bare from the
sand in the desert beyond Hanguya. The site had not
been known at the time of my former journey, and possibly
might prove one of promise. So by a liberal Bakhshish I
engaged Roze to revisit it with a view to ascertaining local
conditions, and with other old confrères to collect from the
desert similar antiquarian indications which might be
useful for the start of my autumn campaign.

The great heat during my stay at Khotan clearly
demonstrated the impossibility of work in the desert at
this season. So as soon as I had arranged for the
'treasure-seekers'' reconnaissances I felt free to set out
for the mountains. My zealous Chinese secretary could
not be of any help in a region where human beings are
exceedingly scarce and things Chinese altogether unknown;
so I left him to freedom and comfort at Khotan. I also
lightened our *impedimenta* by handing over to Badruddin
Khan's care all equipment not immediately needed. In
order to maintain the connection with Ram Singh's recent
surveys about Pusha it was advisable to start work
from the mountains near Nissa ; and to reach this small
Alpine settlement the only available route was the one
I had followed in November 1900, on my way down to
the plains.

On the morning of August 11th we started for Langhru,

53. TESTING RAFT OF INFLATED SKINS ON A TANK OF NAR-BAGH.

54. TANK AND ARBOUR NEAR RUKNUDDIN MAZAR, YOTKAN.
For the interior of this shrine see Fig. 312.

the large village near the debouchure of the Kara-kash, from which we were to enter the mountains. During the long day's ride I took occasion to revisit the Yotkan site. A start had just been made with the annual operation of washing the soil containing the deeply buried culture-strata of the ancient Khotan capital for the sake of extracting leaf-gold and small objects of value. It was pleasant to see the village, which stands on ground so full of historical interest, with its orchards and arbours now decked out in rich foliage, instead of the autumnal bareness which reigned here during my stay in November 1900 (Fig. 54).

My old host Khuda-berdi, the jovial Yüz-bashi of Yotkan, received me in great style. Though Fate has endowed him with only a modicum of natural gifts, he had manifestly prospered during the years intervening ; and the spacious new house where his Dastarkhan was spread for us, showed that he knew how to use the good things which Fortune had granted him. The trees in his much-enlarged garden hung full of delicious peaches and plums, while huge bunches of grapes were also ripening. Khuda-berdi had duly collected for me from his villagers whatever of ancient terra-cottas, old coins, seals, etc., remained in their possession from last year's washings. So after making my purchases I could send bags full of interesting old pottery back to Khotan as the first-fruits of my new collection.

My ride from Yotkan to the south-west edge of the oasis took me past several of the sacred sites of Buddhist Khotan which Hsüan-tsang had visited, and which I had succeeded in identifying with popular Muhammadan shrines of the present day (Fig. 55). The satisfaction of covering ground, the *topographia sacra* of which could still be clearly established in spite of all changes of time and religion, made the burning heat of the mid-day hours seem less trying. On the barren gravel glacis which stretches down from the foot-hills along the right bank of the Kara-kash I then sighted once more the *morne* conglomerate cliffs with the sacred cave of Kohmari, famous in ancient Khotan as the shrine of Gosringa, 'the Cow's horn Mountain,' and a site of curious legends. Below rolled the Kara-kash as a mighty river swollen by the melting ice of its distant glacier sources, very different from the insignificant stream I had crossed in November 1900.

After the intense heat and glare of the Sai, it was a relief to ride up the narrow fringe of cultivation formed by the fields of Nussia and Faizabad, which extend for some miles along the right bank. Then followed again barren plateaus of stone and rubble overhanging the river, until near the east edge of the fields of Langhru I came upon the remains of a ruined fort vaguely connected by popular belief with a demon 'Konsasmoma.' The walls, badly decayed, form an irregular quadrilateral, about a hundred yards long on the north-east, and built of sun-dried bricks of large size. There was no trace of structural remains inside, nor did the rough construction of the enclosure supply evidence as to relative age. So much, however, was clear, that the little stronghold was intended to close whatever routes led down from the mountains. Night had fallen by the time I reached camp at a comfortable old farm at Langhru. The vicinity of the river and a fine grove of trees gave but little protection against the torrid heat thrown out by the barren sandstone cliffs enclosing the valley. So through the stuffy night I felt doubly glad for the near escape to the mountains.

55. MOSQUE WITH TANK NEAR WEST GATE OF KHOTAN TOWN.

56. IN TOPCHA GORGE, SOUTH OF ULUGHAT PASS.
The few trees here are Toghraks (wild poplars).

CHAPTER XV

THE only route available for approach to the westernmost head-waters of the Yurung-kash was the one I had first followed on my expedition of 1900, but in the inverse direction. So no detailed account need be given here of the four long marches which took us from Langhru across a succession of high transverse spurs and through barren gorges to Nissa. Nothing had changed in the desolate look of these curiously eroded rugged ranges and the mighty strata of detritus and loess dust which cover their higher slopes. But the narrow strips of vegetation at the bottom of those gorges which push their heads close enough to the snow-line to receive running water during the summer months, looked greener now than I could have expected from the impressions left by my autumn passage six years before (Fig. 56). On the top of the first pass, the Ulughat, close on 10,000 feet above the sea, where an exceptional chance of clear weather had then given a day so profitable for our triangulation, I found the little mound of loose earth and scrub we had heaped up as a ' station mark ' perfectly intact, a fresh proof how favourable the conditions of this dry region are to the preservation of even the most insignificant structures. The fame of the ' Pao-t'ai ' we had built on the mountain-top had spread far and wide among the scattered little settlements of Taghliks; for Ram Singh had heard it talked of even in the forlorn valley of Pusha.

But if nothing had changed in the weirdly arid look of these mountains, it was different with the atmospheric conditions. Instead of the brilliantly clear sky which in

1900 had enabled me to secure that series of fine photo-theodolite panoramas of which I was now carrying with me reproductions, since published by the Royal Geographical Society in a separate volume, a haze of aggravating constancy hid all the more distant snowy peaks on the main range southward. Still it was an interesting experience to let my eyes wander over the maze-like succession of fantastically serrated ranges, to study the extraordinary surface formations etched out by erosion, and to be able at the same time to record on faithful reproductions of this strange mountain waste whatever information about topographical details within the actual horizon could be gathered from my Taghlik guides.

On approaching the Yagan-Dawan, the second pass crossed by the route, I was delighted to find among the coarse grass covering the loess slopes a fair display of Alpine flowers, the first I had seen since Kashmir. Among them were edelweiss, bluebells, and a few other familiar flowers, known to me, alas! by look only and not by name. The tracks leading through the fantastically eroded gorges and over the boulder-strewn approaches of the passes were as trying for animals and baggage as before. But whether it was a result of the 'lifting of the Purdah' effected by my previous passage through these mountains, or due to more stringent orders from the Amban which overawed these hill-men, suspicious by nature and averse from all foreign intrusion, the tiny semi-nomadic settlements we met with in the valleys of Mitaz and Chash seemed 'tamer,' and yaks were duly forthcoming for the baggage. Thus Nissa was reached without delay or mishap by the afternoon of August 15th.

At the point where the gorge descending from the Brinjak Pass debouches upon the Nissa River, and a short distance above the collection of twenty mud hovels which form the winter quarters of the hill-men grazing and cultivating in this high valley some 9000 feet above the sea, I was obliged to halt for a day in order to make preparations for the work I had in view. It included two main tasks. In the first place, I was anxious to supplement our survey of 1900 by ampler topographical details about the great glaciers which we had then sighted at the heads of the side valleys draining the high Kun-lun range south of the Yurung-kash, but had been unable to approach owing to the advanced season and the want of adequate transport.

Another object I had kept my eyes upon was to clear up the doubts about the difficult and long-disused route by which Johnson in 1865, on his plucky visit to Khotan from the westernmost Tibetan plateaus, had been taken across the high snow-mountains south of Karanghu-tagh. Our explorations of 1900 had revealed very puzzling discrepancies between the sketch-map illustrating Johnson's journey and the actual orography of this region, and the obstinate reticence of the Karanghu-tagh hill-men had prevented any clue to the true location of his route. There was little reason to hope that their obstructive attitude would have undergone any material change. But now we had at least succeeded, by prolonged cross-examination of the herdsmen at Mitaz and Chash, in eliciting that there was 'behind the mountains' a high valley called Brinjaga, to which the 'Bais of Karanghu-tagh' were believed to send their yaks for summer grazing. The admission seemed encouraging; for this local name, of which all knowledge had been stoutly denied on occasion of my first explorations, actually figured in Johnson's route sketch as the designation of a valley he had passed through before reaching Karanghu-tagh.

On Karanghu-tagh, as the chief place of the small settlements of Taghliks and criminals exiled from Khotan who form the only population in this desolate mountain region, we depended for supplies, transport, and guides. So I lost no time in summoning its head-man. The old Yüz-bashi, whose passive resistance had caused so much worry in 1900, had died in the interval. But his successor, a good-looking young fellow, who duly arrived in the evening of our day's halt near Nissa, seemed equally inclined to such tactics. I confronted him with the admission made by the Mitaz men as to Brinjaga, and tried to convince him that continued professions of ignorance would only result in our prolonged stay in his valleys and additional trouble to himself. The argument seemed to make some impression ; for the Yüz-bashi now remembered having heard the name, though on the score of his youth he maintained he could not be expected to know anything more about it.   But his reiterated protestations of ignorance as to any route southwards and of inadequate influence over his refractory crew of herdsmen and exiles left ground for misgivings.   However, I felt glad that no objections were raised against my intended visit to the glaciers at the head of the Nissa Valley.   It might serve as a convenient respite for the men of Karanghu-tagh to come to a better frame of mind, and in order to familiarize the Yüz-bashi with our work and ways I decided to take him along.

On August 17th a short and unexpectedly pleasant march brought us to the head of the Nissa Valley.   Narrow as the valley was for the first four miles or so above our camping-ground, an almost unbroken string of fields extended along its bottom.   The river, fed by the numerous glaciers southward, supplies water in plenty, as we could easily judge from the difficulty the repeated crossings caused us.   Yet only a small portion of the carefully terraced fields was actually bearing crops of oats ; for owing to the poorness of the soil and probably also from want of sufficient labour, cultivation of individual fields was said to take place only in turns of four or five years.

We had passed the highest of these fields at Püsh-ünga at an elevation of about 10,000 feet and were just emerging from a barren rocky defile above the side valley of Tor, when suddenly there opened out before us a vista of Alpine scenery such as I had never expected to meet in this barren region (Fig. 57).   From an amphitheatre of high snowy peaks southwards there stretched down a broad valley basin with green meadows at its bottom and a picturesque succession of high grassy ridges in its centre. As the route ascended these ridges, I soon recognized that they were formed by ancient moraines of huge size which had been left behind by glaciers of earlier periods, far exceeding those still to be found in the valley.   Yet even the present glaciers were extensive enough to give to its uppermost part abundant moisture and verdure.

The view of these ice-streams in the panorama obtained

57. HEAD OF NISSA VALLEY SEEN FROM TAM-ÖGHIL, ABOVE TOR.

Loess-covered old moraine ridges in foreground

in 1900 from our survey station above the Brinjak Pass
had been impressive in spite of the distance, and the
successful triangulation subsequently carried out had shown
that among the many imposing peaks rising above them
there was at least one exceeding the height of 23,000 feet.
For us down in the valley this high peak was now hidden
from view by a satellite of about 20,000 feet rising just in
front. But even without the photographic panorama in
my hands it would have been easy to locate its position by
the exceptional length of the glaciers which we soon found
descending from that direction to the head of the valley.

It was delightful to ride over the grassy slopes with which
a thick mantle of loess, showing in places rounded down-
like forms, had covered up these ancient moraines. After
all the barrenness of sand and crumbling rock I had passed
through for months, I felt myself carried back now almost
to the Alpine plateaus of my beloved Kashmir Margs.
The glaciers descending from the huge amphitheatre of
snowy peaks and ridges drew nearer and nearer, and at
last we had to pitch camp on a fine grassy spur known
as Kashkul, just opposite to the snout of a big glacier,
at an elevation of some 13,300 feet. Its terminal wall
of dark ice rose at least 150 feet above the boulder-
strewn slope on which the glacier finally deposits its
detritus. Enormous masses of rock débris completely
covered the crest and sides of the glacier. Yet big ice-
falls and gaping crevasses of great size disclosed the mighty
stream of ice which carries them downwards. All through
the afternoon and evening I could hear the rumble of the
boulders sliding down over the ice-wall at the snout and
sides as the sun loosened the grip of the surface ice.
Louder still and continuous was the roar of the ice-fed
streams which leaped down the slopes all round our ridge.

It was an Alpine camping-ground such as I could
scarcely hope to find again in these forbidding mountains.
So I was doubly glad to be caught just here by a big and
long-expected mail bag carried up with no small trouble
from Khotan, and to be able to use a day's halt, needed
anyhow on account of survey observations, for its disposal
in such cheerful surroundings. With this Dak had come the

concluding proof-sheets of *Ancient Khotan*. An auspicious chance thus allowed me to finish my last task on that work in an Alpine *entourage* singularly recalling Kashmir, where its first plan had been formed, and yet within the true confines of Khotan.

The reconnaissance survey of the Nissa Valley and the high range southward brought back from my previous expedition was based solely on the view, extensive and clear though it was, which we had then obtained from a single plane-table station above the Brinjak Pass. In order to supplement and rectify it by more exact details, it was absolutely essential to climb to some commanding height above the head of the valley. The latter bifurcates about a mile below the Kashkul Glacier, and only by ascending the high rocky spur which flanks the latter on the east could we hope to get a view of the higher peaks south-eastwards and of the glaciers likely to descend from them.

The morning of August 19th, when we set out for this purpose with full survey equipment, was delightfully clear, with neither clouds nor that ominous dust-haze which on previous days usually about noon had swept up from the north to hide all distant mountains. The wish to visit *en route* also the crest of the ice-stream induced me to attack the spur with Ram Singh from the side of the Kashkul Glacier. It took us more than an hour to traverse the glacier, though its width was scarcely more than three-quarters of a mile near its end; so troublesome were the confused masses of rock débris travelling slowly downwards on its surface among which we had to pick our way. The ice of this terminal portion, even where exposed in steep wall-like falls and by the side of small pits filled with half-frozen green water, looked almost black.

Once across the glacier we found ourselves at the foot of what looked like a huge wall composed of enormous rock fragments. They seemed as if torn out from the mountain by a colossal explosion, or heaped up by the hands of Titans. Their size and the sharpness of their edges strikingly illustrated the forces of disintegration at work on these mountain slopes, where they are not protected by a permanent cover of snow or ice, and thus are left exposed to the effects of extreme variations of temperature. In curious contrast to the eastern slope of the same spur where we subsequently found plentiful small detritus, the decomposition of the rock had not advanced here further than to produce cyclopean blocks. The greater frequency of rapid variations of temperature on the side which is heated by the morning sun, may perhaps supply the explanation.

It was a hot climb before we escaladed the top, some 1200 feet above our starting-place on the glacier edge, and the Taghliks who accompanied us, carrying plane-table, theodolite boxes, etc., were with difficulty induced to come on. Once on the crest, the ascent towards the spire-like culminating points of the spur promised to be easier. But we soon found that this arête was nothing but a succession of huge fissured rocks quite impracticable in a straight line or from the west, and providing gymnastic exercise of a trying sort even on their more accessible slope. For an hour and a half we clambered along them, refreshed only by the grand view of the snowy peaks both to the east and west. When at last we drew near to the point where the first great rock-pinnacle rose above the crest of the spur, it became evident that to scale it with our instruments was wholly impossible for the men. The east and west faces seemed almost vertical, and the narrow couloirs running more or less in the direction of the crest were not only extremely steep but, in addition, rendered unsafe by falling stones which the melting of the ice or snow in the higher fissures was loosening. So we were obliged to fix the plane-table on the highest accessible part of the grat (Fig. 58). The aneroid showed its height to be close on 15,000 feet.

To the south-west there lay before us the grand amphitheatre of steep ice-crowned ridges and névé-filled valleys which contribute to the Kashkul Glacier. Westwards we commanded a view of the less high but equally rugged side range trending to the north, which sends down the drainage of its own separate glaciers to meet the stream fed by the former. In continuation of a very striking snowy pyramid,

well over 20,000 feet in height, there rose like a huge wall
of ice the watershed towards what Ram Singh's recent
surveys led me to surmise must be the head of the Panaz
Valley draining into the Kara-kash.   Little I thought when
examining this ice-clad arête through my glasses and trying
to form an idea of the lie of the valleys beyond, that my
quest of Johnson's Yangi Dawan would lead me two years
later to climb from the south the main range of the Kun-
lun at a point not very far from that very pyramid, and let
me take farewell here, for a period at any rate, of this wild
and grand mountain-world of the Kun-lun.

The whole length of the Kashkul Glacier, some six
miles from the firns below that ice wall to the snout facing
our camp, lay stretched out before or below us.   Immediately under the steep névé slopes of the head, the uppermost reach of the glacier, with a closely packed succession
of schrunds, still showed up white.   But, farther on,
enormous masses of rock débris sent down from the bare
rib-like lower ridges smothered the ice-stream, and made
its surface look like that of a huge dark river flowing in
rapids and suddenly petrified in its wild course.

On the other side of our ridge the view for survey
purposes was far less comprehensive and defined.   The
fantastically serrated ridges before us to the east and
south-east formed manifestly but a big transverse spur
completely hiding the axial range of the Kun-lun.   We
could clearly see that the stream coming down in the
valley below us was far larger than the one issuing from
the Kashkul Glacier.   But of the proportionately bigger
ice-stream which feeds it, only a small portion of the
terminal moraine was visible about two miles higher up,
the rest being hidden by the rocky spur on which we
stood.   The plane-table made it evident that this, to us,
invisible great glacier must descend in a big bend from
the east or north-east slopes of the triangulated snowy
peak of 23,071 feet, and the panorama taken from above
the Brinjak Dawan in 1900 seemed to confirm this assumption.   But, to complete our survey with reasonable accuracy,
an advance towards this eastern and main head of the
Nissa Valley was indispensably needed.

58. HEAD OF KASHKUL GLACIER WITH ITS NÉVÉ-BEDS, LOOKING TOWARDS NORTH-EAST.

Photograph taken from great about 15,000 feet above sea-level.

When we had clambered down over the somewhat easier east slope of our spur and had rounded its foot towards Kashkul, return to camp was still seriously obstructed by the glacier streams intervening. In the early morning they had been crossed without any trouble. Now in the afternoon the increased volume of greyish-white water sent down by the melting ice and snow of the higher slopes had swollen them into raging torrents which even yaks could not face without risk of being swept off their feet for some distance. Luckily the yaks brought up from Nissa seemed accustomed to fords with rolling boulders under their feet and to swimming too. By having ropes taken across from the opposite bank and attached to their nostrils, sufficient guidance was secured for the sluggish beasts to carry us and our instruments through the racing torrent without more damage than a ducking up to the waist.

CHAPTER XVI

ON THE OTRUGHUL GLACIER

EARLY on the morning of August 19th I had our camp moved to the very foot of the previously surmised great glacier filling the true head of the Nissa Valley. I called it the Otrughul Glacier, from the chief grazing-ground lower down. The bottom of the valley leading up to it proved for the last few miles so broad and open that the general course of the glacier could be fixed from a distance by intersections of the high snowy peaks flanking it. Its length as thus ascertained proved over twelve miles; but only a small portion of this was actually visible from the valley below, owing to bends caused by the spurs descending to the glacier's edge.

So after indicating a camping-place at the last plot of coarse grass below the terminal moraine, I set out with Musa, whom his Chitrali descent and his youth seemed to mark out for climbing, and a few very unwilling Taghliks to ascend the glacier as far as time and conditions would permit. The Surveyor remained behind to nurse a bad cold and—the stiff joints resulting from the previous day's rock-scrambling. The big glacier snout rising before us showed a crescent-shaped ice wall, over half a mile across and fully 200 feet high, exposed and yet almost dark with fine detritus (see the panorama in Plate II., taken farther up). Over the huge terminal moraines in which the snout was embedded, and which imperceptibly merged with the débris masses overlying the flanks of the ice wall, access could have been gained to the crest. But the previous day's experience had shown me how greatly an advance on the glacier itself

PANORAMIC VIEW OF END PORTION OF OTRUGHUL GLACIER, AT HEAD OF NISSA VALLEY, TAKEN FROM DETRITUS SLOPE FACING THE WESTERN FLANK OF THE GLACIER.

The foreground in centre and on left shows the glacier flank completely covered with débris masses of moraines (see i. p. 188). The ice wall behind is exposed, darkened with fine detritus. On extreme right is seen the foot of the precipitous rock-spur past which the route of our ascent on the glacier lay (see i. p. 189). The panorama was taken at an elevation of circ. 14,800 feet.

was likely to be impeded by its covering masses of rock and detritus. So I decided to try a route along its western edge, where the main drainage had cut itself a way between the lateral ice wall of the glacier and the steep boulder-strewn slopes rising above it. To cross this stream of greyish ice-water where it debouched near the snout was not easy on yaks, even so early in the day, and the apprehension seemed justified that by the time of our return in the evening the melting snows might have made the passage quite impracticable. The eventual prospect of being cut off from camp and its comforts after a tiring day's work was not encouraging. But there was nothing for it but to face it.

For about a mile onwards the slope to the west was practicable for yaks, in spite of the confused masses of rock detritus which covered it. But soon we were forced to pick our way over huge blocks of rock heaped up wall-like and almost as bad as those over which our climb of the previous day lay. An hour's toil had scarcely advanced us more than a mile when there came in view, a short distance ahead, a precipitous rock-spur which would have effectively barred farther progress, at least for the accompanying Taghliks. Between the foot of this spur and the ice of the glacier, pressing in contorted masses against it, the stream was rushing down in foaming cataracts (Plate II.).

But fortunately at a point below we saw it spreading in several branches over a small delta-like basin formed by the detritus washed down from a glacier-crowned side valley. So we crossed here to the side of the glacier, the big lateral ice walls of which had faced us all along. In many places the masses of dark-coloured ice, from 120 to 200 feet in height, rose almost vertically above the side moraine and the stream closely skirting it. But just where our crossing had been effected a slope of detritus facilitated access to the top of the glacier. We found it here comparatively clear of encumbering boulders but fissured by many deep cavities. Between these we picked our way, grateful that there was no fresh snow to hide the dangerous crevasses.

For a mile and a half we had advanced, using the

ice-axe that Naik Ram Singh had prepared at Kök-yar from a design I had given him, wherever small ridges of ice required step-cutting. Already from a distance I had viewed with misgivings the mighty ice-falls which stretched across the whole breadth of the glacier a little above the point where the spur just mentioned projected into its bed, probably forming a hidden ledge below it. As we got nearer I saw that these torn masses of dark ice would leave us no possible passage. They seemed to be piled up in still wilder confusion against the barring rock-spur on the west. But just as we cautiously approached this, I noticed that a little higher up the lateral moraine reappeared and that we could make our way to this without serious difficulty or risk. Once on the crest of this moraine, progress was easy in spite of its narrowness, and for nearly two miles we moved along it upwards, impeded by nothing but the increased difficulty of breathing. I estimated that we had ascended to an elevation of over 16,000 feet when, after a total climb of four hours, the lateness of the day warned me that it was time to come to a halt.

A series of well-defined snowy peaks previously sighted, rising precipitously above the glacier on the east and north-east, made it easy to fix our position on the plane-table. For a round of photographic views, too (Figs. 59, 60), the point we had gained was excellent. But, alas! a great bend of the glacier to the south-west, about three-quarters of a mile ahead, shut off the view of our guiding star, the great triangulated peak, and of the névé beds by its side where the glacier must take its start. The extremely precipitous rock slopes of the peaks to the east and south-east, and the equally steep hanging glaciers scouring them lower down, were a deeply impressive sight.

As this panorama of silent Alpine grandeur, which no human foot is ever likely to have disturbed before, crowded upon me, I scarcely had time to give much attention to the curious fact that due south, where our previous mapping would have made me look for an array of high peaks of the main range, there extended a flat-topped, snow-covered spur rising only two or three thousand feet above my

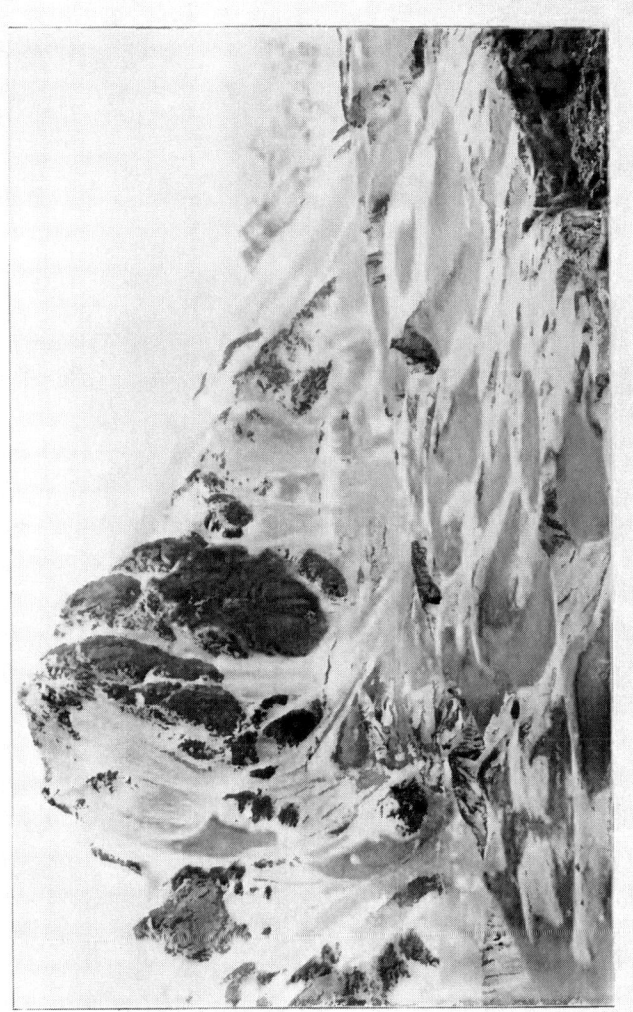

A

B

59. VIEW OF OTRUGHUL GLACIER, LOOKING TOWARDS SOUTH-EAST.

Photograph taken from moraine at elevation of about 16,000 feet above sea-level ; joins Fig. 60 near line A B.

60. VIEW OF OTRUGHUL GLACIER, LOOKING TOWARDS EAST.

Photograph taken from moraine at elevation of about 16,000 feet above sea-level; joins Fig. 59 near line A B.

point of observation.   It looked strangely low and uniform
for the Kun-lun watershed.   But only two years later
could I realize its significance, when our surveys, carried
from across the Tibetan side of the mountains, supplied
evidence that, between the head of the Nissa Valley and
the main range, there lay another high valley as yet
unexplored, which must drain the ice-crowned east slopes
of the great triangulated peak.

Farther ascent on the glacier might have helped to
give an inkling of this, and progress for a mile ahead was
probably easy; but it was getting too late to attempt it.
An ominous haze, rolling up the valley from the north,
warned me that the dust from the desert would help to
shorten the daylight available for the descent.   So as
soon as the plane-table work and photographing was
concluded, by 4 P.M., I gave the order for the return.   The
four Nissa men greeted it with unusual animation.   Before,
they lay stretched out on the detritus mud, complaining
of headache and other symptoms of mountain sickness,—
another proof of the observation, previously made with
Kirghiz, how little continued residence in high valleys
prepares these hill-men for any exertion at great elevations.
The Nissa herdsmen had never moved beyond the grazing-
ground at the foot of the glacier, and nothing but the fear
of the 'Ulugh Mihman' could have induced them to advance
so far.   They little suspected how much the thought of
moving over ground which no human feet had ever touched
added to my enjoyment of this short exploration.

The return to camp was effected without incident.
We had taken the precaution of marking our route up
the glacier, and could now follow it with full assurance in
the reverse direction.   The cloudy sky of the afternoon
and the gathering haze had checked the melting of the
snow on the higher slopes, and thus we found the stream
where we had to cross it above camp, though swollen,
still safely passable with yaks.   A liberal allowance of
tea restored the spirits of my companions from Nissa, and
from a distance I could hear them boast of their exploits
that day when gathered with the other local men round the
camp-fire.

The haze continued heavy next morning, and precluded all hope of sighting further topographical details of importance from any height within climbing reach. I had to reckon with the probability of such unfavourable atmospheric conditions continuing for some days, and decided to use these for the shifting of our base eastwards to Karanghu-tagh and the Kash River drainage. On the march back to Nissa I missed, indeed, the grand vistas of snowy peaks and ice-streams. But as the survey of the valley and its enclosing ranges was already completed, I was content to find compensation in the coolness which this veil of yellowish fog assured. By mid-day we had safely effected the several crossings above Nissa, though not without serious trouble from the swollen river, and an hour later my tent was pitched on a narrow grassy plot just below the last hut of the village. It was barely ready to afford shelter when a light but steady rain began to descend, the first which these valleys had known for many weeks. The rain continued for some four hours, and rarely had I heard the patter of its drops on the fly of my tent with more satisfaction; for I fondly hoped it would clear the atmosphere of those floating dust-clouds which had as yet interfered with distant views in these mountains.

My march on August 22nd towards Karanghu-tagh took me over ground seen already in November 1900. But the difference of the season materially affected my impressions. The valley below Nissa, confined between barren and extremely steep rock walls, 3000 to 4000 feet high, through which we had then groped our way in the dusk of an autumn evening, proved now quite rich in low jungle along the narrow river-bed. Our route had then lain by the side of the river; but now the water was so deep as to make the seven crossings within a distance of about five miles difficult even for us on horseback. For the baggage this portion of the route would have been quite impracticable, and it was fortunate that a pass, reached through the side valley of Boriz, was open to the yaks. Ponies could not have crossed it.

The loess slopes of the Pom-tagh Dawan, about 11,500 feet high, over which we crossed into the valley of the

Kash River, the next feeder of the Yurung-kash eastwards, were now clothed with plentiful coarse grass. The night's rain had visibly revived the vegetation of these waterless spurs, and had also washed down the dust haze. Yet the grand vista of snowy peaks and glaciers eastwards which had greeted me at that height in 1900, was now completely hidden by hovering clouds.

On my descent into the Kash Valley that evening I was not surprised to find my progress to Karanghu-tagh barred by the swollen river. Yet I scarcely anticipated what time it would take to surmount this obstacle. In front of the small alluvial fan known as Ushlash, on which I pitched camp after descending the gorge from the Pom-tagh Pass, the river raced past in a mighty torrent; even the hardy yaks could swim it only with difficulty. The few village elders from Karanghu-tagh who arrived in the evening had crossed by a rickety foot-bridge thrown across the river gorge at a point farther down, and so risky that the Beg who had started to meet me did not venture upon it. The hill-men were unanimous in declaring that no loads could be passed across. So it was evidently a case to bring into requisition my raft of inflated goat-skins from India. But to use it without the ⅜th-inch steel wire rope which the forethought of Major H. T. Sherwood, R.E., had provided, would have been an impossibility; for any raft or boat not thus secured was sure to be dashed to pieces on the numberless boulders by the torrent.

An inspection of the river-bed, made early in the morning with Naik Ram Singh, convinced me that the only point within reach where the steel wire could be fixed across the stream and our 'Mussuck' raft worked from it as a ferry, was at the lower end of a rift which the river had cut for its passage through a ledge of sandstone cliffs some two miles above Karanghu-tagh village (Fig. 61). Just where the river issues like a mill-stream from this rock-cut channel into a deep pool of whirling water, we found it spanned by the frail structure which the men of Karanghu-tagh called their bridge. Three roughly hewn poplar trunks had been jammed in between the rock faces, some twenty-five yards apart at this point. But from warping or otherwise the rudely joined timber pieces had parted company years before. Only one of the trunks was sufficiently broad to serve singly as a foothold; but as this, too, curved greatly downwards in the middle and was badly split, an attempt to use it for crossing would have been very dangerous had not another of the beams kept sufficiently near to serve as a support for the hands.

Seeing the contrivance I understood why even these nimble Taghliks fought shy of carrying any loads over it. To fix the wire rope, from which the raft was to hang by a travelling pulley, on the rocky sides of the gorge was not easy; but fortunately it was found possible to dig out safe anchorages without blasting. To secure the wood needed for the anchors took hours, and it was only by 2 P.M. that the rope was firmly fixed by Naik Ram Singh and ready to guide the rapidly floated raft by means of its traveller. Grass packed between two waterproof sheets had been bound as a platform over the light bamboo framework, eight feet square, to which the twelve goat-skins were lashed. But even thus the top of the raft rose only a foot or so over the tossing water. By much coaxing and some mild coercion Musa, my plucky Chitrali, had induced a young Taghlik to accompany him on the first experimental crossing. It was an exciting affair; for the force of the current shook the tiny craft violently, while the shortness of the rope by which it was attached to the steel wire made its front rise at an uncomfortable angle. But the two men hung on to the lashing and were safely pulled across.

For the return passage Ram Singh decided to lengthen the guiding rope in order to allow the raft to ride well on the water. But the result of the change proved disastrous. Scarcely had the raft been pulled from behind the shelter of a projecting rock when the waves began to break over it. I was just beginning to think how risky it would be to expose the baggage to such a ducking as young Musa, now the only occupant of the raft, was getting, when there was a loud report as of a pistol shot and a violent jerk on the rope by which the men on my side were pulling the raft across. Under the great strain of the current the twisted wire rope had snapped just above the anchorage.

61. 'BRIDGE' ACROSS KASH RIVER ABOVE KARANGHU-TAGH.

In foreground baggage being hoisted across by wire rope.

The force of the five or six men on the pulling rope by my side was not sufficient to stem the gliding raft. But luckily no one had been struck by the snapped wire, and they were holding on pluckily, though the rope cut into their hands, and the jerk had nearly precipitated them into the river some thirty feet below the vertical rock bank. We all rushed to their aid. For seconds which seemed terribly long I feared the worst for poor Musa; but then the previously slack rope from the right bank helped to hold back the raft. The men on that side, realizing the danger, pulled away with all their strength, and, aided by the bearing of the current, succeeded, after some anxious minutes, in dragging the raft safely ashore. Musa lost no time in divesting himself of his dripping fur coat, and soon to my comfort I saw him drying himself on a rock and composedly munching an oat cake.

Experience had shown that our wire rope, though tested for great weight, could not resist the terrific force of the current, and that the raft, however sound in design, could not be used here in safety. So we decided to trust to the wire alone, of which there was still a spare length intact, and to hoist the loads across by its means. This changed procedure necessitated fresh anchorages; for between the steep rock walls where the wire was first fixed the loads could not have been safely unslung. Hours passed over this, and when the newly fixed wire had at last been tried by the transport of a big boulder it was too late to commence the passing of loads. So camp had to be pitched once more by the side of the roaring river.

The evening passed in long and fruitless enquiries from the wily Taghliks as to any route for reaching the grazing-grounds suspected to exist on the upper Yurung-kash or for crossing the great mountain barrier southward. To all questions that surly '*bilmaiman*' ('I do not know'), to which the tactics of the men of Karanghu-tagh six years before had accustomed me, was the stereotyped answer. There could be no doubt that the pretended ignorance of Brin-jaga, which even the people of Mitaz and Nissa had heard of, was the result of a systematic conspiracy. It was difficult to guess the reason of this so long as the position of that valley could not even approximately be determined. But there was only too much reason to believe that the stout denial of any knowledge of a passage over the mountains southward to the high Tibetan plateaus from which Johnson had descended, was due to the fear that the rediscovery of that long-closed route might expose the dwellers of these forsaken valleys to passing traffic and— fresh imposts and corvées.

CHAPTER XVII

IN THE KARANGHU-TAGH MOUNTAINS

On the morning of August 24th it took three long hours to pass our baggage piece-meal across the Kash River by the wire rope. It included this time also my lively little terrier tied up ignominiously in a bag; for he could not possibly have crossed the so-called bridge, and none of the Taghliks felt plucky enough to carry him over it. Then one by one we clambered over the frail beam. It swung uncomfortably towards the middle, and the other tree was too low down to afford a firm hold for one's hands; but in the end all of us were safely across.

A walk of two miles, mainly along cultivated terraces, brought me to Karanghu-tagh, the collection of some forty mud hovels which during the winter months shelter the majority of the herdsmen and select malefactors from Khotan banished to these forbidding mountains (Fig. 62). The look of these habitations was quite as wretched and uninviting as when I first saw them in October 1900, and the changed season could not affect the depressing barrenness of the bleak steep slopes of rock or detritus shutting in the valley. But there was at least the green of a narrow band of oat fields and the foliage of a few poplars to give temporary relief from the gloom of what the exiles called their 'town.'

I found neither supplies nor transport ready in the village. So I preferred to move my camp a few miles farther down to Khushlash-langar, where the Kash River is joined on the right by the stream from the Busat Valley. Our survey of 1900, effected from a considerable distance, had shown this valley to terminate at its head in a large glacier branching out like the spread fingers of a hand towards what we took to be the main Kun-lun watershed. The hill-men stoutly denied the existence of any track leading hence across the great snowy range southward. But there was a special reason for me to test their statement by a closer survey. Six years before I had been greatly puzzled by the topographical features of the sketch map illustrating the route which Johnson claimed to have followed on his descent to Khotan in 1865. According to this map Johnson had made his way across the Kun-lun main range by a very high pass, which he called 'Yangi diwan' (i.e. 'Yangi Dawan,' 'the New Pass'), to an affluent of the Yurung-kash, and thence by a second pass, designated as 'Naia Khan Pass,' to another valley joining the main river from the south close to Karanghu-tagh.

It was true that the position assigned to the latter as well as other topographical features were found to differ widely from the actual configuration of these valleys as revealed by our survey, while none of the names of passes, etc., shown south of Karanghu-tagh were known to the hill-men. No help could be got from the very meagre record published of Johnson's remarkable feat. There was no reason to doubt the general fact of his having crossed the Kun-lun main range from the head-waters of the Kara-kash southwards, and it was thus a matter of considerable interest to ascertain where his actual route lay.

But owing to the wide discrepancy between his map and the real topography of these mountains only conjectures could guide me in the search for this route. And a number of conjectural indications, which it would be impossible to explain here without analysing in detail the relationship presented by certain features of Johnson's rough sketch map to the ground as our surveys had shown it, seemed to point to the Busat Valley as the most likely approach to his 'Naia Khan Pass.' If it were possible to trace from it a practicable crossing to the head of the nearest valley eastward, the Chomsha Jilga of our survey, we might then be justified in looking from the south-western end of the latter for that mysterious 'New Pass' by which Johnson at an elevation of

62. EXILED MALEFACTORS FROM KHOTAN AND TAGHLIK HERDSMEN AT KHUSH-LASH-LANGAR,
KARANGHU-TAGH.

19,500 feet claimed to have penetrated the great barrier of the main Kun-lun.

My start for the head of the Busat Valley was not effected without serious trouble. The Yüz-bashi and greybeards of Karanghu-tagh did not deny that it was one of their grazing-grounds and that the approach to it was easy. But when I demanded, with a view to possible further exploration, that the men who were to accompany the few yaks needed for what little of baggage was to be taken ahead, should be provided with food for ten days, the answer was a *non possumus* clamorously uttered in chorus. The dozen men or so who had been collected, declared that more than a day's bread was not within their reach, while the ' Bais ' of the settlement, men owning plentiful cattle, were equally emphatic in assurances that there was no spare grain in their houses, however tempting the rates I might offer for its purchase. In the end the suave town-bred Beg of the hill tract who assisted at these preparations undertook to arrange, by fair means or otherwise, that the men should start with adequate provisions. But it was easy to see that his authority was not equal to enforcing this victualling task, and equally clear also that the prospect of ten days' work in the high mountains had completely scared the men who were to benefit by my solicitude. Islam Beg and the Naik were left behind in charge of the ponies and spare baggage.

The march next morning up the valley proved easy, when once the light loads had been put on the yaks and their unwilling drivers set in motion ; for after some five miles of steep tracks along the sides of a rocky defile the bottom of the valley widened to a series of down-like plateaus covered with short but thick grass. Here, as in the upper Nissa Valley, I could recognize ancient moraines covered by loess deposits. We had just ascended the grassy slope of the first plateau when the clouds that hung about the spurs on either side descended in drizzling rain.

It was a fit prelude to the weather which we were to experience throughout our stay in the valley. In the rain and driving mist the dirty small felt tents or ' Kara-ois ' in which the families of the herdsmen on these uplands

were sheltering, looked doubly miserable. To the dismay
of my yak-men I pushed on to the highest of these Alpine
meadows, close to where the high detritus walls of terminal
moraines were looming through the mist above us, before
pitching camp at an elevation of about 12,300 feet. In
order to lighten all loads I had left my own little tent
behind and instead brought up the Naik's, just six
feet square. With my camp cot squeezed into it there
remained barely room for a mule-trunk and the smallest of
camp tables. But against the rain, which continued well
into the night, the shelter was complete, and I soon got
accustomed to stowing myself away in so confined a
space.

Early next morning the clouds were still low, hiding
almost completely the rugged spurs which I knew encircled the head of the valley. Only the huge moraines,
stretching down from the south and from both sides of the
valley towards our camping-place, showed that we were
near the big glaciers sighted six years ago from across the
main Yurung-kash Valley. At first thick mist descended
and delayed our start on the reconnaissance I had decided
upon in spite of the threatening weather. But by half-
past eight the Surveyor and myself with a few men were
on the move up the moraine slopes to the south-east where
I surmised a large ice-filled side valley. The point to be
ascertained was whether it could offer a practicable route of
access to the head of the Chomsha Valley eastwards.

As soon as we had left the slope covered with grass
and moss, progress became very slow. We had to pick
our way over accumulations of fissured rock débris lying
in the wildest confusion, and the rain of the night had
made the surfaces very slippery. Soon the yaks brought
behind us for experiment's sake had to be halted, as the
barricades of sharp-edged boulders grew too difficult to
cross, even for their sure feet. For nearly three hours we
toiled on, scarcely realizing at the time in the mist which
again enveloped us that we were ascending the rock-strewn
surface of an ice stream.

At a height of about 13,600 feet by aneroid we had
just surmounted a huge transverse ridge of piled-up rocks,

when we found ourselves on a smooth slope of hard snow. Though the mist around scarcely allowed one to see ahead more than a few hundred yards, I rightly guessed that we had reached the névé beds feeding this branch of the glacier. To ascend transversely some 500 feet higher up was not particularly difficult, since the ice-axe, brought with us, cut steps with ease and rapidity. But the tracks worn by stones and big snowballs which had glided down warned me that we were on a slope by no means safe from avalanches. Just then the mist lifted a little, and I was beginning to hope for a full view of our surroundings, when rumbling sounds above announced the fall of softened snow or ice. None of it passed near us, but the sound was enough to make the four Taghliks, carrying plane-table and cameras, bolt downwards in terror. They had already, while we were crossing the moraine walls, declared their fear to move over ground that was wholly strange to them, and the dread of an avalanche now completely demoralized them. There was nothing for it but to follow them downwards, though in a more cautious fashion. Not far from the topmost limit of the débris accumulations encrusting the glacier proper we found a bit of level ground in a cirque, completely sheltered by huge masses of split rock. Here we might have hoped to advance our camp, but the preparations we made for clearing this space sufficed to fill the Taghliks with renewed terrors. To pass a night in such surroundings evidently appeared to them a step dangerously near to destruction.

For a short while, as we descended, the mist scattered before a brisk breeze and revealed above, to the south-east, an imposing amphitheatre of névé-covered slopes, crowned by a crest of bare and most precipitous rock walls, reaching to an estimated height of about 17,000 feet. With due precautions I thought the crest might be gained through one of the several snow-filled rock couloirs. But even these short glimpses sufficed to convince me that there was here no possible route for laden men such as these Taghliks. Still less was it to be believed that the party of Habibullah's men, whom Johnson had accompanied, could have brought their numerous yaks down over snow and rock slopes like these. The vista vanished rapidly, after disclosing also mighty falls of dark-coloured ice at several points of the glacier. Then the drizzling rain of the previous day enveloped us once more, and made us all eager for shelter.

In the course of the afternoon I received evidence of the effect produced by the day's reconnaissance on our yak-drivers and prospective coolies, most of whom had kept under shelter at the Kara-ois lower down. The demand, communicated through the Yüz-bashi, for a few days' supply of dry yak-dung, the only available fuel, sufficed to drive them into a state of utter dismay. In a mass the excited crowd came to my tent to clamour for a speedy return. I had not had time to ask them their grievances when two young fellows threw themselves upon the Yüz-bashi and the Darogha, who had tried to reason with the men. In an instant the fighting couples were on the ground, while the rest of the Taghliks were preparing to join in the fray.

The shouting had brought up my own men, and with their help the much-battered victims of this onslaught were soon put on their legs again. I had just time to identify the aggressors, when the whole body moved away, threatening to decamp with their yaks. The prospect of being left here without transport, and soon also, perhaps, without fuel, was not exactly cheering. So I let the Yüz-bashi depart for the night, to try and bring his violent-tempered yet timorous Taghliks to reason. The conduct of the rest was to be forgiven if the two assailants, who had laid hand on the Darogha and their own head-man, were produced to receive due punishment thereafter at the Khotan Ya-mên.

The night was again a wet one; but for a short time at daybreak the clouds cleared, and I could sight the snowy peaks above the main glacier southwards illuminated by the rising sun. Imposing as the spectacle was, it failed to give me the impression that I was facing here a part of the main range: the peaks seemed somehow too near and their heights scarcely great enough. But there was no time for closer observation before the curtain of mist again descended. Only the dark detritus wall of the great terminal moraine, about three-quarters of a mile broad, was visible between the foot of the flanking spurs when at 8 A.M. the sulky band of hill-men reappeared behind the Yüz-bashi. A self-complacent smile seemed to indicate that the young ·man was quite satisfied with this display of reasserted authority and had already forgotten the blows he had suffered yesterday.   The offenders whose punishment I demanded were still at large; but I lost no time in setting out with a few men to survey the main glacier as far as possible.   Of its wall-like end I obtained a good view from the top of an old moraine overlooking the wide boulder-strewn flat where the streams draining the glacier first collect after cascading down the detritus slopes (Fig. 63).

Like a huge dark river of rock débris and mud the glacier stretched towards us, its end wall fully 200 feet high.   But as far as the gathering clouds let us see, no ice appeared on the surface.   Yet its presence under these enormous masses of detritus was clearly revealed by small greenish lakelets filling depressions and by the streams of greyish water issuing from the sides.   Though it was still early in the day, and the main stream draining the glacier on the west side had not yet gathered its full volume, we found some difficulty in crossing it in order to proceed higher up the valley where stretches of moss-covered ground promised easier going. But scarcely had we thus skirted the glacier for about half a mile when the mist rolled up again heavily from below, and after a useless wait we had to descend in steadily drizzling rain.   It was evident that our stay in these mountains coincided with the period when the monsoon current succeeds in passing the tail end of its moisture across the high Himalayan ranges southward to this part of the Kun-lun.

It was a miserably wet day, and its discomfort was not much relieved by the arrival of Islam Beg, whom I had summoned from Karanghu-tagh.   He brought a mail-bag from Kashgar which had found its way through.   The two 'wanted' offenders had been duly secured, and were now produced with a rope round their arms, more as a symbol of their status than as a means to prevent their escape.   For hours I was busy in my tiny tent answering the newly arrived mails, and glad to let my thoughts travel from my few feet of dry ground to dear friends far away in the West and to my plans for the winter campaign in the desert.

The rain did not stop till late at night, and next morning the masses of clouds were still hugging the peaks at the head of the valley and also the slopes of snow and ice below them. But our reconnaissances of the previous days had sufficed to convince me that this valley offered no possible outlet south or south-eastwards which Johnson could have used with yak transport. Trained mountaineers from Europe might, indeed, make their way over more than one col I had sighted on the crest overhanging the glacier to the south-east. But for load-carrying men, let alone yaks, the barrier was quite impassable.

There could be no doubt that our prolonged stay at this height exposed the wretched dwellers of Karanghu-tagh to a great deal of privation and suffering. So on August 28th, after a fresh climb to a side glacier westwards, I did not hesitate to give the order for our descent. The rain was not slow to overtake us; but while it still held off I secured a photograph of one of the felt tents pitched on the lower plateau and of its inhabitants grimy with smoke and dirt (Fig. 64). Among the few weather-worn Karanghu-tagh women who pass their summer here, I found to my surprise an old acquaintance, a quaint woman of great age to whom I had given six years before some alms on my passage through Omsha. My charity, no doubt a rare thing among these harsh surroundings, had evidently left an impression; for the shrivelled age-bowed woman had made her way here with a view to a fresh appeal, in spite of all the difficulty of the summer route. The swollen river had closed the direct tracks from Omsha to the Busat Valley; and in order to reach the bridge below Khushlash-langar, by which alone the Yurung-kash could be crossed, the old lady had to follow a rock path which was declared to be quite impracticable even for unladen yaks.

The march down the valley did not pass without an incident which showed me what little chance there was of getting help from the Taghliks for further work in these mountains. I had intended to halt some four miles above

63. SNOUT OF DETRITUS-COVERED GLACIER AT HEAD OF BUSAT VALLEY.

64. TAGHLIK FAMILY FROM KARANGHU-TAGH, AT FELT TENT IN BUSAT VALLEY.
On extreme left the old woman from Omsha.

Khushlash-langar, in order to visit next day the smaller valley of Tashwa, which there joins in from the south-east. Our previous survey had made it clear that this valley did not lead up to the main range; but there was the possibility of its offering a lateral approach to the next large valley eastwards, which might have served for the route followed by Johnson from the watershed range. The order to stop at the mouth of the Tashwa Valley had been clearly explained to the yak-men; but when the baggage animals came up, their leaders frantically protested against halting there. They had been starving, they declared, for the last two days, and unless they could get back there and then to their ripening oat-fields they could not hope to stay their hunger.

The allegation was palpably false; but neither reasoning nor the offer to procure food for them from our own store, left at Karanghu-tagh, availed. On they dragged the yaks, threats and blows from our Beg and Darogha failing to stop them. Some of the men became wild with excitement, and swore in their headlong rush that they would rather be killed than spend another day camping with us in the mountains. It was only about two miles farther down that I managed to stop the rush myself by getting ahead of the string of yaks on the narrow track and forcibly detaining the front men. At the first point where the steep slopes overhanging the river would allow of a tent being pitched, I hastened to call a halt. With difficulty we got the men to unload the yaks, and then we had to let them go off in quest of what my own people called the 'Taghliks' fodder'; for they had seen them munching oat sheaves, freshly torn from the fields, without crushing or boiling the grain.

Everything indicated that the hill-men had got quite out of hand and were in a dangerous mood, while my time available for work in the mountains was getting too short for a protracted struggle with such obstruction. My main concern now was to make sure of the transport we needed to reach Pisha, the valley nearest to the north of Karanghu-tagh, where I planned to make a halt of some days and to collect local information independent of what the Karanghu-tagh men had vouchsafed—or rather concealed from me. Islam Beg, whom I had sent to the village to represent to the 'Bais' there the risk of serious punishment from the Amban, and to assure the return of the absconded men, arrived back in the morning with some of the latter showing a less truculent mood. But the yaks had been allowed to stray, no doubt purposely, and for hours we waited in vain to see them brought back from the distant hillsides they had ascended. At last I set out on foot with some of the men towards Tashwa. But heavy rain overnight had rendered the Busat stream impassable without yaks, and when, after long hours of waiting, a couple of yaks were brought up, it was too late in the day for a useful reconnaissance of that side valley. I had little doubt that the delay was intentional, and took note of it as an indication that there might be some route that way which was to be kept hidden from us. But neither promises nor threats could elicit from the Taghliks anything but assertions of complete ignorance reiterated with yak-like stolidity.

My surmise was confirmed by the view revealed on the next day's march to Pisha. It was a gloriously clear day, and I was doubly glad for the splendid vistas it gave us, up the Yurung-kash Valley and towards the great spurs which descend to it from the south; for when I had followed this route on my first visit to Karanghu-tagh the dusk of a late autumn day had overtaken us on the brink of the precipitous rock slopes overlooking the Yurung-kash cañon from the north, and we had painfully struggled down those five thousand feet in darkness. Now after more than a week of clouds and mist the sun broke forth in full radiance, giving to the grey and brownish tints of the steeply eroded rock walls which confine the Yurung-kash course a warmth I had never expected.

The gorge was still in gloom when we crossed the river early in the morning by the crazy bridge, made of rudely joined tree-trunks, which spans its rock-passage, only some forty-five feet wide, a few miles below Khushlash-langar and close to the junction with the Kash River (Fig. 65). The mighty volume of glacier water brought down by the

65. BRIDGE ACROSS YURUNG-KASH RIVER IN GORGE NEAR
KHUSHLASH-LANGAR.

Yurung-kash rushes through this narrow channel, cut in the solid cliffs, with such violence and rapidity that no attempt at measuring the depth would succeed: the speed of the current being nearly four yards per second. My thoughts went back to the story graphically told by the Moghul historian, Mirza Haidar, in his *Tarikh-i-Rashidi*, how the tyrant Aba Bakr, his own uncle, when on his flight from Khotan to Ladak, had from the bridge then existing at the identical spot thrown down all his riches of gold and precious objects; finding that they could not be carried beyond Karanghu-tagh over the extremely difficult tracks alone offering a chance of escape.

His ill-gotten treasures, of which the Moghul historian records an extravagant estimate, have been often searched for since, but in vain. Looking down into the whirling water of the chasm, it was easy to realize that the fugitive prince could not have selected a safer place for depriving his pursuers—or future treasure-seekers—of whatever wealth he had himself to abandon. Nor was I surprised to find that the story, however little of historical truth there may be in it, still lives in local tradition. How could it be otherwise in a region like Khotan where the thought of 'treasure,' whether in the form of gold, or jade, or riches hidden by those of old, has been the chief object to exercise people's imagination for untold generations?

The ascent of the extremely steep track which leads up to the edge of the Tope ridge, close on 13,000 feet high and overlooking the Yurung-kash, was a tiring business. But luckily the rain of the previous days had laid the deep loess dust which covers the rock frame of the slopes. From a height of about 10,500 feet on the Kara-kir spur I could follow the whole gorge of the Yurung-kash from where it winds round the mighty buttresses of Peak K.5 (Fig. 66), to the cañon-like chasm into which the river disappears lower down near its junction with the river of Nissa.

I knew that the gorge itself could offer no possible passage to the Tibetan plateaus south-eastward. But across the Yurung-kash I scanned with no small interest the precipitous slopes of the spurs which descend to the river between the Busat and Chomsha Valleys. The Surveyor's keen eyes had sighted a clearly marked track leading along these slopes from the Boinak ridge above Khushlash-langar towards the mouth of the Chomsha Valley, and my binoculars soon showed that it was manifestly practicable for yaks (Fig. 67). Was this then the stoutly denied approach to the Chomsha Jilga? In itself it was a proof that the latter was, indeed, visited by herdsmen.

Nothing but an actual march along this track could show whether it debouched into the Chomsha Valley at a point where this would offer a route farther on towards the watershed range. There appeared, indeed, a dip in the ice-crowned chain at what seemed to be the head of the valley. But the view before me also left no doubt as to the extreme narrowness of the latter. With our experiences in the gorges of the Nissa and Kash streams still fresh, it was impossible to hope that the Chomsha Valley could be ascended as long as the summer flood from its glaciers filled the tortuous stream-bed. And thus, I thought, I could account for the tenacious obstruction by which the Karanghu-tagh men had striven to keep us from attempting the route. Near the top of the valley probably lay the Alpine grazing-grounds of Brinjaga. But to reach them while the swollen stream filled the gorge was evidently impossible, and the fear of being obliged to run risks in attempting the passage might, more than anything else, have goaded the Taghliks into their obstinate resistance.

Even now when we were turning our back on their mountains it was impossible to get from them anything but a surly assertion of entire ignorance of any and every route. But I consoled myself for this by the splendid opportunity which the clear weather and the commanding position of the Kara-kir ridge gave me for a complete series of panoramic photographs of the Karanghu-tagh region. The great peak of 'K.5,' with its triangulated height of 23,890 feet, was, alas! shrouded in clouds, and so also was the highest of the glacier-crowned summits on the watershed southwards. But these my photo-theodolite panorama

66. VIEW UP YURUNG-KASH VALLEY FROM KARA-KIR SPUR.

67. VIEW FROM KARA-KIR SPUR ACROSS YURUNG-KASH RIVER GORGE TOWARDS
CHOMSHA VALLEY.

A track is seen leading along slopes of spur in centre.   Below a short bend of river is just visible.

of 1900 had already retained, and for whatever lay below them my new 'station' offered a far better point of observation. At a height of about 13,000 feet we attained the top rim of the great plateau which slopes up with broad down-like undulations from the Pisha Valley. It was a striking contrast to the tortuous gorges and towering walls of rock and ice we had left behind. Before losing sight of them on the almost imperceptible watershed, I turned round in the saddle and privately registered a vow that the head-waters of the Yurung-kash were yet to see me from the east or the south, despite all obstructive forces of nature and man.

The high mountains seemed loth to let me depart; for their clouds kept still with us, and in pouring rain we accomplished the long but easy descent. I had decided to stop for some days in the Pisha Valley, partly with a view to collecting, if possible, that local information which I had failed to secure from the Karanghu-tagh people, and still more in order to use this last halt in the cool of the mountains for recording explanatory notes on the photographic panoramas brought back from this region, while all details regarding its orography were fresh in my recollection.

I had no reason to regret my decision. On the very first morning after my arrival there turned up a queer-looking individual who claimed to have found a man "knowing the way to Brinjaga." The look and manners of my informant did not inspire confidence. He claimed to be a Badakhshi by descent, and to have been a wanderer from his early youth. Where and how he had picked up his tolerably fluent Hindustani he did not explain, nor how he had found his way to these mountains. Having heard from my Dak man of my enquiries about Brinjaga, he had thought he could make himself useful; and now he had come to produce a gold-washer from the Kara-tash Valley eastwards, who had himself been to the place. All he claimed in return was some recommendation which might help him along to reach his old home in safety.

How much of this story was true I had no means of ascertaining. But after an hour or two the Kara-tash

miner actually turned up. He looked far more reliable
than the shifty adventurer who introduced him, and what
he told of his visit to the 'mouth of Brinjaga' tallied
remarkably well with topographical facts. He and eight
associates, also gold-washers, had some ten years before
been tempted to try their luck at a 'Kumat' situated by
the bank of a stream that falls into the Yurung-kash east
of the Busat Valley. They had proceeded there by a
route that skirted the spurs overlooking the main valley
from the south, evidently the track we had sighted from
Kara-kir. They had thus reached the debouchure of a
side valley which they heard designated as the 'mouth of
Brinjaga'; but the latter itself they had not seen, and
access to it, they were told, became possible only in the
late autumn or winter. The sand they washed did not
prove very paying, and the party therefore soon retraced
their steps to Khushlash-langar. It was a simple straightforward account, unmistakably pointing to the Chomsha
Valley as the location of that 'Brinjaga' which had seemed
to keep ever floating in mythical haze. Daud, the gold-
seeker, was ready to guide us to the place he described,
only one day's march from Khushlash-langar, and I thought
it best to let him repeat his statements in the presence of
the Karanghu-tagh people still with us.

The result was by no means encouraging. The
Karanghu-tagh men obstinately clung to their cherished
affirmations of complete ignorance, and declared that their
yaks were worn out, and they preferred to drown themselves rather than start on fresh climbs! I left their Yüz-
bashi the choice of either bringing his men to reason or
of being taken to Khotan to answer to the Amban for
disobeying his orders. In the presence of the recalcitrant
crowd our would-be guide had grown uneasy, and I was
not surprised when an hour or so later the Badakhshi
disconsolately reported his disappearance. The adventurer
naturally felt grieved at the prospect of losing a reward
and hurriedly set off to hunt for the fugitive. But the
latter knew how to keep out of the way, and neither him
nor his pursuer did I see again.

The Yüz-bashi's case was settled less promptly. He

failed to induce the men to offer their services for a short visit to the mouth of the Chomsha Valley, and when asked to procure fresh yaks stoutly maintained that there were none. So there was nothing for it but to keep him under watch and to arrange for his despatch to the Amban's Ya-mên. The half-crazy Taghliks, who previously seemed inclined to assault their so-called head-man, now threatened to starve by his side and clamoured to be sent also to Khotan. But the threat was not one to impress me greatly, and the interposition of the Pisha elders, who did not much relish seeing their crops despoiled by unscrupulous neighbours, soon cleared them away from the vicinity of my camp.

Apart from the clue which I thus obtained while at Pisha, but which want of local help, and still more of time, did not allow me to follow up there and then, my four days' stay there fulfilled all I had looked for. The little meadow by the side of the Pisha stream, in the middle of a broad open valley about 9000 feet above the sea, proved an ideal working place. The slopes of the reddish sandstone ridges which line the valley were bare enough to suggest the desert, but there was a narrow yet continuous belt of cultivation stretching along its bottom to give relief to the eye. Above the south-eastern end of the valley there towered in grand isolation the ice-covered massif of K. 5, only some twenty miles away as the crow flies; and, in spite of the dust raised by the strong wind blowing each afternoon and evening, I could daily feast my eyes on its noble form crowned by the Phrygian cap of its highest peak, nearly 24,000 feet above the sea. I could not have wished for a more suitable place for writing my paper on the photo-theodolite panoramas of the Pamirs and of the rugged Alpine regions just revisited.

Short walks in the evening took me along the carefully irrigated oat-fields which occupy every level stretch of ground in the valley, and visits paid to the modest homesteads scattered along them at wide intervals brought me into friendly touch with several of the leading cultivators. Such wealth as they possessed was derived mainly from their flocks of sheep and yaks. Yet it was sufficient to have enabled two among them to effect recently the expensive pilgrimage to Mecca. Talking to these worthy Hajis about their experiences on their long journey *via* Samarkand, Baku, Constantinople to the Red Sea, and thence back *via* Bombay, Kashmir, and Ladak, it was pleasant to hear them expatiate on the comforts of Indian travel and on the good treatment they had received on the wonderful 'rail.' The numbers of pilgrims from Chinese Turkestan is rapidly increasing each year, from Khotan, perhaps, even more than from other parts; and I wondered inwardly what gain in the way of enlarged ideas, experience of Western comforts, etc., was being carried back to the country in return for the financial drain which these constant pilgrimages entail. Sums equal to rupees 200-300 were named to me in different places as the cost of the Haj even to pilgrims of the humblest class.

Two days after my arrival I despatched the recalcitrant Yüz-bashi to Khotan under the escort of a Darogha and one of my own men, who was to report to the Amban the story of local obstruction. At the same time I sent the Surveyor to follow a new route to Khotan, skirting eastwards the slopes of the outer range known as Tikelik-tagh, which we had not previously mapped in detail. I myself set out on September 5th for the same goal by the direct track which crosses a western spur of that range over the Ulugh Dawan. I had followed it already in 1900, and so need not describe the four rapid marches which took me down to Khotan. No 'Sahib' of any sort had since travelled through these arid hills and gorges (Fig. 68), and consequently I was not surprised to find every little incident of my former visit faithfully remembered at the few scattered 'Langars.'

Even in such uninviting surroundings, where the water-supply is of the scantiest, I noticed a distinct increase in the small patches of cultivation. At Bizil where the Yurung-kash River leaves the hills for the great alluvial fan of the Khotan oasis, I was greeted on the morning of September 8th with a cheerful Dastarkhan including a profusion of long-missed fruit. But the river there at its debouchure was still far too high to be forded.

69. GATE WITH VOTIVE OFFERINGS ON PATH TO SHRINE OF IMAM JA'FAR SADIK.

On left Ibrahim, 'the miller,' on right, mendicant with son; see page 297.

68. GORGE OF KIZIL JILGA, BELOW TARIM KISHLAK, ON ROUTE ACROSS TIKELIK-LAGH.

So I had to follow its right bank through the fertile Beg-ship of Yurung-kash, past Chalmia, Altila and an unbroken succession of flourishing villages, before I could cross to Khotan at the usual ferry place and seek quiet shelter for the fresh work before me.

CHAPTER XVIII

A FEAST AT KHOTAN

My Khotan camp had been pitched in old Akhun Beg's suburban garden, which before in the autumn of 1900 had offered me peace and shelter since gratefully remembered. But the absence of my host sadly dimmed my pleasure at this renewed hospitality. Already during my visit in August the most genial of my Khotan friends had talked of his intention to proceed on the Mecca pilgrimage. Seeing how little fitted for such a trying journey the aged gentleman looked, with his asthma of yore increased and also his portly form, I had done my best to dissuade him. To confess the truth, I had refused to take seriously the worthy old Beg's eagerness to earn such saintly merits; for with satisfaction I had noted that he was still fondly attached to the good things of this world of which Fate—and a well-employed career in the service of the heathen 'Khitai' no less than of that champion of the faith, his first master, the rebel Yakub Beg—had given him plenty.

Now I learned with grief that, in spite of his family's well-founded remonstrances, Akhun Beg had set out in earnest. Only two days before my arrival he had started in company of half a dozen lesser people from his own Mahalla or suburb. He had received news of my early return and evidently regretted as much as I did the missed chance of meeting once more in life. But the stars had been consulted earlier about an auspicious time for the start, and regard for his fellow-pilgrims had precluded a change. With tears in his eyes, Akhun Beg's only brother, also well advanced in years, delivered to me my host's message of welcome. He, too, feared like myself that the hope of seeing the old man return from the Haj was small.

To all objections of his wife and family Akhun Beg had steadfastly answered that, if death was to come, it might just as well find him on the way to the sacred sites as at home. His own argument was that, having been a Beg for so many years to serve worldly masters, he might now do well to serve God, too, at the close of his life. Remembering his genial ways and unfailing kindliness I found it difficult to believe that his conscience could be burdened by any sins needing expiation by such a sacrifice. And the greatness of this I could estimate by all the comforts and possessions on which my old friend had now turned his back.

Sitting in the airy Aiwan of his house, on his favourite carpet, and surrounded by choice fruits from his garden, Akhun Beg had more than once entertained me with a loving account of his cherished possessions : his fat well-farmed lands in Tosalla, his vineyards in Borazan, and the thousands of sheep and cattle he owned in the Hasha mountains. Compared to the honoured ease of his home, a journey to Mecca meant for him hardships such as would never confront the modern European traveller wherever he went for a similar purpose. I had to go back to the Middle Ages and to their Palestine pilgrimages in order to realize what such an undertaking meant for the old Beg. Eagerly I availed myself of the chance of sending by some belated pilgrims, who were just leaving Khotan to catch up the party, my heartiest wishes for his welfare and a sort of recommendatory letter intended to assure him attention at Kashgar and on his eventual return through India. Whatever the effect might be, I had the satisfaction of knowing that the provision of this ' Khat ' gave comfort to the disconsolate family.

Multifarious preparations for the archaeological campaign now about to open kept me hard at work from the day of my arrival, and made it rather difficult to spare time for the claims of polite intercourse with my Chinese friends. My visit to Ch'ê Ta-jên's Ya-mên on the first morning was a function as cheerful as it was solemn. The genial

Amban received me like an old friend, but yet with all honour and ceremony. Nothing was wanting in preparations. On passing through the inner gate I found the whole establishment drawn up in due order of precedence, from the red-clothed executioners upwards, and all in the newest of garments. Never in dear old P'an Ta-jên's days had the Khotan Ya-mên seen such display.

Yet my reception by the Amban was not the less hearty for this. I had to tell him in detail of my experiences in the mountains and, of course, did not screen from him all the wiles of Karanghu-tagh obstruction. Ch'ê Ta-jên manifestly grasped the curious mixture of timorousness and dogged *vis inertiae* in those hill-men, and how difficult it was to cope with it. His own attitude was that of a sensible administrator who realized that his means of coercion could not safely be put to a test there. If such obstruction occurred anywhere in the district proper, he declared, he would beat those who tried it into obedience even if he had to move out with his troops for the purpose. But what was to be done in the mountains? I thought of the gorges I had passed through, of the rivers which formed almost impenetrable bulwarks, and felt glad that there was no need to expose peaceable Chinese soldiers to such trials.

Ch'ê Ta-jên requested my presence at a garden-party he was anxious to give in my honour to the assembled dignitaries of the district, and pressed his invitation so warmly that there was no escape from the function. It took place on the afternoon of the second day of my stay, soon after I had received the Amban's return visit at my garden. With Badruddin Khan's help an open pavilion where Akhun Beg used to enjoy himself on warm summer days, had been gaily decked out with red felt rugs and Khotan carpets. To give colour to the human *entourage* I made Naik Ram Singh in his scarlet and blue uniform of the 1st Sappers and Miners take his place by the side of the Amban's attendants. The towering height of his burly figure did not fail to make an impression. I presented the Amban on this occasion with a copy of the *Travels of Fa-hsien*, the earliest extant record of a Chinese

Buddhist pilgrim to India, in the neat edition of the Clarendon Press, and with the account of a more recent traveller in search of Buddhist sanctuaries—my own *Sand-buried Ruins of Khotan*. That the illustrations of the latter were more eagerly scanned and interpreted by the Amban than the difficult text of old Fa-hsien might have flattered my literary vanity, had I not known how much of this attention was to be attributed to Chinese politeness.

The feast to which I proceeded a few hours later was an experience sufficiently novel to compensate for the time it cost—and for the trial it necessarily implied for a European digestion. But a few rapid notes must suffice here. Ch'ê Ta-jên had planned hospitality on a large scale, and had invited whatever of Begs, Qazis and other notables he could gather at headquarters. The old garden palace of Nar-bagh was the scene of the treat. But what change was worked in this familiar place! The crowds filling the spacious outer courts, the bustle of numberless cooks and attendants seemed to revive the days when Niaz Hakim Beg sat there in state. The central pavilion of the garden, where I had found a peaceful retreat during previous stays, served now as the Amban's reception-room for his Chinese guests and myself. The whole of the civil staff at headquarters was invited, and with the eight Ssŭ-yehs representing it there came also a jovial-looking relative of the Amban, no doubt a candidate for office, who had recently arrived on a visit from Urumchi.

The long paved causeway serving as approach from the Aiwans of the residence to the pavilion was allotted to the Muhammadan guests, and through the double row of Begs lining this broad causeway shaded by vines and fruit trees (Fig. 70) I was conducted in solemn procession. In two of the other avenues radiating crosswise from the pavilion the crowd of lesser dignitaries was entertained. In the third, discreetly hidden, I discovered arrangements for letting those of the Chinese guests who cared for it enjoy the pleasures of an opium smoke. I should never have suspected them, had I not been led to this quiet corner in search of a convenient place from which to take the photographs desired by the Amban. Bands of Khotanese musicians were scattered through all the avenues, and a specially large body, with guitars, tambourines, and flutes, was posted close to the front verandah of the pavilion where the table was laid for us special convives of the Amban. The noise was great at such close quarters; yet there was rhythm and a curious captivating verve in the airs played by these ragged men. The performance, the first I had heard in Khotan, seemed to justify even to my untrained ears the special reputation which the music of Khotan has enjoyed from early days.

I am not competent to give an account of the wonderful menu to which the hospitable Amban treated us. Nor can I find time to record now all the amusing incidents which helped me to enjoy the long dinner-party. Only one must be mentioned. Ch'ê Ta-jên had courteously noted the well-deserved praise I gave at my first visit to Islam Beg's services in the mountains. He promptly showed his appreciation of my remarks by promoting my faithful local factotum to the fat Beg-ship of Kayash, and already that morning Islam Beg had brought me the great news and thanked me with an air of grateful emotion. He now approached the Amban towards the close of the dinner to receive the formal announcement of his new dignity. His threefold prostration was in conformity with Chinese etiquette as adopted by Turki officials throughout the country. Yet its performance was done with such ease and grace as befitted a descendant of that old Khotan race, the courtly politeness of which had already struck the earliest Chinese observers. But Ch'ê Ta-jên, too, knew how to rise to the occasion. The gesture with which he held out his hand to his *protégé* in order to raise him, was full of dignity and paternal kindness. Any dignitary of the Church, whether Western or Eastern, might have studied the pose with advantage.

That the Amban with his genial *bonhomie* knew all the same how to keep his Begs in their place was curiously illustrated by a little incident while I took my photographs. It was easy to get the group showing him and his Chinese staff. But when he was to be photographed with all his

70. AMBAN'S GUESTS FEASTING ON TERRACE LEADING TO 'MY' PAVILION IN NAR-BAGH.

71. CH'É TA-JÊN, AMBAN OF KHOTAN, WITH LOCAL BEGS.
On extreme right Islam Beg, Beg of Kayash.

crowd of Begs (Fig. 71), the size of a quarter-plate naturally proved far too small. So I suggested closer grouping by making some at least of the local dignitaries sit on the bare ground by the side of the Amban's chair while the rest were to stand behind. The alacrity, good-natured yet decided, with which the Amban shrank from the idea of allowing any of his native myrmidons to sit in his presence, was quite amusing. I have little doubt, the Begs would have known better than to fall in with such a ' Firang' notion !

It was getting late in the afternoon when the longed-for bowls of rice, marking the close of the feast, appeared on the table, and I felt grateful for the sensible rule of Chinese etiquette which makes the chief guest take his leave as soon as the table is cleared. After such an entertainment a little ride might well be indulged in, and the city Bazars and suburban lanes in the soft twilight afforded a pleasant diversion. Everywhere I noted new comfortable houses with elaborately carved timber façades, new Sarais and other improvements, unmistakable signs of the rapid increase of prosperity which had taken place since my visit five years before, in Khotan town as in the entire region.

For the rest of my six days' stay I had barely time to emerge from my busy retreat in Akhun Beg's garden. My preparations for the desert campaign were inaugurated by the early appearance on the scene of the party of Yurung-kash ' treasure-seekers' whom I had sent out in August under the direction of Roze Akhun, old Turdi's step-son, to look out for likely sites to explore. It was a queer-looking band which marched up the day after my arrival, ragged and haggard men most of them, fit recruits, I thought, for a Falstaff's commando (Fig. 72). But the specimens of antiques they brought, including fragments of manuscripts in Indian script, were of promise ; and with the experience gained on my former campaign I could gauge the relative importance of the places described, and the time the exploration of them might claim. It took long cross-examination to get exact indications as to distances, routes, etc., and what with these and the preparation of accounts, arrears of correspondence, repairs of equipment, etc., I was busy from dawn until close on midnight. Luckily clouds kept the air cool, and just before my start a two days' intermittent light rain laid the dust of many months and refreshed the air.

But there was a cloud, too, gathering on the mental horizon. One of the camels which I had brought from Kashgar, and which early in August I had sent off to the mountains for a good rest and cool grazing, had then already been ailing. Now when that portion of my transport rejoined me at Khotan I learned with dismay that this as well as another of the camels had succumbed while away on their holiday, and that two more were showing signs of weakness. Hassan Akhun, whose grief at this affliction to the fine-looking beasts put under his care was genuine, ascribed the loss to poisonous plants abounding in the mountains above Hasha which my camels, accustomed to the northern ranges, had not learned to avoid. But I knew well that diagnosis and treatment of camels' diseases was wholly beyond the ken of the most experienced Turkestan camel-men, my energetic factotum included, however great their insight into the mysteries of managing camels while they were well. I had heard much of the rapid spread of infection to which camels seem particularly liable, through a sort of fatalistic inertia, and wondered anxiously whether the true cause of that loss were not some disease, lurking unsuspected, which the hot marches from Kashgar, relatively few as they were, might have sufficed to ripen. There was need for all care—and eventual resignation.

CHAPTER XIX

BY THE DESERT EDGE OF KHOTAN

On the morning of September 15th I set out from Khotan. I had decided first to revisit the interesting large ruin of Rawak, the scene of my last excavations in 1901, partly in order to ascertain whether any change had since taken place in the condition of the surrounding dunes, and partly for the sake of inspecting some remains newly reported in that neighbourhood. At the same time Ram Singh was to start independently for the foot of the Kun-lun south of Keriya, in order to carry triangulation along the range as far as possible eastwards. I was busy long before daybreak. But the division of baggage and a host of other tasks, such as settling accounts, which local insouciance delights to leave to the very last, delayed me sufficiently to allow the Amban ample time to effect his announced intention of offering a grand official farewell.

The rain had just stopped when I left my garden camp, and a little sunshine breaking through the clouds gave additional colour to the scene awaiting me on the high road eastwards. I found it lined with the whole Chinese garrison, some two hundred men in bright red and blue, carrying picturesque banners, and the whole scene looking delightfully Eastern. The fanfares blown from horns of imposing length were discordant enough to alarm my Badakhshi pony. There was the kindly Amban in full state, and by his side the military staff with which visits had been exchanged in due form during both my stays. Our chat in the gaily decked reception hall by the road-side was more than a sacrifice to etiquette. I felt glad to be able to thank Ch'ê Ta-jên once more for all his friendly help and attention, and his wish that we may meet again found sincere response in my heart. But was it to be at Khotan or somewhere far away in the north where my energetic Amban friend might be looking out for early promotion?

A large posse of Begs accompanied me across the Yurung-kash to the boundary of the newly established sub-district of Lop, formed out of those cantons of the old oasis which are watered by canals on the right bank of the river. There I bade farewell too to honest Islam Beg, in whose eyes I could read true regret that he was not to share my wanderings farther. Directing my heavy baggage in charge of my Chinese secretary to Yurung-kash Bazar, I myself set out northward. A ten miles' ride took me through the fertile village tract of Jiya to the edge of the desert near Suya. There ponies for the baggage and supplies for the next few days awaited me. Roze Akhun, too, had collected there his band of labourers who were to take their share in prospective excavations.

The bare gravel Sai with high dunes on either side on which we emerged almost immediately after leaving the shady groves of Suya and Imam Asim's Mazar, looked strangely familiar, in spite of the five and a half years since I returned here from my Rawak labours, and the total absence of landmarks. The cloudy grey sky, so rare in this region, had been the same then, and this exact reproduction of the atmospheric conditions largely accounted for the feeling. The broad gravel belt, clearly marked as an ancient bed of the Yurung-kash and still known as 'Kone-darya,' offered easy going in spite of occasional low dunes. Yet it was dark long before I could hope to reach Rawak. So we camped in the desert by a small brackish well which 'Otanchis,' or men bringing fuel from the riverine jungle farther north, had dug by the roadside. Next morning we struck due north and, after crossing for some six miles a belt of steadily rising dunes, I sighted once more the white brick pile of the ruined Stupa of Rawak.

My thoughts had dwelt often on this imposing old ruin and the fine series of sculptures brought to light by my excavations around it in 1901. All the more striking was the change in its surroundings which the first glance revealed. The mighty dunes which then covered fully three-quarters of the great quadrangle enclosing the relic tower, had moved on considerably farther east. The south-west wall, where I had excavated some of the best-preserved colossal statues of the shrine, was now almost completely hidden under a ridge of sand some twenty feet high. Of the south-east face, too, less emerged from the sand than before, yet enough to show me the destruction which had been dealt here by the hand of man since my visit. The wall, which I had found lined with a continuous row of large relievos in stucco, shown in the plates of *Ancient Khotan*, now displayed bare brickwork. A large party of Chinese jade-diggers from Kumat, so I was told, had come here two years before to try their luck at seeking for 'treasure,' and attacking the only accessible part of the enclosing wall had stripped it completely of its friable stucco images. My care in burying these again under sand just as I found them had proved in vain.

The movement of the dunes had curiously changed the aspect of the Stupa itself. Whereas its imposing base of three stories was five years before almost entirely covered by drift sand except to the south-east, its uppermost portion now emerged free on all sides (Fig. 73). But below this there still remained some seventeen or eighteen feet of sand filling the court, and a complete clearing of the latter was now quite as impracticable, without a disproportionate expenditure of time and money, as when I first explored the great ruin. The exact comparison of the sand conditions with those recorded on my previous visit had a special interest; for it fully supported the view already suggested that the high dunes observed in this part of the desert are the direct product of the fine alluvial deposit left behind by the river floods along its banks and thence carried into the desert in the direction where the alternating east and west winds have most play.

The patch of eroded bare ground westwards where I had camped in those hot and dusty April days, was now entirely buried beneath a dune. Yet not far off another small Nullah had formed where there was just room for my tent and my servants' camp. Leaving Naik Ram Singh in charge of the labourers' party which was to clear one corner of the intact Stupa base, and to enable him to take an elevation of the elaborate stucco mouldings still adorning it, I pushed southwards where a ' treasure-seeker ' from Suya had reported some 'Tims' and a ruined building. It was of interest for me to supplement my previous knowledge of this tract by the survey of whatever minor ruins might still survive besides Rawak.

After five miles up and down closely packed dunes rising to forty feet and more, we reached the two much-decayed brick mounds reported. They proved to be the remains of small Stupas, about twenty-four feet square at the base, half buried below the sands and, alas! completely stripped of all architectural decoration. A bare depression between the dunes running southwards showed plentiful pottery débris, an indication of ancient dwellings; but for the latter one would look in vain on ground so completely eroded. In the course of a short search several tiny Chinese coins, without legend but of ancient look, were picked up here; their square holes enclosed by the narrowest of rims attested long circulation. Farther on we came upon clear traces of an irrigation channel eight or nine feet broad, well known to Kasim, my guide, as reappearing at several points temporarily left bare by the high dunes. There was the mark of a small tank, too, not far off; its earth embankment, once hardened by moisture, still rose above the level of the surrounding ground which wind erosion had lowered. Even the little earth-cone known as ' Dömbel,' which the villagers to this day invariably leave in the centre of their tanks, was clearly recognizable.

The ruin which I had come in search of, was hidden away in a curious bay-like depression between steep dunes a short distance eastwards. With the experience of my former labours it was easy to see that the scanty remains were those of a temple cella built in timber and plaster, about twenty-seven by twenty-four feet, enclosed on its

72. ROZE AKHUN'S BAND OF KHOTAN 'TREASURE-SEEKERS.'
Roze Akhun on extreme right.

73. RUINED STUPA OF RAWAK SEEN FROM DUNE ABOVE SOUTH-WEST WALL OF QUADRANGLE.

four sides by a passage after the fashion of the Dandan-oilik shrines. The rapid clearing effected by the small party brought with me, soon showed that the walls rose nowhere more than two feet above the original floor. Their timber framework had completely perished under the influence of damp from subsoil water, but had left distinct matrices. But even these modest remnants sufficed, by their fresco decoration in red and black outlines and the mode of construction, to furnish some clue to their date.

Like the Rawak Stupa, this structure manifestly belonged to the period from the fourth to the seventh century A.D. Chinese coins of the ancient uninscribed type picked up under my eyes on the neighbouring 'Tati' ground confirmed this conclusion. With it agreed, too, the considerable depth (from ten to twelve feet) to which wind erosion had lowered the adjoining ground unprotected by ruins. It thus became evident that this whole tract, within a few miles of the right bank of the Yurung-kash, must have been abandoned centuries before the sands were allowed to overrun the settlement of Dandan-oilik some sixty miles farther out in the desert north-eastward. Here we have another proof that the progress of general desiccation cannot by itself supply an adequate explanation of all such changes in the extent of cultivated areas.

I devoted the following morning, September 17th, to a careful survey of the dunes in relation to the ruined walls still exposed, and then once more said farewell to Rawak, earnestly hoping that the dunes will keep watch and ward over the sculptures on those sides of the great Stupa quadrangle which are still completely buried. I wondered whose task it might be years hence to spend here the months and—the money needed for a final exploration.

My next object was the ruined site of Kine-tokmak, from which Roze's men had brought to Khotan small pieces of stucco relievos once serving for wall decoration, of exceptional hardness and yet withered and cracked by long exposure to the summer heat and the fierce winds of the desert. The condition of the ruin, reached after a march of only three miles over gradually lessening dunes to the north-east, corresponded exactly to the indications I had deduced from these scanty relics. There were the remains of ancient brick walls, traceable for about forty feet on what had once been the south-east and south-west faces of a quadrangular temple cella (Fig. 74). But they rose only some two feet above the old ground level, and on the other sides had disappeared completely through deep wind erosion of the soil. What was once the interior of the cella now showed as a hollow lying more than six feet below the bottom course of bricks in the extant wall remains. The soil washed out under the latter, as if by a current, told plainly how the erosive power of the wind was proceeding in its work of destruction. The bleached fragments of carved timber and the small fissured fragments of stucco relievos showing familiar floral designs of Graeco-Buddhist art, which my men collected from the eroded ground, curiously recalled relics from some ancient burial-place.

The clouds which had given welcome shelter during the preceding two days had receded to the horizon and, though still clinging to the mountains southward, no longer mitigated the force of the sun. So it was hot work tramping over the glaring dunes in search of the other 'houses' which Ahmad, the Suya treasure-seeker, had still to show me in this neighbourhood. They proved to be the remains of modest dwellings built with timber and plaster walls, first destroyed by erosion and finally by the burrowings of those who have searched for 'treasure,' whenever the march of the dunes left them exposed during the course of long centuries. In one of them we could still trace the ground plan marked by the remains of walls made of plastered reed matting, the position once occupied by large jars sunk into the mud floor, and so on.

Farther east, where the dunes were getting lower and erosion had run its full course, the ground showed a distinct approach to the familiar 'Tati' type. Pottery débris reddened large stretches of eroded ground. Yet here and there the light drift sand still protected more distinctive marks of ancient occupation. There were the low stumps of fruit trees and poplars which once had surrounded the vanished

74. ERODED REMAINS OF TEMPLE RUIN AT KINE-TOKMAK.
Arrows mark original ground level and lowest masonry course of south-east and south-west walls.

75. ENTRANCE GATE TO PILGRIMAGE SHRINE OF IMAM JA'FAR TAIRAN, CHIRA.

houses. In one place I could still make out a row of Jigda or Eleagnus trees as planted in an orchard. An old 'Taklamakanchi' myself, I had no difficulty in distinguishing the fissured trunks of apricot and other fruit trees from the bleached débris of poplars once enclosing these orchards. A fine piece of decorated cut-glass was the best among the finds of small objects picked up on that evening's wanderings. Even its hard smooth surface showed grinding by the corrosive force of driving sand.

Camp was pitched some three miles to the east, where a belt of flourishing Toghraks, tamarisks and desert scrub marked the line of an ancient river bed traced on my first visit to Rawak. There was a gorgeous sunset, and after the heat of the day the distant vista of the great snowy range southwards was doubly refreshing. The night brought quite a sensation of chill, and next morning I enjoyed a gloriously clear view of the whole Kun-lun from Sanju to the mountains about Polur. With the help of my binoculars I could distinctly recognize the glaciers to which my climbs from the Nissa and Karanghu-tagh valleys had taken me, the grand peaks triangulated in 1900, and the fantastically serrated lines of the outer ranges between Kara-kash and Yurung-kash. This splendid mountain panorama kept dazzlingly before my eyes as I rode steadily southward towards the tract of Hanguya. After ten miles or so I arrived at the ruined Stupa of Arka-kuduk Tim, already visited in 1901, and on the strength of old Turdi's teaching could enlighten Roze as to its true name. For the route to the Ak-terek site, however, which was my goal, I had to trust wholly to Roze himself; for though I knew it to be situated somewhere on the Tatis which fringe the desert towards Hanguya, a search for it might have cost long days,—so extensive are the pottery-strewn areas marking ancient occupation which crop up over square miles wherever the dunes leave the ground bare.

The six miles' ride over absolutely sterile dunes, closely packed here and rising to twenty-five feet or so, was made very trying by the fierce heat with which the sun beat down through an atmosphere of such clearness as Khotan rarely sees. Reflection from the glittering sand full of mica particles greatly increased the glare, and before long a sensation recalling my experience on the glacier of the Darkot made me aware that my face was getting blistered.

The resulting discomfort was soon forgotten when I arrived at the site of Ak-terek. Of the temple ruin, from which Roze had brought me some interesting decorative relievos in what seemed terra-cotta, no structural remains whatever were visible above ground. But plentiful fragments of the same type could be picked up near a small dune which my guides had taken the precaution to mark by a rag-topped staff. There were small seated Buddhas surrounded by lotus-leaves, flower scrolls and flame-bundles, and other relievo fragments exactly similar in style to the *appliqué* stucco decoration of the halos which I had discovered at Rawak round the colossal images (Fig. 76, 2, 7). Their appearance here, scattered among the pottery débris of a 'Tati,' seemed puzzling; for of structural remains, such as temple walls which might once have borne a corresponding adornment, the level surface of sand showed no trace whatever. Like the potsherds around, these relics of the wall-decoration of an ancient temple rested now on nothing but soft eroded loess.

To search for more substantial remains of the shrine seemed like a piece of true treasure-seeking, without any of the archaeological guidance on which I had learned to rely during my excavations at Dandan-oilik and elsewhere. For a systematic trial trench to show the possible location of walls, the dozen men of Roze's party who had tramped after us in the broiling heat were an inadequate force. But in order not to lose time I let them start digging near the north foot of the dune where the terra-cotta fragments lay most numerous. Chance favoured us more than I could reasonably expect; for after burrowing down in the loose sand for only two feet, Roze himself struck the remains of a fairly thick wall in reddish clay, and the débris layer near it, covering a plastered floor some two feet lower down, began to yield in rapid succession more relievo fragments of the same description. I made the rest of the men clear the wall thus discovered as far as they could follow it before dusk overtook us; and the continuity of finds rewarding the work assured me that the wall indeed belonged to a temple.

That this temple had undergone almost total destruction in its structural features, was, alas! plain enough from the lowness of the wall laid bare and the entire disappearance of its original facing. Yet if I could not hope to bring to light here larger sculptures or frescoes, such as the well-preserved walls of Dandan-oilik or Rawak had yielded, there was some compensation in the abundance of decorative details and the ease with which their remarkable hardness allowed them to be recovered. At Rawak the same relievo decoration consisted of unbaked clay so friable that many of the pieces broke in the very attempt to remove them, and the safe arrival of some which I managed to carry to London seemed nothing short of a miracle.

The prospect of gaining fresh materials for the study of that sculptural art which my Rawak finds had first illustrated was not the only reward of the day's work at this site, which had promised so little at first sight. Again and again the practised eyes of my diggers noticed pieces of *appliqué* relievo still retaining tiny flakes of gold, —unmistakable evidence that the greatest part of the wall decoration must once have been gilded. For the first time I had here before me definite confirmation of the hypothesis which I had formed in explanation of the gold washed from the culture-strata of the ancient Khotan capital marked by the Yotkan site. In that gold I had recognized the remains of that profuse gilding which the old Khotanese, according to early Chinese records, were fond of using in their sacred buildings. But Yotkan had not furnished so far a single intact object with gilding, the friable stucco which alone appears to have been used there having completely decayed in a soil kept ever moist by irrigation.

It was with the feeling of a novel and gratifying archaeological experience that I started in the dusk for my camp pitched at a farm close to the edge of cultivation near the village of Ak-kul. Though it proved to be only two and a half miles away, yet the dunes to be crossed on the way were so high and sterile as to make me feel as if I were back again in the depth of the desert. The area of moving sands is here steadily being pushed back by resumed cultivation. The lands of Ak-kul had been brought under irrigation only some fifteen years before, and my return march next morning showed how cultivation was now being gradually extended over ground abandoned for centuries to the desert. In the fertile loess soil to which new cuts carried ample water, the poplars, willows, and Jigda trees usually planted along the edges of fields were shooting up rapidly. Hence it was easy to note at a glance the new conquests made each year from the desert sands. Already the belt of luxuriant reed beds and tamarisk scrub in which the overflow from the Ak-kul canal finds its end, was approaching from one side the ground where ancient occupation has left behind its pottery débris. And I wondered whether, in spite of slowly progressing desiccation, the time was not near when, under the pressure of increased population and a growing need of land, the oasis might victoriously recover most of this desolate waste of the Hanguya Tati.

I felt grateful for this advance of human activity, since the vicinity of cultivated ground made it easy for me early next morning to attack the ancient structure with an adequate posse of labourers and without any worries about their commissariat and water-supply. Within a few hours we laid bare what proved to be the north wall of a temple cella, sixty-four feet long, adjoined by a passage which must, as in the case of the Dandan-oilik shrines, have extended all round the four sides of the cella. All along the walls of this passage the finds of small terra-cotta relievos were plentiful, and the deeper they lay buried the more frequent were the remains of the original gilding. Of the larger sculptures and of the frescoed plaster surfaces of the walls, which in all probability adorned the enclosing passage, only the scantiest indications remained in the débris covering the original floor to a height of about two and a half feet. The friable clay of which they were made had evidently crumbled away just as in the strata of Yotkan.

But the careful examination of that débris revealed

76. REMAINS OF STUCCO RELIEVOS FROM WALL DECORATION OF VARIOUS
BUDDHIST RUINS NEAR KHOTAN.

Scale, three-tenths.

1, 3. Figures of flying Gandharvis, from Khadalik. 2. Head and breast of haloed Buddha, from Ak-terek.
4, 7. Appliqué figures of Buddha seated within halo and lotus, from Khadalik and Ak-terek respectively. 5, 8.
Figures of standing Buddha in 'protecting' pose, from Khadalik and Kara-sai respectively. 6. Figure of
divine attendant in act of worship, from Khadalik.

that this complete decay had been greatly aided by a destructive factor of another kind. The general reddish colour of the clay in débris and wall remnants alike, the discovery of small fragments of completely charred wood, and a number of other indications I cannot here set forth in detail made it clear that the shrine had first suffered by a great conflagration. The heat produced by it had sufficed to give a terra-cotta-like colour and consistency to the smaller *appliqué* relievos of the walls, originally (like those of Rawak) merely of sun-dried clay, as well as to such detached fragments as fingers, ears, etc., manifestly belonging to life - size sculptures of the same material. But it had not been great enough to protect the clay masses of the sculptures themselves by a sort of regular burning. Excepting those fragments, they had completely decayed under atmospheric influences while exposed, and subsequently through moisture when the ground was levelled and brought under cultivation. That some time had elapsed between the first destruction of the shrine and the complete levelling of its walls was proved by the fact of a stratum of loess-like soil about one and a half feet thick intervening between the débris layer over the original ground and a second thinner layer of débris with many small relievos.

This same accumulation of fine alluvial dust still proceeds all over the oases wherever there is enough moisture to retain it, and, as I have explained before, steadily raises the ground level. On the top of it fell the hardened relievos when the walls were finally pulled down to make room for some later structure or for cultivation, and fresh layers of loess had protected them until occupation finally ceased, and the ground was abandoned to the desert dunes. Wind erosion, ceaselessly proceeding between the shifting dunes, had now begun to lay bare again this upper layer of relievos on the exposed loess surface ; and to it was due the discovery of the ruin in the midst of these vast 'Tati' areas, with pottery débris coming down probably to much later periods.

Whatever objects might have survived the combined effects of burning and moisture must have been long exposed to those repeated burrowings which threaten all ruins near the inhabited area. Hence one could not expect here finds of objects such as only ruins abandoned once for all to the desert sand could preserve. Yet a careful search of the débris layers did not fail to supply indications of distinct chronological interest. The conclusion already drawn from the style of the relievos, that this temple must have been approximately contemporary with the Rawak Stupa, received confirmation by the discovery close to the floor of a Chinese coin of the uninscribed type belonging to the Han period. On the other hand, finds of grotesque figurines in true terra-cotta of the type familiar to me from the culture-strata of Yotkan representing monkeys in human attitudes, as well as of decorative pottery, furnished the first definite evidence as to the period when this branch of old Khotan art flourished. It was curious, too, to observe how much more frequent were fully gilt relievo pieces in the débris layer resting on the floor than in the upper stratum. The explanation was not far to seek when we noticed how easily the light breeze blowing during the day would carry off the thin flakes of leaf-gold from the gilt fragments excavated if left too long exposed on the surface.

The height of the dune rising southwards over the greater part of the area once occupied by the cella proper would have made the complete excavation of the latter a difficult and protracted task. The clearing of the northwest corner and part of the inner north wall face showed that the remains of terra-cotta relievos were few here, and in no way different from those which had come to light so plentifully from the enclosing passage. So I did not feel justified in spending some weeks on removing the sand which covered the rest of the cella to a maximum height of some eighteen feet.

It was all the easier for me to forgo this sacrifice of time and money as a visit paid during the middle of the day to what my Yurung-kash guides called the 'little But-khana,' acquainted me with a ruin illustrating in a typical fashion all the architectural features I was anxious to ascertain. Going for about two miles to the south-

west over ground where low dunes alternated with extensive stretches of 'Tati,' I found there the outlines of a
small quadrangular Buddhist temple, about twenty-five by
twenty-three feet, clearly recognizable by clay walls almost
flush with the flat eroded loess soil around. Fragments
of plaster relievos exactly similar to those which once
adorned the walls of the larger shrine could be picked
up on the surface; and some more turned up when I had
the interior of the cella cleared down to the original floor,
only one and a half feet below the present surface. Here,
too, the enclosing quadrangular passage could be traced
with certainty.

The remains of this little shrine lay fully exposed on a
flat débris - strewn area clear of dunes, which my guides
knew by the name of Siyelik, and it was easy here to study
the present conditions which account for the appearance of
the ruin. Vegetable fibres and roots permeating the layer
of earth and mud-brick débris which filled the cella, proved
plainly that the ruin after its abandonment must have been
buried for a time under a gradually accumulating and
cultivated loess layer. When cultivation retreated from
the site, wind erosion must have been at work for a prolonged period. Small loess banks up to six feet in height,
generally bearing on their top heavy pottery débris which
seemed to have protected them, rise as 'witnesses' over
the general level of the 'Tati' quite close to the shrine,
marking the extent to which the surface of the ground has
been lowered. From the mass of human bones which
mingled with pottery débris around the ruined cella, it was
certain that the soil, now again carried off by the winds, had
once served for interment. The inference seems justified
that a burial-ground had been established here in early
Muhammadan times, because the site once occupied by a
Buddhist sanctuary continued to receive local worship as a
Mazar. Also quite close to the ruined temple first discovered I noticed between the dunes large stretches of
eroded ground thickly strewn with human bones, to which
the same explanation would apply.

Plentiful matter for antiquarian speculations of this kind
was offered by the silent Tatis extending here to east and

west in a line of over twelve miles. I felt glad that the
interesting remains excavated had supplied data such as I
had scarcely hoped for when I first touched in 1901, between
Ak-sipil and Hanguya, this vast tract of ancient occupation now abandoned to the desert. During the hours of
broiling heat spent over my survey of the Siyelik remains
and some small ruined Stupa mounds in the vicinity,
the grand view of the snow-covered mountains to the
south furnished a refreshing background. Rarely, indeed,
can they be seen from the plains of Khotan, and I wondered
as I stood watching the progress of the excavations at the
large temple, whether the ice-crowned peaks of the Kun-lun
had ever looked down upon labours such as mine.

But there was little time for thoughts of this sort or for
enjoying the brilliant colour effects of a perfectly clear
sunset over the desolate waste of yellow and red. All the
hundreds of small stucco relievos required to be sorted,
numbered, and packed. Though Naik Ram Singh and
my Chinese secretary slaved away like myself, it was quite
dark before I could return to camp. Chiang-ssǔ-yeh had
from the start taken to excavation work with wonderful
keenness and zest. In spite of the heat beating mercilessly
down upon us and of the smothering dust rising from the
trenches, he made a most watchful and energetic overseer.
Then, with a versatility doing credit to the quick eye and
hand of the true literatus, he promptly learned to copy with
his brush the distinguishing letters to be painted on all
'finds.' Though he could not read a single one of my
English characters and figures, the thoroughness of his
Chinese scholar's training enabled him to copy them with
such unfailing exactness that I never felt the slightest
doubt about their perfect legibility when the 'finds' should
come to be unpacked in the British Museum.

We spent the greater part of September 20th, too, at
the Ak-terek site. Only in the afternoon, when all the
sculpture fragments worth removing had been safely packed
and the deep trenches along the temple walls carefully
filled in again as a protection against 'treasure-seeking'
exploration, could I follow my baggage through the rich
agricultural tract of Hanguya to Lop town. There, at the

headquarters of the new district carved out some three years before from the eastern portion of the Khotan oasis, I spent a busy day's halt over final arrangements. The Amban, a somewhat heavy dignitary, ponderous alike in mind, body, and manners, insisted on treating me and Chiang-ssŭ-yeh to a small luncheon party, and though the culinary preparations were fortunately for myself only of a modest type, the slowness of conversation made the time spent over this entertainment appear longer than ever. An initial want of attention on the Amban's part had offended my good-natured and usually so genial secretary, who knew, however, what return to claim for his own punctilious politeness; and the efforts required to make up for the *faux pas* did not exactly shorten the proceedings.

After making up a big mail-bag for Kashgar, I had still to settle accounts with my faithful friend and factotum Badruddin Khan, who had insisted on following me to Lop, and on offering practical assistance to the last. I did not dread those accounts without reason; for honest as they were, my old helpmate's sole scribe and accountant, his boy of some twelve years, invariably managed to present them as a confused and barely decipherable jumble. So that night brought few hours of sleep for both of us.

CHAPTER XX

On the morning of September 22nd I set out for the thirty-five miles' march through gravel Sai and desert to Chira. It was dark by the time we reached the first outlying portion of the oasis and with it the limit of the Keriya district. There a most cheering welcome awaited me from Ibrahim Beg, my old Darogha, who had helped me so valiantly in the desert campaign of the winter 1901. On my recommendation he had subsequently, as Mirab Beg, been put in charge of the canals of Chira, but had managed to retain this comfortable berth only until a few weeks before my return. Whatever might have caused him to lose the new Amban's favour—whether complaints of Chira cultivators who had found his régime too strict, or a false accusation by a bribing rival—Ibrahim Beg's deposition had not lowered his social status. For the cavalcade of local Begs who had also come out to receive me, readily allowed my fidus Achates the place of honour by my side.

I on my part was glad to note that those years of ease and dignity had neither added bulk to his wiry figure steeled by many hardships, nor in the least impaired his tried capacity for summary execution of orders. Ibrahim, remembering my taste for camps pitched in quiet gardens, had prepared the right place far away from the Chira Bazar. But it was only by torchlight that I could admire the fine walnut-trees and elms of my camping-place, and it was near midnight when dinner appeared.

Since my former journey certain manuscript finds had reached Badruddin Khan and through him Mr. Macartney ; and during my stay at Khotan I had been able to trace these to diggings carried on by a certain Mullah Khwaja at a ruined site in the vicinity of the Domoko oasis. Through Badruddin I had myself secured some interesting leaves of Sanskrit 'Pothis' which Mullah Khwaja had found, and by sending out an old associate of Turdi I had managed on my return from the mountains to bring the man himself to Khotan together with some further specimens.

Mullah Khwaja proved to be no regular 'treasure-seeker,' but a respectable village official well advanced in years whom Ahmad Merghen, my old guide to Dandan-oilik, had some five years previously taught to look out for 'old Khats' such as he had seen me excavate. Mullah Khwaja, being badly in arrears with revenue dues to the Ya-mên, had thought of a chance here for getting out of his debts. By using his local influence he had induced men accustomed to collecting fuel in the desert jungle to the north and east of Domoko to guide him to some 'Kone-shahrs' not far off. Scraping among the ruins at one of these small sites, known to the wood-men as Khadalik, he had come upon the hoped-for 'Khats.' Having realized some money by their sale at Khotan, he had intermittently carried on his burrowings for the last three years or so. Of the true 'treasure-seeker's' love for a roving life there seemed little or nothing in the age-bowed little man, nothing also of that fraternity's cunning shiftiness and exuberant imagination. So when, on the promise of a good reward and my intercession at the Keriya Ya-mên, Mullah Khwaja undertook to show me his find-spot, I felt free from worrying doubts as to whether I might not be starting on a wild-goose-chase.

Domoko, which I had passed through in 1901 on my search for Hsüan-tsang's P'i-mo, lies a day's march east of Chira. The site I was bound for was said to be situated only about one and a half 'Pao-t'ais' or roughly three miles from Malak-alagan, the northernmost colony of that village tract. In order to reach the latter I chose a route away from the high road, which enabled me to enfilade as it were the belt of scrub-covered ground where the outlying hamlets of Chira, Gulakhma, and Ponak carry

on their struggle with the desert.   The ride through
the amply irrigated and fertile Chira oasis was delightful.
Nowhere in Turkestan had I seen such shady lanes and
luxuriant hedges.   Riding between the latter I found
myself absent-mindedly looking out for honeysuckle as
if back again in my old Hampshire haunts.   I also feasted
my eyes on the imposing tomb and mosques of Imam
Ja'far Tairan (Fig. 75), a favourite pilgrimage place and
probably successor to that famous old Buddhist shrine of
P'i-mo which I had traced at Ulugh-Mazar in the desert
due north of Chira.

The northern portion of Gulakhma, separated from
Chira by a stretch of scrubby waste, did not offer so
cheerful a picture.   Here irrigation depends mainly on
springs ; and, as a good deal of this water is apt to escape
into a deep Yar, or ravine cut into the loess, which the
villagers cannot effectively cope with, much fertile ground
is left uncultivated, to be overrun by luxuriant Kumush
beds.   But even here increasing prosperity and consequent pressure of population are pushing the limits of
cultivation northward.   About the scattered holdings of
Ponak, too, which fringe the desert edge towards Lachin-
ata, I made the same observation.   It was curious, in the
midst of luxuriant tamarisk scrub, to come across new
clearings for maize fields, and to note the numerous
tamarisk-covered sand-cones left in the fields as silent
witnesses of the desert jungle here dispossessed.

At Malak-alagan, reclaimed from the desert only
fifteen years ago, I pitched my camp once more at the
large farm of Ismail Beg where I had halted in 1901 after
my march from the Keriya Darya.   The change worked
since then by the rapid growth of the young fruit trees
into shady orchards, by the avenues of poplars, willows,
and Jigda trees which had sprung up around, was very
striking.   Malak-alagan had expanded into a regular village
of some 150 households.   Nor was I surprised to learn
that cultivation was now steadily recovering from the
desert the abandoned fields towards 'Old Domoko,' the
earlier village site described in my *Ruins of Khotan*.

Leaving all heavy baggage at the farm, and having

recruited twenty men for trial excavations, I started on the morning of September 24th for the site of Khadalik. The limit of cultivation eastwards was soon reached at the Domoko Yar, a lively little stream at this season spreading itself in a wide grass-covered Nullah. Beyond I entered once more that maze of closely packed sand-hills overgrown by tamarisk scrub which I well remembered from my march from the Shivul swamps. After wending our way through them for about three miles eastwards, we came to more open ground; and, forewarned by the appearance of pottery débris, I found myself presently at the old site I had come to explore.

Its appearance at first by no means encouraged archaeological hopes. There was a little plain about 400 yards from east to west and less than half across, fringed all round with high tamarisk-covered sand-cones. The ground, partly eroded by the winds and elsewhere overrun by low sand dunes, showed no indications whatever of structural remains. Considering how near the site was to the oasis and how exposed its remains must have been from early times to constant exploitation, I did not feel surprised at the absence of those gaunt remnants of timber-built houses and ancient orchards, which had at once struck the eye at sites previously explored far out in the desert. But what filled me with misgivings was the thoroughly-dug-up surface of the low but extensive mound pointed out by Mullah Khwaja as his find-place of manuscripts. It seemed as if all its layers must have been disturbed by such multifarious burrowings.

This feeling did not last long when, after a rapid preliminary survey of the whole site—not a protracted affair, seeing how small were its limits—I set the men to work where an eroded depression approached the south face of the mound. The first clearing of the slopes brought to light broken pieces of a frescoed wall manifestly belonging to a Buddhist shrine, and with them little fragments of paper manuscripts written in bold Indian script of the type known as Central-Asian Gupta. Within half an hour there emerged from the loose sand the first important 'Khat,' for the discovery of which I had promised a special reward. It consisted of three large leaves, fifteen inches long by five in height, belonging to a manuscript book or Pothi of some Buddhist Sanskrit text, in excellent preservation. More finds of the same kind, consisting of detached leaves or sometimes small packets, more or less intact, or mere torn fragments, in far greater number, followed in rapid succession. All these manuscript remains were in Indian Brahmi writing, but manifestly belonged to half a dozen or so of different texts, either in Sanskrit or that unknown language of ancient Khotan for which the examination of earlier discoveries seemed to indicate an Aryan origin. With them mingled rarer finds of oblong wooden tablets inscribed in the same non-Sanskritic language of old Khotan. By the evening the number of individual 'finds' exceeded a hundred, and I could scarcely keep pace with the diggers while extracting and marking them.

Fragments of stucco relievos, too, and of painted panels turned up in plenty, all closely recalling in style and decorative motives similar finds made in 1901 among the Buddhist shrines of Dandan-oilik (Fig. 76). Yet vainly did I watch all through the afternoon for the appearance of any structural remains *in situ*. The excavation had, indeed, been carried down through the layers of sand and plaster débris to the original floor of the building; but still I remained without guidance as to its shape or extent.

One thing only was clear, that the temple had been a large one, and that the diggings of Mullah Khwaja and his associates had barely done more than scrape the débris heaps left behind by destructive operations of a far earlier time. Fortunately the experience gained during former explorations saved me the doubts which might otherwise have arisen from this want of structural finds. From the first I felt certain as to the character of the ruin and the origin of the rich manuscript finds which it yielded. Lying close to the floor or in the loose sand from six inches to eighteen inches above it, they could only be votive deposits of those who had last worshipped here.

The vicinity of Domoko, some five to six miles off, enabled me to summon rapidly an additional contingent of labourers; so next morning by daybreak the work could be resumed with increased vigour. It needed a large number of men to clear away the big heaps of sand accumulating behind the line of actual diggers. With satisfaction I greeted the first indication of the structural disposition of the building, a line of low broken posts marking the position of a timber and plaster wall. It was plainly the south wall of a quadrangular cella or of its enclosing passage, and I soon ascertained that it extended to the length of about seventy-four feet, more than three times that of the largest cella wall at Dandan-oilik.

As the clearing proceeded within the line of this wall, the manuscript finds became so frequent that I soon had to give up the attempt to number all the fragments individually. The ground was divided into sections, and the fragments collected in separate paper-bags marked accordingly. All large collections of leaves or finds otherwise important I tried to extract myself and to sort and pack on the spot. But the task proved almost too much, so constant were the summons from all points of the front line of searchers announcing the discovery of fresh 'Khats.'

The day's work was truly exciting, but like the rest of the labours which were to follow here it also meant a test of endurance. The heat of the sun was still great and the glare and the dust most trying. During the half-hour's recess which I had to allow to the men and myself about mid-day, it was difficult to get rid even superficially of the thick crust of fine sand which covered me from head to foot. There were reasons for pushing on the work as rapidly as possible, and I felt glad that my physical fitness allowed me to stick to it without any consideration of health or comfort. I was grateful, too, for the sturdy labourers who cheerfully kept at their work for nearly twelve hours each day, wielding their 'Ketmans' with a vigour that astonished my trained sapper Ram Singh. Ibrahim Beg was indefatigable in urging on the men when they showed any signs of flagging; and by picking out the most intelligent of Roze Akhun's party which had followed me from Hanguya, I soon obtained efficient foremen for the several gangs.

In spite of all efforts, and of the large number of men kept at work, the excavation of this temple was not completed until the evening of the third day,—so great was the mass of sand and débris which had to be shifted, and so rich the yield of manuscript leaves, relievo fragments in stucco and wood, and pieces of frescoed wall plaster, which had to be collected with care and marked. For the detailed examination of them there was no time then. Tired out as I was by the long day's work at the ruin, I had to labour well into the night cleaning the sand crusts off the manuscript remains—they could not otherwise have been packed safely—and recording exact details as to the place and conditions of all the more important finds. Among striking observations thus gathered on the spot only a few can be mentioned here. Again and again I came upon leaves from the same texts in Brahmi writing which had turned up in widely separated parts of the building, a proof that the worshipper depositing them had, as in the case of the shrine excavated at Endere in 1901, tried to please with his offerings as many as possible of the divinities represented among the sculptures and frescoes of the temple.

That there had been Chinese, too, among the pious visitors was proved by the discovery of two well-preserved rolls of paper, one fully thirty-six by ten inches, evidently parts of the same manuscript, showing a neatly written Chinese Buddhist text on one side and an equally extensive text in cursive Brahmi script on the other. Closer study of the latter was impossible at the time. Yet the mere hope that it might be a translation of the Chinese text on the obverse, and thus prove thereafter in the hands of an expert collaborator to furnish a key for the decipherment of the 'unknown' language of Buddhist Khotan, was by itself no small encouragement. The total number of separately marked manuscript packets, containing larger portions of texts or else collections of fragments, amounted in the end to over 230.

In the course of the second day I found my architectural conclusions confirmed by the discovery of a large central image base and of remains of frescoed walls which had belonged to double quadrangular passages enclosing the cella. There was plentiful evidence that the walls of timber and plaster had been almost completely destroyed at an early period for the sake of abstracting the wood-work. The larger posts and beams must have been worked upon the spot for facility of transport elsewhere; for again and again I came upon heaps of carpenters' chippings, often showing remains of delicate painted repre-sentations of Buddhist saints, etc., with which the surface of columns and other exposed woodwork had evidently been covered.

Of the sculptures in stucco which must have once risen on a central platform about nine feet square laid bare within the cella, no trace remained *in situ*,—a proof of long-continued exposure and the havoc wrought by quarrying operations. But of the elaborate relievo decora-tion in hard white stucco which had formed vesicas behind those statues and others, set perhaps against the cella walls, many small pieces had escaped those early vandals. They represented figures of Bodhisattvas or flying Gand-harvis, and showed excellent workmanship (Fig. 76). The friable plaster of the wall surfaces must have been entirely broken when the timber framework was being abstracted.

Yet fortunately large fragments of the wall frescoes up to five feet in length had got detached before this destruc-tion, and lying buried near the floor had escaped (Fig. 77). They showed close resemblance to the frescoes of the Dan-dan-oilik shrines in style, but marked superiority in design and colour. Most of the wall-surface seems to have been occupied by stencilled representations of small Buddhas, seated in rows and varied only in the colours of dress, halo, etc. But large fragments of individual fresco panels showing Buddha in different poses—teaching, fasting, or worshipped by attendants—fortunately came to light also. The colours had survived in remarkable freshness; and, if the pieces selected for transport could safely reach London, I felt sure of their offering plenty of details to the trained eyes of an artist such as my devoted friend and helpmate Mr. F. H. Andrews, to feast upon.

Though among the mass of manuscript remains there were no datable documents, I could not feel in doubt as to the age of the ruin. All pictorial and relievo remains pointed clearly to the period when the shrines of the Dandan-oilik site were abandoned, *i.e.* the close of the eighth century A.D. The discovery of some Tibetan lines on the Chinese Brahmi rolls previously mentioned agreed with this conclusion; but definite chronological evidence was to come from the remains of the ruin which I next proceeded to excavate on September 27th. This was a temple marked by a low débris heap some fifty yards to the south-west. Here the cella proved smaller, twenty-seven feet square, with a single quadrangular enclosure; but the destruction of the walls had not been quite so thorough, and finds of artistic interest were relatively more numerous.

Small painted panels, as well as excellently modelled small relievos in hard plaster (Fig. 76), turned up near the north wall containing the entrance. The relievos had undoubtedly formed part of decorative halos around life-size stucco images; but of the latter, modelled in much more friable plaster, only sadly broken fragments such as hands and parts of heads, survived. Of technical interest were finds of moulds in 'plaster of Paris,' which had served for casting small relievos of figures and floral ornaments such as formed part of the wall decoration in these shrines, as well as for portions of the larger stucco images. Some fine wood carvings, in relievo and in the round, also turned up, besides little clay models of Stupas in plenty.

Among manuscript finds I was fortunate to recover here large pieces, including several complete leaves, of a Sanskrit Buddhist text written on birch-bark and probably, on palaeographical evidence, to be attributed to the fourth or fifth century A.D. The brittle birch-bark sheets became wonderfully fresh in appearance when I gave them a good bath, such as they needed after the scorching they had manifestly undergone and their twelve hundred years of burial in arid sand. I could greet them as friends from Kashmir, which the material clearly indicated as their place of origin. Some of the paper manuscripts found here showed traces of having been exposed to great heat,

77. LARGE FRAGMENT OF FRESCOED WALL FROM BUDDHIST TEMPLE, KHADALIK, WITH
STENCILLED BUDDHA FIGURES.

The foot-measure in top left corner indicates the scale.

78. INTERIOR OF SMALL RUINED DWELLING EXCAVATED TO THE NORTH OF MAIN
TEMPLE SITE, KHADALIK.

Aziz, the Ladaki servant, seated on bench near ancient fireplace.

and some of the stucco pieces were blackened by smoke, a clear proof that the ruin had suffered from fire. Wooden tablets inscribed in Brahmi; boards used for holding Pothis, with remains of leaves still adhering; fragments of a text illuminated with miniatures, also emerged from this small shrine in gratifying variety.

But the discovery which pleased me most was a numismatic one. Deep down on the floor of the passage through which the entrance to the cella had led, there came to light first a scattered batch of Chinese copper coins of the T'ang period, and then, as if to satisfy my craving for exact chronological evidence, from a corner two completely preserved rolls of coins, counting some twenty and fifty pieces respectively, still held together by the original string which the last owner had passed through their square holes. Rapid examination showed that the rolls were made up, apart from some older uninscribed pieces, of T'ang coins only, the latest being issues of the Ta-li period (A.D. 780-783). As votive deposits of this sort must belong to the period immediately preceding the abandonment of the shrine, the date of this event in the case of the whole group of ruins could thus be definitely fixed at the close of the eighth century.

Of the excavations which followed, and which kept me incessantly at work until October 1st, I can only give the briefest account here. They laid bare a series of small dwellings close to the west and north of the large temple which had probably served as abodes of monks (Fig. 78). Here the walls, partly of sun-dried bricks and partly of timber and plaster, still stood over six feet high, the sand accumulated within having evidently been high enough from the first to hide and protect them. Once more I could sit down on a bench by an ancient fireplace and collect in numbers humble domestic implements, such as wooden locks and keys working with a curious arrangement of movable pins which has its exact parallel in a system of locking still traceable from Khotan to Egypt; brooms, bags with raw cotton wool, etc.

By running trial trenches through the surrounding sand I traced other small shrines and monastic quarters close to the main temple, and gathered from them a plentiful harvest of manuscript remains and inscribed tablets.   The walls had almost completely disappeared, but the plastered floor and the manuscript deposits above it sufficed to show the position of these smaller structures. There were exciting finds, too, here, such as that of some twenty fragmentary leaves of a Pothi in Sanskrit, nearly two feet long, written in fine bold Brahmi characters like the hymn-book for some abbot or canon.   The discovery of Tibetan records on wood supplied clear proof that the presence of the Tibetan invaders, attested by the Chinese Annals for different periods of the eighth century A.D., was not confined in Khotan territory to mere inroads, as might otherwise have been supposed.   One of the rooms adjoining the main shrine northward seemed to have been used as a sort of workshop by those who had quarried the deserted shrines for timber, and among the chippings and other materials left behind as useless I was glad to unearth richly moulded balustrades, columns, finials, and other pieces of fine architectural wood carving (Fig. 79).

The careful search of all ground which had escaped erosion, and thus could be supposed to retain débris of buildings, was a big task.   It took the unremitting labour of ten days to accomplish it, though we worked with a large number of diggers and in spite of heat and smothering dust practically without interruption from daybreak until nightfall.   For many years past I had not felt so thoroughly tired evening after evening.   But success kept my spirits refreshed, and my eagerness to move on eastwards to sites farther away in the desert and hence likely to have been abandoned far earlier urged me to additional exertions. In the end I felt doubly glad that I had spared at the outset the time and labour for Khadalik ; for, when nearly eighteen months later I returned to this tract, I found that the area containing the ruins had, after long centuries, again been brought under irrigation from the stream, the vicinity of which had been such a boon to us all during those long hot days of hard labour—and their destruction completed.

79. WOODEN COLUMN WITH MOULDINGS EXCAVATED IN ROOM NEAR MAIN SHRINE, KHADALIK.

Chiang-ssŭ-yeh and Ibrahim Beg in background supervising diggers ; Roze Akhun on right.

80. MY SEVEN CAMELS FROM KERIYA, IN WINTER DRESS, MARCHING IN GRAVEL DESERT.

CHAPTER XXI

SITES AROUND DOMOKO

WHILE Naik Ram Singh was directing the opening of trial trenches, and my ever alert Chinese Secretary carefully watching for any remains which the diggers might light upon incidentally, with note-book and brush ready to record their position, I managed to pay visits to some smaller ruined sites scattered among the sand-cones and tamarisk scrub of the neighbouring desert at distances varying from one to three miles. Apart from Tati areas strewn with potsherds, their only remains consisted of almost wholly eroded ruins of modest dwellings built of plaster and rush walls which were easily cleared and searched.

But at the southernmost of these little sites known to Mullah Khwaja as Darabzan-dong, I succeeded in tracing the position of a Buddhist temple on the top of what, owing to wind-erosion of the surrounding ground, presented itself as a small clay terrace or 'witness,' to use the geological term. Though the layer of sand and débris covering the top was nowhere over one foot thick, we here unearthed fragments of fresco wall decoration and stucco relievos together with badly decayed pieces of a Brahmi manuscript. Insignificant in themselves, the finds sufficed to establish the important chronological fact that this site, too, though within less than a mile of the stream of Domoko, was abandoned about the same period as Khadalik and distant Dandan-oilik. The discovery had its own special interest, as it strengthened my doubts as to whether this simultaneous abandonment of settlements dependent on the same water-supply and yet widely separated in distances could adequately be accounted for by progressive desiccation alone.

These surveys gave me plentiful opportunities for instructive observations on the physical changes which had come over this desert area around Khadalik, once evidently occupied by numerous villages. Again and again I noted how the patches of open ground, probably marking the positions where the dwellings of small agricultural settlements had clustered, were being broken up and scooped out by the erosive force of wind and driven sand. Small terraces of fairly hard loess soil, rising to heights of six to thirteen feet above the eroded depressions close by, served as 'witnesses' indicating approximately the ancient level of the ground. Thin layers of pottery fragments and similar hard débris on their surface helped to explain why these terraces had withstood the unceasing attack of wind erosion. How the latter was proceeding could be clearly seen from the sides of the terraces, which everywhere showed the effects of under-cutting as plainly as the bank of a river towards which the current sets. What remains of modest dwellings could still be traced here, consisted usually of low rush walls or fences, which by their very weakness offered less scope to the grinding force of driven sand, and on the contrary were apt to catch and retain it as a cover.

The closely packed sand-cones, encircling such open areas and rising to fifteen feet or more above the original ground level, illustrated in their structure the same phenomenon. Tangled masses of tamarisk scrub, usually dead at the foot but still flourishing on the top, invariably covered these small hillocks. There could be no doubt that the latter owed their origin to the tamarisk bushes, which had first overrun the fields when cultivation ceased, and had then served to catch and collect the drift sand passing over the ground. It was this initial stage of the process which I had seen exhibited by the low tamarisk thickets spread over the abandoned fields of Ponak and 'Old Domoko.' The struggle for light and air, which the tamarisk bushes once rooted on level ground had to carry on against the sand steadily accumulating around them, forced their head branches to rise higher and higher. The sand, the smothering embrace of which they tried to escape, naturally followed this rise, and the cones formed by it thus grew correspondingly in height and size.

The time taken over this building-up process was brought home to me with quasi-chronological exactness by an interesting observation made at the edge of a small area of open eroded ground about half-way between Khadalik and Balawaste. Here a few fragments of small relievos in hard stucco were seen emerging from the slope of eroded loess soil immediately at the foot of a big tamarisk-covered sand-cone. Such excavation into the side of the hillock as the masses of sand sliding down permitted us to make, brought to light more stucco fragments originally forming part of the relievo decoration of some big halo in a Buddhist shrine, which undoubtedly belonged to the same period as the temples of Khadalik.

The abraded condition of the relievo pieces representing small standing Buddhas and floral borders, left no doubt that they had been exposed for centuries to 'grinding' by driven sand, until the expansion of a neighbouring sand-cone came to provide protection for these humble remnants of a shrine otherwise completely destroyed by erosion. The level on which they were found was about three feet higher than the top of the nearest 'witnesses,' while the latter themselves rose six to ten feet above the bottom of the eroded depressions adjoining them. This difference of about three feet manifestly represents the progress made by erosion since the relievo fragments came to be buried beneath the slope of the sand-cone. This itself rose now fully sixteen feet above the level indicated by this débris.

Like the explorations over neighbouring ground just referred to, the careful packing of all relics capable of removal, the photographing of others which had to be left behind and reburied, the filling up of all ground excavated, etc., had to be effected simultaneously with the general clearing of the main ruins. It was only by such constant and varied exertions that I was able by the morning of October 3rd to leave Khadalik, where, in spite of unpromising aspects, I had gathered a rich harvest. The manuscript remains carried away nearly sufficed to fill a good-sized mule-trunk, and probably exceeded three or four times all the finds in Brahmi script of my former journey.

Before leaving the Domoko tract I decided to search a spot south of the oasis where, according to an old villager's statement reported by Mullah Khwaja, 'old papers' had been found some forty years before by men engaged in searching for saltpetre to supply Yakub Beg's powder factories. They were said to have been thrown away again on the spot as useless rubbish. It seemed a true 'treasure-seeking' business to follow so vague a clue, especially as Mullah Khwaja knew nothing of ruins there. But the march to the alleged site proved of interest.

It gave me the desired opportunity of visiting the main oasis of Domoko, and also of clearing up the peculiar irrigation conditions to which its latest colony, Malak-alagan, owed its rise. When in 1901 I first touched the northern edge of this tract, I was struck by the shifting which its irrigated area had undergone within living memory. From the site of 'Old Domoko' in the zone of desert vegetation immediately to the north-west of Malak-alagan, where I then came across abandoned fields and dwellings, the area of cultivation had, according to the villagers' uniform statements, been transferred to its present position, eight miles farther south, near the Khotan-Keriya high road, only some sixty years before. The gradually increasing difficulty of conducting the irrigation water sufficiently far was indicated to me as the cause of the shift. This had undoubtedly served to bring the cultivated area nearer to the springs in which the water of the mountain streams about Nura and Tört-Imam comes to light again at the foot of the great glacis of Piedmont gravel southwards, and upon which the oasis entirely depends for irrigation before the summer floods.

It was thus natural to connect the shift with that general desiccation or gradual drying up of the climate which, as is becoming clear to competent observers, has affected the physical conditions of Central Asia so extensively during the historical period. The merit of having first systematically investigated this great physical change over widely distant parts of Asia belongs to my friend Mr. Ellsworth Huntington. After having with this object in view in the autumn of 1905 carefully studied the physiography of the region east of Khotan, he did not fail to lay special stress in his fascinating volume, *The Pulse of Asia*, on this well-authenticated change in the area of cultivation, for which shrinkage in the amount of available water-supply seemed to offer the simplest explanation.

Yet there were also indications of special local conditions which might have influenced the change. I remembered what a tradition heard on the occasion of my first visit in 1901 asserted about such shifts of the cultivated land, backwards and forwards, having occurred repeatedly in the case of Domoko. The opening of the Malak-alagan colony fully six miles to the north of the centre of the present oasis looked curiously like an illustration of the reverse movement northward having already set in. That the number of settlers at Malak-alagan had increased considerably since 1901, and that its irrigation was now being extended even towards the long-abandoned fields of Old Domoko, I had learned when stopping there on my way to Khadalik. But of the peculiar conditions of water-supply to which this interesting colony owed its origin and development I could obtain a clear idea only as I marched from Khadalik south to Domoko and the alleged old site near Mazar-toghrak.

Going westwards from Khadalik we soon struck the Domoko Yar close to the point where its stream, lively but shallow, is dammed up in order to feed the canal leading to Malak-alagan. Then we followed upwards the broad reed-covered depression of the Domoko Yar, flanked on either side by closely set tamarisk cones and looking, with its numerous branches now all dry, like the bed of a stream once far larger. After about three miles we reached the eastern edge of the present oasis, and exchanged the dreary waste of scrub-covered sand-hills for scenery far more cheerful. The ground we had to pass through for the next few miles on our way south was all 'yangi kent' ('new land'), having been brought under cultivation only

for about twenty to twenty-five years. Many old sand-
cones, once, no doubt, covered with tamarisks, but now
bared by seekers for fuel, still rose above the levelled
fields, and had often been made use of as building ground
for the scattered homesteads. Otherwise the soil seemed
very carefully cultivated, and the lanes were all lined with
dense hedges. Then we skirted on our right the older
part of the oasis as transferred here about the forties of the
nineteenth century, until the line of the Shakül canal we
were following struck the high road leading to Keriya.

All the cultivated ground south of the road was declared
to be 'new land,' gradually added to the oasis in the course
of the last thirty years, and there in the hamlet of Dash I
found a large and delightfully shady garden near a well-to-
do villager's farm in which to leave my camp. Riding
southward along the canal for another one and a half miles
I reached the great 'Tugh' or dyke by which the waters of
the Domoko stream are safeguarded for the main oasis.

It was quite an imposing piece of engineering, as
things go in the Tarim Basin, which I saw before
me. A dam nearly 200 yards long and of very solid
construction closed the head of the Domoko Yar, rising
more than thirty feet above its marshy bottom. The
whole dyke consisted of stamped earth with thick layers
of brushwood at short intervals. Its top was broad
enough to permit a wide road to pass. On the south
thick rows of willow trees guarded its side towards a large
sheet of water, formed by the stream of Domoko close to
the point where the canals of the oasis absorb its water.
The depression southward holding the stream looked
broad and shallow. Very different was the appearance
of the Domoko Yar which formed the natural continuation
of this stream-bed northward. It presented itself here as
a well-marked winding ravine, deeply cut into the loess
soil between steep banks fully sixty to eighty feet high.
Thick growth of reeds and coarse grass in the basin
forming its head indicated the presence of springs; but
there appeared no course of flowing water.

I had heard of this dam during my stay at Khadalik;
but only on the spot could I realize properly its signifi-

cance for the history of the oasis, past and present.
Seventeen years before my visit, I was told, an exceptionally big summer flood had come down from the mountains
in the bed of the Domoko stream and had converted a
small channel, generally dry, into the broad and deep-
cut ravine now extending towards Malak-alagan.

There was serious risk of the whole water-supply of
Domoko being drawn off into this deeper 'Yar,' where the
difference of level would have made it useless for the
irrigation of the extant oasis. So after a year's interval,
during which the tendency of the stream to be absorbed
in the new bed had seriously interfered with the service
of the canals watering the fields of Domoko, the local
Begs, acting under the orders of the Keriya Amban, whom
the prospective abandonment of the oasis threatened with
loss of revenue, set about by a joint effort to erect the
present dam. About fifteen hundred labourers, drawn
from all the neighbouring oases, were said to have been
kept at work on it for close on two months. Considering
how widely scattered and scanty was the population, and
how divergent the interests of the several oases, the collection of so much labour, all *corvée*, of course, must have
been a serious undertaking. Nor could the dam have
been maintained in effective condition without large con-
tingents of men being employed annually on its maintenance during the summer floods.

By these efforts Domoko was assured its former supply
of 'Kara-su' ('black water'), or water from springs, which
is indispensable for irrigation during the months preceding
the summer floods. But in addition a fresh and constant
supply was obtained from the springs which came to light
near the head of the newly formed 'Yar.' This led to the
formation of the Malak-alagan colony. The steady growth
of the latter was attributed to the water of these springs
having remained uniformly ample, and rendered the new
settlement less dependent than Domoko itself upon the
amount of the 'Ak-su,' or summer floods. It was interesting
to note the uniform assertion that the volume of 'Kara-su'
water available for the canals of Domoko had not been
reduced by the formation of the new springs. The evident

explanation was that the latter were draining strata saturated with subsoil water far lower than those feeding the sources of the Domoko stream some eight or nine miles higher up on the Sai.

The observations thus gathered at the great dam of Domoko helped to bring out clearly two facts of wider geographical interest. It became evident that the opening of the Malak-alagan colony was the direct result of a movement by which the Domoko stream had endeavoured to carry its water once more towards the old village site abandoned about 1840 A.D. Had it not been for the timely construction of the dam, practically all the available water would have turned into the Yar, leaving the canals irrigating the present village lands to run dry. In that case, it is safe to assume that the settlement would have been shifted back again to the position occupied by 'Old Domoko.' In proof of this it is sufficient to point out that, as I convinced myself on the occasion of a subsequent visit in 1908, the old village lands are now being gradually approached again by the surplus water of Malak-alagan brought northward along the old canal alignment, still traceable, even without any aid of water from the Domoko stream.

The fate of abandonment which threatened the extant oasis and was averted only by an engineering feat of unusual importance for this region, shows plainly that changes in the cultivated area may take place on ground peculiarly situated without necessarily being occasioned by desiccation and a consequent diminution of the water-supply. But more important still is the lesson we may draw from it as to the influence which a quasi-historical factor, the assertion of human energy, must have in respect of such changes. Had it not been for the effective administration introduced on the Chinese reconquest of the country and the economical development which it has fostered, the damming up of the Domoko Yar would certainly have proved too great a task to be attempted with local resources. The villagers of Domoko would have been left to face their calamity as best they could, and everything points to the probability of their adopting the remedy indicated by local tradition, which tells, as I have mentioned above, of repeated shifts of cultivation backwards and forwards.

When I had inspected the dyke my guides took me south along the left bank of the reed-covered depression in which the Domoko stream meanders, and after little over one mile we reached the popular shrine of Mazar-toghrak, marked by a fine grove of old Toghraks of great size. A little to the west of it and less than half a mile from the stream was the spot of 'old Khats,' which Mullah Khwaja had cast his eyes upon but never touched.

When on the morning of October 4th I began to clear the little plateau, about 200 feet by 130 feet, rising above what was manifestly eroded ground, I soon realized that I was opening an ancient rubbish mound with all the unsavoury associations I remembered so well from the diggings of my first journey. From the layers covered only with a foot or two of drift sand there came the same pungent smells of long-decayed animal refuse, old rags of coarse fabrics and felt, broken implements of wood, especially such as weavers use to this day, etc. But instead of the promised great haul of ' Khats,' I had to be satisfied at first with little scraps of documents on paper, in Chinese and cursive Brahmi script, presumably in the old language of Khotan. Their material and writing gave evidence of approximately the same date as the Khadalik ruins. Of the small structures which must have once stood amidst these refuse accumulations, only the floors, with here and there a mud-built sitting-platform, could be traced.

The day's reward came late in the evening when near the west edge of the plateau one of the diggers hit upon a confused heap of narrow wooden tablets, or rather sticks, bearing on their flattened surface Chinese records in single line. Owing evidently to prolonged exposure to atmospheric influences many had become more or less rotten, and all were thickly encrusted with decayed matter and salts drawn from the layers of refuse. Their wood had become so exceedingly friable that many got broken during removal in spite of all the care used. But with

the help of my Chinese secretary, who, of course, turned
with special eagerness to these finds, I ultimately managed
to piece together again most of the fragments.

In the end over fifty wooden documents of this sort
were collected, their size and shape varying greatly. Some
are flat, showing two smoothed surfaces covered with
characters ; a few are stick-like, with four inscribed sides.
Others are written on what is nothing more than the split
half of a branch, usually of tamarisk, with one surface
roughly smoothed, showing the writing, and the other
left in the original round and sometimes retaining the
bark. As far as Chiang-ssŭ-yeh was able to examine
them, all seemed acknowledgments, brief orders, and
similar miscellaneous petty ' papers ' connected with
village administration and matters of irrigation. A few
are bilingual, bearing, besides Chinese, inscriptions in
cursive Brahmi script and that ' unknown ' language of
Khotan which seems of Aryan type.

There could be no doubt that I had recovered here
' waste paper' remains of some little office. Their poor
state of preservation was accounted for by what Haidul
Khwaja, an aged villager and Mullah Khwaja's informant,
told us of how the rubbish deposit had been dug into by
villagers who searched here for saltpetre some forty years
earlier. Disappointed in their quest they abandoned the
' site' after a day, leaving the documents incidentally
brought to light to rot on the surface. Curiously enough,
local tradition seems to have preserved some inkling of
the official character of the ruined structure ; for Mullah
Khwaja and other greybeards of Domoko knew the spot
by the name of Kone-ötang, ' the old postal station.'

Several of the Chinese records on wood bear dates in
months and days only, and the detailed examination now
proceeding has not yet disclosed any documents with the
desired full dating. But even in the absence of this the
character of both Chinese and Brahmi writing, and the
close agreement between the art-remains unearthed
eighteen months later at the closely adjoining ruins of
Kara-yantak, and those of Khadalik, suffice to indicate
that the relics of Mazar-toghrak belong to the closing

period of Chinese rule in the Tarim Basin under the T'ang dynasty, *i.e.* the second half of the eighth century A.D. The probability thus presented of sites at opposite edges of the Domoko oasis,—Khadalik, etc., below, and Mazar-toghrak with Kara-yantak above, the present area of irrigation—having been abandoned about the same time is in itself of considerable geographical interest.

But the problem raised as to the cause of this abandonment is thrust more forcibly upon our attention when we remember that the same period must have seen the desertion of the large ruined settlement of Dandan-oilik which I explored in 1900 and which, as recognized by Mr. Huntington, had received its water from the same drainage system. Dandan-oilik is situated fully fifty-six miles farther north in the desert; and if shrinkage of the water-supply needed for irrigation were to be considered as the only possible cause of abandonment of these sites, the chronological coincidence in the case of localities dependent on the same streams and yet so widely separated would be very curious.

That such shrinkage of the available water-supply has taken place in the Tarim Basin during historical times, and that it must be connected with a general desiccation period affecting the whole of Central Asia and probably most regions of the earth, is a conclusion to which we are forced by a mass of evidence steadily accumulating from ancient sites examined in the desert or near the present oases. Nobody has done more than Mr. Huntington to bring out this central fact. Taking the tract which extends along the southern edge of the Taklamakan between Chira and Keriya, it is certain that the water now brought down by its rivers would be quite insufficient to reach the more distant ruined sites, such as Dandan-oilik. Nor would it be adequate to irrigate, besides the actual oases, the whole of the area adjoining them that was once cultivated.

But this fact by no means justifies the assumption that, because desiccation has rendered once cultivated areas incapable of reoccupation after the lapse of centuries, their original abandonment must have been due to the same cause. Where man's struggle with adverse conditions of nature is carried on by a highly civilized community, such as archaeological exploration reveals to us at these ancient oases of the Tarim Basin, human factors introduce elements of complexity which must warn the critical student to proceed warily and to look for definite historical evidence before drawing his conclusions. Where cultivation is wholly dependent upon careful irrigation and the maintenance of the latter on any scale is possible only by organized co-operation of an adequate population, as in these oases adjacent to and surrounded by the most arid of deserts, a variety of causes apart from the want of water may lead to the gradual shrinkage or complete abandonment of cultivation. Amongst them I need only mention reduction of population through invasion or pestilence, maladministration and want of security through prolonged disturbance of political conditions, etc.

In order to gauge correctly the most probable causes in each case, we need definite historical records which neither silent ruins nor learned conjecture can replace, and reliable materials of that kind are still exceedingly scanty for any period of the history of Chinese Turkestan. But even thus it is well to remember that the end of the eighth century A.D., during which the settlements of Dandan-oilik, Khadalik, and probably also the other small sites near Domoko were abandoned, was the period when the T'ang dynasty's rule in the Tarim Basin came to a close, and with it the ordered conditions dependent on an effective central administration.

CHAPTER XXII

TO KERIYA AND THE NIYA RIVER

WHILE my camp rested peacefully in Dash at a well-to-do villager's homestead, two days' continuous work allowed me to clear completely the deposits of ancient refuse at Mazar-toghrak. So by the morning of October 6th I was able to start on the march to Keriya which my successful work about Domoko had put off longer than I had expected. Twice in 1901 I had followed the high road to Keriya, and I now took occasion to vary the route by visiting Achma, a flourishing new oasis to the north of the road. It owes its existence to the sudden appearance of springs some fifteen years ago, which added so largely to the water of the Kara-kir Yar that an area now sufficing for some 800 households could rapidly be brought under irrigation. For fully three miles I traversed ground thus newly reclaimed from the desert, and felt cheered by the vista of young avenues of poplars and Jigdas stretching away to the north as far as the eye could reach. It was an interesting instance of that successful fight with the desert which this portion of the Taklamakan edge seems to have witnessed at recurring intervals, but of which it is difficult now to secure definite records.

A curious incident of the day was the appearance of a Punjabi Muhammadan from near Guliana in the Salt Range, who joined us at Achma. According to his story he had wandered, with a Mullah as his spiritual guide, from Kashmir to Ladak, and thence to the shrine of Imam Ja'far Sadik. His 'Ustad' having died he had settled down at Achma some six years ago, obtaining land there with the Turki wife he married. His dress and mount showed that he had fared well, and he had nothing but praise for the way in which as a Saiyid he had been helped by the villagers.   Nevertheless he seemed home-sick for his barren Salt Range hills, and talked of soon setting out for them.   It was a queer Punjabi he talked, and I wondered what welcome he would find in his old home. He declared that during all these years he had never thought of getting news about his parents or relatives !

From Achma and the adjoining small oasis of Laisu I struck south-east through a belt of luxuriant Toghrak jungle to the edge of the marsh of Shivul.   After a night's camp there near a desolate little Langar I visited a small Tati with old pottery débris, known as Jigda-kuduk, some five miles away to the south-east, where the dune-fringed marsh approaches the bare gravel glacis descending from the foot of the Polur hills.   The edge of the Keriya oasis proved only a little over two miles away from this dreary waste, which once, no doubt, had formed part of the cultivated area—how long ago I could not determine. From its glare and heat I was glad to gain the broad, well-shaded road which passes through the oasis to the town and district headquarters of Keriya.

There a halt was indispensable in order that I might make the acquaintance of the Amban, and secure his assistance for whatever explorations I might have to carry on within his district, mainly desert, which stretches for nearly five degrees of longitude eastwards to beyond Charchan.   But my stay would certainly not have extended to five days, had the necessity of obtaining fresh transport not detained me.   Keriya was the last place where I could make sure of replacing the camels which, by a succession of deaths due to some unexplained illness, I had lost since August.   We had taken all possible care of the fine-looking animals acquired at Kashgar, and used every chance for giving them rest and plentiful grazing.   Yet, as already related, I had the mortification of seeing them return to Khotan from the Kara-tash Valley, where they had been grazing at ease during my absence in the Karanghu-tagh mountains, reduced by two in number. During my work about Domoko two more succumbed in rapid succession, and it scarcely needed the death of a fifth while on the march to Keriya to convince me that some infectious illness had evidently taken hold of the lot.

Keriya is full of ' Bais' owning camels, and information of my wish to purchase fresh animals there had been duly sent to the Ya-mên weeks ahead. Yet the selection of a suitable set proved a protracted business. Ho Ta-lao-ye, the Amban of Keriya, showed from my very entry into his district all possible attention and willingness to assist. When I paid him my visit on the day following my arrival, I was received in full state and treated to a well-arranged luncheon. I soon realized that my host, in spite of his strikingly young looks, did not in vain enjoy a reputation for learning and a wide mental horizon. He seemed fully aware of the historical interest attaching to the researches which had brought me to these parts, and the many questions he put about my finds, etc., even when interpreted in more familiar terms by my excellent Ssŭ-yeh, taxed my incipient colloquial knowledge most severely. Ho Ta-lao-ye had been the Urumchi Governor-General's chief secretary, and there was much in his ways and talk which reminded me curiously of clever young Civilian friends in Indian Secretariats. Of his professed desire to protect the people of his district against exactions I had heard at Khotan. But his solicitude in this direction, whether genuine or otherwise, was not likely to stimulate the zeal or strengthen the hands of the local Begs.

The latter had received explicit injunctions to hunt up and produce camels suitable for my journey. Yet even when the Amban's order was emphatically repeated in my presence during the return visit he paid me, the supply of animals for selection was by no means as prompt and satisfactory as it would have been under a more experienced though, perhaps, less learned district head, such as e.g. my old friend Huan Ta-lao-ye, who had helped me so well in 1901 from this very Ya-mên. For two days I was treated to the wearisome inspection of long strings of camels either too young or past work, while it was evident that more serviceable animals were being carefully kept out of sight. To buy camels in the open market would have been against all precedent at Keriya, and there was nothing for it but to put pressure on the Begs charged with the task of producing acceptable animals. That they had been receiving *douceurs* from those who owned the right sort of camels, but first hoped to force me into bad bargains, was common talk in the little Bazar which had soon formed in the road outside the garden I occupied, and Abdullah Khan, the picturesque old Afghan trader, who had helped me in 1901 (Fig. 51), confirmed it. But perseverance and repeated complaints in the Ya-mên prevailed in the end, and by the fifth day seven big and strong animals had been picked out in spite of all dilatory tactics.

To judge of camels' points requires the experience of a lifetime, or rather the inherited knowledge of a born camel-man. So it was no small comfort to feel that in a matter of this sort I could rely on Hassan Akhun's honesty quite as much as on the effect produced among the wily owners by his sharp tongue. The result justified my reliance. The camels I purchased at Keriya, for which I paid in the end an average of thirty Taels (then equal to about five pounds) per animal, together with another which Hassan Akhun subsequently acquired from Niya on private speculation, proved the mainstay of my transport thereafter (Fig. 80). However great the cares and difficulties about 'transport and supplies' on my archaeological expeditions into the desert, my brave camels from Keriya never caused me worry. They held out splendidly against all privations and hardships, and after nearly two years' travel were so fit and fine-looking that, when at last I had to dispose of them before my return to India, they realized over seventy per cent. profit—of course, for the Government of India.

When it came to fixing the animals' price I requested the Amban's mediation in order to arrive at a fair estimate without additional loss of time implied in the usual bargaining. Ho Ta-lao-ye promptly seized the occasion to pay me an informal visit, not so much with a view to assisting in any practical settlement as to enjoy a scholarly talk about old T'ang-sên and antiquarian lore in general. As soon as I had become aware of his learned propensities, I had presented him with copies of the original Chinese text of the Hsi-yü-chi and Fa-hsien's Travels.   That the gift had gone to the right man was evident from the profuse thanks now offered and the numerous topics of old geography, etc., which my visitor raised in discussion.   His scholarly interest, of course, touched me ; yet I should have appreciated better a little business-like decision about the ostensible object of his visit.   After confessing that he knew nothing whatever about camels, the well-meaning young Amban lavishly wasted his own time and mine by a personal inspection of all the animals originally brought for selection. Of course, as we stood in the road the opportunity was taken for petitions and complaints of all sorts by the assembled idlers, until the benevolent district head became fairly bewildered.   I did not envy the Ya-mên interpreter who had to translate all these clamorous representations. In the end Ho Ta-lao-ye could save himself only by retreating to my tent in the garden and leaving the settlement to be effected by myself, as it was in the end with all fairness.

However, the long visit did not pass altogether without progress in business.   For old Mullah Khwaja I managed to secure from the Amban discharge from certain long-standing accounts about petty village dues which had caused much trouble to my honest Domoko guide and threatened to ruin him.   Ibrahim Beg, too, whom the Amban had only a few weeks before ignominiously deprived of his office on complaints of a weak nature, saw his case prepared for reconsideration.   As I urged my need of Ibrahim's practical help on the onward journey, the Amban readily agreed to let him accompany me in a sort of *sub. pro tem.* function.   For efficient services such as I could confidently expect from my old desert factotum, he was to be rewarded thereafter by some suitable vacancy.

Frequent changes in Begships form an essential part in the local administrative system, for reasons which suit equally well Chinese political interests, competition among the local petty aristocracy, and the pockets of officialdom. Hence Ibrahim could start with me confident of a speedy restoration to the place he had gained years ago on my recommendation.   An additional piece of business achieved

was the strengthening of my cash reserves by taking over
a quantity of silver equivalent to fifty-one 'horse-shoes,' or
2550 Taels, from the Keriya Ya-mên against money to that
amount paid on my behalf by Mr. Macartney into the Tao-
tai's treasury at Kashgar.   It was a convenience to me to
have been saved the transport of that heavy weight of
silver, and equally also to the Keriya Amban, who could
reduce correspondingly the cash payments due from him
at Kashgar.

All through my stay at Keriya I had been kept hard at
work writing up arrears in records and correspondence
inevitable during the high pressure of the preceding weeks.
So I felt relieved when on October 13th, after a night
spent mostly over letters, I could set out for the two long
marches to Niya.   My next objective was the ancient
site in the desert beyond Imam Ja'far Sadik, where on my
first visit in 1901 I had made important discoveries among
ruins deserted in the third century A.D., and where I knew
of several ruins still awaiting excavation.   Its great distance
from any larger settlement, and the difficulty of assuring
an adequate supply of water far out in the desert, demanded
careful preparations.   In order to gain time for them I
covered the sixty odd miles from Keriya to Niya in two
days, keeping ahead of the heavy baggage.   What with
fresh transport, accounts to settle, etc., a late start from
Keriya was inevitable.   So it was close on midnight
before we got to Yes-yulghun, the tiny half-way oasis.

It was late, too, when next evening, after a twelve
hours' tramp and ride over most desolate wastes of gravel
overrun in parts by light dunes, I reached the familiar
oasis of Niya.   But my reception made me forget all
fatigue and a dinner delayed beyond midnight.   Rai Ram
Singh, the Surveyor, had duly arrived there to join me for
the new expedition, and the account he could give of
the triangulation work successfully accomplished in the
mountains south of Keriya and Niya since our separation
at Khotan, was as satisfactory as I could hope for.   Local
help, too, was forthcoming with a will from the small oasis,
thanks largely to the influence still possessed there by
Ibrahim Beg, who had been in charge of Niya for two

years after my former journey. Last, but not least, there
was information about fresh ruins discovered in the vicinity
of the old site.

From Ibrahim, "the miller," my old guide, who had
first come upon inscribed tablets there, I learned that
a party of Niya villagers and ' Kalandars,' or religious
mendicants, from Imam Ja'far Sadik, stimulated, no doubt,
by the success of my previous explorations, had gone out
in the winter of 1902 to search at the ' Kone-shahr ' for
' treasure.' The hoped-for gold did not reward their enterprise; but in the course of several days' roaming some of
the adventurers had come upon ruins which were described
as situated a day's march to the north-east of those I had
been able to sight and explore. Ibrahim himself had been
tempted back into the desert two years before my return,
and striking westward had traced a large group of ' old
houses ' hidden away among sand-hills some miles beyond
the western edge of the area previously surveyed. It was
gratifying to hear that on both occasions prolonged snowfall had kept the treasure-seeking parties from any serious
attempt at burrowing into the ruins.

Guided by this information, I decided to take with me
as large a band of labourers as my available iron tanks and
goat-skins would allow me to keep supplied with water, and
to push on excavations rapidly. All of the diggers who
had accompanied me on my first expedition and were still
at Niya, a dozen in number, joined again at the shortest
notice. What with the example set by my ' old guard,'
the prospect of fair pay, and the assurance derived from
the arrangements of my first expedition, the rapid recruit-
ment of nearly forty additional men was accomplished without much difficulty. Muhammad Yusuf, the Beg of Niya,
a pleasant old man, worked hard to procure within a single
day's halt all the supplies and additional camels needed.
He proved a relation of Islam Beg of Kara-kash, and,
having heard of the latter's promotion through my good
offices, was doubly eager to help. What, as a new arrival
at Niya, he lacked in local knowledge was amply made up
by Ibrahim Beg. The gratified looks of the villagers, who
thronged to my camp to welcome Ibrahim Beg back again

in their midst, were proof of the good name left behind by his administration.

By such willing help and dint of friendly pressure the 15th of October sufficed to collect the duly equipped column of diggers, together with a month's supplies for them and my own men.   I took care to include among the labourers a few carpenters and leather-workers who, besides wielding the Ketman, could give professional help in regard to packing-cases, repairs of water-skins, and the like (Fig. 81). The camels arrived with the baggage that evening ; and after making a depot of all boxes, etc., not actually needed I was able to start northward next morning.

The three marches which brought me to where the Niya River dies away beyond Imam Ja'far Sadik's Mazar, lay through the broad jungle belt described in my former narrative.   But the difference of the season materially affected the landscape.   When I had passed here before, the trees of the luxuriant forest tract stood in wintry bareness, and snow covered all shaded ground.   Now the whole of the jungle was glowing in brilliant autumn tints.   The leafy Toghraks, in their short-lived splendour of bright yellow and red, made a delightful setting to the broad reaches covered with golden reeds, which, moved by a pleasant breeze, rose and fell like fields of ripe corn. Here and there an Eleagnus, or specially big wild poplar, still retained its green foliage, while the purple tufts of the omnipresent tamarisk bushes completed this revel of colours.

The picturesque parties of pilgrims returning from the lonely shrine of Imam Ja'far Sadik added a touch of human interest to the sylvan scenery (Fig. 82).   Most of them were cheerful Khotanliks, whom it was pleasant to talk to about people and places I knew near their homes, or to entrust with greetings for friends in the distant oasis. There was bracing freshness in the air as on a clear autumn day in Europe, and with the minimum thermometer showing 17 to 20 degrees Fahr. in the morning all trouble from heat and glare was forgotten.   Everything in nature seemed to tell that this was the season of the hunter. With long marches to be accomplished each day, and a large convoy of men and animals to look after, I could not

81. MY DIGGERS FROM NIYA IN JUNGLE NEAR ENDERE RIVER.

Ibrahim, 'the miller,' second from left, standing; next to him on right, Mullah, the carpenter; Rustam, third from right, squatting.

think of going into the forest after the game which seemed plentiful. But my little terrier was ever on the alert, chasing hares, foxes, and deer with the same unremitting energy. ' Kardash Beg's ' activity seemed to puzzle greatly the young shepherd dog whom the Surveyor had brought down from the Karanghu-tagh mountains as a travelling companion of his own.

Though the route to Imam Ja'far Sadik's shrine had not varied since I last followed it, there were conspicuous changes in the dying course of the Niya River. Already on the first march we suddenly came upon the river, and had to cross it at a point near Yoghan-toghrak, where our former survey showed it several miles away to the east. On enquiry I learned that during the summer floods of 1904 the stream had greatly altered its course. From the first I suspected that this deflection westwards would carry the river back into the clearly marked old bed which in 1901 we found completely dry. This assumption proved true by what we saw next day. The reversion of the stream had assured a fresh lease of life to the splendid forest which grows along this old bed, and which six years before seemed doomed to wither slowly away.

On the third day I sighted once more the picturesque group of Sheikhs' houses, pilgrims' shelters, and ' Ziarats,' marked by rag-decked bundles of staves, which make up the holy place of ' Padshahim,' or ' My Lord ' Imam Ja'far Sadik. Being ahead of the men and the baggage, I could find time for a visit to the bare gravel hillock which bears on its summit the supposed resting-place of that holy warrior, and on its slope the innumerable little earth-heaps intended to mark the graves of his host of fellow-martyrs. In one of the shady poplar groves at the foot, where roughly-set-up staves, meant to symbolize gates, are profusely hung with quaint collections of rags, yak-tails, and other votive offerings (Fig. 69), I came upon a queer-looking Diwana from Kashgar who had settled down to live upon the Sheikhs' charity. Along with his little son he acted as my cicerone on this pious perambulation. Like most of these devotees he showed only too plainly the effects of the Charas habit.

I did not give my men a chance of wasting time at the Sheikhs' flesh-pots, but pushed on the same day, October 18th, to the farthest point where water was obtainable. The customary sheep bought from the sacred establishment and returned to it as an offering sufficed to allay any religious scruples. The Niya men were quite content to pay their respects to the saint's tomb from across the small lake which fringes the foot of the hillock. Most of their land is held from the shrine, and I could only conjecture that, perhaps, the tithes they have to pay to the Sheikhs were not calculated to develop in them such feelings of special awe and attachment as may animate pilgrims attracted from afar.

At Tülküch-köl, four and a half miles below the Mazar, a fertile little oasis, cultivated by some fifteen men, had been cleared in the luxuriant jungle. There we pitched camp near the last of the small lakes which give to the place its name, and which the river of Niya feeds during the summer floods before finally losing itself in the sands. The filling of the four water-tanks and of most of the twenty-five goat-skins I had brought from India was accomplished in the evening. But the selection of supplies to be stored here in a depot, arrangements with the local shepherds about our ponies' grazing, etc., kept me busy far longer. In order to economize water and transport, and also to save my learned Chinese secretary weary tramps over high sands, for which his previous career had not given him physical fitness, I was obliged to leave him behind in charge of the depot.

82. KHOTAN PILGRIMS RETURNING FROM IMAM JA'FAR SADIK'S SHRINE.

83. ROW OF DEAD MULBERRY TREES IN ANCIENT ORCHARD NEAR RUIN N. XVIII., NIYA SITE.

Under first tree Naik Ram Singh with 'Dash'; to left a sand-cone with dead tamarisk.

CHAPTER XXIII

AT THE NIYA SITE RUINS

On the morning of October 20th we left behind the last abode of the living, and also the present end of the Niya River. Five camels carried the first supply of water for my column, counting in all over fifty labourers. I was bent upon moving that day as far as possible ahead towards the ancient site to which my thoughts had turned so often since those happy days of labour in the winter of 1901. Yet unexpected finds en route delayed my arrival at the ruins which had then served as familiar landmarks. I had just passed, some five miles beyond Tülküch-köl, the last deserted shepherd's hut in the gradually thinning jungle, when Ibrahim and his fellow-guides suddenly told me of some remains they had discovered since my visit among the high tamarisk-crowned sand-hills east of the route.

On reaching the hidden spot I found a small open area about 340 yards from north to south, and about half that distance across, covered with unmistakable traces of ancient avenues and fenced gardens, and much-eroded remains of some dwellings constructed in timber and plaster. Owing to far advanced erosion of the open ground around, there was no cover of sand or refuse to protect these scanty relics of ancient houses. All I could still distinguish in the least damaged of them was the foundation beams which had once borne the rush and plaster walls of several small apartments. Yet even thus my familiarity with constructive peculiarities previously observed sufficed to convince me that the remains dated back, like those of the main site ahead, to the third century A.D. Long centuries of exposure to the desert winds had left nothing for me to dig here. But the mere fact of the area of ancient occupation stretching so far south was important. In any case there was the joyful sensation of finding myself once more among the shrivelled trunks of poplars and fruit trees which had flourished when there was still an Imperial Rome.

After regaining the route we again passed for more than a mile through a belt of big living Toghraks. Most of them, by the size of their trunks and their much-fissured bark, seemed of great age, and plenty of dead trees were lying in the thickets between them. Here and there I caught sight of a narrow and tortuous channel emerging from the sand, probably cut by the last summer flood which the dying river had succeeded in pushing out to this border area of dead and living forest. But that may have been centuries ago, since the great depth to which such large specimens of the wild poplar are known to send down their roots would make them independent of occasional surface watering. We had left these trees with their bright-coloured foliage behind us, and wound our way for a mile north-westwards through a sombre maze of tamarisk-covered conical sand-hills, when I found myself once more at the spot where rows of completely bleached trunks of poplars and mulberry trees, much splintered yet upright, mark an ancient orchard or farm-yard already noticed in 1901. The sand here seemed now less heavy, and for a distance of some sixty yards I could follow the line of ancient trees planted at regular intervals.

From here the route followed by Saduk, the shepherd guide from the Mazar, who had marched ahead with the water-carrying camels, seemed to strike slightly more west-wards than the one I had taken in 1901. After less than half a mile it emerged, to my surprise, upon a small open plain, about 300 yards long from south-east to north-west, where, by the side of bare, eroded ground strewn with hard débris, substantial rush-built fences and avenues of poplars could clearly be traced in the low sand. Near the centre of this area a small plateau rising island-like above the eroded ground bore the remains of a house, constructed partly of the familiar timber and plaster walls and partly of mere rush walls once covered with clay. The walls nowhere stood more than two feet above the original mud floor, and the rooms traceable were all small.

Yet even ruins of such a modest description had before yielded interesting finds, and chance willed it that the experience should repeat itself here. The few labourers with me had scarcely begun to clear the corner of a small room only eight feet square, as a kind of experimental scraping, when there emerged several well-preserved wooden tablets inscribed in that ancient Indian Kharoshthi script, and of the curious type with which my former excavations had rendered me familiar. I greeted these remains of ancient correspondence yielded up by so humble an abode with real joy. They held out cheering promise at the outset, and also furnished the conclusive proof I was looking out for that this area, fully four miles south of the first ruins reached in 1901, held remains belonging to the same period.

The need of marching my caravan that day as close as possible to the large group of ruins reported by Ibrahim forced me to tear myself away from this encouraging find-place. Nor could I do more than rapidly survey a group of ancient houses upon which we came three-quarters of a mile ahead. They had remained hidden by a line of high tamarisk-covered cones from the more easterly route previously followed. It was strange to see old, but still amply-leafed Toghraks growing here and there near these ruins. Most of their companions were dead, and raised their gaunt trunks and branches in varied states of decay. There could be little doubt that this jungle, now approaching extinction, had grown up long after the dunes had overrun the deserted ancient settlement. But as I looked upon these patriarchs, still flourishing at their crowns, however splintered and fissured their trunks, I felt respect for them too. What struggles against constant aridity and the extremes of the desert climate these last outposts of the riverine jungle must have passed through!

After a weary tramp of another three miles we passed the two large residences which were the southernmost of those explored in 1901. It was true comfort to see that the years since passed had dealt gently with the ruins. Scarcely a detail in the state of erosion or in the decay of their timber differed from the picture as recorded in my photographs and in my memory. Only a few inches of sand covered the large wood-carvings which I had found in the 'Ya-mên' along with the ancient chair, and which I had been obliged to leave behind. Rapidly I pushed on northward to where the brick structure of a small Stupa had formed my first landmark. The winds appeared to have cleared much of the treble base then hidden under drift sand; but there was no time for closer examination.

The long shadows of the evening made the high swelling dunes to the north-west look doubly imposing. Yet I managed to drag my straggling column onwards for close on two miles before falling darkness compelled us to halt. From my detailed map of the site I knew that we were now close to some ruins which I had sighted on the last day of my previous stay, and had then reluctantly been obliged to leave unexcavated as a reserve for another visit. While my tent was being pitched, I set out to find them, and soon set foot amidst their sand-buried timber (Fig. 91). The distance and other difficulties overcome made me feel like a pilgrim who has reached his sacred goal after long months of wandering. At the ruin I had struck, a large wooden bracket, decorated with carvings in Gandhara style, lay exposed on the surface. As I sat on it listening to the great silence around me, and thought of the life which seventeen hundred years ago had thronged this ground, now disputed only by the rival forces of drift sand and erosion, I enjoyed the happiest moments of rest I could wish for that evening.

Next morning I divided my party. Ram Singh, the Surveyor, was despatched north-eastward with three camels and an adequate supply of water to search for the ruins which Islam Akhun, a Niya villager, had offered to show at the distance of one march from the site as we knew it.

84. NORTH ROOMS OF RUIN N. XIII, NIYA SITE, AFTER EXCAVATION.

In foreground remains of ancient household furniture and implements. The photograph shows the construction of wall with timber framework and wattled matting.

He was then to push due north into the desert as far as he could in a day without exhausting the camels. I myself with the rest of my column tramped on under Ibrahim's guidance over the high sands to the north-north-west, in quest of the ruined dwellings upon which my old guide had lighted in his wanderings two years previously. Progress was slow over the steep dunes closely packed amidst a maze of tamarisk-covered sand-cones, and it took fully an hour before I reached the nearest of these ruins. It proved that of a timber-built dwelling, half covered by a big dune, just beyond the line to which living tamarisk scrub extended.

Marching on over absolutely bare dunes for another two miles, I passed one after another of the ancient houses reported. They lay in a line along what must have been the extreme north-western extension of a canal once fed by the Niya River. The line proved to be situated only about two miles to the west and north-west of the northernmost ruin we had been able to trace in 1901. But the swelling ridges of sand intervening had then kept them from view. For my camp I selected a patch of open eroded ground near the northern end of the ruins, and lost no time in commencing my day's work at the farthest ruined structure we could trace.

It was a comparatively small dwelling covered only by three to four feet of sand, and just of the right type to offer an instructive lesson to Naik Ram Singh and the men (Fig. 84). It occupied a narrow tongue of what, owing to the depression produced around by wind erosion, looked like high ground, extending in continuation of the line of a small irrigation canal still marked by fallen rows of dead poplars. As soon as the floor was being reached in the western end room, Kharoshthi documents on wood began to crop out in numbers. After the first discovery of a 'Takhta' had been duly rewarded on the spot with some Chinese silver pieces, I had the satisfaction of seeing in each of the three living-rooms of the house specimen after specimen of this ancient record in Indian language and script emerge from where the last dweller, probably a petty official, about the middle of the third century A.D., had left behind his 'waste paper.'

Rectangular tablets, of the official type, with closely fitting wooden covers serving as envelopes ; double wedge-shaped tablets, as used ordinarily for short demi-official communications ; oblong boards and labels of wood containing records and accounts of all kinds, were all represented among the remains of this first ruin.

The men soon learned to scrape the sand near the floor in the approved fashion and, content with announcing their finds, to leave the careful removal of them to me. Familiar as my previous explorations at the site had made me with the outward shapes of these records, I could not help feeling emotion, when I convinced myself on cleaning them from the fine sand adhering, that a number of the rectangular and wedge-shaped letter tablets still retained intact their original string fastenings, and a few even their seal impressions in clay (Fig. 95). How delighted I was to discover on them representations of Eros and a figure probably meant for Hermes, left by the impact of classical intaglios! To be greeted once more at these desolate ruins in the desert by tangible links with the art of Greece and Rome seemed to efface all distance in time and space.

Equally familiar to me were the household implements which this ruin yielded (Fig. 85). Remains of a wooden chair decorated with elaborate carvings in Graeco-Buddhist style, weaving instruments, a boot-last, a large eating tray, mouse-trap, etc., were all objects I could with my former experience recognize at the first glance, while the various methods employed in building the plaster and timber walls could be demonstrated at once for the practical instruction of Naik Ram Singh. In spite of the wind-erosion which had lowered the adjoining ground to a depth of fifteen feet below the original level and destroyed a portion of the structure, the kitchen and the remains of out-offices and rush-wall enclosures were still traceable.

Laden with the spoils of these first few hours' work, we retraced our steps in the afternoon to the ruins of a far larger structure quite close to our camping-place. Here the walls and any objects which may have once been left between them proved completely eroded, though the

85. REMAINS OF HOUSEHOLD FURNITURE AND IMPLEMENTS (3RD CENTURY A.D.),
EXCAVATED IN RUIN N. XIII., NIYA SITE.

A. Eating-tray with ornamented border. B. Decorated double bracket and jar. C. Pitchfork and mouse-trap.

86. ROOM EXCAVATED IN RUIN N. XXVI., NIYA SITE, WITH ANCIENT CARVED CUPBOARD
IN WOOD.

massive posts, bleached and splintered, still rose high, marking the position of the timber framework. But when I examined the ground underneath what appeared to have been an outhouse or stables about fifty feet square, I realized quickly that it was made up of the layers of a huge refuse heap. Previous experience supplied sufficient reason for digging into this unsavoury quarry; though the pungent smells which its contents emitted, even after seventeen centuries of burial, were doubly trying in the fresh eastern breeze, driving fine dust, dead microbes, and all into one's eyes, throat, and nose.

Our perseverance in cutting through layer upon layer of stable refuse was rewarded at last by striking, on a level fully seven feet below the surface, a small wooden enclosure about eight by six feet and over five feet high, which had probably served as a dustbin for some earlier habitation. In the midst of coarser refuse, mixed up with various grains, we found there curious sweepings of all sorts—rags of manifold fabrics in silk, wool, cotton, and felt; pieces of a woollen pile carpet, embroidered leather and felt, plaited braids and cords, arrow-heads in bronze and iron, fragments of fine lacquer ware, broken implements in wood and horn. But more gratifying still was a find of over a dozen small label-like wooden slips inscribed with Chinese characters of exquisite penmanship, which Chiang-ssŭ-yeh's subsequent interpretation made out to be forwarding notes of various presents (Fig. 119, I, II).

But it was only through the scholarly analysis and translation furnished to me years later by M. Chavannes, my learned Sinologist collaborator, that I became aware of the special antiquarian interest attaching to these small records. He has shown that not less than eight among them were originally fastened to presents consisting of a jewel which members of the royal family made to each other, or received from their subjects, perhaps on occasion of the New Year. On one side of the slip the donor inscribed his name and the mention of his present and good wishes, on the other the name or title of the recipient is indicated. In one case it is the mother of the king who presents her gift and salutations to her son; in another the wife of the hereditary prince sends them to one of the king's wives, etc.

Most of these 'royal' personages are designated by name; but seeing that they probably belonged to the family of some small local chief ruling over but a few oases, it seems doubtful whether they will ever be identified from Chinese historical records. In the meantime it is interesting to find that one of the royal wives is described as 'the princess from Chü-mo,' the territory which, as we shall see, corresponds to the present Charchan, some ten marches away to the north-east. Was it from the large residence not far off and, unfortunately, thoroughly eroded that these quaint relics of a royalty as yet unrecorded found their way into this dustbin? Or did the latter, before it was covered up by stable refuse, belong to a more imposing structure of an earlier period which had completely disappeared?

Quite at the bottom of the enclosure there turned up a small heap of corn, still in sheaves and in perfect preservation, and close to it the mummified bodies of two mice which death had overtaken while nibbling at this store.

The clearing of these rubbish deposits continued during part of the second day of my stay, but even before it was finished the number of available men had enabled me to commence the excavation of the chain of smaller ruins stretching south, Naik Ram Singh supervising. When I was free to bring the whole of my men to this task the progress was as rapid as I could wish. Some of the dwellings had suffered a good deal from erosion, and within their broken walls but little sand had accumulated. Others had been better protected, and the clearing of the high sand which filled their rooms, in one or two instances to the very ceiling, cost efforts (Fig. 88). But the men wielded their Ketmans with surprising perseverance, and Ibrahim Beg's rough-humoured exhortations, together with the encouragement of small rewards paid for the first finds of value in each structure, sufficed to keep them hard at work for ten to eleven hours daily. The making of exact plans and the record of all observations and finds held me busy even longer.

87. RUIN OF SAND-BURIED DWELLING, N. XX., NEAR NORTHERN END OF NIYA SITE,
BEFORE EXCAVATION.

Trunks of dead mulberry trees in foreground.

88. ROOM IN RUINED DWELLING, N. XX., NIYA SITE, IN COURSE OF EXCAVATION.

Kharoshthi records on wood, whether letters, accounts, drafts, or memos, turned up in almost every one of these dwellings, besides architectural wood-carvings, household objects, and wooden implements illustrative of everyday life and domestic industries, such as weaving instruments and boot-lasts (Fig. 86). Though nothing of intrinsic value had been left behind by the last dwellers of this modest Pompeii, there was sufficient evidence of the ease in which they had lived, in the number of individual rooms provided with fireplaces and comfortable sitting platforms (Fig. 89). Remains of fenced gardens and of avenues of poplars or fruit trees could be traced almost invariably near the houses. In some cases where dunes had afforded protection, the gaunt, bleached trunks in these orchards, chiefly mulberry trees, still stood upright as high as ten to twelve feet (Fig. 83). Elsewhere they lay prostrate, or only the stumps survived, as in the case of the big poplars which had once lined an oblong tank near the southernmost of these dwellings, and the positions of which I could still accurately trace at the foot of a big tamarisk cone.

With so much of these ancient homesteads in almost perfect preservation it was soon easy to feel quite at home in them. No great efforts of imagination were needed to restore their original appearance, and consequently there was no sensation of awe to impress one. Being constantly reminded of identical features in modern Turkestan houses, I often caught myself wanting in antiquarian reverence for these relics of a past buried for nearly seventeen centuries.

But what at first fascinated me most was the absolute barrenness and the wide vistas of the desert around me. The ruins at the northern end of the site stretch beyond the zone of living tamarisk scrub. Like the open sea the expanse of yellow dunes lay before me, with nothing to break their wavy monotony but the bleached trunks of trees or the rows of splintered posts marking houses which rose here and there above the sand crests (Fig. 87). The feeling of being in an open sea was ever present, and more than once those remains seen from a distance curiously suggested the picture of a wreck reduced to the mere ribs of its timber. There was the fresh breeze, too, and the great silence of the ocean.

For the first few days I found it difficult to confine my thoughts to the multifarious tasks which claimed me, and not to listen inwardly to the Sirens' call from the desert northward. How joyful it seemed to be free for pushing farther and farther into that unknown waste beyond the last dunes on the horizon ! Though a number of matter-of-fact observations did not allow my archaeological con-science to indulge in dreams of 'buried cities' far away to the north, nevertheless I was longing to leave behind all *impedimenta* and cares for a long plunge into the sand ocean.

I felt this temptation more than ever when, on the second evening after my arrival, I marched under Ibrahim's guidance across the dunes south-eastwards in order to visit the northernmost ruins explored in 1901, and to test the position of my new camp by their distance and bearing. It was a gloriously clear evening, and the colour effects of the red light diffused over the semi-lunes of yellow sand were quite bewitching. I had just reached my goal when my guide's keen eyes discovered the Surveyor's camels steering towards us. On this great expanse of uniformly high dunes even the figure of a man standing on the crest makes a landmark. When Ram Singh had joined me I learned with some dismay that the guidance of Islam Akhun, the Niya villager who had offered to show ruins newly discovered away to the east, had failed completely.

He persisted in marching northward in manifest contra-diction to his own previous indications, and when no ruins of any sort were met with after a long day's march, confessed to having lost his bearings. He then on the next day endeavoured to pick up some guiding points by steering south-eastwards. But his confusion became so manifest in the end that the Surveyor thought it prudent to head again for my camp before the camels, which showed signs of exhaustion, broke down. Ram Singh on this Odyssey had reached a point fully thirteen miles farther north than my last camp of 1901, and his testimony as to the complete absence of ancient structural remains in that direction

89. RUIN OF LARGE SAND-BURIED HOUSE, N. XXVI, NIYA SITE, IN COURSE OF EXCAVATION.

Foot measure on left against fire-place.

helped greatly to keep me to the ample antiquarian tasks in hand and before me. Curiously enough, though the dunes were steadily rising, the Surveyor had found at his northernmost camp a group of living Toghraks, evidence, perhaps, of the subsoil water from the Niya River coming nearer to the surface there than over the greater part of the ancient site.

It seemed highly probable that Islam Akhun, like his great namesake, the Khotan forger of happy memory, had indulged in romancing. Yet his statement as to ruins to the east of those previously explored by me could not be left untested merely because he had chosen a wrong bearing. So next morning Ibrahim, with two enterprising companions and a goat-skin full of water, was sent out to reconnoitre independently eastward. I myself had advanced so far with the clearing of the ruined dwellings in the north-western group that I could avail myself of the camels bringing the first fresh convoy of water to shift my camp farther south on the fourth day. Three camels were not enough to move all baggage and food supplies; but, fortunately, there was the large band of labourers to fall back upon. So they dragged what loads the camels could not carry to the ruin which was on the day's programme, and when we had cleared it by the evening, shouldered the heavy loads again without a murmur and marched on with them to the new camp. It was quite dark when we reached it, and I sat long by the blazing fire fed with ancient timber before all the men had come in and my tent could be pitched.

CHAPTER XXIV

RECORDS FROM A HIDDEN ARCHIVE

For my new camp I had chosen the group of ruins on the extreme west edge of the site which on my previous visit had been discovered too late for systematic exploration. For the sake of them I had wished ever since to return to the site, and I soon had gratifying proof that these remains I had so long kept *in petto*, as it were, deserved my faithful remembrance. From a small and almost completely eroded structure to the south of the group nearly three dozen official letters on wood were recovered during the early morning of October 24th, besides interesting pieces of lacquer and basket-work in what looked like bamboo.

Encouraged by these finds I next turned my men to the large ruined residence situated nearest to the dwelling N. xii., with which my excavations of 1901 had concluded (Fig. 90). Here a rich haul awaited me such as I had scarcely ventured to hope for. Already when clearing the rooms north of the large central hall I had come upon some fine pieces of wood-carving (Fig. 92), including an architrave in excellent Gandhara style, which proved that the dwelling must have been that of a well-to-do person. His having been an official of some consequence was suggested by the fact that a long and narrow apartment to the east of the hall, and communicating with it by a series of panelled windows, once probably closed with lattice work, yielded finds of well-preserved Kharoshthi records on wood of respectable size, including a tablet measuring fully three feet in length, and bearing on both sides what seemed to be drafts for various letters.

The hope of finding more in his office was soon justified

90. RUIN OF ANCIENT RESIDENCE, N. XXIV., NIYA SITE, SEEN FROM REMAINS
OF DEAD ARBOUR ON EAST.

91. DOOR WITH ORNAMENTAL WOOD-CARVING IN SAND-BURIED RUIN OF DWELLING
N. XII., NIYA SITE.

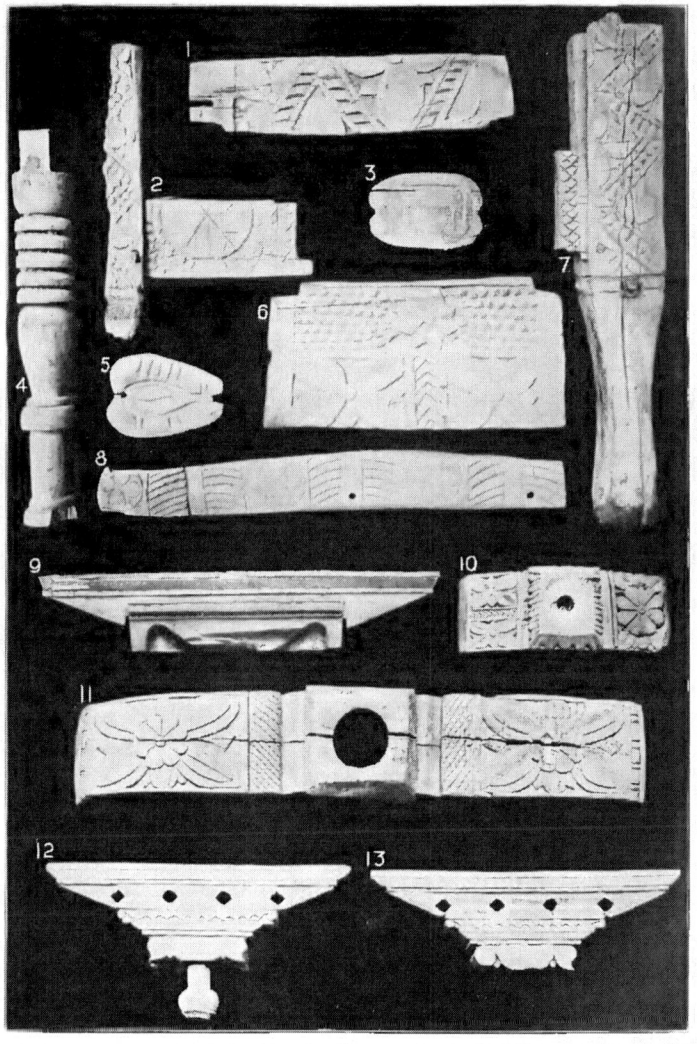

92. REMAINS OF ORNAMENTAL WOOD-CARVING, MAINLY FROM RUINS OF
NIYA SITE.

Scale, one-seventh for Nos. 1-8; one-sixteenth for Nos. 9-13.

1, 2, 6, 7, 8. Portions of cupboard decorated in Gandhara style. 3, 5. Wooden stamps with ornamental designs. 4. Turned leg of chair or cupboard. 10, 11. Double brackets or architraves with floral ornament in Gandhara style. 9, 12, 13. Architraves of later design from ruins at and near Khadalik.

when the first strokes of the Ketman laid bare regular files of documents on wood near the floor of a room about twenty-six by twelve feet adjoining the central hall on the south (Fig. 93). Most of them were 'wedges,' such as were used for the conveyance of executive orders ; others, on oblong tablets, were accounts, lists, and miscellaneous 'office papers,' to use an anachronism. Evidently we had hit upon files from an official's 'Daftar' thrown down here, and excellently preserved under the cover of sand which even now lay five to six feet deep. In rapid succession over threescore documents of these kinds were recovered here within a few square feet, and a subsequent careful search of the rest of the room added to the number. Some emerged from the top of the mud-flooring, having been thrown into corners and below the walls probably long before the abandonment.

The scraping of the floor was still proceeding when a strange discovery rewarded honest Rustam, the most experienced and trusted digger of my 'old guard.' Already during the first clearing I had noticed a large lump of clay or plaster, looking like a fragment of a broken wall, close to the north wall of the room just where the packets of tablets lay closest. I had ordered it to be left undisturbed, though I thought but little of its having come to that place by more than accident. Now when Rustam extracted between it and the wall a well-preserved double wedge, still retaining its clay seal and fastening, I could not prevent its removal ; and scarcely had this been effected when I saw him eagerly burrow with his hands into the floor thus laid bare, just as when my little terrier is at work opening rat-holes. Before I could put any question, I saw Rustam triumphantly draw forth, from about six inches below the floor, a complete rectangular document with its double seal intact and its envelope still unopened (Fig. 94). Rustam's fingers now worked with feverish energy at enlarging the hole, and soon we saw that the space towards the wall and below the foundation beam of the latter was full of closely packed layers of similar documents.

It was clear that we had struck a hidden archive, and my excitement at this novel experience was great ; for, apart from the interest of the documents themselves and their splendid preservation, the condition in which they were found was bound to furnish valuable indications. I had to master my impatience in order to have the ground in front opened out so as to permit safe and orderly removal of the tablets, and when this had been done darkness came on long before I could extract the whole of the records which lay exposed below the wall. As one large rectangular double tablet after another passed through my hands and was cleared of the adhering layer of dust, I noted with special satisfaction that with one or two exceptions they all had their elaborate string fastenings unopened and sealed down on the envelope in the regular fashion.

It was not only the state of perfect preservation of these documents and their value as fresh materials for the study of the language and the conditions of the period which delighted me. What pleased me equally was the manifest confirmation they afforded of a conjectural explanation I had arrived at in the case of a few previous finds of this kind. Several considerations had led me to suppose that these were agreements or bonds which had to be kept under their original fastening in order that in case of need their validity might be established in court. As long as the clay seal impressed in the centre of the covering tablet, and the string passing under it and holding the under and covering tablets tightly together, remained unbroken, all chance of tampering with the text written on the inner surfaces was precluded. Here was a large series of documents exactly in the same condition, carefully hidden away as deeds, bonds, and the like would be, and all of them bearing docketings which were clearly not of the usual address style. Were they deeds or agreements which the official residing in the house had in safe keeping, or did they refer to land or property of his own?

Only a full decipherment of the documents, not to be hoped for till years hence, could give the answer. But in the meantime I noted that the very exceptions seemed to support my conjecture. For when late that evening I examined the two letters on wood which alone in the

93. CENTRAL HALL AND OFFICE ROOM IN RUINED RESIDENCE N. XXIV., NIYA SITE, AFTER EXCAVATION.

A marks spot where hidden archive was discovered below floor; on the right of it Rustam, the digger

whole series had turned up open, I found that both were
private letters addressed in due form to the Honourable
Cojhbo Sojaka, 'whose sight is dear to gods and men.'
That this worthy officer had resided in the house I had
already ascertained, from the address invariably borne by
the office orders on the wedge-shaped tablets which
had come to light in such numbers during the afternoon
from above the floor of the same room. I wondered what
the contents of those two letters might have been to induce
Cojhbo Sojaka to keep them along with the deeds, etc., as
papers of value.

I felt like a real 'treasure-seeker' as I extracted in the
growing dusk, and later on by the light of a candle, one
wooden document after another. But as the operation
required much care in order to save the clay sealings from
any risk of damage, I realised that my task could not be
finished that night. So in order to protect the deposit
against any attempt at clandestine digging on the part of
the men who might be tempted to look in such a hiding-
place for objects of more intrinsic value than mere wooden
'Khats,' I had the excavation in the floor carefully filled
up again. Over the opened space I then placed my little
camp table topsy-turvy, and by tying its legs with string
to the wall posts and sealing the fastenings, I produced a
sort of wire entanglement which the cleverest poacher
could not have removed without betraying himself. Honest
Ibrahim Beg was made to mount guard over the treasures
still left behind for the night. He had to sleep in Sojaka's
old office room, and as no fire could be lit from fear
of igniting the timber framework so brittle and dry, I
fear that my Beg had to pass a cold night. Our minimum temperatures were already ranging about 18 degrees
Fahrenheit.

As I put the seals on to the entanglement with my
electrotype reproduction of a beautiful gold coin of
Diodotos, the first Bactrian Greek king, showing Zeus
hurling the thunderbolt, I thought how victoriously the
art of the Greek die-cutter had survived all the vicis-
situdes of the ages. It was true, too, at this distant
and strangely desolate site. For when at night I came

to clear the clay sealings on the documents which I had carried away to my tent carefully wrapped up, I discovered that almost all remained as fresh as when first impressed, and that most of them were from intaglios of classical workmanship representing Pallas Promachos, Heracles with club and lion-skin, Zeus, and helmeted busts (Fig. 95).

The fact that the majority of these tablets bore in the sunk socket of their covers or envelopes the impressions of two, or in a few cases even three, seals strongly supported the assumption of their containing agreements or bonds executed before witnesses. Among the tablets with single seal impressions there were two showing the official title of the Chinese commander at Shan-shan or Lop-nor in Chinese lapidary characters (Fig. 95, 6). The importance attached to the preservation of the sealings was illustrated by the silk wraps found tied closely for protection over the clay-filled seal sockets of several tablets.

The clearing resumed early next morning brought the total number of perfectly preserved documents close up to three dozen, by far the largest series of complete records which any of the ruins had yielded. I wondered when the time would come for having the strings cut which still fastened them as securely as when they were first sealed down. It was strange to find myself the *de facto* possessor of Sojaka's deeds probably referring to lands and other real property. True enough, they had all lain buried for centuries under the silent dunes or those sombre sand-cones covered with tangled tamarisk scrub dead or dying. Yet so fond had I become of this great dead waste, fascinating and peaceful, that I should have felt sorely tempted to assert legal claims to any part of it, had there been but an Amban ready to read 'my' deeds and recognize their validity !

The circumstances in which these documents had come to be buried were, as I recognized from the first, deserving of the closest consideration ; for it was evident that they might throw light on the important question as to how this settlement was deserted. The care which had been taken to hide the deposit and at the same time to mark its

94. KHAROSHTHI DOCUMENT ON RECTANGULAR DOUBLE TABLET, FROM
HIDDEN ARCHIVE IN N. XXIV.

Scale, one-half.

A. Double tablet fastened and sealed.   B. Obverse of under-tablet.   C. Reverse of covering tablet.

position—for that, no doubt, was the purpose of the clay lump, as Rustam had guessed when he started his burrowing—plainly showed that the owner, Cojhbo Sojaka, in all probability, or his heir, had been obliged to leave the place in an emergency, but with a hope of returning. The absence of any provision for a covering or receptacle to protect these valued records while buried clearly suggested hurried departure, an indication with which the scattered condition of the other files of tablets left above the floor close by well agreed.

In any case it seemed difficult to account otherwise for such a *cache* and the method of marking its place. If the hole below the foundation beam had been used regularly as a sort of safe, some receptacle would have been provided, and it would scarcely have been necessary to mark its position in so obvious a fashion as long as its existence was remembered. If, on the other hand, the departure of the owner had been connected with a systematic abandonment of the site caused by a gradual failing of the irrigation water-supply through desiccation, we should have expected this collection of specially valued records to be removed with other cherished possessions, neither bulk nor weight presenting any difficulty.

It would be useless now to conjecture what particular emergency gave occasion for this hurried deposit; nor can we ever hope to learn what prevented the owner's return. But so much is certain, that a re-occupation of the settlement must have subsequently become impossible through the action of that great physical change, desiccation, which has so widely affected the scene of man's struggle with the desert all along the Taklamakan. This change, however, was gradual, and did not prevent the abandoned site from being visited and exploited during centuries before the sands finally covered up its dwellings. They must have continued to be searched, probably from the very time of the abandonment, for any objects of value or practical utility left behind. And so it was scarcely surprising that when we completed the clearing of Sojaka's residence on October 25th, some wooden utensils, such as a plainly carved cupboard and a four-footed large eating-tray, earthenware jars, remains of a few farmyard implements and of rugs, were the only spoil added to that plentiful harvest of inscribed tablets.

The value of the rich haul of ancient records we had made in this ruin (N. XXIV.) lay not merely in the number of individual documents, but even more, perhaps, in the remarkable state of preservation which almost all of them showed. The labours of my friend Professor E. J. Rapson, who, aided by two distinguished French confrères, MM. Senart and Boyer, undertook the decipherment and partial publication of the Kharoshthi materials brought back from my first journey, have revealed only too clearly the serious difficulties presented both by their script and their language. The obscurities arising from the very cursive form of Kharoshthi writing, otherwise known to us only from inscriptions and coins of the Indian North-West, have proved scarcely less troublesome than those due to the use of an early Prakrit dialect which differs considerably from the forms represented in Indian literature. The fact, recognized from the first, that we have in these inscribed tablets of the Niya site mainly official records or correspondence dealing with the *menus détails* of local administration and daily life, was bound to increase greatly the difficulties of interpretation.

In order to overcome these difficulties with a good chance of ultimate success, my philological collaborators needed further materials, and in particular an adequate supply of complete documents in which the state of preservation should leave no room for uncertainty as to the actually inscribed characters. The finds made in the course of my renewed explorations at this site supply such materials in plenty. But the necessity of first concentrating their efforts upon the publication of the Kharoshthi records already in hand has so far prevented Professor Rapson and his fellow-savants from giving any detailed analysis of the contents of the documents newly recovered. I must therefore content myself here with a rapid sketch of the most curious features in the 'wooden stationery' on which they are written, and with hints as to what the progress of elucidation is likely to reveal about their subject matter.

95. CLAY IMPRESSIONS OF INTAGLIO SEALS ON KHAROSHTHI DOCUMENTS
FOUND AT NIYA SITE.

Scale, two-thirds.

1, 2, 4. Impressions from classical seals showing figures of Pallas Promachos, Hermes, Zeus, and a bearded head. 3, 5. From Oriental seals showing classical influence. 6. From seal of Chinese commander at Shan-shan, in Chinese lapidary characters.

In the case of the wedge-shaped tablets forming so large a portion of the records brought to light, a series of complete 'double wedges' found intact under their original seal and fastening afford the clearest possible illustration of the manner in which documents of this class were used and despatched (Fig. 96). A pair of pieces of wood, pointed at one end and cut off square at the other, were fitted exactly to match each other. There is evidence that the carpenter engaged in producing this kind of stationery usually facilitated his task by first shaping the 'double wedge' as a whole, and then separating its two pieces by sawing or splitting. The under tablet of the pair was made quite flat, and received on its smoothed obverse the text, arranged in lines parallel to the upper long side of the wedge and never exceeding four in number. The upper or covering tablet rested on it as a kind of envelope to protect the writing, which could be continued on the reverse of the upper tablet whenever the length of the communication required it.

The wood of the upper tablet was kept thicker near the square end, and in this raised portion of its outside surface a square socket was neatly cut for the purpose of holding a clay seal impression. A hole drilled through both pieces near the pointed end received the string that was to unite the pair of tablets. The ingenious method used for fastening this string of hemp is best illustrated by the diagrams of Mr. F. H. Andrews' drawing in my *Ancient Khotan*. After having been passed through the string-hole of both tablets and drawn tight by means of a cleverly devised running loop, the string was drawn towards the seal-socket near the square end of the double wedge. There it was laid in regular cross folds over the seal-socket, three grooves cut through the edges of the latter serving to hold it in position. The socket was then filled with clay covering the folds, and the signet seal of the sender impressed into the clay. Subsequently the pair of tablets could be separated only by either breaking the clay of the sealing or by cutting the string.

By the ingenious arrangement here briefly indicated the communication written on the inner surfaces of the pair of tablets was completely protected against any attempt at unauthorized inspection or tampering before delivery to the addressee. The latter, after satisfying himself that the seal impression was intact, could get access to the contents either by cutting the string near the string-hole, and then sliding out the under tablet from the folds of string running beneath the seal, or else by severing these folds. In the former case he retained a convenient fastening for the two pieces, being able to pass the under tablet back again into its original position, as we can still do now with a number of double wedges first opened many centuries ago. The name and title of the addressee are invariably shown to the right of the seal cavity on the obverse of the covering tablet, while a corresponding entry found ordinarily on the reverse of the under tablet records the name of the messenger or other person entrusted with the document.

Curiously enough none of the wedge-shaped double tablets so far deciphered seems to bear a distinct indication of the sender. But this peculiarity, so strange at first sight, becomes intelligible in the light of what information is already available about the general character and contents of these missives. Their official origin was made clear to me from the first by the introductory formula found invariably at the commencement: *Mahanuava maharaya lihati*, " His Excellency the Maharaja orders in writing." Since then the researches of Professor Rapson and his collaborators have brought out the fact that the wedge-shaped double tablets were generally, if not always, intended for the conveyance of brief orders which concerned the bearer, or in the execution of which the bearer was to co-operate. Thus all the fully translated tablets of this class prove to contain directions about the supply of transport and escort to official messengers, about aid to be given to them in certain enquiries, or for the apprehension of fugitives, etc.

It thus becomes highly probable that these ' wedges ' represent warrants issued for the purpose of accrediting persons charged with the execution of administrative orders, and of securing for them the needful assistance of the local authority. The clay impression from the seal of the superior officer sufficed to attest the order which his

26. KHAROSHTHI DOCUMENTS ON DOUBLE-WEDGE TABLETS FROM RUIN N. XIII. NIYA SITE.

Scale, three-sevenths.

A. Reverse of complete double-wedge tablet with fastening intact.   B. Double-wedge tablet opened after cutting string passed under clay seal.

C. Obverse of double-wedge tablet retaining seal and string intact.

messenger or agent would be expected to set forth verbally with all requisite details. Perhaps we may take it as a sign of the superior importance attached to these verbally transmitted orders that several of the double wedge tablets were discovered unopened. In the case of a well-known official messenger presenting his warrant with its seal intact, examination of the brief and formal mention of his business within the document might well have appeared superfluous.

Of the rectangular double tablets I have already had occasion to discuss the probable purport. The fact of so many of them having been found unopened and with seals intact in that hidden deposit of the ruin N. XXIV. is significant, as also is the frequency of double and treble seals impressed upon them. If such tablets were used ordinarily for agreements, contracts, bonds, or other official records intended eventually to serve as legal evidence, we can understand the care and ingenuity bestowed upon their make and method of fastening. The under tablet, as can be seen from the illustration given of a complete document (Fig. 94), was provided with a raised rim on either of the shorter sides. Between these rims fitted exactly a covering tablet, the obverse of which, in its raised centre, had a square or oblong socket for the reception of one or more clay seals. In order to assure exact fitting the pair of tablets seem always to have been cut out of one piece.

The obverse of the under tablet served for the reception of the text written in lines parallel to the longer side. Where necessary it was continued on the reverse of the covering tablet. The latter was then fastened securely to the under tablet by means of a double-stranded string passed tightly over both in successive folds, which were firmly kept in position by three grooves cut on the obverse of the covering tablet and communicating with the seal-cavity. When once the folds of string laid through the socket had been secured under a clay seal inserted there, it became quite impossible to separate the covering and under tablets without either cutting the exposed folds or completely breaking the seal. Thus any unauthorized opening of the document written on the inner sides of the two tablets or tampering with its contents was effectively prevented. At the same time it is clear that only as long as the string fastening remained intact could the seal impression on the covering tablet be appealed to as proof of the genuineness of the written contents within; for nowhere do we meet in the latter with anything that could be taken as a signature or other means of authentication.

I must refrain from touching here upon any of the fascinating questions which naturally suggest themselves in connection with finds of records such as I have just described. The area of the travels and labours which my present narrative has to cover is too great to permit space for recapitulating the conclusions to which I was led by my first explorations at this site five years earlier, and which I endeavoured to indicate in my *Sand-buried Ruins of Khotan* and subsequently to set forth more fully in *Ancient Khotan*. The elaboration of the literary remains brought back from this site has not advanced sufficiently in the interval to yield fresh details which could be discussed with advantage in a personal narrative like the present. But I may note with satisfaction that neither my later work on the spot nor the researches of my philological collaborators have disclosed any features which could throw doubt on the justness of my main conclusions of historical interest.

In the light of my new finds it can still be asserted with confidence that the ruins belong to a widely scattered agricultural settlement which flourished in the third century A.D. and was abandoned when Chinese supremacy in the Tarim Basin came to an end towards the close of that century. The essential observation still holds good, that the administration of the tract was carried on in an Indian language and script. Their use lends support to the old local tradition recorded by Hsüan-tsang which tells of Khotan having received a large portion of its early popula-tion by immigration from Takshasila, the Taxila of the Greeks, in the extreme North-West of India. But since my subsequent explorations yielded proofs of Kharoshthi

97. KHAROSHTHI RECORDS ON OBLONG AND LABEL-SHAPED WOODEN TABLETS FOUND AT NIYA SITE.

Scale, one-half.

script and Prakrit language having been known as far east as the Lop-nor region, the question will claim attention hereafter whether their far-spread use was not partly due also to the powerful influence of that Indo - Scythian dominion which during the first centuries of our era seems for a time to have brought the Tarim Basin into direct political relations with Afghanistan and the distant Indian North-West.

CHAPTER XXV

LAST DAYS AT A DEAD OASIS

THE ruin (N. XXIV.) where we had discovered the small hidden archive was adjoined eastwards by three smaller dwellings half smothered by dunes. The excavation of them, which occupied us on October 25th and 26th, was not rewarded by similarly striking finds, but revealed various interesting details of domestic architecture. In one of these dwellings, buried under fully seven or eight feet of drift sand, we came upon a fine double bracket in wood which once supported the ceiling of the main room (Fig. 98). It measured nearly nine feet in length with a height of about one and a half feet, and bore on each side well-designed carvings in bold relievo. Monsters of the composite type, which Gandhara borrowed from the West and which ancient Khotan art seems particularly to have cherished, with winged bodies, crocodiles' heads, and the legs of deer, filled the end panels. The panel in the centre showed a vase holding branches with leaves and flowers pendent, the whole arranged after the fashion of an Indo-Corinthian capital. To move this massive piece of carved timber as a whole would have been quite impracticable. So I was glad that my Sapper corporal's skill permitted me to have the panels carefully separated along the bead ornaments marking the divisions. Then the weight of each portion had to be reduced by hollowing out the core in order to make up loads which a pony could carry. The sawing was effected so neatly that I felt sure that when this fine specimen of architectural carving was set up again in the British Museum it would need skilled eyes to discover the joining.

98. ROOM EXCAVATED IN ANCIENT RESIDENCE N. XXVI. NIYA SITE. WITH DECORATED DOUBLE BRACKET IN WOOD

The room at the south-west corner of the same house was so deeply buried under a dune that it had preserved its walls and roofing practically intact. The smoke-begrimed plaster of the walls, the two outer ones of which were built of solid stamped clay, and the absence of any opening except a narrow window below the ceiling showed that it was an apartment specially affected as a warm corner during the winter months. It was, perhaps, due to the darkness which prevailed here that I found, lying on the top of the fireplace, a collection of small but perfectly preserved Kharoshthi records on wood, apparently in the main domestic accounts and memos (Fig. 97). Otherwise the room had been cleared completely. But the last occupier evidently forgot to look to the high mantelpiece which he had used as a shelf for petty 'papers.'

From this camp I also revisited the ruin containing that precious rubbish heap (N. xv.) which I had cleared with such rich rewards in 1901. My thoughts had dwelt so often from afar on this small ruin that I was relieved to find that neither the winds nor other destructive agencies had as yet worked any appreciable change. I came back with the special object of looking out for some items from that refuse heap which I remembered with some feeling of shame to have thrown aside in 1901 as valueless. They were small pieces of very hard leather, rounded at one end and peculiarly punched with holes, in which I had since learned to recognize pieces of scale armour.

I found the refuse we had cleared out still lying undisturbed by the side of the room, and my conscience felt relieved when after some careful scraping, done by Ibrahim, my old guide, an expert in such hunting, the missing scales were recovered. Another tramp over the dunes was directed to a spot about a mile northward at which Ibrahim and a companion had, while 'treasure-seeking' two years before, come upon remains of skeletons, and which they had promptly christened the 'Mazar.' There by the side of an isolated small tamarisk cone I found, indeed, unmistakable indications of an ancient cemetery—not only plentiful human bones scattered over the eroded slopes of a small plateau, but also the bleached and splintered boards which once had formed coffins. Unfortunately the force of erosion had left no intact skeleton, not even a complete skull for measurement. Were these the remains of good Buddhists who preferred to be buried instead of being committed to the pyre after the Indian fashion, or was I here facing the burial-place of some heterodox community? There was nothing to give me the answer.

While I was still at this camp a select band under Ibrahim after three days' search succeeded in tracing a number of ruined dwellings south-eastward which, hidden away amidst high and closely packed sand-cones, had escaped discovery five years before. A reconnaissance by the Surveyor had fixed their position in a line stretching east and south-east of the southernmost ruins explored in 1901, and supplied sufficient reason for shifting my camp thither on October 27th. No camels were available, and once more I had to fall back upon my labourers for the transport of the most needful camp-kit and what water we had left in tanks and skins. Then after a tiring tramp of some five miles under loads we set vigorously to work, and by the end of a second day these eight or nine dwellings with their out-houses and cattle-sheds had been searched.

Most of them were small and poorly built, as befitted the homesteads occupying what was evidently the eastern-most fringe of the ancient settlement   Others on island-like 'witnesses,' rising over ground which had been lowered by wind erosion fully twenty feet below its original level (Fig. 99), were too clear of drift sand to retain much of antiquarian value. One large ruin, how-ever, had fared better and, having evidently been occupied by a person of some consequence, yielded up Kharoshthi tablets in numbers. Fences and groves of fruit trees near it were remarkably well preserved; in one of the latter I found the bleached trunk of a mulberry tree still rising to some fourteen feet in height, while remains of thick vines lay twisted beneath the sand.

A strong north-east wind was blowing during these days, and the fine sand driven before it made the work of

99. RUINED DWELLING, N. XXVIII., ON ERODED CLAY TERRACE, NIYA SITE.

Fence of ancient garden and more erosion 'witnesses' in foreground. Figure of man in centre
indicates extent of erosion.

100. RUIN OF ANCIENT DWELLING, N. XXXVI., AT SOUTHERN END OF NIYA SITE,
IN COURSE OF EXCAVATION.

excavation very trying and the air laden with haze. As our work proceeded to the south the surroundings grew, if anything, more sombre and lugubrious, in spite of the appearance of still living scrub. The ruins had to be searched for amidst closely packed sand-cones raising their heads covered with tangled masses of tamarisk, dead or living, fully forty feet high or more. Ruins with splintered timber just emerging from the foot of sand-hills and deeply eroded ground on the other side made up a weird picture of solitude. Nowhere did I feel the desolation of the dead oasis so intensely as while wending my way through this maze of mournful tamarisk cones and searching the confined deep hollows between them, the whole shrouded in murky grey mist like a landscape in the world of the dead.

It was almost with a feeling of relief that I emerged at last upon somewhat more open ground towards the southern end of the site. Here the dunes were quite low, tamarisk scrub plentiful, and, as I had noted on the day of my arrival, living Toghraks still lingering among the far more numerous dead trees. The half-a-dozen ancient dwellings we could trace scattered in this jungle which still struggled against death, were all roughly built and of no great extent (Fig. 100). Thus a day of steady digging with the men, whom the eager hope of returning to their homes from this arid wilderness urged to extra exertions, sufficed for the clearing of them and the recovery of what modest store of Kharoshthi records they proved to contain.

The frequent appearance of thick layers of sheep-dung within what must have been living quarters was at first sight puzzling. But in the end it became evident that these ruins, long after their abandonment, had been used to shelter flocks grazing the jungle, which had grown up around them while the summer floods still reached this nearest portion of the old site. I wondered how many of the shrivelled old Toghraks still alive in their crowns were ancient enough to have seen the flocks once grazing amongst the ruins of this strange Campagna.

The last ruin was not cleared until the morning of October 30th. It was the same modest dwelling from which, on the first day of my return to the site, I had extracted three tablets. Its badly eroded remains, which also showed traces of recent burrowing, refused to yield up more than some wooden mouse-traps, carved locks, and similar domestic utensils. But a careful inspection of its surroundings, as shown by the panorama in Plate III., revealed some features of special interest. Only some sixty yards off there still stood a square of dead mulberry trees, raising their trunks up to ten feet and more, which had once cast their shade over a tank still marked by a depression. The stream from which the canal once feeding it must have taken off was not far to seek; for behind the nearest ridge of sand to the west there still lay a foot-bridge about ninety feet long, stretched across an unmistakable ancient river-bed.

The extant parts of this bridge were formed by two sets of roughly smoothed Terek trunks, each over forty feet long and sufficiently broad for foot traffic. Of the trestles which had carried the bridge two still stood upright, half buried in the dune that hid the eastern bridge-head. The trunks lay stretched out in a straight line over the slopes and the bottom of a steeply eroded Nullah some fifteen feet deep—a strange and almost uncanny memento of the distant period when a lively stream had filled the depression. Beyond the left bank stretched shrivelled remains of orchards for upwards of two hundred yards to where deep banks seemed to mark a large square reservoir. For over two miles to the north-west we could follow the traces of the ancient river-bed, in places completely covered up by drift sand, but emerging again at short intervals with steep-cut banks amongst low dunes and patches of dead forest. At times the traces were so faint that without the plain indication of the bearing furnished by the Nullah near the bridge it would have been scarcely possible to recognize them.

Finally, the winding bed seemed to join a broad valley-like depression stretching far away, with living poplars and tamarisks. There the Surveyor on an earlier reconnaissance had come across steep banks like those of a river. From the top of a sand ridge some fifty feet high the view

III.

PANORAMIC VIEW TAKEN NEAR SOUTHERN END OF NIYA SITE SHOWING REMAINS OF ANCIENT DWELLING (A), TANK WITH SURROUNDING ARBOUR (B), AND OUTBUILDINGS (C) STRETCHED ACROSS DRY RIVER-BED, ALL ABANDONED DURING THIRD CENTURY A.D.

The panorama, seen taken from the top of a tamarisk-covered sand-cone, and reads from right (S.E. field) to W. (right). In the foreground behind the ancient dwelling (N. viii.) of mud and brick (see p. xxx pp.), are seen the remains of dead trees and fences marking lines of ancient avenues and gardens. The layer of a tank mer reveal bridge (C) indicates the height of the terrace to which material beyond, half built of clay, once broke on the extreme old clink attached (?) trees which appears to have been a large structure. In the background, no single mud sand-bank, chains of Columnas tree, help slopes of tamarisk distance.

extended over miles of this strange silent valley, flanked by big 'Dawans' of dunes rising to two hundred feet or more, and looking over this flat expanse like chains of true hills. Ibrahim who stood by my side had vainly searched this great Nullah and others west of it for several marches in the hope of more ruins. Here was clearly the depression into which the flood-water of the Niya River had once been diverted below the head of the canals irrigating the ancient settlement. But certainly it had seen no water for long ages. Over all this strange ground desiccation was most plainly written.

Though the minimum temperature of the night before had fallen to 20 degrees Fahrenheit below freezing-point, the sun at mid-day shone with such force as to make the tramp across the dunes by the side of the parched-up river quite trying. So a short rest after our return to the southernmost ruin was welcome. As I sat by the side of the small tank in the shade of its bleached and splintered trees, I thought the time opportune for securing a souvenir of those who laboured with me at this oasis of the dead. So a group of my Indian helpmates, with the most familiar figures from among our Niya diggers, was quickly formed under the trees which seventeen centuries of desert storms had failed to uproot (Fig. 101). Worthy Ibrahim Beg was made to sit in the centre swinging an ancient rod, as was his wont in urging on the lagging. 'Kardash Beg,' my little terrier, who seems always happy to pose before the camera, was, of course, by my side showing his interest in the proceedings.

The ponies summoned from Tulküch-köl then met us, and the ride back to Imam Ja'far's Mazar through the forest, first dead and then gradually changing into a sylvan wilderness still alive with all the glow of autumn tints, was delightful. Never had I seen in Turkestan such blazing colours under a deep blue sky. With a feeling of respect I passed the deep 'Yars' furrowing the jungle. Might they not have seen floods that had once brought water into the distant desert valley I had toiled through that morning? The trees about Tulküch-köl seemed giants, a picture of what the dead trunks of the ancient colony may have been when their roots still drank the water of canals. An illusion which I have often enjoyed made the waving expanses of reed beds look exactly like fields of ripe corn. It was almost with a feeling of disappointment that I emerged on the bare lands actually under cultivation by worthy Nurullah, the guardian of the Mazar's flocks, and his uncouth shepherd myrmidons.

Then under a star-lit sky of exceptional brilliancy we wended our way to the holy settlement, where I pitched camp for a day's halt, needed to settle the labourers' accounts and to collect fresh supplies and transport. The night hid mercifully all that is ragged and mean about the quaint desert shrine. Yet it needed careful search, and removal to a respectful distance, to prevent my tent being pitched on the numerous fields of refuse which encircle the pious colony of priests, 'stranded' pilgrims, and professional mendicants. Even then a strange mixture of sounds from the shrine's stable-yards made me realize in the darkness that I had come back once more to the purlieus of the living.

My stay there was to be only of the shortest. The success of my excavations at the old site northward had been most cheering. But even greater, perhaps, at the time was my satisfaction at having been able to push them through so rapidly; for my thoughts were eagerly turning all the time eastwards to the Lop-nor region which was to form the true scene for the winter's explorations. The distance separating me from it was still great—some four hundred odd miles, practically all through desert—and an early arrival was important for a variety of practical reasons. There were ancient remains, too, I knew, waiting for examination *en route*.

So I almost grudged the single day's halt which, on October 31st, I was obliged to sacrifice at the Mazar to a host of urgent tasks. The majority of the Niya men, who had laboured so valiantly under trying conditions and on the scantiest of water rations but were now fairly worn out, had to be paid off to their homes. Fresh supplies, brought down from the oasis for those of them who were to remain with me and for my own party, had to be

101. TRUNKS OF DEAD TREES ENCLOSING ANCIENT TANK, NIYA SITE.

The group shows sitting on left Rai Ram Singh and Ibrahim Beg, on right Naik Ram Singh and Ibrahim 'the miller', in middle author with 'Dash.

distributed.   The new 'finds' needed careful packing in rapidly-made-up cases and, with the exception of precious Kharoshthi tablets, despatch to my Khotan depot for safe keeping.   In addition to all this, there arrived opportunely in the evening my faithful Dak carrier Turdi with the mails from Khotan, three bags full.   Small wonder that the attempt to cope with these postal accumulations kept me busy writing till about 3 A.M.   An icy east wind had sprung up that evening, and the bitter cold in my little tent made me realize that winter was already upon us.

CHAPTER XXVI

TO THE ENDERE RIVER

ON the morning of November 1st our camp separated. Ram Singh, the Surveyor, was sent south to Niya and Sorghak with instructions to resume his triangulation along the foot of the great Kun-lun range, and to carry it as far east towards Lop-nor as time and conditions would permit. The Charchan oasis, where the two available routes eastward meet, the one skirting the mountains and the other through the desert, was the nearest point where touch could be resumed between us. I myself with the rest of my party set out for the high sands due east in order to revisit the Endere tract before moving on to Charchan. In 1901 I had explored there the ruins of an ancient fort and Stupa. Time had been wanting then for a thorough survey of the whole site, and as various indications suggested the existence of other remains, my archaeological conscience would not have allowed me to forgo a fresh visit, even if the shortest route to Charchan had not led quite near. But a curious acquisition made during my stay at the Niya site supplied also a special reason.

Sadak, a young cultivator from the Mazar working with my party, had on hearing of my intended move to Endere told me of a ' Takhta ' he had come upon a year or two before while prospecting for ' treasure ' close to the old fort of Endere. When he brought it for my inspection I was surprised to find that it was a fairly well preserved under tablet of a rectangular Kharoshthi document. The writing clearly proved that it belonged to the same early period as the wooden documents of the Niya site, *i.e.* the

third century A.D.   Yet my own finds in the ruined fort
of Endere in 1901 had established the fact of this site
having been occupied at the beginning of the eighth
century A.D. and abandoned to the desert soon after.
Assuming Sadak's statement to be true—and he as well
as his father Samsak, a queer-looking old shepherd, clung
to it stoutly, in spite of all my critical questionings—there
was here an interesting archaeological puzzle which could
only be solved on the spot, and which, as I shall soon have
occasion to show, has a wide historical bearing.

The necessity of saving our hard-worked camels and
men any additional trials and risks, and also of effecting an
early junction with the heavy baggage portion left behind
at the Niya oasis, would not allow me to strike across the
desert to Endere by any other route than that explored in
1901.   So my description of these marches may be brief.
The first two led across a dreary succession of high ridges
of sand absolutely bare.   The intervening belts of level
ground, covered with scanty scrub, mostly dead and
marking ancient river-beds, were equally desolate.   All
the way we were faced by a cutting north-east wind which
kept us in a dust-laden and depressingly foggy atmosphere.
So it was not surprising that, when on the evening of
November 2nd we arrived by the dying course of the
Yar-tungaz River, all trees in the narrow jungle belt lining
it had already shed their leaves and stood in wintry bareness.   The contrast with the autumnal splendour of the
forest passed through only three days earlier was most
striking.

Marching down the river where it gradually loses itself
in a deltaic maze of dry water-courses and widening
Toghrak jungle, we reached next day the small terminal
oasis of Jigda-bulung.   My old host Abdul Karim Akhun,
the owner of the main farm, was still there to welcome me,
bent by increased age, but yet hale enough to look after
his property.   He was complaining of bad harvests caused,
as usual, by the vagaries of the river; which, after threatening to shift westwards at the time of my former passage,
had for the last few years returned once more to its old
bed.

Though Abdul Karim had no longer the energy needed to attract fresh settlers, and to extend cultivation as the available water-supply would permit, he had prospered sufficiently to meet an increased assessment and to lay by a good deal of surplus produce. So we could secure adequate supplies not only for our own party and the men I had brought along from the old site, but also for the additional fifteen labourers who now opportunely reinforced us from Niya. Ibrahim Beg's energy managed in addition to raise overnight a small local contingent of labourers from among the thirty odd scattered males of this outlying settlement.

The immediate goal for which I set my column in motion on the morning of November 4th was not the old site across the Endere River whence Sadak had brought away his Kharoshthi tablet, but another 'Kone-shahr' which his father Samsak alleged to have visited years before in the desert between the Yar-tungaz and Endere rivers. Information about it had been kept from me on my previous visit, and the assertion of complete ignorance would have been, no doubt, maintained also on this occasion, had I not been able to quote in support of Samsak's statement the testimony of my friend Mr. Huntington, who during his survey of this area a year earlier visited ruins manifestly corresponding to the Mazar shepherd's description. So after a good deal of shuffling at last one Yar-tungaz man, Kutluk, a withered old herdsman, owned up to a knowledge of the ruins about Bilelkonghan.

In spite of this local guidance the search proved a troublesome business. On November 4th our heavily laden caravan toiled all day eastwards over successive huge ridges of sand rising up to 300 feet and running parallel to salty depressions between, which manifestly had once served for river-beds. After crossing the fourth we camped in a narrow waterless plain known as Yantakchaval, where dead tamarisk scrub supplied fuel. Next morning our guides led us in a winding course towards the Endere River, and when after six miles across Dawans of less height we reached the edge of a wide area covered with fairly thick Toghrak jungle growing amidst low dunes, they set out to locate the ruins.

Three hours passed in weary waiting. Though the atmosphere had now cleared sufficiently, and isolated high tamarisk cones gave a wide outlook, I vainly scanned the horizon with my glasses for any sign of ruins. At last the guides returned crestfallen with the report of having failed to discover them. It was past mid-day by that time, and as our animals had tasted no water since Yar-tungaz and the supply brought from there for my men was wellnigh exhausted, I thought it safest to strike due east for the Endere River, and to await the result of the fresh search on which I sent out our 'guides.' Leading the caravan by the compass I had scarcely proceeded a little over two miles when high trunks of dead poplars standing on more open level ground attracted my attention. Presently we stumbled on the 'Kone-shahr,' only a couple of hundred yards off the course I was actually steering!

There were ruins of houses, rough in their timber construction but well preserved on the whole, crowding an area comparatively clear of tamarisk growth and overrun only by slight dunes (Fig. 102). The first look at the site was far more suggestive of an 'old town' than the usual appearance of the widely scattered ruins or insignificant Tati remains to which the term is indiscriminately applied by all dwellers along the edge of the desert. As soon as, in eager expectation, I had hurried up to the ruins, I realized that they were all contained within a roughly oval circumvallation formed by a clay rampart still traceable at most points. Subsequent measurement showed the enclosure to be about 263 yards long at its greatest axis from north-east to south-west and about 210 yards across where widest.

My satisfaction was great at having been saved by lucky chance a protracted search on such deceptive ground and with ignorant 'guides.' But a rapid preliminary inspection sufficed to damp any over-sanguine archaeological hopes. A number of observations suggested from the first that the remains of this 'deserted village'—for as such it could properly be designated in spite of its modest rampart—could not claim any very high antiquity. Neither within nor without the enclosed area could I trace any sign of serious wind erosion, that inevitable impress left by time upon all old sites in this region. In spite of very scanty protection by sand, the rough posts and roof beams exposed in the ruins, invariably wild poplar trunks unhewn or but partially planed, showed little of that far-advanced bleaching and splintering which experience had taught me to recognize in timber of old sites as the infallible mark of long-continued exposure.

But all antiquarian yearnings apart, how little could a thousand years more or less matter, compared with the strange fascination of such a scene where human activity unrecorded had struggled with, and succumbed to, the desert? I entered the circumvallation from the south-east where a gate some eleven feet broad still kept its folds of rough timber ajar. As I passed between the many ruined dwellings scattered in irregular groups, the abundance of these silent witnesses of a life long departed seemed almost uncanny by contrast with the total absence of signs of human occupation outside. But could I succeed in securing from them definite evidence as to the origin and age of the settlement?

The uniform roughness of construction in these dwellings held out little promise, and their number was embarrassing at the start. Luckily I had brought with me an adequate posse of labourers, and as soon as the baggage had been unloaded on a patch of bare clay outside the west wall, I set them to work at two of the less coarsely built structures. The drift sand which filled them did not reach the low roofing made of rough trunks of the wild poplar, with brushwood and earth above. Yet it had sufficed to protect the walls, which here consisted of vertical bundles of reeds faced outside with a layer of mud. The timber framework supporting the whole showed none of the careful carpentry displayed by all ruins of the Niya site, but mere unhewn Toghrak posts with other trunks laid horizontally across the gable ends. The two or three rooms contained in these huts were absolutely bare of fittings. There was not even the comfort of a mud-built

162. INTERIOR OF RUINED VILLAGE AT BILEL-KONGHAN, SEEN FROM CIRCUMVALLATION ON NORTH-EAST.

sitting platform or fireplace, such as poor cultivators' houses in the modern oases ordinarily display.

When next day we proceeded to clear one after the other of the small ' houses ' built with walls of stamped clay or coarse sun-dried bricks, the experience was repeated. Nowhere did we come upon the remains of furniture or household implements, however humble.   Fragments of broken pottery, elsewhere the commonest marks of earlier occupation, were strangely absent.   Most curious feature of all, nowhere within or without the ruined dwellings and sheds did we strike any of those accumulations of refuse or dung which in this region invariably adjoin any group of habitations tenanted for some length of time, whether ancient or modern.   It was clear that we could not hope here for datable archaeological evidence.   But in the end closer observation of the general conditions prevailing helped to reveal something about the origin and abandonment of this curious site.

As already stated, I was struck from the first by the absence of marks of wind erosion.   This fact was not merely a definite indication of relatively recent date for the ruins, but also gave significance to certain negative features.   Though there were near the circumvallation considerable patches of ground clear of drift sand, I looked in vain on their flat expanse for any traces of that careful terracing and division for purposes of irrigation which ancient cultivated soil retains for long periods wherever surface erosion is absent.   Nor could I find anywhere the remains of fruit trees or Tereks, such as are invariably planted along fields and roads in an oasis, though the trunks of dead Toghraks rose in plenty both within and without the enclosure.   Characteristically enough the big Toghraks inside the wall were to be found mostly in open spaces left between the dwellings, having evidently grown up there before these were erected and having been spared for the sake of their shade when clearing and building began.   The good preservation of the branches in these patriarchs of the desert jungle, as seen in the illustration (Fig. 102), suggested that their death did not date back to any very distant period.

As I pondered over these observations and compared them with what could be inferred from the uniform roughness of the dwellings, and from the absence of refuse heaps, the following suggested itself as the most likely explanation. At a time when the Endere River was following a course west of its present bed, and thus bringing water to the wide open plain now covered with scrub and Toghraks mostly dead, a colony had been planted here in the hope of utilizing the chance offered for an agricultural settlement. The provision of a circumvallation and the crowding together within of numerous dwellings, all of a uniform type and manifestly provisional, point to a scheme of colonization very different from the haphazard growth of scattered holdings usual in the smaller oases.

This is fully accounted for by the special importance which the area of vegetation along the terminal course of the Endere River must always have claimed in historical times as the only possible position for a half-way station on the desert route, some 220 miles long, between Niya and the oasis of Charchan. The ruins to be described presently of older fortified stations near the east bank of the Endere River undoubtedly date from successive attempts to establish here a settlement which would help to facilitate and protect traffic on the route leading eastwards along the Taklamakan to Lop-nor, and thence to China proper. It thus seems but natural to connect the unmistakably later ruins of the fortified village with a systematic endeavour made in Muhammadan times for the same purpose. The change in the site chosen for the new settlement was, no doubt, due to a temporary shifting of the Endere River course. The attempt must have failed soon, as was shown quite clearly by the absence of all traces of agricultural development near the site and by other indications already mentioned.

In the absence of more definite evidence we cannot make sure of the immediate cause of this abandonment. Under the peculiar physical conditions prevailing, another shift of the river to where it now flows, fully five miles to the east, would have sufficed to make irrigation impossible. But that other causes might also be thought of was brought home to me by a curious observation. The oval enclosure of the ruined village consisted of a mud rampart, about sixteen feet broad at the base, carrying at a height of about eight feet a platform of rush bundles fixed on rough beams. Over this again on the outside rose a parapet of rough bricks and clay about $1\frac{1}{2}$ feet in thickness. Almost the whole of this circumvallation was still traceable, except on the north segment where tamarisk - covered dunes overlaid it, and throughout the exposed portion of the wall showed marks of having been subjected to fire. Charred fragments of wood lay about on the rampart, and the clay was reddened by burning. Considering also that a number of the huts cleared in the course of our two days' digging had their timber partially burned, it was evident that a conflagration had played its part in the early end of the deserted settlement.

On November 7th I visited, about one mile north of the ruins, a small salt marsh, said to be fed by springs, in a depression which seemed to have once formed part of an old river-bed coming from the south-east and long completely dried up. Then after a last look at the silent village I marched due east towards the actual river course by the broad track which our camels had trodden when bringing water. After about three miles we crossed a high ridge of sand marking the western edge of some 'Kone-darya,' and another two miles farther struck a succession of shallow beds which the river had filled during the last summer flood. In the newly formed main channel, half a mile beyond and about ten yards broad, the water was flowing with a depth of over three feet and a strong current.

Tokhta Muhammad, the owner of the forlorn small colony of Endere Tarim struggling with the vagaries of the river some distance lower down, had joined me at the ruined village. From his statement and that of some of the Niya men who had worked there, I knew that the river's move into this new bed some three years before meant in reality a return to the western channel which I had seen in 1901 completely dry, and which was then locally known as the 'Kone-darya.' The 'new river' of that date was reached about a mile farther east, and presented itself now as a deeply cut Nullah, winding between forest where the young trees had already begun to wither from want of water.

We ascended this dry bed for some distance to the point known as Kokul-toghrak, where the river had branched off to the north-west. There we came upon a newly constructed embankment intended to keep the summer flood from breaking back again into the deserted channel. As I looked at this precarious barrier on which some sixty men were said to have toiled for over two months, I realized the hazard implied in cultivation at the Endere River end. The water I saw flowing past the 'Band' was the supply of 'Kara-su,' said to come from springs higher up, where the river-bed leaves the foot of the great gravel glacis of the mountains. The amount of water thus permanently available seemed ample for a fair-sized oasis. The men from Niya estimated it at ten 'Tash,' i.e., sufficient for moving ten millstones, and declared it more plentiful than the supply of 'Kara-su' available in their own river.

But all the advantage for irrigation derived from this abundance of water during the early part of the year is effaced by the risks which arise from the shifting of the river course at the time when the 'Ak-su,' or 'white water' of summer floods, comes rushing down from the snowy range. The cultivated area is then either exposed to flooding, or to being left without irrigation altogether through the river moving away from the canal head. The latter calamity had occurred during the preceding summer, and the small party from Endere Tarim, which hospitably came to meet me at Kokul-toghrak, complained bitterly of the assessment of a thousand Tangas still exacted for the acreage of two thousand *mou* supposed to be under crops.

I had no time to spare for a visit to this hapless 'Tarim,' but marched up the river for another six miles until nightfall compelled me to pitch camp amidst the luxuriant Toghraks of the shepherd-station known as Kara-öchke-öltürgan ('where the black goat had sat'). The carelessness of some of our labourers, who had set huge heaps of dry foliage and then a couple of big trees ablaze, provided towards midnight a grand illumination at imminent risk to tents and baggage.   Luckily there were plenty of hands ready to shovel sand and stop the conflagration from spreading.

CHAPTER XXVII

ON the morning of November 8th I shaped my course into the desert south-eastwards, and after eight miles across low dunes and dreary wastes with tamarisk scrub and salt efflorescence, reached the high Stupa ruin which mounts guard over the ancient site at Endere first visited by me in 1901.

Want of time then had obliged me to confine my exploration to the interior of the ruined fort about one mile to the south-east of the Stupa (Fig. 103), and even within it to leave uncleared some apartments which were too deeply covered with drift sand. So it was with an eased conscience that I once more pitched my camp by its side. A rapid inspection assured me that the remains of the little temple in the centre, which had then disclosed interesting manuscript relics and a Chinese sgraffito inscription of some importance, had not suffered in the interval.

Then I hurried outside to where, only a quarter of a mile to the south, Sadak declared he had found the Kharoshthi tablet which he had shown me at Imam Ja'far's Mazar. The ground there was covered with conical hillocks of sand bearing tamarisk dead or living, eroded banks of bare clay showing up between them. The spot to which Sadak took me without any hesitation looked like one of these terraces, only lower. But on approaching closely I recognized that what rose a few feet above the easy sand slope was not a mere 'witness,' but a solid mass of rubbish with the broken brick walls of a small house emerging through it.

This unpretending ruin had probably been laid bare by

103. INTERIOR OF RUINED FORT OF ENDERE SEEN FROM EAST.

In foreground walls of large dwelling, E. III, excavated in 1901. A marks position of ancient rubbish heap under fort wall, B that of Buddhist temple in centre.

a slight movement in the adjoining dunes since my first visit to the site, and Sadak knew that some 'treasure-seekers' from Niya had been attracted to it a few years later. But they had contented themselves with digging holes here and there, and had left the refuse thus extracted lying close by. I had scarcely begun to examine it when, amidst plentiful fragments of pottery, rags of felt and coarse fabrics, and clods of stable refuse, I came upon a small piece of wood bearing traces of Kharoshthi characters. So the men were set promptly to work, and most of the ruin was cleared before nightfall. On the top there was a thick layer of stable refuse and straw, extending uniformly over the remains of brick walls, only about three feet high, and over the débris which filled the two rooms clearly traceable between them. From their floor and that of an adjoining apartment, which erosion had almost completely destroyed, I recovered, besides several fragmentary Kharoshthi records on wood and leather, a large and perfectly preserved oblong tablet showing a curiously elongated variety of that script, and ending with a series of curious monograms of Indian look manifestly meant for signatures. Another noteworthy find was a piece of flexible bark inscribed with a line of very cursive characters bearing no resemblance to any of the known Central-Asian writings.

But of far greater antiquarian interest than any of these epigraphic relics was the new light which the discovery of this small ruin began to throw on the history of the site. When in 1901 I excavated the ruins within the circular fort, I had recovered from its temple a Chinese inscription dated in 719 A.D. and a number of manuscript remains in Tibetan, Brahmi, and Chinese. These proved the fort to have been occupied about the first decades of the eighth century A.D. and abandoned during the Tibetan occupation soon after. Now it was curious that Hsüan-tsang, who on his return journey to China about 645 A.D. passed along the desert route from Niya to Charchan, found no inhabited place on the ten days' march ; but he mentions, in a position exactly corresponding to the Endere site, four marches after leaving Niya and six from Charchan, ruins of abandoned settlements which the tradition of his time

described as 'old seats of the Tu-huo-lo' or Tukhara,
famous in Central-Asian history. This country, he tells
us, had long been deserted, and "all the towns presented
the appearance of an uninhabited waste."

It had before seemed a problem how to reconcile the
results of my excavations of 1901 with the pilgrim's reference to ruins seen in the same locality but abandoned to
the desert centuries earlier. But as soon as I had verified
Sadak's find by the discovery of more Kharoshthi tablets
in the same ruined structure, and under my own eyes, the
right explanation dawned upon me. Clearly we had here
a definite historical instance of an old site in the desert
having been reoccupied after the lapse of centuries. The
Kharoshthi records on wood, like those of the Niya site
which they closely approach palaeographically, undoubtedly
belong to the second or third century A.D., and thus to the
very period of the ascendency in the Tarim Basin of those
Indo-Scythians whom Hsüan-tsang, from the main seat of
their power on the Oxus, knew as Tukhara. The small
house yielding the tablets must have belonged to the
earlier settlement which Hsüan-tsang found completely
deserted and in ruins.

That the area had subsequently come under occupation
again, probably in consequence of the improved conditions
which followed the establishment of Chinese authority
throughout Eastern Turkestan within a little over ten
years after Hsüan-tsang's passage, was conclusively proved
by the ruined fort which my former excavations had shown
to have served for a Chinese garrison at the commencement of the eighth century A.D. But even the condition
of the earlier structure itself furnished evidence for this reoccupation; for only thus did it seem possible to account
for the layers of straw, plentifully mixed with wheat grains,
and of stable refuse which uniformly extended both over
the broken walls and the mud-brick débris filling the rooms
between. Evidently some one among the new settlers of
the seventh or eighth century had found it convenient to
erect his humble homestead over the mound formed by
the tumbled-down ruin.

A curious find from the latter, which at first did not

receive due attention, was a canvas bag holding two narrow and flat pieces of wood, about six inches long, showing along one edge a series of small cup-like holes evidently blackened by smoke. It was only when these pieces came to be examined at the British Museum that Mr. H. G. Evelyn-White, then one of my assistants, recognized them as regular fire-blocks meant for the production of fire by the churning of small wooden sticks which fitted the holes. Even then I might have doubted the survival of this primitive method as late as the third century A.D., had not the subsequent discovery of an exactly corresponding block at the ancient site north of Lop-nor, which dates from about the same period, furnished confirmatory evidence.

The search for other old remains in the vicinity of the T'ang fort was continued with care on November 9th; but only in one of the several badly eroded dwellings which I managed to trace, did we come upon datable relics in the shape of two fragmentary Kharoshthi tablets. The ruins of a small Stupa and of a square tower, still rising about eighteen feet high, both built with sun-dried bricks of large size (Fig. 105), were the only surviving remains of more substantial structures near the fort which could be connected with the earlier settlement. The havoc wrought by far-advanced wind erosion was, no doubt, mainly responsible for this scarcity of older structural remains; for pottery débris of very ancient look appeared plentifully on all patches of bare soil for nearly one mile south of the fort, and whatever copper coins were picked up about the latter belonged to the Chinese currency of the Han dynasty.

The most striking evidence, however, of the often-proved accuracy of my Chinese guide and patron saint came to light, when a chance find led me to discover that the clay rampart of the fort, built within a generation or two of his passage, was in one place actually raised over a bank of consolidated refuse which belonged to the first centuries of our era. At a point about a hundred feet to the west of the fort's single gate, wind erosion had badly breached the circumvallation of stamped clay. Searching on the surface thus laid bare, one of the men came upon the well-preserved portion of a Kharoshthi document still folded sticking out from a layer of rubbish. The writing and arrangement of the fragment agreed precisely with similar documents on leather recovered by me on my former journey from the richest refuse heap of the Niya site.

When searching the bank of ancient refuse which had yielded it, I ascertained that it extended right down to the natural soil of hard loess, six feet lower, being embedded on either side between stamped clay layers of the later rampart. From among the miscellaneous contents of the small rubbish heap thus preserved there emerged bagfuls of rags in a variety of fabrics, including fine silks, fragments of rugs, and a knife-hilt in bone. Seeing what the builders of the Chinese fort in the 7th century had taken here for a foundation, I wondered how much more of the débris of the earlier site might still rest safely covered up under other portions of the rampart.

Whatever the defensive value of the latter may have been against human attacks, it had served to catch and retain heavy accumulations of drift sand which protected the structures within. So the complete excavation of those dwelling quarters in the fort, which I had not been able to touch before, proved a heavy task for my labourers. We now cleared them all, including a large hall; but our only finds were some fine wooden pillars with rich mouldings— clearly produced by the turning-lathe in spite of diameters exceeding one foot—and some elaborately modelled fireplaces in underground rooms which must have served for shelter in the winter. While my diggers were thus hard at work under the Naik's and Chiang-ssŭ-yeh's supervision, I found time to visit certain remains farther away about which information had reached me. Going north beyond the large Stupa, I ascertained that the shapeless mounds of stamped clay, already noticed on my first arrival, had originally formed part of a large walled enclosure decayed by erosion almost beyond recognition and half buried amidst dunes.

It was only by closely observing the alignment of the wall fragments still traceable here and there that the area

B

104. REMAINS OF ANCIENT WALL ON EROSION 'WITNESS,' ENDERE SITE.
The line A B marks original ground level. In background portion of ancient walled enclosure.

105. RUINED TOWER WITH REMAINS OF WIND-ERODED DWELLING IN FOREGROUND,
ENDERE SITE.

once enclosed, an oblong about 540 feet from north to south and about 340 feet across, could approximately be determined. The stamped clay rampart, about thirty to thirty-five feet thick at the base, seemed to have borne a super-structure formed by courses of large bricks set in thick layers of clay. But there appeared little regularity in the construction, or else repairs had been frequent, and few of the extant wall portions retained enough of their height to permit of exact measurement. Pottery débris, mostly black or dark brown, thickly strewed the ground within where not covered by broad dunes. Wind erosion had evidently first breached the outer walls and then scoured the remains of whatever buildings the interior once contained (Fig. 104). The east wall had suffered particularly in this process, while the wall to the south had practically disappeared. The whole made up a weird picture of desolation, impressive even in the desert surroundings to which I had grown accustomed. For excavation there was no scope left here. But the far-advanced decay of walls once so massive, and the much-worn appearance of the débris inside, strongly suggested that these ruins, too, went back to the period of the earlier 'Tu-huo-lo' settlement.

Other excursions acquainted me with whatever old remains my Endere guides knew of amidst the closely set tamarisk cones to the south. One among them was the ruin of a small fortified post built in a solid square with walls of stamped clay, about eight feet thick (Fig. 106). They had suffered relatively little damage and still rose to eighteen feet in places. A projecting square bastion protected the gate on the south. The interior court, about forty-eight feet square, was completely bare, except for accumulations of straw and dung left undisturbed by erosion under the lee-side of the east wall. Some of the posts of Toghrak wood once flanking the inner gate still stood upright, and on clearing the débris filling the latter we came upon big pieces of timber which my men recognized as carved from mulberry and Eleagnus trees.

So cultivation at the time of the fort's construction was proved. But I searched in vain for distinct antiquarian evidence as to the period of its occupation. The fair preservation of the walls might have been taken as an indication of late date, had not the fact of a huge sand-cone covered with living tamarisk on the top adjoining the west wall, and rising fully twenty feet above it, suggested the possibility of another explanation. Judging from what experience has taught me at other old sites by the southern edge of the Taklamakan, I should find it easier to account for the height attained by the tamarisk cone if this ruined fort, too, dated back to the time of Tukhara occupation. In the case of some badly eroded small dwellings traced within half a mile to the south and south-east, the large size of the bricks used and similar structural details distinctly pointed to the earlier epoch; but here, too, the search for exactly datable relics was fruitless.

It was on my return from these surveys southwards that I traced quite clearly the line of an ancient river-bed running from the present course of the Endere river to the north-east, and passing within half a mile on the east of the ruined fort of the T'ang times. A close search along it showed here and there bleached and much-decayed remnants of ancient fruit trees. But no more structural remains could be traced, and as the excavation of the last dwelling-places within the fort was now concluded, on the evening of November 12th I moved my camp back to Korgach higher up the river.

On the frosty but brilliantly clear morning of the next day I paid off my Niya labourers, new and old, and saw them set out in great glee for the four days' tramp to their homes. Then crossing the river, which in spite of the winter's close approach still filled a channel some forty yards broad and two feet deep in the centre, flowing with a current of about a yard per second, I visited what old remains Mihman, our shepherd guide from the Endere Tarim, could show me in the riverine jungle belt westwards. The closeness of the luxuriant tamarisk thickets made orientation very difficult. But in the end, after many détours, we succeeded in tracing the débris of a roughly made water-mill by the side of a shallow canal bed, and at a distance of nearly two miles from the river the almost completely eroded relics of a hut built with Toghrak

106. RUIN OF ANCIENT FORTIFIED POST, NEAR HIGH TAMARISK-COVERED SAND CONE, ENDERE SITE.

107. 'DASTARKHAN' OFFERED ON DESERT ROUTE TO CHARCHAN.
On left Chiang-ssŭ-yeh and my caravan-men enjoying the treat brought by Beg from Charchan.

beams. The only 'find' rewarding the clearance of it was some wheat straw embedded in the flooring, a proof that cultivation was once carried on here. It was of interest, too, to discover that a deeply cut channel took off from the river above Korgach and passed through the dense jungle to the north-west. Mihman declared that he had followed it to the vicinity of the abandoned fort village beyond Bilel-konghan, a distance of some eighteen miles.

It was late in the evening before I recrossed the river above the grazing grounds of Tokuz-köl, and found my camp pitched amid Toghrak groves and luxuriant Kumush beds at Kök-jilga-öghil not far from its right bank. There a mass of urgent correspondence, which needed despatch to Kashgar and India before I started on the long trek eastwards, kept me busy at work all next day. It was pleasant to feel that the halt meant a long day of luxurious ease for my men, with abundance of water and fuel, and un-limited grazing for my hard-tried camels and ponies. Four of the Endere people were sent ahead to clear the wells at our prospective halting stages.

Then on November 15th we set out for the journey to Charchan, which we were to cover in six marches, just as old Hsüan-tsang had done. It was the same silent uninhabited waste he describes between Niya and Char-chan, with the drift sand of the desert ever close at hand. " The tracks of wayfarers get effaced, and many among them lose their way. On every side there extends a vast space with nothing to go by; so travellers pile up the bones left behind to serve as road-marks. There is neither water nor grazing, and often hot winds blow. Then men and animals lose their senses and fall ill." Nor was it strange for the pious pilgrim in such lonesome wilds to give credence to the stories he heard about demons which with their singing and wailing caused people to go astray and perish. But for those who like myself had already passed over worse ground, there were other and less forbidding features to observe along this ancient desert high road.

The greatest part of its length, some 106 miles from the Endere River to Charchan, and almost all bearing to the north-east, carefully hugs the line where the glacis of absolutely sterile Sai, sloping down from the foot of the Kunlun and overrun in parts by high dunes, is fringed northward by a zone of desert vegetation. Here the subsoil drainage of the streams lost higher up on the Sai again approaches the surface, and, besides supporting the growth of wild poplars, tamarisks, and other desert plants, provides occasional wells. Without them this desert route would be quite impossible for caravan traffic. As it is, the water of these wells is throughout brackish, and at some points so salt as to be scarcely fit for drinking. This, coupled with the great summer heat, the mosquitoes then bred in the flood-beds, and the risks arising from Burans, practically closes the route from May till September.

But wherever the amount of subsoil water is larger, owing to the size of the rivers which debouch from the mountains on to the glacis of Piedmont gravel, the belt of sandy scrub and jungle spreads out. Thus for two long marches beyond the Endere River, to the stages of Shudanöghil and Chingelik, we passed through large areas of relatively abundant desert vegetation. They were said to extend considerably northward and to afford winter grazing for some of the flocks belonging to the Endere Tarim. Moving along these dreary pastures I thought of what Marco Polo tells us in his brief account of the ' Province of Charchan': " The whole of the Province is sandy . . . and much of the water that you find is bitter and bad. However, at some places you do find fresh and sweet water. When an army passes through the land, the people escape with their wives, children, and cattle a distance of two or three days' journey into the sandy waste; and knowing the spots where water is to be had, they are able to live there, and to keep their cattle alive, whilst it is impossible to discover them; for the wind immediately blows the sand over their track."

After we had on the third day left behind the numerous and steeply cut summer flood-beds of the Kara-muran River, the stretches of absolutely bare desert crossed by the route steadily extended, while what vegetation could be found between grew thinner and thinner. A cutting

wind from the north-east faced us for the latter half
of the journey, and with the dust haze and cold much
increased its discomforts.   When after toiling over heavy
dunes we arrived on the evening of the fourth day at
the stage appropriately known as Yantak-kuduk, 'the
Well of Thorns,' I was cheered to find a gourd of milk
and a basket of eggs hospitably deposited.   It was a
mute greeting thoughtfully sent ahead by the Beg of
Charchan.   Nowhere else on this 'high road' did we
come in touch with humanity.   The ground onwards now
changed to a barren gravel Sai overrun at intervals by
low dunes of coarse sand.   Only a few depressed patches
held vegetation of the scantiest sort, and at one of these,
called Kalasti, from a robber's skull once exposed there as
a warning—or an assurance—to wayfarers, we made our
last halt before Charchan.

Next morning I had scarcely covered five miles when
a big cavalcade met us to offer welcome.   It was Sidik
Beg of Charchan, with a posse of local notables, and four
sturdy Pathan traders who were temporarily settled at the
oasis, and eagerly asserted their right to share in the
reception of a 'Sahib' from their own land.   I was doubly
pleased with the presence of these enterprising pioneers
of Indian trade, when I found that all had their homes
in such familiar trans-border tracts as Swat, Buner, and
Bajaor.   They were accustomed to take small caravans
with Indian goods from Khotan *via* Charklik to Kara-
shahr and on to Turfan in the north-east, and had found
Charchan a convenient half-way station on their ventures.
They had much needed information to give about routes,
distances, supplies, and the like.

But there was little chance for quenching my thirst for
such practical knowledge, until a big Dastarkhan, brought
up by the Beg's people, including meat dishes and dried
fruits, had been duly disposed of by the joint efforts of my
hosts and my own men who had long missed such rich
fare (Fig. 107).   I had plenty of time to gather local
information as we rode on, for the whole march to the
oasis lay over an absolutely bare level plain with not one
feature to distract attention.   At last, when the dark patch

made up of trees and homesteads showed clearly on the haze-covered horizon, we came upon the line of an old canal completely dry, yet marked by tamarisk scrub. This was all that survived of the attempt which an enterprising Beg of Charchan had made, some twenty years before, to utilize an irrigation channel of some earlier period for founding a new colony below the present oasis. The water had flowed all right for some years, but the endeavour to assure cultivation had failed from want of adequate labour. It was an apt illustration of the main difficulty which seems ever to have dogged the chequered fortune of this the most isolated of Turkestan oases.

Then followed a rapid ride to what remains of former settlements my local guides could show me, in the shape of a few broken walls of clay on the west, and of an extensive débris-strewn 'Tati' on the south-west edge of the oasis. The dusk was upon us when at last, to the relief of my cortège, who were eager for their flesh-pots, and yet too attentive to accept an earlier discharge, I passed within the cultivated area. Fields and gardens alike bore the look of recent colonization. Yet the fine growth of trees and hedges, and the substantial look of the homesteads, made me feel that I had come again to a place of rural plenty ; and in fact I had heard all day praise of the fertile soil of Charchan, and still more of the abundance of water brought down by its river. By the light of torches we rode through the large new Bazar, and then comfortable quarters received me at Tursun Bai's house, which after the dreary wastes passed through seemed almost like a mansion.

CHAPTER XXVIII

ALONG THE CHARCHAN RIVER

CHARCHAN fulfilled whatever promises my first impressions of the place had held out. The two days' halt, which was all I could afford, proved a pleasant and refreshing change from the last five weeks' desert journeyings for both men and animals. There was plenty of dry lucerne for the ponies to revel in after all the hard fare on reeds and thorny scrub. The camels, too, found a treat after their own fashion on the foliage of the Jigda trees, withered as it was by the frosts. The men had the means provided to get ready all sorts of supplementary winter clothing, and, what they probably enjoyed quite as much, could indulge in a court full of gossiping idlers and a lively Bazar within easy reach.

Already on the march I had gathered information which showed that Charchan was now a steadily growing oasis. The time when it was a dreaded place of exile, used by the Chinese in pre-rebellion days as a settlement for malefactors from Khotan, had passed away long ago. From a wretched collection of hovels, such as it was described some thirty years earlier, it had gradually developed into a lively oasis now manifestly bigger than Niya. It is difficult throughout Turkestan to obtain approximately correct statistics of population, etc. But in oases of such recent growth as Charchan even the help of conventional figures derived from earlier settlements fails one. So much, however, seemed clear, that the number of households among the settled cultivators could not well be less than five hundred.

Arable land there was, of course, as much as the most

extravagant colonization scheme would require. All my informants agreed that the water-supply available in the Charchan Darya, which drains a number of high snowy ranges, was more than sufficient for an oasis quite as big as Keriya. All that was wanting were fresh settlers, and for these all the land-holding Bais of Charchan were wistfully waiting. The influx of labourers from the Khotan region was steady but slow. Facilities on the long desert route were manifestly needed to quicken it, and to overcome the reluctance which poor cultivators would necessarily feel about migrating to so distant a place.

The geographical position of Charchan, about half-way between Lop-nor and Keriya, was enough to ensure importance to the oasis at any period when the route south of the great desert was frequented. Hsüan-tsang and Marco Polo had not failed to mention Charchan; and travelling as I was along the very route which had taken them into China, it was a special satisfaction to me to see with my own eyes how after centuries of neglect and abandonment the vitality of this ancient settlement was vigorously asserting itself. When on the day after my arrival I escaped from my quarters and the petty cares about repairs, transport arrangements, etc., which kept me busy there, for a ride through the central portion of the oasis, I was pleasantly surprised by the big crowd which thronged the newly built roomy Bazar. It was not the market day nor a particular day of feasting. But Ramazan had ended some four days before, and this, at a season when agricultural labour rested, was enough to draw a throng of holiday-makers, scarcely less than four or five hundred, before the few shops and booths that were open.

Just beyond the end of the Bazar street where Wang Ta-lao-ye, the Chinese sub-magistrate of Charchan, had his official residence,—modest, indeed, but pleasingly clean and new,—some crumbling mud hovels were shown to me as the old market. This juxtaposition made it easy to judge of the change which is coming over Charchan. It was a bleak and bitterly cold afternoon with a fog-like dust haze hiding all distant views. But there was plenty to see in close proximity along the lanes by which Sadik Beg, the youthful Beg of the oasis, guided me. The comfortable-looking homesteads, the plentiful but young orchards, and the abundance of well-dressed men and women I passed on the road, riding home from their Bazar 'Corso,' all told the same story of prosperity and expansion. What else could be the main cause but a rise in the economic conditions of the whole Tarim Basin brought about by peace and tolerably good administration?

The case of Charchan illustrates in a striking fashion the *péripéties* to which isolated settlements along the southern edge of the great Turkestan desert have been particularly liable at different periods. In the Annals of the Han dynasty Charchan is described as a petty chiefship, with a population of two hundred and thirty families, the Chinese rendering of its name being Chü-mo. It is probably meant also by the 'Chalmadana' repeatedly referred to in my Kharoshthi documents from the Niya site as a place of some consequence. When in A.D. 519 Sung Yün, a Chinese Buddhist pilgrim, passed here from Lop-nor to Khotan, he found the oasis, which he calls Tso-mo, inhabited by only a hundred families. Hsüan-tsang, following the same route more than a century later, mentions in a position exactly corresponding to Charchan "the old kingdom of Chê-mo-t'o-na which is the territory of Chü-mo." He saw there the walls of an old town still standing, but there were no longer any inhabitants. Yet when Chinese rule had been re-established soon after his passage, Charchan or Chü-mo figures once more in the T'ang dynasty's Annals as a place duly garrisoned. In Marco Polo's description of the 'Province of Charchan,' fully verified on other points, we read of "numerous towns and villages, and the chief city of the Kingdom bears its name, Charchan." But cultivation had completely disappeared by the end of the eighteenth century and probably long before.

It was only after the first third of the last century that the Chinese commenced to settle Charchan once more as a small penal station. The growth of the new settlement seems to have been slow at first, and the disturbed conditions during the Muhammadan rebellion must have sadly interfered with it. But since then the tide of renewed development has continued; and though many of the colonists brought from the western oases under official auspices, *recte* pressure, have escaped back to their old homes, the population is steadily growing. When I crossed the river, still flowing, in spite of the late season, in four or five well-filled channels with a volume far in excess of that of the Khotan Darya as I had seen it in the autumn, I recognized the possibilities which nature affords for the Charchan oasis. But who can foresee whether they will ever be fully realized, or how near or distant the time may be when desolation will again reign here supreme?

These glimpses of the present Charchan had their best counterfoil in the silent 'Tatis' which I visited on the second day to the south-west of the extant oasis. These débris areas of bare eroded soil, where nothing but small potsherds, broken pieces of glass, and metal and other fragments of hard material indicate former occupation, extend in patches from the present edge of cultivation for nearly five miles to the south-west. The ground presents itself as an almost level Sai of fine gravel, with here and there some island-like 'witness' of loess indicating the height of the overlying soil which has been eroded and carried away by the winds since cultivation had ceased. Near the Mazar of Yalghuz-tug ('the lonely Yak-standard') new fields are again invading the area of what the people of Charchan know as the 'Kone-shahr.' Any remains besides pottery débris which the ground may have once retained, have, of course, long ago been searched for treasure and destroyed.

The line of an old canal running towards this nearest of the 'Tatis' was followed by me for nearly two miles to its point of junction with the irrigation channel which Musa Beg some twenty years before had endeavoured to put to fresh use and which I had crossed on my approach to Charchan. Old pottery débris cropped up also in extensive patches west of this ancient canal, as far as the banks of a shallow depression which receives water from the Ayak-tar stream during the summer floods. Judging from the configuration of the gently sloping alluvial fan, it seemed clear that the water of the Charchan Darya could still be brought here without difficulty. But far-advanced deflation has left on these southern Tatis only a soil of fine gravel without the fertile loess layer which once covered it, and with many thousands of acres of fertile ground available along the river lower down, renewed cultivation is not likely to take this direction.

None of these 'Tatis' which my guide distinguished by quaint fancy designations offered scope for systematic archaeological labour. Nor did I succeed in discovering among their small débris anything affording a definite clue as to their age. So great appears to be here the force of wind erosion that intact Chinese copper coins, so common at most of such sites, are said never to be found now. Only tiny fragments retaining the characteristic rim attest their former existence. Some gauge, however, as to the different age of the débris areas is afforded by the fact that, while to the south the ground once cultivated has been denuded right down to the underlying Piedmont gravel, the 'Kone-shahr' Tati adjoining the present oasis which may represent the site of mediaeval Charchan shows its remains resting on loess soil, the process of erosion being still in progress. As an indication of the eroding force at work I may mention that a huge solitary 'witness' of loess in the middle of the Tati adjoining the Ayak-tar bed rises to a height of twenty-three feet and is covered with very hard potsherds of ancient look on its slopes.

All day a strong wind was blowing from the north-east, and its icy blast made me glad in the evening for the shelter of my room in Tursun Bai's house. By dint of great efforts the freshly hired camels and the supplies we needed for the journey to Charklik had been secured in good time along with the men's winter equipment. There were no antiquarian tasks to retain me, and thus I could keep to my programme and set the caravan on the move again by the morning of November 23rd. For Ram Singh, who was still away triangulating the range to the south, I left instructions to rejoin me at Charklik and carry his surveys eastwards as far as possible by the foot of the mountains.

The caravan route towards Lop-nor on which I was now eager to push forward, leads for the greatest part along the banks of the Charchan Darya. The facility thus afforded for the supply of water, grazing, and fuel must at all times have been appreciated by travellers bound east of Charchan. Yet with the exception of Tatran, a small hamlet some twenty-four miles lower down, there is no inhabited place along the hundred and fifty odd miles of jungle and desert which have to be crossed before Vash-shahri is reached, the westernmost settlement in the Charklik or Lop-nor district. We had accordingly to carry seven days' supplies for both men and ponies.

For the first two days the route on the right bank, which is now more in favour than the one shown in previous maps, closely hugs the actual river-bed. Under a misty grey sky the succession of tamarisk cones, reed-covered steppe, and thin Toghrak jungle offered little to the eyes to relieve a sense of monotony. I had secured at Charchan an excellent guide in the person of Ismail, a cultivator of Tatran, whose reputation as a hunter was great. Whatever feats he might have achieved with his quaint old matchlock, there soon remained in my mind no doubt as to his keen sight and astonishingly accurate sense of locality. The unfailing ease and correctness with which he found our bearings over ground offering so few landmarks, made my work on the plane-table quite a pleasure in spite of the benumbing cold to which it exposed my fingers.

That Ismail 'Pawan' had also the pluck befitting a hunter, I learned when on the morning of the third march I proceeded to visit the small brick mound known as 'Tim' which I had found marked in Hedin's map. It lay on the opposite side of the river, and when I proposed to cross over Ismail had his doubts on the subject. The bottom of the river-bed is formed in many places by treacherous oozy mud which would not bear ponies, and might prove dangerous for men on foot. The difficulty was increased by the young ice floes which now came floating down the river in daily increasing size. When we reached the shepherd-station of Shor-kölöghil, where Ismail proposed to find a ford, the ice-crust lying over the extensive mud banks proved too thin to carry men.   But they were safely crossed all the same by Ismail and the Charchan man whom I had taken along to push my cyclometer for road measurement.   Then the two men waded pluckily through the two channels of swift-running water, each approximately fifty yards broad and nearly four feet deep in the middle.   To look at their shivering bare legs, cut by the ice cakes in more than one place, as they tried to warm themselves by a fire after returning from their reconnaissance, made me think of the French pioneers who, working to their waist in the ice-filled Berezina, built the bridges that were to save the fleeing remnants of the Grande Armée.   Ismail, in spite of his trying experience, volunteered to carry me across, and, feeling much in doubt as to whether my feet were equal to such a passage, I gladly accepted his offer.   The crossing on my hardy mount was effected in safety though not without trouble ; for when Ismail came to climb the steeply cut bank towards the shallow which divided the two channels, he failed to secure a foothold on the slippery ice and came down on his face and hands, giving me a fair ducking.   So I, too, had something to dry by the roaring fire which the men kindled amidst the thick reeds of the opposite bank.

The 'Tim,' found quite close to where we had crossed and only some hundred yards off the river-bank, proved to be the ruin of a small square structure in solid masonry which in all probability had served as a Stupa base.   The extant portion was only eleven feet long, standing at a height of about seven feet above the present ground level. The great size of the bricks and their careful setting attested the antiquity of the structure.   Its interest lies in the fact that it proves the existence of a Pre-Muhammadan settlement in the immediate vicinity of the present river course, and thus supports the presumption that the latter has changed less in its main direction than the many dry branches and lagoons met with on either side might otherwise lead one to suppose.

The route, where we regained it after this excursion,

led no longer along the river but past the southern edge of a series of extensive marshes which run parallel to the general direction of the river and probably mark lagoons once formed by flood-water. Dense beds of reeds covered these depressions and allowed but rarely a glimpse of clear water. Toghrak groves were met with at intervals, generally on small tongues of sandy ground projecting into these 'Köls.' The rest of the ground through which the route led for fully two marches, some forty-three miles, was mainly salt-impregnated steppe with a scanty growth of reeds or tamarisk. Had it not been for the delightfully clear sky which the increasing cold had brought us—on November 26th I registered a minimum of 34 degrees Fahrenheit below freezing-point—and visions of the distant snowy range south, the landscape would have been more depressing to my sense than the region of absolutely sterile dunes northward. For there the graceful wave-lines of the dunes and the great ridges of sand which rise between them, create an ever-changing horizon and keep the eye occupied.

I had an opportunity of gaining a good idea of the nature of these marshes and of the tangled jungle which extends between them and the river, when on the morning of our fourth march I proceeded to visit under Ismail's guidance some ruins I had heard of while at Charchan. From camp on the bank of the Chong-köl or 'Big Lake,' we struck north-eastward to where Ismail knew a safe crossing through the marsh belt. The water being fed by springs had not yet frozen, and without our guide's amazingly sure local sense we might have long searched in vain for a track across the treacherous marsh bed. Where we eventually crossed, it narrowed to a channel only four or five hundred yards broad. But even here the ground was too soft to carry laden animals. The reeds grew to ten feet or more, and to break through their thickets was no pleasant experience even in the wake of Ismail and his pony.

The latter was a small wiry thing which I never ceased to admire on these marches. Besides its tall rider it had to carry his food supplies and its own fodder for some ten days, a matchlock of imposing size and weight, not to reckon felts and other kit which would allow Ismail to camp out in the jungle during the severest season. Yet the pony never lagged for a moment and was ever ready to take the lead in awkward places. Of such there were many indeed, before we approached the ridge of tamarisk-covered sand-cones which Ismail pointed out from a distance as marking the site of the ruins. In the intervening depressions which probably are reached by occasional summer floods, the tamarisk and other scrub grew in such tangled luxuriance as to be often quite impassable on horseback. Toghraks of great size and frequently of curiously twisted appearance studded patches of ground between these depressions so closely as to force us to make détours. Everywhere there abounded tracks of deer, boars, and smaller game, and I could well realize what execution Ismail's antique weapon might do here.

The ruins of Yalghuz-dong, 'The Lonely Hillock,' consisted of three isolated small structures, showing oblong walls of very soft brickwork and built on the top of tamarisk cones which lower sand ridges connected. The walls stood only a few feet above the ground, and though partially protected by the sand which the tamarisk scrub had detained, they nowhere showed remains of any superstructures. On the slopes of the hillocks rising about thirty feet above the plain, there lay some large beams or planks of splintered Toghrak wood which Ismail thought might have belonged to coffins. But there was nothing to show their original position or use. Altogether these poorly preserved walls and their strange situation looked puzzling. But the small size of the bricks and their softness suggested no great age. The puzzle was not solved when about one and a half miles to the north-east Ismail showed me a second group of small rectangular structures closely resembling the first, but built on low ground by the side of what was manifestly an old irrigation canal. Here, too, the walls stood only two to four feet above ground and retained no trace of superstructures.

But when, following the traces of this canal for a little over half a mile eastwards, Ismail took me to the principal group of the 'old walls,' 'Kone-tamlik,' as he called the site, the true explanation very soon revealed itself. Here I saw a row of over a dozen rectangular enclosures, built in the same brickwork but more completely preserved, stretching from east to west along the top of a low ridge. Their size varied greatly, the largest measuring fifty by forty-two feet; but each showed on one side a narrow arched gateway standing to a greater height than the rest of the walls. Everything recalled the walled enclosures so frequently met with in Muhammadan cemeteries farther west, and the discovery of a grave outside one of the enclosures near the edge of the ridge confirmed the conjecture.

A row of rough Toghrak branches covered the coffin, which was formed of a hollowed tree trunk; and when the men with me had scraped away enough of the soil to display the feet of a skeleton turned due south, it became quite certain that we were at a resting-place of the Faithful. So satisfied about the character of the ruins, I could let the dead remain undisturbed in this desolate cemetery. The portion of the grave exposed was properly covered up again before we left for the long march still before us. Finds of chronological value could not be expected in Muhammadan graves, and to collect anthropological measurements from the dead buried here would have implied prolonged stay and such labour as neither the men nor myself would have cared for.

Even without more definite evidence as to date, the discovery of these remains had its geographical value; for it made it quite clear that at a period not very remote, when the Charchan River followed a more southerly course, perhaps the one marked by the line of marshes we had been skirting, an agricultural settlement had been able to maintain itself here for a time under physical conditions probably not very different from those about Tatran. Now the shift of the river northward and the probable progress of desiccation in the meantime had brought a dismal change over the adjoining ground. We had to cross extensive stretches of soil encrusted with hard cakes of salt, and to pick our way warily between *morne* salt lagoons where even the reed beds were dying, before we regained the line of spring-fed marshes and the camels' track leading past their southern edge. The air was perfectly calm and clear, and the brilliant colours thrown by the setting sun upon the snowy range southward, rising like a huge rampart with peaks over 18,000 feet high, only helped to deepen by contrast the mournful gloom of the foreground.

On the following day a wearisome march protracted until late at night brought us back to the actual river-bed. But owing to its very sinuous course it was impossible to keep by it, and our track led again and again along deserted dry channels and across extensive stretches of salt-encrusted steppe which, like much of the ground on the preceding marches, tried the camels' feet sorely. Several of them had developed bad cracks on their soles and delayed still more our heavily laden baggage train. At Ak-ilak where we camped under a splendid Toghrak grove, it was midnight before dinner appeared.

The experience was repeated next day when we first followed the river down to the grazing ground known as Lashkar-satma from a small guard once stationed here in Yakub Beg's days, and then struck across a belt of high and completely sterile dunes to the south-east. The big semi-lunes of drift sand rose up to about 120 feet, and all pointed with their concave face to the south-west, the first intimation of that prevailing north-east wind with the frequency and force of which in the whole Lop-nor region we were soon to become familiar. At Yaka-toghrak darkness obliged us to halt by the edge of some desert jungle which subsoil drainage from the mountains keeps alive. There was fuel in plenty to protect us from the bitter cold of the night; but the water from a shallow well proved quite undrinkable, thus giving foretaste of one of the chief amenities awaiting us round Lop-nor.

CHAPTER XXIX

WITH the footsore camels painfully lagging behind and the ponies, too, showing signs of exhaustion, it was impossible to cover on November 29th the thirty odd miles which still separated us eastwards from Vash-shahri, the first little oasis of the Lop-nor region. For a considerable distance we had to surmount, too, a succession of big sand 'Dawans' which stretch inlet-like northward from the submontane belt of true desert. So I was glad when by nightfall we found a spot with some grazing and a well of tolerably fresh water, not far from the point by the roadside known as 'Pailu' where a wooden post with a Chinese inscription, protected by a tiny hut, marks the boundary between the districts of Keriya and Charklik.

The latter depends from the Tao-t'ai-ship of Ak-su, which had only some three months before passed into the charge of my old friend P'an Ta-jên. Already from Khotan in the summer I had through Chiang-ssŭ-yeh's elegant brush addressed a suitably worded epistle to my learned friend and patron asking official help for my explorations in his new dominions. The distance between us had been too great for an answer to reach me. But now it was a good omen and like the sign of a friend's hand stretched out from afar that here, on my very arrival within the border of P'an Ta-jên's most remote district, local assistance promptly appeared. Weary with a fresh attack of that mild malarial fever which had clung to me on and off since my tours on the Indian N.W. Frontier, I was waiting for signs of the baggage approaching, when quite unexpectedly the Beg of Vash-shahri rode up, the first man we had

sighted since Charchan. I knew the place to be still some
ten miles off and nothing but a small hamlet. So the
apparition on the scene of this worthy Muhammadan
wearing his Chinese cap of office and followed by a son
of Kepek, the original settler of the place, carrying a big
gourd with milk, was a pleasant surprise. I welcomed his
coming not merely as an earnest of the friendly reception
awaiting me at Charklik, but also because it allowed me to
secure without loss of time guides and labourers for a
survey of the ancient site of Vash-shahri which I was
anxious to examine *en route*.

A march of less than four miles brought me next
morning to the centre of the débris-strewn area which
marks the position of the earlier settlement. The patches
of eroded ground extending between large tamarisk cones
for about one mile both north and south of the route
showed all the features of a typical Tati. Among the
fragments of pottery which profusely covered the loess soil
where bare of sand, pieces of finely glazed ware in a variety
of rich colours from translucent brown to celadon green
were numerous. Fragments of coarse opaque glass and
of small objects in bronze, such as buckles and arrow-heads,
with beads of all sorts in paste and stone, were also
abundant. What copper coins I could pick up on the spot
or acquire from the villagers of Vash-shahri, all belonged
to the coinage of the T'ang and Sung dynasties, and thus
pointed to the site having been occupied down to the
thirteenth century or the time of the Mongols.

By the side of tamarisk cones, and thus partially protected, half-a-dozen small structures still showed their brick
walls to heights of from four to seven feet. I had the
one or two rooms which each of them comprised cleared
with care, but without coming upon 'finds' of any sort.
One little ruin attracted my attention by being built in
hard burnt bricks, a material nowhere else met with among
sites south of the Taklamakan. In another I noted that
the sun-dried bricks, which throughout the ruins showed
a fairly uniform size of about fifteen by eight inches with
a thickness of four inches, were carefully laid with the
long and short sides facing in alternate courses, a practice

subsequently observed in Kan-su in the masonry of many buildings old and new.

The general impression left by my inspection of the remains was that of Chinese influence more direct than that observable in the ruins of the Khotan region. This has since been confirmed by Mr. R. L. Hobson's expert analysis of the glazed stoneware, among which he has recognized pieces belonging to bowls known to have originated at the Chunchow factories of Ho-nan during Sung times. But there was nothing to indicate whether this increased Chinese influence was due merely to a position so much farther east on a once much frequented trade route from Cathay, or to the presence at this point of a small Chinese settlement during the early middle ages.

The abandonment of the village site since that period was proved by the height, ten feet and more, to which tamarisk-covered sand-cones had risen above some ruined structures, and equally also by the erosion, down to six to seven feet, which unprotected ground near others had suffered. The much-fissured trunks of dead poplars and fruit trees lay scattered not merely within the narrow belt occupied by the remains of old homesteads, but also for a short distance over the bare gravel Sai extending eastwards. An original top layer of fertile soil had evidently been blown away altogether, and this accounted for the raised line of the canal still clearly traceable across it. This canal, after skirting the old site, seemed to turn to the north-north-east, in exact conformity with the summer flood-beds of the actual river which we began to cross amidst luxuriant Toghrak jungle some three and a half miles farther east. At last after another couple of miles we reached by the side of the main bed the new colony of Vash-shahri, the growth of barely a generation and still a very weakly plant.

The history of this curious colonizing venture was strikingly illustrated by the contrast between the few ramshackle dwellings we passed and the brand-new and comfortable small rest-house or ' Kung-kuan ' which to my surprise I found ready for my reception. For years past the Chinese district administration, under higher official

orders, had endeavoured to utilize the water supply available in the Vash-shahri River for the creation of a small
oasis which would serve to facilitate and develop traffic on
the route between Charchan and Charklik.   The strategic
and commercial importance of this ancient route had
manifestly appealed to the keen topographical sense of the
rulers ; but the execution of their order had been no easy
task.

The three sons of Kepek, the original settler from
Keriya, who first took up land here some thirty years
before, had indeed kept to their little colony and prospered.
But the destitute agriculturists whom successive Ambans
had tried to attract to the new settlement from distant
oases by advances of food, seed-corn, etc.—by fair
promises, too, as well as by the application of some gentle
pressure—had in almost all cases decamped whenever the
harvest did not come up to their expectations, or the
question of refunding advances arose.   With the keen
competition for agricultural labour going on all along the
widely scattered oases in the east of the Tarim Basin, there
was little chance of detaining such roving folk at an outlying place like Vash-shahri.   At the time of my passage
some twenty families had been brought there by the
'Beg' who had last contracted for this official 'development scheme.'   But feeling little confidence in the per-
manency of the human material supplied, he had taken the
sensible course of investing some of the grant received
in 'bricks and mortar.'   The building of a rest-house,
granary, and Bazar would serve as a most effective official
'eye-wash' and allow his patron, the Amban of Charklik,
to send great reports of colonizing achievements to headquarters at Ak-su and Urumchi.

However this may be, I felt as grateful as did my men
for what comforts in the way of shelter and supplies Vash-
shahri could offer.   The most useful of the latter was a
stout ox-hide from which to prepare fresh soles for those of
the camels whose feet had been worn sore by the hard
salt-encrusted ground encountered along the old inundation
beds of the Charchan River.   The new soles, alas, had to
be sewn on to the live skin of the poor beasts' foot-pads—

a very painful operation which without the skill and pluck of Hassan Akhun, my experienced camel-man, would scarcely have succeeded. As it was, it took hours for each of the injured camels to be duly 're-soled,' and half-a-dozen men to hold down the huge writhing patient.

Early on the morning of December 1st I started my caravan for the two final marches to Charklik, a distance of close on fifty miles. Almost the whole of this distance lay over a desolate glacis of gravel, fringed only here and there by patches of scanty tamarisk growth and thorny scrub stretching northward. We halted in a narrow belt of marshy vegetation by the side of the Tatlik-bulak stream, and next day, after a long dreary ride under a hazy sky, sighted at last from afar the trees of the Charklik oasis. *En route* we had met the first travellers since leaving Charchan, a couple of traders clad in heavy furs taking some fifty donkeys laden with wool to Khotan. Now, as twilight descended, I was received at an outlying patch of cultivation by the Begs of Charklik. Their attention left no doubt as to the assistance which P'an Ta-jên's recommendation had assured me at the local Ya-mên.

Refreshed by the tea of a modest Dastarkhan I rode on for another six miles, past straggling fields of poor aspect and over intervening wastes, to the broad river-bed where the thin streaks of water already carried ice. The new well-built Bazar beyond looked large as we crossed it in darkness, and soon I found comfortable quarters in the spacious house of Tursun Bai, a settler of substance. My host was one of those 'Lopliks' who, as more or less nomadic fishermen, have lived in isolation for centuries by the marshes and lakes of 'Lop' and had taken to agriculture only within a generation or two. The comfort of his large brick-built homestead gave striking proof of the progress since made. Yet a look at his quaint Mongolian features would by itself have sufficed to remind me that I had now indeed reached Lop, Marco Polo's "town at the edge of the Desert, which is called the Desert of Lop."

It was this desert which offered the goal for my

eagerly sought explorations of the winter. Ever since my plans were first formed I had fixed my eyes on the ruined sites north of Lop-nor, discovered by Hedin on his memorable journey of 1900. After exploring their remains and whatever else of ruins we might trace in this region, I proposed to take my caravan right across the great desert north-eastwards to Sha-chou or Tun-huang by the ancient route which Marco Polo followed, and which has since been abandoned for centuries. The information I had so far succeeded in gathering about it was scanty in the extreme. But everything pointed to the need of careful arrangements about transport and supplies, if serious risks and losses were to be avoided. Had not the great Venetian traveller recorded his caution? "Now, such persons as propose to cross the Desert take a week's rest in this town to refresh themselves and their cattle; and then they make ready for the journey, taking with them a month's supply for man and beast. On quitting this city they enter the Desert."

It was not a single crossing of the desert alone for which I had to provide, but a series of expeditions partly over ground quite unknown, and — most serious feature of all—implying prolonged stays at desert sites with a considerable number of labourers. The greater the uncertainty about the extent of the operations before me, the more important it was to husband my time as carefully as possible. I knew well that I could make sure of work in waterless desert only during the few months of winter when the cold would allow me to transport water in the form of ice. It was equally certain that, in order to obviate delays in a region so exceptionally devoid of resources, it would be essential to have adequate transport and supplies ready beforehand for all likely contingencies.

Thus the tasks I had to cope with during my short stay at Charklik were bound to be exacting. Within three days I had to raise in the small oasis a contingent of fifty labourers for proposed excavations; food supplies to last them for five weeks, and my own men for at least a month longer; and to collect as many camels as I could for the transport, seeing that we should have to carry water, or rather ice, sufficient to provide us all on a seven days' march across waterless desert north of the Lop-nor marshes, and then during a prolonged stay at the ruins as well as on the return journey. The problem looked indeed formidable when I found that, by exhausting all local resources, I only could raise the number of camels to twenty-one, including my own and six animals hired from Charchan. It would have been still more complicated had I not been able to reckon upon the small fishermen's hamlet at Abdal, near where the waters of the Tarim empty themselves into the Lop marshes, as a convenient depot. There I could leave behind all baggage and supplies not immediately needed, as well as our ponies, *à cheval* as it were, on the desert route to Tun-huang.

Fortunately Liao Ta-lao-ye, the Chinese magistrate of this forlorn district (Fig. 109), counting in all between four and five hundred homesteads, proved most attentive and helpful. When on the morning after my arrival I called upon him in his modest Ya-mên transformed from a local Bai's house, I was received with an *empressement* which betokened not merely deference to my Tao-t'ai friend and patron, but personal goodwill and interest. Liao was a slightly built man of about thirty-five, with pleasant and refined features of a typical Chinese cast. His charge was more of an exile, and an unprofitable one in addition, than that of any Chinese official of his rank I had yet met. So the state reception was simple enough, two Turki villagers, disguised as executioners in long red gabardines, being the chief *figurants*, besides a Chinese clerical attendant and the Begs escorting me.

But I had not long been seated on the Amban's left, upon the chair of honour, in his cosy and neatly kept small living-room, before I was struck very pleasantly by my host's remarkably well-bred manners and quiet air of authority. With the help of Chiang-ssŭ-yeh, ever the liveliest *causeur* on such occasions and a true fountainhead of genealogical knowledge in regard to every Chinese dignitary of the 'New Dominions,' I soon discovered that Liao was a younger brother of Liu-chi Ta-jên whom I had met in 1901 as Amban of Yarkand. The intelligent grand-

A   B   C

108. WESTERN GROUP OF RUINED STUPA AND TEMPLES, MIRAN SITE.
A. Stupa mound.   B. Buddhist shrine M. V.   C. Buddhist shrine M. III.

109. LIAO TA-LAO-YE, CHINESE MAGISTRATE OF CHARKLIK.

seigneur bearing and amiable grace of the latter had then
impressed me favourably, in spite of widespread reports
of his unabashed exactions and rather unscrupulous ways
in general. But then was not his uncle the great Liu
Chin-t'ang, the famous general who, after the rebel Yakub
Beg's death, had in 1877 reconquered Turkestan, and
whose services to the Empire I had on my first visit to
Kashgar seen honoured by a stately temple dedicated to
his memory?

The family of such an 'organizer of victory' might well
claim exceptional privileges under a grateful Government;
and indeed I was not surprised to learn during my previous journey that the great Liu Chin-t'ang's relatives, close
and distant, held a conspicuous share in the most lucrative
official posts of the Province. Much-talked-of reforms had
not yet seriously affected the time-honoured state of affairs
under which the civil administration of the Province was
considered as a kind of reserved ground for the relations
of Liu Chin-t'ang and his redoubtable confrère Tso Tsung-
t'ang's relations, as well as for their Hunanese friends.
Chiang-ssŭ-yeh's inexhaustible flow of Ya-mên stories and
scandals, diverting subjects of talk on our long weary
marches, had fully assured me on that score.

But, alas! Liu-chi Ta-jên's official fortune had, through
causes which need no relating, suffered serious eclipse.
Deprived of administrative functions, he was at this time
living in proud retirement at Urumchi, preparing for the
long journey back to his native Hu-nan, where he wished
to end his days in philosophic seclusion. And through his
elder brother's disgrace Liao Ta-lao-ye's official prospects
too had been blighted. After various charges in Urumchi
and Kashgar his Ambanship of Ê-tun-hsien, as modern
administrative nomenclature, reviving a very early Chinese
name, designates the Lop-nor tract, spelt nothing less than
impecunious exile. The official pay, of course, as throughout the Province and the Empire, would barely provide
for the unfortunate magistrate's absolute necessities and
the maintenance of a modest but indispensable staff.
In this poor and undeveloped tract, still needing all possible administrative nursing, there were absolutely no

chances for feathering his nest by perquisites more or less excusable. So a man of Liao's refined taste and scholarly turn of mind was entitled to my sympathy in this dreary Tomi of Lop-nor.

He seemed unfeignedly grateful for the pleasant diversion which my secretary's gossip brought him, and for the stimulus, too, which he drew from such old Chinese books of travel, photographs, maps, and antiques as I could show him on his repeated visits. But best of all was it that Liao still knew how to give orders and to see them obeyed. In a small oasis like Charklik, where the total of the settled agricultural population was estimated at about three hundred families, but probably did not reach that figure, it was no easy task to raise the fifty labourers I needed for excavations in the desert. Without the Amban's stringent orders it would have been quite impossible.

Whether descendants of colonists brought from Keriya and the northern oases, or of Lopliks who had taken to agriculture, all the men were thoroughly frightened by the prospect of having to leave their homes in the depth of winter for a distant and wholly unknown journey in the waterless desert north-eastward. I for my part was only too well aware of the hardships which awaited us in that desolate region, and of the risks which might have to be faced from want of water if we should fail to locate the ruins promptly, or should find the salt-springs of Altmish-bulak still unfrozen. So I was doubly anxious to enlist only men of thoroughly sound physique, and to assure their starting fully equipped with adequate winter clothing and ample supplies.

The difficulties arising over the selection of suitable men were great. Full of apprehensions themselves, and disheartened by the wailings of their relatives who were lamenting them as already doomed, they tried their best to get off by shamming disease or by other subterfuges. I was wistfully longing for such moral support as the presence of some of my old 'treasure-seeking' guides from Khotan or Niya would have given me, when help opportunely arrived on the second day in the persons of two hardy hunters from Abdal. Old Mullah and Tokhta Akhun, his burly companion, had in 1900-1901 seen service with Hedin around Lop-nor, and I had already from Vash-shahri sent a request ahead for them to be summoned from their homes. The Amban's messenger had fortunately found them at Abdal, and now, after having covered over sixty miles by a hard ride through day and night, they turned up cheerfully to take their places by my side.

It was true that neither of them had ever approached the ruins by the direct route from Abdal, and therefore could not be expected to act as guides beyond the point where we should leave the marshes. But they knew the nature of the ground we should have to traverse, and, inured to hardships of all sorts by their life as hunters, they were ready to face the wintry desert like men. Their prompt appearance on the scene and calm willingness to share my fortunes in the desert served as an excellent tonic to the fluttered hearts of Charklik. What with the cheerful assurance of the hunters, the offer of generous pay, and a promise from the Amban of exemption from the usual *corvée*, my selected victims seemed in the end sufficiently encouraged to look upon themselves as the pick of the manhood of Charklik and bravely kept their fears to themselves.

To myself it was a relief to have such companions by my side, trained by their calling to the endurance and self-reliance which the desert demands, and tested by the hard work which Hedin's expeditions had given them. Each of them was a character, rough but clear-cut. Old Mullah, who seemed close on sixty, was a quaint, wiry figure, with much-furrowed features of a distinctly Mongolian type, and a squeaky, high-pitched voice which recalled that of an elderly lady not in the best of tempers. He could remember quite well the times when all his fellow-Lopliks still lived by fishing along the Tarim and the riverine lakes which it feeds; when what little cultivation had been started at Charklik was confined to spasmodic sowings of oats and barley, and when the luxury of mud or brick-built dwellings was quite unknown. His own heart was in the chase of wild camels, whose haunts along the barren foot of the range southward he knew well. The sale of their meat at Charklik brought him profit. He knew also the desert stretching north-eastwards along the edge of the Kara-koshun, as the Lopliks call the great area of terminal marshes and salt lakes which the dying Tarim feeds, and which we, like the Chinese, are accustomed to designate by its Mongol name of Lop-nor. So when, some twenty-five years before, efforts were made by the Chinese administration to reopen the forgotten old caravan route leading from Abdal to Tun-huang, it was Mullah who, along with another Loplik since dead, succeeded in rediscovering the difficult desert track and guiding a plucky Chinese official through.

Tokhta Akhun, the other 'Pawan' from Abdal, was a figure from a different mould, personifying as it were the adaptation of the hardy old Loplik stock to the new phase of civilization which was coming over this region. He was of a younger generation and about thirty-five years of age. In his burly, square-built body and heavy, broad face, with strongly projecting cheek-bones and the scantiest of hair growth, he still showed all the physical characteristics of that Mongolian race which had survived unmixed among these isolated fishing nomads on the Tarim, as it has farther west among the Kirghiz of the Pamirs. His speech was the thick-spoken, deep-vowelled Loplik dialect with its archaic vocabulary, which was often scarcely intelligible even to my Turki-speaking followers from Yarkand and Khotan.

But Tokhta Akhun's mental horizon ranged far beyond the customary haunts of the Lop men by the river and in the desert. He had travelled along the line of pre-carious new settlements northward as far as Kara-shahr, and had followed Hedin far away on the Tibetan plateaus southward and among the Mongols grazing in the high Chimen-tagh. He had something of the newly tamed barbarian's interest in all contrivances and technical com-forts of civilization, and proved handier about pitching my tent or camp bed than my staid old servants for whom such 'Firang' dodges had long lost all novelty. But he gave me even more useful proof of intelligent observation at the outset when he presented me on arrival with a fragmentary leaf of paper showing early Tibetan writing on both sides. He had discovered it some time before by scraping among the ruins of the old fort of Miran, which the Russian map showed as situated near one of the routes leading from Charklik to Abdal. The 'find' looked decidedly promising, and in conjunction with the fairly detailed description Tokhta Akhun could give me of what manifestly were remains of old shrines in the vicinity of the ruined fort, it induced me so to shape my programme that I might visit Miran *en route* for the sake of trial excavations.

But even at Charklik itself, engrossed as I was day and night by practical preparations, I could not keep my thoughts altogether from antiquarian interests close a hand. A number of considerations convinced me that the oasis of Charklik represented the chief place of this whole Lop-nor region in old times as it does now. The river to which it owed its existence was certainly the largest descending to the Lop-nor depression from the Kun-lun east of Charchan. The facilities it offers for irrigation on its alluvial fan are far more assured than any which could possibly be derived in this region from the terminal course of the Tarim itself sluggishly winding in low and ever-shifting beds. Broad geographical facts left no doubt for any one acquainted with local conditions that Marco Polo's Lop, "a large town at the edge of the Desert" where "travellers repose before entering on the Desert" *en route* for Sha-chou and China proper, must have occupied the position of the present Charklik.

Nor could I see any reason for placing elsewhere the capital of that "ancient kingdom of Na-fo-po, the same as the territory of Lou-lan," which Hsüan-tsang reached after ten marches to the north-east of Chü-mo or Charchan, and which was the pilgrim's last stage before his return to Chinese soil. It would be impossible to discuss here in detail all the historical evidence, furnished by the Chinese Annals and pilgrims' accounts, which proves that the alternate name Lou-lan or Shan-shan was from Han times down to the T'ang dynasty applied to the whole of the region comprising Lop-nor and the adjacent tracts of desert and riverine jungle, along with what scattered small oases they might then have contained. So much, however, I may mention, that whatever exact topographical indications are furnished by the itineraries contained in those records, clearly point to Charklik as the chief settlement of Lou-lan or Shan-shan.

So it was some satisfaction to me to find that signs of ancient occupation hitherto unnoticed were traceable in the very centre of the present cultivated area of Charklik, even on the surface. Quite close to the east of my quarters stretched one of the walls of a ruined circumvallation built in oblong shape and well known to the people as the 'Sipil.' Its mud ramparts, though badly decayed and completely levelled in places for the sake of cultivation within and without, could easily be made out for just over half a mile from north to south. Its width was about one-third of a mile. The extant height of the ramparts varied from twelve to twenty feet. Though the whole of the interior was occupied by fields and homesteads, a rapid examination disclosed here and there remains of manifestly old structures in large bricks partially utilized by the modern settlers. In one of these I thought I could recognize the surviving portion of a small Stupa with its circular dome twelve feet wide and, of course, long ago dug into for 'treasure.'

Far more imposing was the ancient mound known as the 'Tora,' or tower, to which my attention was called about one mile away to the north-west. There, within about 300 yards from the left bank of the river, rose a large and steep mound to over fifty feet above the irrigated level. The layers of rubbish with plentiful large stones exposed on its slopes left no doubt about its artificial origin. The top bore much-dilapidated remains of a brick structure, about sixteen feet in diameter and still rising to a height of twelve feet on the north side. Below it the brickwork of a much wider square or oblong base was traceable. There could be little doubt about its being the remnant of a Stupa dating from Buddhist times. But the mound below was far too large to be formed by the débris of any single structure, and the strata of rubbish composing it, where laid bare by cuttings, distinctly suggested an origin from prehistoric occupation. The ancient refuse mixed with the stones was being dug for manuring, and this might have accounted for the disappearance of other mounds.

Was it possibly this stone material, evidently brought from a distance, which had induced the Chinese of the T'ang times to designate the place—then occupied by a garrison, three marches south of Lop-nor, and by its position on the route to Charchan clearly corresponding to Charklik—as 'the Stone Town'? The T'ang Annals distinctly place there the capital of the Lou-lan or Shan-shan of the Han period, at least from 77 B.C. onwards. Chinese administration still retains a keen eye for matters of military geography. It was thus scarcely surprising to find that Charklik, as a point of strategic importance where a well-known route from Tsaidam and Tibet joins the roads to Khotan, Kara-shahr, and Tun-huang, had in recent years been held important enough for a small Chinese garrison. The neat little fort, with walls of stamped clay erected some ten years before, now stood empty, greatly to the relief of the people of Charklik, for whom the presence of a garrison of a hundred men had meant additional fiscal obligations. But the appearance on the scene some years after of a body of Tungan rebels, who had fled from Hsi-ning to Tsaidam, and were thence troubling the Mongols grazing in the mountains south of Charklik, well illustrated the wisdom of Chinese precaution.

In spite of all the harassing work my three days at Charklik seemed cheerful. Perfectly calm weather had set in with bright sunlight, and for most of the time I could see the mountains south quite clearly. In addition to all that was needed in the way of men and supplies for the desert expedition to my immediate goals, I had gathered very welcome information from a trader about the route across the desert to Tun-huang, and had laid in accordingly stores of supplies, fodder, and even uncoined silver, in anticipation of my move to that new field. With my depot established at Abdal I should be independent of Charklik and free to strike eastwards whenever my tasks about Lop-nor would allow.

By December 6th all was getting ready for the start; even the camels' winter clothing, patched up from many felt rugs which Charklik, with its abundance of wool from the mountains, afforded at cheap rates, was nearing completion. Only the absence of the Surveyor, of whom I had had no news since Charchan, remained an immediate cause of anxiety. Pleasant, well-bred Liao Ta-lao-ye had returned my farewell visit in the evening, chatted long of things ancient and common friends far away, and given me a last chance of expressing my hearty gratitude for all his help in that queer Chinese of my own which, by dint of Chiang's unremittent conversational flow, I had now learned to use with some freedom. Night had settled over the open-air Bazar which my people were busily holding in the outer courtyard with half the traders and all the idlers of the oasis to attend upon them, when at last Rai Ram Singh too arrived.

It was a great relief to learn that he had successfully carried his separate surveys right through along the foot of the Kun-lun, and had succeeded in extending a net of triangles, from a base measured near Polur and connected with fixed points of Captain Deasy's surveys and of the Indian Trigonometrical Survey, all the way to a peak south-west of Vash-shahri. But the cold which was so welcome to me, as giving me hope of being able to carry our water-supply in the form of ice, had been severe in the foot-hills of the great range, and had caused the Surveyor's old trouble, rheumatism, to reappear in a measure which might seriously handicap him. In any case he had well earned a short rest. So I was glad that the prospective work at Miran made it possible to leave him behind for a couple of days.

CHAPTER XXX

START FOR THE LOP DESERT

ON the morning of December 6th, 1906, I set out from
Charklik. I was up long before daybreak, but it took
four hours' constant urging to tear my big caravan from
its flesh-pots. In its full strength it was not likely to see
such again for a long time. For two miles we passed
between well-tilled fields, and then reached a somewhat
narrower belt of arable land known as Tatran, where
cultivation was said to be carried on intermittently every
third year. Low tamarisk growth was allowed to encroach
on these fields, for the regular cultivation of which either
the available water or labour did not suffice. By the side
of a shallow, ice-covered river branch which divides the
two areas, I found all my fifty labourers duly arrayed, each
couple sharing a sturdy donkey well laden with bags of
flour and heavy furs for the men and their modest utensils.
I made sure that a week's supply of oats had also been
brought for every animal, and that the artisans I had taken
care to have included among the labourers (two carpenters,
a blacksmith 'Ustad,' and a leather-worker) were duly
provided with implements. The whole seemed a work-
manlike lot and resigned to the hardships before them.

As I reviewed my crew the strong Mongolian strain in
most of the faces struck me greatly. Then, as we passed
beyond the last fields on to the bare Sai of coarse gravel,
the relatives of the men and the Begs who had come so
far bade us farewell with shouts of 'Yol bolsun,' 'May
there be a road.' Rarely had this Turki good-bye sounded
to me so pregnant in meaning. Our march of close on
twenty miles led all day eastwards over the monotonous

barren glacis. On our left a distant fringe of low tamarisk cones lined the horizon, with glimpses of Toghraks, living or dead, where the channels of rare rain floods from the mountains expand and at times bring some moisture. To the south the absolutely sterile outer range remained in full view all day, its scarp furrowed by 'Chaps,' which the wild camels were said to haunt.

We halted for the night at Yandash-kak, where amidst high cones of sand covered with dead tamarisk we found two wells about six feet deep yielding plentiful and tolerably good water. Next day a long march, which from the total absence of any distinguishing features seemed never-ending, took us north-eastwards across some twenty-seven miles of uniformly bare Piedmont gravel to the banks of the Jahan Sai. We crossed its broad flood bed, almost dry, as the light was failing, and hurried to kindle a big bonfire on one of the highest tamarisk cones in the belt of sandy jungle which stretches along the east side ; for the column of baggage and labourers was far behind and in need of guidance. Then we who were mounted groped our way ahead in the darkness until we struck first a small canal with some fields, and then a luxuriant growth of Toghraks by the side of a shallow stream.

It was the stream of Miran, a branch of the Jahan Sai, which the people of Abdal have utilized for a generation or two to create a small colony known as the Miran Tarim. Here in a somewhat spasmodic fashion they cultivate fields of wheat without having abandoned their fisherman's life by the river. It was close upon midnight before all our heavy goods-train of camels had arrived. But what did a much-delayed dinner matter? We had fuel and water in plenty, and as I sat warming myself by a well-nourished camp fire, the rosy glow which lit up the young forest around us seemed to harmonize with my hopes of archaeological work before me.

Next morning, December 8th, I left our camp by the stream and, crossing the thin ice sheet which covered it, hurried under Tokhta Akhun's guidance with my full posse of labourers to the ruins he reported as being close by to the east. For about half a mile we passed through a fertile strip of ground, partly abandoned to rank tamarisk growth, and partly cultivated in turns of two or three years. A short distance beyond, on a scrub-covered sandy steppe, the track we were following led past a roughly built structure of timber and reed walls. Some ten years before it had served as a shelter for a Chinese detachment posted here to intercept the body of Tungan rebels who had fled from Hsi-ning to Tsaidam, and were expected to debouch upon Charklik from the mountains. Then we emerged soon upon a bare, gravel-covered waste, absolutely level but for a succession of narrow and low ridges. Their curious look and straight direction, running roughly parallel from south to north, at once suggested that they marked old canals.

Near to where the first of them was crossed by the caravan track leading eastwards—the route to Tun-huang and also to the mountains of the Altin-tagh—I came upon a completely ruined mound showing solid brick masonry and still about fifteen feet high. The tunnel dug into it from one side by treasure-seekers left no doubt about its having been a Stupa. That it was of considerable anti-quity was proved by the difference of level, some seven or eight feet, between the eroded terrace or 'witness' on which the lowest brick course rose and the ground sur-rounding the ruin. Yet the presence of such a 'witness' on what looked like gravel soil not easily attacked by wind erosion puzzled me a good deal at the outset, until I con-vinced myself on my tramp across this strange plain that its apparent gravel soil in reality consisted only of a thin layer of small pebbles covering deposits of fine loose sand beneath. Our footprints sank deep into the ground as they never would do on real gravel, passing easily through the thin surface dressing into the soft sand below.

So I gradually realized that deflation was at work here too, the sharp blasts of the desert slowly carrying away all the finer particles, while the small pebbles mixed up with the original sandy layers, which the winds could not lift, were left behind to accumulate on the surface. This quasi-geological explanation subsequently helped me to account for the apparent disproportion between the great

age of certain of the ruins and the relatively modest height
of the observed ' witnesses.'

The top of the Stupa mound commanded an excellent
view of other ruins cropping up on the wide level flat
eastwards like low islands on an inland sea. The first
group, reached after going for only some 800 yards,
consisted, as seen in Fig. 108, of four small ruined
structures. One among them, on the extreme left, was
readily recognizable as a much-decayed Stupa. Another,
to the right in the middle, showed a small and relatively
well-preserved Stupa, surrounded by the broken walls of
what had manifestly been an enclosing circular building.
The remaining two ruins were those of square structures
solidly built in sun-dried bricks of unusual hardness,
but too much covered by débris to be identified without
excavation.

After a rapid first survey I hurried on to where at
over a mile's distance there rose the old fort which Tokhta
Akhun had spoken of as the principal ruin of the site.
Seen from afar, and over ground almost as flat as a billiard
table, the ruin looked quite imposing. But when I had
approached it and was eagerly clambering over the badly
breached walls of the west face, I could not escape a
feeling of disappointment. The crumbling walls and
bastions were massive enough in dimensions, but their
inferior construction seemed to suggest a relatively late
date.

The whole formed an irregular quadrangle, with the
walls facing east and north-west about 250 feet long on the
outside, and those to the south and west somewhat shorter.
Massive oblong towers jutted out at the corners, while the
curtains between them were guarded by bastions near the
centre. The tower on the south face was particularly
massive, projecting close on ninety feet beyond the line of
wall, and rising even now to forty-three feet in height,
it suggested a donjon (Fig. 110). The construction of
the walls was as irregular as the shape of the whole fort.
Layers of hard stamped clay formed the lower portions;
above rose masonry of coarse sun-dried bricks, smaller in
size than in the ruined shrines first examined, with layers of

110. SOUTH FACE OF RUINED FORT, WITH CENTRAL BASTION, MIRAN SITE.
For scale observe figure of man at foot of bastion.

111. LOPLIK FISHERMEN AT REED HUT, ABDAL.
On extreme left standing the young hunter who accompanied Turdi into the desert (p. 407).

tamarisk brushwood fixed between the courses at intervals of one and a half to two feet. The walls, which on their top seemed to have had a thickness of eleven or twelve feet, were surmounted by parapets where thickly packed tamarisk layers alternated with brickwork at close intervals.

Rough, indeed, the construction of this desolate stronghold looked and lamentably bare its interior. But I could not well doubt its age when I noticed that, within the circumvallation and near the east face, wind erosion had scooped out a depression fully ten feet below what layers of stable refuse marked as the original ground level. The surface sloped down from the east wall, behind which a layer of fine gravel and sand, evidently blown across by the prevailing north-east winds, had accumulated and afforded protection. It was here and not far from the inner north-east angle that a few wooden posts, rising a foot or so above the gravel surface, had attracted Tokhta Akhun's attention when he visited the ruin in the preceding spring.

On digging down single-handed he had then come upon what seemed to be the tamarisk bundles of a roof, and discovered among them the piece of paper inscribed with Tibetan which he had brought to me at Charklik. I could not expect to find a better spot for my intended trial excavation, and lost no time about setting my men to work here on a line stretching along the east wall. The promise of small rewards for the first finds stimulated their energy, and with fifty Ketmans working away lustily a row of small apartments soon emerged from below the cover of gravel and sand. They were all built in brick, with rough posts of Toghrak wood to support a roofing made of tamarisk branches and earth above. Apart from their being ranged more or less parallel to the fort wall, the disposition of these little rooms was extremely irregular. The largest measured only sixteen by eleven feet, and some of the smaller ones had a width of scarcely five feet.

But in inverse proportion to the small size and roughness of the half-underground hovels was the richness of the rubbish which seemed to fill them to the roof. From the very start of the digging pieces of paper and wood inscribed in Tibetan cropped up in numbers (Fig. 136).

The layers of refuse of all kinds left behind by the occupants continued to yield such records, complete or fragmentary, right down to the bottom. The papers varied greatly in size and character, some written on oblong leaves and with regularly ruled lines, being manifestly fragments of Pothis with religious contents, while the majority, written on sheets of rather flimsy paper, which recalled my corresponding finds at Dandan-oilik and Khadalik, represented documents of a secular character.

That the far more numerous records on wood, mostly narrow tablets up to eight inches in length and inscribed on both sides, were also of the latter type was made clear by the small seal cavities found frequently at their left end. But there was no time for closer examination, in fact scarcely for the marking of such finds, so rapid was their succession. The first day's work brought the total up to over two hundred. Similarly the remains of implements of all sorts, articles of clothing, arms, etc., were abundant. There were many curious pieces of scale armour, in hard leather, tastefully lacquered in red and black; embroidered pieces of silk; seals in horn, with Tibetan letters; neatly worked dies in bone, etc. Everything pointed to the conclusion that these deep deposits of rubbish, rich in archaeological plums—and remarkable, too, for their dirt—had accumulated during a protracted period of Tibetan occupation which historical evidence justified me in assigning to the eighth or ninth century A.D.

The profuse antiquarian haul of that first day, which it took me half the night in my tent to clean, sort, and examine, made it hard to leave behind such a mine, even for a time, without exhausting it. But when on the following morning I left the excavations in the fort to be continued under Naik Ram Singh's and Chiang-ssü-yeh's supervision, and proceeded on a reconnaissance to a ruin about 1¼ miles away to the north-east which Tokhta Akhun had spoken of as showing remains of sculptures, I soon realized that I could not possibly settle down now to a complete clearing of Miran without risking indefinite delay in the execution of my raid to the sites in the north of the Lop-nor desert. The ruin proved to be that of a temple, of which the central portion presented itself as a solid mass of masonry about forty-six feet long and thirty feet wide. Above the débris encumbering the sides there still showed remains of fine stucco relievos arranged between architectural decoration, also of good design. On clearing a small portion of the base of the east side with the few men at hand, I lighted upon fragments of stucco sculptures of large size, including a well-modelled colossal Buddha head, closely resembling in style the relievos of the Rawak Stupa, and therefore Graeco-Buddhist work.

Then I felt quite assured that the temple dated from a period far more ancient than that ascertained for the Tibetan fort. A number of observations made it appear *a priori* probable that a site of considerable antiquity had been reoccupied here, as in the case of Endere. The careful excavation of this temple and of the other ruins of earlier origin noted on my arrival would have claimed much labour and time; and as I could not afford this before my start northward, I determined in any case to revisit the site. The vicinity of Abdal, where I proposed to establish my base, and which would have to serve as the starting-point for the desert journey to Tun-huang, would make it easy to shape my plans accordingly.

So, after a further rapid reconnaissance of the whole site, I retraced my steps to the fort. There I had the quarters which we had excavated, and which continued that day, too, to yield up interesting 'finds' in plenty, carefully filled in again. It was a precaution in case any casual traveller visiting the lonely ruin before my return should be ill-advised enough to hunt for 'treasure' in such refuse left behind by poor soldiers. The tramp back to camp was cheerful for me in spite of the cold and the dark, which had settled upon us before 'the burial' in the fort was completed. For did I not carry away unexpectedly rich spoil from a ruin which had looked so unpromising, and the hopes of more to follow?

There was little chance, however, of my being allowed to forget the difficulties which had to be overcome somehow before I might return to this quarry. On arrival in camp I found that Rai Ram Singh had rejoined me in accordance with my programme, but was prostrate with rheumatic fever. This was a poor outlook, indeed, since I badly needed the Surveyor's assistance for my expedition into the Lop desert. To make him march on foot, as we should all have to do after reaching the last point where water was available for the ponies, was manifestly impossible. He would require a camel as a mount, and this meant an appreciable reduction of that ice-supply upon the adequacy of which the extent of our work on this expedition and in a sense our very safety depended.

Our own party numbered fifteen in all, including camelmen and Lop hunters; and after a careful calculation of the weight of the indispensable food-supplies, baggage, and ice needed, I decided that thirty-five was the maximum number of labourers which we could hope to take along in addition, without serious risk of being forced to a premature return owing to water (*i.e.* ice) failing us. So on the morning of December 10th my first task was to select and pay off the fifteen men who were to be allowed to return to their homes. Of course, we took care to pick out those who had proved least efficient during the previous two days' digging. It was curious to watch the wistful faces of those who were to remain and share our venture. But fatalistic acquiescence prevailed, and I must add, to their credit, that not one of them tried to sham disease either then or after. Perhaps their misgivings were somewhat lightened when they found me buying up the spare flour of the dismissed men as a reserve for their own use.

Then we marched off along the Miran stream northward. For about ten miles our track led through gradually thinning jungle where the water of the dying hill-stream disappeared in pools already frozen. Then a dull, saltcovered steppe stretched before us with scarcely a tamarisk to relieve its *morne* monotony. Across this another nine miles had to be covered to Abdal, a wretched hamlet composed of fishermen's reed huts, and the most notable place for those Lopliks who still cling to their traditional manner of life (Fig. 111). I was not altogether astonished when, long before reaching it, I was welcomed by two

Begs masquerading in official Chinese get-up. It is true
that Kum-chapkan, the other hamlet boasting of a Beg,
was only a short distance lower down the river. But after
my experience at Vash-shahri I had grown accustomed to
seeing the official zeal for colonization in this region taking
a turn at Potemkin fictions. In any case there was evidence that, what with their profits from fishing and grazing,
these good Lopliks could afford to make a brave show.

In order to assure a timely start on the morrow I had
taken care to get a ferry constructed well ahead under
Mullah's supervision, and to start off our camels long before
daybreak from Miran. So on reaching Abdal I had the
satisfaction of seeing that the five dug-outs cleverly lashed
together for a ferry and propelled by skilful Loplik paddles
had already succeeded in taking a portion of our transport
and supply column across the Tarim. It flowed here in a
deep and well-defined bed, about fifty yards broad, with a
current of a little under six feet per second. But more
impressive than the river's appearance was the thought
that here in this narrow bed there flowed past me all that
remained of the united drainage which the great snow-
covered ranges of the Kun-lun, the Pamirs and T'ien-shan
send down into this huge thirsty basin of Turkestan.

On the right bank I established my depot of whatever
baggage could be spared in a felt tent or Ak-oi well
removed from the inflammable-looking reed huts. Tila
Bai, the steadiest and most reliable of my servants, who
was to remain behind and keep guard over my boxes,
knew that they contained all my reserve of uncoined silver
intended for Tun-huang, besides the most precious of my
'finds' since Khotan. His care was to extend, too, to our
ponies, which were to return to Abdal after taking us to
the first waterless stage on the journey.

It was far harder for me to leave behind at Abdal my
devoted helpmate Chiang-ssŭ-yeh. But eager as he was to
face the 'Ta-Gobi,' 'the Great Desert,' with me, I knew
well that his feet, unaccustomed to more than short town
walks, would be unequal to the long, trying tramps before
us across dunes and eroded ground. To spare a camel
for him was impossible, and even if, as he pleaded, I could

let his slender weight be carried on the top of a laden
camel there would have remained the insuperable objection
of the increased provision in baggage, supplies, and ice
needed for him and his servant. Besides, my excellent
secretary was too valuable an asset for the spring and
summer campaign which I had planned on purely Chinese
ground for me to expose his health needlessly to such
risks as this desert expedition implied. So Chiang agreed,
as it were under friendly protest, to remain behind in the
most comfortable quarter which the Beg's reed-built huts
could furnish, and to help me from a distance by acting as
my post-office and keeping communications open with our
common friend, the well-meaning magistrate of Charklik.

The arrangements about the division of baggage, the
storage of surplus stores, etc., kept me busy till late at
night, and it was not until the morning of December 11th
was well advanced that I managed to get my big desert
column to start. There was no ice yet anywhere in
the winding bed of the Tarim, which we followed for
about five and a half miles down to Ak-köl, from where
the reed huts of Kum-chapkan were visible in the distance.
But Mullah and Tokhta Akhun, who from their hunting
expeditions knew the ground to the north-east well for
about three marches, were expecting to find ice in one of
the fresh-water lagoons left behind by the northernmost
flood-bed of the river known as Yangi-su, 'the New
Water.'

I was aware that the water of the lagoons and marshes,
collectively known as Kara-koshun, was bound to be more
salty and to freeze later, the farther away from the head of
the delta below Kum-chapkan. And in spite of minimum
temperatures of about eighteen degrees of frost at night
the last few days had felt warmer than any since leaving
Endere, a result no doubt of the much-reduced elevation
and the temporary absence of wind. So when, after
traversing a monotonous steppe covered with reed beds
and occasional tamarisk cones for about eight miles to the
north-east, we arrived by dusk at the banks of the lagoon
known as Alam-khoja-köl, it was a relief to find that its
marshy bed was already hard-frozen. All the men were

set to work cutting ice, and by the light of big bonfires the filling of the huge bags of coarse wool brought for the purpose from Charklik proceeded until midnight.

Next morning I roused the men by 5 A.M.; but it was four hours later before the fully loaded column could be set in motion. The bags of ice, of which each of the eleven camels set apart for this portion of the transport was to carry three, had been made far too heavy. So all of them had to be opened again, and the surplus weight distributed as well as it might between the remaining camels carrying our supplies and indispensable baggage. How glad I was that this troublesome rearrangement could be effected not on the backs of restless camels groaning piteous protest, but on those business-like stacks or 'Shotas'! According to Turkestan practice these are made up of two short ladders lashed at the top, and when once charged with the loads can be lifted on and off the camels' saddles without great trouble (Fig. 126). Ordinarily four men suffice for the operation. But now, when we had to put loads of over four hundred pounds on the back of each available animal, six men were not too many. In addition, we had some thirty donkeys laden with smaller bags of ice. It was my intention to make them march for two days beyond the last point where drinkable water or ice was available, and leave their ice there for a sort of half-way depot. Of course, the donkeys would need water; but with a two days' thirst and relieved of loads they could be trusted to return quickly by the track we had come.

As to the camels, they had under Hassan Akhun's supervision been given a thoroughly long drink, six to seven big bucketfuls each, from a hole cut through the ice, and that would have to last them, for all that we knew, for some weeks. Once we had left the last lagoons and salt pools behind us, no fodder of any sort could be hoped for them until they reached the reed beds of the Altmish-bulak salt springs, well to the north of Hedin's ruins. But Hassan Akhun had not forgotten to include in our equipment a few skins full of rape-seed oil, in order to provide each of our own camels at least from time to time with a pound or so of this evil-smelling luxury. It was "the camels' tea," so my camel factotum declared, in the cold of the winter, and doubly needed when they were to go so long without any grazing. Ever since we started from Charklik Hassan Akhun had shown that he felt being put on his mettle. It would have been too much to expect him to divest himself of his quarrelsome temper and inordinately sharp tongue. But placed in charge of this armada of 'ships of the desert,' he seemed to realize his responsibility and the importance of proving that much-vaunted experience of the desert which he claimed from my Taklamakan expeditions. In any case I felt the instinctive assurance that Hassan Akhun's was the only human soul with me for whom this desert adventure had a real attraction.

Our march on December 12th was long but uneventful. We were following a rough track, evidently frequented by Loplik fishermen. It led north-eastwards through dreary salt-encrusted steppe with scanty tamarisk, mostly dead, or else beside shallow depressions where open sheets of salty water still unfrozen were edged by abundant reed beds. Dusk obliged us to halt near the lagoon known as Yaghizmak-köl, then completely dried up. I was anxious to cover as much ground as possible during the first marches while our camels were still fresh, and was up by 4.30 A.M. next morning. But as the ponies had now to be sent back owing to want of water, those of my men who had hitherto been mounted did not quite relish the prospect of having, in common with myself, to trudge it now on foot. So by one pretext or another they tried to put off that experience as long as possible, and succeeded for once in delaying the start.

In order somewhat to lighten the loads, two of my own men were to be deposited with a portion of the labourers' rations at a kind of advance base a short distance farther on where the hunters expected to find some ice. When I declared my choice of the men, and Muhammadju, my staid Yarkandi servant, found that he was not included, his disappointment was so great that he threw himself on the ground in impotent rage and writhed like a madman. It was a very effective performance, but so manifestly overdone that it failed to make an impression. Even the other men, who like my Kashmiri cook equally dreaded the long desert tramp, burst out laughing—and my worthy old follower soon recovered his senses.

After about four miles we approached the northern extremity of a large sheet of water forming part of the Chainut-köl, which Mullah and Tokhta Akhun declared to be the terminal lake regularly fed by the floods of the Yangi-su branch of the dying Tarim. Here they showed us hidden among high reeds a pool where the water was drinkable for animals and covered with a thin sheet of ice. So the spare rations were quickly deposited in charge of Aziz, the Ladaki, and Karim Akhun, who had so far acted as the Surveyor's pony attendant, with instructions to send them on to our proposed half-way depot as soon as the donkeys should have returned to fetch them. I was glad to see that the donkeys could be given a good drink here; for this made it possible to take them and their ice loads on for another two marches.

The point was a regular camping-place for the ' Balekchis ' or fishermen from Kum-chapkan and Abdal on their expeditions to the lagoons of this neighbourhood. From Hedin's book and the sketch-map of Lop-nor accompanying it I could also make sure that the route we had so far followed was the same which had brought him to Abdal after he had struck the northern edge of the Tarim delta or Kara-koshun on his journeys across the Lop desert in 1900 and 1901. I knew that, in order to reach the ruined sites first discovered by him, we should now have to strike a route to the north-north-east which would necessarily lead near those he had followed in the reverse direction. But there would be nothing to guide us, only the position of the ruins as indicated in his route-map and the compass. Neither of the Lop hunters had ever visited the ruins from this side. But for about one day's march to the north they were still familiar with the ground from former hunting trips, and on one important point they could definitely assure me. The newly formed large shallow lake, which in 1901 had caused Hedin so much trouble to get round, had since almost completely dried up again, leaving only scattered lagoons of salt water. So I could safely steer my course by the compass, provided that Hedin's position for the ruins was approximately correct, without having to fear détours and loss of time.

We had marched for over two miles when we touched the southern end of such a salt lagoon which had formed part of the ' Yangi-köl ' or ' New Lake,' and to the Lop fishermen was specifically known by that designation. Though no fresh influx of water was said to have reached it for three years, fish were still plentiful in it, and near a reed hut we found a great quantity of them stacked for drying. But now they were said to be dying off rapidly owing to the increased saltness of the water, and the men caught plenty of moribund or benumbed fish with their hands from under the thin crust of ice just forming. It meant a pleasant change in the labourers' diet, though the smell was distinctly high.

Large stretches of salt-covered boggy soil surrounding this lagoon and others of smaller size which we passed farther on, attested the rapid shrinkage of these sorry remnants of the ' New Lake.' Most of them had completely dried up, like the large bare basin known to the hunters as Kurban-kullu-köl, near which the ample growth of young reeds and tamarisk induced us to camp for the night. In the course of the day's tramp I had gathered interesting information from Mullah and Tokhta Akhun about the notable change which has taken place in the physical aspects of this dismal ground since Hedin saw it. For three years after his first visit in 1900 the basins of the Yangi-köl area were filled with fresh water from the Yangi-su branch of the river. Since then no water had reached them, and the lagoons had steadily shrunk, while what water was left turned more and more salt.

They knew the Yangi-köl depression since their youth from hunting expeditions after deer and the like, and could recall having seen its western edge where it was marked by rows of dead Toghraks. Their fathers had told them that the basins had also formerly held water for certain periods. So the presence of thin Kumush, dead or living, over extensive patches of ground seemed easy to account for from such intermittent inundations. The total absence of vegetation in certain intervening depressions was attributed by my hunters to the depth of the water once held in them.

On December 14th I succeeded in getting the camels to move off by 8 A.M., and to do a march of close on sixteen miles before nightfall in spite of the increasing trouble which the ground gave to the animals. The succession of salt pools and dry salt-covered lake-beds, large and small, which we passed all day, showed that we were still within the 'Yangi-köl' depression, which the latest inundation period had affected. But we had scarcely covered more than four miles, and just left behind what might be described as the area of scanty but continuous desert vegetation, when we had the first indication that we were now nearing that zone of strongly marked wind erosion which from Hedin's description I knew to constitute so striking a feature of the northern portion of the Lop desert.

It was a belt of narrow ridges or terraces in hard clay, separated by small Nullahs, not deep as yet but showing sharply cut banks, such as only the erosive action of wind and driven sand could produce in this region. The top of the terraces or 'Yardangs,' as we may call them after the Turki term adopted by Hedin, invariably showed shallow parallel furrows, all running like the Nullahs or trenches in the direction of the prevailing winds which had carved them, north-east to south-west. The soil exposed on the sides of the Yardangs was a hard stratified clay, unmistakably the sediment of an ancient lake-bed. Erosion could not have been long at work here, or else returning moisture must have temporarily stopped denudation ; for in places I found dead reeds which had grown between the Yardangs.

Beyond this first outpost line of the true desert northward there came again dry lagoons large and small. The water of the rare pools left behind in these salt-encrusted depressions was so salt that in spite of the cold it had nowhere yet frozen. The fact of only a single patch of living tamarisk and reeds being met with on the day's march after crossing those Yardangs suggested that the period of recent inundation had been too short in this area to allow of the growth of vegetation, or had been altogether exceptional.

The soft salt crust or 'Shor' of the dry lagoons affected the soles of the camels' feet so badly that I hailed it with relief when at last towards the evening we emerged on an area where wind-eroded banks and 'witnesses,' six to seven feet high, rose among low dunes. Bleached remains of dead poplars and tamarisks strewed the bare soil in abundance, silent proofs of a belt of luxuriant riverine jungle having once existed here. Shells of fresh-water snails were also plentiful. A mile or so beyond, the dusk obliged us to pitch camp at the foot of high sand-cones covered with hoary tamarisk growth, some of which was still living. At a point where the sand felt moist I had a well dug which yielded water at a depth of only five feet. But I scarcely felt disappointed when it proved to be utterly salt and undrinkable even for the camels.

CHAPTER XXXI

ACROSS AN ERODED DRY DELTA

NEXT morning, December 15th, I had all the bags of ice which were available on the thirty donkeys carefully stacked on the north side of the highest sand cone, which we marked with a conspicuous signal staff. I arranged that the donkeys, in charge of two extra men brought for the purpose, should return as quickly as possible to the Chainut-köl base. After two days' rest there the men were to march back to our desert depot with as many donkeys as were needed to bring up the labourers' reserve food supplies, also fresh ice in the bags so far emptied, and some loads of reeds for the camels. They were then to await the arrival of the camel convoy, which I proposed to send back to this rendezvous as soon as we had reached the ruins, to fetch up all the remaining supplies. I did my best to assure that these marchings of our divided transport columns should be timed so exactly as to avoid all needless waits; for even donkeys could not be expected to go without water for more than two complete days.

But I knew well how much the success of my plans depended on our locating the ruins promptly. In any case I could not let this chance of communication pass by without despatching a mail cover under a big Chinese official envelope. It was to be sent on through my base camps at Chainut-köl and Abdal to Charklik. Thence the Amban's care would see it sped slowly but safely by the Chinese line of Dak riders on the six weeks' journey *via* Kara-shahr to Kashgar. Adding the six odd weeks of transit from Kashgar *via* India I might reasonably hope for my desert messages to reach friends in Europe some time about Easter. How gratifying it was to learn ten months later that a kindly Providence had seen this, as my other desert mail bags, safely through to their far-off destination!

Our march on December 15th left no doubt that we had now definitely passed out of all recent lake basins and entered a zone of a very different character. Right through the fifteen miles' tramp the surface, where not covered by drift sand, was a very hard greyish clay cut up into Yardangs by wind-eroded trenches running regularly from north-east to south-west. The top of the plateaus left between them was also carved by a network of small furrows showing the same general direction. Corrosion by driven sand was manifestly a powerful factor in this sculpturing of the surface of the ancient lake bottom. The only portions of the ground protected against it for the time being were the successive narrow areas where the drift sand had accumulated in low dunes. I soon found that these drift-sand areas generally corresponded to strips of dead forest usually extending from west to east across the route we were steering. In most cases the withered and bleached trunks of Toghraks and tamarisks, whether lying half-smothered on the ground or still upright, seemed to form more or less regular rows.

In the growth of living riverine jungle I had often noticed this peculiarity of rows of wild poplars ranging themselves parallel to the banks of water-courses, big or small; they gave the impression that these strips of dead forest we passed through at intervals of two or three miles, had once lined channels of running water in what had formed part of an earlier delta of the Tarim. While kept alive by its water they had helped to arrest the drifting sand of the desert, and when they died through loss of moisture, this cover had in turn helped to protect their remains from erosion. Where the rows of dead trees were adjoined by erosion trenches the banks of the latter often seemed particularly steep and high; and the thought has since occurred to me that possibly wind erosion had only continued there the work begun by preceding water action. But only in one place, some three miles from camp, did we come upon a well-marked and far-stretching depression which recalled a river bed, with wall-like banks some fifteen feet high ; and here, too, the general direction seemed to coincide with that of the prevailing north-east wind.

But it was not the physical aspect of the ground alone which suggested that the area we were moving across had once been occupied by extensive riverine jungle—at some early period, intervening between the time when the lake sediments of its soil were deposited and the present stage, when, owing to complete desiccation and consequent denudation, it was undergoing rapidly progressing erosion and deflation. Curiously enough, we had scarcely moved for more than a mile from camp, across eroded ground, when implements of the Stone Age began to appear in numbers. The first which I picked up myself were a rudely worked small axe-head in stone, then an arrow-head and knife-blade in flint. More finds of similar implements, especially of knife-blades, files, and miscellaneous flakes in flint, followed in frequent succession, as the men with me were encouraged to keep a look-out for such small objects. Honest Jasvant Singh, the Surveyor's far-travelled cook, had been since my first journey an experienced searcher for small antiques, such as eroded ground near ruins displays to those who are keen-eyed and patient. For the sake of his ever cheerful ways and well-bred manners I liked to keep him by my side now that Chiang was not with us ; so I could watch his hunt proceeding steadily under my own eyes. Fragments of very coarse hand-made pottery, grey, brown, or red, together with slags, were also met with at intervals over most of the march.

As our route had to be kept as straight as possible, and search to right or left was practically excluded, the frequency of these finds is conclusive evidence that this tract must have been occupied by men in prehistoric times. Down to what period the physical conditions continued to allow of such occupation it was impossible to be sure. Some of the arrow-heads found that day were so carefully worked that even without expert knowledge I felt certain of their being neolithic. From what I had seen and heard of the Lopliks' traditional ways of living, it was easy to picture this ground, when it was covered by water-courses from the Tarim and by riverine jungle, affording a sufficient livelihood to a scattered semi-nomadic population of herdsmen, hunters, and fishermen. But that it had seen at least occasional visits of man during early historical times was proved by a well-finished bronze arrow-head which was picked up within five miles of our last camp. Judging from its workmanship, which agrees closely with other specimens found subsequently near the ancient site northward, it is likely to have been left behind by some hunter or soldier in the early centuries of our era.

These unexpected finds were calculated to turn my thoughts to many fascinating problems. Did the Stone Age remains belong to widely separated periods, and was it only the erosion of the successive layers originally containing them which had brought them to lie side by side on the present surface? Would it be safe to assume that the difference in level between the latter and the top of the terraces protected by dead trees and drift sand gave the measure of the extent to which wind erosion had done its work of scouring and lowering since the Stone Age? Or had moisture continued to reach here down to a much later epoch, and had the formation of alluvial loess in the meantime actually helped to raise the ground-level until the progress of desiccation led to the death of all vegetation and consequent denudation?

It was hard to attempt the solution of such questions at the time, or even the collection of sufficiently accurate measurements of levels, etc., while my attention was being constantly distracted by practical cares about the proper direction and safe progress of my desert column. Now when we were proceeding over ground so much broken, even the maintenance of a correct course towards the compass point by which we were steering became a matter of some anxiety. It was impossible to get any distant outlook or well-defined landmarks, and the constant succession of steep-cut Nullahs between terraces crowned by rows of dead trees and dunes was very confusing. Regard for the camels, which could not negotiate steep banks, and whose feet were sorely tried already by the hard soil of the Yardangs, necessitated incessant little détours. The Surveyor, whom rheumatism severely taxed both in physical endurance and *moral*, was more or less *hors de combat*, and the guidance of our course by the needle fell entirely upon me.

But this was not my sole care of navigation, as it were. It was not enough to bring my big convoy as straight and as quickly as I could to the scene of operations. I had to make sure, also, that the party which I proposed to send back as soon as we had reached the ruins for our reserve supplies of ice and food, should be able to guide itself without risk or fail to the depot left at Camp CXXI. On the hard clay of this trying ground no footprints would show, and I knew that the first heavy gale, such as we had to be prepared for in this wind-swept region even during winter would quickly efface our track in such drift sand as covered Yardang terraces or lay at the bottom of trenches. To provide easily recognizable road-marks became all the more important because, after our excavation task was done, I had planned to divide our party and eventually to make my way to the Tarim by a new route through the desert. So I took care to have our track marked at points easily seen from each other by sign-posts built up of dead wood or detached blocks of clay, Naik Ram Singh with Islam, the blacksmith, and a few lightly laden labourers being employed on this duty. What a relief and comfort it proved afterwards to have taken this precaution!

The day's tramp across those terribly hard clay-banks and trenches, with belts of drift sand intervening, had tired men and animals badly. The heavily laden camels could not do more than about a mile and a half an hour over such ground, nor safely cross it in the dark. Where dusk obliged us to halt, there extended a perfect maze of low Yardangs, so hard on their top that to drive in the iron pegs for the tents cost great efforts. Dead wood was very scanty. But, luckily, there were plenty of men to send out for collecting needful fuel. By the light of the fires they kept blazing, Hassan Akhun was busy at work with his acolytes 're - soling' unfortunate camels whose foot-pads, what with the trials of salt 'Shor' and sharp-edged clay-banks, had got badly cracked. I heard the poor beasts still groaning when I went to rest about midnight.

Two hours later I was awakened by violent gusts of wind shaking my tent and driving in sand. To secure the tent-pegs by slabs of hard clay piled up over them was unpleasant work in that icy blast from the north-east. Though the fall in the minimum temperature, which had ranged about 12 degrees Fahrenheit since leaving Abdal, was but slight, the cold seemed suddenly to have doubled. I did not know then how much of our stay in this region was destined to be spent in the clutches of this freezing and unrelenting north-east wind! I was up by 5 A.M. ; but the men crouching round the fires were, with the exception of my two hardy hunters, so benumbed that I did not manage to get the transport started until towards nine.

Cutting as the wind continued, its velocity was not great enough to lift high the sand which from here onwards seemed to become of somewhat coarser and heavier grain. So on fixing the plane-table above our camp in the morning, I was able to sight a low reddish-brown ridge far away to the north, the first sign of the desolate barren hills of the Kuruk-tagh at the foot of which our goal lay. To the south the high snow-topped range of the Altin-tagh could still be made out quite clearly under heavy cloud banks. So for a while I could cheer myself with the thought that my eyes were resting alternately on those two great chains of innermost Asia, the T'ien-shan and the Kun-lun. Somehow it seemed to relieve that sense of overpowering vastness which the desolation of this lifeless Lop desert produced. I now decided to shape our course due north, so as to strike the area of ruins discovered by Hedin somewhere near its centre, and thereby reduce the chance of missing its landmarks altogether owing to some difference in the reckoning of our position. Another reason was that I should thus, as I had tried to do ever since leaving the last fishermen's camping-place, be able to keep about midway between the two routes Hedin had surveyed on his successive journeys south from the site, and to approach it by a new track.

The ground over which this course took us on December 16th bore the same general character as on the previous day. The closely packed Yardangs all showed a uniform direction from north-east to south-west, and their tops were all intersected with furrows having the same bearing. Now with their creator, that icy north-east blast, at work, it was interesting to watch how the scouring and scooping was proceeding. It was easy to see that the erosive effect of the wind was greatest on the sides of the trenches, which the sand driven before it was steadily undermining just like running water. The closeness of the relation between this north-east wind and the surface configuration would have forcibly been brought home that day even to the least observant of men. For tempting as the trenches, cut down to twelve feet and more, looked as places of shelter, it was quite useless to seek a short rest there from the wind which seemed to cut to one's marrow. The blast was, if anything, greater there. Vainly would one search for a protecting bank at the end of a Yardang terrace. Invariably it ran out into a sharp edge, where piercing currents of air would catch one from both sides as if in an eddy. Rows of dead Toghraks and tamarisks running apparently west to east were met with again and again, usually over hard gypsum-like banks and adjoined by ridges of low dunes. Also some five miles from camp we passed extensive patches of ground where the tops of Yardangs were covered with dead reed stubble.

Remains of flint implements and coarse pottery, manifestly neolithic, continued to crop up in plenty at frequent intervals. There could be no doubt that we were still passing over ground which had seen human occupation during prehistoric times. These finds presented an increased interest, since we were now well within the area where Hedin had been led to locate his earlier Lop-nor lake depression. From about the sixth mile onwards I thought I could recognize fragments of pottery of distinctly better make, showing a uniform black surface over a red core. Nevertheless I was scarcely prepared about three miles farther to come upon what at once suggested the appearance of a small Tati of the historical period.

For nearly half a mile the hard soil was strewn everywhere with pieces of slag and potsherds, red and black, showing relatively finer grain and distinctly recalling the pottery débris met with about the Niya and other early sites. There were pieces among them, such as part of the neck of a large vase, which bore evidence of having been made with a wheel. My impression was soon confirmed when Tokhta Akhun, who with a few men then kept by me, picked up a large and well-preserved bronze signet ring, which in shape and design unmistakably tallied with similar finds of the first centuries A.D. obtained from those early sites of the Khotan region. A fragmentary square-holed Chinese coin, uninscribed, but of a type associated with the Han dynasty, furnished definite proof of the débris marking the site of some settlement of the historical period. High sand-cones held together by dead tamarisk growth gave a familiar look to the little Tati, and had restricted the carving out of Yardangs. Mullah's sharp eyes discovered that on the top of three cones the tamarisk was still living, and on approaching we found near them droppings of wild camels which at times must come to feed upon it.

By that time we all felt half-frozen by the cutting wind under a grey, sunless sky. When the wind dropped slightly about 2 P.M. light snow fell for half an hour, and almost gave comfort by limiting the dreary outlook. It lay only to the depth of half an inch or so, and, after the next morning's sunshine, disappeared altogether except on Yardang slopes where protected by corniced clay edges. Even thus it helped us to economize ice for a couple of days, and afforded a chance for the camels to moisten their tongues. To let them have a good drink off this snow was impossible; for it was dark before they could be unloaded, and it would have been unsafe to let them stray about on ground to which their legs were so ill-adapted. A mile or so before dusk obliged us to halt, we had crossed a long row of big dead poplars still rising to ten feet or more and clearly marking an ancient water channel.

Beyond we struck a thin belt of cones with dead tamarisk which seemed to promise some shelter, and there I had camp pitched. Our reckoning would make us within eight miles of Hedin's big ' Pao-t'ai ' ruin, and eagerly I scanned the horizon from the top of a large sand-cone with my prismatic glasses for that or any other landmark. But in vain.

The men from Charklik had started with a heavy heart and many misgivings at the outset. Now the exposure and fatigue of six weary marches over ground which seemed steadily to get worse, had increased their dejection. If I did not succeed in guiding them within a day or two to the ruins which I had definitely announced as the goal of this trying expedition, they would despair altogether and be likely to give trouble by attempts to desert or force a return. So I thought it right to show a face of sanguine confidence, though I knew well that on ground such as this, and at the rate we were obliged to move, no amount of care in taking our bearings with forward and backward rays, etc., could be absolutely depended upon to assure a true course.

The night was made miserable by the violent gale which swept down from the north-east about 1 A.M. and nearly blew my tent down. I had previously got the outer tent-pegs secured as well as we could. But under the strain of the rapidly swelling blast one rope broke, then another, while the inner fly of the tent was bodily lifted off the ground, together with the iron nails which fastened it down. I woke up half-smothered with sand, and not until I had piled up large lumps of clay all round the edges of the outer fly, with the help of the men brought from their distant camp-fires by my shouts, was a precarious stability secured for my shelter. It was as well that with my heavy woollen underclothing, intended for semi-Arctic wear, fur-lined vest for night use, and big fur boots of 'Gilgit' type, I was equipped for such outings. The men were all well provided with sheep-skins, padded 'Chappans' of cotton beneath, and felt socks and leather 'Charuks' which never came off their feet; but had it not been for the plentiful fuel supplied by the bleached tree trunks, they would have suffered even more from exposure than they did. The gale lessened somewhat after daybreak, and once the driving of sand ceased, it was remarkable how quickly the atmosphere cleared. But, of course, what food I got that morning was permeated with sand—as on many occasions thereafter.

It was nearly nine by the time I had got my convoy started, and we had not marched far before the sun broke brightly through the dust haze. Yet with that irrepressible wind steadily catching us from the north-east the cold seemed to grow more intense as the day wore on. Even a double supply of my warmest caps and gloves failed to keep head and hands warm. But if that day the conditions felt Arctic, there was exciting expectancy to keep the heart warm. We had advanced only three and a half miles northward across Yardangs and low dunes when in quick succession three Chinese coins of the Han type were picked up along our route. They, with some bronze arrow-heads and small fragments of metal objects of uncertain use which now cropped up, were a clear indication that we were nearing a site of the historical period. After another four miles, we struck a broad and well-marked depression running with a slight bend from west to east and lined with rows of dead Toghraks and decayed tamarisk cones. Mullah, without hesitation, recognized in it the ancient river course which he remembered having seen south of Hedin's ruined sites. Once beyond this belt the eye ranged wider, and soon the outermost low range of the Kuruk-tagh, all red and yellow barrenness, came into full view across a flat expanse terribly scoured and furrowed by erosion.

I had promised that morning a good reward in silver to the man who should first sight a ruin. Impelled by the hope of earning it and the wish to allay their anxiety as to the end of this quest, labourers and all were moving ahead with wholly unwonted alacrity. Great was the excitement therefore when, from the top of a plateau-like Yardang which he had climbed in advance, while his animals were halted and we were setting up the plane-table about a mile from the dry river bed, one of the

younger camel-men shouted that he could see a ' Pao-t'ai '!
All eyes were directed eastwards where he pointed, and
soon I verified with my glasses that the tiny knob rising
far away above the horizon was really a ruined mound,
manifestly of a Stupa. What a relief it was to us all!
The men from Charklik were all buoyed up with sudden
animation, and beamed as if they were already arrived at
the beginning of the end of their troubles, while my own
men affected a look of self-complacent assurance as if
things could not possibly have happened otherwise.

But the most curious thing to me was to watch the
triumphant figure and pose which Hassan Akhun, my quicksilvery camel factotum, presented. There he stood on the
top of the Yardang, with his right arm stretched out and
supported on a staff like that of a triumphator, while his
left rested akimbo. He was addressing his audience of
labourers, whom on the march he loved alternately to
cheer and to bully, with a mien half that of the prophet
proved true and half of the exultant demagogue. Had he
not always tried to drum it into their thick heads that
under the guidance of *his* Sahib, who could fathom all
hidden places of the dreaded Taklamakan with his ' paper
and Mecca-pointer,' *i.e.* map and compass, all things were
bound to come right? Now by the appointed day he had
brought them to the promised ' Kone-shahr,' just as he
had hunted up plenty before. What more could they wish
now than to earn their ample wages and the rewards
offered for old ' Khats '?

I always knew that my troublesome and mercurial
myrmidon had his uses, especially for any tough bit of
desert work. But never had it struck me so clearly that
in him lived the spirit and manners of an old Greek
adventurer. As he stood there, full of jubilant conceit and
heroics, in his bright red cloak and high-peaked purple cap,
his moods of dejection and petulance clean forgotten, he
called up to my mind a vision of one of Xenophon's Greek
mercenaries who shouted: *Thalatta! Thalatta!* More than
once after this day in the Lop desert I felt haunted by the
thought whether it were not from a drop of Levantine
blood, bequeathed by some remote ancestor who had found

his way to Seric regions like those agents of Maës, the Macedonian, that Hassan Akhun derived his strange jumble of versatile ingenuity and exuberant temper, fitful energy and classical impudence.

There was every reason to believe that the mound sighted belonged to the eastern or main group of Hedin's ruins. So I decided, without hesitation, to steer for it. The direction differed but little from that of the Yardangs, and thus favoured progress; but the distance proved nearly five miles, and though all the men moved on with alacrity, it took us two hours to cover them. On arrival I convinced myself that the large brick mound was that of a Stupa, undoubtedly the same near which Hedin had first camped on his return in 1901. Chinese coins of the Han type were picked up in numbers around, and finds of arrow-heads and other small objects in bronze became frequent.

Among the three mounds which now had come into view, the one to the south-east and largest was quickly recognized by Mullah as the place where Hedin's camp had stood. The ground separating us from it was frightfully eroded, and the succession of steep clay banks and sharply cut trenches between them, twenty and more feet deep, had to be negotiated at right angles. These last three miles were like an obstacle race, and most tiring. But just as darkness came on I had the satisfaction of reaching the foot of the ruined Stupa, which stands out in this weirdly desolate landscape as the landmark of the main group of ruins.

The abundance of ancient timber strewing the ground where structures had been completely eroded, allowed us to light a big signal fire on the top of a high clay 'witness,' and, guided by it, the convoy of our much-tried camels safely arrived nearly two hours later. I, likewise, had been fairly worn out by the exertions and anxieties of this week of hard desert marching. Yet as I sat warming myself with the men by the glowing bonfire, which threw ruins and Yardangs alike into fantastically bold relief, all that remained was elation at the goal successfully reached. In the letters which I wrote that night in my little tent until

112. RUIN OF ANCIENT STUPA, LOP-NOR SITE, FROM SOUTH-EAST.

In foreground remains of ancient dwelling, L.A. IX., on wind-eroded terrace covered with dead tamarisk.

the ink was freezing in my fountain pen, to carry to distant friends the news of my safe arrival, that feeling was duly reflected.

Sincere was my gratitude, too, to Hedin for his excellent mapping which, in spite of a difference of routes and the total absence of guiding features, had allowed me to strike these forlorn ruins without a day's loss, and exactly where his route map had led me to look for them. Since the results of our own plane-table surveys, checked by triangulation as far as the mountains south-west of Charklik and by ample astronomical observations, have been fully computed and plotted, I have convinced myself with no small satisfaction that Hedin's position for this site differs from ours only by about one and a half miles in longitude and less than half a mile in latitude, a variance truly trifling on such ground.

CHAPTER XXXII

FIRST EXCAVATIONS AT THE LOP-NOR SITE

DELIGHTFUL was that first night's rest at the ruins which it had cost such exertions to reach, and with the minimum thermometer showing about zero Fahrenheit on the morning of December 18th the temptation was great to keep between warm rugs and furs a little longer. But there were many reasons for making the most of our time in this region. So I was up by daybreak. An hour later the various detachments into which I had divided our transport were ready to start in accordance with the programme I had decided upon while on the march. All loads were to be left in our camp at this main group of ruins, the precious bags of ice being carefully stacked close to my tent in a place conspicuous and safe from poaching. Five camels were to march back to our half-way depot and to fetch supplies left there and such fresh ice as had been brought up since by the auxiliary donkey column.

The main convoy of camels was to be taken north to the salt springs of Altmish-bulak, in order to get a rest and much-needed grazing there. Tokhta Akhun, who was to guide them, had a year before accompanied Huntington on his plucky march to Altmish-bulak across the salt-encrusted old lake bed east of the Kara-koshun marshes. Having thence visited the two groups of Hedin's ruins, he could be relied upon to find the nearest spring quickly. He estimated that even unladen it would take the camels two days to get there. He was subsequently after a short rest to return himself with a camel to the western group of ruins, and to reconnoitre thence west and south-west for any other remains which might await exploration.

A

B

113. VIEW TO THE SOUTH-EAST FROM RUINED STUPA, LOP-NOR SITE, ACROSS WIND-ERODED GROUND.

Ruined dwelling L.A. IX. in foreground. A B marks line of joining with Fig. 114.

A

B

114. VIEW TO THE SOUTH FROM RUINED STUPA, LOP-NOR SITE, ACROSS WIND-ERODED GROUND.

Part of ruin L.A. I. in foreground. A B marks line of joining with Fig. 115.

A shorter reconnaissance in the same direction was entrusted to Rai Ram Singh, whom I expected to make an exact survey of the positions occupied by the ruins which Hedin's popular narrative mentions west of the group we had reached, but which the small-scale route map attached to it could, of course, not show. I thought that the large number of men at my disposal would enable me to deal quickly with the ruins I had rapidly inspected in the morning. So Hassan Akhun was instructed to send back by December 23rd a batch of camels sufficient to shift our camp then to new ground near the western ruins.

Free of loads the camels and those with them seemed eager to get clear of our desolate camping-place, and shortly after 8 A.M. I was left with my labourers to the undisturbed peace and solitude of the site. As I looked round from the high base of the Stupa below which my tent stood, while the men for once were finishing their morning meal in broad daylight, the scene of our prospective labours struck me like a view strangely familiar and at the same time novel (Figs. 113, 114). The ruins of timber and plaster-built houses rising with their splintered and bleached posts, like the last remnants of wrecked boats, on terraces high above the eroded ground, bore an unmistakable likeness to the structures I remembered so well from the Niya site. But how different was their setting!

Instead of the soft-lined expanse of swelling dunes and sand-cones, the eye here caught nothing around but an endless succession of sharply cut Yardangs of hard clay, all running exactly the same way, as sculptured by that relentless north-east wind. They too, like the dunes, called up a picture of the sea, not, however, a sea in free movement, but one frozen hard and buckled into innumerable pressure ridges. The view ranged freely over many miles. But apart from the closely packed cluster of ruined dwellings to the south and south-west of the Stupa, my powerful prismatic glasses showed no trace of structural remains elsewhere excepting a few scattered mounds, manifestly brick-built, in the distance northward. It seemed hard to believe that any isolated house of the usual timber construction could have survived such frightful erosion.

Familiar and novel aspects mingled curiously, too, in the work to which I now settled down. The clearing of the ruined structures of the sand accumulated within them, the searching of the débris strewing the eroded slopes below, and so forth, would not have seemed strange to my 'old guard' from Niya. I knew, in fact, beforehand that the remains at both sites dated from exactly the same period. But to me it was a novel sensation to have to conduct these wonted operations at a site which had already been searched by an earlier European explorer. Hedin's fascinating book had, by its chapter on 'The ruins of ancient Lop-nor,' and its excellent illustrations, sufficed to acquaint me with the general features of the ruins, which a lucky chance had led him to discover in 1900, and with the remains he had been able to bring to light there on his second visit in 1901. His 'finds' had been important, indeed, and the antiquarian evidence which they furnished was in many respects quite assured. Yet Hedin, out of a total stay of six days, had been able to give only three to actual excavation at the eastern group of ruins, and a fourth at the western. He had the services of only five men besides himself, and not one among them had previous experience of such work, while the number of ruins to be searched was relatively large. Thus from the first it was clear that a thorough exploration of the site by an archaeologist was needed in the interest of science. But who could feel sure in advance of how much a site thus 'researched' would still yield in new facts, observations, and 'finds'?

Chance would have it that the very first ruin on which I set my men gave cause for encouraging hopes. It was the remnant of a house once manifestly much larger, occupying the top of a small and steeply eroded terrace due south of the Stupa and only some fifty yards off (Fig. 115). Four rooms, including one over thirty feet long, could still be clearly made out by the broken walls, built of timber and wattle exactly as at the Niya site. Plentiful débris of timber strewing the slopes of the terrace, especially to the east and the south, marked the positions where other parts of the building had once stood, and where

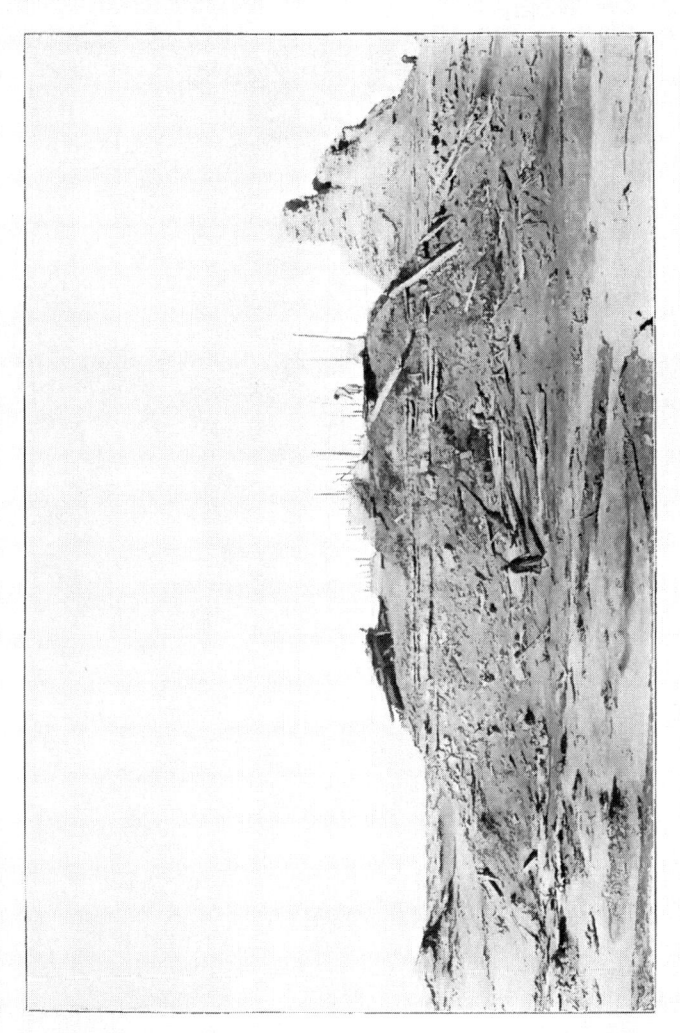

115. RUIN OF ANCIENT DWELLING L.A. L., AND OF STUPA, LOP-NOR SITE, SEEN FROM SOUTH.

all the soil had been carried away by wind erosion. Thus on the south the original ground level had been lowered fully eighteen feet. The sand which covered the floor of the rooms still extant was only one to two feet.

But even this had sufficed to protect a number of interesting small relics. The first was a narrow slip of wood, about half an inch broad, inscribed with a column of Chinese characters, and exactly conforming in its dimensions to those ancient Chinese records which I had brought to light on my first visit to the Niya site in 1901. Similar finds of Hedin in a ruin presently to be mentioned had prepared me to find more of such Chinese 'slips' at this site. But it was a very gratifying surprise when this was followed almost immediately by two oblong tablets in wood bearing four or five lines of faint but still perfectly legible writing in Kharoshthi. I had scarcely ventured to hope for records in ancient Indian script and language so far away to the east.

A second Chinese slip emerged from the corner of an adjoining room; and subsequently, when we began to clear carefully the miscellaneous rubbish which had found refuge amidst the fallen pieces of timber on the eroded slopes, successive shouts of 'Khat' soon announced the discovery of Chinese records on paper. They were fragments large and small, evidently of documents, and half-a-dozen in number. But better preserved and more curious were the closely packed layers of papers inscribed with a Chinese text, which seemed to have served as a backing for what had manifestly formed part of a large Buddhist painting executed on a thin ground of plaster. Little survived of the colouring, and the subject could not be made out with any certainty. The regular columnar writing on the backing leaves suggested some text or official record.

From the débris-strewn slopes came two more Kharoshthi records on wood which even on their first hurried examination offered some points of interest. One was the covering tablet of a wedge-shaped document which, though all the writing had become badly effaced through driving sand, still showed by its seal-socket, string-hole, etc., that the elaborate system of ancient stationery was exactly the same in this far-off eastern corner of the Tarim Basin as in the Khotan region. But the other document on wood, far rougher in appearance, helped to call my attention to an essential difference. It was an oblong piece of thick bark, cut apparently from a tamarisk trunk and inscribed with two long lines of Kharoshthi. Its material looked curiously uncouth when I thought of the neatly finished and smooth tablets of the Niya site; and when I examined more closely the other Kharoshthi records just recovered, I noticed that their rough and much-cracked surface was due not so much to corrosion and exposure as to their wood being that of the Toghrak or wild poplar, instead of the Terek or cultivated poplar invariably used for the Niya records.

It was an important indication, supported by plentiful observations thereafter, that arbours and avenues must have been rare in the vicinity of these ruins. Everywhere in the structures of what for the present I prefer to designate as the eastern of the Lop-nor sites, the timber employed proved to be taken from the wild-growing poplars of the riverine jungle; nor did I succeed in tracing near it any remains of garden trees such as the Terek, Jigda, mulberry, so common at all old sites from Khotan to Vash-shahri. When I subsequently explored the western of the Lop-nor sites I found that there, too, it was only a single ruin, and that manifestly a residence of some importance, which showed the dead tree trunks of an ancient arbour. So it became evident from the first that the resources of local cultivation could not have been sufficiently important by themselves to account for these ancient settlements.

But the finds at this first ruin were not confined to written records, and among the relics of another sort were several claiming special interest. From the corner of one of the rooms there emerged two fragments of a well-woven pile carpet in wool (Fig. 116, 4). Where not too hard worn, it had preserved its colours, several varieties of brown, a rich claret tint, buff, and bright blue, in remarkable freshness. The technique in the arrangement of warp, weft, and pile closely resembles that of the modern cheap Japanese rug; but no detailed description can be given here. It was the first ancient specimen of a true pile carpet I had so far been able to trace in Chinese Turkestan, and my satisfaction at its discovery was not small. Yet I had scarcely had time to examine it closely before a find scarcely less important for the history of ancient fabrics rewarded the scraping of a piece of ground, adjoining the north side of the ruin and showing no extant remains of superstructure. It was a small bale of yellow silk, lightly rolled and evidently unused, which had become so dry and brittle that when first lifted it broke in two (Fig. 116, 3). Its complete width was just under nineteen inches, its diameter over two.

It was strange thus to light at the very start upon so well preserved a relic of that ancient silk trade from China which, as many considerations had long before led me to believe, moved westwards during the early centuries of our era along the very route marked by this ruined settlement. Small pieces of silk in various colours, undoubtedly shreds from garments, turned up plentifully among the rubbish both at this and some other ruins of the site. But this find alone could show us the actual form in which that most famous product of the silk-weaving Seres used to travel far away to the classical West. It was useless to speculate why it had been left behind when the building was deserted by its last dwellers, or how it had escaped those who during a succeeding period were likely to have searched the abandoned settlement for any objects of value or practical use. But all doubt about the width of the silk being the regular one adopted for China's early export trade was set at rest when, on my return to Miran, I recovered from one of the ancient ruins of that site a large piece of silk preserving its original edges and also measuring accurately nineteen inches across.

I cannot describe here in detail a number of small implements such as spoons, eating-sticks, fragments of dishes in bronze or lacquered ware, which also emerged from among the débris of the first ruin cleared. Nor can I find space for more than a reference to the very abundant crop of small objects in metal, glass, or stone which were collected that first day from eroded soil in the immediate vicinity of the ruins (Fig. 117). This was a happy hunting-ground for the few attendants who were not kept busy digging; and they were eager to earn some pocket-money by rewards for chance finds. There were fragments of bronze mirrors in abundance, sometimes showing excellent relievo decoration at the back, rings and pieces of buckles, clasps and other well-worked personal ornaments in bronze, stone seals with geometrical designs, neatly finished small bells of the 'grelot' type, etc.

The rich harvest in beads, made of glass, paste, or stone, and often of brilliant colours, pointed to the fair sex having been amply represented at this station from which life and all its pleasures had departed so long ago. But still more striking, perhaps, was the profusion of Chinese copper coins, square-holed, and all without exception belonging to the types which were current during the Earlier and Later Han dynasties. It was impossible to escape the impression that this settlement, small in its extent and limited in its local resources, had yet seen a plentiful circulation of petty cash and that lively traffic which this usually indicates.

But on the spot I had little time to spare for such antiquarian trifles. As soon as the clearing of the isolated structure was completed, I moved my band of labourers across to the south-west, where, at a distance of about one hundred yards from the Stupa, there rose the ruins of a larger structure. It occupied the easternmost portion of a terrace-like piece of ground, about two hundred yards wide, which, owing to the protection afforded by these ruins and the remains of half-a-dozen less substantial dwellings, had escaped being cut up into Yardangs and now stood out as the centre of the whole ruined area. All around it the soil was eroded to a depth of twelve feet or more.

In the main structure, which appears to have had an enclosure of large sun-dried bricks, the thick walls of three narrow apartments still rose to a good height. I easily recognized the spot where Hedin had come upon his 'find' of Chinese records on paper and wood. He had recovered forty-two narrow tablets or rather 'slips,' and about two

116. REMAINS OF ANCIENT WOVEN FABRICS FROM LOP-NOR SITE.
Scale, one-third.

1. Hemp shoe from ruin L.A. VI.   2. Slipper from L.B. IV., in wool material, woven in coloured pattern.
3. Small bale of ancient silk (see p. 381).   4. Fragment of pile carpet in wool from L.A. I.

hundred pieces of paper, including many small fragments, from the rubbish layers which filled the easternmost and narrowest of these adjoining apartments. In the refuse which had been thrown out of this and left to litter the slope immediately south, a thorough search still revealed quite a mass of fragments of inscribed paper and wood. In the thin curled pieces of wood which formed the majority, it was easy to recognize 'shavings' from Chinese slips originally of the regular size, about nine and a half inches long and half an inch wide, which had been scraped down in order to serve again for writing. Since the material used for these slips seems to have been mostly a very pliable and smooth pine wood which could not possibly have been obtained locally, the economy practised by the fresh use of this old stationery was easy to account for.

Leaving a few men under Ibrahim Beg's supervision to sift carefully this refuse, I next turned my attention to the remains of a large but badly eroded structure in timber and wattle which had originally formed a kind of western wing to the building marked by the brick walls just mentioned. Huge Toghrak beams lay scattered over the eroded east slope, and some of the posts which appeared to have once supported a sort of central hall still stood upright to a height of over thirteen feet. The information available about the contents of the documents brought away by Hedin made it highly probable that this block of rooms had once contained an official Chinese residence. The careful clearing effected here yielded no finds beyond some large volutes carved in Toghrak wood, which probably served for the adornment of a bracket supporting the roof.

But when I turned the men to a piece of ground closely adjoining westwards which seemed to have been occupied by an outhouse or open court, Chinese records, mostly on wood but some also on paper, were recovered in quick succession (Fig. 119). Among the thirty odd wooden slips a number were quite perfect; others were only charred at one end, having evidently been used as convenient tapers. Alas! there was no Sinologist by my side, not even lively Chiang-ssŭ-yeh, to enlighten me as to the contents. Yet it was easy to guess the purport in the case of a slip still retaining at one end the string of twisted hair which had evidently been used to attach it to some object. M. Chavannes' interpretation three years later showed that it had once marked the bag containing a certain quantity of grain issued to worthy Kuan, a soldier of the detachment in garrison.

With the stimulating finds of this first day I spent a happy evening when at last darkness drove me to the shelter of my little tent. The icy north-east wind always grew sharper in the evening, and it was pleasant to think that the men, by the side of their roaring camp fires lit within the brick-built ruins, were really warmer than I in my snug tent. For heating it depended upon the two candles I kept burning and upon the embers which I allowed to be placed in my small Arctic cooking-stove until the need of fresh air forced me to turn this contrivance outside. No one was so comfortable as ' Dash,' my little terrier, when, clad in his own fur coat, he could seek warmth and oblivion of all privations amidst the rugs of my bed. The Jaeger blanket which lay lowest, he claimed as his favourite bedding, and invariably would dig down to it whenever I was not at hand to tuck him up myself. With night temperatures now rapidly sinking to 13 degrees below zero Fahrenheit, I could scarcely have kept myself out of bed as long as I did in the evenings, had I not been able to ensconce myself, big boots and all, in the fur-lined sitting-bag which I had brought from Kashmir.

CHAPTER XXXIII

On December 19th, in the bitter cold of the early morning, work was started with the clearing of a fairly well preserved ruin some sixty yards to the south-west of what we called the 'Ya-mên.' Neither the dimensions of the dozen rooms still traceable nor the size of the timber pieces were large here. But drift sand had accumulated within the broken walls to a height of three or four feet, and this, together with the familiar look of the ground plan and the wattle and timber construction, exactly as at the Niya site, raised hopes. They were not disappointed. It is true the first room, evidently intended with its thick walls of stamped clay, big fireplace, and broad sitting-platforms for use as a warm corner in the winter, yielded only small pieces of a carpet of well-woven ingrain material, and showing a delicate floral pattern in colours still vivid.

But in a passage dividing this from a larger room westwards we came upon three large rectangular tablets complete with their wooden covers and seal-sockets, and still retaining most of their Kharoshthi writing in excellent preservation. Two of them lay wrapped up in a piece of well-woven brown fabric, with about three feet of sand below them, having manifestly fallen into this position from some receptacle higher up on the wall. Except for the wood, which was of Toghrak instead of the cultivated poplar, these documents conformed in all details of arrangement, script, etc., to the features made so familiar by my Niya finds. As official records these rectangular tablets were sure to show a date in their opening portion, and as I looked for this eagerly I soon convinced myself

that here, too, the dating was by the year of the reigning
Maharaja; but his name, apparently Dugaka, entirely
differed in formation from the names of rulers recorded by
the Niya site documents. It was evident that here, too,
Chinese control, military and political, had allowed the
indigenous administration to continue undisturbed in the
hands of the local ruling family.

That the house we were excavating had once sheltered
some representative of this native ruler of the Lou-lan
region became highly probable when we discovered that
the rubbish on the top of a small débris heap, quite close
to the north end of the main structure, and perhaps
marking an outhouse, held not less than twelve Kharoshthi
tablets. Rectangular and wedge-shaped letters, memoranda,
and account records on oblong tablets were all represented
among them. The wood of some of these records had
become badly bleached and cracked by exposure. But
enough of the writing remained to prove that the whole
collection had once belonged to the 'Daftar' of some
petty native official. Along with the finds of Kharoshthi
documents at other ruins of the site, and the observations
I was able to make as to their places and conditions of
discovery, this justified the important conclusion, that the
same early Indian language as found in the records of the
Niya site was in use also in the Lop-nor regions for
indigenous administration and business. Considering how
far removed Lop-nor is from Khotan, this uniform
extension of an Indian script and language to the extreme
east of the Tarim Basin offers a special historical interest.

But like many new discoveries which seem simple and
obvious, it also raised fresh problems. In the Khotan
region it was possible to account partially, at least, for
this official use of an Indian language by the old local
tradition recorded by Hsüan-tsang, which mentions early
immigration from India as an important element in the
local population. But so far away to the east, at the
very threshold of China, the identical use of this foreign
administrative language seemed to indicate rather a
political dominion exercised by invaders from the Indian
side and for a time embracing the whole of the Tarim

Basin. Was it then, perhaps, a lasting impress left by that Indo-Scythian conquest from the side of Bactria, of which we catch dim glimpses through Buddhist tradition in China, and which seems temporarily to have broken Chinese imperial control in these parts during the first or second centuries of our era? Or could this influence of a power which had its base on the north-western confines of India be traced still farther back?

It was impossible at the time to give much thought to such fascinating problems. Leaving Naik Ram Singh in charge of the labourers who were to clear the remaining rooms of the 'Beg's house,' as we promptly christened it in distinction from the 'Ya-mên,' and the adjoining ground, I set out myself for a closer inspection of the immediate surroundings of the main group of ruins. As I moved along the south side of the latter my eye was caught by a long terrace which rose above eroded ground just like the Yardangs close by, but differed from their absolutely regular bearing by stretching from east to west. On approaching the terrace and examining its top I soon noticed that it bore the much-decayed remnants of a rampart in stamped clay, still rising to a height of four and a half feet in places with a maximum thickness of five feet. The longest continuous stretch I was able to trace on the south side measured about ninety yards.

These scanty remains of an enclosing wall—for as such they could clearly be recognized—had helped to protect from erosion a narrow terrace which was covered with an unusual quantity of pottery débris. Built against the inside of the wall remnant at one end I found the badly eroded traces of a rush-wall structure; but otherwise the rampart ran clear of adjoining buildings. Guided by the indication here furnished I soon discovered corresponding wall fragments, shorter but equally distinct in bearing and construction, extending in a straight line along the north side of the main group of ruins. In places the wall still stood to a height of eight feet, and the layers of tamarisk twigs inserted at regular intervals to strengthen the stamped clay could be made out with ease. The distance between the north and south walls I had thus traced was just a little under a quarter of a mile.

It now remained to ascertain the position of the east and west walls which must once have completed the defences of this small fortified station. This proved no easy task. On the east side of the ruins, beyond the Stupa mound, I searched in vain for any sign of a continuous wall among the close-set Yardangs which furrowed the ground with the regularity of a ploughed field. Ultimately I was forced to the conclusion that the constant scouring of that terrible north-east wind and the sand it drives before it, must first have breached this eastern wall face at every point now marked by a Yardang trench, and in the end have broken down and carried off any fragments of the clay rampart that had at first survived on the tops of the erosion terraces. As these were quite narrow here and streaked by sharp-cut smaller ridges, the process could be fully explained ; yet its result looked very puzzling at first, until the badly breached eastern walls of ruined Chinese towns about An-hsi, surveyed half a year later, revealed to me the intermediate stages. That powerful wind, which had first breached and then completely effaced the east wall, had, of course, been at work on the west wall, too, which equally lay in the line of its progress. After the first obstacle had been literally blown away altogether, the force of its scouring attack on the second must have increased still further.

So the total disappearance of the western face of the enclosing wall proper was a fact which did not surprise me. But luckily I could still determine the line it had once occupied by two decayed mounds of stamped clay which rose facing each other exactly half-way between the extant northern and southern wall faces and to the west of the main group of ruined dwellings. A close examination showed that they were the remains of two massive bastions or towers which had once flanked the main gate of the little fortified station. They must have been over twenty-four feet in thickness, and still rose to sixteen feet or so above the intervening ground. This was strewn with pieces of heavy timber, evidently the remains of a large gate. The distance between the northern and southern wall faces was about 370 yards. Assuming that the area enclosed by the rampart had a square shape, as usual in the case of fortified Chinese towns, all remains still recognizable as those of dwellings at this group of ruins would just fall within it.

Outside only two ruined structures had survived in the immediate vicinity. Both were low mounds of solid masonry which appeared to have served once as bases for shrines and by their massive construction had so far escaped complete erosion. The one about half a mile to the north-east of the station was reduced to a small pyramid about ten feet high and measuring about thirty-five feet on each side at the bottom. This, as in the case of every large structure at the site, rested on a foundation of two layers of tamarisk brushwood, embedded in clay. The other mound not far from the south-east corner of the walled area was larger, and must have measured originally over fifty feet along each of its orientated sides. The height of the erosion terrace on which it stood, fully sixteen feet, added to that of the extant mass of masonry, close on fourteen feet, made it look quite imposing. That wind erosion had been aided here by human activity was clearly proved by a tunnel which treasure-seekers, no doubt of an early date, had cut from the centre of the mound right through to the west face. No trace was left of the superstructure which this mass of masonry must have borne, nor of the stucco revetment likely to have adorned its sides.

It was curious to note here, and also among the ruins within the enclosure, the plentiful remains of tamarisk scrub which had once managed to subsist both at the foot of the débris and on the eroded slopes below. It must have helped greatly to protect the ruins, and its dead branches strewed the slopes of most of the terraces. Also within the erosion trenches small tamarisk cones and single dead bushes could occasionally be found. Not far from the ruin of the 'Ya-mên' I even discovered a small clump of tamarisks still alive. All this suggested that water might have found its way again to this ground at some period long after the station had been abandoned, and even after the jungle vegetation surviving human occupation had completely died away.

To the east and south Mullah and my own men sent out on reconnaissances entirely failed to trace any structural remains. But on the north side, from the commanding position which the ruined Stupa of the main site supplied, two broken mounds could be made out clearly above the Yardangs, and these I proceeded to survey. About two miles to the north-north-east I found the ruin of a solid brick structure rising in two stories to a height of fifteen feet. Its sides, which must have measured over thirty-six feet in length, were too badly decayed through erosion to permit the character of the building to be determined with certainty. In all probability it had formed the base of a shrine. This base was constructed of sun-burnt bricks of the large size usual at this site, about nineteen by eleven inches and three inches thick, and besides these, smaller ones lay scattered below, very hard and undoubtedly fired, which may have belonged to a superstructure. Some hundred and thirty yards to the north-west I traced the position of a relatively large structure by the débris of massive timber, including Toghrak beams of over twenty feet in length, which littered the bare eroded soil.

After crossing frightfully cut up ground for about one mile and a half north-west-by-west I came upon the remains of a smaller brick mound and adjoining timber structure showing similar features. Here, too, erosion had proceeded too far to leave us anything to excavate. But on my way back to camp, I crossed, about half a mile south, an old river bed which afforded some interesting observations. It ran with many windings in the general direction from west to east, and seemed to connect with the bed we had crossed when approaching the ruined area on December 17th. Its width varied from about fifty to sixty-five yards. The banks, distinctly marked by dead Toghraks and tamarisk cones, descended steeply to a depth of fifteen to twenty feet.

The bed showed a fairly level bottom covered with

light sand and quite free from Yardangs. It seemed as if the originally low position, together with the direction of the bed—which differed from that of the prevailing north-east winds,—had prevented any excessive scouring by wind and driving sand; possibly erosion had been retarded by the heavy drift sand which had accumulated in the bed while desiccation proceeded. Nor was it easy to make sure in the absence of direct antiquarian evidence whether this bed existed at the time when the site was last occupied or had been formed subsequently during some temporary return of the river.

CHAPTER XXXIV

IT is impossible to describe here in detail the progress and results of the excavations which for the rest of December 19th and the next three days kept us all hard at work among the ruins of the little walled 'town.' The remains of the half-dozen dwellings left for clearing varied greatly in extent in accordance with the protection from erosion they had enjoyed. But in almost all of them there was enough drift sand or consolidated refuse to preserve wooden records inscribed in Chinese or Kharoshthi and other interesting relics. In a small but carefully built structure in wattle and timber adjoining the north wall of the 'Ya-mên,' the communication between two rooms showed a very curious feature. The western room had along its east side a broad platform nearly three feet high and approached by three steps from one corner. The wall behind this platform was broken in its centre by a panelled opening, about seven feet wide, which looked into a larger room eastward. Could the platform have been meant to seat a personage holding his court, while the adjoining hall accommodated applicants and attendants? In the latter the timber and wattle of the walls was found charred.

But close to the steps of the platform in the other room a wooden measure, eleven and a half inches long, had survived in excellent preservation, showing a 'foot' divided into ten 'inches' according to the decimal system of Chinese metrology. Taking into account the chronological evidence to be discussed presently, it is certain that we have in this curious relic an exact representa-

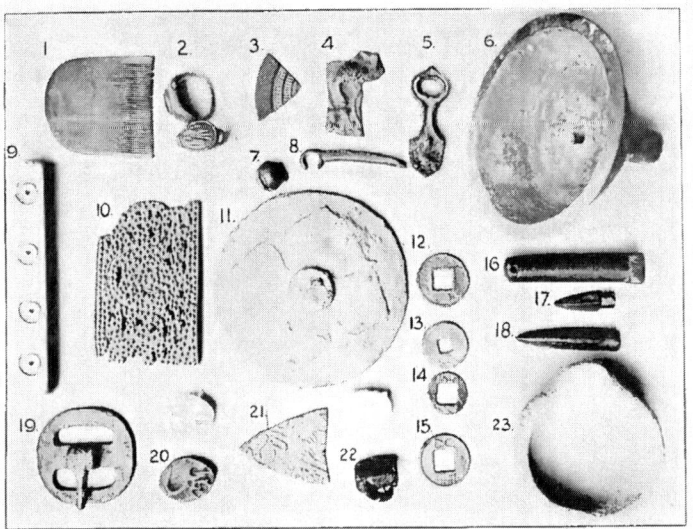

117. SMALL ANTIQUES, MAINLY IN METAL, COLLECTED FROM WIND-ERODED
GROUND AT LOP-NOR SITE.

Scale, two-sevenths.

1. Wooden comb. 2. Signet ring in bronze. 3, 4, 21. Fragments of bronze mirrors with relievo decoration.
5, 8, 19. Metal clasps. 6, 11, 16. Decorated metal objects of uncertain use. 7. Small bronze bell. 9. Ivory die.
10. Fragment of bronze buckle, perhaps intended for cloisonné work. 12-15. Copper coins of Han period.
17, 18. Bronze arrow-heads. 20, 22. Lignite seals. 23. Lamp in burnt clay.

118. LARGE REFUSE HEAP IN CENTRE OF ANCIENT STATION, LOP-NOR SITE, IN COURSE
OF EXCAVATION.

Mullah, of Abdal, on extreme right ; Ibrahim Beg supervising diggers.

tion of the standard measure prevailing in the third century A.D. under the Western Tsin dynasty. As the standards of measure in Ancient China are known to have varied a good deal at different periods, and their determination from literary sources is difficult, this find possesses distinct archaeological interest.

By the side of so much evidence of a highly organized civilization, it was strange to come upon a small block of wood which had undoubtedly served for producing fire in the manner current at all periods among savage races. Along one side it showed four charred holes partially sunk through the thickness of the wood and communicating with the edge by means of flat grooves which were intended to convey the spark to the tinder. Threaded on a strip of white leather, and still attached to the block through a hole was a small peg, having at one end a blunt point which just fitted the holes. It was manifestly this peg which had to be revolved in the holes. But to do this quick enough for the friction to generate fire must have required a drill apparatus, and of this I could find no remains. However this may have been, it is clear from the fire blocks I discovered here and at the sites of Niya and Endere, and subsequently along the ancient frontier wall west of Tun-huang, that this primitive method of fire production prevailed during the early centuries of our era all along the line of Chinese advance westwards.

In none of the ruined dwellings, however, did we strike such a rich mine as in the large rubbish heap extending near the centre of the walled area, and close to the west of the 'Ya-mên' (Fig. 118). It measured fully a hundred feet across with a width of about fifty. On the south to a height of four to five feet, gradually diminishing northwards, lay a mass of consolidated rubbish consisting of straw and stable refuse. But we had scarcely commenced digging up this unsavoury quarry when Chinese records on wood and paper cropped up in great number, especially from layers two to three feet above the ground level. The careful sifting of all these accumulations of dirt occupied us for nearly a day. The odours were still pungent, with the icy north-east wind driving fine particles impregnated with ammonia into one's throat and nose. Our labour was to the end amply rewarded by finds, and the men, whose attention and care I stimulated by appropriate Bakhshish for objects of special interest, reaped a good harvest for their trouble. Of Chinese records we recovered over 120, not counting small fragments (Fig. 119). The great majority were wooden 'slips' of the regular size, nearly ten inches long and half an inch wide, and many of them complete. Of Chinese paper documents, all torn pieces, but some of large size, we counted over forty. The Kharoshthi records were few, but comprised a perfectly preserved large document on paper exactly resembling in arrangement those on leather which another precious heap of refuse had yielded at the Niya site in 1901.

There was a novelty, too, in the shape of a strip of white silk inscribed with Kharoshthi. It furnished the first tangible confirmation for that Chinese antiquarian tradition which knows of silk as one of the ancient writing materials preceding the invention of paper. Two small rectangular lids in wood, provided with a seal-socket and adjoining string-grooves (Fig. 119, 13, 14), exactly like the 'covering tablets' of official Kharoshthi documents, afforded special satisfaction to my archaeological conscience; for the Chinese writing they bore, evidently addresses, proved clearly that I had been right when years before I conjectured a Chinese origin for all the essential technical features of that ancient wooden stationery first brought to light at the Niya site.

But still more welcome, perhaps, on account of the new problem it raised, was a small strip of paper showing two lines in an 'unknown' writing I had never seen before. It manifestly ran from right to left, and several of the characters distantly recalled Aramaic. No decipherment could be hoped for from such a fragment. Yet the script, with its clearly Western look, forcibly drew my thoughts to people from ancient Sogdiana or even more distant Iranian lands who might have travelled and traded by this old high road to the country of the silk-weaving Seres. As I put the precious fragment carefully

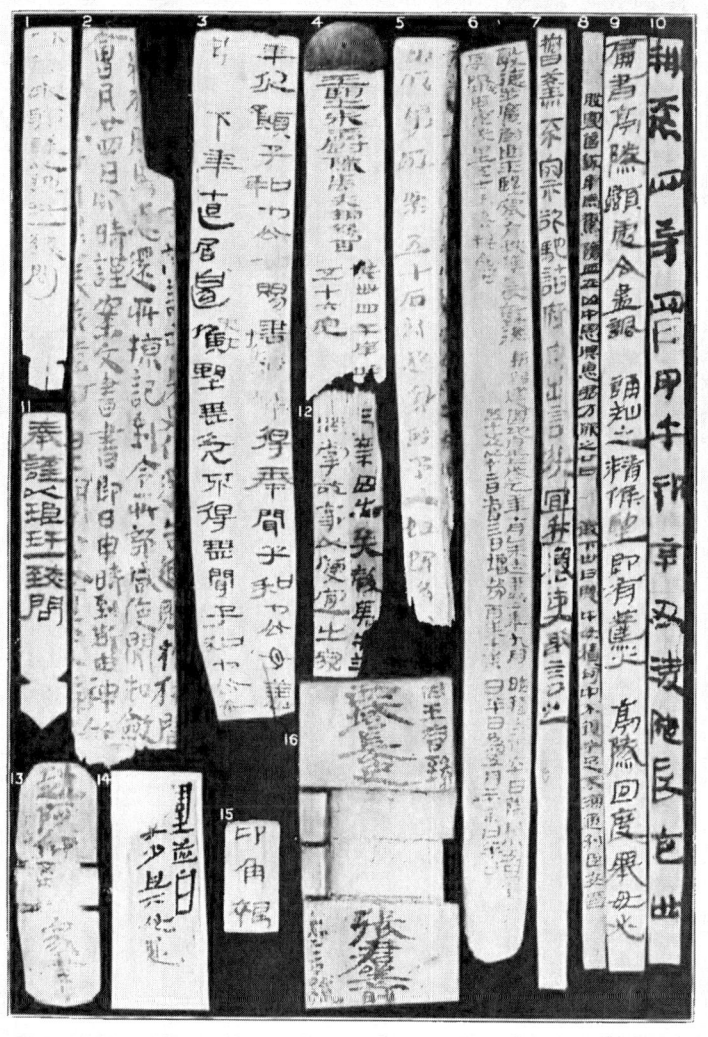

119. ANCIENT CHINESE DOCUMENTS ON WOODEN TABLETS, FROM RUINS OF
THE NIYA AND LOP-NOR SITES, AND OF THE TUN-HUANG *LIMES*.

Scale, two-thirds.

1, 11, from N. xiv., Niya Site; 2, 13, 16, from L.A. vi., Lop-nor Site; 3-10, 12, 14, 15, from various watch-stations
of ancient Chinese *Limes*. Nos. 3, 16 are covers with seal-sockets; No. 14 is a 'shaving.'

away, I had little inkling of the great find of complete letters in the same script which was waiting for me in a forlorn watch-station at the eastern end of this ancient desert route.

That all these miscellaneous records had found their way to the large refuse-heap as sweepings from the surrounding offices and dwellings, was plainly shown by the plentiful remnants of worn-out articles of clothing and broken implements which we found mixed up with the refuse. The collection of rags in all kinds of fabrics, from fine silk and brocade to felts and coarse homespun ; of old shoes and sandals in leather, woven string, etc., brought home to me, more vividly perhaps than anything else, the petty realities of a life long departed.

The discovery of these ancient refuse layers added so greatly to our stock of Chinese records from the site that from the first I felt encouraged to hope for historically interesting data to be gleaned among them. This expectation has been justified by the painstaking and thorough analysis which M. Chavannes, the eminent Sinologist, has made of these documents. The difficulties presented by their archaic and often very cursive script, by their contents too often fragmentary and always bristling with obscure administrative details, have been great even for such a master of Chinese antiquarian lore as my learned collaborator. But in most cases he has succeeded in overcoming them, and his kindness in communicating his translations and notes, as far as documents on wood are concerned, makes it possible for me, even before the appearance of his full publication, to offer some glimpses of what the records reveal as to the character and local conditions of the site.

To begin with the main point, they clearly prove the ruins to belong to a small fortified station garrisoned by Chinese troops and intended to guard an important ancient route which led from Tun-huang on the extreme west of Kan-su to the oases along and north of the Tarim River. We knew in a general way from the early Chinese Annals that a route opened about 110 B.C. through the desert west of Tun-huang to the Lop-nor region served for the first expansion of Chinese political influence westwards, and remained in use through the whole period of the Han dynasty. But the indications available in those texts were by no means sufficient to determine its exact direction ; and for the topographical and archaeological observations, which in the course of the winter and spring I was able to collect at what I believe to have been the starting-points of the route east and west of the absolute desert intervening, confirmation by documentary evidence was highly to be desired. So every scrap of information gleaned here from original local records acquires special importance.

There is abundant evidence in the Chinese Annals to prove that during successive periods of China's supremacy in the Tarim Basin it was always the great route leading along the southern foot of the T'ien-shan and through the string of big oases from Korla westwards to Kashgar, which claimed the chief attention of its soldiers and admini-strators. It was by this route that the bulk of the silk trade moved to Farghana and Samarkand, the ancient Sogdiana. The protection of it against the inroads of the Huns and other nomadic tribes north of the T'ien-shan was the main purpose for which the Tarim Basin was held. Now a glance at the map shows that the shortest way to reach that line of oases, the Pei-lu or 'Northern Road' of the Chinese Annals, from the westernmost parts of Kan-su and China proper, lay along the foot of the Kuruk-tagh just north of the Lop desert and past the ruined site I was engaged in exploring. Yet at the present time the total want of drinkable water along this route would make it impossible for any caravan traffic to cover the two hundred and forty odd miles of direct distance intervening between the Tarim and the nearest well on the Tun-huang-Charklik track.

Nowhere, perhaps, in Central Asia is the change in physical conditions so strikingly brought home to us, and our interest in determining the limits of time within which this took place must therefore be all the greater. Now among the records so far dealt with by M. Chavannes there are fifteen fully dated from years corresponding to

A.D. 263-270. This is exactly the time when we know the Emperor Wu-ti, the founder of the Western Chin dynasty, to have reasserted Chinese control over these distant confines of the empire after the period of internal disruption known as the ' Epoch of the Three Kingdoms' (A.D. 221-265). We may safely conclude from the prevalence of those dates that the route and the station guarding it had then experienced years of exceptional traffic and activity. But that the post remained in Chinese occupation for at least sixty years longer is proved by a slip from the first ruin I excavated, which records a payment to a certain barbarian in the year A.D. 330.

Curiously enough the very way in which this date is expressed conveys a clear indication of the final abandonment then being near. The year is stated as the sixteenth of the ' Nien-hao' or regnal title Chien-hsing, which commenced in A.D. 313. But as the reign of the last emperor of the Western Chin dynasty, which it designates, came to a close in A.D. 316, it is certain that the little station must then have been completely cut off from official intercourse with the central authorities of the empire. Else it could not have continued using the obsolete ' Nien-hao' for fully fourteen years longer.

That this condition of administrative isolation was not merely local, but must have also affected other Chinese garrisons surviving in the Tarim Basin, is made highly probable by another significant observation. The ruined site could not have been a mere outlying post; it must have lain on an important line of communication for the refuse of a few closely adjoining structures to furnish half-a-dozen fragmentary documents which directly emanate from, or are addressed to, the ' Commander-in-Chief of the Western Regions'—i.e. the chief representative of Chinese imperial power in the Tarim Basin. One of them conveys the ' Chang-shih's' order to a certain officer to set out for some specified localities still identifiable in Kan-su. Another names as the writer the ' Secretary in charge of official correspondence under the orders of the Commander-in-Chief.' Of particular interest is the sealed wooden lid which must once have closed a small box containing an

official report or petition, addressed in due form 'to Mr.
Chang, Commander-in-Chief of the Western Regions, by
me Yüan, for transmission through Superintendent Wang.'
The document itself, which is likely to have been written
on wooden slips in accordance with conservative office
tradition, may have been carried away elsewhere by the
Commander-in-Chief's *chancellerie*. But the cover was left
behind on the rubbish heap, and for us attests the great
man's passage.

There are slips, unfortunately mere fragments, which
give us glimpses of military action on a stage manifestly
not local and probably far away on the north or west.
But the great majority of the records are such as plainly
indicate the modest range of the duties and interests
looked after by those whose offices fed the rubbish heap
with their 'waste paper' (*recte* wood). Theirs was the
business of looking after the maintenance in food-supplies,
arms, and arable land of a small Chinese military colony,
which was intended to guard and keep open one of the
main routes linking China proper with the far-flung
Central-Asian outposts of imperial policy.

Yet even the petty records of administrative routine
acquire a distinct interest for the historical student by the
light they throw on practical details of organization, which
had their importance in the story of Chinese political expansion, but are never noticed by the dynastic Annals. Most
numerous are the statements and orders relating to the
storage and issues of cereals by the officials in charge of the
local military magazine. The elaborate system of control
in vogue is illustrated by the list of those who had to check
inventories and countersign orders. Detailed statements
of issues to individuals or small detachments acquaint us
with the daily rations of grain sanctioned per man, and
with the way in which the keep of camels and donkeys
placed at their disposal for marches was provided for.
Difficulties must often have attended the provisioning
of the local garrison, besides keeping supplies available for
those who passed through. This is curiously illustrated
by repeated orders urging the reduction of issues in due
proportion for the several classes of officers and men.

The necessity of 'making both ends meet' is more than once emphasized in a fashion which allows us to realize how hard the task must have been. Yet in accordance with an administrative policy which seems to have been followed by the Chinese from the very beginning of their military activity in the Tarim Basin, there was a systematic effort kept up to make the local garrison self-supporting by turning the soldiers into military colonists. We have indisputable proof of this in the numerous inscribed tablets which specify allotments of lands, either already under irrigation or prepared for it, or yet to be cleared, to small sections of troops for purposes of cultivation. The kinds of cereals and fodder crops which were to be grown on particular areas are sometimes set forth in detail.

A superintendent of local agricultural labours is referred to, and he was probably the official responsible for the issue of agricultural implements, such as spades, saws, and ropes, receipts or requisitions for which are numerous among the records. A special officer in charge of irrigation is mentioned. Elsewhere we read a report of the flood having broken through an irrigation embankment in several places, an apt illustration of the danger which always threatens agriculture in low-lying deltas of Turkestan rivers. Of another ever-present risk we catch a glimpse in a letter which was to assure its recipient that certain shepherds sent south with their flocks had after several marches reached water. It was evidently a case when particular tracts of riverine jungle had become useless for grazing owing to their water-courses running dry or getting diverted.

Reports from or to an inspector of the armoury about articles of military equipment lost, materials required for leather armour, helmets, crossbows, etc., show that the peaceful preoccupations of those responsible for the small colony did not altogether efface its military purpose. But characteristically enough, in the great majority of the cases where individual soldiers, apart from officers, are specified, we find them described as 'Hu' or barbarians. It is of considerable interest that their nationality, wherever more exactly indicated, is stated to be 'Ta Yüeh-chih' or Indo-Scythian. It is evident that the mercenaries employed under Chinese officers at this post, and probably also at other and more important garrisons of the 'Western Kingdoms,' were mainly drawn from that foreign nation which in Chinese eyes had the merit of representing the hereditary foe of the Hsiung-nu or Huns.

We know from the Han Annals that the 'Great Yüeh-chih,' the later Indo-Scythians, had been driven by the Huns in the second century B.C. from the plains north of the T'ien-shan, first to Sogdiana and thence to the Oxus region which remained the main seat of their power for centuries, even after their conquest of Northern India. While established north of the T'ien-shan the Huns were by their inroads a constant danger to the oases of the Tarim Basin and the great route leading through it. Finding the local population then probably as unwarlike as it is now, and much divided by internal rivalry, Chinese political wisdom naturally fell back upon the expedient of enlisting troops from its western neighbours, the Indo-Scythians, whom the common danger threatening from the Huns was likely to make trustworthy. A comparison with the conditions prevailing about this very period along the northern borders of the Roman empire might furnish curious parallels.

It is, however, not of such general aspects of China's Central-Asian policy that we can expect direct information in our office records from this site. The military incidents which they mention relate mainly to petty cases of individual soldiers. Thus we hear in some detail of the unhappy end of a man who through the negligence of his officer was drowned in deep water, severe punishment being meted out to the guilty superior. Elsewhere we are furnished with a list of all the kit in clothing and felts, issued to a 'barbarian' soldier on joining, and so on.

One of these brief reports on matters of discipline is of interest, as it mentions Lou-lan as a place to which a certain man had proceeded and from which his early return was to be secured. The way in which the matter is brought to the addressee's notice makes it clear that his residence, presumably the site itself, was distinct from the locality meant by Lou-lan. Above I have already indicated the antiquarian reasons derived from the Chinese Annals which point to the oases of Charklik and Miran as the most likely positions for the seat of the old native chiefs of the ' Lou-lan kingdom.' So, if after the usual Eastern fashion the writer of that report meant by ' Lou-lan ' the chief place of the whole Lop-nor tract, we can account without any difficulty for the way in which the local reference is introduced.

Since the above notes were written M. Chavannes' translation of the Chinese records on paper has also become available. Most of them have proved to be private letters, some complete and occasionally throwing curious side-lights on the conditions of life prevailing along the line of these small Chinese garrisons. But considerations of space forbid here the addition of details.

Perhaps it was fortunate that my complete want of Sinologist training saved me from occupying my mind at the time with the many knotty points of detail which arise in the interpretation of these records ; for there was more than enough work to keep body and mind busy during those bitterly cold days. Even in the evenings, when I could seek shelter in my little tent from that unceasing icy north-east wind, the hours available before the ink would freeze in my pen barely sufficed for writing up notes and cleaning, numbering, and storing away ' finds.'

I was pushing on the excavation of all traceable ruins as hard as I could ; for our ice-supply was diminishing rapidly, and the report of the Surveyor, who had meanwhile returned from the western group of ruins, had shown me that there, too, work for several days was awaiting us. My anxiety about retaining an adequate margin of time for it increased considerably when on December 22nd Tokhta Akhun, who had taken the camels to the springs south of Altmish-bulak, arrived with the information that the water there was so salt that practically no ice had as yet formed. For the same reason the poor camels, even with the thirst of ten days, had refused to touch it. With the hoped-for supply of ice from the springs failing, I could not feel particular regret that Tokhta Akhun's search for more ruins, during a two days' reconnaissance around the western site, had proved fruitless. And when by the evening of that day the exploration of all structural remains and refuse heaps traceable at the eastern site was completed, I felt something like relief.

CHAPTER XXXV

DISCOVERY OF ART REMAINS

THE opportune arrival of the camels which I had sent back to our half-way depot for the men's reserve supplies and ice, allowed me to arrange for shifting camp to the western group of ruins by the evening of December 23rd. As the distance was only about eight miles I was able to use the whole forenoon for getting the remains we had cleared buried again by the men for the sake of protection. I myself was busy in taking a careful plan and elevation of the Stupa, which with its height still rising to over thirty feet seemed to stand guard over the scene of our past labours (Fig. 112). The task was not easy, owing to the destruction of surface features caused by erosion and some digging operations of Hedin's men. But in the end I succeeded in determining the dimensions of the three square bases, of the octagonal drum and the dome, all in masonry of sun-dried bricks, which made up this orthodox Buddhist structure.

It was in the course of this examination that I came upon a metal tape-measure lying on the second lowest base just where Hedin had forgotten it in 1901. Of course, there was nothing specially remarkable in its having been left undisturbed on the ruined mound which no human being was likely to have visited in the few years' interval, and where it was out of reach of drift sand and its corrosive action. So when over two years later I had the pleasure of returning the little instrument to its distinguished owner at an informal dinner party of the Royal Geographical Society in London, it caused me some quiet amusement to find that the incident, which to me on the spot had seemed rather trivial, supplied matter for newspaper paragraphs.

The tramp to our new camp constantly crossing the ridges and furrows of Yardangs was trying for us all. The labourers were burdened with articles of supplies and baggage which the few available camels had not sufficed to carry, while I myself felt shaken with an attack of malarial fever which the exposure and exertions of these hard days had caused to reappear with fresh force. But early on the morning of December 24th I was able to start work at a small group of ruins, including the Buddhist shrine which one of Hedin's men had accidentally discovered in 1900, and from which he himself had brought away in the following year a number of fine wood-carvings. As his visit then had been paid from the camp established at the eastern site, and had necessarily been confined to the hours available between the tramp to and fro, there was reason to hope for more spoil here. The ruins comprised the badly eroded remains of the shrine already referred to (Fig. 120), and flanking it to the north-east and south-west two larger structures which manifestly had been dwellings. The whole occupied the top of an island-like terrace over 200 feet long, and rising fully twenty-eight feet above the eroded ground immediately at its foot northward (Fig. 121).

The two dwellings which I cleared first proved of interest, mainly owing to the ease with which the constructive details of the timber and wattle walls could still be studied in several large rooms. The walls, originally ten feet high, had at some early period fallen bodily inwards, and lying flat on the floor had thus escaped erosion. Their thickness was made up to eight inches by plaster layers on either side of a wattle, which in its lower portion consisted of horizontal bundles of reeds, and higher up of a sort of tamarisk matting woven diagonally. The buildings must have been thoroughly cleared out soon after their desertion, for in spite of the excellent cover offered by the fallen walls, the 'finds,' apart from some copper coins of the Han period and rags of plain silk, wool, and felt fabrics, were confined to portions of a large cupboard constructed after a model still in common use in Turkestan oases for the storage of

120. REMAINS OF ANCIENT BUDDHIST SHRINE L.B. II., LOP-NOR SITE, BEFORE CLEARING.

121. RUIN OF SMALL STUPA NEAR SHRINE L.B. II., LOP-NOR SITE, RISING ON 'YARDANG'
WHICH WIND EROSION IS UNDERCUTTING.

victuals. But the excellent wood-carving displayed on the front legs, more than seventeen inches high, and in some pieces of panelling, was of interest by its unmistakable Graeco-Buddhist design.

When in the afternoon the turn came for clearing the heap of timber débris which covered the small eroded terrace in the centre and marked the position of the shrine, my hope of other artistic remains of the same sort was soon fulfilled. Even among the woodwork which lay on the top practically without any sand to protect it, just as Hedin's people had left it, I discovered carved panels and posts which still retained portions of beautifully designed floral decoration in relievo. In others, which had lain fully exposed to the force of sun and wind, the surface of the wood had become badly bleached and splintered. But even among such withered pieces my eye lit here and there upon familiar outlines of flower ornaments known to me from the sculpture of distant Gandhara.

How great was my relief when I discovered that, on the south-east slope of the terrace, where sand had since its erosion accumulated to a height of three to four feet, numerous fine pieces of ornamental wood-carving had found a safe place of refuge! (Fig. 122). From here emerged several thick beams, over seven feet long and eight inches wide on their carved face, showing rich festoons of eight-petalled lotus flowers of a type I remembered well from the fresco decoration of one of the residences I had excavated in 1901 at the Niya site. Other beams up to twelve feet in length, which might possibly have served also as uprights, were decorated with a very tasteful relievo pattern of large lozenges filled by open four-petalled flowers common to the art of Gandhara. Even more classical in design was a beautiful piece of wood-carving over five feet long, which might originally have served as the top part of a door frame, showing intertwined garlands of acanthus leaves and clematis (Fig. 122,9).

All these pieces must have belonged to the decoration of a structure nearly square and mainly built in timber; its outer foundation beams on the south-east and north-east sides, nineteen and a half and eighteen and a half feet long, respectively, were still *in situ* on the top of the terrace. In front of the south-east beam there lay stretched out on the eroded slope a portion of the timber framework of the wall which it had once borne, just as the wind must have thrown it down after centuries of exposure. The roof beam was still intact, showing the dowels into which posts and lintels had fitted. At the eastern corner two posts were still in their position joined together by horizontal pieces.

That a considerable portion of the wall space of the little shrine—as other finds conclusively proved it to be—must have been left open for lighting became highly probable from the very numerous panels, mostly broken, of open relievo work which we discovered in the sand (Fig. 122, 8). Apart from pieces of geometrical trellis-work, there were panels showing flowers of varying design and size, or the heads and bodies of different grotesque animals. In some of these, *e.g.* a strange beast with the mouth of a crocodile, long neck, and twisted horns, clever modelling and imaginative power are conspicuous in spite of poor preservation. It is evident that all these open-work panels had formed part of screens intended to ward off heat and glare in the summer.

From the interior of the shrine came undoubtedly the many elaborately turned balusters, over one and a half feet high, which fitted four each into a kind of top railing intended to represent a succession of small double brackets (Fig. 122, 2). Other relics of interior adornment were small models of Stupas up to three feet in height carved in wood, complete with base, dome, and a string of mushroom-shaped umbrellas; large blocks of wood with carved rosettes, designed probably for a tympanum decoration, etc. But of the images which the shrine was likely to have contained, only the scantiest relics had survived, such as the fore-arm and hand of a relievo figure carved in wood; and small pieces of fine 'plaster of Paris,' showing remains of relievo decoration, as if from the jewelled arm of a life-size image. The stucco fragments all turned up on the north-east slope where the layer of sand was far too light to afford effective protection. The conditions were equally unfavourable on the two remaining sides of

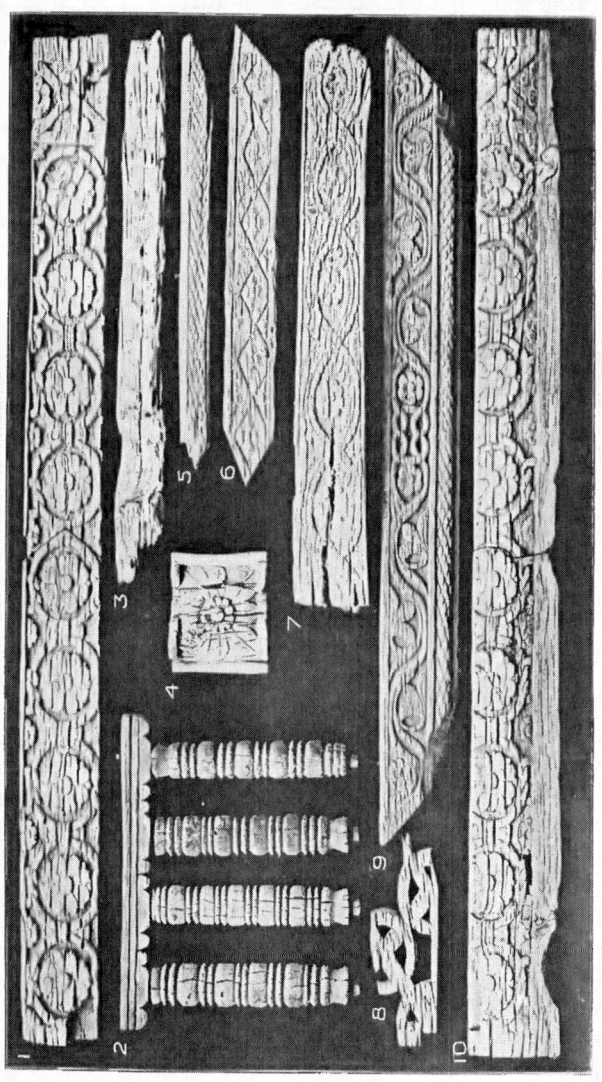

122. PIECES OF ARCHITECTURAL WOOD-CARVING DECORATED IN GANDHARA STYLE, FROM RUINED BUDDHIST SHRINE, LOP-NOR SITE.

Scale, one-thirteenth.

1, 5-7, 10. Ornamented beams and posts. 2. Balusters supporting small double brackets. 3. Panel with decayed relievo representation of seated Buddhas. 4. Large rosette filled with lotus. 8. Fragment of geometrical trellis work. 9. Portion of ornamental door frame.

the structure; but, curiously enough, a few feet down the south-west slope a small refuse heap had survived, which yielded some fragmentary Chinese records besides the usual miscellaneous rags of silk and canvas.

The clearing of the ground which yielded those fine architectural wood-carvings was still proceeding when the dusk began to descend upon us. Absorbed by the interest of my find I was not as likely as the tired labourers to have my attention distracted by the approach of some men from the camp side. But suddenly I noticed a commotion among the groups of diggers, and shouts of 'Dakchi keldi' ('the Dak-man has come') struck my ears. I could not believe them. But as I looked up, my eyes fell in amazement upon the familiar figure of honest Turdi, wearily trudging towards me with a bag over his shoulder, and accompanied in great glee by Muhammadju, Jasvant Singh, and the strange figure of a Loplik hunter.

At first the sudden apparition of my faithful 'Dakchi' from Khotan seemed miraculous. On November 15th I had seen him last setting out from the Endere River with my mail bag, which he had strict orders to deliver personally to Badruddin Khan at Khotan. He had done so twelve days later. Since parting I had marched over 500 miles in the opposite direction almost without a halt—and yet here he was in the midst of this awful Lop Desert to deliver to me Badruddin Khan's devoted Salams and three Kashgar Dak bags tucked away into one! All work stopped at once, and in the midst of an admiring circle of labourers, grateful like school-boys for an early closing of class, honest Turdi was besieged with questions. Yes, he had trudged it to Khotan and duly seen the Khan Sahib; slept a night in his house, and been peremptorily sent off next morning with this fresh Dak, but mounted on a hired pony this time, and provided with a good fur coat. Twenty-one days had sufficed for my hardy postman to cover the thirty usual marches reckoned between Khotan and Abdal. There he found that I had left for the desert without instructions for any one how to follow me. With a mind which had more than the usual share of dog-like fidelity—and simplicity, he took this for a reason to push on and join me.

The Beg of Abdal, seeing his determination, thought it safest to give him as companion the young hunter who was keeping up the connection between Abdal and my servants left at Chainut-köl. Donkeys took them to the latter place in one day, and thence for the last five days they had followed our marked track on foot as best as they could. They had started without any clear notion how far I had moved in search of the ruins, and by the evening of the fifth day from Abdal the little supply of ice which they had been able to carry along from my half-way depot was exhausted. So when by the middle of the sixth day they had reached our camp at the eastern group of ruins and found it deserted—the Surveyor with a fresh detachment of camels returned from the salt springs had finally cleared it of ice-bags and supplies that morning—their anxiety was great. They had no idea how far ahead we had moved and where they might hope to catch us up. But, thirsty as they were, they preferred the risks and chances of a move ahead to the certainty of a three days' tramp without drink back to the ice depot. And now that by Allah's grace they had found me and escaped the peril of dying of thirst in this strange desert of clay, said Turdi, would I look at the bags from Kashgar and see that the seals of Macartney Sahib were intact in the little wooden seal-cases attached to the ends of the fastening strings? For then he could leave them in my hands and take a good sleep by the camp fire.

It was a delightful surprise for my lonely Christmas Eve in the desert to have this big load of letters from distant friends suddenly descending upon me as if it had been brought through the air. Returned to camp I ordered my men to treat Turdi to tea and what other little luxuries my own larder could afford. But as I retrospectively realized the risks which he had run of losing himself and his companion in the desert, I felt sorely tempted to treat him at the same time to a sound scolding for his unjustifiable rashness. That evening, however, I was too busy feasting on letters and papers of all sorts, which, though four months old, seemed to efface for the time all feeling of isolation and distance. How grateful I felt to Turdi for the happy

Christmas he had brought me, when the last cover was opened by the flickering light of my candle and nothing but good news emerged! As usual on such occasions of suddenly resumed touch with a distant world, sleep was slow to come to me that night, and long I lay awake vainly trying amidst my rugs and furs to forget the bitter cold and the discomfort which badly chapped fingers gave. But the absolute peace around was a comfort, and my thoughts were free to visit in turn all the places where I knew dear friends were gathered for Christmas, from Kashgar to far-away Oxford.

Next morning all glamour of his heroic performance seemed to have departed from Turdi. He looked again what he was—an honest, rather stupid and, except when on Dak duty, hopelessly sluggish fellow. But the sensation of a true red-letter day still continued for me in spite of plentiful work, and was fanned afresh by the promising results which it yielded. After finally clearing the remains of architectural wood-carving from the ruined shrine last described, I took the men by mid-day to the ruins of two closely adjoining structures about a mile away to the east-south-east. One of them, by the almost complete erosion of the ground it once occupied, had been reduced to a heap of much-splintered timber. But the remains of decorative wood-carving, including turned balusters, brackets of a small railing and panels of open screen-work, which we picked up on the exposed slopes, made it appear highly probable that a small Buddhist shrine had stood here closely related in type and date to the one previously explored.

Facing it some thirty yards off to the west was the ruin of a much larger building occupying the top of a terrace which fortunately had not been much affected by erosion (Fig. 123). Our subsequent excavation proved that the protection enjoyed by this piece of ground was due to a thick and well-consolidated layer of sheep dung which had accumulated in and around the rooms of an ancient dwelling; evidently for a considerable number of years the abandoned building had served as a shelter for the flocks of shepherds.

That the house had once been occupied by some person

of consequence was made clear by a succession of interesting finds which came to light from below that protective cover. There were Kharoshthi tablets of official shape in excellent preservation; pieces of elaborately woven rugs in delicate colours; wooden panels once evidently belonging to cupboards or similar pieces of furniture, and decorated with floral designs in relievo unmistakably derived from classical models. Of articles which plainly suggested use by some clerical establishment, there were writing styles in wood; several detached seal-cases, no doubt used in the manner employed by Mr. Macartney to secure my mail bags; a curious almost square tablet, with its surface slightly sunk between narrow borders as if for the reception of wax or some similar coating after the fashion of classical note tablets; and a flat stone for rubbing Chinese ink on.

In one hall, measuring twenty-eight by twenty-five feet, the roof had been borne by four elaborately turned pillars which still rose in their original places (Fig. 124). Above they were badly withered and splintered; but below, where hard layers of dung were encrusted around them to a height of nearly two feet, they retained their fine mouldings. A large trough, such as used for the feeding of cattle, dug out roughly from a tree trunk, was found here embedded in the dung layer. It strikingly illustrated the contrast between the original character of the building and the base use to which it had been put when the ancient colony had fallen to the state of a primitive pastoral station.

The clearing of these consolidated crusts of refuse cost far more care and time than mere digging in sand would have. Thus it was not until December 27th that the large ruin yielded up some of its finest relics. Among these were two exquisitely modelled and painted pieces of wooden furniture, probably arm-rests from chairs, which vividly demonstrated the close and varied relations of all local art with the Far West (Fig. 125, 2, 3). One carved in relievo and elaborately lacquered showed the representation of a grotesque beast, probably meant for a conventional lion. The design is distinctly of Persepolitan style and suggests Assyrian ancestry, down to the many-coloured spirals which indicate the hair round the claws. The other, larger

123. PORTION OF RUINED HOUSE L.B. IV., LOP-NOR SITE, SEEN FROM EAST, BEFORE CLEARING.

124. HALL IN RUINED HOUSE L.B. IV., LOP-NOR SITE, WITH TURNED WOODEN PILLARS,
AFTER EXCAVATION.

and worked almost in the round, represents a composite figure having below the leg and hoof of a horse, and above the bust and head of a human being, with a face curiously reminiscent of the Greek sphinx. The transition is effected through a half-open lotus, while behind the breast small wings are indicated, which still further emphasize the descent from the classical monster.

Equally Western was the decoration of a small slipper, which must have once seen better days on the foot of some lady (Fig. 116, 2). Its 'upper,' mounted on a thinnish sole of leather, consisted of a fine cream-coloured wool material, which showed a delicate pattern woven in brocade fashion. All round the front part ran a band woven in elaborate geometrical design with exquisitely matched colours, and curiously recalling Coptic or early Byzantine models. An ugly patch of leather, sewn across one side of the front where the material had suffered from long wear, contrasts strangely with the tasteful elegance of the original work.

What with plentiful fragments of balustrades and openwork panels, showing floral decoration in acanthus and laurel leaves and other classical motives (Fig. 125, 1, 4-6); with a large oblong ivory die of distinctly Indian origin ; with Chinese records on wood, silk rags, and lacquered work on bamboo material, which must manifestly have come from the Far East, the 'finds' of this ruin seemed like a Christmas present specially prepared to bring home to me in the desolation of the desert how this forgotten dead corner of Central Asia had once been linked by relations of art, trade, and culture with all the great civilisations of the ancient world.

While the excavation steadily proceeded in the bitter cold of these grey, sunless days, I had opportunities for plenty of curious observations on the ground immediately adjoining. But of these I can only mention here the discovery of an extensive rush fence to the north and northwest of the ruin, evidently enclosing what must have been a large orchard or garden. The pliable rushes, so weak by themselves, had succeeded in catching and binding the drift sand, which, formed into a clearly marked low ridge, had effectively kept off erosion. So within and under its lee side trunks of dead mulberry and Jigda trees could still be traced. About a hundred yards to the west I came upon eight big trunks of the cultivated poplar lying in a row, the only specimens I saw at the site. Their size—one measured forty-seven feet in length and six feet in circumference—suggested that at this point, at least, cultivation had proceeded for a long time before the site was abandoned.

Repeated reconnaissances made with the help of Rai Ram Singh and my Loplik hunters failed to reveal within striking radius any other structural remains beyond some already seen by Hedin. These were so badly eroded that their exploration, though revealing some features of interest, e.g. the use of burnt bricks, did not occupy us for more than a day. I had made my arrangements accordingly, and felt heartily glad when, by the evening of December 28th, all the camels from the salt springs northward arrived. It was just as well that eleven days of constant toil, carried on under exceptionally trying conditions, sufficed for the completion of our tasks. With the hoped-for supply from the springs failing, our ice store was running very low. It would have been even lower but for the blizzard on our arrival, the snow of which lay long enough at the foot of the hills near the springs for a small quantity to be melted down to refresh the animals. Recurring cases of illness among the men showed how exposure to the continuous icy blasts, with hard work by day and inadequate shelter at night, was telling on them. The Surveyor's rheumatic pains had placed him *hors de combat* for most of the time. I myself, amid constant exertions and strain, had renewed attacks of malarial fever to contend with.

It was time for us all to regain ground where there was water and with it life. I decided to effect this move in two separate columns. The main camp was to march back to Abdal with the 'archaeological proceeds,' nearly four camel loads, by the track we had come. The Surveyor could take charge of this column, since his ailing condition made him unfit for topographical work on any new route I should otherwise have liked him to take through the desert.

125. FRAGMENTS OF DECORATIVE WOOD-CARVING, PARTLY WITH CLASSICAL
MOTIFS, FROM RUINED HOUSE L.B. IV., LOP-NOR SITE.

Scale, one-fourth.

2. Painted arm-rest, carved in the round, representing composite figure in style derived from Hellenistic art.

3. Lacquered arm-rest, representing grotesque beast in Persepolitan style.

I myself, with half-a-dozen picked men still fit for digging if the opportunity offered, was preparing to strike through the unexplored desert south-westward, and thus to make for the Tarim. I had been bent from the first upon taking a new course across the Lop desert, and was looking forward keenly to this chance of moving for once free from the *impedimenta* presented by a heavy convoy and specific archaeological tasks.

Various considerations combined to settle the direction of my course. It would have been most tempting to move to the east along the foot of the Kuruk-tagh hills, and thus to trace if possible the ancient trade route which the ruined Chinese station had once guarded, right through to the point where it diverged from the desert track still connecting Charklik with Tun-huang. But I knew well that for a direct distance of at least 120 miles no drinkable water could now be found along the line which that route must have followed. Owing to the presence of salt bogs and otherwise difficult ground the marching distance to the nearest well was likely to spread out a good deal more, and without a fresh supply of ice and animals thoroughly rested any attempt to cross it would have involved grave risks.

There was little chance of novel observations westwards, where the old trade route could be followed along the foot of the Kuruk-tagh to the Tarim; for Hedin had marched by that line on his first visit to the ruins, and since then Mr. Huntington had passed through the desert strip immediately south of the Kuruk-tagh hills in the reverse direction. He traced, indeed, the old river bed, a continuation of the present Konche Darya, which had once carried water to the site, but came nowhere upon structural remains such as might have supplied a motive for me to follow that direction. Now by striking through the desert to the south-west I should be able to survey wholly unexplored ground. At the same time this route offered the further attraction of taking me straight to the ruined fort of Merdek-shahr, which Hedin had seen in 1896 not far from the eastern lagoons of the Tarim, and which I was anxious to examine before resuming my excavations at Miran.

So with my plans well settled beforehand it was easy to push on rapidly the arrangements for our respective moves. The careful packing of the ancient wood-carvings, etc., with whatever materials I could improvise, cost time and labour. But all the men, my Indians included, showed unusual alacrity at the prospect of leaving behind this desolate working-ground, and to complete the task worked cheerfully by the light of bonfires till late at night.

CHAPTER XXXVI

ACROSS THE DESERT TO THE TARIM

THE morning of December 29th, a bright day and the first fairly calm one, saw our departure from the ancient site (Fig. 126). All the Charklik labourers who were returning *via* Abdal had their accounts for wages and donkey-hire duly settled in silver and Russian gold, with an ample Bakhshish in addition. Rai Ram Singh, for whom we had a comfortable couch prepared on the back of a camel, and Mullah, who was to look after the dismissed labourers as Yüz-bashi, *sub. pro tem.*, received my final instructions. Then, after seeing the big convoy safely started by 10 A.M., I was free myself to say farewell to the ruins and set out for the desert south-westwards. By comparison with the camp I before had to manage, my party now seemed delightfully small. Besides Ramzan, the sullen Kashmiri cook, now looking darker than ever with the grime and dirt of weeks, and Muhammadju, my personal attendant, it comprised Naik Ram Singh, Ibrahim Beg, Tokhta Akhun, lazy, good-natured Turdi, and six picked men from Charklik, who might prove useful, were a chance for digging to offer. Knowing that we should have to be prepared for much heavier going amidst the ridges of high dunes likely to flank the Tarim, I took care to keep ten of the hired camels for our transport so as to make the loads as light as possible.

We had moved through familiar ground of wind-eroded trenches and clay terraces for about four miles when our track brought us to the well-marked old river bed which we had first sighted on the day of our arrival at the site, and which here, too, was running from west to east with a broad winding course. The depressions of the Yardangs lying exactly in the direction in which we were steering had, up to this point, made progress so easy that it caused us a downright feeling of dismay when we noticed how within a couple of miles from the dry river bed they gradually forsook us. The hope of turning to our advantage these strange scourings of the bitter north-easter for part at least of our new tramp had proved futile. A close succession of low dunes kept the ground covered with sand, and erosion had manifestly lost much of its power here. For about three miles we crossed numerous belts of dead trees, all Toghraks of small size, which must have died young; they marked courses which the river had followed only for short periods. Their lines seemed to run more or less parallel to the old river bed. Then followed bare eroded ground overrun by dunes only six to ten feet high, until dusk obliged us to halt by the side of a line of dead poplars still running west to east.

No doubt all this area was in the times of the Han occupation jungle-grazing, subject to inundations from the river. Hence the finds of small bronze objects, such as a fine arrow-head, were very scanty, once we had passed the main river course. A Han coin picked up close to that evening's camp was our last datable relic. But, of course, where erosion had free play it had laid bare also remains of far earlier periods. Thus we met on that first march rare patches of very coarse pottery, which was manifestly neo-lithic; and when nearing camp I picked up a fine celt or axe-head of jade four inches long, undoubtedly belonging to the later phase of the Stone Age. How near the latter approached our earliest historical epoch in this region is a question which it is quite impossible to answer at present.

Our march on December 30th, under a cloudy sky and with the wind for a change blowing from the west and north-west, was still easy. But certain significant observations suggested that we were passing into different ground. The characteristic direction of erosion from north-east to south-west was no longer observable on such bare banks and surfaces of clay as we met with. The dunes, at first quite low, grew slowly in height, while the flat, bare

126. CAMELS BEING LOADED FOR START FROM LOP-NOR SITE.

127. WIND-ERODED CLAY TERRACES (YARDANGS) RISING AMONG DUNES, LOP-NOR DESERT.

patches between them narrowed more and more. After about eight miles we came frequently upon groves of dead Toghraks enclosed by semi-lunar dunes up to twenty-five feet high. The depressions thus formed assumed a regular bearing from north to south, but were as yet only 100 to 200 yards long. In the midst of the dunes continuous belts of Toghraks could still be made out at intervals of three to four miles. The old river beds marked by them came from the west-north-west, evidently branches of the river which watered the ancient settlement, and my plane-table sheet showed clearly that they connected with the lines of dead jungle which we had crossed at right angles farther east when marching towards the ancient site. Curiously enough, at the first of the belts of dead Toghraks, some four miles from Camp CXXVI., I found some dry leaves exposed in the sand as if a few of the trees had lived on until recent times. Near the next belt a ridge of old tamarisk cones displayed a few gnarled stems still alive.

A short distance before this, and about nine miles from our last camp, one of the labourers picked up the fragment of a bronze mirror, bearing on its back relievo ornamentation in a style which showed close resemblance to work found at the ancient site. It was the last trace I could find of this ground having been visited during the historical period. With the increasing height and closeness of the dunes the ground became so trying for the camels that, after having covered only a little over thirteen miles, we were obliged to halt by nightfall at a point where a narrow strip of eroded ground emerged between heavy ridges of sand. It looked like the bank of a very ancient river bed smothered thousands of years ago, and the big trunks of Toghraks, bleached and splintered almost beyond recognition, burned like tinder. How grateful we felt for their blaze in these cheerless surroundings!

The following morning opened more brightly than we expected. The air was brilliantly clear, and the horizon showed up distinctly the barren ridges of the Kuruk-tagh north and the snow-covered range of the Chimen-tagh south. It seemed a comfort to have visible assurance in these distant hill lines that the great dismal depression which we were traversing had its bounds. After half a mile the closely packed ridges of sand gave way to a wide expanse of flat ground evidently eroded. It showed a soft surface as if of disintegrated clay or loess, and over extensive patches was thickly covered with snail - shells. I had often before noticed the latter embedded in the layers which erosion had exposed on the slopes of Yardangs; but nowhere yet had I seen these proofs of ancient fresh-water marshes or lakes spread out so uniformly and in such profusion. Erosion during long ages seemed to have done its work of levelling so completely here that but few Yardang ridges had escaped. They rose island-like among low dunes (Fig. 127). About three and a half miles from camp we came upon a grove of dead Toghraks, surrounded by dunes rising to about thirty feet.

At two points beyond, each three to four miles farther, we found our route crossed by continuous ridges of sand, like the Dawans of the Taklamakan, rising to about fifty feet above the flat eroded expanse (Fig. 128). But otherwise the latter continued and offered relatively easy going. My satisfaction at this was, however, soon damped by the observation that after the patch with dead Toghraks above mentioned the remains of ancient trees completely disappeared. The ease with which we had so far been able to obtain fuel, and the need for keeping the camels lightly laden, had made us overlook the necessity of being prepared for this emergency. I got the men to pick up carefully in bags every scrap of decayed wood débris we could sight. But the total crop thus gathered weighed only a few pounds when dusk began to descend.

It was a bad outlook for the night, the last of the year 1906, and though I was glad to spend it in the solitude and peace of the desert, the prospect of having nothing to prepare warm drink and food with was distinctly unpleasant. How should we fare in the bitterly cold nights still to be faced before we could strike the jungle belt of the Tarim? I had resigned myself to a fireless camp after a fourteen miles' tramp with the wearied camels when, from the height of a curious eroded clay 'witness' rising to twenty-five feet or so between low dunes, I spied a small darkish cone.

It proved to have retained a few roots of tamarisk scrub dead long ages ago. The men dug them out keenly, and had a tiny fire to crouch round for the night and to prepare our meal by.

Immediately near this old tamarisk cone the soil felt moist, and a thin crust of salt covered the surface. So subsoil water must still find its way there. But where did it come from? There could be little doubt about the day's march having led mainly over what had been a lake or marsh bed at some distant period. But how far back did this lie? In the present state of our knowledge there is neither geographical nor archaeological evidence to supply a clear answer. Implements of the Stone Age and neolithic pottery débris cropped up at intervals along the day's route. Had the people who used them occupied this area before it was last under water, and how long ago? Before such questions can be discussed with any prospect of settlement much minute survey work will be needed all over the Lop Desert, and the time for that does not seem to be at hand yet. In the meantime the total absence over this area of the lines of dead forest and of the old river beds which they mark, is a feature deserving special notice.

The temperature of the night had fallen to a minimum of 13 degrees below zero Fahrenheit. So I felt doubly grateful that the morning of the New Year 1907 dawned upon us not merely in brilliant clearness, but without wind. There was no fire to warm myself by in the morning, and even in the sun the temperature of the day did not rise more than a few degrees above freezing-point. The march proved tiring to men and beasts alike; for at intervals of two to three miles broad Dawans up to sixty feet and more in height had to be surmounted, and even most of the depressions between them were covered with a succession of smaller dunes. The occasional patches of hard ground met with in narrow, trough-like valleys would have offered better going. But they were rarely more than thirty or forty yards long, and running just like the Dawans and individual dunes from north to south, could not be utilized for our progress.

Steering as steadily as I could to the south-west I was glad to avail myself of such saddles as offered in the successive lines of Dawans. Even thus the track to be practicable for the camels had each time to wind up and down again for half a mile along the crests of the main dunes piled up on the Dawan, and across the isthmus-like ridges connecting them (Fig. 129). Tiring as it was to have almost constantly to negotiate these sand escarpments, big and small, running diagonally across our route, the regularity of their bearing seemed a propitious sign; for from my experiences gained by the rivers which lost themselves in the Taklamakan, I concluded that we were now passing into the region of the high riverine sands, which would keep as usual parallel to the Tarim. And the latter's course here lay from north to south.

Wherever the ground between the Dawans was flat, soft shells of fresh-water snails abounded; and at one point, about twelve miles from Camp cxxviii., we crossed what looked like the bed of an ancient lagoon about a mile broad with a clearly marked shore-line westwards. We came upon neolithic remains in half-a-dozen places; but the rarity of dead wood continued so extreme as to cause us a good deal of anxiety. The few fragments we discovered here and there were so completely shrivelled up and decayed that it was quite impossible to determine from what trees they had come or where these might have grown. It was a great relief when, after more than half of the day's weary tramp was done without yielding fuel, we came upon a few armfuls of much-perished tamarisk roots on a patch of hard gypsum. This just sufficed to save us from a camp without warm drink or food. It was not a cheerful spot where darkness obliged us to halt at the foot of a big Dawan, and the night, with a perfectly clear star-lit sky, proved the coldest of the winter. The minimum temperature dropped to 48 degrees Fahrenheit below freezing-point; yet we had to do without a fire to warm us after ice had been melted for tea and for the simplest cooking.

Next morning we sacrificed a couple of packing 'Shotas' from the camels' gear to get tea and a little warmth,

128. DAWAN OR RIDGE OF DUNES, RISING TO ABOUT FIFTY FEET, LOP-NOR DESERT.

129. CAMELS CROSSING DAWAN OF DUNES, LOP-NOR DESERT, NEW YEAR, 1907.

and set out for what proved an encouraging day's march.
It is true there were four Dawans of big size to be crossed;
but the areas of relatively open ground between them,
with low dunes and occasional erosion terraces cropping
out, seemed to get gradually broader.   What dead wood
we had come across for the last two and a half days had
invariably lain in small fragments on eroded hard soil
without any indication of its original place of growth.   So
it was cheering when, after ten miles, a few low cones with
dead tamarisk *in situ* were sighted.   Their wood looked
extremely decayed and of great age.   Close by we found
pottery fragments of very coarse make, probably neolithic,
as we had noticed before at intervals.

I tried to keep up the men's spirits by offers of rewards
for the first tree sighted or sign of animal life; and soon
shouts announced the discovery of dead Toghraks.   Some
shrivelled trunks still stood upright amidst the low dunes.
About the same time with great satisfaction I myself
noticed ahead a 'sign of land,' *i.e.* of living vegetation and
water, in the shape of fine hairy seed-pods of reeds floating
in the air.   The Lopliks knew them as 'Pakawash.'   After
surmounting a broad Dawan we pitched camp that evening
at its west foot, in a depression over a mile broad.   There
were plentiful dead trees, all Toghraks, and many of them of
large size, stretching in lines from north to south.   It was
clear that we were now nearing ground where lagoons and
beds fed by the Tarim might have existed within historical
times.   But the look of the dead tree trunks seemed
decidedly more ancient than, *e.g.*, near the Niya site.
There was good cheer for us all in the huge flaring bonfires we were able to kindle that night, and I felt as if I
were beginning to have a little holiday after all the fatigues
and cares of the last month.   But the men felt the pinch
of supplies running out, and some of the camels had begun
to show increased signs of exhaustion.   When should we
strike the line of lagoons fringing the east bank of the
Tarim?

Our march of January 3rd brought no striking change
in the aspects of the desert, such as the men hoped for;
and they were becoming impatient for a sight of the

riverine jungle. But though the succession of Dawans seemed now again closer together, and the going was accordingly heavy, there was no want of encouraging signs. About three miles beyond camp there appeared on dune-girdled cones a few tamarisks still alive. We had come before upon patches of flat ground covered with the stubble of dead Kumush stalks, still eight to ten inches in height.

Frequently we passed cones with dead tamarisks rising amidst the dunes; and when after about twelve miles I fixed my plane-table on the top of a high sand ridge, I could make out through my glasses far away to the west a dark line running north to south, clearly made up of tamarisk cones bearing living bushes. Such bushes were met with, in fact, very soon after, though in isolation, and by the time we were nearing the end of our tiring fourteen miles' tramp, the spirits of the men had been raised by the sight of a patch of living reeds. The camels had kept up with us all day remarkably well. Had they scented the approach to water and grazing? Close to the small Yardang where we pitched camp, two fine old Toghraks raised their gnarled trunks still alive, and the top branches we cut off were eagerly chewed by the camels for their sap. All day snail-shells had littered flat sand and bare clay alike; but pottery débris had become very scarce, and of bronze only a small fragment was picked up.

Next morning, in spite of the bitter cold, the men got ready for an early start with unusual alertness. At first progress was slow; for the dunes before us were high, up to thirty or forty feet, and showed no grouping into successive ridges and depressions. A huge Dawan of sand, probably over one hundred feet in height, which loomed in front stretching from north to south, was avoided by keeping a more southerly course as we had done repeatedly during the last few marches. Then we skirted the northern edge of a similar big ridge which showed on our left, and met more and more tamarisk cones and groups of Toghraks still living. At last the dunes got lower and lower, and after nearly seven miles gave way to an inlet-like depression covered with dead Kumush stubble and fringed by big cones with living tamarisks. Here we first noticed the droppings of hares and deer, and the tracks made by them and smaller jungle animals. We followed the depression, manifestly the bed of a recent lagoon with traces of a flood channel cutting through it to the south-west, and after another three miles were attracted by a luxuriant bed of reeds.

While the camels fell to grazing on this with the hunger of some ten foodless days (Fig. 130), we ascended a low sand-ridge close by in order to get a look-out. Suddenly Aga - bergan, the ' Kharat ' or carpenter, recognized a Toghrak grove in which only a year before he had helped to make a Loplik's ' dug-out,' and assured us that the lagoon of Köteklik-köl with its fishermen's station was quite near ! The men shouted with joy, and we all pushed on westwards through the thick scrub and reeds until less than half a mile beyond we stood on the north shore of the hard-frozen winding lake.

CHAPTER XXXVII

It was a strange sensation to have dropped so suddenly upon water in abundance and upon traces of human habitation. The latter, however, was manifestly intermittent; for neither our united shouts nor a shot fired from a carbine succeeded in drawing any sign of life from the hut visible in the distance. It was of importance to make sure of our exact position; and as the chance of catching a guide was greater if we approached the main bed of the Tarim and the route leading along it, we decided to move straight across to the west. The sheet of perfectly transparent ice before us looked most inviting in its smoothness. Before taking to it I had the camels' loads lightened by emptying the last two bagfuls of ice which remained, though after nearly a month's strict economy it seemed sadly wasteful to scatter fine lumps of ice on the sand of the lake shore.

Marching westwards for about a mile and a half we crossed successive arms of the lake, all covered with ice so clear that we could see right down to the bottom, six to eight feet deep, and watch the fishes moving. Its thickness was about one foot, as measured at occasional holes which fishermen had cut to insert their nets. According to Tokhta Akhun's account, it was customary for the fishermen to form a ring on the ice and to drive the fish into the net by stamping in a gradually narrowing circle. It was curious to watch the effect which the novel experience of crossing this ice-sheet had on honest Naik Ram Singh. None of the strange sights he had shared in our travels through mountains and deserts had so far made anything like such an impression on his solid Jat artisan's brain. Again and again he expressed doubt whether his fellow-villagers far away in the Punjab would believe him when he returned and told this tale. Poor fellow, how lucky he was not to know that the big lustrous eyes which had witnessed this wonder of camels walking over deep water were never to see his Indian home again !

By sunset we pitched camp under high tamarisk cones by the north-west corner of the lake, and there late at night we were visited by the solitary fisherman of Kötek-lik-köl whom Tokhta Akhun and Aga-bergan had at last succeeded in tracking down. He had no supplies to spare for our labourers beyond a few fish which they devoured half-raw ; but the information elicited from him made it easy for me to locate our position on the chain of riverine lagoons which stretches along the east of the main Tarim bed and is connected with the flood channel of the Ilek. The attraction we had unconsciously undergone on our desert crossing, owing to the easier ground between the high Dawans stretching north to south, had tended to make us steer a somewhat more southerly course than the one I was bent upon. Thus on striking the Tarim, or rather the Ilek, we found ourselves fully a march to the south of the Merdek ruin.

This made it necessary to recover what we had lost in latitude by marching up the Ilek on January 5th. The night had been perceptibly warmer than any of those passed in the desert ; as we moved along sheltered depressions and under a bright sky, the day's tramp was quite enjoyable. It took us along a succession of frozen lagoons to the fishermen's reed-huts by the Sadak-köl abandoned for the winter. Then through wide expanses of reed-beds, in which the channels of the Ilek seemed completely to lose themselves, we reached a belt of luxuriant Toghrak jungle where we decided to halt for the night. Under the shelter of the magnificent poplars the evening seemed almost warm, and next morning the minimum thermometer showed only twenty degrees of frost. Luckily the small foraging party I had sent out towards the fishing station of Tokum by the Tarim now returned with a supply of flour and a guide. So no time was lost in striking across the reed-covered flood bed of the Ilek, here fully two miles broad, towards the hut of Arzan, an old fisherman who had been settled here with some cattle and sheep for six years past, and who was likely to guide us to ' Merdek-shahr.' So far all Lopliks met with had stoutly denied any knowledge of the ruins.

By good chance we caught the quaint old herdsman 'at home' in his hut at the foot of a conspicuous sand-ridge, and found him ready to conduct us to the ' Tim ' as he called the ruin. Soon leaving behind the narrow belt of living jungle, we marched eastwards 'for about two and a half miles over fairly high dunes and across depressions with salt pools, until by the side of a dry lagoon I sighted the clay rampart of a small circular fort overgrown with reeds (Fig. 131). Pitching camp there I devoted the day to a close examination of this modest ruin and soon found evidence of its early origin.

The very construction of the rampart, stamped clay below with sun-dried bricks above, both strengthened by layers of tamarisk twigs and horizontal Toghrak beams, suggested antiquity. The rampart measured some fourteen feet on the top, and at its base, now mostly covered by sand, showed a width of probably twice as much. Its total height above the present ground level was about ten feet. Measured from the centre line of the rampart the little stronghold had a diameter of about 132 feet. On clearing away the sand which covered the masonry portion of the rampart, I ascertained that its large bricks showed exactly the same dimensions as those found in the structures of the ancient sites north of Lop-nor, eighteen by eleven inches, with a thickness of four inches. The conclusion which this close agreement suggested as to contemporary origin was soon confirmed by finds of Chinese copper coins, all belonging to Han types, and two bearing a legend which we know to have been first introduced by the usurper Wang Mang at the very commencement of our era.

There could be no reasonable doubt that this small fortified post had been occupied during the earliest period

130. CAMELS GRAZING ON FIRST REEDS AFTER CROSSING LOP-NOR DESERT.

131. CIRCUMVALLATION OF SMALL FORT OF MERDEK-SHAHR, OVERGROWN WITH REEDS.

of Chinese control over the Tarim Basin. Insignificant as was the ruin itself, its date invested it with a definite antiquarian and geographical interest; for its existence at this place proves that a branch of the Tarim must already in the early centuries of our era have flowed close to the present line of the Ilek, and this is a fact that was worth establishing in view of much-discussed theories about earlier wanderings of the Tarim and its terminal lake beds. Whether the deep Nullah, passing close to the south of the ruin and in line with the marsh known as Bayi-köl, went back to the time of its occupation, it was impossible to determine. But it was said to have received water during the summer floods until quite recent years.

We observed an unmistakable effect of this when, digging down in the centre of the circumvallation where some withered Toghrak posts lay exposed, we came upon moist sand at a depth of only four feet. It was clear that none of the usual débris in perishable materials could here have survived subsoil moisture. And in fact, on subsequently clearing the gate passage, which once led into the small fort from the south, I found that the massive Toghrak posts originally flanking it had completely rotted away, except for three or four feet on the top where they showed marks of having been exposed to fire. To the vicinity of water was due, too, the complete absence of wind-eroded ground near the ruin, and the consequent want of the usual débris in hard materials. Nor did the search which I made around that day and on the following morning reveal the survival of any other structural remains.

Therefore, satisfied with the chronological evidence which our rapid work at Merdek-shahr had yielded, I was free by mid-day of January 7th to start again southward. The main object drawing me back was, of course, the excavation of the ruins of Miran. But before settling down to this task I decided to visit the ancient site which Roborowsky's survey, as embodied in the Russian Transfrontier map, marked under the name of Kötek-shahri, near the terminal course of the Charchan Darya. Regard for the men whom all these weeks of hard work in the wintry desert had tried severely, and whose supplies were now rapidly running out, obliged me to keep as far as possible to the route which connects the several fishing stations along the main bed of the Tarim, and is utilized also in parts for the Chinese postal service from Charklik towards Tikkenlik and Korla. Seeing that the route is well known, I can be brief in my account of these marches.

We had just recrossed the wide marshy depression of the Ilek, and were moving across the interfluvial belt of sandy jungle to the south-west, when to my pleasant surprise we were met by the ponies which I had ordered Mullah to send up from Abdal in charge of Aziz and Musa. So progress became suddenly easy, for us mounted men at least, and I confess that the comfort of being in the saddle once more helped me greatly to appreciate the pleasant change the scenery underwent as we neared the Tarim. With rows of living Toghraks becoming more and more frequent, the ground we passed through assumed quite a park-like appearance. Once by the bank of the hard-frozen river we had a magnificent natural avenue of wild poplars to ride along. It was like a vision of those distant ages when the lines of fallen dead Toghraks we had passed in the desert still rose high by river beds long since dry. We halted at Tokum, where my followers found shelter against another bitterly cold night in a picturesque cluster of reed huts, ensconced in a thicket of poplars and occupied by five or six Loplik families. I could buy the men flour and a sheep for a big treat, and myself indulge again in the long-missed luxury of milk.

Next day we moved down to the fishing-station of Shirghe-chapkan; passing the Köteklik-köl again, and a succession of smaller lagoons all connected at flood time by the channel of the Ilek, now dry. The ice was delightfully smooth everywhere, and I longed for skates to warm myself by a good run against the cruel north-east wind which blew all day. The Niaz-köl, which the six or seven reed huts of Shirghe-chapkan adjoin, forms the last widening of the Ilek bed, and a few miles lower down, the latter unites with the present main course of the Tarim.

But in earlier times a big branch of the river turned off here sharply to the east in the direction of the Kara-koshun marshes, and its bed, still lined in parts with living trees, and occasionally reached by water in years of exceptional floods, serves as the direct route to Abdal. I used this to send off some of the camels to Abdal, with orders for the Surveyor and much-needed stores from my depot to join me *via* Charklik.

I myself, with the rest of our transport, moved off to the south-west, and after a couple of miles crossed over the ice of the Tarim, here about 130 yards broad, to the right bank. A mile or so beyond we struck the Charklik-Tikkenlik high road, and marched along it to the south without sighting the river until we reached the postal station of Kurghan for the night's halt. The ground, a bare sandy steppe, with scanty tamarisk growth and devoid of trees, looked far more dreary than the true desert, and the desolate little 'Ötang,' built with timber and mud bricks from a ruined small fort of Yakub Beg's time, harmonized with these wretched surroundings. The poor livid-faced Chinese 'Ssŭ-yeh' stationed here to look after the mail service, seemed a picture of misery, but gave me the kindliest welcome in his tumble-down hovel. To the hospitality of the filth-littered travellers' room I greatly preferred my tent, and here in due course I treated my polite visitor to tea and what apology for a cake my cook could produce. His interest in all I could tell him of my desert wanderings and diggings seemed keen, and my only regret was that with my stores practically exhausted, I had nothing but a small packet of candles to offer as a souvenir. It was a comfort to find the passage of my several letters to Kashgar duly recorded in the postal register.

Our march on January 10th to the station of Lop was if anything still more depressing. The track representing the 'high road' to Charklik now turned to the south-west and finally forsook the Tarim. The wearisome succession of marshes which we skirted all day manifestly formed the northernmost edge of the Charchan river delta. At first the depressions were dry; then we came upon shallow lakes divided by strips of 'Shor,' and could take short cuts across their hard-frozen surface. Finally, close to Lop we encountered channels of running water which came from the south-east, and undoubtedly were fed by the present end of the Charchan Darya. Lop Ötang was a miserable place, if anything even less inviting than Kurghan, with lagoons and salt-impregnated hummocks closing in all round. But from the fishermen's hamlet about a mile eastward we succeeded in securing a number of men who might act as diggers; and so I was able to pay off and dismiss the last of my Charklik labourers, who had held out so pluckily by my side during those hard weeks in the desert, but were now worn out and anxious to regain their homes. Nobody at Lop would aver that he knew anything of Kötek-shahri. But luckily, late at night, there turned up from Abdal Osman Bai, one of the 'Mirabs' of Charklik, whom the Amban had sent on in response to an earlier message, and who was able to guide us.

So no time was lost in setting out next morning. At first we followed the 'road' leading south to Charklik, and close to Lop crossed by a rickety bridge what manifestly was for the time being the main channel of the dying Charchan Darya. Then after a few miles we struck off to the right for a south-westerly course, and followed a well-marked shepherd's track across a singularly bare and desolate waste. It showed unmistakable proofs of forming part of the inundation area of the Charchan River; but for four or five years past no water was said to have passed into any of the channels south of the main bed which we had crossed near Lop, and the scanty Kumush in the depressions we passed was dying. Only in two small lagoons did we find any water. At last, after about ten miles we reached a belt of thriving reed-beds and subsequently crossed a well-marked river bed known as Sulagh Darya. I could see no trace of its having carried water recently; but abundant vegetation attested that sub-soil water was near, and rows of Toghraks could be seen lining it for a long distance westwards. Here we met a large flock of sheep guarded by two boys. Finally we reached another dry river bed surrounded by luxuriant tamarisk scrub, where a rude enclosure made of high bundles of reeds afforded convenient shelter for the night. Attracted by the light of our camp fires four shepherds joined us late in the evening. From them I learned that in order to water their flocks they had to drive them a long distance north to the channel known as Lop Darya, the only one which then held water or ice. This diversion of the whole Charchan Darya into the northernmost bed accounts for the large lagoons we had crossed north of Lop, and also for the reported drying-up of the Kara-muran marshes which the Russian explorers had found at the eastern end of the delta.

Our march on January 12th to the vicinity of the old site proved long but pleasant. First we moved along the dry river bed through low jungle steadily increasing in luxuriance, came on isolated Toghraks farther on, outposts of the true riverine forest, and finally, after eleven miles or so, struck a narrow ice-covered channel near the dried-up lagoon of Yekinlik-köl. The channel was only some fifty yards wide, and, a short distance to the north-east, seemed to end in a small, ice-covered expanse. Along the bank of this channel westwards we passed miles of fertile grazing lands which the shepherds were manifestly bent on improving by taking off regular irrigation cuts. At last our channel led us up to the main river bed, which suddenly came into view as a continuous sheet of glittering ice fully four hundred yards wide. No such imposing sight had met my eyes anywhere on the Tarim.

Splendid, too, were the groves of big Toghraks lining the banks; and the beauty of the silent sylvan scenery, as it presented itself in the light of a brilliant sunset, made me forget all the fatigue and cold. Just as darkness came on we pitched camp in a fine poplar grove between the river-bank and a dry lagoon to the south known as Shah-Tokhtaning-köli (Fig. 133). There was shelter from the biting breeze, with good water and plenty of fuel. But our contentment became still greater when the men sent out to reconnoitre for shepherds, came upon a small convoy of supplies which the Beg of Charklik, in response to a message despatched from Tokum, had sent out to meet

us near the 'old town.' There was at last abundance of
flour, rice, and fat for the men; and such small luxuries
as eggs, frozen milk, and dried fruits brought home to me
likewise the advantage of resuming touch with a 'base of
supply.'

Next morning, leaving my men and animals behind to
enjoy a well-earned holiday, I set out with Osman Bai and
the Lopliks for the old site. It proved far nearer than
expected, but disappointing, too, at the same time. For a
mile or so we crossed to the south-west a belt of luxuriant
reed-beds, with traces of dried-up lagoons. Then we came
upon a line of sand-hills up to thirty feet high, covered
with tamarisks and wild poplars mostly dead, and clearly
marking the direction of a former river bed. It was about
half a mile broad, and ran parallel to the present course of
the Charchan Darya. Beyond, there extended an open
eroded zone of alluvial loess steppe, from one to one and a
half miles wide, and covered with many low 'witnesses'
rising four to six feet above the general level.

Fragments of coarse and brittle pottery, also pieces
of stone showing marks of grinding, could be picked up in
plenty; but vainly did I search for any trace of structural
remains or even a single coin or piece of worked metal.
All the potsherds were hand-made, and in their gritty
coarse substance resembled the pottery I had grown
accustomed to associate with neolithic remains. Judging
from the extent over which this ancient débris was scattered and the relative thinness of its distribution, I was
led to conclude that a settlement, sparse but perhaps
long continued, had existed here in times earlier than any
to which our present historical evidence reaches back.
It seemed probable that similar remains might survive
at many points along the whole river course, but were
hidden from view by vegetation or drift sand. South of
the eroded area there spread a belt of true desert. But
the dunes were low, and a well-marked sheep track showed
that herdsmen on their way from and to Vash-shahri were
accustomed to move across it. Before mid-day I was
back in camp, and with the sun shining brightly through
the leafless trees settled down to busy work on a long-

132. HABDAL LABOURERS FROM CHARKLIK.

See page 502.

133. MY TENT AT SHAH-TOKHTANING-KÖLI, BY CHARCHAN RIVER.

On left, Ibrahim Beg of Keriya ; on right, Loplik with cyclometer.

delayed mail. It was by no means yet finished when the bitter cold, in spite of fur sitting-bag and the rest, drove me to bed about midnight.

The rest in this riverine camp was badly needed for my men and beasts alike, and the peace which reigned for once around me was so ideal that I decided to make a halt on the next day and finish the most urgent writing tasks before starting for fresh work at Miran. I had no reason to regret the delay; for it allowed me to enjoy at full ease the finest revel of colours which the heavens could ever prepare by surprise. I had scarcely despatched faithful Ibrahim Beg with my Dak bag to Charklik, when, after 11 A.M., a sensation of growing darkness forced me to rise from my little table and look outside the tent. The sky appeared strangely yellow and brown, and my first thought was of a sand storm coming from the east to sweep down upon us. But the air was calm and not a sound to be heard.

Then I looked at the sun and saw his ball half-hidden behind a thick veil. I realized we were in for an eclipse, and by good luck it proved total in this far-off corner of innermost Asia. I shall not attempt to describe the wonderful illumination effects to which we were treated. But for a few fleecy clouds above the mountains southward the sky was clear and allowed me to watch them to perfection. Never shall I forget the deep lustrous tints of yellow and blue in the sky to the west, with the belt of intense green lining the horizon. No words of mine could paint them, nor the silvery glory of the corona, while the eclipse was complete. The waves of yellow light flitting over the wide silent landscape were weird. Tinted by them the broad glittering ice-sheet of the river, the brown belts of riverine jungle, and the lines of dunes beyond looked all alike unreal. Then, as the sunlight gradually returned, fresh life seemed to rise in the lonely strip of forest, and the birds were heard again. My men and the Lopliks had, with the prosaic nonchalance of their race, remained quietly seated round their camp fires, and not one of them troubled to ask me any questions. An icy wind sprang up in the afternoon, this time from the west, and soon forced me to lace up my little tent and seek warmth for writing by the light of candles.

Early on the morning of January 15th I started again down the Charchan River with the intention of making eastward for Miran. We had left behind the point where the track to Charklik branches off southward, and were moving across a level scrub-covered plain towards the grazing-ground of Koköl-satma, where we were to halt for the night, when our caravan was caught up by a mounted messenger despatched from the Charklik Ya-mên. The cover which he brought proved to be a telegram from Macartney, sent to Kara-shahr in reply to my letter of November 15th, informing me that the sum of 1500 Taels in Chinese silver, which I had asked him to place at my disposal through the good offices of the Tao-t'ai of Ak-su, was to be available for me, not at Charklik where the local administration was manifestly unable to raise such a sum, but at the treasury of Kara-shahr.

Now this place, the headquarters of a district situated on the great high road from Kashgar to Urumchi and into China proper, lay some three hundred and fifty miles away to the north. The telegram had taken over a fortnight to reach me from there, and while I fully appreciated the saving of time effected by the use of the wire between Kashgar and Kara-shahr, I could not help feeling disappointed on finding from an accompanying Chinese-Turki epistle that the prefect of Kara-shahr, evidently fearing risks about the transmission of the silver, had left it to me to arrange for fetching it. It was practically impossible to achieve this without returning first to Charklik; and as it was important that I should receive my reserve of Chinese silver horse-shoes before setting out through the desert for Tun-huang, I decided to make my way to Miran *via* Charklik.

A number of other reasons also urged this change of route. Ram Singh, the Surveyor, had reported his arrival at Charklik, but added that increased rheumatism wholly incapacitated him from work. Several of my men had suffered severely under the hardships of our desert work; Muhammadju in particular had never ceased groaning for some days past, complaining of pains which suggested pleurisy—or a creditable imitation of it. A few days' rest

under comfortable shelter might restore the physical
endurance of my caravan, and only Charklik could afford
that.

So on the morning of January 16th, to the great
relief of my myrmidons, I changed our course at right
angles and headed for Charklik due south. It was a long
and dreary day's march. The portion of the Charchan
river delta through which we first passed had received
no water for six to seven years; I noted how scrub and
low jungle was dying away to the south. Then came
miles and miles of bare waste, with the surface clay or
loess showing slight wind erosion. The dry river beds
which we crossed in this belt seemed to come from the
direction of Vash-shahri. After eleven miles we struck
the broad bed of the Charklik Darya, here some fifty yards
broad, but holding only scanty water, and passed into a
loess steppe with gradually increasing vegetation. Finally,
we reached in the dark the edge of Charklik cultivation,
and after a total march of some twenty-six miles found
a hearty welcome and shelter in our old host's house.

CHAPTER XXXVIII

THE RUINED FORT OF MIRAN

My stay at Charklik gave my men the rest which they amply deserved and needed. But I myself found the five days to which, in spite of my efforts, it dragged out, almost too short for all the tasks there were to get through. An early visit to the Ya-mên, where Liao Ta-lao-ye greeted me with the cordiality of an old friend, allowed me to arrange for the rapid progress of Ibrahim Beg, who was to proceed to Kara-shahr and fetch my silver reserve with all possible speed. Using freely all official resources, the journey to and fro could not be accomplished in less than a month, and it was important that my own start for Tun-huang should not suffer delay on that score.

Ram Singh's rheumatism, in spite of a week's rest at Abdal, had shown no sign of abatement; and I realized that, even if we could get him fit again for more field work, it would be useless to expect him to face the hardships of another desert campaign next winter. So I used Ibrahim Beg's despatch to Kara-shahr for addressing to the Surveyor-General in India a telegraphic request *via* Kashgar to send another native surveyor in relief of Ram Singh. It was due to this accelerated appeal and prompt compliance with it on the part of the Survey Department that Rai Lal Singh could join me nine months later far away in Kan-su. Then I was kept busy with securing fresh labourers for my excavations at Miran, and collecting all supplies my large party needed, not merely during our protracted work there, but also for the long desert journey to Tun-huang. I knew that Abdal had no resources to offer, and that all arrangement for the additional transport we should need would have to be made weeks ahead at our Charklik base.

In addition to all these preparations I had to concern myself about adequate packing materials for the many antiques, prospective and already secured, which would require secure despatch to Kashgar before we set out for the desert eastwards. With a couple of skilled carpenters, my precious supply of iron nails and screws brought from India, and a few needful tools, Naik Ram Singh could always be relied on to produce packing-cases out of dead trees at any old site. But experience had shown me that felts, cotton wool, stout sheets of Khotan paper, and other materials badly needed for securing my finds from damage, could not be improvised on the spot. And how necessary it was for me to examine all this stuff in person if the supply of inferior materials and consequent embarrassment in the field were to be prevented! So, what with a fresh Dak opportunely arriving from Khotan, and preliminary accounts of my explorations to be written up, I found it hard to spare sufficient time for the mutual visiting which the Amban's friendly attention exacted. The ancient Chinese records and other relics I had brought to light from the Lop-nor sites were to his cultured mind a source of unceasing interest. When I thought of what life in the isolation of Charklik meant for this well-bred official exile, I could not grudge the little sacrifice which our antiquarian confabulations cost me. Still less do I regret it now when I recall how my poor Amban friend was destined some eight months later to close his life in this dreary Central-Asian Tomi.

On the morning of January 22nd I was free at last to start back to Miran with diggers and supplies all complete, but my caravan slightly reduced in men and animals. Two veterans from my first journey, Muhammadju and Karim Akhun, the Surveyor's attendant, were down with internal complaints. They were probably the two oldest men of the party, and were now so worn out by the preceding fatigues and hardships as to be useless for the rough work which lay before us. So I decided to leave them behind under care at Charklik, trusting that while

we were digging at Miran they would recover sufficiently
to be able to take charge subsequently of the convoy of
antiques I intended to send back from my Abdal depot,
and to escort it safely to Kashgar. Half of the hired
Charchan camels, too, were no longer fit for work,
and had to be paid off to return to their oasis. Those
raised at Charklik similarly showed signs of exhaustion,
and could not be reckoned upon for the long journey
through the desert.

Our marches to Miran lay along the route followed
before and were uneventful. There was but little wind,
and that from the south, where the view of the mountains
was now completely effaced by a dust haze. On approaching Miran late in the evening of January 23rd I was
surprised to find that we had to cross a thin sheet of ice
spread out for more than a mile's width before we reached
the edge of vegetation. This wide and shallow bed of
gravel had on our passage in December been completely
dry and bare. Tokhta Akhun explained that this happens
every winter. Evidently when the water in the actual
river bed gets frozen hard, the supply furnished by springs
rising in the bed at the foot of the gravel glacis is
forced to make its way laterally, and being protected from
evaporation by the cold spreads itself more widely than it
can at any other season.

It was again in complete darkness that we made
our way to the jungle belt by the river. But we had
spied a fire to guide us, and by its side there waited
dear Chiang-ssŭ-yeh, quaint old Mullah, and a dozen of
Lopliks from Abdal to give us a joyful welcome. In
obedience to my original order they had camped here
patiently for a week past in readiness for fresh excavations. It was delightful to be reunited once more to
my devoted Chinese helpmate. Since, alas! no correspondence mutually intelligible could pass between us,
there were plenty of details to tell him of our work and
experiences as I sat by his camp fire, and, refreshed by
his hospitable ministrations, waited and waited till the
baggage arrived late at night.

The night, with a minimum of only 15 degrees of frost,

seemed quite close, and in the early morning I found myself with surprise in an atmosphere full of mist and hoar-frost.   As we marched out to the ruins the mist lifted, and when the clouds in the south also cleared off for a short time, we could see that snow was steadily falling on the distant mountains.   It was strange to be reminded in this terribly barren plain that there was still such a thing as atmospheric moisture.   Arrived at the ruined fort I had the camp pitched close under its walls (Fig. 135), in the hope that they might afford us some protection soon, when the icy winds should be loose again to sweep the desert glacis.   The camels were sent back to the narrow jungle belt by the Miran stream to find there such grazing as dead leaves of wild poplars and dry roots could offer. The ease with which an ample supply of ice could be assured here meant a great advantage for us all, and spared me the usual anxieties about water transport. Then we set promptly to work to continue the systematic clearing of the interior where my trial excavation had stopped a month and a half earlier.

It did not take long to get proof that the ruined fort was likely to fulfil the promise held out by the first experimental digging.   When I examined the ground between the row of apartments previously excavated and the eastern fort wall behind them, another line of small rooms was laid bare, built casemate-fashion partly into the rampart, and also crammed to the roof with refuse of all sorts (Fig. 134). In the midst of inconceivable dirt, sweepings from the hearth, litter of straw, remnants of old clothing and implements, and leavings of a yet more unsavoury kind, there were to be picked up in plenty Tibetan documents on wood and paper, fragments in many cases, but often quite complete (Fig. 136).   From a single small apartment, measuring only some eleven by seven feet, and still retaining in parts its smoke-begrimed wall-plaster, we recovered over a hundred such pieces.   The amount of decayed animal and vegetable matter which had found a resting-place in these walled-in dustbins had often caused the remains of written records to be encrusted so thickly that it required much attention and care to spot and extract them.   An all-pervading smell of ammonia brought home the fact that each of these little rooms, after being used as quarters by dirt-hardened Tibetan soldiers, must also have served them intermittently for purposes far more offensive.

The rooms and half-underground hovels which had sheltered the Tibetan garrison during the eighth to the ninth century A.D. were all rough in design and construction. In those which extended along and near to the east wall of the fort, and the clearing of which kept us busy for the first three days, it was possible to discover attempts at some regular planning and disposition. But as our excavations extended farther towards the centre of the circumvallated area and along the north face, the agglomeration of hovels, built quite irregularly one against the other with thin walls of mud or coarse brickwork, and often showing considerable differences of floor-level, was apt to remind one of a rabbit-warren. Many of those on the north side showed no entrances, and had evidently been approached from above; some with bottoms four or five feet deeper than the rest had probably served as places of storage for the supplies and chattels of the motley collection of soldiers and petty officials which the stronghold had sheltered. In these archaeological 'finds' were often scanty. But it was different with the rooms which had served as living quarters at some time or other; and the refuse accumulations contained in them proved in some respects the most remarkable it has ever fallen to my lot to clear.

The rubbish reached in places to a height of close on nine feet, and right down to the bottom the layers of refuse yielded in profusion records on paper and wood. With one remarkable exception to be described farther on they were all in Tibetan. The total number of documents amounted in the end to more than a thousand. The seal sockets attached to many of the wooden 'slips,' and the seal impressions in vermilion often found below the better-preserved pieces of inscribed paper, made it clear to me at the outset that the majority of these Tibetan records were likely to contain official correspondence. The paper documents showed sizes up to eleven inches in length, and all were closely covered with lines of often very cursive writing.

134. SOUTH-EAST CORNER OF INTERIOR OF MIRAN FORT, IN COURSE OF EXCAVATION.

135. CAMP BELOW WALLS OF RUINED FORT, MIRAN.
On right of Chiang-ssŭ-yeh's tent a Mongol visitor (see page 467).

But the paper was of a peculiarly flimsy kind, fit for writing only on one side.

These peculiarities and the predominant use made of wooden 'stationery' at that relatively late date suggested that paper must have been difficult to obtain, the supply not being local. This conclusion was strengthened by comparison with the rarer sheets of well-made strong paper, manifestly of a different substance, which by their regular big writing, the ample space between lines, and the string-holes, could be recognized at once as leaves from 'Pothis' containing canonical texts or prayers. I thought of how similar leaves discovered by me in 1901 in the fort of Endere as relics of the Tibetan occupation had, on Professor Wiesner's microscopical analysis, proved to be made of paper for which the fibres of the Daphne plant, quite unknown in the Tarim Basin, had supplied the material. So I wondered whether these relics of the pious reading practised by members of the Miran garrison, or for their spiritual benefit, had not also been brought from monasteries far away to the south adjoining the Himalayan watershed.

My want of Tibetan knowledge prevented any attempt on the spot to learn from this wealth of written remains about the local conditions prevailing at the site during the period of Tibetan occupation. But no information to be gathered from them could compare in convincing direct-ness with the impression obtained at the find-spots as to the squalor and discomfort in which those Tibetan officials and braves must have passed their time at this forlorn frontier post. Evidence of a varied and often very un-savoury kind seemed to indicate that the rooms continued to be tenanted to the last, while the refuse accumula-tions on the floor kept steadily rising. Nothing but absolute indifference to dirt could have induced the occupiers to let room after room of their closely packed quarters be turned into regular dustbins, choked in some instances up to the roof.

It was indeed a thoughtful provision for the anti-quarian interests of posterity to establish these big deposits of miscellaneous refuse and records in the place where they were safest from erosion. But what a life it must have been, spent amongst them ! I have had occasion to acquire a rather extensive experience in clearing ancient rubbish heaps, and know how to diagnose them. But for intensity of sheer dirt and age-persisting 'smelliness' I shall always put the rich 'castings' of Tibetan warriors in the front rank. The recollection of these Miran Fort perfumes was fresh enough a year afterwards to guide me rightly in the chronological determination of another site ; but that is a story to be told later.

Apart from desiccated pure filth and interspersed miscellaneous records, these rubbish layers contained remains of implements, articles of clothing, and arms. Modest, indeed, they all were in make, and much worn in condition. But this uniformity throughout the deposits, which must have taken a long time to grow to that height, was additional evidence that they faithfully reflected the local conditions of life. There were in abundance pieces of coarse woollen fabrics, canvas, and felt, which must have once belonged to the braves' personal outfit. The colours varied greatly, dark browns and deep shades of red prevailing. But not a rag had found its way into the rubbish until it had become hopeless for use. The scarcity of silk pieces was significant. Fragments of elaborately woven rugs had survived ; but the patterns, like the weaving of the woollen fabrics used for clothes, strikingly varied from those of the corresponding relics brought to light at the earlier sites of Niya and Lop-nor.

It is impossible here to give details of particularly curious finds, such as a small bag made up from a piece of delicate silk brocade ; a well-preserved felt pouch which might have formed part of a soldier's equipment (Fig. 138, 27) ; a quilted shoe of buff cloth stitched all over in elaborate geometrical designs. An exceedingly filthy pigtail of coarsely strung black hair did not look as if its quondam owner had troubled much about the use of the combs in wood and horn of which we recovered numerous specimens (Fig. 138, 25). Remains of nets in stout string suggested that fishing in the stream of Miran had been a more productive pursuit than at present, or else that the marshes of the Kara-koshun

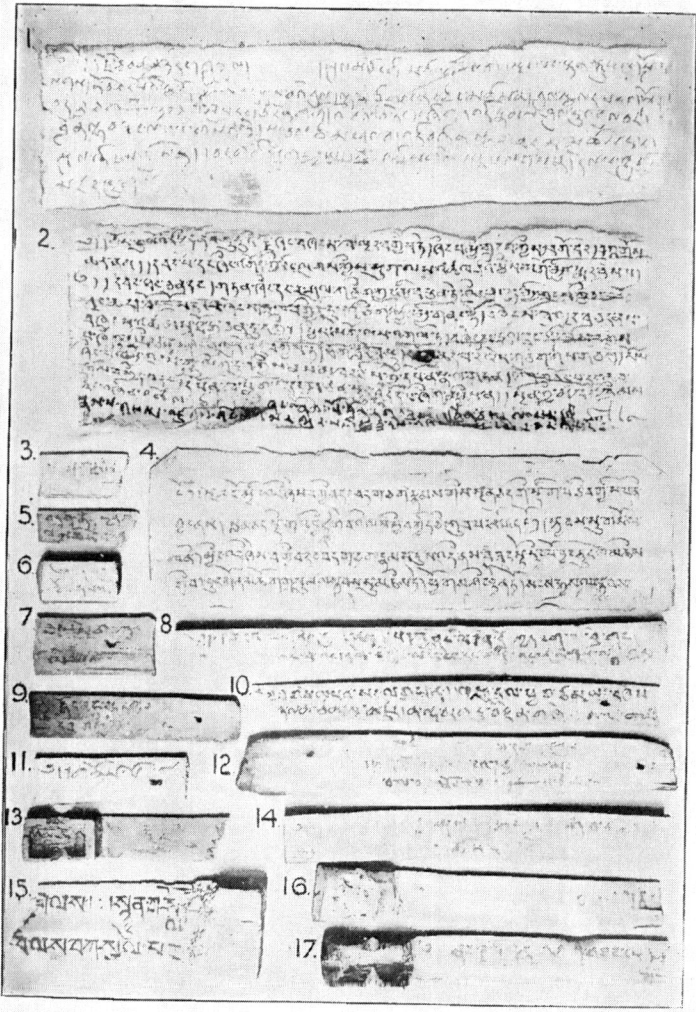

136. OLD TIBETAN DOCUMENTS, ON WOOD AND PAPER, EXCAVATED FROM RUINED QUARTERS OF MIRAN FORT.

1, 2. Documents on paper.   4. Religious text on paper.   3, 5-17. Records on wood, complete or fragmentary, some showing sockets for clay sealings.

perhaps approached nearer than they now do. More
warlike occupations were indicated by broken shafts of
reed arrows and iron arrow-heads. A sling of strong
and carefully woven goat's hair had found its way there
evidently after prolonged use.

But far more abundant were the relics of defensive
armour in the shape of lacquered pieces of leather, varying
in size, but all oblong (Fig. 138, 26). That I could recognize
them at once, even though the first finds were quite
detached pieces without any definite indication of their
original position or purpose, was my reward for having
years before correctly identified a small piece of hard
'green leather' from an ancient rubbish heap of the Niya
site as having once belonged to scale armour. Subsequently, in a suit of mail brought to the British Museum
from the Lhasa expedition, my devoted helpmate, Mr.
Andrews, discovered scales, shaped and laced exactly
after the fashion suggested by that single little piece of
leather; and this had strikingly confirmed my conjecture.
And now finds of scales, detached or still joined to their
neighbours by the original fastening of narrow leather
thongs, followed one another so rapidly that even without
painted or relievo representations of ancient scale armour
to refer to, such as some of the temples excavated in 1901
had displayed in their frescoes and stuccoes, it was easy to
reconstruct the appearance of the leather mail which had
once protected those Tibetan warriors. Judging by the
way in which the scales had been 'shed' in the different
rooms and by their number, armour of lacquered leather
must have been commonly worn at the period.

Though the scales undoubtedly belonged to a number
of different suits of armour, and varied in size as well as
in ornamentation, there was much uniformity in technical
make and style as well as in methods of lacing. The
slightly curving pieces of hard leather, perhaps of camel-
skin, bore thick lustrous lacquer on both sides, generally
applied in successive coats of brilliant red and black up to
the number of seven. Decorative effects were produced
by scraping small ornamental designs, such as rings,
ellipses, double hooks and the like, through the various

top coats of lacquer after the fashion of *sgraffito* paintings. The bronze rivets found in some pieces also served for ornamentation. For the purpose of lateral fastening the longer sides of the scales, which measure from about two and three-quarter to four and a quarter inches in different sets, were placed so as to overlap, and were then laced closely together by means of thongs passed in a cleverly designed fashion through sets of holes which are always placed near to the edges, but vary in number. The vertical attachment was effected in a similar fashion by thongs running through two pairs of holes cut near the top end and towards the middle of each scale.

In all probability the scales overlapped upwards, in a fashion curiously differing from the classical and mediaeval examples of Europe, but in accord with the specimens of scale armour which Central-Asian and Graeco-Buddhist art reproduces. The illustration given in Fig. 138, 26 of such a set of scales, found with its lacing still intact, will help to explain these details. Curiously enough, all the scales, being oblong, appear to have belonged to the skirt part of mail coats. Probably this suffered most from wear. Of the breast portion, which judging from frescoes and relievos seems to have always been made up of scales having their top ends rounded, not a single piece was found. But an elaborately worked fragment of large size, which manifestly was meant to protect the throat or arm-hole (Fig. 138, 24), proves that the armour also for the upper portion of the body was worked in lacquered leather.

137. TRADING CARAVAN PASSING MIRAN SITE EN ROUTE FOR TUN-HUANG.

138. REMAINS OF SCALE ARMOUR AND MISCELLANEOUS OBJECTS FOUND
IN TIBETAN FORT, MIRAN.

Scale, two-sevenths.

24, 26 a,b,c. Scales of lacquered leather from suits of armour, the last two showing method of lacing outside and inside.
25. Horn comb.   27. Felt pouch.   28, 29. Chinese copper coins of T'ang period.   30. Shaft of arrow.   31. Wooden key.

CHAPTER XXXIX

It was hard to find time or the right mood for the examination of antiquarian details during the five days of trying work which the clearing of the old fort cost us. Icy gales, mostly from the north-east but veering at times to north or east, were blowing almost without interruption. The misery which they caused to all of us was severe. In order to watch the excavations proceeding in different places, I had to keep most of the time on the top of the dominating east rampart, where the force of the constant onslaught of the wind was felt to the full. Whenever I descended to the diggings I enjoyed my share of the blinding dust, made up largely of disintegrated filth, which that same wind was constantly blowing into one's eyes and all exposed parts of the face. It seemed hard to decide which was worse.

But for concentrated discomfort I shall always remember the time we spent in emptying the rich mine of refuse and records presented by two fairly large rooms near the south-eastern angle of the fort (Fig. 134). Here the protecting-wall curtain had fallen, and on the surface of the rubbish exposed in this breach the gale asserted its full force. To work or to stand here for any length of time meant worse than merely facing an icy blast which cut to the bones. With the fine gravel driven across the breach and the abraded particles of refuse which rose from the surface, it felt as if one were undergoing wind erosion in person. It was impossible to keep the dozen or so of men for whom there was room, at work here for more than half an hour at a time, and I arranged to have them relieved in shifts. But documents were constantly emerging, and for most of the time I had to keep close at hand in the breach to note finds of importance and prevent loss or theft. While cleaning and opening documents my hands had necessarily to be exposed, and my fingers felt as if they were frost-bitten. Yet it had to be done, if only that the lucky finder of specially well preserved records might be rewarded on the spot—and *pour encourager les autres*.

How glad I felt that at least ever alert and devoted Chiang-ssŭ-yeh was ready to take my place at intervals! The Surveyor was down with rheumatism and passed painful days lying in his tent under whatever extra furs and rugs could be spared for him. Soon after I was obliged to let him depart for Abdal. Naik Ram Singh suffered from attacks of fever, and when not actually on the sick list could not be expected to do more than look after the labourers in some better-protected corner. Matters stood equally badly with the servants. Muhammadju had remained behind at Charklik like a worn-out veteran looking out for a convoy homewards. Ibrahim Beg, the most trustworthy of my people, was, as already related, sent off to distant Kara-shahr to bring fresh horse-shoes of silver. Ramzan, my dusky Kashmiri cook, was prompt to take the cue, and on a declaration of illness in general settled down to hibernate among his furs for the rest of our stay at Miran. As he was at the time suffering from a fresh outbreak of a malignant skin disease of old standing, I should have less minded the cessation of his cooking functions had Aziz, his *soi-disant* substitute from Ladak, developed the slightest capacity for turning out tolerably digestible food. But no amount of association with Ramzan's work could teach that tough young pony-man the modicum of skill needed for the humblest European *cuisine*.

In the shelter of my little tent, which the gale was shaking and more than once nearly brought down, I used to be busy till late at night cleaning and as far as possible numbering the day's finds of records. While handling them with half-benumbed fingers I often thought of the difficulties which interpretation of them was likely to cause thereafter, quite apart from the closely packed writing and the very cursive script. Tibetan literature, while abounding in canonical Buddhist texts and works of a devotional nature, possesses exceedingly few specimens of early secular writing. For the full elucidation of documents such as the fort of Miran has yielded, philological acumen is needed combined with intimate knowledge of the living language and the ways of Tibet. The Rev. Dr. A. H. Francke of the Moravian Mission, Leh, one of my former collaborators and the recognized authority on the antiquities of Western Tibet, is the scholar best suited for the task, and to my great satisfaction he has agreed to undertake it. But obligations arising from recent exploratory tours of his own prevent him for months to come from making a complete examination of my Tibetan records. In the meantime I must content myself here with a brief summary of such indications as emerge from his preliminary scrutiny of some documents on paper and wood, and similar notes kindly communicated to me by my friend, Dr. F. W. Thomas, the learned Librarian of the India Office.

The information so far available leaves no doubt that the great mass of the Tibetan records from Miran consists, as suspected by me from the first, of miscellaneous 'office papers,' reports, applications, etc., addressed mainly to the officers commanding the Tibetan garrison. Topics of a military interest seem to predominate, affording glimpses of the disturbed condition of things in that region. Out of the dozen and a half of documents so far translated in extracts, six distinctly refer to encounters with hostile troops. In one tablet addressed to the chief officer at 'Great Nob' we hear of a convoy having been captured and of troops being ordered to move against the attackers. In another the 'council of the fort of Little Nob' report to 'the great Lord, the general officer' how, while they were engaged in strengthening the defences, the enemy made an attack, killing their families and destroying certain supplies. There is a tablet from some small oasis calling for quick assistance to defend the threatened northern frontier and reporting disturbances in Western

Tibet. "With long lungs make haste" is the graphic close of the appeal.

Curious, too, is the petition of an old officer, complaining of not having received yet the promised reward for his services and hinting at their being needed again to repel certain fresh inroads. Elsewhere we have reports on a punitory expedition, movements of hostile cavalry, directions about the transport of supplies, etc. The urgent issue of reminders to certain dignitaries is solicited under orders from the supreme Government; and expenditure authorized on certain specified items of wages and transport. In one of the wooden tablets a certain Jehu-lho, 'servant of the four Tiger ministers,' reports his presence at Little Nob after executing his mission, and in much distress from want of further instructions asks for his marching orders. In a paper document, still difficult to read owing to incrustation with dirt, we have a private letter to a high official recommending for his use a certain medicine to be prepared of boiled sheep's dung mixed with butter, barley-flour, and other savoury ingredients. From scarcity of writing material, the reverse of the same sheet has been used for a long-winded application by some one else for a sealed passport to return to his home. A more imposing record, dated in a year of the Twelve Years' Cycle and bearing the red impressions of nine seals, contains curious court proceedings concerning the sale of a slave taken in a recent war, whom a priest disposes of to a purchaser under certain guarantees in case of his escape.

About the many points of interest which, according to my collaborators' opinion, the palaeography, spelling, and dialectic peculiarities of these records raise, it would be out of place to speak here. They belong to the earliest written monuments of the language, and are bound to throw much new light on the social and military organization of a period when Tibet played a powerful rôle in the political history of Central Asia. The identification of the numerous local names mentioned in them will prove an interesting and fruitful task. Here it must suffice to point out that among these names we have 'Cher-chen,' the earliest reference to the Charchan oasis by its modern name, and that the name 'Nob' occurring in the above-quoted documents manifestly supplies the long-sought phonetic link between the form 'Na-fo-po' used by Hsüan-tsang when describing the Lop-nor tract, and the 'Lop' of Marco Polo which Sir Henry Yule had already recognized as its mediaeval derivative. If the site of Miran, as the wording of the tablet first quoted strongly suggests, was known to the Tibetans as 'Great Nob,' it appears very probable that by 'Little Nob' they meant Charklik. This distinction would closely correspond to that which the Han Annals indicate between the two main places of Shan-shan or Lou-lan, Yü-ni, 'the Old Town,' to the east, and I-hsün or 'the New Town,' these two being now repre-sented, as I believe, by the sites of Miran and Charklik respectively.

Whatever details of historical interest may yet be gleaned from this rich garner of documents, it can be considered already certain that the occupation of the Miran fort, and in all probability also its construction, must belong to the period of Tibetan domination in Chinese Turkestan and the regions immediately eastward. Scanty as our historical materials for this period as yet are, we know that it must have extended from the downfall of Chinese power westwards in the last third of the eighth century to about the latter half of the ninth century A.D. The total disappearance of Chinese influence and control in the Tarim Basin, which marks this epoch from its commencement and largely accounts for its obscurity, is reflected by the significant fact that, among the odd thousand of written pieces which the excavation of the Miran fort yielded, not the slightest scrap of Chinese writing could be discovered.

But, curiously enough, towards the close of my diggings there came to light, from an apartment adjoining the inner face of the north rampart and filled only with a shallow layer of rubbish, a non-Tibetan record of considerable interest. It was a crumpled-up packet of paper which when opened out resolved itself into a large sheet nearly one foot square, and two torn pieces of another covered with a bold lapidary-looking writing. I recognized it at once as Runic Turki, the earliest Turkish script, first discovered some twenty years ago in certain bilingual inscriptions of the early eighth century A.D. on the Orkhon and Yenissei Rivers.

Professor V. Thomsen, the distinguished Danish savant, to whom belongs the merit of having first deciphered the script and language in those famous monuments of Mongolia, has been kind enough to undertake the publication of my Miran record. The provisional translation supplied by him shows that the document contains a long list of men, all bearing Turki names, to whom, either in person or through representatives, warrants, in all probability passports, were issued. A number of terms used in designating the recipients seems to prove that most if not all of them belonged to a Turkish military force, and thus the idea suggests itself that we have here a relic of the period preceding Tibetan occupation, when the Tarim Basin was being overrun by various Turkish tribes from the North over whom the Chinese endeavoured with varying success to assert some political control.

Neither in nor around the Miran fort could I trace any evidence of the site having been inhabited in any permanent fashion during the rule of the Uigurs, who drove out the Tibetans about 860 A.D., or during the succeeding Muhammadan period. Considering that even now a stream capable of being used for irrigation passes within a few miles of the site, progressive desiccation would scarcely suffice to explain this rapid abandonment soon after the period of Tibetan occupation, whatever the changes it has since worked on this ground. But it becomes easier to understand the abandonment when we remember the geographical facts which rendered the position of Miran so important for the Tibetans and for them only. At Miran they were guarding the key of the direct route from the southern oases of the Tarim Basin to Tun-huang. Like the branch previously mentioned as leading north of Lop-nor, this route must have been a main line of communication into China from the last centuries B.C. onwards, and must have grown in importance when the former became impracticable through desiccation about the fourth century of our era.

But a still more essential reason for the Tibetans to garrison Miran probably lay in the fact that at this little oasis debouch the two most direct routes leading from Central Tibet and Lhasa across the high plateaus and ranges of the Kun-lun to the easternmost part of the Tarim Basin. Thus Miran must have been for them a *point d'appui* of strategic value. Once the Tibetan power had disappeared from the north of those great inhospitable mountain wastes, Miran must have rapidly sunk into insignificance ; since for whatever traffic passed along the ancient route from Khotan and the other southern oases to Tun-huang and China during Uigur, early Muhammadan, and Mongol times, Charklik offered a far better base.

Thus it is easy to understand why there is no mention of Miran in Marco Polo, whose ' town of Lop ' undoubtedly represents Charklik. No doubt, when the Venetian's caravan passed the old fort on its way into the ' Desert of Lop,' the crumbling walls which looked down upon it were quite as silent and deserted as now. Once, late in the evening when the icy gale was howling its wildest, a large caravan numbering sixty or seventy camels, all laden with brick tea from Tun-huang, made its way past our desolate camp by the fort wall. The enterprising Kashgar traders who owned them were eager to reach water and fuel, and would not stop for more than a hasty greeting even though we were the first people they had met for twenty-three days past. So the whole tinkling train soon vanished again in darkness like some phantom from an age long gone by.

CHAPTER XL

THE abundance with which the ruined fort yielded up materials illustrating the conditions of the later occupation of the site, only increased my eagerness to get at remains which might help me to trace its earlier history. So I felt heartily glad when on January 29th the advanced state of the fort excavations allowed me to take a portion of my band of diggers across to the ruined temple a little over a mile away to the north-east, where experimental clearing in December had disclosed some sculptural relics of manifestly early type. It was a bitterly cold day. The minimum temperature was 37 degrees below freezing-point ; and in the piercing north wind it seemed as if this would never rise at all. But all the discomforts from cold, wind, and the dust clouds attending work in the trenches were forgotten at times over the interesting results of the digging.

The ruin, which on my first visit I had recognized as that of a Buddhist shrine, presented itself before clearing as an oblong mound of masonry in sun-dried bricks, measuring about forty-six feet on its longer sides and a little over thirty-six feet on the shorter. The corners were roughly orientated towards the cardinal points. Two stories could be clearly distinguished, one about nine feet high above what proved to be the original ground level, and on the top of it another and far more decayed one, about fifteen by seventeen and a half feet in ground plan, and in its broken state still over eleven feet high. Destruction caused by wind erosion had completely removed the plaster covering and decoration from the upper story

139. BASE OF ANCIENT BUDDHIST SHRINE M. II. MIRAN SITE, FROM NORTH-EAST, AFTER EXCAVATION.

as well as from the north-west and south-west faces of the lower one. But along the foot of the north-east face and partially along the south-east there emerged remains of decorative relievos just above the masses of débris.

As soon as these were cleared away, it was seen that the lower story or base had been adorned with niches about two feet broad and eight inches deep between projecting wall surfaces about as broad, all heavily coated with plaster (Fig. 139). Projections and niches alike survived only to a height of about four feet. But this was enough to show that the former had been decorated throughout with relievo representations of columns of strikingly Persepolitan look, bearing large capitals with turned-down volutes and at their foot a succession of round, knob-like bases separated by bold mouldings. The style distinctly recalled the elaborately carved wooden pillars brought to light in ruins of the Niya site. The niches had once contained life-sized statues in stucco; but of these only one, in the centre of the north-east side, had survived to the hips, while of others I could trace *in situ* only scanty remains of the feet besides many detached fragments.

Already when on my first visit I probed the débris of broken clay and plaster, which lay heaped up against the north-east side of the structure, there had come to light the detached head of a life-sized statue in stucco. In spite of the damage it had suffered when it fell and while buried under débris, the good modelling and proportions showed the influence of Graeco-Buddhist sculpture quite as plainly as the relievos excavated by me in 1901 in the court of the Rawak Stupa near Khotan. Now, as the heavy masses of débris were being carefully removed all along what subsequently proved to have been the north-east side of a passage once enclosing the whole central fane, we soon came upon a colossal head in stucco, representing a Buddha or Bodhisattva, on a level still fully three feet above the original floor. It had fallen with its face downwards on a layer of sand which had accumulated within the ruined passage, and thus retained traces of the original colouring on its well-modelled features. Across the temples it measured fully seventeen inches.

The material was merely a coarse clay mixed with straw and faced on the surface with a finer though very soft plaster, which, however, derived some consistency from an admixture of vegetable fibres. To lift this heavy mass of friable material in safety was no easy task. But when it was accomplished without serious damage and I found that the wooden core, though rotten, still survived within, I decided to risk its removal. Subsequently another colossal head emerged from the midst of the débris near the centre of the north-east passage, even larger and somewhat heavier in type, but in spite of all damage displaying with equal clearness features of Graeco-Buddhist style.

The origin of these colossal heads was revealed when, late in the afternoon, the clearing of the north-east passage had proceeded sufficiently to show that its outer wall was lined by the torsos of huge figures seated with folded legs, which, judging from the surviving portions of the drapery, manifestly represented Buddhas (Fig. 140). On completing the excavation next day I ascertained that this side had accommodated altogether six of these colossal statues. Across the knees they measured a little over seven feet. One near the middle of the row still retained the hands folded in the 'Dhyanamudra' or pose of meditation. Its head had fallen with the face upwards when débris filled the passage to a height of nearly three feet, and had been badly battered.

On its left knee we found placed another head, of life size, which manifestly belonged to one of the images filling the niches on the opposite passage wall. This smaller head had survived relatively well. Remembrance of similar observations in the course of my Rawak work supplied the explanation that it had been removed to this position of safety by the pious hand of one of the last worshippers when it threatened to fall off. Enough survived of the ample drapery of these colossal seated Buddhas to prove how closely the sculptor far away at Lop-nor had followed the elaborate arrangement of the folds, which the Graeco-Buddhist style of Gandhara derived

140. REMAINS OF COLOSSAL FIGURES OF SEATED BUDDHAS IN NORTH-EAST PASSAGE
OF RUINED SHRINE M. II., MIRAN SITE.

141. STUCCO HEAD OF COLOSSAL BUDDHA FIGURE, AS DISCOVERED BETWEEN STATUE
BASES IN RUINED SHRINE M. II., MIRAN SITE.

from classical models. Even the wavy edges of the festoon-like plaits hanging from the arms were reproduced with exactness. It was impossible to doubt that the construction of this ruined temple dated back to a period long anterior to the Tibetan occupation.

But that even its abandonment must have taken place centuries earlier became highly probable when I discovered in front of and close to the base of one statue a fragment about six inches long of a palm-leaf manuscript written in Sanskrit with Brahmi characters of an early Gupta type. The material showed that the Pothi-shaped manuscript, containing apparently a Buddhist metaphysical text, had been written in India; and, judging from the palaeo-graphical features of certain characters, it was safe to conclude that it could not have been written later than the fourth century of our era, and possibly somewhat earlier.

The position in which the detached leaf was found made it almost certain that it had been deposited as a votive offering on the neighbouring image base after the fashion first seen by me in the ruined shrine of Endere. On several grounds it appeared very unlikely that the manuscript could have been of great age at the time, or that a leaf of such brittle substance could have lain thus exposed for a prolonged period before the débris of the crumbling shrine came down to cover and protect it. As another curious instance of the shelter from the pressure of heavy débris, which the proximity of the massive image bases could afford, we discovered the colossal head, which once had belonged to the third statue from the north corner, firmly wedged between its own base and that of its right-hand neighbour, still upright and with its front quite uninjured (Fig. 141).

It seemed a puzzle why the shrine should have retained these remains of its sculptural decoration just on its north-east side, the one most exposed to the destructive power of the winds; but it was soon solved when our continued excavation showed that the outer passage wall was adjoined here at a few feet's distance by the massive enclosing wall of another and larger building. While helping to ward off wind erosion, this itself had suffered badly. It might have been a chapel court or monastic structure; and one solid brick wall, which lay exactly in the direction of the prevailing north-east wind, still rose for a length of close on sixty feet. But of the apartments once adjoining only one could be traced, and that merely in its ruined foundations. It was a massive small structure, measuring about nineteen feet outside and enclosing a circular chamber which recalled to my mind the domed chapels so often seen amidst the ruined Buddhist sites of the Indian North-West Frontier.

Unfortunately no antiquarian remains whatever survived within the low broken walls; and when I subsequently cleared the narrow space intervening between the walls behind the north-east temple passage, we discovered only deep layers of dung from sheep and horses. In places this also formed a thick cover over broken wall portions, thus proving that the ground must have retained vegetation fit for some sort of grazing long after the decay of the shrine. It will be remembered that my excavations at the Niya and Lop-nor sites revealed exactly corresponding evidence of a transitional period through which the area of ancient cultivation must have passed before becoming the utterly desolate waste it is now.

The safe packing of such sculptural remains from the ruined shrine as could be removed was no easy task, considering their weight and exceedingly friable substance. So I was kept hard at work while the men were laboriously 're-burying' everything else that our excavations had exposed. I could not deny the same measure of preservation to the quarters dug up in the fort, late as everything seemed there by comparison. But meanwhile I lost no time in starting work on January 31st at a group of ruined mounds which remained unexplored (Fig. 108), about a mile and a quarter west of the fort. The cursory inspection I had made of a cluster of five of them on my first approach to the site, had left the impression that they were much-decayed ruins of Stupas of the usual type. But even then I had been struck by the curious appearance of the smallest mound, which showed a remarkably well preserved little dome emerging from much débris above what seemed a disproportionately large base.

At first the clearing of this revealed nothing more stirring than the broken remnant of a narrow terrace or passage which seemed once to have run round the sides of this supposed main base, about twenty-nine feet square. I left the few men with me to complete, under Tokhta Akhun's supervision, the removal of the débris outside, while I made a preliminary survey of the adjacent masonry mounds. But on returning I realized quickly that the brickwork then laid bare was not a base at all but the remains of a solid structure, square outside but circular within, which was once, no doubt, domed and meant to enclose the small Stupa in its centre (Fig. 142). Heavy masses of débris fallen from the vaulting and the upper portions of the walls had completely blocked up the circular passage four feet eight inches wide which was left around the Stupa base, this, too, circular and measuring nine feet in diameter. The débris lay to a height of six feet and more from the original floor; but its removal was facilitated by the broad cutting which treasure-seekers, probably at an early date, had made from the west right through the massive masonry of the cella and, as we soon found, into the base of the Stupa itself.

The clearing was still proceeding in the afternoon when from the north and east segments of the circular passage fragments of painted stucco cropped up rapidly. It was evident that the interior walls of the cella had once been adorned with frescoes. Yet, when the digging there had reached a level of about four feet above the floor and a delicately painted dado of beautiful winged angels began to show on the wall, I felt completely taken by surprise. How could I have expected by the desolate shores of Lop-nor, in the very heart of innermost Asia, to come upon such classical representations of Cherubim! And what had these graceful heads, recalling cherished scenes of Christian imagery, to do here on the walls of what beyond all doubt was a Buddhist sanctuary?

As in eager excitement I cleared head after head with my bare hands in order to prevent any chance of damage,

I rapidly convinced myself that the approach to purely classical design and colouring was closer in these frescoes than in any work of ancient pictorial art I had seen so far, whether north or south of the Kun-lun. Much in the vivacious look of the large, fully opened eyes, in the expression of the small dimpled lips and the slightly aquiline nose, brought back to my mind those beautiful portrait heads of Egyptian Greek girls and youths which I remembered having seen long years before in the Graf collection on panels from Fayûm mummies of the Ptolemaic and Roman periods. Perhaps the faint trace of Semitic influence recognizable in the features presented by one or other of the frescoes helped to suggest this linking. But then, again, there was a note of the quatrocento in the lively directness of gaze and pose, the simple ease of the outlines, conspicuous even in the graceful upward curve of the short fluttering wings. One thing was quite certain at the first glance : work of such excellence could not possibly have originated in the time of Tibetan occupation nor in the period of Chinese rule immediately preceding it. As well might we look for the decorators of Pompeian villas among those who ministered to Theodoric's Goths.

I was still wondering how to account for the distinctly classical style in the representation of these Cherubim and the purport of this apparent loan from early Christian iconography, when the discovery of a ' Khat,' announced by a shout from the men, supplied definite palaeographic evidence for the dating. From the rubble of broken mud-bricks and plaster filling the passage on the south there emerged in succession three large pieces of fine coloured silk, evidently belonging to what had once been a votive flag or streamer, and each bearing a few short lines inscribed in Kharoshthi. These pieces measured about twenty-two inches in length, with a width of six to eight inches. Other fragments of the same excellently woven silk turned up later, but without writing. In all the material showed a ground colour of delicate cream, with numerous narrow stripes in harmonizing tints of buff, brown, and purple.

The Kharoshthi inscriptions on these pieces and on a

Plate IV.

FRESCOES OF WINGED FIGURES FROM DADO OF RUINED
BUDDHIST SHRINE M.III., EXCAVATED AT MIRAN SITE.

(CHAP., XLI., XLII. SCALE, ONE-FIFTH).

A B marks line where the two fresco panels join.

142. RUIN OF DOMED BUDDHIST SHRINE ENCLOSING STUPA M. III., MIRAN SITE, SEEN FROM EAST.

fourth subsequently unearthed, showed the same neat and clerical handwriting which is found on the leather documents excavated by me at the Niya site; and as these belong to the latter half of the third century A.D., the conclusion seems justified that the deposition of these votive offerings must have taken place here about the same period. The writing on the silk had remained remarkably fresh and black even without a protecting cover, such as folding provided, in the case of the leather documents or wooden envelopes in that of the Kharoshthi tablets. Hence it appeared very unlikely that the gift of the inscribed streamer could have preceded the abandonment of the shrine by any great length of time. And from this, again, the assumption would follow with good reason that Miran, like the sites of Niya, Endere, and north of Lop-nor, must have been deserted about or soon after the close of the third century A.D. For its subsequent reoccupation during Tibetan predominance the case of the Endere ruins furnishes an exact parallel.

[I may add here that since this chapter was written, the Abbé Boyer, my learned collaborator in Paris, has communicated to me the result of his decipherment of these Kharoshthi inscriptions. They contain prayers for the health of a number of persons and their relatives, all the names given being, significantly enough, of either Indian or Iranian origin.]

Twilight was setting in soon after the first of those delightful angel-busts on the north passage wall had emerged from their long interment. It was hard to have to stop work here for the day; but when, digging a little farther on the north-east side, we came upon frescoed plaster surfaces, which had evidently peeled off from higher wall portions of the little rotunda, and now lay closely packed against the painted dado, I realized the need of most careful procedure, and had to refrain from uncovering them. On the west and south-west, where treasure-seekers of old had breached the wall and nothing of the fresco decoration survived, the clearing of the débris was continued until nightfall.

Here, besides numerous pieces of silk in fine carmine,

yellow, etc., evidently once belonging to streamers, and fragments of wood-carving in Gandhara style, which had perhaps once adorned the 'Tee' or decorative umbrella above the Stupa, I recovered curious relics of what may have been votive offerings of the last worshippers at the shrine. They consisted of a mass of artificial flowers, cleverly cut out of stiff woollen fabrics, coloured cream, blue, saffron, purple, etc., and provided with small stems of wood supporting a clever imitation of stamina. Two large pieces of a stout material resembling buckram, and showing a diagram of black and white painted on a surface layer of wax or plaster, turned up with some of the flowers still stuck on to them ; of others there remained the punched holes. Evidently these painted fabrics had served to hang up offerings of artificial flowers.

I felt warmed inwardly with elation as I sat in my bitterly cold tent till a late hour that evening, trying to record in orderly fashion the facts and impressions of the day's work, and to find the true perspective and import of the vista which this unpretentious ruin had begun to reveal of classical pictorial art strangely transplanted to Lop-nor. It meant an illuminating discovery, but also the source of new problems. I should have to face practical difficulties, too, and these almost at once. For the fine wall-paintings now about to rise from their grave there was no other chance of thorough study and protection but removal. But I knew well, it would be a very difficult task to effect this and the distant transport in safety. The backing of the fresco panels was nothing but a layer of friable plaster, *i.e.* dried mud, which in many places showed ominous cracks even where still adhering to the wall. The method and means of detaching them, as well as of packing them, had still to be improvised, not to mention the making of cases sufficiently large and strong out of such materials as the jungle of the Miran stream could supply.

CHAPTER XLI

A DADO OF ANGELS

On the morning of February 1st the clearing of the circular passage was resumed as early as I could get the men to leave their fires. It was soon ascertained that the passage had been lighted by three windows, besides the entrance passing through the completely destroyed west side. The north and south windows were found to be almost exactly orientated and to reach down to about two feet eight inches from the floor. The fresco frieze or dado decorating the wall segments between each pair of windows, or between door and window, consisted of six closely adjoining lunettes; from the hollow of each there rose the head and shoulders of a winged figure nearly life size (Plate IV.). Below the row of lunettes, which were about one and a half feet high, and ranged with their chord or top line nearly four feet above the floor, there ran a broad band of wave lines boldly painted in black, and suggestive of the sea. This filled also the spandrels left between the curving sides of the lunettes. Each of the latter measured two feet two inches at the top, where a thick black line separated this 'dado of angels' from an upper fresco frieze almost completely perished.

Owing to the damage which the enclosing circular wall had suffered, little survived of the lower dado outside the north-east and south-east segments. But the débris accumulated in the latter soon proved to have protected a considerable quantity of fragments of frescoed plaster which had once decorated the higher wall faces. The larger pieces among them were found leaning in closely packed layers against the wall-portion still standing. The preservation of them was manifestly due to their having slid down at a time when sufficient débris from the vaulting had already accumulated below to stop the fall of the gradually loosened fresco pieces. Thus in one place the dado was at first completely hidden behind three successive layers of frescoed stucco. It was reasonable to assume that the innermost piece was the first to be stopped in its fall, and thus to have originally belonged to the frieze nearest the dado.

To remove any of these pieces of painted stucco, some several feet large and all very brittle, was an exceedingly delicate task. The stucco backing consisted of nothing but very friable clay, mixed with short straw of cut reeds, but not sufficiently to give it coherence or elasticity. Nowhere did it show a thickness of more than half an inch. When touched without the greatest care it was apt to break away at the edges. There was a very thin facing of finer clay to receive the painting, but it had no admixture of fibres, as often found in later fresco backing, and its greater firmness seemed only to increase the liability to cracks when once removed from the wall surface. There was the risk, too, of losing sight of the connection between fragments which had fallen close together, and might form parts of the same composition. So it was essential to secure as exact a record as possible of the condition and place in which these superimposed fragments of fine wall painting were found before attempting their separation and rescue.

Detailed descriptive notes and photography were the means available; but both offered difficulties of their own. All day it was bitterly cold, and icy gusts from the north soon benumbed my hands as I kept crouching in cramped positions, busy with endless measuring and scribbling of pencilled notes. These had then in the evening to be worked out and transferred in ink to my diary under the shelter of my tent. Photographic work was scarcely less trying. The whole width of the circular passage was only four feet eight inches, and the consequent want of space necessitated extraordinary positions for the camera, and still more troublesome twistings for myself if a sufficiently

143. FRESCO PIECE FROM FRIEZE OF RUINED BUDDHIST SHRINE
M. III., MIRAN SITE.

Scale, one-sixth.

The piece, originally found in several fragments, represents Gautama Bodhisattva in teaching pose, with
princely worshipper. Painted on background of Pompeian red.

large surface was to be covered with my wide-angle lens and bad distortion avoided. As I grovelled amidst the sand and clay débris on the floor adjusting the levels of the camera, focusing the lens, etc., the temporary protection from the wind which the focusing cloth secured for my face seemed but a scant comfort; but even for that I felt grateful.

It was no easy task to complete these preliminary records within the short hours while the winter day gave adequate light low down in the confined passage of the ruined temple. In the meantime the men from Abdal had been kept busy under old Mullah's direction in dragging from the riverine jungle trunks of dead Toghraks which were to be sawn up and turned into serviceable cases. The carpenter included in the crew from Charklik had, with some of the more handy labourers, been made to set up his workshop on the bare Sai by the ruin, and there planks, etc., were being manufactured as rapidly as the limited outfit of tools and the men's natural slackness would permit. I had big bonfires lit to give light and warmth to my improvised craftsmen, and encouraged them by handsome 'overtime pay' to continue their labours after nightfall. So next morning I had a sufficiency of tolerably well joined boards at hand to commence the clearing of the fallen fresco pieces.

There still remained the ticklish question how to lift these terribly brittle panes of mud plaster on to my boards without letting them break into fragments or injuring the delicately painted surface. Any attempt to handle them direct would have meant almost certain destruction. Naik Ram Singh, in spite of severe attacks of fever and the bitter cutting wind, roused himself sufficiently to come to my assistance for part at least of these days, and utilizing his professional skill I soon arrived at a system which answered remarkably well. A board lightly padded with cotton wool, under large sheets of that tough Khotan paper, which I never ceased blessing as the best packing stuff produced in Central Asia, was pressed gently and evenly against the front surface of the fallen fresco. Next a large sheet of stout tin, which Ram Singh had managed to improvise out of carefully stored empty cases and to stiffen with thin iron bands, was slowly introduced with a saw-like action at the soft back of the broken panel, care being taken not to injure the frescoed layer behind. When once firmly held from front and back, the piece of wall plaster, however large, could be safely tilted forward until, with its painted surface downwards, it came to lie flat on the padded board, and could be moved without risk.

Thus layer after layer of frescoed wall-surface was recovered from the débris without widening even the cracks of centuries. Great was my joy whenever, behind the outer layer, there came to light additional portions previously unsuspected of some fresco composition. The brilliancy of the colours all painted in tempera was a treat for the eyes. But there was no time then, nor after, to indulge in enjoyment at this resurrection of fine art work, so wonderfully preserved on most perishable material amidst all this ruin. As little could I occupy myself with attempts at grouping and joining the fresco pieces which by position and subject were likely to have belonged together. With hands half-benumbed by the icy blast, and chapped fingers rendered doubly painful by constant contact with the salt-impregnated plaster and débris, I had to concentrate my thought and attention on the ever-recurring manual difficulties of our work of rescue. But at the same time careful record had to be kept of the position of individual pieces, and of indications furnished by the subjects, condition, etc. All these might help hereafter to determine details as to the original arrangement of the fresco decoration represented by these *disjecta membra*.

It was thus that I came to note down also a little find of quasi-pathetic interest, the discovery at the foot of one of the larger fresco pieces of the feathers and bones of a pigeon, together with the remains of a nest. The bird must evidently have been killed by the collapse of the higher wall portion in which it had built its nest, and the fresco pieces found near it had probably adjoined the vaulting. By a strange irony of fate the poor bird, destined to become an archaeological witness, had found its last resting-place just under the bust of a Buddha figure holding up his hand in the gesture which Buddhist iconography knows as that of 'protection.'

The technical difficulties were quite as great, and the feeling of responsibility certainly increased, when it came to cutting out and removing those fine fresco panels of the dado showing winged figures. Seven of them were well enough preserved to justify an attempt at rescue by removal; but in the case of these also there were sufficient cracks present to cause apprehension as to whether they would not crumble into dry mud even before the long transport westward began. It was fortunate that in the north-east segment, which contained five of these panels, there remained *in situ* scarcely any of the frescoed wall surface above the dado, and that the north window offered a convenient starting-point on the side. Thus it became possible to insert a large flexible steel saw, included in our Indian equipment, at the back of each successive fresco panel, and then to cut through between its plaster backing and the brick wall surface. The plaster was here somewhat thicker, and not quite as brittle as in the detached pieces of fresco.

But unforeseen difficulties arose here more than once, as when behind several of the panels we came upon a layer of salt concretion, very hard and firmly binding the plaster to the interstices of the brick-work. It might have resulted from subsoil water having penetrated into the brick-work and brought out the salts originally contained. Continued practice taught us to meet incidents of this sort with novel expedients, however slender our available stock of tools and the allowance of time. Yet I confess I never set to work on the removal of a fresh panel without fearing that my eyes might never again behold the graceful features, the bright, impressive gaze of the figure represented. To whatever pantheon these strangely fascinating 'angels' might trace their origin, I felt as if I ought to ask their forgiveness for taking such liberties and risks with their portraits!

The odds against these brittle panes of mud plaster travelling safely to London seemed terribly heavy. But at least I was resolved to spare no precaution and trouble to make their transit as secure as conditions would permit, and thus to save my archaeological conscience. The question as to how best to attempt the seemingly impossible task had been revolved in my mind all through these busy days; and when by the evening of February 2nd all the frescoes capable of preservation lay safely spread out on their wooden boards, carefully protected against wind, driving sand, and other agents of mischief, I had my plan of packing ready.

The problem was how to combine the rigidity and compression which alone could keep the friable plaster from breaking up into dust and straw, with an elasticity which would counteract the innumerable buffetings and tumbles the packages were bound to undergo from camels, yaks, ponies, and loading men on their journey of months. It would have been worse than useless to think of materials such as European dealers might employ for delicate antiques. But I remembered how helpful the bundles of reeds, brought for camel fodder, had been for packing fragile wood-carvings at the sites of Niya and Lop-nor, and decided to make the most of the Kumush beds within reach by the dying Miran stream. Plentiful loads of their produce had been brought up over-night, and old Mullah sent to Abdal had managed to collect a supply of sheep's wool to replace my reserve of cotton wool already giving out.

The details of my method of packing were not evolved until repeated experiments which cost labour and much pain to one's chapped hands. But in the end I arrived at a *modus operandi* which left, at least, some hope that I might not have laboured in vain. I had reeds, dry but still fairly supple, cut down in regular fascines to a uniform length, somewhat greater than the longitudinal dimension of my fresco panels. Above a fairly thick layer of these I spread crosswise a substratum of shorter reeds cut to correspond to the width of the frescoes. Then came a thick bedding of the soft feathery tips of reeds containing their flowering parts, admirably suited to hold and protect the exposed rough plaster surface on the back of the fresco panel. The difficulty about reversing the latter and bringing it to lie safely on the top of these several layers of packing was solved by the use of the board and sheet of tin originally employed in removing the frescoes from the temple wall.

The smooth painted surface of the panel now lying face upwards was covered with a thin layer of cotton wool which was kept from moving by sheets of Khotan paper. On the top of these came again cotton wool, and then a second fresco panel, but this time with its painted surface downwards. The same successive layers of reed packing were used for its protection, but now in reversed order. The thick oblong packet of reeds which had thus been built up round each pair of fresco panels was next completed along the edges by additional fascines. The whole was then fastened by ropes drawn as tightly as possible over pairs of thinnish planks which were placed below and above the packet to keep the reeds in position and to assure uniform distribution of the pressure. Finally, the packets thus secured in a practically rigid condition were inserted two and two in stout cases of Toghrak wood made to fit them exactly. The elastic reed bundles were bound to expand in time in spite of our tight roping; but this would only help to render the 'fit' of the contents more close.

This careful, methodical packing which, owing to the Naik's condition, I had to carry out practically with my own hands—none of our Turkis could have been trusted with any but the most mechanical tasks about it—kept me busy for the best part of three bitterly cold days. In the course of it I had the satisfaction of assuring myself that the transfer so far effected had caused no damage to the frescoes. But what was this transport of a few yards carried through under my own eyes compared with the risks which those frail panes of plaster would have to face on their journey of thousands of miles across deserts and ice-covered ranges to railhead? There were moments when it seemed to me almost futile to expect success in the end. Then my proceedings would look to myself quite as strange as they had, no doubt, to the burly big Mongol who passed our camp one morning (Fig. 135), taking five camels laden with flour from Charklik to his far-off encampment on a high plateau of the Chimen-tagh. He was a delightful barbarian figure buried in enormous sheepskins and carrying a heavy straight sword with a brass hilt studded with corals and green jade. He talked no language any of us could understand, would on no account face the camera, and looked altogether of another age. My trouble over all this rotten old plaster seemed to amaze him a great deal. I for my part felt very much as a classical archaeologist might who, while uncovering the remains of a Roman villa somewhere near Hadrian's wall, suddenly saw himself watched by a clansman from across the border in full panoply of the Middle Ages.

Some assurance came to me eighteen months later at Khotan when I had to open the cases brought away from Miran on camels, some weighing nearly two hundred pounds, and to repack their contents into lighter loads for ponies and yaks. Apart from slight cracks here and there, which were easily accounted for by the panels taken from slightly curving wall segments having necessarily been packed flat, no damage had occurred so far. By applying then a net-work of narrow bandages heavily steeped in carpenter's glue to the back of the plaster, I provided a very useful stiff backing, and thus an additional safeguard, for which at Miran there had been neither materials nor shelter available. But the time for true relief arrived only when, just three years after that trying exploit at Miran, the cases came to be opened at the British Museum. Then all doubts about the success of the hazardous experiment were lifted from my mind. How delighted my eyes were to behold these fine art relics, probably the most fragile ever transported over such a distance and over such ground, brought to safety practically in the same condition as when I had the good fortune to see them rise from their grave of long centuries in that dismal wind-swept desert of gravel!

CHAPTER XLII

IT is more than the mere thought of difficulties successfully overcome, or of art pleasure afforded to others, which makes me look back upon the result of my toil at the Miran temple with special gratification. Subsequent examination of the fresco remains thus recovered has made me realize fully how little my notes and photographs, even if taken under less hampering conditions, would have sufficed for an adequate record of all points of artistic interest presented by these remarkable paintings. Only by bringing the originals before the eyes of such expert students of Graeco-Buddhist and Central-Asian art as my friends, Mr. F. H. Andrews and M. A. Foucher, was it possible to prove the impression I had gained on the spot that these frescoes marked an *étape* of exceptional interest in the history of classical pictorial art as transplanted to innermost Asia under Buddhist auspices.

Owing to the total loss on Indian soil of remains of pictorial work corresponding in date and origin to the Graeco-Buddhist sculpture of Gandhara, our knowledge of the earlier stages of that art development is exceedingly scanty. This explains the special importance of the new light thrown upon them by the frescoes of the Miran temples, particularly since the date of these can be so closely determined. But it would need a far more elaborate disquisition than can find a place in a narrative like the present, to indicate all the evidence which the frescoes furnish as to the classical and other Western elements embodied in Central-Asian Buddhist painting, So I must content myself here with reproducing a few typical specimens of the frescoes recovered from the temple, and briefly explaining some of the specially interesting points they present.

The fresco composition reproduced in the colour plate (Pl. v.), broken as it is, serves as a good illustration of what the wall decoration must have been in the friezes which once encircled the rotunda. The two pieces of painted plaster now united in the panel about three and a half feet wide were discovered in a detached condition at the foot of the north-eastern segment of the dado. Their position there, nearest to the wall and behind two other layers of frescoed plaster, makes it probable that they had fallen from the wall portion immediately above the dado. The outer fresco layers, which a photograph taken at the time of excavation clearly shows, are likely to have belonged to a second frieze on a higher part of the wall. The broad black streak which runs across the red-brick background on the top was evidently intended to separate the two friezes. The permanent preservation and joining of the badly broken pieces from the lower frieze could be effected only by replacing the friable mud and straw at the back of the painted clay surface with a fresh backing of plaster of Paris. This delicate operation was effected at the British Museum by my artist helpmate Mr. F. H. Andrews, and my second assistant Mr. J. P. Droop, with extreme care and skill. The slightest attempt at supplementing missing bits of the original fresco surface or at other 'restoration' has been rigorously avoided. Even the mud of the original backing was removed only in order to prevent the salts contained in it from exuding on the coloured surface under the influence of the moisture which it would otherwise have absorbed from the plaster of Paris needed to strengthen and join the whole.

The panel thus safely preserved represents the upper portion of a typical scene of Buddhist iconography. On the left we see Buddha standing, dressed in a simple robe of that dark red-brown colour which Indian tradition since ancient times prescribes for ascetics and saintly preachers of all sects. The halo and the characteristic top-knot of hair, partly broken, make it quite certain that the teacher

is meant for a Buddha. Whether Gautama or some earlier 'Enlightened One' it is impossible to decide. The right hand is raised in the pose or 'Mudra' technically known to Buddhist iconography as that of 'Abhaya' or protection; the left held low in front probably supported drapery. Behind the teacher and to his left we see six Arhats, or Buddhist saints, ranged in two rows and wearing robes in a variety of bright colours. The shaven heads mark them as leading the life of monks. One on the left end of the upper row carries a white fan, probably meant for a yak-tail or Chauri, the traditional emblem of sovereign power. M. Foucher points out to me that this figure would be Ananda, the favourite disciple of Gautama Buddha, if the latter is intended by the haloed figure. To the left again of the saints, who manifestly appear here as Buddha's disciples, there rises an elliptical mass, probably part of a tree, studded with red and white flowers and poppy-like leaves on dark greyish-green ground. Against this background is seen an upraised right arm grasping a handful of white buds or flowers, apparently in the act of throwing them. This background and a corresponding one with well-drawn leaves and flowers behind Buddha's right hand clearly indicate that the scene is laid in a garden or grove, as in so many legends of Buddha's life story.

Not enough is left of the frieze to determine which particular legend this portion was intended to illustrate. However, it is the artistic treatment in composition, design, and colouring, not the iconographic purport, which gives to this fresco fragment its great value and interest. Strictly Buddhist as the subject is, all the details in its presentation point to adaptation from classical models. The head of Buddha is of a type unmistakably Hellenistic, in spite of a slight Semitic touch in the nose and of compliance with Indian Buddhist convention in regard to the top-knot and long-lobed pierced ears. The large straight eyes of the teacher and disciples alike have nothing of that elongated, slanting look which all painted figures, as yet known in Central Asia and the Far East, invariably display as a particular point of beauty. If we could possibly doubt whence the artist derived those big eyes with their frank

European look, assurance is provided by the peculiar pose of the curving fingers on the left hand of the last Arhat below on the right, which appear at the neck from inside the robe. It is the familiar place for the left hand, as hundreds of classical statues of the Roman period show it emerging from inside the toga.

The Graeco-Buddhist sculpture of Gandhara has long been known to abound in exactly corresponding examples of poses and drapery borrowed straight from classical modelling. But it was reserved for the fresco fragments brought to light at this most distant corner of the Tarim Basin to prove that this dependence on Western art was at first equally close as far as painting is concerned and traceable even in methods of technique. In the latter respect no more striking testimony could be desired than that supplied by the regular employment of methods of 'light and shade' wherever flesh is painted in these frescoes. The use of 'chiaroscuro,' so well known to classical painting, had never before been observed in the old pictorial work of India, Central Asia, or the Far East.

The frescoes of Miran display it invariably in all exposed portions of the body. The usual method, as seen both in the frieze panel just described and in the 'Angels' of the dado, consisted of applying over the flesh tints different shades of grey, pale or warm, for the shadows round the face, under the eyes, or elsewhere. But occasionally the effect of 'high lights' is skilfully obtained by allowing the lighter tint of the flesh to show through in the proper places from under the stronger pink outlines of the lips or similar features. In some cases these 'high lights' are cleverly laid in by bold brush-work in white. Here and there this is thick enough to catch a real 'high light,'—a method distinctly reminiscent of the treatment which is natural to encaustic painting, and is actually illustrated by the surviving examples of classical painting in wax. These and many other details of technique make it obvious that the painters of these Miran frescoes had inherited from their Western masters well-established methods of producing a finished effect with such economy of work as constant application demanded.

Another example showing how the forms derived from late classical, *i.e.* Hellenistic, art were adapted to the representation of subjects from Indian Buddhism is seen in Fig. 143. This reproduces, but without the harmonious colours of the original, a fresco piece about three feet high, which probably had belonged to a higher frieze, and was discovered broken into several fragments near the panel last described. Here we see seated on a low throne the figure of a teacher meant in all probability for Gautama Bodhisattva. A dark red under-garment reaches from the hips to the ankles, and a buff-coloured cloak is thrown over the left shoulder, leaving most of the upper part of the body bare—an arrangement which conforms entirely to the traditional description of Buddha's appearance as gathered from early Indian texts. But just as in Graeco-Buddhist sculpture, where similar representations of Buddha in the attitude of teaching are frequent, the drapery is treated in a fashion that is unmistakably classical.

We note the same dressing of the folds in the smaller adoring figure to the right, which, however, has its princely character clearly marked by a curious white conical hat encircled with rings and two lunette-shaped red flaps. This head-dress, which recurs in a number of the Miran frescoes, has been traced by me neither in the Buddhist sculptures of Gandhara nor in any later Buddhist shrines of Eastern Turkestan. It possibly represents a feature introduced for a time from one of the more westerly territories, like Bactria or Sogdiana, through which this classical adaptation of Buddhist iconography must be supposed to have found its way to the Tarim Basin. Of a second adoring figure on the left only parts of the knee and arm survive. In the foreground the representation of two tanks or tesselated terraces suggests that a scene in a palace or royal garden was intended, such as often figures in the stories of Buddha's life as a preacher.

Varied and instructive from different points of view as are the surviving fragments of those frescoed friezes, they cannot compare in artistic interest and iconographic significance with the fine winged figures of the dado.

From the first they held my archaeologist's eyes spell-bound as it were, and now when I can see them under less trying conditions and in safety, this fascination has in no way diminished. As already related, all the seven panels recovered from the dado travelled remarkably well, considering the distances and risks overcome. It has thus been possible to reproduce here the two seen in the colour plate (Pl. IV.) exactly as they reached the British Museum, and before the friable clay and straw at the back was replaced by plaster of Paris. Since this was effected, the cracks suffered by the painted surface, partly when still on the wall, have closed up almost completely. The two selected panels, which originally adjoined in the middle of the south-eastern segment of the temple wall along the line marked *A B*, characteristically illustrate the variety of expression introduced by the painter into this cycle of Cherub-like figures. While in all externals, such as the type of head, the wings, and the simple but effective dress, the aim manifestly is at a homogeneous effect befitting a heavenly fraternity, nevertheless a strong individual element prevails in the faces.

The skill with which this is obtained will be best realized by a close examination of the two neighbouring panels seen in the plate. The upper one shows us against a greenish-blue background, probably meant to indicate the sky, the head and shoulders of a youthful figure manifestly rising upwards. The delicately round contours of the face, the large and wide-open eyes, the three-quarters turn of the head, the aquiline nose, and a number of other features, are also exhibited in the panel below and in others. Yet a glance suffices to distinguish the peculiar firmness of the mouth marked by the straight line dividing the curving red lips, and the steady, eager gaze which is emphasized by the pronounced upward tilt of the head. The rippling black love-lock hanging in front of the slightly elongated right ear helps to reduce the fulness of the face and to give it a slightly more serious look. With this the bold painting of the outlines and the plain band of drapery in rich red accord remarkably well. A curious feature, common to all these figures of the dado, is the peculiar tuft of hair arranged in resemblance to a two-lobed leaf with stalk, which appears on the otherwise shaven front of the head. The origin of this fashion still remains to be traced.

In the panel below an extraordinary vivacious character is imparted to the whole by the clever way in which the general left inclination of the lines of the figure is counter-balanced by the steady gaze of the eyes to the right. The head is here round like that of a Cupid and the cheeks plump, but not with the baby puffiness of the Renaissance. The large, fully opened eyes bear a happy, ingenuous expression, the lively effect being heightened by the skilful painting of the nut-brown iris, not circular, but vertically elliptical, to mark the foreshortening of the gaze turned aside. The lips are full, smiling, and painted in open lines of bright vermilion, allowing the pink under-tint of flesh to appear and express 'juicy' high lights. Tiny spots at the angles of the mouth emphasize the dimples. All features and contours have been drawn freely with the brush over a wash of pale flesh tint. The general effect is delicately softened by the careful applica-tion of warmer pinks on the cheeks and elsewhere, and of well-graduated greys for the shadows.

By the side of such command of colour and chiaroscuro technique as these dado paintings display, there remains in all of them a distinct aim at boldness of outlines and general effect which was admirably well suited to the sub-dued light in which they were placed. Where so much must be mere reproduction of art forms developed far away in the West, it is of interest to note indications of the artistic feeling and skill with which the painters at Miran managed to adapt their often practised designs to peculiar structural conditions. Clear evidence of this is afforded, I think, by the clever way in which the whole pose of the winged busts in the dado is devised for the position they occupy on the wall of a circular passage and about three feet from the floor. Their gaze, whatever its direction, to the right or left or straight in front, is raised just suffi-ciently to catch the eyes of the worshipper as he passes along in the traditional circumambulation of the Stupa.

With the same aim they are given the air of rising towards him; this is expressed by the inclination of the shoulders and the graceful upward curve of the wings, which with their long feathers separated at the extremities distinctly suggest fluttering.

But where did the conception of these youthful winged figures originally take shape, and how did they come to be depicted here on the walls of a Buddhist temple? The first of these questions is more difficult to answer with precision than might appear at first thought. If we take into account the general classical basis of all this art and the winged forms occasionally met with in Graeco-Buddhist relievos as representations of certain divine attendants, we can scarcely resist the conclusion that it is the young winged Eros of Greek mythology to whom these figures of the Miran dado must be traced back as their ultimate ancestor. But there is plenty to warn us that this descent cannot have been without intermediate stages in which an infiltration of Oriental conceptions has left its mark. To put it quite plainly, the figures before us, with their youthful but not childlike looks, their low-cut garments and quasi-sexless features, suggest far more closely the angels of some early Christian Church than the love-gods which originally served as their models.

If the possibility of influence exercised by early Christian iconography should seem too startling, it will be well to remember that the idea of angels as winged celestial messengers was familiar to more than one religious system of Western Asia long before the rise of Christianity, and was in particular firmly established within the region of ancient Iran through which all elements of classical art and culture must have passed before being transplanted to Central Asia. Nowhere in the Hellenized East, not even in Egypt, have graphic representations of angels survived from a sufficiently early period to throw light on the question as to where and when the Cupids of classical mythology underwent transformation into that type of winged figures which the painter of the Miran fresco dado made use of for the decoration of a Buddhist shrine. Yet there is so distinct a suggestion of Semitic traits in most of these faces that one's thoughts are instinctively carried to regions like Syria, Mesopotamia, and Western Iran as likely ground for that original adaptation.

It would be tempting, and yet for the critical student useless, to carry such speculations further at present. But fortunately we are on safer ground when considering the question how those angels came to figure in the fresco decoration of a Buddhist shrine on the very confines of true China. The Graeco-Buddhist sculpture of Gandhara furnishes examples proving beyond all doubt that figures copied from the winged Eros were actually used on Indian soil to represent that class of celestial attendants which Buddhist mythology, borrowing from still older Hindu lore, knows by the name of Gandharvas.

So if ever a Central-Asian Herodotus had visited this temple of Miran and had cared to enquire from the priest in charge about the significance of the winged beings so strangely reminiscent of figures he might have seen before in regions where Buddhism had never effected a foothold, the local guardian would not have felt in the least embarrassed about labelling them Gandharvas. Admissible as this interpretation would be from the purely iconographic point of view, it yet seems to me very doubtful whether we need it at all; for on excavating a closely adjoining mound, as described in the next chapter, we discovered there a Buddhist shrine of exactly this type and displaying, below a frieze with pious scenes from orthodox Buddhist legend, a dado decorated with figures of an altogether secular and frankly Western character.

CHAPTER XLIII

THE work of packing the frescoes just discussed was still far from complete when a closer inspection of the other ruined mounds near by revealed to my delighted surprise a piece of coloured stucco just showing from the débris of the square ruin some sixty yards to the north-west. It was a badly decayed mass of brickwork, rising to a height of about fifteen feet and marked M. v. on my plan (Fig. 144); its shape and the flatness of the top had from the first suggested that it could not, like several other neighbouring mounds, be the remains of a solid Stupa tower. Its close vicinity allowed excavation to be started while the packing of the frescoes was still proceeding, and before long I felt sure that the ruin was that of a temple in plan exactly resembling the one last cleared and having for its centre a small Stupa built within a rotunda. Of the outer passage, which was square, there survived only a small portion on the south side, and here the remnant of a wall fresco was soon laid bare. It showed below in a dado the boldly painted bust of an angel, and above in a narrow frieze the gladiator-like figure of a man defending himself with a club against a monster with the body of a lion and the head and wings of a bird, exactly like the classical griffin. The painting, though somewhat coarser in execution, was so closely akin in style and design to the frescoes first recovered that the fact of this second temple dating back to the same period was settled from the outset.

The circular passage round the Stupa within was choked by heavy débris of large bricks which had once

144. RUINED MOUND CONTAINING REMAINS OF BUDDHIST SHRINE M. V., MIRAN SITE, BEFORE EXCAVATION, SEEN FROM SOUTH-EAST.

145. INTERIOR OF ROTUNDA AND STUPA IN RUINED BUDDHIST SHRINE M. V., MIRAN SITE, AFTER EXCAVATION.

belonged to the fallen vaulting. The clearing of it took two full days of hard work, though I set all hands to dig and sent off Mullah to Abdal to bring up every available man to help. But enough progress was made before nightfall to reveal the dimensions of the interior and to prove the wall of the rotunda to have been adorned with a frescoed frieze and dado. The Stupa, though badly broken on the top, still stood to about eleven feet in height (Fig. 145). It measured twelve and a half feet in diameter and showed a series of boldly projecting mouldings meant to represent circular bases. Like the relic tower in the small 'temple of the Angels,' it had been dug into at its foot in early times, no doubt from a hope of 'treasure.' The circular passage had a width of seven feet, thus giving to the dome which once rose above the Stupa a total span of twenty-six and a half feet.

There was no definite evidence by which to estimate the height of the dome. But the discovery among the brick débris of fragments of fine wood-carving made it clear that the vaulting must have been high enough to enclose not merely the Stupa itself but also an elaborate 'Tee' or wooden superstructure representing the succession of Chhattras or umbrellas which the miniature reproductions of Stupas in Gandhara sculpture and the actual Pagodas of Burma and other Buddhist lands invariably show. Among the delicately carved pieces which had once decorated this 'Tee' were an eight-petalled lotus in wood still retaining in parts a rich cover of gold foil, and a portion of a well-designed capital and shaft displaying the acanthus ornament well known from Graeco-Buddhist art of Gandhara. More remains of architectural wood-carving in the same classical style came to light when we cleared the entrance to the shrine which lay on its east face. Stucco images appear to have once stood on the platform flanking this entrance outside; but of these only pairs of wooden stumps survived, manifestly remnants of the core or framework for the legs, and a few plaster fragments richly painted in a pattern suggesting brocade.

The clearing of the circular passage on either side of this entrance first revealed the fresco decoration I had hoped to find on the enclosing wall. By good fortune there emerged some short inscriptions painted in Kharoshthi script and Indian language by the side of the two figures of the upper frieze first laid bare. What better proof could I have wished in support of the conclusion to which my previous finds had already led me, that these temples and frescoes dated back to the time when the sites of Niya and Lop-nor still flourished? But even thus I was little prepared for the sight which the frescoed wall remnants presented when at the end of two days of hard digging, in an icy gale and whirling dust clouds, I could proceed to the clearing and closer examination of the paintings.

On the west side a segment of the circular wall, once probably containing a second entrance, had been levelled right down to the floor by early treasure-seekers; and owing to this destruction the frescoes were found now extending over two detached hemicycles broken at either end. The wall decoration in the one to the north had for some reason suffered so badly that of an upper frieze nothing could be made out but half-effaced groups of small figures. But in the frescoed dado below, which reached to a height of about three feet from the floor, it was easy, in spite of faded colours and plentiful cracks of the plaster, to recognize a remarkably graceful composition almost classical in design and details. Its connecting feature was a broad festoon of wreaths and flowers which youthful supporters carried on their shoulders with the ease and abandon of true Putti. Among them wingless Erotes alternated with young figures wearing the Phrygian cap and of a type which, in spite of a certain girlish cast of face, unmistakably recalled the Mithras worshipped throughout the Roman empire.

But more remarkable still were the portraits which filled in succession the hollows of the undulating festoon. In each of them there rose the head and bust of a man or girl, presented in classical outlines and yet with a freedom of individual expression which made the effect most striking. The types of men's heads differed. Some were quite Roman in look, others with their peculiar cut of hair and beard suggested barbarian races. But it was clear at a glance that neither they nor the few portraits of beautiful girls interspersed among them, could have any relation to Buddhist worship or mythology. The pose of the hands, where it could still be made out, confirmed the conclusion to be drawn from the frank enjoyment which was expressed in the faces and the lustrous wide eyes. Thus, one girl, richly adorned, was resting her hand on the neck of a three-stringed musical instrument, while in another festoon lunette close by a gay youth, curiously reminiscent of some quatrocento figure in dress and features, raised his right hand with some fingers stretched out and others bent under, just as if engaged in the classical game of ' Mora.'

But all doubts as to the purely secular nature of this dado vanished as soon as I could examine more closely the portraits in the southern hemicycle. Here the wall still rose in parts to a height of nine to ten feet, and towards the south-east its frescoed stucco surface was in better preservation. The lunette immediately adjoining the east entrance was filled with a large eight-petalled crimson flower which its strongly marked seed pods clearly showed to be meant for a lotus. The next upward bend of the festoon depended from the shoulders of a well-drawn wingless amorino, whose forehead displayed the peculiar leaf-like lock which we had already come across in the angels of the neighbouring temple. The portrait in the following hollow of the festoon, as seen in Fig. 146, was that of a graceful girl playing on a four-stringed mandoline and looking demurely downwards. A wreath of white flowers sat on her rich black hair, which was bound by a crimson ribbon and gathered in a bunch behind the neck. A diadem made up of red beads and pendent jewels stretched across the forehead. A crimson flower or ornament of that shape hung from each ear, before which a curly love-lock descended. The full sensual lips harmonized with the elaborate adornment of this mature beauty, the glowing effect being heightened by the rich crimson cloak shown on her shoulders and over part of her slate-coloured vest.

Next to the right came a Phrygian-capped figure draped in green carrying the festoon ; beyond this, facing the girl, was a bearded male bust striking in features and dress. The heavy curled hair, the moustache, and long beard at once clearly distinguished this head from the almost classical male faces seen elsewhere in this dado. But there was something in the expression of the eyes, the low forehead, and broad lips curiously suggestive of the type by which classical art of the later period represented northern barbarians such as Gauls and Scythians. The right hand raised against the breast held a goblet of transparent material, evidently glass. The coat of pale bluish-grey was covered in front by a scarf laid crosswise and showing bold arabesques in black and red over cream ground. Everything about the face, pose, and dress seemed to convey that frank devotion to the good things of this world which seems always to have been the predominant note in the character of Turkestan people. Was it not an appropriate association which made the painter place a purple grape in the hand of the Phrygian-capped figure supporting on its shoulders the festoon immediately to the right ?

Beyond it my eyes rested on a male bust which the first glance showed to be intended for a young Indian prince (Fig. 147). It was a youth clean shaven, except for a curling moustache, and exactly conforming in type and dress to the figures which in the fragments of the frieze from the first temple had appeared in the attitude of worshipping Buddha. An unmistakably Indian expression of softness was conveyed by the features and the dreamy-looking eyes. The characteristic head-dress consisted of a conical cap, like the peaked ' Kulla' still worn on the North-West Frontier of India, with two red-lined flaps turned upwards over the forehead, and a white Puggree wound round it. The end of the Puggree was gathered behind into a sort of hood, exactly as seen in many Gandhara sculptures representing Prince Siddhartha and other royal figures. A large ornament in the ear, a broad jewelled band round the neck, and two heavy armlets over the right wrist, seemed to symbolize that naive delight in

146. PORTION OF FRESCO FRIEZE AND DADO ON SOUTH-EAST WALL OF
ROTUNDA IN BUDDHIST SHRINE M. V., MIRAN SITE.

The frieze shows Prince Vessantara with his wife and children leaving the palace gate (p. 490). In the dado below
are seen a girl playing the mandoline, a garland-carrying figure, and part of bearded male bust.

147. PORTION OF FRESCO FRIEZE AND DADO ON SOUTH WALL OF ROTUNDA
IN BUDDHIST SHRINE M. V., MIRAN SITE.

The frieze represents Prince Vessantara making an offering of the magical white elephant (pp. 487, 490).
In the dado the bust of an Indian prince between two garland-carrying Putti. Inch-measure on right below.

jewelry to which Indian manhood of high rank has always been prone, as the relievos of Gandhara abundantly show us. An ample cloak of light green was thrown over the left shoulder, leaving the rest of the breast bare. The right hand appeared to raise a fruit which by its shape suggested a pomegranate.

The next pair of busts by their strikingly Western look carried me far away from India. Beyond a wingless amorino there showed first the portrait of a young girl, carrying in graceful pose on her left shoulder a narrow-necked jug of transparent ware and in her right hand a patera (Fig. 148). In her delicate face Greek features seemed to mingle strangely with others which called up a Levantine or Circassian type of beauty. To the Near East or Iran pointed the white turban which, trimmed with a red band and held by a large black knot on the right, rested on the rich black hair. From the latter descended long ringlets in front of the ears, while a fringe of hair came down on the forehead decorated with three bead strings of coral. The ears bore graceful pendants in pink. A close-fitting vest with sleeves in a deep red brown covered breast and shoulders, and from the head-dress there hung a veil of a delicate pale green.

What a startling apparition of beauty and grace it all seemed in this desolate ruin! But strange it was, too, to find this fair portrait balanced on the opposite side by that of a male head of a type distinctly Roman (Fig. 148). It was the head of a young man, with a broad low forehead and square jaws. The strongly built face was clean shaven, close-cropped black hair covering the head. The dress, a dark red coat with a pale green cloak thrown over the right shoulder, had faded badly. But across the breast I could still make out the right hand raised in the peculiar pose which suggested a player at ' Mora,' with the second and fifth fingers outstretched and the two between turned downwards.

Beyond this portrait the frescoed surface had suffered too much to show more than the outlines of heads and Putti, even where the wall still stood to the height of the dado. But just close to where the breach in the western wall segment began, there survived the head of a garland-carrying girl with a face of rare beauty under the white Phrygian cap. The right hand with shapely fingers was clasping the patera of wine against the breast. This fine head, narrowly preserved from destruction, impressed me at the time like a fit embodiment of that classical joy of life which seemed to animate the whole composition.

Amidst the ruin of this ancient place of worship the painter's art had survived triumphant. But could he ever have foreseen how much the effect of his gay figures, representing as it were the varied pleasures of life, would be heightened by the utter desolation around, when after their burial of long centuries they again saw the light? The contrast between the warm bright life which these paintings reflected and the bare Dasht of gravel was inexpressibly weird. Nor could I help thinking how different from this atmosphere of happy enjoyment was the existence we had been leading for months past. For my eyes, which had so long beheld nothing but dreary wastes with traces of a dead past or the wretched settlements of the living, the sight of these paintings was more than an archaeological treat. I greeted it like a cheering assurance that there really was still a region where fair sights and enjoyments could be found undisturbed by icy gales and the cares and discomforts of desert labours. The distance which separated me from it seemed to shrink as I examined again and again the fascinating figures of this dado, so Western in conception and treatment.

Hence it was scarcely surprising that during the next days I often felt tempted to believe myself rather among the ruins of some villa in Syria or some other Eastern province of the Roman empire than those of a Buddhist sanctuary on the very confines of China. And yet the winter climate of this desert was just then doing its best to keep me painfully alive to our true situation. The bitter winds blew almost constantly and stiffened at times to real gales. Their force was quite as cutting amongst the ruined walls as it had been amidst the wind-eroded

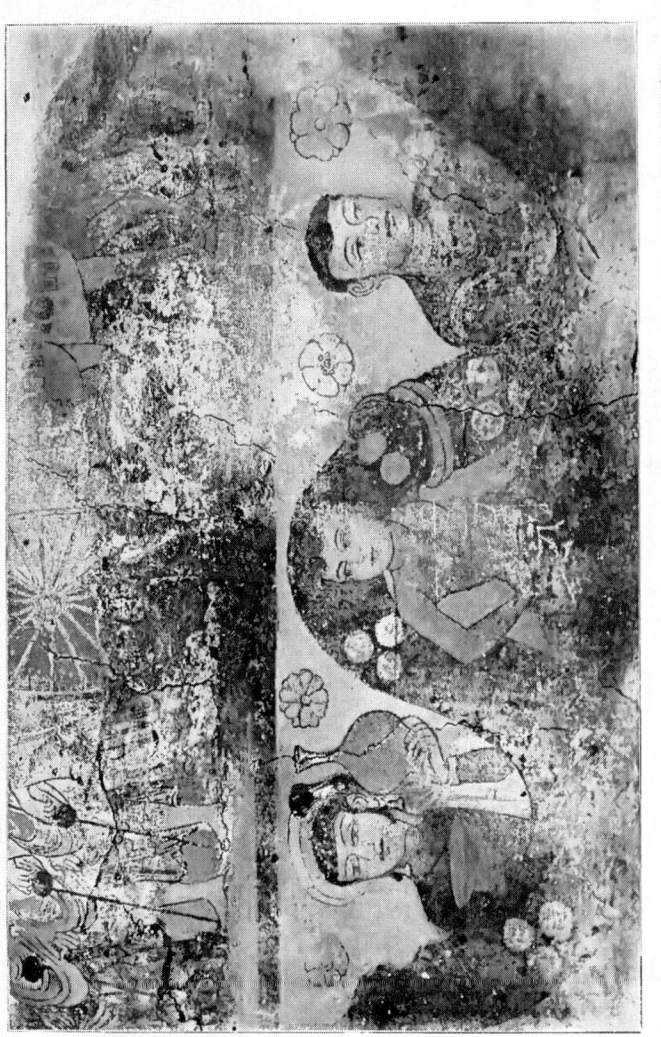

148. PORTION OF FRESCOED DADO, WITH LOWER PART OF FRIEZE, ON SOUTH WALL OF ROTUNDA IN BUDDHIST SHRINE M. V., MIRAN SITE.

The dado closes on left a girl carrying jug and patera; on right the bust of a young man; between them a wingless amorino carrying garland. In frieze the lower portions of four draped male figures and quadriga.

Yardangs of Lop-nor, and the thick dust clouds made photographic work practically impossible for a couple of days. Luckily these could be used for detailed study and the taking of elaborate notes, even though the fingers felt benumbed and the ink in the fountain pen froze.

CHAPTER XLIV

MURAL PAINTING OF BUDDHIST LEGEND

THIS cycle of youthful figures, proclaiming as it were the rights of the senses, seemed a strange decoration for the dado of a Buddhist temple, and the problem presented by the contrast between it and Buddha's orthodox preaching made me turn with increased interest to what remained of the fresco decoration above. The wall of the northern hemicycle had suffered much damage, and of its frieze only detached groups of figures, mostly broken, were to be seen, which, though full of interest in themselves, could give no key to the general composition and subject. But on the south-east the frieze immediately above the dado was intact over a segment more than eighteen feet long, and the picture there presented was the most striking I had yet set eyes upon in the course of my explorations.

On a field of true Pompeian red about three feet wide and marked off above and below by a symmetrical succession of narrow bands in black, slaty green, and cream, there extended a procession which at first sight suggested a Roman triumph more than anything else. Starting from the left and passing over the partially broken piece of the frieze near the eastern entrance, I saw a princely figure on horseback riding out of a palace gate (Fig. 146). The wooden framework of the walls and decorative carving on the gate was elaborately indicated, while on the lintel and above the rider's head a line was inscribed in large Kharoshthi characters. The horseman's costume was very much like that of the 'Indian Prince' in the dado. A crimson cloak descended across the left shoulder to below the waist, while a green garment resembling the

Indian Dhoti covered the lower parts of the body. A rich jewelled armlet and a broad necklace painted in red marked the high rank of the rider. His horse, remarkably well drawn, was white. Its head-stall and bridle were decorated with red tufts; passing across its breast and apparently reaching to the saddle was a broad belt made up of three strings or straps, over which were fastened conspicuous round and square plates. The whole suggested saddlery such as seen in Roman sculpture of the later empire.

In front of the horseman was a chariot with four white horses abreast bearing harness of the type just described. The trotting movement of the team was indicated with ease, as if a familiar model had been copied. The body of the chariot was painted purple in front with a top band of elaborate tracery work in yellow, probably meant for gold. Above it there appeared the head and shoulders of a beautiful woman, evidently in the act of guiding the reins with her right hand. Her hair descended in black tresses below the neck, with two love-locks in front of the ears. The face bore a ' Houri '-like type, suggestive of Iranian influence on some late classical model. Her dress consisted of a mauve bodice open in front and held together by two bead strings across the breast, and of a green mantle laid in heavy folds over the left shoulder. Behind the fair charioteer appeared standing two children, rather poorly drawn, but recognizable as boys by the peculiar double leaf-shaped lock on the forehead.

In front of the chariot and evidently intended to suggest sylvan scenery, there appeared a tree drawn as a dark green cone with yellow flowers sprinkled over it, exactly in the manner which the fresco from the temple M. III. (see Plate V.) displays. Beyond was seen marching a richly caparisoned white elephant, drawn with remarkable truth to life and probably the best modelled figure in the whole frieze (Fig. 147). The expression of the animal's eye and face was caught with great skill. The elaborate adornment of the forehead and trunk, consisting of a diadem of leaves, bands, bosses and rings, cannot be described here at length. Nor can I give details of the carefully painted saddle-cloth and the carpet-like covering spread over it which showed clearly the pattern and colours of the diaper. On the quarter, above the right hind leg, was a small but neatly written inscription of two lines in Kharoshthi, to which I shall have occasion to refer presently.

The elephant was being led by a personage who, judging from the characteristic dress, exactly as in the dado, and the rich jewelry shown on neck, ears, arm, and wrist, was manifestly meant to represent an Indian prince. The left hand supported the elephant's trunk, while the right carried a peculiarly shaped jug. Very narrow at the base and with a straight snout, it closely resembled the vessel which is known to the Hindus of Northern India as 'Gangasagar,' and is in traditional use for sacrificial offerings of water. Moving forward in a row to meet this procession there appeared next four plainly dressed figures, which by their bushy hair and beards and the long staffs they carried could readily be recognized as typical representations of Indian anchorites (Fig. 148). The one on the extreme right of the group was an old man with white beard and simple white Puggree, the second and fourth middle-aged, and the third a beardless youth. Their dress varied only in colour; a Dhoti-like garment was wrapped round loins and legs, the 'Sanghati' thrown across the left shoulder, leaving the breast bare. Behind the group to right and left were painted two blossoming trees with branches and leaves, drawn with such freedom as to suggest copies from nature. Beyond this the wall surface was badly injured or completely lost. But part of another chariot, apparently driven by a male figure, could just be distinguished.

What was the meaning of the animated procession which unrolled itself before me on this fascinating frieze with its background so strangely reminiscent of Pompeii? The scene was clearly taken from some sacred Buddhist story, so much I felt sure of on the spot. But my knowledge of Buddhist hagiology failed me for the identification of it; nor could I have found time for a systematic search even if the needful books had been at my disposal. Puzzled as I felt at the time about the interpretation of the frieze, there was something that exercised my attention even more. It was the difference, unmistakable and yet difficult to define, between the artistic treatment of the frieze composition above and that of the figures in the dado. In the latter almost everything, the general scheme, the ease of design, the technique of colouring with its light and shade, the freedom with which each figure was treated, pointed strongly to work by the hand of a painter who was mainly reproducing types fully developed by Western art, and yet was sufficiently familiar with its spirit and methods to give an individual air to each of his portraits. Looking at his work in the dado I had no need to ask myself what these panels and decorative features meant. The beauty and joy of life pervading almost all of them would suffice to please Western eyes.

In the frieze it was very different. The many points of resemblance in technique, etc., left no doubt about the same hand having been at work here. Yet, though many features, such as the drapery and the quadriga, were manifestly borrowed from classical art, there remained for me the impression that the painter was following models which had already passed through the far stiffer moulds of a distinctly Indian tradition. Where so much is still obscure, it may be premature to hazard explanations. But it seems to me likely that, whereas in the frieze the painter, wherever his original home may have been, was obliged by the sacred subject to cling closely to the conventional representation which Graeco-Buddhist art had centuries before adopted for that particular legend, he was left free by the decorative and quasi-secular character of the dado to yield to art influences from the West more direct and more recent. To put it quite briefly, the Graeco-Buddhist style of India gave its impress to the frieze, and the contemporary art of the Roman Orient as transmitted through Persia was reflected in the dado.

The puzzle as to the subject of the frieze was solved when in the summer of 1910 I was able to submit it to the expert judgment of my friend Professor A. Foucher, the leading authority on the Buddhist iconography of

India, and the kindest of helpmates. From my photographs and description, he very soon recognized in the scene a portion of the legend of King Vessantara, one of the hundreds of Buddhist 'Jatakas' or 'Stories of the Buddha's former births.'

As related at great length in the canonical Pali version, it tells how Prince Vessantara, in whom the Lord Buddha had incarnated himself during a previous existence, being exceedingly devoted to making pious gifts, had fallen into disrepute in his father's kingdom through giving away to Brahmans a magical white elephant which could produce rain. He was thereupon banished with his family into the forest. On leaving his royal city with his wife Maddi and his two young children mounted on a chariot, he gave away many loads of precious things. When he was subsequently met by Brahman beggars who had come too late for the distribution, he parted in succession with horses, chariot, and all the rest of his personal property. Finally, in the retirement of a hermitage he was made by the gods to give away in pious gifts even his wife and children. After having thus tried his inexhaustible charity, the gods ultimately restored to him wife and children, and all ended in earthly happiness.

With the legend once identified it was easy to recognize the prince leaving the palace gate with Maddi and his two children 'in a gorgeous chariot with a team of four Sindh horses,' just as the Jataka describes them. The four figures of mendicants, who in the frieze come to meet them amidst sylvan scenery, represent, no doubt, the four Brahmans to whom the gift of the horses is made in the story. By a kind of anachronism, which is common in all pictorial representations of sacred lore (mediaeval saints' pictures included), the gift of the magical elephant by the prince, being one of the most striking incidents of Vessantara's story, is introduced in the centre of the scene, though it really preceded his departure from his royal home and all the incidents which followed during his banishment in the forest.

At the same time close adherence to the legend is shown in minor features, such as the rich adornment of the elephant's head and body with jewels, and in the equally significant detail of the sacrificial jug carried by the prince to mark the pouring out of the water on the right hand, an Indian symbol of donation distinctly mentioned in the story. Some of the later incidents must have been depicted in the upper frescoes of the north hemicycle; for M. Foucher's luminous identification enables us to recognize certain characteristic figures, such as the wild animals encountered by Maddi in the jungle, even among the badly injured remnants of the lowest part of the frieze.

With the meaning of the whole fresco once solved I felt doubly eager for a precise interpretation of the two short inscriptions in Kharoshthi already mentioned which appeared on the well-preserved part of the frieze. I had taken careful tracings of them and convinced myself from a few words easily identified on the spot that their language was the same Indian Prakrit in which the documents of Niya, Endere, and the Lop-nor site are written. I had also had my attention attracted by a curious fact about the inscription which was written in black ink over the right thigh of the elephant. It consisted of three short and slightly curving lines; the neatly painted characters, though only about one-third of an inch high, were particularly legible against the white background of the elephant's skin.

For a record naming the scene or actor represented this inscription seemed too long, and its writing also wanting in that lapidary size and ductus which the other above the palace gate showed. On the other hand, it did not look like a mere *sgraffito* of some passing visitor, especially as the place for it had evidently been selected with care. So by a combination of rather slender arguments I was led at the time to conjecture that this little inscription might possibly prove to contain some conspicuously placed brief record about the painter himself.

To my surprise this guess, almost forgotten by me by the time, was curiously confirmed three years later when the photographs and tracings of this inscription were examined by the Abbé Boyer, the distinguished Paris Indologist, and one of my most competent collaborators on the philological side. According to his repeatedly checked reading, the text has to be interpreted: "This fresco is [the work] of Tita who has received 3000 Bhammakas [for it]." The only elements of doubt in connection with this rendering arise from a crack of the plaster which passes through the first two syllabic signs of the word 'Bhammaka,' and from the absence of textual confirmation for the meaning 'piece of money,' recorded by Indian lexicographers for the Sanskrit term *bharma*, of which it appears to be the correct phonetic derivative.

But leaving aside the question as to this possible mention of the painter's wages, there remains quite enough to justify the reference I have made here to this curious little inscription and the Abbé Boyer's rendering; for if we are right in accepting the latter I should feel no hesitation about recognizing in 'Tita,' the painter's name, the familiar Western name of Titus. Tita is a noun form which, as an indigenous growth, we could not etymologically or phonetically account for in any early Indian or Iranian language. On the other hand, the analogy of a considerable number of Greek and other foreign names borrowed by ancient India from the West, proves that Tita is the very form which the name Titus would necessarily assume in Sanskrit and Prakrit.

We have abundant evidence for the fact that Titus as a personal name was, during the early centuries of our era, in popular use throughout the Roman Orient, including Syria and the other border provinces towards Persia. Recent archaeological discoveries in India have also accustomed us to the knowledge that men with good classical names, like Agesilaos and Heliodorus, found employment as artists and royal servants, not on the Indus alone, but far away in the Indian peninsula, down to the times of Indo-Scythian rule from the first to the third century A.D. That the date of the Miran temples cannot be far removed from the end of this period we have seen already. Of the strength and directness of the influence then exercised by classical art in this remote corner of Central Asia the frescoed walls of the temples give eloquent testimony.

What surprise need we feel, then, that one of the artists there employed should have borne a name which must have been common among Rome's Oriental subjects from the Mediterranean shores to the Tigris? It is as a sort of Roman Eurasian, half Oriental by blood, but brought up in Hellenistic traditions, that I should picture to myself that painter-decorator whom his calling had carried to the very confines of China. That men of much the same origin had travelled there, to the 'land of the Seres,' long before him, we know for certain from a classical passage of Ptolemy's *Geography*, where he tells us, on the authority of Marinus of Tyre, of the information obtained from the agents whom " Maës, a Macedonian, also called Titianus, a merchant by hereditary profession," had sent for the purposes of trade to the distant capital of the Seres.

I must refrain from dilating further upon the fascinating glimpse into the art history of innermost Asia which this epigraphic relic opens for us. Nor is this the place to give details about the second short inscription which appears in a more lapidary writing on the lintel over the palace gate. It, too, is in a form of Prakrit, and according to M. Boyer's reading refers, as its position from the first suggested, to the prince seen riding beneath it; though, curiously enough, it calls him Ishidata (for Sanskrit Rishidatta), a name not hitherto known among the several designations of Vessantara.

It was easy to make sure of exact and permanent copies of these inscriptions by means of repeated tracings. But for the frescoes it was practically impossible to secure a record equal to their artistic and archaeological importance. To do justice to the harmonious but often faded colours of these paintings with the camera would have taxed the skill of a professional photographer working with special plates and appliances in his studio. But for an amateur like myself, the conditions under which the work had to be done were almost prohibitive. It was sufficiently difficult to squeeze myself in my bulky fur kit into a position low and distant enough to photograph a frescoed dado just above the floor and on the curving wall of a passage barely seven feet wide. For days the dust haze raised by the violent winds made the light so poor that prolonged exposure was needed, with the attendant risk of seeing the result spoilt by the camera shaking in the gusts. To examine the correctness of negatives so exposed would have required development of each plate on the spot. But in the intense cold still prevailing this could not be done at night without risk of the plate freezing while drying in the tent. In order to reduce the risk of total failure I laboriously took several complete rounds of the frescoes with varying light and exposure,—only to find in the end, when development became possible, some four months later, that my efforts had failed to secure an adequate record.

But even if the photographs had been more successful, I should still have keenly regretted that I had no means of reproducing those fine paintings in colour. The only alternative was to remove the frescoes themselves. In spite of my reluctance to cut up these fine wall paintings into panels of manageable size I should have felt bound to attempt it, had not a carefully conducted experiment proved that, with the means and time at my disposal, the execution of such a plan would have meant almost certain destruction.

The plaster of this wall differed materially from that in the other temple. It consisted of two layers, of which the outer one was remarkably well finished and smooth, but only a quarter of an inch thick and exceedingly brittle. The inner layer, about three-quarters of an inch thick and softer, had very little admixture of straw, and consequently broke far more easily than the wall surface of the other temple, where the plaster, being uniform in substance and full of chopped straw, possessed a good deal of cohesion. When with all due precautions I had removed a detached Putto head and one of the already injured male busts from the dado, I found it impossible to prevent parts of the thin outer layer breaking off in fragments as the plaster behind was being loosened. So I reluctantly realized that there was here no hope of safely detaching any larger piece of frescoed surface, unless the wall behind were systematically tunnelled and special appliances used for lifting off and strengthening the curving planes of stucco.

Italian fresco restorers, working with the accumulated

skill of generations and all technical facilities, might have accomplished the task in the course of months. Even they could not have solved the problem of to how to divide the crowded fresco frieze without risking vandalism, nor have assured its safe transport over such a distance. But how was I to improvise in the desert the skilled help and appliances needed, or even to secure the time required for such a task? Whatever local information I had been able to obtain about the route through the desert to Tun-huang told me that it would not be safe to delay the start of a caravan counting so many men and ponies beyond the close of February, owing to the dependence on ice for a number of stages where the water was too salt for consumption except when frozen. The desert journey was reckoned to last not less than three weeks even at a rapid rate of marching.

As it was impossible to secure extra camels, the difficulties about the transport of adequate supplies for men and beasts were sufficiently serious to preclude any thought of marching at a later season when additional animals would have been needed for the transport of ice or water. And besides all this, an early start eastwards was urged by my hope, built on slender foundations, but all the same strong, that I should find ruins deserving excavation along that ancient desert route. To reserve adequate time for the exploration of them before the summer heats was an imperative consideration.

It was not with a light heart that I could bring myself to abandon the temples which had yielded such a harvest of ancient art work. As long as possible I kept their interior open to the sunlight they had not seen for so many centuries, while going on with the packing of the frescoes which it had been found possible to remove, and the survey of the remaining scattered ruins of the earlier settlement. Most of these proved to be decayed Stupa mounds of the usual type without enclosing rotundas, but had been dug into long before by treasure-seekers. A few others were probably the remnants of substantial dwellings, built partly in hard bricks, but in a far advanced state of erosion.

There were finds of interest here too, but I cannot spare space now to detail them. The general impression I gained was that the area occupied by these older ruins, though adjacent to the Tibetan fort, must have been completely abandoned and practically clear of vegetation when the latter had its garrison ; for only thus did it seem possible to account for the remarkable difference seen in the effects of wind erosion. Near some of the earlier structures this had excavated the soil down to seventeen feet below the original level, while round the fort walls the maximum result of the erosion nowhere exceeded six feet.

After our long weeks of exposure to the bitter cold and incessant winds it was a real relief when my practicable tasks at the site were concluded. And yet it cost me a wrench to give the order for that final duty of all—the filling-in again of the interior of the temples, which was to assure fresh protection for the frescoes. This heavy piece of earthwork was, with the help of extra men from Abdal, accomplished on February 11th. It was a melancholy business to watch those graceful wall-paintings, on which my eyes had so fondly feasted in the midst of the wintry desert, as they slowly disappeared again under the dust and clay débris. It seemed like a true burial of figures still instinct with life. Nothing could relieve its gloom but a vague hope for their eventual resurrection, and the thought that if they could but take a look at the desolation around, they might prefer to rest again in the darkness. I could not foresee what was written by Fate, that fifteen months later they would again emerge to light from beneath their protective covering—only to witness a bitter human tragedy, darkness falling for ever on the eyes of my brave Naik Ram Singh !

But for the time being it felt like a difficult task accomplished with abundant reward, and as I rode off late that day, guided by honest Tokhta Akhun, to rejoin my base at Abdal, my heart was kept buoyant in the darkness with hopes for the new field which was to open eastwards.

CHAPTER XLV

THE excavations at Miran had completed my archaeological tasks in the Lop-nor region. But there was plenty of hard work in the way of packing and preparations to be got through at Abdal before the actual start for Tun-huang and the westernmost parts of true China. Yet after all the exposure undergone at Miran the halt necessitated was pleasant, however humble the shelter which the wretched reed huts of Abdal offered. I was glad to find the depot left behind there quite safe under Tila's care and the ponies well rested. Rest and a warm corner had put the Surveyor on his legs again, and to some extent cured his rheumatic pains and dejection. But for myself, had I not been kept busy with practical tasks of all sorts, I could not have put up so easily with the closely packed quarters, the zone of filth hemming in the fishermen's winter quarters, and the inexpressibly dull look of the landscape. The dismal marshlands on the southern side of the dying Tarim, where salt-encrusted ground mingled with ice-sheets in unending flatness, made up a scene fit for a Cathayan Tomi.

But what did such surroundings matter when I could only spare half an hour daily for a stroll in the open! There was all the sorting and packing of the archaeological finds of the last four months, the bulk of which I now decided to send back to Kashgar for Mr. Macartney's safe-keeping. Apart from the documents which I decided to keep by my side, and which filled four boxes, all the rest of the antiques, including the bulky and often fragile wood-carvings from the Lop-nor sites, required special repacking in order that they might survive the long journey during which my presence would no longer protect them from rough handling. It was important, too, in view of the long travels before us, to reduce the baggage as much as possible. So I took the occasion to send back to Khotan two of the galvanized iron water-tanks, along with spare stores and all papers and books no longer needed, to await my return next year.

The heavy loads of antiques made up quite a respectable convoy of camels and ponies. I entrusted the care of it to two veteran Turki servants, Karim Akhun, the Surveyor's pony-man, and Muhammadju, my own servant, whom, as already related, I had been obliged to leave behind at Charklik sick, in reality, or only of desert hardships. Whatever the truth may have been, both men were no longer fit to follow me farther. A judicious adjustment of pay arrears and rewards to be disbursed at Kashgar gave hope that my convoy would be safely delivered. But in spite of continuous driving and pushing it was only on the seventh day from my arrival at Abdal that I saw the caravan, which included also Turdi, the plucky Dak-man, start for their two months' journey to Kashgar (Fig. 150).

To get my own caravan ready for the long desert crossing cost simultaneous and quite as great efforts. It is true that after our expedition of December my men were not apt to think much of the weeks in 'the Gobi' ahead of us, when they heard that water and some sort of precarious grazing were available along the greater part of the route. But the provision of a month's supplies for men and animals was a big job, and still more the arrangements for their transport. My united party counted in all thirteen persons, eleven ponies for mounts, and eight camels. The latter, fit again after all the hardships of the Lop-nor Desert, and, as always, the mainstay of my caravan, would just suffice to carry our baggage and a part of our food stores. They themselves—brave, frugal beasts—needed nothing except a few skinfuls of rape-seed oil to serve for an occasional smack of that 'camel's tea,' as Hassan Akhun used to say, which was to keep up their stamina. But the

149. SPRING OF LOWAZA WITH ICE SHEET AT FOOT OF OLD LAKE SHORE AND VIEW
NORTH-EASTWARDS ACROSS SALT-ENCRUSTED LOP-NOR BED.

150. CONVOY OF ANTIQUES STARTING FROM ABDAL FOR KASHGAR.
On left Karim Akhun, one of the 'veterans'; in the middle Turdi, the Dak-man.

ponies could not do without fodder, and how to carry enough of this for a month with the rest of the men's food was the crux. To procure camels for the purpose proved impossible. The few Charklik camels which I had secured for the march across the Lop-nor Desert were still too weak from the fatigues undergone to be taken along without imminent risk of a break-down, which would have seriously hampered us when once started on the long desert journey.

So I fell back upon those patient donkeys which had proved in December so useful a supplement to the ice-carrying column. There were plenty of them at Charklik, and through the effective magisterial pressure exercised on my behalf by excellent Liao Ta-lao-ye there was no difficulty in raising the twenty odd animals which we needed. But, naturally, the hardy little beasts would have to be fed themselves, however modest their demands, and equally also the men to take charge of them. Their united rations for a month would make up loads for almost as many donkeys again, and so on and so on. Thus when I first started, while still at Miran, calculating my transport requirements, these donkey estimates seemed to swell out alarmingly.

Of course, I recognized very soon that the only method would be to make detachments of the donkey train return to Abdal by relays when their loads were consumed. But even thus the safe calculation of the numbers needed on this plan and their fodder supplies was a troublesome mathematical operation. Worst of all, I had good reason to fear that the shrewd householders of Charklik would try hard to let me have on hire as many unsound animals as possible, in the hope that they would break down on the journey, and either be promptly sent back or else earn substantial compensation for their owners by dying on the route. In order to protect myself against such schemes and their hampering consequences, I had arranged early to have a large number of donkeys, considerably in excess of our real needs, sent down to Abdal for selection. It was no easy task to pick out a fairly reliable lot of animals, and almost as troublesome to assure that they were properly looked after before our start, and fraudulent substitutions prevented.

What with these ceaseless commissariat transactions, the
'Ustads' brought from Charklik for much-needed repairs
of equipment (some of my heavy winter garments showed
sad signs of the roughing), and all the packing, the scene
in front of our quarters was as lively as any Bazar. Within,
the Beg's reed dwelling was like a Sarai filled to overflowing, and there I worked away obsessed with long-delayed
writing tasks and accounts of all sorts. My men, though
giving little thought to the long desert march immediately
before us, were feeling curiously uneasy how we should
fare among the 'Khitai infidels' on the other side of the
desert. After all, wherever my strange hunts for 'old
towns' might take them within the limits of Turkestan,
they felt they were within their 'God's own land,' and my
Indians, appreciative of the ease of the oases, were inclined
to sympathize.

But beyond we were to enter the unknown, the strange
lands of the 'heathen Chinee,' and they knew enough by
hearsay to apprehend how different were the ways of
life there, and how little inclined the people to meet
the customs and needs of strangers like themselves. So
all my men were eager to draw arrears of pay and provide themselves with extra kit and little luxuries. An
enterprising trader, who had come down from Charklik
with wares for an improvised booth, enjoyed profitable
custom. But I ought to add that almost all my Turki
myrmidons bethought themselves of the occasion to make
remittances to wives and families left behind, through pay-
orders I was able to make out for Khotan, Yarkand, and
Kashgar.

In the midst of all this bustle which the resident Lopliks,
young and old, seemed to enjoy hugely, there arrived to
my relief honest hard-riding Ibrahim Beg with the fifteen
hundred Sers of silver in Chinese 'horse-shoes,' for which
I had despatched him less than a month before to the
Kara-shahr Ya-mên. He had covered the distance there
from Charklik, more than 330 miles, within seven days on
post-horses, but was obliged to spend fully twice as much
time on the return journey owing to the company of two
Chinese Ya-mên attendants. The timorous old Amban

had forced this escort upon him for safety's sake after much hesitation whether he ought to pay out at all.

The timely arrival of the 'horse-shoes' was for me a matter of importance; for reliable information had warned me that nothing in the way of coined silver or gold was received into circulation at Tun-huang, only silver bullion in the traditional Chinese shape. Before taking over the quaint 'horse-shoes,' big and small, I had them, of course, weighed, though I knew that I could trust Ibrahim Beg implicitly in a matter of this sort. The operation was performed with one of those neat and cleverly designed pairs of ivory scales which work on the adjustable lever principle, and are in general use for precious metals wherever Chinese methods of business extend. I had bought a pair at Khotan in anticipation of the primitive currency conditions farther east, but soon realized how little it would save me from the troubles and endless intricacies of a monetary system, or want of system, which seems to have survived from hoary antiquity.

When Chiang-ssŭ-yeh with nimble hands and inexhaustible patience had finished all the weighing, it was found that the number of ounces of silver was short of the expected total by an amount equivalent, at the rate of exchange I had last heard of at Khotan, to something over rupees 40, or roughly £3. It was scarcely possible to suspect Ibrahim Beg of such petty larceny; besides, the official seals on the bags containing the silver had been found quite intact. The correct explanation was soon revealed when Chiang on reference to the Amban's letter ascertained that payment had been made on the official scale of weights accepted at Turkestan treasuries, whereas my own scales were supposed to conform to the weights in use for trade transactions in the 'New Dominion.' What the difference exactly amounted to I did not succeed in extracting from my financial advisers. But, anyhow, I had received a foretaste of those monetary or rather metrological complexities which were in store for me in Kan-su, and which before long made me dread that innocent pair of scales like a highly refined and effective torture instrument.

I scarcely know now myself how I managed in the

evenings to find peace for taking down language specimens
from two Habdals whom I had discovered at Charklik,
brought along to Miran amongst my posse of labourers, and
reserved for a sort of philological dainty (Fig. 132). They
belonged to that very curious gipsy - like tribe known
generally in Turkestan as ' Habdals,' small semi-nomadic
colonies of which, living by begging, mat-weaving, and the
like, are to be found at several of the larger oases in the
western portion of the Tarim Basin. Their language is
full of Persian words, and points unmistakably to immigration from the side of Iran ; but, in addition to these and
the prevalent use of Turki forms and inflexions borrowed
from their new neighbours, it contains a considerable
admixture of strange elements, the origin of which has not
yet been traced. My two Habdals, quaint, shifty-looking
men, had come from Tam-öghil near Khotan many years
before, and having married Charklik women had forgotten
a good deal of their own tongue. But what linguistic stock
remained was duly extracted in our night sittings.

They also left me their anthropometric records, like all
the local Lopliks I could get hold of (Fig. 111). Again
and again I noted how strongly marked in the latter were
those peculiar ' Tartar ' features, like projecting cheek-
bones, narrow slit eyes, scanty beards, by which the more or
less pure Turkish elements occupying outlying parts of the
Tarim Basin are distinguished from the far more ancient
and good-looking population of the southern oases. Until
a generation ago these Lopliks were practically nomadic ;
and owing to their hardy ways of life they all seemed a
healthy stock, quite impervious to the many drawbacks
of their execrable climate, with its extremes of cold and
heat, its icy winter gales, and its summer pest of mosquitoes,
relieved only by dust storms. As a consequence, Abdal
seemed full of queer gout-bent and shrivelled-up octo-
genarians.

Quaint old Mullah himself had such an ancient couple
of parents still living, and on their account prayed to be
excused from sharing the journey to Tun-huang, much
though I wished to keep him as a guide for the ancient
desert route he had himself helped to re-discover. Tokhta

Akhun, too, had to be left behind at the prayer of his aged mother. So deprived of the services of these two excellent Loplik followers, I was doubly pleased when faithful and energetic Ibrahim Beg, my old Keriya Darogha, who had so far accompanied me only on a kind of 'deputation' from his district chief, came of his own accord and asked leave to share my fortunes wherever work would take me among the distant 'Khitai.' Yet, a *rara avis* among Turkestan followers, he never once raised the question of his pay. Of course, it meant throwing up for a couple of years all chances of a new Begship in his district. But Chiang-ssŭ-yeh's brush was at hand to indite an elegant epistle to young Ho Ta-lao-ye, the Amban, and with polite compliments to explain away Ibrahim's preference for my own service.

At last on February 21st I was able to set out with my caravan for the long desert journey. It had taken us a little longer to get ready than the travellers of old of whom Marco Polo, in a passage already referred to, tells us : " Now, such persons as propose to cross the Desert take a week's rest in this town [of Lop] to refresh themselves and their cattle ; and then they make ready for the journey, taking with them a month's supply for man and beast." But then it is true, Abdal was not a town, nor had Marco's travellers gone through the preliminary of an archaeological campaign in the wintry desert. The distribution and loading of the baggage took long hours in the morning, and it was ten o'clock before I could get the whole column, including close on forty donkeys, to move off. The settling of final accounts and claims kept me back for another three hours. But at last I, too, could ride off, after giving much-prized little European presents to the women-folk and children of my host. Chiang-ssŭ-yeh during his long stay in December had made himself a great favourite with the little ones and was visibly affected by the parting. The Beg himself escorted me across the marshy ground to the south-east up to a point where the reed huts of his chief settlement showed up merely as a low line above the flat horizon.

It was our last glimpse of Turkestan habitations for a

long time. A dismal monotonous waste, salt-encrusted, extended as far as the eye could reach around this Ultima Thule of the Tarim Basin. We sighted on our left a succession of small, reed-fringed lakes, all connected with the dying Tarim, and visited at times by fishing canoes. But the dry, salt-covered ground which the track crossed, no doubt part of a relatively recent lake bed, showed not a trace of vegetation until after riding close on twenty-four miles we approached in the dark the meandering dry beds of a tiny stream appropriately known as Achchik-bulak, 'the Bitter Springs.' At the point called Donglik where the caravan had halted, I found the narrow water-course covered with ice and a plentiful growth of tamarisks with some reeds. These were welcome for the animals, ponies and donkeys having been watered by melting ice. I, for my part, was glad for the peace of my tent, which allowed me to struggle with a big mail to Europe for two hours or so after midnight.

Next morning I noticed, from the small hillock of gravel and salt where we fixed the plane-table before our start, that about three miles to the west there rose a high and massive mound recalling a Pao-t'ai. Mullah and Tokhta Akhun, who had come so far to bid me farewell, assured me that it showed no brickwork. Nevertheless, it seemed *a priori* very probable that it was of artificial origin and meant for a road-mark or watch-station. The gravel of which it was said to be composed would naturally be bound together into a sort of conglomerate or marl by the salt contained in the soil and seen everywhere efflorescent. The direction which it indicated was exactly that of Miran and of the straight caravan route to Charklik leading past it. In spite of all efforts my mail-bag was not yet completed, and as the despatch of it could not be delayed beyond the next halt and time was pressing, I had reluctantly to forgo a visit to the mound, which would have implied a great détour.

A look round Donglik revealed close to our camping-place another historical relic of the route, though dating only from its most recent past. It was a wooden Stêlê set up on a tamarisk hillock, with a Chinese inscription written on it to record the exploit of the Chinese official who, in the seventeenth year of the reigning emperor, had been commissioned by the Fu-t'ai or Governor-General of the ' New Dominion ' to explore and report on the route right through to Tun-huang.

The day's march, close on twenty miles, led to the north-east, keeping for most of the way along the edge of a barren gravel Sai with a thin belt of tamarisk cones showing northward. This, too, disappeared after about two-thirds of the march, and the rest lay across low ridges of gravel with no trace of vegetation dead or living. So I was glad to make for a patch of scanty tamarisk cones which came in sight when the light failed, and to halt where at least fuel was assured for the night. We knew from Tokhta Akhun who still kept with us, and from one of the Charklik donkey-men who had followed the route once before and was to act as our guide, that no water could be found on this march nor until the close of the next one. So ice had been brought along from Donglik for us men.

Till 2.30 A.M. I laboured that night finishing my big mail-bag for Kashgar and Europe, and felt no small relief when at last I saw it safely started next morning in charge of Islam, the Dakchi from Khotan, whom I had picked up in January on my passage through Charklik and ever since kept by me. Considering all conditions it was a reasonably early 'return of mail,' and as Islam was no doubt eager to get back to his home at Khotan, I had the satisfaction of learning next winter that this my last Turkestan mail reached England in the record time of about three and a half months. We had a hearty farewell from honest Tokhta Akhun, the burly Lop hunter, who had served me so well since December. He was to escort Islam and my mail-bag to Charklik, and now departed much pleased with the twenty Sers of silver, equivalent to about fifty rupees, which I gave him as wages. For Abdal, which until thirty or forty years earlier had practically known no money, only barter, this was quite a big sum.

The day's march was long and tiring especially for the animals which had gone without water. But it was favoured by an unusual calmness of the air, and was of interest as introducing me to certain characteristic features of the southern shore of that ancient lake bed along which the greater part of our journey was to lead. Already on setting up the plane-table in the morning on one of the tamarisk cones, I noticed beds of reeds forming a belt to the north, and beyond them as far as the eye could reach a bare level plain of whitish colour, evidently encrusted with 'Shor' or salt efflorescence. We saw this quite clearly when after about two miles' march to the north-east the route began to skirt an unmistakable old lake shore marked by a steep fall northward of the low gravel-covered plateau over which we were moving. The route, now taking a more easterly trend, seemed to keep closely to this ancient shore line, but to cut off its sinuosities. In one place it crossed a former bay where the flat of the old lake basin was broken by curious isolated clay terraces up to thirty feet high, which looked as if carved out by erosion. Was it the action of wind alone or had water and wind been successively at work here? I had plenty of occasions to ask myself this question thereafter.

Farther on, a stretch of tamarisk cones appeared again on our left, a clear sign that life-giving moisture was being still received at least periodically by the subsoil. The explanation soon appeared when about the middle of the march we crossed a succession of dry flood channels marking the course of the Lachin stream. It was said to bring down occasional floods from rain or melting snows in the barren high mountains of which the outer spurs were dimly visible to the south. But there was no vegetation by its side where we crossed it, only a narrow belt of drift sand and then once more the same monotonous gravel Sai we had skirted all the way from Donglik.

It was getting dark when we found ourselves on the edge of this *morne* low plateau with the route descending to the foot of the steep clay cliffs, forty to sixty feet high, in which it falls off to the dried-up lake bed. The old bank above us made a good guide as we moved on to cover the last five or six miles of our march. In the moonlight I could see a narrow strip of reed-beds hugging the shore line, and beyond it the gleaming white of the salt-encrusted lake bed, a vision of nature in death. At last we arrived at the halting-place of Chindailik, where in the midst of boggy ground we found a fairly large ice sheet formed over a salt spring. The distance had been close on twenty-four miles, and the last of the hard-tried donkeys did not come in until midnight. We did all that was possible to get ice melted in sufficient quantity for all the ponies and donkeys to get the sorely needed drink. But the process was necessarily slow, and some of the donkeys were so utterly exhausted that I was not surprised when next morning three were reported to have died.

Our march on February 24th proved longer and even more trying for the animals. We had followed the foot of the old lake shore, showing steep cliffs of clay forty to fifty feet high, for barely two miles when its line turned off to the south-east, manifestly to bend round a big bay. To avoid this great détour the track we were following now entered the absolutely flat, salt-encrusted waste which extends over what in an earlier phase of the present geological period was a bay of the lake and probably down to historical times remained an impassable salt marsh. In fact, were it not for the narrow track which the traffic since the reopening of the route has worn into the hard salt-cake surface, caravans would probably find it easier to skirt round the bay and thus save fatigue and sore feet to their camels. I was therefore by no means surprised to learn subsequently that Mr. Huntington, who passed along the first five stages of the route a little over a year before me, had with his usual keen observation noted traces of such an earlier track following the lake shore. There were, of course, no means of judging when its use had been discontinued, whether recently or long ago.

For fully sixteen miles we moved in a straight line across this great bight of what was the true dead sea of the Tarim, the crumpled salt surface recalling that of a river over which the ice-pack had set and got compressed in the freezing. The going was so rough that I greeted with relief the first sight of 'land' when it showed at last in the shape of large isolated clay terraces fringing

the ancient lake shore.   They were from fifty to eighty
feet high, and as we passed between them I noticed that
their slopes showed salt efflorescence at different levels,
thus proving that these terraces had been formed during
periods preceding the present desiccation of the great
lake.   But that they had originally been carved out of
the low gravel-covered plateau which fringes the salt
marsh on the southern side of the basin was quite clear.

In the evening we moved across the top of this Sai
for about a mile and a half where it projects northward,
forming a kind of promontory.   Finally, we descended
again to the foot of the shore cliff, and along it completed
in darkness the remainder of the twenty-six miles to the
stage of Lowaza.   Already I had for some distance
noted isolated tamarisk cones and moist patches with
salt efflorescence.   On reaching the spring we found its
water drinkable and the ground all round covered with
a plentiful growth of reeds and low scrub (Fig. 149).
Next morning I saw that the water was issuing in a
thin but steady flow from a narrow cutting of the terrace
behind, and that its course at the foot of the latter was
covered with a thick sheet of ice for a distance of fully
a hundred yards.   It was a great boon for the animals
to have water in plenty, but for some it came too late.
It was again midnight before all the loads were in ; but
not till next morning did I learn that two of the donkeys
had been left to die on the road.   Three more were
reported unable to get on their feet.

It was evident that, if such losses continued, there
would soon be not enough transport left to carry our
supplies through to Tun-huang.   There was reason to fear
that the men sent with us to look after the donkeys from
Abdal and Charklik were getting indifferent to the fate
of their charges.   So I arranged that the animals' feeding
should be looked after by my own men, all fodder being
issued from a common store, and the whole donkey train
placed under Ibrahim Beg's supervision.   To encourage
the donkey drivers I promised to pay them a special
reward, distinct from the hire due to the owners, for each
animal brought through safely.   These measures proved

effective.   Two of the reported invalids were coaxed into eating some oats, and, having been got to move close to the spring where reeds and scrub were abundant, could be safely left behind with a hope of subsisting at ease until the men returned from Tun-huang to take them home again.   The third poor beast, however, was doomed, and died before I could come round to shoot it. Thus the total roll of victims rose to six, and to that figure, I may state at once, I had the satisfaction of keeping it down in spite of all the fatigues which still confronted us before Tun-huang.

It was certain that all our beasts, the brave camels included, were in need of a rest.   But from the information previously gathered I knew that Koshe-langza, the next stage, would be the best place for this.   So I decided to push on.   The march brought little change in the physical aspects of the ancient lake bed which the route continued to skirt.   For the first seven miles or so we crossed another bay, less wide than the former, and with a soil which, though covered with 'Shor,' still showed remains of old reed-beds.   Then we struck again the line of more or less continuous littoral terraces and moved along their edge, forty to fifty feet above the level of the flat salt-encrusted lake bed which stretched away northward as far as the eye could reach.

The deathlike torpor impressed on this landscape was broken only by the distant view of a high mountain range to the south, and by a shallow Nullah with plentiful tamarisk growth which was crossed after about seventeen miles.   A stretch of salt marsh fed by springs and covered with reeds extended here at the foot of the clay terraces, and numerous footprints showed that animals, including wild camels, were in the habit of descending to the Nullah for water.   They probably came from the sandy desert, vaguely talked of by the Abdal hunters as Kum-tagh, which extends over the higher glacis of the mountains south.

Finally the route dropped down to the foot of the old lake banks, which here rose very steeply to a height of 100 to 120 feet, and after a total march of some

twenty-two miles we reached Koshe-langza by 7.30 P.M.
The donkeys once more did not arrive until midnight,
and half-a-dozen of the loads had been left behind by
the track to be recovered next morning.   But when a
muster of the animals showed that they at least had all
been brought in safely, I knew that I had not in vain
trusted to Ibrahim Beg's perseverance and energy in
wielding authority over transport.

CHAPTER XLVI

ON OLD TRAVELLERS' TRACKS

FEBRUARY 26th was spent in a refreshing halt, of which men and beasts were sadly in need. Koshe-langza, not without reason, is a favourite halting-place. There were a number of springs with tolerably fresh water oozing out from the reed-covered peaty soil, and grazing was abundant. The day began calm and relatively warm, with a minimum temperature of not less than 23 degrees Fahrenheit. But, unsuspected by us on arrival at night, close to our camping-ground lay the carcass of a camel left behind by the last caravan which had started for Tun-huang some three weeks before us. So I had reason to feel glad when, in the course of the morning, there sprang up a steady south-east wind which raised a strong haze and kept the air cold. While the animals were peacefully grazing and the men enjoying their *dolce far niente* by the camp fire, I was busy under the shelter of my little tent writing up notes and accounts for which neither the strenuous days at Abdal nor the fatiguing marches since had left time. Then after my modest *déjeuner*, I was free to indulge in a mental treat, and refresh my memory as to the accounts which have come down to us of this ancient route from Lop-nor to China.

The array of books to be dug out from the mule trunk which held my camp library was not great ; yet it was a comfort to have the few known records of the route at hand for fresh reference. The earliest of them is contained in that precious chapter of the Imperial Annals of the Han which has preserved for us a survey of the 'Western Regions,' and the story of the first expansion of Chinese power to them towards the close of the second century B.C. I knew well that, in spite of the mass of precise and important historical data there recorded, I could not look for topographical details or picturesque glimpses of the route which had made that expansion possible and which I was now endeavouring to retrace. But even thus it was of great interest to review the few broad facts which emerged with clearness.

Ever since the remarkable mission of Chang Ch'ien (*circ.* 136-123 B.C.), whom the Emperor Wu-ti had sent west-wards to open communications with the Great Yüeh-chih tribe (the later Indo-Scythians, then settled on the Oxus) for an alliance against their common enemy, the Hsiung-nu or Huns, the Chinese knew of two main routes by which to reach the 'Western Regions,' *i.e.* the Tarim Basin and the countries on the Yaxartes, or Syr-Darya, and Oxus. One, known then as the 'Northern' route, led from the territory of Tun-huang past Chü-shih (corresponding to the present Turfan) and through the northern oases of the Tarim Basin to Kashgar, and thence across the mountains to Farghana and Sogdiana, *i.e.* the present Russian Turkestan. The other, or 'Southern' route, also starting from Tun-huang, passed first to the territory of Lou-lan or Shan-shan in the vicinity of Lop-nor, and thence along the northern foot of the Kun-lun mountains through Khotan to Yarkand, whence the country of the Great Yüeh-chih in the Oxus Valley was gained.

We are not told exactly how the 'Northern route' reached Turfan and the northern oases. But a number of significant passages in the Han Annals show that, during the earliest period of direct Chinese intercourse with the 'Western Regions' which followed a great victory over the Hsiung-nu or Huns in 121 B.C., the main approach to the former for all Chinese missions, whether diplomatic or military, lay as a matter of fact through Lou-lan, *i.e.* the Lop-nor region. The king of the latter, at the instigation of the ever hostile Huns, is reported to have repeatedly waylaid and robbed Chinese envoys. At last an imperial general, despatched at the head of a small force of light horse, about 110 B.C., seized the king of Lou-lan, subjugated Turfan, and overawed the small states westwards.

When subsequently, in 104 B.C., an envoy to the chiefs of Ta-wan or Farghana had been killed, and the Emperor Wu-ti was obliged to send an expedition to chastise that distant territory, it was again at Lou-lan that a body of Hun horsemen endeavoured to cut off the return of the victorious Chinese leader. Thereupon a relieving force of Chinese troops advanced from the 'Jade Gate,' the end of the fortified frontier line which some years earlier had been pushed forward beyond the newly occupied territory of Tun-huang. Its appearance forced the king of Lou-lan to break finally with the Huns and "to place his State within the bounds of the Chinese empire." In conse-quence of this successful expedition "resting stations were erected at intervals, from Tun-huang westward as far as Lake Lop."

At the same time two military colonies were established and a 'Deputy Protector' created to exercise Chinese political control in the Tarim Basin, and this must have made the maintenance of a practicable line of communica-tion doubly important. The difficulties with which the Chinese advance beyond Tun-huang had to contend, both from nature and man, are curiously reflected in a passage of Chang Ch'ien's biography contained in the Annals. Before the chiefs of Farghana decided to repel the imperial mission they are said to have reflected: "China is at a great distance from our country, and travellers thence are frequently lost in the Salt Desert. If they leave by the northern route they are exposed to the Hun raids; if they take the southern route they suffer from want of water and pasture, and at many parts of the road, where there are no settled inhabitants, great scarcity prevails. If the Chinese envoys come with a retinue of several hundred persons more than half of them usually die of starvation on the way. How then can they possibly send an army?" There can be no doubt that the physical obstacles here alluded to must have been greatest on that part of the route which lay east of Lou-lan.

By the time we reached Koshe-langza I felt certain

that by the 'Salt Desert' was meant the great salt-encrusted lake bed we had been skirting for days, which seemed to extend interminably to the north and north-east. Of the difficulties of transport, too, I had had my experience; and when I thought of the trouble my preparations for this desert crossing had brought on the people of Charklik and Abdal, I could appreciate what another passage of the Han Annals records of the attitude which the people of Lou-lan adopted towards this traffic early in the first century B.C. "Now the extreme eastern border of the Kingdom of Lou-lan, where it approached nearest to China, was opposite the Pih-lung mound, where there was a scarcity of water and pasture; and it always fell to its share to provide guides, to carry water and forward provisions to meet the Chinese envoys; but being frequently exposed to the oppressive raids of the soldiery, they at last resolved that it was inconvenient to hold intercourse with China."

But such local grievances did not save the petty chief-ship, placed on the most direct line from Tun-huang to the Tarim Basin, from becoming an important link in the chain of garrisons and politically controlled states by which Chinese power asserted itself in the 'Western Regions,' with varying energy and success, during the first century before and the first two centuries after Christ. Though the Annals of the later Han dynasty mention Shan-shan or Lou-lan repeatedly in connection with events that took place in the Tarim Basin between *circ.* 25 and 170 A.D., they have preserved no details about the routes which led thither from the extreme west of China proper.

But, fortunately, M. Chavannes' researches have made accessible to us brief yet interesting information on the subject in the Wei-lio, a fragmentary historical work on the immediately succeeding Wei dynasty, composed between 239 and 265 A.D. Yü Huan, its author, tells us that instead of the two routes previously known and referred to above, there were in his time three lines of communication leading from Tun-huang and the 'Jade Gate' to the Western Regions.

The southern one passed from Tun-huang first through

the territory of the nomadic Jô Ch'iang tribe, who grazed in the hills to the south-west, and then reaching the southern rim of the Tarim Basin about Charklik, led westwards to the Pamirs. A look at the map shows that the route meant is the one which skirts the high Altin-tagh range, and still serves as the usual connection between Tun-huang and Charklik during that part of the year when the shorter desert route is closed by the heat and the absence of drinkable water. In the autumn of 1907 Rai Ram Singh surveyed it on his return to Charklik.

The second route, which the Wei-lio calls the central one, started from the 'Jade Gate' westwards and, after passing a number of desert localities which I shall have occasion to discuss hereafter, turned to the north-west and arrived at 'old Lou-lan.' This bearing, and the subsequent mention of Kuchar as a point reached by going west of Lou-lan, make it clear that by the latter must be meant here the ruined site to the north of Lop-nor with its fortified Chinese station which I had excavated in December.

The third route, which is called 'the new,' was directed to the north-west and, passing some localities which are not yet identified, debouched on Turfan. With this last route lying so far away to the north I had no concern for the time. But there were strong grounds for assuming that the track we were actually following to the north-east would after a few further marches bring us on to the ancient route which in the Wei-lio figures as the route of the centre. It was equally evident, as recognized already by M. Chavannes, that the latter route was the same as 'the northern route' of the Han Annals, and that the change in its designation was merely a result of the opening of the 'new' northern route *via* Turfan which took place about the year 2 A.D.

I was fully prepared to appreciate the historical value of these early notices, though on a brief day's halt in the desert I could scarcely give them that close study which critical analysis needed. But, I confess, I felt still more grateful for the records which wove something like human interest round the bare facts of historical geography. Many a pious Buddhist pilgrim from China must have trodden this ancient desert track, and luckily one of the earliest known among them, worthy Fa-hsien, has left us a graphic account of it.   He and four other monks, all bent on seeking spiritual guidance in distant India, started in 399 A.D. from Tun-huang in the suite of an envoy.

The learned prefect of that frontier district "had supplied them with the means of crossing the desert before them, in which there are many evil demons and hot winds. Travellers who encounter them all perish to a man.   There is not a bird to be seen in the air above, nor an animal on the ground below.   Though you look all round most earnestly to find where you can cross, you know not where to make your choice, the only mark and indication being the dry bones of the dead left upon the sand.   After travelling for seventeen days, a distance of about 1500 Li, the pilgrims reached the kingdom of Shan-shan—a country rugged and hilly, with a thin and barren soil."   As the settlement north of Lop-nor was by that time already abandoned, there can be no doubt that the pilgrims' route must have taken them towards Miran and Charklik.   Their subsequent journey of fifteen days to Kara-shahr with its north-westerly bearing confirms this location.

Two and a half centuries later the route we were following had seen a Buddhist pilgrim of still greater fame, Hsüan-tsang, of pious memory, returning from India to China laden with Buddhist relics and sacred books after his many years' wanderings.   Unfortunately, the great pilgrim's own *Memoirs of the Western Regions* stop short with his arrival in the territory of Lou-lan.   He evidently considered the remaining portion of his homeward journey as lying within the borders of the Chinese empire, which just then had commenced its fresh expansion westward, and hence as outside the scope of his record.   But we know from his biography, written by a disciple, that Hsüan-tsang actually accomplished this final part of his travels by crossing the desert from Lop-nor to Tun-huang.

Often had I thought of him during those hard days at Miran, and liked my ruined temples all the more as I remembered how in all probability their walls, then no doubt already sadly decayed, must have seen my Chinese patron saint with his caravan of sacred relics pass by. I sometimes wondered behind which of the Stupa mounds he might have sought shelter during a brief rest. In a region where all is dead and waste, spiritual emanations from those who have passed by long centuries ago, seem to cling much longer to the few conspicuous landmarks than in parts where life is still bustling.

But the old traveller always nearest to my thoughts on this desert journey was Marco Polo, and in my peaceful camp by the edge of the dreary salt plain it was a treat to read again in Ser Marco's immortal book what he has to tell us of the great ' Desert of Lop.' Even to handle the volume was a refreshing assurance; for was it not Sir Henry Yule's edition, replete with all his wide learning and literary charm, and did I not owe this copy to his daughter's kind remembrance of my life-long devotion to the memory of that great elucidator of early travel? Chiang-ssŭ-yeh had joined me in the meantime for my Chinese lesson, which was a fixed item of daily routine whenever time permitted. As I could neither miss it nor tear myself away from the Venetian's fascinating narrative, I set myself to translate his account of the desert into my best Chinese, a solution which I knew would satisfy dear Chiang's keen interest in the old traveller.

Thus it runs in Sir Henry Yule's version: " The length of this desert is so great that 'tis said it would take a year and more to ride from one end of it to the other. And here, where its breadth is least, it takes a month to cross it. 'Tis all composed of hills and valleys of sand, and not a thing to eat is to be found on it. But after riding for a day and a night you find fresh water, enough mayhap for some fifty or hundred persons with their beasts, but not for more. And all across the desert you will find water in like manner, that is to say, in some twenty-eight places altogether you will find good water, but in no great quantity; and in four places also you find brackish water.

" Beasts there are none; for there is nought for them to eat. But there is a marvellous thing related of this desert, which is that when travellers are on the move by night, and one of them chances to lag behind or to fall asleep or the

like, when he tries to gain his company again he will hear
spirits talking, and will suppose them to be his comrades.
Sometimes the spirits will call him by name ; and thus
shall a traveller ofttimes be led astray so that he never
finds his party.   And in this way many have perished.
Sometimes the stray travellers will hear as it were the
tramp and hum of a great cavalcade of people away from
the real line of road, and taking this to be their own
company they will follow the sound ; and when day breaks
they find that a cheat has been put on them and that they
are in an ill plight.   Even in the daytime one hears those
spirits talking.   And sometimes you shall hear the sound
of a variety of musical instruments, and still more commonly
the sound of drums.   Hence in making this journey 'tis
customary for travellers to keep close together.   All the
animals, too, have bells at their necks, so that they cannot
easily get astray.   And at sleeping time a signal is put up
to show the direction of the next march.   So thus it is that
the desert is crossed."

It did not need my journey to convince me that what
Marco here tells us about the risks of the desert was but
a faithful reflex of old folklore beliefs he must have heard
on the spot.   Sir Henry Yule has shown long ago that
the dread of being led astray by evil spirits haunted the
imagination of all early travellers who crossed the desert
wastes between China and the oases westwards.   Fa-hsien's
above-quoted passage clearly alludes to this belief, and
so does Hsüan-tsang, as we have seen, where he paints
in graphic words the impressions left by his journey
through the sandy desert between Niya and Charchan.

Thus, too, the description we receive through the
Chinese historiographer, Ma-tuan-lin, of the shortest
route from China towards Kara-shahr, undoubtedly corresponding to the present track to Lop-nor, reads almost
like a version from Marco's book, though its compiler, a
contemporary of the Venetian traveller, must have extracted
it from some earlier source.   "You see nothing in any
direction but the sky and the sands, without the slightest
trace of a road ; and travellers find nothing to guide them
but the bones of men and beasts and the droppings of

camels. During the passage of this wilderness you hear sounds, sometimes of singing, sometimes of wailing ; and it has often happened that travellers going aside to see what those sounds might be have strayed from their course and been entirely lost ; for they were voices of spirits and goblins." I had only to watch the eager interest with which Chiang-ssŭ-yeh listened to this latter part of the account I translated, in order to realize how the awe of these desert solitudes was working its spell on him too, sceptic as he was in most matters beyond the senses.

As Yule rightly observes, "these Goblins are not peculiar to the Gobi." Yet I felt more than ever assured that Marco's stories about them were of genuine local growth, when I had travelled over the whole route and seen how closely its topographical features agree with the matter-of-fact details which the first part of his chapter records. Anticipating my subsequent observations, I may state here at once that Marco's estimate of the distance and the number of marches on this desert crossing proved perfectly correct. For the route from Charklik, his 'town of Lop,' to the 'City of Sachiu,' i.e. Sha-chou or Tun-huang, our plane-table survey, checked by cyclometer readings, showed an aggregate marching distance of close on 380 miles.

By special exertions amounting practically to a succession of forced marches, we managed to cover it within three weeks, indispensable halts included. But traders still reckon the journey ordinarily at twenty-eight stages for fully laden animals, and considering that at this reckoning the average for each march works out at thirteen miles, I much doubt whether any large caravan could do it in less than a month without risking serious loss of animals. Experience showed that the number of stages where water was either unobtainable or too salt for drinking were four, exactly corresponding to that of the places which Marco notes to have brackish water. In the same way his warning as to the limitation of the water-supply available elsewhere proved well founded. Nor had we to travel far before we came upon 'the hills and valleys of sand' which his description mentions.

CHAPTER XLVII

On the morning of February 27th we resumed our journey, with an icy wind blowing in our faces from that usual quarter, the north-east. For some ten miles the route skirted the still clearly marked lake shore over bare wastes of gravel and coarse sand, or else crossed in places small salt - encrusted inlets. Then the ground through which the track led onwards changed to a broad belt of vegetation with plentiful tamarisks and other scrub. On the south the cliffs of the ancient lake shore altogether disappeared, giving way to a gently sloping Sai with numerous wind-eroded clay terraces. Far away to the south the snowy range of the Altin-tagh was just visible in the clear atmosphere. Northward there still extended the level greyish flat of the salt-covered lake bed as far as the eye could reach. But at last there appeared a dark line on the horizon to the north-east, which before the day's march was ended could clearly be recognized as a projecting angle of the Kuruk-tagh. I greeted it with relief.

Where the scrub-covered belt along which we were moving narrowed, it was easy to see that its level lay ten to twenty feet above that of the salt-encrusted bare plain. To the mournful desolation of the latter my eyes had by now grown accustomed. Yet it served to heighten the effect of the fantastically eroded clay terraces which towards the end of this march cropped up in increasing numbers on our right and curiously resembled ruined buildings. At the halting-place known as Panja, which we reached by nightfall, we found springs with water that tasted quite fresh and plentiful scrub for the animals.

The peculiar features of the ground just described appeared still more pronounced during the next march. All day we followed a narrow strip of marshy ground plentifully covered with tamarisk, reeds, and scrub, and unmistakably marking the edge of an old lake basin. The bare salt-encrusted plain stretched unbroken to the north of the track, but the terrace-like fall towards it grew less distinct after the first four miles, and in parts disappeared altogether. Curiously enough the ground adjoining the marshy strip from the south showed now a similar crust of hard salt cakes, and was so difficult for the animals to move over that we had to keep to the track, water-logged though it was, almost throughout. A slight rise in the ground level was generally observable between the marsh belt along which we were moving and the barren salt steppe southward; and as the hardness of the salt crust increased the farther off I reconnoitred from the line of springs and of the route, I took this for an indication that the level of moisture here had been gradually shrinking.

In any case I felt justified in assuming that this narrow belt of marsh and vegetation, which we skirted for about thirty miles altogether, marked a 'shore line' of far more recent date than the one which we had followed along the littoral clay terraces up to Koshe-langza. In this connection I may mention that the elevation indicated for Panja by our aneroid observations, 2400 feet above sea-level, was the lowest noted in the Lop-nor basin. The water in the marsh springs was brackish, but not altogether undrinkable for animals. Plentiful tracks and droppings amidst the scrub along the route showed that wild camels, deer, and other animals used to come here from the foot of the mountains for water and grazing. The presence of the springs themselves is fully accounted for by the direction of the Altin-tagh drainage, which, as the map shows, sends a main bed, no doubt mostly dry, into the sandy desert just south of this portion of the route.

The level bareness of salt steppe and marsh had been relieved only by a single isolated clay terrace which we passed about eight miles from Panja. But on approaching the end of the day's march we found the route flanked right and left by large groups of such 'witnesses' rising with fantastically eroded steep faces to forty feet and more. In the twilight their reddish clay walls suggested castles and mansions. They seemed the remnants of low ridges stretching from north to south. But it was too late that evening to trace their relation to the long sand-covered foot-hills visible on the horizon to the south. We had left the end of the marsh belt behind us for some miles when the night's halting-place was reached near a well of rather brackish water appropriately known as Achchik-kuduk.

All night an icy wind was blowing from the north-east, which made preparations for the start next morning very trying. But the sky for once was clear, and the view obtained from a clay ridge close to camp showed a distinct change in the scenery. Due north of us a salient angle of the low Kuruk-tagh chain was now full in view, at a distance which our intersections showed to be only about twenty-two miles, and from it the barren hill range seemed to trend steadily towards the north-east. Parallel to it, but on the south of the route and of the belt of vegetation it was hugging, extended a long ridge overlain by huge dunes of drift sand which seemed to attain heights of 300-400 feet. The bearing of this ridge was also unmistakably to the north-east, and as its distance from the route was only about eight miles or less, I could easily make out that the base was formed of clay, just like that of the eroded terraces which could be seen at intervals stretching out from its foot across the plain northward.

Our route followed all day the direction of the latter to the north-east. For some twelve miles the track skirted the line of dried-up marshes with tamarisks and reeds growing on salt-impregnated soil, while north of them still extended the *morne* salt lake bed bare of all vegetation dead or living, and limited only by the equally sterile glacis of the Kuruk-tagh. But from there onwards the barren salt crust disappeared, and its place was taken by an expanse of reed-covered steppe as far as the eye could reach. So at last we seemed to have reached the eastern-most end of that inexpressibly dreary, dry lake bed, the true 'Marsh of Salt,' as the Chinese of old called Lop-nor. For twenty-two miles, the whole length of the day's march, we passed at intervals through strings of isolated clay terraces jutting out from the foot of the dune-covered ridge on our right in the direction of the Kuruk-tagh.

These terraces rose to fifty feet and more in height, and on all their steeply cut faces showed horizontally deposited strata. That their isolated appearance on this level plain marking the eastern end of the ancient lake basin was somehow due to erosion, I recognized on the spot. But their peculiar significance in connection with lacustrine features of this desert region and the erosive forces at work on its surface was only brought home to me by subsequent observations farther east.

I fared similarly in regard to the curious resemblance which most of these boldly carved clay mounds bore to structures by human hand. Again and again from Achchik-kuduk onwards the men as well as myself were tempted to see in them ruins of walls, towers, and houses, until close approach dispelled all illusion about the strange form which wind erosion had produced. But not until long afterwards did I become aware of the fact that this optic deception had impressed travellers many centuries ago, and left its distinct trace in early Chinese records of this desolate region.

In a commentary, dating from the beginning of the sixth century A.D., on that famous Chinese classic, the *Book of the Waters*, M. Chavannes has found a very interesting description of the course of the Tarim River. We read there that the river finally empties itself into marshes which correspond to the lake P'u-ch'ang or Lop-nor of the *Book of the Waters*, and are situated to the north-east of Shan-shan and to the south-west of the 'Town of the Dragon.' Shan-shan, as we have already seen, corresponds roughly to the present tract of Charklik and Miran.

The 'Town of the Dragon' is described as the site where once stood the capital of a great barbarian kingdom. An overflow of the Lop-nor is said to have destroyed this town. "But its foundation walls are still preserved; they are very extensive; if one starts at daybreak from the western gate one reaches the eastern at nightfall." Its name is accounted for by a legend, according to which the wind constantly blowing had given the shape of a dragon turned westward to what was once the line of a canal skirting the ancient town. Whatever may have been in reality the particular feature in which the imagination of those early wayfarers recognized their favourite monster, the dragon, I have little doubt that the whole story of the ruined town was first suggested by those fantastically eroded clay terraces encountered along the route from Panja onwards. We know well how large a part popular imagination, stimulated by peculiar topographical features, has played in the ancient folklore both of the East and the West.

Our location of this imaginary 'Town of the Dragon' is strongly supported by the detailed reference which the text makes in connection with it to a vast salt-covered area. " This region extends for a thousand Li (or roughly two hundred miles); it is made up entirely of salt, but of salt in a hard and solid state. The travellers passing there spread pieces of felt for their animals to take their rest upon. On digging down below the surface one finds blocks of salt, big, like large cushions, heaped up regularly. Haze and floating clouds rarely allow the stars and sun to be seen; of living creatures there is little, but plenty of demons and strange beings." It is quite certain that this graphic description refers to the vast salt-encrusted old lake bed which the traveller from Abdal or Miran skirts almost all the way to beyond Achchik-kuduk.

This conclusion is confirmed by the matter-of-fact account which the commentator appends as to the position of the region containing the 'Town of the Dragon.' On the west it is said to touch Shan-shan, or the Charklik district; on the east side it extends to the 'Three Deserts of Sand,' which we know otherwise to represent the desert west of Tun-huang. " It forms the northern extremity of the lake; it is on this account that the P'u-ch'ang or Lop-nor also bears the name of Salt Lake." A glance at the map will show how closely these bearings agree with our identification of the 'Town of the Dragon.' Nor can it be mere chance that the Wei-lio's notice of 'the route of the centre,' already referred to, places the Lung-tui, or 'Mounds in the shape of Dragons,' immediately before the station of old 'Lou-lan' for a traveller coming from Tun-huang. Once more a look at the map proves that the most direct route to the ruined site north of Lop-nor which represents that station, must have branched off from the Tun-huang–Abdal route somewhere near the march I have just been describing.

This march ended at Kum-kuduk, the 'Sandy Well,' where we found slightly brackish water in a well only four feet deep. The name was appropriate; for some miles before we arrived there, light drift sand covered the ground amidst thinly scattered tamarisk cones. Our journey next day, March 2nd, showed that we had now finally left behind the ancient salt-covered lake bed we had skirted so long. It was a broad but well-marked valley in which we were moving north-eastward, with the sombre, serrated hill range of the Kuruk-tagh in full view on our left, and the low dune-covered desert ridge on the right keeping within three or four miles of the route. The bottom of the depression between them, some twelve to fifteen miles across, seemed one flat, sandy steppe covered with reed-beds and less plentiful tamarisks, the whole looking quite cheerful by contrast with the dead marshes behind us.

Here and there ridges of clay and isolated terraces jutted out from the ridge on the south to the route and beyond it. All day scarcely any trace of salt efflorescence was noticed, a great comfort for the sore feet of our camels, several of which had been in need of re-soling. After seventeen miles we halted behind a boldly projecting clay promontory where scrub was abundant, and unexpectedly succeeded in getting at plentiful water after digging down only some three feet. It tasted far less brackish than that of the preceding wells; and what with this discovery and camp pitched for the first time before nightfall since the start from Abdal, men and beasts were content. Luckily the bitter north-east wind, which had been blowing into our faces for days past, stopped that afternoon, and without it a minimum temperature of 20 degrees

Fahrenheit below freezing-point seemed quite pleasant that night.

On the following day, too, these easy conditions of the ground continued. For about ten miles the route skirted the northern ends of several finger-like offshoots from the clay ridge on our right, all rising with boldly carved faces to eighty or a hundred feet. In one of the scrub-covered little bays between them we passed the well of Yantak-kuduk, the usual halting-place. But as the distance was too short for a day's march, I decided to push on, in the hope of digging a new well farther on. The dune-covered ridge we had followed from Achchik-kuduk now approached quite close to the track. The coarse sand of its lower slopes, showing clearly the effect of constant grinding by the winds, gave good going. The reed-covered steppe north of it seemed to stretch right across to the foot of the Kuruk-tagh, the crest line of which could now be fixed by intersections as eighteen or nineteen miles off.

Towards the end of the march I thought I could recognize a perceptible rise of the valley bottom to the north-east, an observation for which the slow but steady rise of the aneroids during the last two days had prepared me. We halted for the night amidst low tamarisk cones, and at a point where the sand felt moist within a foot or so of the surface succeeded in sinking a well. At a depth of only four feet it gave an ample supply of water, but slightly brackish, gathering from a hard clayey soil. There could be no possible doubt that this desert valley, forbidding as its approaches seem on all sides, receives a good deal of underground drainage. But where does it come from?

Our march on March 4th was long, but was covered under a perfectly clear sky and in good spirits. We knew that it was to bring us to Besh-toghrak, the best of the halting-places before touching the marshes north-west of Tun-huang, and that a day's rest there would refresh men and beasts. For some five miles the track kept close to the foot of the high dune-covered ridge, with a sandy steppe of reeds and scrub stretching away on our left to the glacis of the Kuruk-tagh. A far-swung line of reddish clay terraces, all cut up by erosion, appeared to mark its edge. Plentiful tracks of wild camels crossed the route from the south. Did they lead to grazing or to water? After about twelve miles we passed the wells known as Kosh-kuduk; but before this the dunes and fine gravel slope on our right had given way to an almost level expanse of reed-beds. Visible from a long distance before us was a low gravel ridge, which seemed to stretch right across the flat valley bottom. But on approaching it I found that this was an illusion, due partly to a slight bend in the direction of the valley.

The ridge, about 120 feet high, jutted out for only two miles or so from a gravel plateau now fringing the valley on the south. Yet after all the dull flatness of the ground behind us it looked quite an impressive feature, and as I crossed its top with Chiang-ssŭ-yeh over a narrow saddle we felt both as if we had reached at last the outermost gate of Kan-su. So we promptly baptized the ridge as 'K'ai-mên-kuan,' 'the Station of the Open Gate.' Much had we talked already on our long lonely rides from Lop-nor of that famous watch station of Yü-mên or the 'Jade Gate' which once stood on the Kan-su border closing this ancient desert route, and the true position of which I was eager to clear up after the oblivion of ages.

Curiously enough the view from the top revealed a distinct change in the landscape. An unbroken expanse of reed-beds, level like a yellowish lake, seemed to stretch away eastward. It was bordered on the south no longer by a high sand-ridge, but by almost vertically cut clay cliffs which looked as if eroded by the currents of some ancient river. The vegetation immediately to the east of the ridge bore a distinctly more flourishing look. Thickets of thorny scrub and round knolls of a reed-like plant not previously noticed became abundant. What a treat to tempt our poor camels and donkeys! It was hard to keep them going.

A black spot far away in the distance was recognized by Ata-ullah, the guide, as Besh-toghrak. But it was quite dark by the time we reached the five wild poplars which have given the place its name (Fig. 151).

Modest specimens they seemed and of no great age, standing in a row some 150 yards from the foot of the cliffs and all bent westward by the prevailing wind. Yet I could not help approaching them with respect. For were they not the hardy advance guard thrown out into a forbidding desert from the jungle of a river system which failed to struggle through to Lop-nor? Near them we found two wells about five feet deep, which, after being cleared, yielded water less brackish than any we had tasted since Panja.

151. CAMPING-GROUND OF BESH-TOGHRAK, ON ROUTE TO TUN-HUANG.

152. ERODED CLAY TERRACE NEAR WESTERN EDGE OF OLD TERMINAL BASIN OF SU-LO HO.
The small figure of the man standing at the foot of the terrace helps to give an idea of its height.

CHAPTER XLVIII

A STRANGE OLD LAKE BED

THE day's halt which I allowed at Besh-toghrak was turned to good use by us all. Fortunately the east wind dropped in the forenoon, and the delicious calm and warmth which followed helped us greatly in our several tasks. The thermometer registered a maximum of 72 degrees Fahrenheit in the sun at 2 P.M. Not since our halt by the Endere river on November 14th had I felt such comfort in my tent. Camels and ponies needed careful examination for treatment of sore backs and other ills. Of saddlery repairs there was enough on hand to keep a shop going.

The hardy little donkeys, which had held out so bravely, and were now holding high feast on reeds and thorns, had to be carefully mustered. For our much reduced stores they were no longer all needed, and I decided to leave the eight weakest behind in charge of an Abdal man who was to look after them until the rest of our hired transport should return from Tun-huang. What with the warmth and the abundant grazing, all the animals seemed to pick up fresh life, except one poor donkey, which somehow had managed to fall into a well over-night and was rescued next morning half-frozen. But even he was warmed to life again with the fires I had lit around him and some vigorous rubbing. By the afternoon I saw him on his legs again, and contentedly munching his extra ration of maize. Ram Singh, the Surveyor, was busy with theodolite observations for latitude, taking clinometrical heights and careful readings of the mercurial barometer to check our aneroids, and to obtain more exact records of our elevation and that of the Kuruk-tagh range. The subsequent computation of those readings showed the height of Besh-toghrak camp as 2620 feet above sea-level.

This was a distinct confirmation of the slight but steady rise of level I thought I had observed during the last two marches, and to me the geographical interest of this observation was great. The depression in which we were moving since Achchik-kuduk had gradually narrowed into a regular valley descending from the north-east. The ease with which water was reached along its bottom by digging wells, and equally also the appearance of the high banks of clay edging it, suggested that this valley might once, and that within the present geological period, have served to carry surface drainage down to the ancient Lop-nor lake bed we had traced as far as Achchik-kuduk. But from where could this have come in sufficient quantity to erode such a valley? Not from the utterly barren Kuruk-tagh hills north, which, as our clinometrical readings showed, in the so far visible chain rose nowhere above *circ.* 4200 feet, and nowhere disclosed the debouchure of any important side valley. Nor from the high range of the Altin-tagh, a hundred miles or so away to the south, with its scanty drainage running at right angles to the direction of our valley, and lost long before reaching it on the huge gravel glacis and amidst the big drift-sand ridges of the Kum-tagh.

Naturally my thoughts turned eastward, up the direction from which the valley seemed to trend to Besh-toghrak. I knew that two large snow-fed rivers, the Su-lo Ho and the Tang Ho, united north of Tun-huang, and after flowing for a short distance to the west were supposed to end their course in the Khara-nor lake. The latter was to be looked for some eighty miles to the east of Besh-toghrak, judging from the Russian map embodying Roborowsky's and Kozloff's reliable surveys. A series of isolated small lakes and marshes shown there west of the Khara-nor, and thus in our direction, seemed to tempt the conjectural explanation that they might be connected somehow with a far more ancient line of drainage towards our valley and the dried-up Lop-nor lake bed. But Colonel Kozloff's manifestly careful route sketch indicated no connecting links between these lakes and marshes. This was a serious objection, and left me in puzzling doubts about the problem before me.

Chiang-ssŭ-yeh joined me in the evening for our Chinese reading, and on finding me still poring over maps and absorbed in this geographical question, with his usual keenness set forth a puzzle of his own. He well remembered having seen Chinese cartographical works in which Lop-nor was made to extend far away to Tun-huang. Ever since Abdal he had eagerly looked out for the great 'Lake of Salt.' Now when we had finally passed out of the dried-up basin, he was more than ever exercised by the difference between that traditional representation and the small size of the marshes he had actually seen. It was but a poor substitute for enlightenment when I told him that recent European literature about 'the Lop-nor problem' was threatening to fill book-shelves, and that there was little hope of our finally emerging from all its controversial lucubrations until the whole of that dreary region had been mapped with a mesh of accurate surveys such as we had just endeavoured to carry out along the least formidable of its possible route lines.

It was by no means the first time that I had occasion to appreciate my excellent secretary's lively interest in geographical matters and his keen eye for surface forma-tions. His place was invariably by my side or that of the Surveyor whenever we set up the plane-table. With that natural aptitude for orientation and map reading which seems common even among less educated Chinese, he had long before made himself familiar with the use of the diopter and the rudimentary principles of plane-tabling. Gladly would he have applied himself to the theodolite, too, if only Ram Singh had found time to teach him the practical handling of it for star observations, and I had possessed the requisite Chinese knowledge to expound the theoretical basis of the operation. More than once he surprised and nonplussed me by the acute questions he put about the 'reasons why,' when confronted by novel topographical features. Altogether I often thought what excellent material the Survey of India would command, if it could but enlist and train for its service 'field literati' of such topographical sense, painstaking care, and intelligence as displayed by Chiang-ssŭ-yeh.

Luckily for me he was as lively a *causeur* on things and people in general as he was keen in enlarging his knowledge. So many a weary hour of these long desert marches was lightened by the endless flow of stories he would tell me from the varied experiences of his wandering life as a petty official from Lan-chou-fu to Urumchi, from Karghalik to distant Tarbagatai. There was always a plentiful admixture of good-humour in his stories, in spite of pathetic little incidents and irrepressible raillery at all the defects of the administration he knew so well. What amusing confidences he told me of all the unholy profits with which various Ambans of Chiang's far-spreading acquaintance were credited in the intimacy of their Ya-mêns, and about the methods more or less shady by which these quick fortunes were made! But that would be 'another story,' and—I know, Chiang would like me to be discreet.

On the morning of March 6th, a brilliantly clear day, when the minimum thermometer registered twenty-three degrees of frost, we set out from Besh-toghrak. The Abdal man we left behind in charge of the eight donkeys needing rest seemed to face his solitude with stolid resignation, comforted by a twenty days' supply of rations, a box of matches, and the prospect of unlimited sleep until the return of the donkey caravan. After moving about four miles to the east I was surprised to find the soft reed- and scrub-covered ground giving way to dunes of coarse-grained sand which stretched northwards across the valley from a high ridge of sand on our right. The dunes rose to twenty or thirty feet where we crossed the belt, but seemed a good deal higher both to the north and south; their surface had a curious crusted appearance suggesting the presence of binding salt grains.

The vegetation became exceedingly scanty. At a distance of about nine miles from Besh-toghrak we found ourselves on the western edge of an absolutely bare and uniformly level depression covered with salt efflorescence, and manifestly part of a dried-up lake basin.   It proved about two miles broad, and extended from south-west to north-east, where it seemed to join on to a larger basin. From its eastern edge the direction of our march under Ata-ullah's guidance took a decided turn to the south-east, and after crossing a second promontory of drift sand, rising to a ridge of forty feet or so, brought us to another bay of the great dried-up basin northward.

The most striking feature of the latter consisted of hundreds of high clay ¦terraces, unmistakable ' witnesses ' of erosion, which could be seen scattered ih clusters or rows over the wide depression.   All shapes and sizes were represented; but most rose like islands or towers with very steep walls, looking in places almost vertical.   Their top level seemed fairly uniform, and the evident variation in relative height was mainly due to unequal erosion of the ground at their feet.   A big terrace near which I halted on reaching the second bay, and which is seen in Fig. 152, rose to fully eighty feet.   It showed clearly horizontally deposited strata of fine and hard clay with thin layers of compressed wind - ground sand between. Owing to wind erosion proceeding more rapidly in the latter the walls of the terrace were under-cut in many places, and large masses of débris at its foot showed that erosion and detrition were still actively proceeding.

Our onward route continued to skirt the southern edge of the great eroded basin from which these huge ' witnesses ' rose.   In the course of seven miles from where we had left the eastern edge of the first, we crossed two more ridges of sand projecting from the south - west into the salt-encrusted depression.   At their foot some scanty reed stalks were found, mostly dead.   Farther on we came upon a few low cones covered with scrub, and then passed again amidst a belt of clay terraces, where the only trace of vegetation consisted of dead and completely withered tamarisk wood cropping out over drift sand.   Here darkness obliged us to halt, though the attempt to dig a well failed completely.   The water brought in one tank gave out before dinner was cooked, Hassan Akhun in his care to lighten the camel's load and from over-confidence in our well-sinking luck having unduly limited the supply. But at least there was plenty of fuel to give warm camp-fires to the men when the bitter wind rose in the evening—this time from the south-east—and there had been just enough water for tea to go round.

Notwithstanding a missed dinner I sat content in my little tent; for the day's march, fatiguing as it was, had yielded interesting observations in abundance. It had served to illustrate strikingly Marco Polo's account of the difficulties and dangers of the route. The track, soon after leaving the Besh-toghrak grazing, had become practically effaced over long stretches of sand, and as the Kuruk-tagh range recedes here northward and flattens, it would have been easy to lose the right route. By continuing too long eastwards travellers coming without guides from Besh-toghrak might easily stray away into the hopelessly barren desert north of the depression to which we had to cling. This wilderness of fantastic clay terraces and sand dunes would necessarily impress those who tried to make their way across from the side of Tun-huang. In fact, it is like a curtain, and most effectively hides the well-marked valley which leads south-west from Besh-toghrak and affords the natural route to Lop-nor.

The most interesting feature, however, of the day's march was the discovery of the large lake bed along and through which we had been passing for fully ten miles. Its aspect and its position relative to the Khara-nor made me already feel convinced that it must have served once as a terminal basin for the Su-lo Ho and Tun-huang rivers. But when did the latter's waters cease to reach it? Parts of the lake bed we had crossed showed a thin salt crust which looked quite recent. Yet the lake shown as Khara-nor in the maps, where the Su-lo Ho and Tun-huang rivers were hitherto believed to end, and from which alone sufficient water could come, lay, according to Roborowsky and Kozloff's map, still more than a degree farther to the east.

What seemed a puzzle at the time luckily found its explanation two months later. Then, in the course of resumed surveys to be related hereafter and illustrated by inset *A* of Map I., we discovered that a considerable river flows out of the Khara-nor during the spring and summer floods; after draining a series of smaller lakes and marshes lower down, it carries its water right through to the southern portion of the great lake bed which we had passed so much farther west, and had then thought finally dried up. But like most new facts, this discovery, too, raised its crop of fresh problems. I cannot set them forth here in detail, nor have they all yet found their solution.

How was the maze of high clay terraces scattered over the lake bed to be accounted for? That their clay was built up by lacustrine sediments, deposited perhaps in some earlier geological periods, was clear, and equally also that their separation was the result of erosion which gradually broke up the ancient lake bottom. But was this erosion solely the work of the winds during periods of excessive desiccation, or had the cutting action of running water prepared and helped it on? Only close examination on the spot by a competent geologist could furnish a definite answer. But in the meantime it may be well to record here that I observed exactly corresponding clay formations in abundance around the Khara-nor and other lake basins. In their direction and grouping I often found proof of the fact that ridges originally cut out by the erosive action of drainage had subsequently been subjected to the grinding force of the prevailing east winds and the sand driven before them, and in due course been broken up into those curious isolated terraces.

Another problem with which my thoughts were closely concerned at the time was suggested by the obvious relation between the true terminal bed of the Su-lo Ho just discovered and the unmistakable valley we had traced ascending to within a few miles of it near Besh-toghrak, from the north-eastern extremity of the salt-encrusted Lop-nor basin. It was impossible not to draw the conclusion that once, and that probably within the present geological period, the waters of the Su-lo Ho flowed out of the newly discovered terminal basin westwards, just as they still pass out of the Khara-nor, and that entering the Besh-toghrak–Achchik-kuduk valley they reached down to the Lop-nor depression. The aneroid readings at our camp within the lake basin showed clearly that the bottom of the latter lay at least 200 feet above Besh-toghrak.

Our survey had revealed no surface formation which might be considered a permanent drainage barrier between the lake basin and the valley. The belt of dunes which we had found intervening, nowhere exceeding fifty feet in height and only two and a half miles wide where we crossed it, was not a barrage in any sense. Instead of being the cause of the Su-lo Ho waters coming to a standstill in the present terminal basin, it was only a sign and result of the latter getting partially dried up; for manifestly the sand materials contained in those dunes were but the silt deposited by the dying river in the basin and the erosion products scooped out from the dry portions of the latter, both carried away by the prevalent east winds and heaped up on the opposite lake shore. It is exactly in the same way that I invariably found the dried-up terminal courses of rivers in the Taklamakan flanked and headed by ridges of sand or Dawans particularly high. These, too, were built up with the silt which the dying rivers could carry no farther, and to some extent also with the products of the wind erosion proceeding over the area once protected by moisture and vegetation.

So, if my interpretation be right, I was confronted here at the very threshold of our new ground of exploration by evidence of that dominating factor among physical changes in the Tarim Basin, desiccation. I had learned by practical observation how much its effects could alter the surface aspects of an area within the relatively short space of historical periods. But at the same time repeated experience has taught me how clearly subsoil drainage often preserves, even in these parched-up regions, distinct traces of river courses which have long ago ceased to carry life-giving moisture into otherwise arid wastes. I was thus prepared to give due weight to the evidence which the relative abundance of desert vegetation between Kum-kuduk and Besh-toghrak afforded as to drainage still finding its way underground from the present terminal lake bed of the Su-lo Ho down the valley leading to Lop-nor.

Indirectly this assumption is supported by the scantiness of the salt efflorescence which I observed in this lake bed. Were all the waters brought down by the Su-lo Ho floods finally to disappear there by evaporation, we should reasonably expect the surface of the lake bed to be thickly encrusted with salt cakes just like that of the ancient Lop-nor bed. It is impossible to give here further details. But enough has been said to justify my belief that the well-marked valley we had surveyed on our way to Besh-toghrak was the passage through which the waters of the Su-lo Ho and its chief tributary, the river of Tun-huang, had once made their way down to Lop-nor, and that this period was, geologically speaking, quite recent.

The geographical importance of this observation scarcely needs to be set forth at length ; for if it be accepted, the true easternmost limit of the great Turkestan basin is shifted from about 91° 30′ to *circ.* 99° of E. longitude, where it touches the extreme western limit of the Pacific drainage. I may add here, in passing, that my subsequent explorations fully confirmed this observation by showing the close affinity which exists between practically all physical features in the Tun-huang–Su-lo Ho drainage area and those of the Tarim Basin.

CHAPTER XLIX

THE interest of the ground we had now reached was so great that for the sake of closer exploration I would gladly have left our camp where it had been pitched at nightfall, though dismal were its surroundings. But the total want of water and grazing obliged us to push on next morning. For two miles or so we continued to thread a maze of steep clay terraces and then emerged on the north edge of a lagoon-like dry bed which stretched away to the south-west. Though bare of all vegetation, it showed shallow but unmistakable shore lines as if it had held water quite recently. Our guide held on to a south-east course, and after another mile or so we found ourselves at the mouth of a broad and deeply cut flood-bed, recalling an Arabian or Egyptian Wadi. As we moved up its bottom, here close on a mile wide, the sandy soil changed rapidly to a coarse gravel. In the haze raised by the windy night the scenery looked doubly sombre and desolate.

As the Wadi could be seen steadily ascending eastward, I soon realized that we had reached a terminal bed of the Su-lo Ho. But we were not to follow it long; for when the guide espied a narrow gorge opening into the Wadi from the south he struck for it as if at last quite assured of his bearings, and with relief pointed to the well-marked track we found leading up it. After a sharp pull up between steep cliffs of consolidated gravel, we found ourselves on a flat pebble-covered plateau fully one hundred feet above the bottom of the Wadi. The latter was cut in so abruptly that, continuing our course to the south-east, we soon completely lost sight of it. This old river bed now shown on the map was, in fact, not mapped until two months later.

Progress over the flat expanse of gravel was easy, but also strangely monotonous. For nearly ten miles the only features to be noticed were two or three shallow depressions covered with reed-beds which the route crossed. If my attention was kept fully alert on this march it was due now to expectations of an archaeological nature. From the brief account which M. C.-E. Bonin, of the French Diplomatic Service, had published of a journey made in 1899 right across China, I knew that he had attempted to follow the desert route from Tun-huang to Lop-nor. He had been obliged to turn back owing to the want of reliable guides, or the reluctance of his Chinese escort to proceed farther, apparently after having reached the first marshes west of the Khara-nor. In the course of this unsuccessful attempt he had passed ruined watch-towers, and even observed some remains of a wall running near them. But though the distinguished French traveller had expressed a shrewd guess as to the probable antiquity of these ruins, and even as to their historical importance as proof of an ancient route, his passing notice of them could not help me, in the absence of any map or route sketch, to locate them beforehand. Fortunately I had been able to enquire about them from Mullah of Abdal, the true pioneer of the route, and what that observant old fellow had told gave me hope that I might come across the first 'Pao-t'ais,' as he called them, on this very march leading to Toghrak-bulak.

My hope was not disappointed. It is true, the first tower-like mound which attracted attention when we had covered about thirteen miles of march, lay too far off to the north, and was noticed too late to turn back to it. But the second mound, approached after another couple of miles, proved to my joy an unmistakable and relatively well preserved watch-tower. It rose in a solid mass of brick-work, about fifteen feet square, to a height of some twenty-three feet. About its early age I felt no doubt when I examined its well-made bricks of fairly hard clay, some fourteen by seven inches and four inches thick, and found familiar layers of tamarisk branches inserted at regular intervals between the courses.

The tower rose in an easily defended position flanked by steeply eroded small Nullahs, and on the very brink of a deep-cut dry river bed, with its bottom showing streaks of salt efflorescence some eighty feet below the level of the Sai. Adjoining the tower on the west side I could trace the foundations of some small and badly decayed structure, probably the watchmen's quarters as I thought. The small fragments of iron implements, with a few pieces of carved wood and some stout woollen fabric, which I quickly picked up on the slope, confirmed this conjecture. For more there was no time as darkness was beginning to descend. With the deep shadows in the Wadi below, the desolation about this first relic of human agency in the desert was intense.

Yet my heart was buoyed up by cheering thoughts of fresh archaeological work as I hastened after my caravan along the track now luckily well marked in the gravel. After about three miles it brought me to a sharply scarped little valley with plenty of reeds and scrub by the side of a narrow streamlet hard frozen. A fire quickly lit by the men showed the place where the guide had halted. There was no need to search for springs among the flourishing reed-beds; for us men there was abundance of good ice, and for the animals slightly brackish water wherever holes were cut through the thin ice of the marsh. Salt-encrusted dead Toghrak trunks lay by the side of the stream, and living trees were said to exist farther north. So the name of the halting-place, Toghrak-bulak, was no fiction. But we had no inkling either that night or in the light of the morning that this was the bed of a live river which before two months had passed would become almost unfordable.

It broke with a dull dust haze raised by the cutting wind which had blown all night, this time, for a change, from the north-west. But my eagerness to get at more ruins made me press for an early start. We had followed the track leading eastwards across an absolutely barren gravel plateau for barely three miles, when I noticed a ruin rising on what looked like a low ridge to the south-east. I promptly directed the caravan to move on by the well-marked track to the springs where our next camp was to be, while I rode off straight for the ruin, taking along the Surveyor, Chiang-ssŭ-yeh, Tila Bai, and two of the men provided with Ketmans.

The distance was greater than I thought, the apparent flat level of the Sai being broken by a broad depression which showed luxuriant tamarisk scrub and many dead poplars. From its bottom we had to ascend a steep scarp of about a hundred feet to the edge of the gravel-covered plateau where rose the ruin we had sighted. It proved a solid square tower built with carefully set courses of hard sun-dried bricks, and at regular intervals thin layers of reeds inserted between them. The ruined watch-tower, for only as such could it have served, still rose to a height of over twenty feet. Except on the north side the wall faces had suffered little; but as they receded slightly inwards, this gave to the whole the look of a truncated pyramid as seen in Fig. 153. Except for some scanty traces of broken brickwork adjoining the south face, there was no indication of any structural remains besides the solid tower itself, and all round spread a uniformly flat gravel surface.

But, as I prospected around, my attention was attracted by a line of reed bundles cropping out from the gravel soil about twenty yards north of the tower and close to the plateau edge. As I followed this eastward to the top of a low knoll close by, I saw the line stretching away perfectly straight towards another tower visible some three miles to the east, and assuming in the distance the form of an unmistakable wall. It was manifestly part of that early ' Chinese wall ' for which M. Bonin's observation had made me look out, and a little ' prospecting ' on the knoll soon revealed with clearness that I actually stood on remains of it!

On clearing away the fine gravel and the drift sand accumulated below on the side sloping towards the Nullah, we soon came upon a regular wall or *agger* constructed of horizontal bundles of reeds placed at regular intervals over layers of clay mixed with gravel. On the outside and placed in the direction of the wall, but at right angles to the packed bundles within it, were found other reed bundles bound with bark twists after the fashion of fascines and forming a facing.   The thickness of the reed bundles was about eight inches and their length uniformly eight feet. The extant height of the wall, where our experimental digging had revealed it, was about five feet.

There was no time now to investigate constructive details about this strange wall, nor could they by themselves furnish a clue to its date and origin.   But a lucky chance rewarded this first scraping with finds of manifest antiquity.   Within the reed bundles exposed on the top of the wall remnant there turned up a rag of coarse white fabric resembling hemp, such as found at the Lop-nor sites ; a birch of Toghrak twigs ; several small rags of gay-coloured silk ; fragments of wooden boards ; and, finally, a carefully cut piece of hard wood about four inches long, mortised on the back and bearing on its flat obverse five Chinese characters of remarkable clearness and good penmanship.

Even to me in my Sinologist ignorance the writing looked strikingly old, and a sort of intuition made me suggest to Chiang-ssǔ-yeh that it must be of Han times. But my devoted helpmate, modest in spite of his learning, confessed that palaeography had not been his special field of study, and would commit himself only to the cautious statement that the characters looked decidedly older than those used under the Sung dynasty in the tenth to the twelfth centuries A.D.

Often I chaffed my excellent literatus thereafter about the learned restraint he had shown on that occasion, and how my own antiquarian ' bold shot ' was destined to prove right !   Though Chiang quite correctly read the short inscription, there was nothing in its contents to give a chronological clue.   It simply stated that the object to which the little wooden label had been attached was " the clothes bag of one called Lu Ting-shih."   This and the other small relics had turned up within a few square feet, and clearly showed that the ground along the wall, in spite of its desert character, must have been occupied at points. But at the time it was less easy to form a definite

153. RUIN OF ANCIENT WATCH-TOWER T. III., NEAR WESTERN END OF TUN-HUANG *LIMES*.
The spot where the first discovery of an early Chinese record on wood was made is marked by the two men in foreground.

154. RUIN OF ANCIENT CHINESE FORT T. XIV., MARKING THE POSITION OF THE
'JADE GATE,' SEEN FROM NORTH-EAST.

conclusion as to how they had got into the wall just where a fortunate chance had made me first examine it. Either the little objects dated from a working party encamped here at the first construction of the tower and wall, and had been accidentally mixed up with the materials for the latter; or else, perhaps, they were relics from a small post once maintained near the watch-tower, and had found their way into the wall adjoining on occasion of some later repairs.

But of far more importance than any such details was the view of the line of wall revealed to the east, and of the succession of watch-towers which we could sight in the distance. Luck had favoured me in this respect, too. The tower we had struck, T. III., in my subsequent close survey, proved an excellent station for the plane-table owing to its commanding position. It stood, apparently, close to a bend of the line defended by the watch-towers. Only about two miles to the west, on a small spur of the identical gravel ridge or terrace, rose another tower. To the south-west at least two more could be made out at greater distances. Eastwards at the end of the visible line of wall a tower showed quite clearly, and beyond it another seemed to indicate a turn of the line to the north-east.

It was too late in the day to attempt a reconnaissance south-westwards. Instead, I decided to follow the line of wall and towers as far as I could to the east. I had not to regret it. The remnants of the wall cropped out higher and higher as we descended over steep gravel slopes to the southern extension of the scrub-covered Nullah already noticed. For over a mile here the extant wall portion was continuous, and showed a height of five to six feet above ground. Its base seemed to be buried for several feet more under drift sand which the winds had heaped up against it.

The peculiar method of construction could be examined with ease, and not even scraping was needed. Except for the horizontal fascine revetting which wind erosion had removed in most places, the alternate layers of stamped clay and reed bundles were here in perfect preservation. The former, about seven inches in thickness, showed much cohesion in spite of the coarse material full of gravel and small stones. The reed bundles, of about the same thickness, were strongly tied, and with their neatly cut stacks and careful anchoring resembled rows of fascines. The average thickness of the wall was between eight and nine feet.

The wall farther east had become eroded in many places. Yet the remnants of the reed layers could be traced in the sandy, scrub-covered depression to within a quarter of a mile of the next tower. This proved of similar construction to the last, though more injured. A special feature here were vertical pieces of Toghrak set into the brickwork to strengthen the corners, and held at short intervals by ropes of twisted reeds which again were embedded in the masonry. The whole, like the materials used in the wall, seemed to tell plainly how little the surrounding physical conditions and the resources of this desert ground had changed since the line of towers was erected. Incidentally light was thrown on the purpose of the latter when I noticed on the southern face a line of rough footholds spared from the masonry, as if to assist a person climbing to the top by means of a rope. Manifestly the small space on the top was meant to be occupied by a man or two for watching and signalling.

Beyond this tower the continuation of the wall seemed to be lost completely. Crossing the bare gravel plateau to the north-east, we then regained the caravan track leading eastwards in the direction of the next tower which now came in view far away. We had followed the track for scarcely more than a mile when the Surveyor's keen eye caught a slight swelling of the gravel soil running parallel to the route, and half-petrified reeds cropping out from its side and top. By merely scraping the surface I made sure that we were moving once more by the line of the old wall, the reeds clearly belonging to the foot layers of a portion now almost completely eroded.

Farther on the almost imperceptible swelling grew into a perfectly straight ridge, six to eight feet high, where the extant wall lay covered under heaped-up gravel and drift sand. At a point about three miles distant from the last

tower we passed a low mound some twelve yards to the
south of the wall line. It did not require much archaeological insight to recognize in it the débris of a completely
ruined watch-station, as excavation later on proved it to
be, nor to draw the obvious conclusion that the wall must
have been meant to face north.

From here onwards the rest of the day's task was easy.
A perfectly straight line of wall, clearly traceable throughout, brought us after two miles to a massive tower already
sighted from a distance. T. IX., as I numbered it, looked
quite an imposing structure, rising on a commanding knoll
of the plateau edge to a height of over twenty-five feet. Its
remarkably solid masonry showed a base about twenty-three
feet square. The bricks here too were sun-dried; yet the
admixture of salt in the soil or in the water with which
they had been made, seemed to have given them unusual
hardness.

The bare gravel plateau now fell off to a wide scrub-
covered depression, across which we could follow the line
of wall for another three miles to the north-east without
much trouble in spite of the growing dusk. A big ' Pao-
t'ai ' perched on a high isolated clay terrace served as an
excellent guide-mark. I reached the ruin at nightfall, and
had just time on scrambling up to its base to ascertain a
marked difference of construction. Instead of courses of
bricks there were here regular layers of stamped clay, each
receding somewhat from the edge of the lower one, and
the whole thus presenting the effect of a small truncated
pyramid. Heavy impregnation with salt made the structure
shimmer in the darkness.

The very mode of construction suggested that water
could not have been far off at the time of building. Nor
did it prove distant now; for looking out from that height
we caught a flicker of light coming from the camp-fires lit
by our caravan. We reached them after a couple of miles'
ride through high scrub and large groves of luxuriant
Toghraks. About half-way we crossed a small and very
salt stream; but on arrival we found that camp had been
pitched by the side of a small lake which, though itself salt,
had several springs of quite drinkable water on its margin.

There was abundance of grazing on dry reeds and thorny scrub of all sorts for our hard-tried animals, with big Toghraks to feed the camp fires and to shelter us all from the cold which now with the rising elevation seemed to increase again. It was a picturesque camp, and the warm glow which the fires cast on the Toghrak thickets around seemed the very reflection of the contentment felt by men and beasts alike. No doubt they all rejoiced at the end of their long desert journey getting within sight. But what cheered my own heart most that night, and makes me still look back to that camp with delight, was the prospect which I now felt sure was opening before me of novel and fascinating work in this desert.

END OF VOL. I

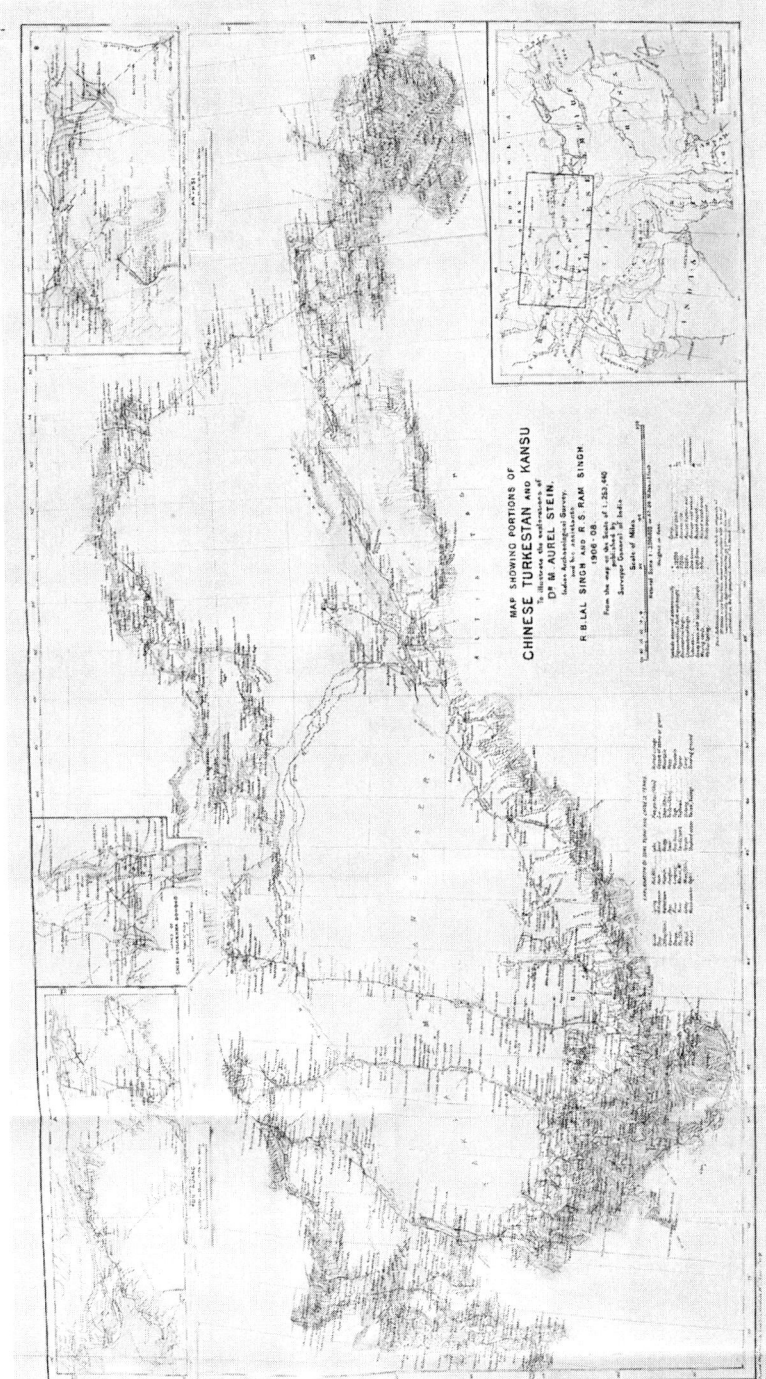

MAP SHOWING PORTIONS OF

CHINESE TURKESTAN and KANSU

To illustrate the explorations of
Dr M. AUREL STEIN,
Indian Archaeological Survey,
and his assistants

R. B. LAL SINGH and R. S. RAM SINGH
1906-'08.

From the map on the basis of 1:253,440
published by
Surveyor General of India.

Scale of Miles